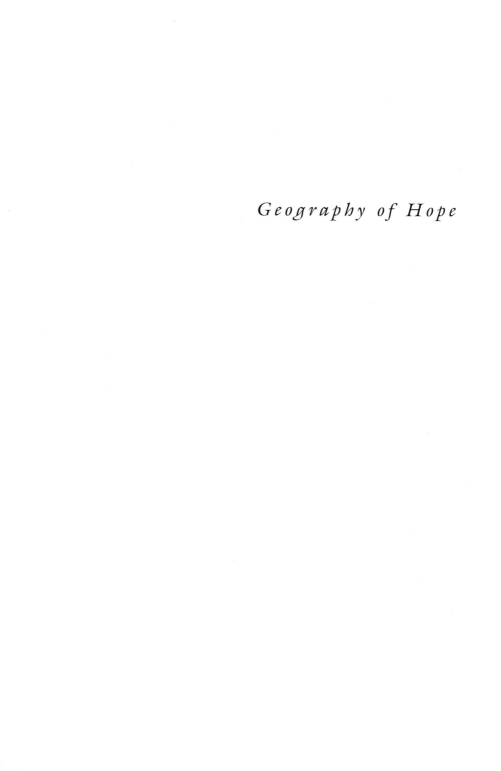

*Geography of Hope*

STANFORD STUDIES IN JEWISH HISTORY AND CULTURE

EDITED BY *Aron Rodrigue and Steven J. Zipperstein*

# Geography of Hope

## *Exile, the Enlightenment,*
## *Disassimilation*

*Pierre Birnbaum*

TRANSLATED BY CHARLOTTE MANDELL

STANFORD UNIVERSITY PRESS

STANFORD, CALIFORNIA

Stanford University Press
Stanford, California

*Geography of Hope* was originally published in French under the
title *Géographie de l'espoir. L'exil, les Lumières, la désassimilation*
© Editions Gallimard, Paris, 2004.

Assistance for the translation was provided by the French
Ministry of Culture.
Ouvrage publié avec le concours du Ministère français chargé
de la culture.

Published with the help of the Fondation pour la Mémoire de la
Shoah, Paris.

Printed in the United States of America on acid-free,
archival-quality paper.

Library of Congress Cataloging-in-Publication Data

Birnbaum, Pierre.
 [Géographie de l'espoir. English]
 Geography of hope : exile, the enlightenment, disassimilation / Pierre
Birnbaum ; translated by Charlotte Mandell.
  p. cm.
 Includes bibliographical references (p. )
 ISBN 978-0-8047-5293-0 (cloth : alk. paper)
 1. Jews–History–Historiography. 2. Jews–History–Philosophy. 3. Jews–
Intellectual life. 4. Jews–Identity. 5. Jewish philosophers. I. Title.

DS115.5.B5713 2008
909'.0492408–dc22                          2007041163

Typeset by Bruce Lundquist in 10.5/14 Galliard

# Contents

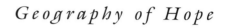

*Geography of Hope*

# Introduction

*Toward a Counterhistory*

Who controls American intellectual life? Sociologists, fond of this kind of question, published a rigorous study in the 1970s comparing the reputations of various figures of the intellectual elite: Daniel Bell is at the top of the list of the first ten names, arranged in alphabetical order, along with John Kenneth Galbraith, Norman Mailer, and Edmund Wilson, while both David Riesman and Hannah Arendt are also mentioned.[1] When, not long after, in the spring of 1981, six hundred intellectuals, scholars, and politicians in France were asked what person most strongly influenced them, almost a quarter of those polled unhesitatingly named Claude Lévi-Strauss, who received nearly twenty votes more than his friend Raymond Aron, who himself was slightly ahead of Michel Foucault, Jacques Lacan, and Fernand Braudel.[2] Daniel Bell in the United States, Claude Lévi-Strauss in France, as well as most of the people mentioned, bear witness to the privileged influence the social sciences have today in the life of ideas.

Although both Bell and Lévi-Strauss were penetrating observers of modern or traditional societies, everything separates them. Both descended from European Judaism; Claude Lévi-Strauss, deeply assimilated according to the French universalist logic of integration, deliberately distanced himself from it, whereas Daniel Bell represents the quintessence of the New York Jewish intellectual whose points of reference remain those of the Eastern European Jewish world of long ago. The author of *Tristes Tropiques* belongs to the Jewish upper-middle

I

class that was in its time received with honors by Napoleon III and the court. It is true that during his adolescence in Versailles, he lived for a few years in the home of his maternal grandfather, who was a rabbi; although he did have his Bar Mitzvah, he still decidedly distanced himself from Judaism, following the example of his parents, for whom Judaism "was already no more than a memory." Of course, Lévi-Strauss "knows he's Jewish"; he belongs to a specific milieu, all the more so when in 1932 he married Dina Dreyfus. Moving from Marseille to Martinique in February 1941, he confessed, "I already felt I was prey for the concentration camp," and he discovered, too, that other passengers on board were Jewish "like me."[3] And, if he emphasizes that "the abominable, devastating catastrophe that has destroyed a fraction of humanity to which I belong . . . has substantially affected my destiny,"[4] it's rather the ways of thinking of the Bororos or the Nambikwaras he sets at the heart of his existence and his work, and it's the virtues of Buddhism he celebrates, not those of Judaism.[5] The cultural relativism that seems to come from his ethnographic approach, from which Jews are excluded, provoked the severe condemnation of Emmanuel Lévinas, who writes, "Modern atheism is not the negation of God. It is the absolute indifferentism of *Tristes Tropiques*. I think this is the most atheistic book written in recent times, this absolutely confused and confusing book. It threatens Judaism as well as the Hegelian and sociological vision of history."[6] If some people persist in adventurous psychological exegeses in seeing Lévi-Strauss not as a prophet but actually as a "Jewish theologian manqué,"[7] it is still true that the theoretician of structural anthropology completely distanced himself from a culture linked to his own past. Commentators think they can include him, despite everything, among the "meta-rabbis" (to use George Steiner's phrase),[8] who since the time of Spinoza reveal in their work an implicit Jewish sensibility, even though they broke explicitly with their culture. Others, in the same sense, are quick to see in him "a non-Jewish Jew," using the questionable image advanced by Isaac Deutscher.[9] Here we will distance ourselves from such haphazard interpretations. On the contrary, the author of *Tristes Tropiques* represents the quintessential thinker, who, in his life as well as in the logic of his scientific method, put an end to a specific past that did nothing to fertilize his imagination.

Daniel Bell, by contrast, remained the child of the Jewish lower classes from the Bronx and Lower East Side slums, with Yiddish as his mother tongue. He was the descendant of those Eastern European Jews attached to a culture and to traditions that were not radically overturned by the Age of Enlightenment, people from that vast continent suddenly transposed almost intact at the end of the nineteenth century into *Goldene America* and never assimilated into the universalist values as most Jews from Western Europe have since. He still belongs to that migratory wave that at the turn of the century carried more than three million Yiddish-speaking people away to the New World, among whom were a number of Orthodox Jews and revolutionaries, poets, writers, musicians—to such a point that "risen up from the sea, deposited on its shores, a language without antecedent in the country. . . . This rift marks the birth of Yiddish modernity."[10] Like so many of these destitute émigrés, Bell fought in the streets, went to *heder*, became a socialist, campaigned for the Jewish proletariat. He met Martin Buber in New York. In the company of Nathan Glazer and Irving Kristol, along with their wives, he would devote long evenings to studying the Talmud, line by line, and the *Mishne Torah* by Maimonides. With his New York intellectual friends, he lived in the heart of the "Upper West Side kibbutz," as he himself calls it.[11] Of Polish origin, his father's name was Bolotsky or Karlinsky—it didn't matter; his mental universe was one of Jewish humor, of *pilpul*, of the Torah, but also of trade unionism and of a socialism hostile to communism. In his eyes, "a foreigner in every country, having no *yichus* [family tree, lineage], stripped of any real home. . . . The main thing was to find one, like every generation in exile, in *galut* [exile, diaspora]."[12] Quoting Maimonides, consulting the rabbi of Berdichev, discussing the work of the most erudite contemporary commentators such as Emil Fackenheim, challenging the "lachrymose" concepts of a sentimental Judaism presenting itself as an eternal victim, Bell adheres to transmission, to fidelity to his father and wants to be responsible for his Jewish past.[13] With Nathan Glazer and Irving Howe, the author of the classic *World of Our Fathers*, which tells the history of Eastern European Jewish immigrants in America, but also with Seymour Martin Lipset and Philip Selznick, Bell participated in the epic of New York Jewish radicalism centered around the journal *Dissent*, which remained proud of the Jewish heritage that resulted "from a tension between universalism and particularism." A child of the Torah and of *Das Kapital*, Bell was rejected by Columbia University, which was at the time openly anti-Semitic. Bell did not follow a normal university path: he received only one doctorate on the strength of his achievements; he preferred to lead worker's struggles in the streets, identified with the Jewish Bund, and rejected the Zionist standpoint for a long time.[14] In this sense, he is one of the last inheritors of that powerful Jewish Eastern European worker's movement that Lenin and Stalin feared, a movement swept aside by history and its communist and Hitlerian cataclysms. Practically wiped out in Eastern Europe, the Bund would scarcely survive in the United States, since "where there is no more Yiddish culture, or Jewish proletariat, or Jewish political activism, there can be no Bund."[15] Steeped as he was in a Jewish universe, Bell nonetheless, apart from a few brief texts where he presents himself as the advocate of a redemptive Messianism,[16] constructed a body of work that is foreign to Judaism, as if involvement in sociology prevented participation in a collective social life, which little by little fades away. He became the theoretician of the end of ideologies, of industrial society and its cultural contradictions, which at length propels him to a professorship at Columbia and then at Harvard.

Daniel Bell and Claude Lévi-Strauss, worlds apart, nevertheless both illustrate an enigma: like a host of other sociologists, anthropologists, political analysts, and contemporary Jewish historians, in their body of work, they both completely abandoned the very fact of being Jewish. Observing society from outside, whether they were of privileged or humble social origins, immigrants or members of the second or third generation, sons of rabbis or assimilated parents, they almost always turned away from it, ignoring, too, the features of a uniquely Jewish historiography that has been in the process of elaboration since the middle of the nineteenth century. Indeed, to take stock of this tropism with respect to the social sciences, one can state, along with Jürgen Habermas, that "the Jews necessarily had to experience society as something one collides with, and this became so persistent with them that they possessed, so to speak from birth, the sociological outlook."[17] Alain Touraine also notes that "it is partly anti-Semitic rejection that made middle-class Jewish intellectuals feel sufficiently distanced from their society to be able to think about it. It is not by chance that sociology in France has been almost completely Jewish—and in the United States too."[18] This state of affairs had already been observed at the turn of the century by Thorstein Veblen, the radical American sociologist of Norwegian origin who emphasized the Jews' "preeminence" in intellectual life as a "hybrid" being, "foreign" to the social system with their dual (*hyphenated*) personality—all characteristics that encouraged them to observe things from a distance and that favored the sociological gaze.[19]

This undeniable quality is not unique to them. Thus Raymond Aron finds that "in the United States, there is a relatively high proportion of Jews and minorities among sociologists. . . . Minorities tend to be at once subjective and objective when they look at their political collectivity, the country or culture to which they belong."[20] In the same sense, Claude Lévi-Strauss also writes:

> I admit that in sociology and ethnology, there is a considerable proportion of Jews. Perhaps we need not attach any more importance to this than to the considerable proportion of hyphenated names among ethnologists, which has also been noted. It seems to me, though, that two types of explanations can be proposed. In the first place, the social promotion of the Jews, in the twentieth century, coincided with the formation of the social sciences as a full-fledged discipline. So there was a "niche" there—in the ecological sense of the word—that was partly vacant, and in which newcomers could establish themselves without confronting stiff competition. In the second place, one has to consider the psychological and moral effects of anti-Semitism, which I, like so many others, experienced intermittently from childhood on, at elementary school and then in high school. To discover oneself suddenly questioned by a community of which you thought you had been an integral part can lead a young mind to step back from social reality, forced as he is to consider it simultaneously from within, where he thinks he is, and from without, where they place him. But that is only one way among many others to learn how to situate oneself in a sociological or ethnological perspective.[21]

"From within, where he thinks he is, and from without, where they place him." Never had the author of *The Elementary Structures of Kinship* so admitted the peculiar origin of his sociological gaze; never had he so evoked that intimate feeling of having been, as a Jew, placed "outside" whereas he "felt he was totally and exclusively French,"[22] he whose family had been established in the Alsace for almost three centuries. This simultaneous position of "insider" and "outsider" is certainly not unique to the Jews, but it might also not be grasped as "one way among others" to situate oneself in a sociological perspective, as the theoreticians of contemporary multiculturalism in turn regard it, who trivialize the notion of diaspora and exile by comparing the fate of the Jews to that of so many other cultural and ethnic minorities, who also find themselves both inside and outside.[23]

If likenesses stemming from similar statuses and positions clearly arise, it still remains true that in the present time the "niche" of the social sciences is more commonly occupied by Jews or intellectuals of Jewish origin who are perceived as such, whatever they might be, than by any other "minority." Already at the end of the nineteenth century, Ludwig Gumplowicz in Poland and Georg Simmel in Germany illustrated this status of foreigner/sociologist. The former, who devoted his thesis to the history of Polish Jews, after being expelled from university explicitly called for the osmosis of Jews into the heart of the populations that welcomed them and regretted that the "decadent Jewish nationality that has for centuries devoured us like vampires, sucked our blood, and destroyed our vitality" didn't disappear more quickly, before being converted to Protestantism.[24] Simmel, though, whose parents also had converted but who still had a brush with the anti-Semitic university, went on to privilege the position of the stranger.[25] During the same period, French-style republican meritocracy made university and research more accessible for Émile Durkheim and, after him, Robert Hertz, Lucien Lévy-Bruhl, and then Marcel Mauss, all of whom became renowned in this domain without, however, devoting any part of their scholarly work to the Jewish issue; Durkheim, moreover, didn't hide the disdain he had for the old time "yüdisch" (sic), who turned their backs on modernity.[26] Finally, a little later on in Hungary, Georg Lukács and Karl Mannheim encountered Marxism and sociology but once again without retaining the slightest hint of their personal history in the development of their work; their dialogue with Martin Buber and the Hassidic world would be short-lived. Lukács writes, "I have always thought that I was Jewish but that has never had any influence whatsoever on my own thinking,"[27] whereas Mannheim "distances himself from Eastern Jews" and "feels no interest in Jewish traditions."[28] They too are caught up by the great assimilationist movement at work in all its forms in both Eastern and Western Europe, but which is revealed to have all the more resonance when it operates in the name of Reason through the intervention of the nation-state. By contrast, in the vast Russian empire and in the distant fringes of the Austro-Hungarian empire, as well as thereafter in the immense decentralized American space, memories live on more easily, in these fragmented worlds.

In the United States, the social sciences have long been dominated by Protestants such as Edward Ross and William Graham Sumner, or Charles Horton Cooley, Franklin Giddings, Talcott Parsons.[29] They all burst on the scene at the start of the Second World War, during which veritable troupes of social scientists immigrated, often assimilated German Jews fleeing Nazism; others during that time came, directly or indirectly, more from those regions of Eastern Europe that were the residential zones allocated to Jews long ago. During that same period, however, the most prestigious Ivy League universities remained almost closed to them, since anti-Semitism was so much in evidence and prevented their hiring. The context changed radically in the 1960s, when anti-Semitism lost all traces of legitimacy. Whereas no Jew had managed to become a professor at Yale by 1946, in 1970, 22 percent of the professors at that university were Jews.[30] A veritable "de-Christianization" of American culture followed,[31] which increased the visibility of Jews in the heart of the most prestigious universities even more since, according to a report by the Carnegie Foundation (1969), Jews then comprised 17 percent of the professorial body of Ivy League universities, while it represented only 3 percent of the population.[32] More specifically, 13 percent of sociology professors were Jews,[33] a fact that gives an entirely different dimension to the statements of Claude Lévi-Strauss or Raymond Aron, and that confirms the viewpoint of Jürgen Habermas as to the specificity of their presence in the various social sciences.

But that is not the main point. It is striking to note that despite their strong representation in these fields of research, rare indeed are the academic Jews who ventured to devote some of their work to the fact of being Jewish itself. In the United States as well as in Europe, there weren't many people who took the risk of being perceived and condemned as Jews who cared only about egocentric ethnicity, thus seeing themselves ever after inevitably relegated to the ghetto of "Jewish Studies," far from the specific and noble field of general sociology.[34] Thus, even in the second half of the twentieth century, their strong presence in the social sciences, especially in the United States, had almost no repercussions on the legitimacy of Jewish studies. Sociology, political science, economy, or history simply seemed like different ways to gain fame, served as springboards for assimilation, facilitated entrance into general society depending on universalist viewpoints and positive methods or even methodological considerations centered on the subject that rightly avoided any excessively culturalist dimension. In a brief but brilliant and already dated article, Seymour Martin Lipset waxed ironic about the fact that "there are a lot of Jewish sociologists but few sociologists who study Jews. . . . Jewish academics would prefer to ignore Jews as an area of study since . . . for most of them, becoming sociologists or even anthropologists was a way to escape their Judaism, since the philosophical and methodological foundations of sociology were universalist rather than particularist . . . from then on, whoever studied the Jews risked being labeled a 'Judaizing Jew.'"[35]

When these specialists in the social sciences did encounter the question of ethnicity during the course of their careers, they almost always focused, for instance, on the future of African Americans, not of Jews, who were supposed to assimilate thoroughly into an open society. From many points of view, this interpretation, iconoclastic in terms of career and integration, but also in terms of self-effacement because of requirements for civility and respectability that imply a differentiation between one's private values and one's behavior suitable to a universalist public space where modernity reigns, has lost none of its pertinence, despite its provocative dimension. The universalist "code of civility," which torments a number of Jewish sociologists, ethnologists, political scientists, and historians in their dealings with "gentiles"—as John Murray Cuddihy once noted in an essay that was as clumsy as it was brilliant, in which he maintained that "the emancipation of the Jews implies their clash with the process of differentiation of Western societies, a differentiation foreign to the subculture of the shtetl and the yiddishkeit"— could only divert them from the fact of being Jewish itself, whether because of a revolutionary choice of a Marxist kind or, on the contrary, of a search for principles that can ensure functional integration into the heart of the existing social system.[36] Entrance into modernity seems to require a distancing, a standing apart from the Jewish milieu, all the more so since in the United States of that time, according to Simon Dubnow, "Yiddish, the vernacular, common to people who came from Russia, Poland, and Romania, naturally constituted the main factor of unity,"[37] as it had in the distant Eastern Europe from which they mostly came, without always having already taken the way of Western assimilation. Their entrance into sociology in the most prestigious institutions, like Chicago,[38] Columbia, and Harvard, where the code of civility reigned supreme through the predominance of the Parsonian model of differentiation,[39] is then conceived as a break with the world of uniquely Jewish identity, with a heavy past of isolation that it has become convenient to forget or reject in order to penetrate on the same level into a reconciled and functional society, or, in the academic community with its principles derived from the Enlightenment, definitively to espouse a vocation that will not tolerate the slightest particularist attachment, which would be considered anachronistic and alienating.[40]

These days, the presence of Jews in the social sciences is undeniable, if more so in the United States than in Europe. In France, for instance, it is almost relegated to the past and is limited to scholars like Claude Lévi-Strauss, Raymond Aron, Georges Gurvitch, and Georges Friedmann,[41] all of whom abstained, like a number of their American colleagues, from devoting any kind of systematic sociological study to the fact of being Jewish.[42] In the United States and to an infinitely lesser degree in Great Britain, the list of such "social scientists" of renown is almost limitless. In ethnology, we find Franz Boas as well as his disciples Edward Sapir, Robert Lowie,[43] Abram Kardiner, and, in Great Britain, Max Gluckman. In sociology, the names abound: from Daniel Bell to Nathan Glazer, Reinhard Bendix, Lewis Coser, Louis Wirth, Alfred Schütz, Erving Goffman, Paul Lazarsfeld, Alvin Gouldner, Joseph Ben-David, Howard Becker, Eliot Freidson, Leon Festinger, Herbert Marcuse, Kurt Wolff, David Riesman, and also William Kornhauser, Herbert Blumer, Kurt Lewin, Erich Fromm, Lewis Feuer, Amitai Etzioni, and Albert Hirschman. Straddling economics as Hirschman does are Karl Polanyi and so many others,[44] as for example in Great Britain: Morris Ginsberg, Karl Popper, Thomas Kuhn, Karl Mannheim, Norbert Elias, Ernst Gellner.[45] In political sciences more generally, we can cite Leo Strauss,

Seymour Martin Lipset, Karl Deutsch, Leo Lowenthal, Hans Morgen-thau, Aaron Wildawsky, Michael Walzer, Franz Neuman, Hannah Ar-endt, Otto Kirchheimer,[46] and, in Great Britain, Isaiah Berlin, Harold Laski, Samuel E. Finer, Elie Kedourie, and Hans Kohn.[47]

These incomplete and disordered lists are full of every imaginable fault. Their usefulness seems doubtful, so deeply based are they in the most varied ways of apprehending an identity that cannot be seriously reified by a simple comparison of disparate names. Any list of names thus organized according to cultural adherence should be viewed with caution, since it artificially gathers together ethnologists, sociologists, and political theorists who have frequently opposed each other in the course of major controversies, since despite a shared cultural heritage they were inspired by conceptions of truth and visions of the world that are radically antagonistic to each other—that could in no way be inferred from one single historicity. Thus Karl Popper and Thomas Kuhn, Morris Ginsberg and Karl Mannheim, Ernst Gellner and Han-nah Arendt clashed strongly, just as theoreticians of symbolic action turned their backs on those who claimed to adhere to functionalism or Marxism. Similarly, we find in this Prévert-like list many scholars of developmentalism favorable to modernization conceived as a linear process productive of roles capable of limiting the amplitude of de-structive internal conflicts: from Karl Deutsch to Marion Levy, from Daniel Lerner to David Apter, from Gabriel Almond to Irving Louis Horowitz, there are many here who offer a pacified vision of history. By contrast, others present themselves as convinced supporters of an approach based on the nature of conflict, confrontation, mobilization, or even revolution as normal—from Lewis Coser to Alvin Gouldner, Gary Marx, and Herbert Marcuse.[48] From many points of view, these lists are thus stripped of any reason for being.

Yet what holds the majority of these social scientists together, be-yond their profound theoretical divergences but also their disparate life stories as well as their varying relationships to the Jewish tradition, is that almost none of them has devoted one single instant of his long pro-fessional life to applying his immense competence to the fact of being Jewish, no matter how this fact is regarded. Their attention is focused instead on studying social stratification, classes, or mobilization; they are concerned with the question of professions, the nature of interaction in totalitarian institutions or in the heart of groups of deviants; at the core of their research they focus on the dimensions of nationalism, ideology, or development, or else on the nature of public politics, bureaucracies, authoritarianisms, electoral behavior, populism. In the favorable context of the second half of the twentieth century, a large number of Jews entered the social sciences, but, like Claude Lévi-Strauss or Daniel Bell, although so different from each other, they systematically neglected the anthropology, sociology, or political history of the Jewish societies of yesterday and today. Even more, from the numerous existing biographies or autobiographies, one could cite the declarations, often the harsh stances of these theoreticians of the social sciences who disclose their wish to do everything they can so as not to appear in the public arena as Jews.

We'll quickly give a few examples. Born in 1858 and raised in Germany in an assimilated Jewish family that had taken up the republican ideas of 1848, living in America in 1884, and having become in 1896 a professor at Columbia, Franz Boas, the master of anthropology, was the first to object, in 1908, to the arrival in the United States of immigrants who were "Hebrew Eastern Europeans," who had "a physical type distinct from that of northwestern Europe," and whose "norms were profoundly distinct from our own." Supporter of a cultural relativism that he sought to make compatible with the universalism of the Enlightenment, an admirer of the customs, traditions, and culture of the Eskimos and of the Indian tribes of British Columbia open to mixed-race marriages, Boas however predicted the disappearance of the Jews through assimilation. He won acclaim for anthropology and became president of the American Anthropological Association. Although he bore on his face the deep scars of the duels he fought in the anti-Semitic Germany of his youth, he deliberately retained none of his own past, although it too was charged with a unique culture—none, except for the rejection of the anti-Semitism he was publicly opposed to, since it prevented the inevitable assimilation he favored. Boas in fact devoted a short text to demonstrating the transformation of the shape of the head of "Hebrews" who adapted themselves to the American environment; in his opinion, "the dispersion of the Jews has considerably increased their mixture . . . their mental reactions correspond to those of the peoples among whom they live"; hence their rapid disappearance.[49]

The same is true for Boas's student Robert Lowie, born in Vienna in 1883 to a Jewish family that was also assimilated. Having become a specialist in the Shoshone Indians, the Washos of Nevada, the Crows of Montana, the Hopis of Arizona, and the Chippewa of Northern Alberta, Lowie was henceforth vastly removed from the Jewish history that continued to unfold in his native Vienna under the iron rule of Karl Lueger. It was only in a few topical texts of a journalistic nature that he spoke of the anti-Semitism that was striking them, comparing it to the lynchings of black Americans.[50] When we know that Marcel Mauss constructed some of his work starting from the culture of the Maoris of the western Pacific, that Robert Hertz was inspired by the example of the tribes of Nigeria or by representations of primitive Christian societies,[51] that Max Gluckman, founder in 1949 of the famous Anthropology department in Manchester, chose to work on the Zulus in South Africa,[52] and that Claude Lévi-Strauss devoted a large part of his life to the Bororos or to the Nambikwaras, it does indeed seem as if anthropological procedure obeys a logic of distancing from and rupture with one's own culture, which has almost been abandoned. It is as if it were a matter of providing oneself with a new culture, at opposite extremes from an age-old history that seems to be coming to an end in Europe and in the United States, thanks to an assimilation that has become realizable. Some have thought that "dominant anthropology has scarcely tolerated studies in which a Jewish dimension is expressed; their authors were most often ghettoized and relegated to Jewish Studies. . . . Does anthropology have 'a Jewish problem'? . . . namely, that a number of American anthropologists come from Jewish families, but almost none of them has undertaken research concerning the Jews."[53]

This remark remains true in many other areas of the social sciences. As with theories of modernization, does attraction to the most sophisticated scientific methods also express the possibility of a certain distancing, a protective neutralization through recourse to truly neutral, objective science, bearer of progress and unarguable knowledge? Thus Paul Lazarsfeld and Karl Deutsch each become prominent in his field through recourse to an extreme positivism. The former, born in 1901 to an assimilated Viennese Jewish family, emigrated to the United States in 1933, became a professor at Columbia in 1941, and became known as the methodologist par excellence in the social sciences. In a long autobiography, Lazarsfeld barely ever mentions the anti-Semitism rife in Austria, preferring instead to discuss his career, during which he never, in his numerous writings, discusses questions having to do with his origin—to the point that the contributions to the festschrift published in homage to him remain almost mute on this point.[54] In a little-known interview, however, he confided his feeling of having remained an "outsider" because of his "Jewish look" and his accent, and he adds, not without humor but faithful to his search for independent variables: "I wasn't too affected by it, since my foreignness won out over my Jewish identity. I think I would have encountered even more difficulties as an American Jew than I did as an Austrian Jew. I think I would never have been appointed to Columbia at that time as an American Jew. No one saw me as a Jew, since I was above all a foreigner: my accent saved my life."[55]

Another example is that of Karl Deutsch, an author quoted 437 times in 1960 by the best specialists in international relations. He was born in 1912 to an assimilated Jewish family in Prague. His mother was the first woman to serve in the Czech Parliament. In 1938, Deutsch and his wife emigrated to the United States, where he became a professor at Harvard in 1967 and president of the American Association of Political Sciences. A supporter of behaviorist methods, his most famous work, *Nationalism and Social Communication*, was based on quantitative data, and later on Deutsch borrowed from cybernetics the concepts that allowed him to write *The Nerves of Government*. Inspired by modernizing perspectives favoring the construction of the nation and integration, his work doesn't preserve any trace of his intellectual origin, which is not even mentioned, except in passing, as a simple piece of information, in works written in homage to him.[56]

There are more examples. In the area of epistemology, we'll cite Karl Popper, also profoundly assimilated, who in 1969 declares, "No, I am of Jewish origin but . . . I hate all kinds of racism and nationalism. . . . I have never professed Jewish faith. I see no reason to think of myself as Jewish," and he adds soon afterward, "I do not consider myself an assimilated German Jew. It's the Führer who saw me that way."[57] And his rival Thomas Kuhn declares in his autobiography, in describing his American childhood, "You have to remember that we formed a Jewish family—not very Jewish, but we were all genuine Jews. Nonpracticing Jews. . . . So it wasn't an important question."[58] Though

Popper and Kuhn furiously debate the question of truth and relativism, they nonetheless agree with each other in not approaching as Jews these questions of the epistemology of sciences, to minimize the weight of their past as much as possible. Popper was born in Vienna, like Paul Lazarsfeld whom he met at that time, as well as Karl Polanyi,[59] all three active in socialist milieus. His parents were married in the main synagogue of the city before they converted to Lutheranism. Excluded from one school because of the prevalent anti-Semitism, Popper pursued his father's assimilationist aims, thinking that "assimilation works: racial pride is both stupid and dangerous, since it provokes racial hatred."[60] Anxious to distance himself from this "racial pride" that according to him too many Jews propagate who refuse "to mingle with the populace,"[61] he married a Catholic woman, and this "determined defender of Enlightenment" came to write that "the Torah is the source of religious intolerance and tribal nationalism," and also confessed that Zionism "makes him ashamed of his origins."[62]

This thorough distancing is expressed by so many renowned specialists in the social sciences that it almost becomes a leitmotif. Thus, Reinhard Bendix, author of studies on Max Weber, bureaucracy, and the construction of the state, thinks of himself, according to the image of Robert Park that he quotes, as a "marginal man" in the process of voluntary assimilation. His grandfather was a teacher of Hebrew in a village near Dortmund and respected all traditions. His father, however, decided to break completely with Judaism and to identify with Germany alone: although he married a Jewish woman, he took up a career as a magistrate, assimilating with German society, refusing all links with Orthodox Jews, since, as he himself writes, "we did not feel at all like assimilated Jews, but rather like Germans identical to other Germans."[63] Arrested in 1933, he was imprisoned in Dachau for almost two years before he emigrated with his wife first to Palestine and then to the United States, where in 1946 they joined their son Reinhard (born in 1916), who had left for America in 1939. Reinhard thought of himself "as a political refugee, not as a Jew,"[64] even if in 1941 he had to go to the German embassy to renew his passport on which an official stamped a capital J, finding himself thus stigmatized as a Jew in the eyes of the Germans but also as a German enemy in the eyes of the Americans.[65] A student of Louis Wirth, Reinhard Bendix became a professor at the University of Chicago, where he found other colleagues, like Edward Shils, Daniel Bell, or David Riesman, who shared a similar background. "For me," he writes, "the link between Ancient Israel and the modern world was broken, and I cannot be a part of the covenant with God . . . if I feel an affinity for the Jewish tradition, it is by sharing its attention to the sick, its respect for life as something precious . . . but its precepts can be found in many religions. They don't allow me to lessen my feeling of being at the margins of the Jewish tradition . . . only exogamic marriage is a small step towards friendship, reconciliation."[66] Here again, in two generations, a link with the past is broken with these profoundly assimilated academics who were German or Austrian.

How many more biographies should we discuss to measure the distance there is for so many renowned specialists in the social scientists with respect to their own past? When David Riesman, author of the classic book *The Lonely Crowd*, died early in 2002, his picture was on the front page of the *Times*, and the *New York Times* wrote about the death "of the last of the sociologists . . . whose work had the greatest influence on the nation."[67] In reading his autobiography, we learn that, born in 1909 in a wealthy neighborhood in Philadelphia, after his father had emigrated from Germany, he thought of himself "as Jewish by birth but not by religion . . . there was neither a religious feeling nor an ethnic feeling in my family." As a devoted sociologist, Riesman studied the nature of crowds and examined the consequences of individualism. Having become a professor at Harvard, he was not on the margins of the Jewish world like Bendix; instead, he had become completely foreign to it, to the point where he converted and joined the Unitarian religion of his wife.[68] Harold Laski, for his part, bluntly declares, "I am English, not Polish; agnostic, not Jewish; I cannot reconcile Maimonides with Mill."[69] In few words, it's all said. His parents, Orthodox Polish Jews very active in the Jewish milieus of Manchester, broke with him: "You are no longer my son," his father said to him when the young Harold married a woman who wasn't Jewish. Having become a socialist, Laski published famous books like *The Grammar of Politics*, *Parliamentary Government in England*, and *The American Presidency*, but despite reconciliation with his family and positions that were hostile to anti-Semitism and favorable to Israel, his scholarly work too was not concerned with the fact of being Jewish.

The conclusion is obvious. Not just the few authors we've just briefly mentioned, but so many others, like Alfred Schütz or Albert Hirschman, Erving Goffman or Howard Becker, Philip Selznick, Alvin Gouldner, Norbert Elias or Karl Mannheim, do not take into account in their work the history they share beyond the dissimilarities, the nature of the specific social facts of which they are the heirs and continuators in new contexts, albeit in different ways. Thus, using his famous typology, Albert Hirschman could have included the classic example of the Jews to discuss the strategies of defecting, of speaking out, or of loyalty, all the more so since he himself "defected" from Hitler's Germany. Moreover, when he focuses on reactionary rhetoric, he could have encountered the question of anti-Semitism that is frequently consubstantial with it, including in the work of a number of authors he discusses.[70] Likewise, when, in pages that have become famous, Alfred Schütz examines marginal figures and the figure of the *homecomer*, he takes care not to discuss examples drawn from a history that is nonetheless familiar to him,[71] like Erving Goffman who only occasionally mentions Jewish examples to support his reflections on the presentation of self. Howard Becker, whose family is originally from Lithuania, works only on jazz or marijuana smokers since, in his eyes, the "outsider" is not connected to a determined historical or social situation; deviance results solely from an interaction between individuals—it's a process whereby an individual is labeled as an outsider, but the outsider can then think that "judges are foreign to his universe." This means that we are far from a historically constructed and less malleable situation where the Jews, for instance, symbolize the foreigner or outsider par excellence, from Georg Simmel's point of view, a historical context that Howard Becker does not remember, even though he studied at Chicago where his direct forebears taught.[72] In the same sense, among all the urban sociologists of the Second Chicago School, many of whom were Jewish, only Herbert Gans, who was born in Cologne and who emigrated to the United States in 1937, dared to take an interest in the world of the Jewish suburbs by calling into question the shortcomings of many of the dominant approaches that were purely assimilationist.[73]

Finally, an author like Norbert Elias, who received a minimal religious education and who, in his youth, was active for many years in the heart of Zionist organizations of a nationalist rather than socialist inspiration,

till he became, as he neared thirty, one of the leaders of a particularly active little group,[74] could also have encountered, for instance, Jews in the
king's court, or else the question of fiscal politics waged by the kings of
France against the Jews when he was studying the society of the court
and the construction of the state, or might have noticed anti-Semitism
and the pogroms when he was developing his thesis on the supposed decline of violence. But that was not at all the case, and when he discusses
the Shoah much later on, it is only to emphasize that in his opinion it
does not call into question his general theory that civility is increasing.[75]
Jewish history actually has almost no place in this historian of modernism from a Jewish background in Breslau (Wroclaw) who fled Germany
in 1933 but who, aside from a brief text of autobiographical nature written later on, never, as a sociologist or as a theoretician, dealt with this
specific aspect of contemporary civilization, even when he wrote an entire book about the Germans. Although, after many other books, he
considered that "it is very probable that the experiences he himself had
as a Jew, in Germany, from early childhood on, contributed to increasing the attraction he felt later on for sociology," since he had to "distance
himself from the dominant society" so much,[76] he was certain that his
reputation would probably not have been so exalted if he had remained
faithful only to the concerns of his youth in the choice of his subjects for
study, even if he had managed to show the same inventiveness.[77]

The observation remains irrevocable: in all the disciplines of the
social sciences, almost all Jews are shown to be careful in the exercise of their profession and in all the themes used for their research
to limit the weight of their own past and to adopt a stance that does
not place them "outside" society. This observation can also obviously be applied a fortiori to the historians who, for instance, devote
their studies to the distant Middle Ages. From Marc Bloch to Ernst
Kantorowicz, from republican patriotism leading to the Resistance
or, at the opposite extreme, the most radical nationalism that is assumed for integration in the Frankish groups—here it is integration in
the republican body that is emphasized, or, conversely, in an organic
and *volkisch* kind of nation. One can in no way compare the separate
fates of these two outstanding historians whose ideals are radically
antithetical—except in their similar desire to refuse categorically the
logic of exclusion that is imposed on them.

Born to an assimilated family in Posen (Poznan), a city concerned nonetheless with traditional, conservative Judaism that would come under Polish administration after 1918, Ernst Kantorowicz protested strongly against his exclusion from university by the Nazis, stating his "enthusiasm for a Reich led in a national direction."[78] Rejected by Vichy France, Marc Bloch writes in the beginning of *L'étrange défaite*, "France, finally, from which some people would like very much to conspire to expel me today and perhaps (who knows?) will succeed in doing so, will remain, whatever happens, the country I could not tear out of my heart. I was born there, I have drunk from its springs of culture, I have made its past my own, I breathe freely only under its sky, and I have forced myself, in turn, to defend it as best I can." A little later on, on March 31, 1942, in a text that is hostile to the creation of the General Union of Israelites in France, an organization imposed by the Germans and their Vichy allies which intended to gather together the French and immigrant Jews, a text cosigned by the sociologist Georges Friedman and by the linguist Émile Benveniste, he declares, "The hopes and sorrows of France are our own . . . the French people is our people. We do not know any other."[79] Then we understand why in the eyes of his son one cannot "find the smallest bit of any so-called Jewish identity in his life or his writings. . . . Marc Bloch was simply French."[80] As Saul Friedlander vigorously observes in comparing these two great historians, "their ideological horizons were in almost complete opposition on every point; and yet, the seemingly complete assimilation of both men, as well as their almost mystical loyalty to their country, would in the end make them face identical dilemmas, and arouse similar reactions in them . . . it seems in both of them that their unconditional faith in this mythical entity, the nation, was expected to heal them, and redeem them from the stigmata of an otherness that is recognized and yet unacceptable, their Jewishness."[81] Becoming a historian of national construction can probably, in the Europe of nation-states, only reinforce assimilation with a collective logic, and distance one from any kind of unique culture, as the example of Felix Gilbert also shows.[82]

On the Old Continent, Jewish historians like Arnaldo Momigliano—probably only in a society like Italy with a weak and profoundly decentralized government, similar in many respects to the profoundly localized Anglo-Saxon model hostile to a strong state, where the most diverse cultures are allowed free expression—were still able to approach the fact of being Jewish in their general work by openly accepting their past, as world-renowned professionals. Originally from a pious family in the Piedmont, a region traditionally open to religious minorities, Arnaldo Momigliano was born in 1908 to an Orthodox Jewish family that observed the rituals and celebrated religious holidays. He received true religious culture from his uncle, a reader of the *Zohar*, to whom he would later dedicate his last collection of essays: "To the one who taught me to study and love the tradition of our Fathers." According to his own words, he received "a strict Orthodox education . . . religion was at the heart of family life. . . . That is why I am incapable of distinguishing what has to do with family life from the religious ceremonies our family celebrated every day."[83] He spent every Saturday in a family country house bought, as he himself writes, according to "the distance an Orthodox Jew can travel by foot from his house on the Sabbath day."[84] Momigliano read the Old Testament, knew the *Pirke Avoth* by heart, had his Bar Mitzvah, married a Jewish woman, and while still very young, when he was barely twenty-six years old, wrote studies on the revolt of the Maccabees as well as on the Emperor Claudius, and on Greek cities during the era of Philip of Macedon. Thus Jewish history is at the heart of his professional research, along with Roman history and Greek history, whose interactions he analyzes by showing "how they [the Jews] stood up to the challenges with which civilizations confronted them."[85] To the extent that Judaism seems like "the most authentic source of his work,"[86] he rejects any idea of assimilation, following the example of the German Jewish Orthodox historian Jacob Bernays, who taught at the Breslau seminary, and to whom Momigliano paid tribute when he declared in a lecture given in 1977 at Brandeis University that "the need to master my Italian side as well as my Jewish side dominated my entire life every day." In another lecture, he adds, "I am Jewish, and I know from my own experience the price the Jews had to pay to remain Jewish. It is not for academic reasons that I am trying to understand what led the Jews to resist being assimilated into the civilizations that surrounded them."[87]

Every day, Arnaldo Momigliano studied the Psalms in Hebrew, along with classical Greek texts; along with Edward Shils, he devoted an entire year in Chicago to analyzing Max Weber's book *Ancient Judaism*. In this city, where according to Peter Burke he encountered a true home in the heart of an American "pluralistic" society that respected minorities, he regularly participated in the ritual of the Seder on Passover.[88] Not long before his death in 1987, he wrote, "I solemnly declare that the Jews have a right to their religion, the first monotheistic, ethical religion in history, the religion of the prophets of Israel. Even today, our moral code depends on it."[89] Finally, he himself chose the epitaph engraved on his tomb in the Jewish cemetery in the little Piedmontese town of Cuneo where his family had a house: "His faith was that of a freethinker, without dogma or hatred. But he loved the Jewish tradition of his fathers with a son's devotion."[90] Having become profoundly integrated into Italy to the point of showing himself open, in 1938, like so many Italian Jews, to fascism,[91] all his life he remained faithful to Jewish history as well as to its memory,[92] the narratives of which play a central role in his whole work.[93]

May we point out too that philosophers—whose mode of questioning is completely different, and whom we will deliberately neglect in the context of this work—like Martin Buber, Karl Löwith, Ernst Bloch, Walter Benjamin, Franz Rosenzweig, or Emmanuel Lévinas, deal with all the various dimensions of their personality more frequently than a number of sociologists, political theorists, and historians? In fact they even give it an essential role in their work, since the messianic plan, concentrated on redemption and hope, which finds so many echoes in Eastern Europe, ignores the logic peculiar to the history of nation-states, their demanding conception of citizenship, the neutrality favorable to assimilation, the self-restraint propitious to integration, the considerations of social integration, the need for "civility." Does this messianic plan on the contrary draw its strength from another vision of the world based on traditional texts, indifferent to rational modernity and to the functional laws that are intended to ensure the smooth functioning of the social system, texts which are utterly impermeable to the characteristic logic of European nations?[94] Heir to this philosophical tradition issuing from the east, between Marxism and Messianism, Erich Fromm, who came from an Orthodox Jewish German milieu and was a textual reader of the Talmud, once he had become a famous American psychoanalyst, did not shrink from singing publicly the same Hassidic songs he had sung before, or from writing an entire work devoted to the Old Testament.[95]

This almost total silence in the contemporary field of social sciences seems to be broken only by Max Weber's book *Ancient Judaism*. One of the founding fathers of sociology, only this non-Jew, in a Germany still in search of national unity, could calmly take the risk of publishing this massive, erudite work largely favorable to the outcast people. Only this undisputed historian of religions, who turned back to Judaism in his book *The Sociology of Religion*, writing, as Simon Dubnow pointed out, that "the particular importance of this 'pariah' people should be capable of being explained mainly from its historical destinies," is not afraid to include such a title within his general work as a sociologist, without, however, imagining that his integration into the German nation might be threatened by it.[96] The rare sociologists of renown who took the risk, for instance in the United States, either chose this path almost imprudently at the beginning of their careers—like Louis Wirth with his book *The Ghetto*, devoted not to American blacks but actually to Jews, something never before seen at the School of Chicago, who then went on to follow other researches until he became president of the American Association of Sociology and even the first president of the International Association of Sociology[97]—or they approached this theme at the end of their careers—like Aaron Wildawsky, who, after also gleaning all honors in the United States in the more neutral field of public policy, left to go live in Israel.[98] The price in terms of their careers seemed too high, since it rightly seemed that the analysis of Jewish themes might dangerously marginalize the few intrepid souls who devoted themselves to it.

Faithful to its universalist logic brought into play by the French Revolution, France greatly facilitated the careers of a number of already assimilated, rationalist Jews who were generally thought of as veritable Israelites, such as Adolphe Franck, Sylvain Lévi, Israël Levi, and Salomon Reinach. These men symbolize a secularized Franco-Judaism that gives 1789 an almost messianic dimension even though, as a general rule, they came from provinces in the eastern part of France. France also welcomed a number of similarly assimilated Jewish intellectuals who came from Christian Germany, where their careers had become impossible, scholars already influenced by the Haskala of the Berlin Enlightenment, like Michel Bréal, Salomon Munk, or Joseph Derenbourg. Both groups were appointed, by the middle of the nineteenth century, along with other Jewish public figures,[99] to prestigious academic institutions, from which they were still excluded in Germany, Great Britain, and the United States. They also had access, without conversion, often after passing the obstacle of competitive entry examinations, to the Collège de France and to the École Pratique des Hautes Études, where they didn't teach contemporary history, which had not yet won a legitimate place, but Greek archaeology and mythology, philology, numismatics, comparative grammar, Sanskrit, law, or even rabbinic Hebrew. But what they did not teach was the study of modern Judaism, which at that time would find no place in the heart of a rationalist and presently republican university whose values were immanent in a universalist citizenship peculiar to the homogenizing nation-state, hostile to group identities, whose historical survival there was reason to fear the Jews might ensure.[100] Thus the Republic opened itself to Jews on the basis of meritocratic criteria from which they did not benefit at that time in the United States or elsewhere while still limiting the official expression of group identities. Can we suppose that at a time when antagonism between church and state was in evidence with such virulence the history or sociology of the Jews found its place any more easily when all references to Catholicism within the public sphere were also prohibited? In this sense, the violent political conflicts that extended in France from the revolution to the turn of the twentieth century, and that led to the almost total expulsion of the religious from the public space, weighed heavily here. From then on, if almost all the scholars recruited for their recognized competence in Judaism continued to write texts on Rashi and the Talmud, or on the Kabbala, or on Jews in the Middle Ages, they were careful in each instance to preserve an interpretation with a universalist aim that did not imply any adherence to a particular history. This era, so favorable to the flourishing of Jewish studies, lasted, however, only for a brief period in the specific context of the French nation-state. Jewish studies would languish not long afterward when so many areas of research, Orientalist for instance, with which a number of these scholars often themselves became involved, would thrive, as if the Jewish dimension, which often caused so much difficulty in that fin-de-siècle France, could not yet benefit from recognition in the heart of public space.[101]

The rare bold ones, the courageous heralds of an always incomplete union that is slowly being realized these days of the social sciences with Jewish studies, of a fusion between disciplines that used to be separated by history and prejudice, had to play the role of pioneers. Many of them, because of their origins or recent emigration, plunged into a past precisely situated east of Germany, in the Polish regions colonized by the Reich, in Russia, or in Lithuania. They bear witness to the life of the shtetls or of the communities of the big cities in Eastern Europe, touched by Western modernity and open to the contradictory trends of socialism and orthodoxy, where socialization is anchored in a culture shaped by Judaic and communal practices organized around religion but also around a language, Yiddish.[102] Can we go so far as to suggest that most contemporary sociologists or anthropologists who decide to devote their talent to specifically Jewish themes come, directly or indirectly, from this Eastern Europe where Jews still shared almost collectively a specific culture and customs formed by traditions as well as by a marginalization that was equally collective, even if individual attempts to escape to large urbanized cities, motivated by the wish for modernity, were frequent, just as adherence to movements of departure, of a revolutionary or Zionist kind, were increasing? It's from this part of Eastern Europe, not yet radically influenced by the Enlightenment, where assimilation often remained an almost inconceivable strategy even if it sometimes took broad strides toward acculturation and urbanization,[103] that a number of the predecessors of contemporary Jewish studies seemed to come, the ones who structure themselves nowadays especially around two dominant centers, the United States and Israel, to which many scholars emigrated who often came from those same regions where the identitarian dimension of Jewish society lasted longer.[104] As if from Vilno (Vilnius) to Kiev or Odessa from that immense Eastern European region influenced by so many Orthodox movements or by the Enlightenment came projects that intermingled but remained distinct and sometimes contradictory. One draws from Yiddish but also and especially from Hebrew, which from David Gordon to Moshe Lilienblum or Ahad Ha'am feeds the cultural Zionism for which, according to Yehuda Pinsker's phrase, "self-emancipation" is the goal:[105] as the poet Chaim Nachman Bialik writes, "By linking itself to Hebrew, the sciences of Judaism will come back to life by rediscovering the people and serving its present needs and future aspirations."[106] The other project attempts to reconstitute, mainly within pluralistic American society, a Jewish culture largely based on Yiddish and to reconstruct in the spirit of Simon Dubnow a historical sociology of the Jewish people capable of giving an account of its values and its methods of social organization in the diaspora.[107]

Is it an accident that Alfred Nossig, the first director of the Verein für jüdische Statistik (Association for Jewish Statistics), created in 1902 by the Zionist movement, a distant source of one of the two contemporary centers for Jewish studies that is currently flourishing in Israel,[108] came from Lvov, in Austrian Galicia? Is it an accident that at the office of this organization devoted to professionalizing the sociological studies of the Jewish populations we find that so many Zionist leaders come from these Eastern-bloc regions, from Chaim Weizmann, eulogist of Hebrew (whereas Leo Motzkin, who also belonged to it, thought on the contrary that "through Yiddish, the very essence of the people has found its language"),[109] to Nathan Birnbaum, who invented the term Zionism and published in 1902 an article entitled "The Importance of Jewish Statistics"? Or that Arthur Ruppin, who became the head of the scientific branch of this organization, author of the classic scholarly sociology text *The Jews of Today*, a work written according to the most objective canons of the discipline, came from Posen, thought of himself as "the anthropologist of the Jews," and undertook in 1903 a long journey to Galicia to "find out more about the Jews who have not yet been affected by Western culture" and preserved their authenticity, a source of comparative materials of a value equal to those that resulted from other quasi-initiatory and romantic journeys to that mysterious East carried out by many explorers of Jewish realities remote from modernizing influences?[110] The ethnographic expeditions financed by Baron Vladimir Ginsbourg and carried out by the Yiddish-speaking writer S. Ansky beginning in 1911 to that same Galicia, with a great number of questionnaires, inaugurated the folkloric and anthropological studies of these Jewish milieus: through the gathering together of songs, stories, paintings, traditions, and superstitions, they tried to collect the materials of a culture threatened by so many massacres. This undertaking was inscribed through the development of a sociology of Jewish reality sketched out in these regions on the cusp of the twentieth century and revealed the fascination about the universe of these *Ostjuden* that Franz Kafka and Martin Buber both shared,[111] at the same period of time.[112] It testifies to the urgency of mapping out this Jewish world beyond national boundaries, to travel through them in order to take a census of its immense wealth, to bring into play the new techniques of the social sciences in order to guarantee their transmission, finally to immerse oneself in them to be able to make a culture reappear that expresses the intensity of the ties of socialization but that belongs to an already distant past of which assimilated Jews are largely ignorant. It seems as if contemporary Jewish studies, the heirs of such an undertaking, resulted from this desire to save this partially preserved world that painters like Isidor Kaufmann or novelists like Samuel Joseph Agnon brought to life in their work.[113]

Is it an accident that during the same turn-of-the-century period but in that other developing center that would be the United States, the land of emigration for European Jews, Franz Boas, who came from a fundamentally emancipated and well-off German Jewish milieu, advocated assimilation, while Edward Sapir, his student at Columbia, born in 1884 in Pomerania (which has now become Polish), who was never of German nationality, devoted all his strength to safeguarding this Eastern European Jewish culture? The Sapirs were Lithuanian Jews; Edward's father was born in Vilkomir and sang in the synagogues; after emigrating to the United States with his family in 1889, he sang in various synagogues in New York, where he also exercised the function of rabbi. His mother was born in Kovno, a famous hub of culture and tradition. In New York, the Sapirs lived in the working-class Jewish neighborhood of the Lower East Side. Edward Sapir's maternal language was Yiddish, and his second language was Hebrew, which he mastered along with German. By contrast, Franz Boas maintained in the United States an assimilationist perspective that had already been developed in Germany and lost interest in the fate of the Jews; Edward Sapir, though, studied the linguistic structures of the Wishram Indians in Washington State or those of the Yakimas, but, unlike Boas (or Lowie), all his life he remained faithful to Yiddish, to the world of the East European diaspora: his article, "Notes on Judeo-German Phonology," published in 1915 in *The Jewish Quarterly Review*, remains a classic. Having become, after Boas, president of the American Anthropological Association and president of the Linguistic Society of America, he joined the Yiddish Scientific Institute in 1933. He even became its president, with Simon Dubnow, Albert Einstein, and Sigmund Freud among its advisory committee. He founded a support committee that included Salo Baron, Horace Kallen, Louis Wirth, and the anthropologist Melville Herskovits, while Franz Boas, whom he personally invited, only reluctantly agreed to be involved in it, since in his eyes the Jews did not constitute a distinct physical or cultural entity: his name was finally not included on this committee.[114] Sapir also became the linguist of YIVO Institute for Jewish Research, created in 1925 in Vilnius, the Jerusalem of Lithuania, an institution that after its creation included one section devoted to "economy and statistics" and another to history: for a long time the portrait of Sapir hung in YIVO headquarters after they were moved to New York. With Hans Kohn and Salo Baron, he also created the Conference on Jewish Relations, which in 1939 and under the direction of Salo Baron produced *Jewish Social Studies*, for which he became one of the members of the editorial board. As David Mandelbaum, one of his students, writes, "Edward Sapir expresses the genius of his people in the finest way. The Jews are, in a certain respect, born ethnologists."[115] That shows to what point access to honors does not necessarily go hand in hand with the search for civility and integration described by John Murray Cuddihy: even if Sapir, who came up against a vigorous anti-Semitism at Yale, especially in the sociology department, did not reject assimilation, he thought that many Jews would continue to live a distinct life in diaspora. Until the end of his life, he conducted linguistic and ethnological studies of the Talmud.

Although Franz Boas contributed greatly to the legitimization of cultures like those of the Indians by posing from the outset the question of a multiculturalism capable of respecting all traditions within the nation, making the United States "a nation of nations," other anthropologists like Edward Sapir, natives of Eastern Europe who kept the use of a language like Yiddish alive even in the heart of American society, managed to preserve Jewish identity in this vast multiculturalism. This perspective is shared by Jewish sociologists like Horace Kallen, the true founder of American multiculturalism, who in 1924 published his foundational text *Culture and Democracy in the United States* and who benefited from the support of Louis Wirth, author of

*The Ghetto*, who also spoke Yiddish. Kallen became the head of the so-ciology department at the prestigious School of Chicago and published in 1926 an article on the Jewish ghetto in the erudite *American Journal of Sociology*.[116] Around Yiddish, Jewish studies, and a strong implication in the identitarian Jewish life distanced from Zionism, which was ig-nored and often even for a long time challenged or combatted up until the Six Days' War, the journal that is even now essential was created, *Jewish Social Studies*, under the leadership of Salo Baron, who since 1930 had held the first chair of Jewish studies at Columbia. Its editorial com-mittee would later comprise many Jewish sociologists like Joseph Blau, Lewis Feuer, and especially Daniel Bell and Nathan Glazer, along with other specialists in Jewish studies like Gerson Cohen or Isaac Barzilay. It was there too that Hannah Arendt, who had become a friend of Baron's, wrote her first article on the Dreyfus Affair.

This coalition of anthropologists, sociologists, and specialists in Jewish studies, distant successors of the German scholars of the sci-ence of Judaism, brought together professors at the most distinguished universities, like Chicago, Columbia, and Yale, scholars recognized by their peers, elected presidents of the American Sociological Association or the American Anthropological Association, who preserved their scientific legitimacy while publishing specialized studies on the Jewish world and its culture. This encounter seems like a unique moment in time, whose fundamental importance no one has yet, from this per-spective, noted. For the first time these two schools of thought met that had always ignored each other by turning their backs on the move-ment of assimilation that most often won over the social sciences as a whole. This original symbiosis directed toward the social sciences pre-served the spirit of the studies undertaken by A. Ruppin and S. Dub-now, while conserving the contribution of the professionalized, general social sciences. It was reinforced by the project of Mordecai Kaplan, the most famous theoretician of reconstructionist Judaism who, at the same period, as a rabbi himself, conceived of Judaism more as a civi-lization than in its sole theological dimension; in this sense, distanc-ing himself from orthodoxy, he undertook to reinforce the identitarian structures of the American Jewish world under the twofold influence of Simon Dubnow and Franklin Giddings, one of the masters of sociolog-ical theory whose teachings he followed at Columbia and whose studies concerned precisely the structure of social groups as vector of socialization. In many respects, Mordecai Kaplan's enterprise is parallel to that of Horace Kallen: both came, like so many others, from the Judaism of Eastern Europe, with Kaplan's father, born in Lithuania near Kovno, a rabbi, just as Kallen's father, also a rabbi, was born in the part of Silesia that became Polish later on. They were both influenced by the decentralizing ideals of Thomas Jefferson or the pragmatism of William James and took on themselves the task of reconstructing a Jewish society in the United States that would take its institutional place within a widening pluralism composed of the most diverse cultural groups.[117]

The two centers were rooted in Eastern Europe and Germany, where *Wissenschaft* was anchored in a consistent Jewish subculture surrounded by a virulent anti-Semitism that limited assimilation.[118] In these two great centers, this unique moment of juncture between the social sciences and Jewish studies remained fragile and almost without a future, since it also testified to the visceral attachment to a past that was becoming ever more distant, to a world before the great initiation into modernization to which the professionals of the various social sciences seemed so devoted. These days, rare are those who take note of the fact of being Jewish in their research, like the founder of social psychology, Kurt Lewin. Native of a small village near Posen in the Polish region occupied by Germany, he emigrated to the United States in 1938; in this veritable compendium that his *Resolving Social Conflicts* remains, he was not afraid to describe at length, with many diagrams supporting his argument, the situation of young Jews in the ghettos or their difficult adjustment because of their identity complex into open American society.[119] Similarly, Seymour Martin Lipset, whose parents, Orthodox Jews, came from Kiev, stood out as the sociologist of political behavior and party politics when he published *Political Man: The Social Bases of Politics*, became a professor at Harvard, president of the American Association of Political Sciences and of the American Association of Sociology, while still regularly writing books on American Jews.[120] Nathan Glazer, who came from a milieu of craftsmen from Poland and who spoke Yiddish at home, published, in the tradition of Wirth, his book on American Jews as well as innumerable articles on the subject, even though he subsequently devoted his professional life to the problems of growth and to those of multiculturalism, for which he became famous.[121] Lewis

Coser, in his famous work *The Functions of Social Conflict*, often used as an example the confrontations linked to anti-Semitism. At the height of his renown as a sociologist and after he had become a professor at Brandeis, he still published in *The American Sociology Review* an article on the court Jews, as well a work on the sociologists and political theorists, almost all of them Jewish and analyzed as such, who fled Nazism to find refuge in the United States.[122] Robert Putnam too, in his book *Bowling Alone*, used terms drawn from Yiddish to recount the sudden and recent decline of group participation in the United States. Careful to explain the collapse of activities within the group (*bonding*) as well as the actions that attached groups to each other (*bridging*), Putnam came to distinguish *machers* from *schmoozers*. The former, the "doers," are active in associations, churches, political activities, demonstrations; the latter, the "talkers," prefer on the contrary to express themselves in informal meetings, cafés, dinners with friends, clubs where they play games, cards for instance.[123] This explicit loyalty, however, occurs increasingly rarely. Thus, Erving Goffman, whose family came from the Ukraine and who talks Yiddish fluently since he spoke this language as a child, remarkably became the celebrated theorist of the presentation of self, of roles that structure the interpersonal links of all social actors. Similarly, Edward Shils, who also speaks this language, following the example of Louis Wirth (who was his professor at Chicago), chose to construct a sociology concerned with ideologies or problems linked to national construction by keeping himself at a distance from the Jewish milieus in Chicago or New York, although he was an active member of the Jewish Publication Society where he regularly rubbed shoulders with the most eminent scholars of Jewish studies.[124]

This unique encounter between the social sciences and Jewish studies lasted for only a short time, since in their emigration from Germany or from Nazi Austria, most social science specialists who were already profoundly assimilated went to the New Continent, with few of them choosing to "dissimilate,"[125] like Hannah Arendt, who wrote to Karl Jaspers in September 1952, "Judaism does not exist outside of orthodoxy on one hand, Jewish people speaking Yiddish and producing folklore on the other."[126] The composition of the present board of *Jewish Social Studies* bears witness to this; it now does not include one single sociologist or political theorist and includes only eminent specialists in Jewish studies. These days, the "social scientists" have often lost the memory of the world of Yiddish, and after many generations, ties with the past have become broken. The "world of our fathers" has disintegrated, the Lower East Side has metamorphosed, spontaneous Jewish socialization anchored in the urban has given way to solitude or, at least, to dispersion in the suburbs: aside from rare exceptions, Yiddish is no longer a naturally spoken language, and only those who have learned it by also mastering Hebrew now have access to the culture for which these languages serve as vehicles and undertake Jewish studies today. Moreover, the present standardization of Jewish studies, a widely growing field in the United States (a subject to which we will return later on), only rarely brings with it a national reputation of the kind Edward Sapir or Louis Wirth enjoyed; it does not lead to the presidency of national or international associations in the fields of sociology, political sciences, or anthropology.[127]

Journals like *Jewish Social Studies* or *Dissent* bear witness, however, to the slow recognition in the United States (far from Eastern Europe and independently of Israel) of the reality of a specific Jewish culture and milieu in the diaspora, in the heart of open and pluralistic societies where multiple forms of socialization, gleaning support from diversified milieus, are recognized as legitimate and, moreover, apprehended as methods of preserving the democratic structure of the society as well as the participation of citizens at the local level through an intense community life.[128] They also express the normality of the fact of being Jewish in the public space. Taking support from a close-knit academic network promoted by the typically private status of a number of the most prestigious American universities that benefit from the financial aid of many private foundations, the recent proliferation of Jewish studies, which arouses only limited hostility in the academic environment, testifies to a visible and accepted presence. Nonetheless it runs the risk, with the multiculturalist wave, of leaving a certain centrality and becoming marginalized among a conglomerate of heterogeneous identities all presented as equivalent and legitimate, all the more so when the specialists in social sciences are notable here more and more by their absence.

A world is becoming more and more distant. The social sciences are separating from Jewish studies by reducing their subject to one field, one that is of course acceptable but that has become marginal again, all the more so since specialists in Jewish studies are sometimes confined to specific departments, and the ones who have only a single appointment within a generalized department are rare.[129] The increasing ethnization is sometimes augmented by a new ghettoization that immediately limits their visibility in the maelstrom of a paradoxical multiculturalism, thus reproducing an earlier situation, "the invisibility of Jewish studies as an academic discipline masked by the strong presence of Jews as academics in numerous fields of research."[130] Is this distance also increasing because the close links between Israel and the milieu of Anglo-Saxon Jewish studies is forming an increasingly complex ensemble of great fecundity,[131] and also at the very time when so many specialists in the social sciences are anxious today to show firmly their distance on this point?

In this sense, a long history is probably coming to an end: that of the encounter between the Jews and the Enlightenment, conceived strictly on the universalist mode and anchored in a demanding vision of regenerating assimilation. Another history, often neglected, is appearing with difficulty, one however which is also inspired by the Enlightenment—Yosef H. Yerushalmi, for example, presents himself as "a Lithuanian rationalist"—without, however, justifying the eradication of cultures or, especially, the end of Jewishness. By unexpected detours, whether claiming to adhere to canonical authors or ones execrated by the dominant republican tradition, in France for instance, this history of the reinvention of a Jewish presence in the West, of the rediscovery of Jewish historicities, of strategies of power capable of ensuring its continued existence, in a mental universe determined sometimes with the best intentions on its disappearance, takes roundabout ways and is the source of many surprises. It involves returning to the diverse sources of the Enlightenment, reconsidering the place of the Jews between those for and against the Enlightenment, searching for the sources of contemporary Jewish studies that attest to a legitimate Jewish existence in the diaspora, reconstructing the contradictory and surprising genealogy that leads from a reconciled humanity (one that has become rational and functional while being deprived of all Jewish life) to a humanity that combines the equality of all humans with the acceptance of their own cultures and memories. It also implies returning to the notion of assimilation, "so disparaged, and rightly so," in Emmanuel Lévinas's powerful phrase, who came from distant Lithuania and who regrets that the Jews after the Second World War were more than ever "sought out" by "the Angel of Reason," concluding that "the Judaism of the Diaspora has no more inwardness. . . . Assimilation has failed. . . . It seems as if assimilation has to end in dissolution."[132]

This book takes us on a journey through disparate diasporic societies, from the Germany of the nineteenth century to the United States of today, passing through France and Great Britain, so many societies with contrary norms and opposing kinds of government. Beyond the history of ideas, we mean to shed light on the historical and cultural base from which emerges either the expected end of the Jews through reabsorption or assimilation, or their simple acceptance, in the margins of society, as foreigners or pariahs, or finally their recognition, as so many individuals endowed, in the diaspora, and here rather than there, with a place of residence thought of as inviolable where a common socialization can be given free rein. A journey through the Enlightenment seems necessary, since it is a source of contrary conceptions of politics more or less open to the idea of pluralism, but also a return to the distant outlines of Jewish studies is required, which, in the context of universalism or of the nationalism of isolation that swept everything away in the nineteenth century, appeared in a chaotic way, often taking the privileged way of Eastern Europe.

In this sense, the path opened by Karl Marx, Georg Simmel, or Émile Durkheim and prolonged in various ways by Raymond Aron, Hannah Arendt, Isaiah Berlin, and Michael Walzer intersects a number of times and often in a surprising way the one that, for their part, was taken by Heinrich Graetz, Simon Dubnow, Salo Baron, and Yosef Yerushalmi, since in a number of respects contemporary Jewish studies, proofs of the legitimacy of the Jewish presence in diaspora, present themselves as the heirs of these giants who confronted in the past century the most varying expressions of the Enlightenment but also of the counter-Enlightenment. As if, from without, carried by areas of socialization not yet lastingly affected by assimilationist aims—from the Eastern Europe of the *Ostjuden* from which came, to varying degrees, Arthur Ruppin and Simon Dubnow, Mordecai Kaplan and Salo Baron, Edward Sapir, Louis Wirth, Daniel Bell, and Morris Ginsberg, but also Isaiah Berlin, whose mental universe plunges us into the Hassidic universe of his distant Riga, Michael Walzer, whose family came from Galicia, Yosef Yerushalmi, whose parents emigrated from Russia—Jewish studies fed on an imagination and a questioning shaped by a Hebraic religious and literary culture but also by a maternal language used daily, typically Yiddish. So it is from the outside, without necessarily taking the path of "disassimilation"—as, in Germany, people like Heinrich Graetz, founder of the historiography of the Jewish people who refused to let his work be translated into Yiddish, were forced to do, or Hannah Arendt, who distanced herself from the world of the *Bildung*—that they fed their ambition by pushing to the limit, to the point of subverting it, the aim of the German *Wissenschaft des Judentums*. Attracted by the Enlightenment, by reforms and assimilation, their aim seems from Mendelssohn on firmly to be the vehicle—even more so since the traditional historiography strongly influenced by the critical vision of Gershon Scholem did not move forward—of another finality, that of relegitimization, in the heart of the German-Jewish osmosis that was so profound, and, in a more general way, within modernity itself, of a cultural and traditional demand, of a radical plan for counterhistory, at the source of a "decolonization," of Jewish history within emancipating and assimilationist European history, of a recapture of its fate intrinsically mixed with global history.[133]

From Eastern Europe to authoritarian and Christian Germany that, by reaction, favored the emergence of this counterhistory, projects of subversion would form, each different in nature but nonetheless open to each other.[134] This counterhistory, which is anchored in the specific histories of nonopen societies, little affected by liberalism, having remained authoritarian and not very accessible to modernity, is like the final snub to the assimilation in vogue in societies that more quickly entered the "Great Transformation,"[135] the global market, pluralism, or in those societies that saw the rapid spread of the nation-state, citizenship, and the public space. These societies, like France, authorized other kinds of processes of emancipation that were even more radical that quickly annihilated the world of *yiddishkeit* and of the intense collective socialization anchored in a distant past.[136] In this sense, Émile Durkheim, Marcel Mauss, Raymond Aron, and many other scholars belonged to families who quickly moved to the capital cities, with their modernity detached from the world of the past and from its culture, greatly nourished by the contributions of migrations from the East.[137]

This counterhistory is like the contemporary echo, on a more sociological and less ideological level, of the imprecations made, in the heart of this old-style world, by Ahad Ha'am (born in the province of Kiev), who for some people embodies the personification of the Slavophile, whose cultural perspective, devoted to the rebirth of Hebrew, impregnates contemporary Jewish studies in Israel, or by Simon Dubnow, anxious to keep Jewish socialization with a predominantly Yiddish flavor in the modern age, and who represents Westernization more, with his influence on these same studies stronger in America, where thanks to an intense Russian emigration a "Jewish America" is rapidly being formed.[138] Both men, in fact, launch diatribe after diatribe against the Jews of the West. They lash out particularly strongly against French Jews who benefit so much from the regenerative Enlightenment, which these prophets, somewhat overstating the case, regard as a new form of servitude, since for these scorners of assimilation "the soul is mutilated" when it is no longer bathed in a collective socialization or a shared culture. For Simon Dubnow, after the French Revolution, "external slavery is replaced by internal slavery . . . assimilation is even worse: the Jew in the Middle Ages bent only his back before the Christian persecutor, he never bent his conscience. . . . We will not sell our national liberty for civic liberty. . . . We will not repeat the fatal mistake of our Western brothers. . . . The awakening of the Western Jew is near: he is now at a turning-point in his history. He must leave the path of assimilation."[139] In the same sense, Ahad Ha'am severely attacks the Society of Jewish Studies and its president Théodore Reinach as well as Salomon Munk, thinking that the French Jews "have publicly abjured their national Jewish identity . . . this intellectual servitude is the price of political freedom . . . if I do not enjoy those rights here, at least I have not sold my soul in return for them." Following his radical reasoning to its end, he plainly adds, "The mask of assimilation has become unbearable for national feeling."[140] Coming from the innermost depths of Eastern European Jewish societies, this radical critique, which makes no concessions to the assimilation from which Western Jews benefit, and which prefers to ignore the positive side of this liberating process, is a resounding appeal for dissimilation on the national or collective level, with the aim of preserving socialization.

This specific counterhistory, coming from different hearths, whether Odessa or Vilnius, Breslau or Berlin, Kovno or Kiev, which is flourishing these days especially within an American society anxious to bring to light a number of counterhistories that all bear witness to the vivacity of various "nations within the nation," would finally achieve recognition when Salo Baron became in 1930 not the first Jew appointed to Columbia, but the first Jewish professor of Jewish history to join this prestigious university, while at the same time the philosopher Harry Wolfson, who also came from a Yiddish-speaking world, was appointed to Harvard. As Baron's friend Hannah Arendt emphasized at the time, "You have become the first professor of Jewish history in this country because you were in fact the first to know how to construct the history of your people as an academic discipline." Heir of the diasporism defended body and soul by Simon Dubnow, this discipline was explicitly asserted, according to Dubnow himself and with many qualifications, as a history that proposes to be "sociological,"[141] in the spirit of Max Weber and not theological or specifically intellectual. It found its complete recognition with the consecration of Salo Baron, Yosef H. Yerushalmi's teacher. Baron begins his major thesis on the Marranos with the statement that the book is "a fascinating contribution to knowledge,"[142] which puts an end to the "isolation" of "an historical sociology" that had been uniquely Jewish now finally becoming scientific, as he himself already described it, by creating its "standardization" allowed by the best national authorities in the institution of the sociological profession. Drawn toward the social sciences, Jewish studies thus experienced a profound "reconfiguration."[143] In that way rival "sociologies" and distinct visions of history are constructed, each animated, from the nineteenth century to the present day, by generations of scholars whose independent genealogies—but also surprising confluences—are retraced here as so many paths leading to a Jewish "geography of hope."

LES PARELLES, SEPTEMBER 2003

*O n e*   Karl Marx:
Around a Surprising Encounter
with Heinrich Graetz

On February 1, 1877, in Breslau, Heinrich Graetz addressed the following letter to Karl Marx:

> Very dear friend
>
> Even if you have committed the greatest crime—even if the last
> of the kings had been hanged with the intestines of the last of the
> priests—I would grant you my pardon. I have had no greater pleasure
> than receiving your letter accompanied by photos as well as *Kapital*,
> and the book by Lissagaray on the Paris Commune. Yes, you have
> given me a great joy which has increased even more by the long wait
> for news from you. The two photographs remind me continually of
> the pleasant time, even if it was short, when we met in Karlsbad. For
> that, for both those things, thank you.
>
> Your *Kapital* requires serious and detailed study, and I'm afraid I
> haven't understood it well. On the other hand, I read your pamphlet,
> *Civil War*, with great pleasure: "Paris all truth, Versailles all lies"?
> When you say that, one has the feeling that the final day of judgment
> of universal history has been uttered. But haven't you found five just
> men in Versailles? Would you also condemn Gambetta? All the same
> I will first go over the book by Lissagaray, which contains a great
> number of details.
>
> But you place me in a difficult situation with all these wonderful
> gifts. I do not know if my *opera omnia* could constitute a compensation
> for you. The contents of my *History of the Jewish People* in twelve
> volumes is far, far from your horizon. Whatever the case may be,
> my work on the subject of Qohelet [Ecclesiastes] might, to a certain
> extent, be more *à votre portée* [in your field]. For its author, according
> to the understanding I have of him, is a coarse realist in a fantastic
> world, one turned toward heaven, who had the courage to say clearly
> that this world, the one that actually exists, is more important than

the other problematic world and who, one thousand nine hundred years ago, preached the rehabilitation of *la chair* [the flesh]. If the text of my commentary was not more filled with Hebrew, and if you had some desire to look at the book, even if only out of interest in the commentator, truly, dear friend, it would be a great joy for me to send it to you.

Your opinion on the subject of the weak aspects of Russia you talked to me about in Karlsbad has been confirmed by events. What a shame! Even the stock markets don't pay much attention to them anymore. . . . I do not know if our German socialists deserve your sympathy. They have, in an obvious way, given themselves over body and soul to the devil, that is to say that they have become allied with ultramontanists. Either they are stupid enough not to see the danger there is for freedom and culture, or they are without principles in thus sacrificing such treasures. In my opinion, there are two enemies that constitute a danger for peace and prosperity: the Jesuits and militarism. Both should be fought by the friends of civilization. You surely know that the democrats in the United States work with the money of the Jesuits.

To finish, allow me, dear Mademoiselle [Graetz is addressing Eleanor Marx here], to write to you. You had surely become engaged already in Karlsbad, judging from your cheerful mood! You should truly be congratulated for having such a fiancé! The book by Mr. Lissagaray is well written, it has style and sense. I thank you with all my heart for sending it to me! Please give your fiancé a greeting from an admirer. This summer, will you again accompany your father to Karlsbad? For I would like to meet him there again and I would not like to miss you. My son, in Berlin, also sends you friendly greetings.

With respect and friendship

your Graetz[1]

A unique moment that defies all logic: it would be difficult to imagine a more unlikely meeting than that between Karl Marx, who devoted his life to building the foundations of scientific socialism, and Heinrich Graetz, who was undertaking a monumental Jewish history, a fundamental work in twelve volumes that left its mark on the nineteenth century and Jewish historiography down to the present day. That such a complicity, even if it was fleeting, could have been established between these two men surpasses understanding: friendly exchanges, wishes of goodwill, personal photos sent, requests for additional meetings, with Marx as "father," all kinds of banter, testify to the reality of this surprising dialogue. After he attained celebrity, Marx, often nicknamed the "red doctor," did not spurn going peacefully with his family to the thermal springs at Karlsbad,[2] a unique place for the most unexpected meetings between the most dissimilar personalities, a middle-class, calm city visited both by Orthodox rabbis and by the historian Heinrich Graetz, heir to the *Wissenschaft des Judentums*, the organization created in 1817 by Jewish intellectuals from the university eager to approach the study of Judaism scientifically. Everything separated Graetz from Marx; nothing predisposed him to this almost incongruous meeting. One of them was at the head of a worker's movement in its struggle against capitalism, defended the cause of the proletariat exploited by the bourgeoisie, and advocated the socialist revolution when he was not practicing it himself; the other, between conservatism and liberalism, devoted his life to retracing the destiny of the Jews in order to evoke the greatness of its spiritual mission, defend its permanence, and reinsert it into their own story. Marx was born in a Jewish milieu but in Trier, far in the west of Germany: all of a sudden, he turned his attention to the Enlightenment, to universalism, to emancipating Reason. Graetz was born far to the East, in Posen, in the formerly Polish part of Germany, like the thousands of more traditionalist Jews from that region that had just been acquired by Germany who emigrated between 1824 and 1871 to the oldest Prussian regions. Following the example of so many other Jewish historians of the region,[3] Graetz was more preoccupied by questions of the future of Jewish identity confronted with modernity, threatened too with disappearing through its growing inclusion within the history of the various adopted nations. Did Graetz try to arouse Marx's "dissimilation,"[4] to cause him to distance himself from the assimilation that Graetz himself rejected? Did he try to fight Marx's profound prejudices about the Polish Jews, to convince him to take into consideration questions of identity without relating them solely to the logic based on means of production that are indifferent to popular values and imagination? What did these two antithetical figures in the history of European Jews, these "brothers" but even more "strangers" to each other,[5] say to each other, how did they confront their different experiences, their knowledge, their conceptions of history? We will unfortunately never know. Only this letter of thanks sent by Graetz a few months after their meeting in the summer of 1876 remains as a trace of their conversations, which figures in the collection of letters by Marx in the archives of the German Social Democrat Party.

Did they truly find "a common field of understanding and discussion, especially about Judaism," as Tcheikover would have us believe, who presents this fabulous document, in Yiddish, which even today has remained almost unpublished?[6] We cannot think so, since the author of *On 'The Jewish Question,'* who knew neither Yiddish nor even the rudiments of Hebrew, was poles apart from Graetz, who was a longtime student of Rabbi Samson Raphael Hirsch, the famous founder of neo-Orthodoxy,[7] and also a disciple and colleague of the reformer Zacharias Frankel, director of the Jewish Theological Seminary in Breslau where he himself taught, devoting his life to the first reconstitution of the history of the Jewish nation. And both men were well aware of this difference, since just as one shows himself politely indifferent to *Kapital*, so the other can only ignore the *History of the Jewish People*, all of whose foundations he rejected, and which was, as Graetz noted, "far from his horizon." As Graetz also politely said, perhaps Marx would be more interested in his commentary on *Ecclesiastes*, which was more concerned with human reality, and, according to him, agreed, in some respects, with Marxist materialism, a text that was thus more "understandable" to Marx, but which unfortunately contained too many "Hebrewisms" that the author of *On 'The Jewish Question'* would not be able to understand even if he was confident of revealing the hidden logic of Jewish fate. As Tcheikover rightly states, it is hardly likely that Graetz read this more than problematic text by the young Marx (1843). We can imagine that had he done so he might have avoided this brief encounter and would have turned away from its author, since this little book is so contrary to his faith in the Jewish people, in its positive inscription in history, which no economic logic could call into question. In his monumental history, Graetz does not quote *On 'The Jewish Question'* and, in his numerous writings, the

name Marx seems to appear only once, after the famous meetings at
Karlsbad: in a rather late text (1883) written against the nationalist and
anit-Semitic historian Treitschke, Graetz thinks in effect that Ricardo,
Marx, and Lassalle, "the three saints of socialism of Jewish origin"
who want to put an end to poverty, are still caught in "a sad illusion"
since they ignore the ethical dimension of social change.[8] Refusing
thus to reduce politics to the brutal confrontation between Right and
Left, between the forces of progress and reactionary forces, challenging any radical dichotomization of the social space that ignores individual choices made in terms of values, Graetz, probably inspired by
*Sodom and Gomorrah*, could not understand that Marx wouldn't admit
the possible presence, in the Versailles camp, of even five innocent
people. Should one really, he wonders, condemn Gambetta too, who,
hostile to the Commune, still became the hero of the Third Republic?
For Graetz, history is more a question of values, of choices that have to
do with fidelity to a moral code.

Karlsbad, then. Unique moment when temporarily, between materialism and idealism, a dialogue was opened that was based on profound
misunderstandings that history will tragically break, a "wonderful" instant that might almost justify in advance the Bund project, the Jewish
worker's party created in 1897, for a long time opposed to any nationalist perspective, working to obtain a cultural, not a territorial autonomy,
that would however evolve, under the influence of Medem, toward recognition of the idea of a nation conceived only in terms of culture, a
project that would meet the fierce opposition of the heirs of Marx like
Lenin and Stalin, who, following Marx's example, fought the idea of a
Jewish nation. A surprising dialogue that would almost give a certain
logic to the project nonetheless doomed to failure of Ber Borochov,
trying to include the Marxist perspective within a Zionist conception
by urging class struggle within the new Jewish nation established on
a territory that belongs to it.[9] These surprising rapprochements would
last only a little while: later on, Simon Dubnow condemned the socialist project of the Bund harmonious with Marxist logic and, taking his
inspiration on the contrary from the history of the Jewish people according to Graetz, to which he gave a more sociological than ideological basis, dismissed the socialist perspective and rejected the Marxist

logic of class struggle. This heir to Graetz explicitly takes issue, more than his master, with *On 'The Jewish Question'* when he writes, "The complete ignorance of the events and movements of Jewish history, a renegade antipathy for the camp he has abandoned, a sophist mode of argumentation, imprint an artificial, hateful quality on Karl Marx's demonstration. . . . The author of the doctrine of historical material-ism was never able to rise to an understanding of the spirit of a nation whose entire history constitutes a refutation of his narrow doctrine."[10] The rupture between the logic of class struggle and the logic of na-tion able to reassert Jewish identity—which had seemed to come close to each other through a surprising friendship between Jewish thinkers that everything separated—was hereafter absolute.[11]

An inexplicable mystery remains: by what strange accident was Graetz able to ignore the work of his friend Marx, *On 'The Jewish Ques-tion,'* published thirty-four years before their meeting? Though Graetz seems not to know of the existence of *On 'The Jewish Question,'* it seems this was, curiously, the case among most of the Jewish thinkers of his time, with none of them going to the trouble of replying to Marx's pamphlet, whereas there were, on the contrary, many ready to take a stand against the book by Bruno Bauer that Marx attacked. The most famous Jewish philosophers of the time (like Abraham Geiger, Samuel Hirsch, Gustav Phillipson, or Gabriel Riesser), whether they belonged to the Reform or distanced themselves from it, wanted to reply to Bauer and not to Marx, since they felt concerned about his concepts hostile to emancipation. The writings of Marx, however, in their economic reductionism and their urgency, affected Jews less, since they were haunted only by the question of assimilation and the cost, from the identitarian point of view, of entering public life, which they thought possible in the framework of the constitutional state to which they were so attached, since, being neither Christian nor atheist, this state would realize their emancipation without pushing them toward disap-pearance. Though these modernist and rationalist Jewish philosophers shared a number of the critiques that Bruno Bauer made of Orthodox Judaism, which they too deemed petrified and too remote from global society, though they found in his writings a distant echo of their own critical statements, they still could do nothing but question his views about the future of Judaism, ending not in the finish of Judaism, but in its necessary transformation to give it life and adapt it to modern society.[12] That was the cause of their haste to refute Bauer's theses, to avoid any ambiguity.[13] Thus, the Hegelian rabbi Samuel Hirsch undertook a severe critique of Bauer's arguments when he published in 1842 *Religionsphilosophie des Judentums*;[14] similarly, Abraham Geiger, the pope of the Reform against which Graetz was at the time struggling (to the point that he published in 1844 a violent article rehabilitating the *Mishna*), attacked Bauer's positions in the same year in his book *Bruno Bauer und die Juden. Wissenschaftlichen Zeitschrift für jüdische Theologie*. In these conditions, one wonders by what strange circumstance Graetz did not get entangled in this controversy that, in the heart of Jewish intellectual circles, was mobilizing his friends, including the ones he was distancing himself from.

This seeming lack of comprehension is surprising when Graetz was party to the quarrel that was troubling the supporters of the *Wissenschaft des Judentums*, and at a time when the emancipation dreamed of by the Reform was called into question by the renewing of anti-Semitism and the closing in of German society, when Kaiser Friedrich Wilhelm had just taken hostile measures using Enlightenment values aimed at expelling the Jews in their particularism by stripping them of their rights as citizens. It was precisely in 1843, when Marx published his *On 'The Jewish Question,'* that Leopold Zunz, the master of the Wissenschaft, definitively broke with the Reform, which he accused of leading Judaism to its end, to its suicide: at the opposite extreme from Marx, Zunz, who was responsible for Jewish history coming to the fore, called for keeping the religious rituals that were unique to Judaism and undertook a new study of the past, rediscovering—contrary to the assimilationist values of the Reform, to which so many intellectuals belonged who were anxious to carry the symbiosis between Germany and its Jewish citizens ever further—the merits of a Judaism of the Middle Ages, which was so often thought of as archaic. The 1840s were a turning point in German Judaism, which Heinrich Graetz would accentuate by playing the role of a new Burke; faced with the modernity of the Enlightenment, as Burke was before with the French Revolution, he was anxious to rehabilitate the traditions, the past, the continuity of Judaism as a nation.[15] It would be difficult to imagine a point of view more unlike that of Marx, who reduced Judaism to selfishness and linked the emancipation of society with the disappearance of Judaism. While Marx published *On 'The Jewish Question'* and in 1845 *The Holy Family*, a work in which he continues his critique of Judaism, Graetz publicly agitated in 1844 against a Reform eager for modernism and assimilation, which he accused of emptying Judaism of its substance. In 1846 he published his first work on Jewish history, which emphasized both its rich continuity through time and the misfortunes and massacres that punctuated it, a concept called, in a profoundly reductive way, "lachrymose," which classical historiography attributed to him a little unjustly, forgetting that though Graetz so consistently emphasized the difficulty of the persecutions undergone by the Jews through the years and the permanence of the anti-Semitism that attacked them, it was above all to highlight the role these things played in reinforcing Jewish identity. The one consequence of martyrology, in Graetz's opinion, was to heighten loyalty to a still-living religion—characteristics of Jewish history that his future friend Marx would choose to ignore.

In these conditions, we can understand why Moses Hess, Marx's friend, his "idol" during his active participation in the communist movement, remained the longtime friend of Graetz. When Graetz received the manuscript of *Rome and Jerusalem* (1862), he found a publisher for it after writing to Hess, "I cannot tell you how much the form and content of your book impressed me." This work rehabilitated the national dimension of the Jewish people, and in it Hess constantly refers to his new friend, Heinrich Graetz, historian of the Jewish people. This intellectual encounter coincided with the time when, unlike Marx, Hess, his constant companion in arms, who had a number of ancestors who were rabbis, returned to Judaism and emphasized, unlike rationalist perspectives, the indestructible link between the Bible and the land of Israel.[16] He even belonged to the Zionist project, but without abandoning the internationalist socialism to which he remained faithful as he continued to be active in workers' movements, where he sometimes spoke in the name of Marx.[17] Though Marx and Graetz exchanged only rare letters in 1877, despite their vividly asserted friendship, from 1862 on, after Hess's turning point, Hess and Graetz struck up a much more

intimate and fertile relationship, which their rich correspondence testifies to, all the more so since both men were distancing themselves
from the Jewish reformist movement, which in their opinion too much
neglected the national dimension of Jewish history.[18] It would be difficult to imagine a greater betrayal in Marx's eyes, who henceforth saw
in his friend Hess (who had remained the friend of Graetz, with whom
Marx was beginning to have the aforementioned brief, friendly correspondence), whom he used to call familiarly his "communist rabbi,"
quite simply an "ass." It is true that in matters of Judaism, everything
separated Hess from Marx when they were involved with writing *The
German Ideology* (1845), while Hess helped Marx in his argument with
Bauer.[19] Everything on the contrary brought him closer to Graetz, for
whom the Jews also formed a nation rooted in history. Like Graetz,
Hess rose up against the Reform, which found favor in Marx's eyes
precisely because it advocated assimilation. Hess, who, following the
example of Marx, married a Christian woman, wrote:

> I myself, had I a family, would, in spite of my dogmatic heterodoxy,
> not only join an orthodox synagogue, but would also observe in my
> house all feast and fast days. . . . No ancient custom or usage should be
> changed, no Hebrew prayer should be shortened or read in German
> translation . . . no Sabbath or Festival should be abolished or be post-
> poned to the Christian day of rest . . . when rationalistic reform denies
> the essence of Judaism, namely, its nationalism, it cannot become a
> creative factor . . . when the third exile will finally have come to an end,
> the restoration of the Jewish State will find us ready for it.[20]

Hess attacked the Reformist rabbi Samuel Hirsch, whose work, favorable to assimilation, Marx on the contrary admired. Hess insisted on
the fact that "Judaism is a nationality, and one is Jewish by birth."[21] The
two socialist friends diverged radically, then, in their understanding
of the Jewish question; whereas Marx was unaware of Graetz's great
work, Hess translated the third volume of *History of the Jewish People*
into French under the auspices of the Universal Israelite Alliance, to the
great satisfaction of its author, who wrote to him, "I rejoice that you
are taking such a large part in my historical conception."[22]

*Rome and Jerusalem*, whose original title was *The Revival of Israel*,
opens with this forceful proposition, which indicates the extent of the

change undergone by the author, who had once strayed so far from Judaism that he foresaw its inevitable disappearance, "Now I am back with my people, after a separation of twenty years,"[23] a public return that explains why Hess openly uses, for the first time, his first name, Moses, whereas before he had signed his name M. Hess, Morits Hess, or, in Paris, Maurice Hess. Although in this work he often quotes Graetz, the name of Marx, whose socialist struggle he had however shared for a long time, never appears. Quite the contrary—without any reference to Marx, we read the following remark:

> The specialty of the German of the higher class, of course, is his interest in abstract thought; and because he is too much of a universal philosopher, it is difficult for him to be inspired by national tendencies . . . in addition to this, the German opposes Jewish national aspirations because of his racial antipathy . . . the publisher, whose "pure human" conscience revolted against publishing a book advocating the revival of Jewish nationality, published books preaching hatred to Jews and Judaism without the slightest remorse, in spite of the fact that the motive of such works is essentially opposed to the "pure human conscience.". . . The "new" Jew, who denies the existence of the Jewish nationality, is not only a deserter in the religious sense, but is also a traitor to his people, his race and even his family. . . . We shall always remain strangers among the nations.[24]

We understand why Hess distanced himself from his friend Marx, author of *On 'The Jewish Question,'* the contents of which can only repel him, since it presupposes the end of a putative Jewish people stripped of all historicity. At the same time he drew closer to his new friend Heinrich Graetz who, after Moses Hess's death, wrote to his widow Sybille Hess to assure her of his "feelings of sadness" at his "friend's" death, which "seems difficult to believe," and he evokes a common "friendship" that lasted for sixteen years.[25]

The historical context in which the writings of Marx occurred is a special one. The Jews were experiencing a difficult time in their history, with hopes born from the Emancipation and the Enlightenment cruelly disappointed. Whereas Napoleon's victory had accelerated measures favorable to the emancipation of the Jews of Germany, leading, in 1812, to the emancipation act passed by Prussia, his defeat marked a brutal retreat. The rise of conservatism, the desire to return to a Christian state, the change in the state of mind of the political and administrative elite, the flourishing of new romantic theories of the state and of the nation all contributed to turning away from the Enlightenment and calling into question the recent rights that the Jews had acquired and thought definitive.[26] This sudden change of course incited a number of Jews to convert, so that they could pursue their careers without being confronted with a growing ostracism: this was the case of Karl Marx's father, who, in 1816 or 1817, became a member of the Evangelical Church, changing his first name from Heschel to Heinrich, which had a particularly Germanic consonance. These attempts at compromise did not prevent the virulent anti-Semitic demonstrations, called the "Hep! Hep!" uprisings, which broke out in 1819 in Bavaria, the same year of the creation of the *Wissenschaft des Judentums*; these spread throughout all of Germany, from Frankfurt to Hamburg, provoking much violence against Jews, who were often forced to flee from the cities.[27] Innumerable books were published at the time that denounced the Jewish poison, the sclerosis of Judaism, its self-exclusion from society—all works comparing Christianity as a religion of love and tolerance to Judaism, apprehended in a completely negative way.[28] It was indeed a matter of a profound movement to try to restore the old oppressive ways.

The Damascus affair, which occurred in 1840, almost at the same time that the huge debate launched by the publication of Bruno Bauer's book began, just a few years after an identical accusation of ritual murder arose (in 1834, near Dusseldorf), and at a time when in Germany severe measures had been passed by Kaiser Friedrich Wilhelm IV against peddlers and Jewish beggars, whose children were compelled to attend Christian schools,[29] once again cast a chill over current affairs and aroused great anxiety among German Jews. The sudden disappearance of Father Thomas and his servant caused the age-old accusation of ritual murder to come to the surface again—a number of Jews were arrested and, under torture, acknowledged their participation in a ritual murder. The grand rabbi was accused of being responsible for this affair, and the Jews of Damascus were thus faced with the direct threat of an actual pogrom. For the first time in modern Jewish history, a high-level collective action was led under the direction of Adolphe Crémieux and Sir Moses Montefiore, who headed a gigantic international protest campaign to challenge the accusation and fight against this anti-Semitic provocation that was throwing Europe into upheaval and causing intense emotional upset in the Jewish people—as well as a newfound and strong feeling of solidarity, which became a source of fresh, more institutionalized actions enabling Jews to come to the aid of their fellows in danger.[30] The Wissenschaft scholars also protested, like Abraham Geiger, who played a crucial role in the refutation of ritual murder. Even Moses Hess was shaken at the time unlike his friend Karl Marx by this return to obsessions and fears from the Middle Ages. Hess's Jewish identity was reawakened and reasserted as he read Graetz's books, completely turning him away from Marx; the Damascus tragedy suddenly reminded him—as he would admit later on—that "he belonged to a pitiful people, slandered all over the world, scattered but still alive."[31] Heinrich Graetz, who devoted more than thirty pages of his *History* to the Damascus affair, observed that through the decisive action of Crémieux and Montefiore, it became credible that the victory of democracies would reinforce the confidence of the Jews in the legitimacy of constitutional and liberal systems, the only ones capable of guaranteeing their rights. This greatly underestimated the feeling of abandonment of the Jews, who had thought they were protected by the process of emancipation, especially in France and Germany; they were literally stunned at finding themselves accused of ritual murder by major newspapers (*Allgemeine Zeitung*, *Times*, and so on) and by a large section of French public opinion, in conformity with the highest government authorities, obedient to the policies decided by Adolphe Thiers.[32]

These tragic events, which threatened the process of emancipation, elicited a resounding response from the Wissenschaft scholars like Samuel Hirsch, who in 1842 discussed them in his work cited above. Hirsch did not, however, want to call into question the emancipation that, despite all the backlashes, still authorized the Jews, by progressively distancing themselves from the perspectives of Mendelssohn to appear as one "spiritual nationality": emancipation favored both their de-ghettoization and their reemergence as a distinctive group.[33] Unlike Graetz, Hirsch underestimated the movement in favor of a pure and simple return to a Christian state, which aroused a new interpretation of the "Jewish question," on which a number of works appeared in Germany from 1838 onward. In the early 1840s, even more books were published that used the titles *Jüdische Frage* or *Judenfrage* over and over again. This famous "Jewish question" kept coming up as a leitmotif among a whole host of anti-Semitic authors who denied the idea that, in a "national Christian society," Jews could preserve their specificity. According to this perspective, the Jews wanted to be emancipated by the state, but they neglected the fundamentally Christian dimension of the nation by preserving their customs and food habits; they sought to become citizens of the state, but they did not want to become integrated into the *Volk*, the Christian nation. Through this condemnation, we can see how nationalism is penetrated through and through with a quasi-racist dimension, which would continue to be ever more evident. As in the 1820s, the "Judenfrage" was now relaunched by a swarm of authors hostile to the presence of Jews within civil society.[34] Reactionary Christian thinkers were not, moreover, the only ones to think of the Jews as a foreign body whose dissolution was desirable; they were joined on this point by the Young Hegelians, adherents of a theory of government by citizens who challenged any particularist identity, all the more so since Hegel himself thought that, in the evolution of the Mind but also of the state, Jewish history should be suppressed (*aufgehoben*), that the Jewish people—whose sufferings he regrets—have no more history, that its alienation can be resolved only by its complete assimilation: thereafter, Hegel "did not know what to do with the Jews *as Jews* in modernity, any more than he could with his system explain their survival."[35]

Unlike the scholars of the Reform, and unlike Graetz, Marx, turning his back on a number of German Jews who in order to pursue their *Bildung* project established themselves in German society while still retaining their own identity, purely and simply ignored his own most recent past, declared he was of Protestant persuasion, and from his youth onward identified with Christianity, starting from the time when his own father decided to convert along with his children, when Karl was six years old. The conversion of Heschel ha-Levi Marx, Karl's father, a lawyer of modest social position, occurred, as did that of so many

Germans of the time, during a period of a reinforcement of prejudices and measures hostile to Jewish presence within German society. He was baptized in the Evangelical Church in Trier, after the Prussian minister of the interior had refused to accept him into the civil service. Six years later, on August 24, 1824, Karl, his five brothers, and his sister were also baptized; Marx's mother, daughter of Isaac Pressburg, rabbi of Nijmegen, in Holland, in turn joined this church in November 1825, after her parents' death.[36] There has been much speculation about the motives for the conversion of Karl Marx's father, with his daughter Eleanor attributing it to his blocked career whereas Laura, his other daughter, on the contrary interprets it as arising from his Kantian or even Voltairean convictions alone. This conversion has been the subject of many studies. Lewis Feuer, in a very detailed article on this essential episode, demonstrates that Karl Marx's deism in no way implied his conversion to Christianity. He also reveals the existence of a document by Marx's father the authenticity of which has been refuted by more recent studies,[37] written in favor of "his co-religionists" for whom he demands justice, challenging all the prejudices that their function as moneylenders overwhelms them with: addressed to the king, this courageous stance in favor of the Jews uttered by a Jew who has separated himself from the religion received no reply. So suddenly (according to Feuer), threatened in his career, Heschel Marx decided on the great leap toward normality through a conversion made all the easier because of the philosophy of the time.[38]

This conversion did not in the least transform Heinrich Marx into a modern Marrano preserving a true fidelity to Judaism in his innermost being. The estrangement was absolute and was also marked by his choice of first names for his children: Moritz, his first son, who died at four years of age; Hermann, who was born a year after Karl and died in 1842; sisters Henriette and Karoline; Karl, to which his parents added, as a middle name, at the time of his conversion, Heinrich, the name of Heschel's father, still alive. This choice came about in opposition to Jewish tradition, as if to arrange things better in terms of generational transmission and to break with Hebraic first names. Karl Marx, whose name seems to be an abbreviation for Mordecai, was nonetheless the son of a long line of rabbis. His paternal grandfather, Meier Halevi

Marx, was the rabbi of Trier; his son Samuel, Karl's uncle, followed him in this position; what's more, all the rabbis, or almost all, of Trier for many generations were direct ancestors of Karl Marx. His paternal grandmother, Raya Moyses Lwow, also belonged to a family that included famous rabbis like Meier Katzellenbogen, rector of the Talmudic university of Padua in the sixteenth century.[39] Marx's mother, unlike her husband, remained closer to Judaism and converted only later on, while still remaining apart from society. The consequences were quick in coming: as a student at the state high school in Trier founded by the Jesuits, Karl Marx wrote a long dissertation in which he proclaimed his Christian faith. Later on, in a letter to his father, he describes with many details the choice of an ideal profession stripped of all "reprehensible" dimensions, even in its "appearance." Some commentators have wanted to see in this wish for normality a desire to procure for himself "a certificate of non-Judaism."[40] While his brothers and sisters all maintained a tradition of endogamic marriages, Karl Marx's union with Jenny von Westphalen, daughter of Ludwig von Westphalen, an important councilor in Trier and a friend of his father, seems to have aroused fears in his new, extremely aristocratic, in-laws and perhaps the open hostility of Karl Marx's mother, who like other members of the family did not attend the ceremony that took place at the church in Kreuznach. Still, Jenny, courted by the all the young men in the city, would be the love of his life and would become involved body and soul, like Marx, in the socialist struggle.[41]

It was in this assimilationist context, eminently favorable to criticism of the persistent Jewish question, that in 1843 Bruno Bauer, following many others, thought that an emancipation of the Jews that allowed them to maintain their particularism was impossible. He spoke even more vigorously against Jewish access to citizenship in the framework of a constitutional state. His book created a considerable stir and provoked Marx's reply, but also, as we have already noted, that of Jewish scholars attached to preserving the process of emancipation. For Bauer, Jews had to abandon both their religion and their claim to constituting a people, since "whoever undertakes the liberation of the Jews as such is carrying out a vain work. Might as well want to try to whiten a black man by washing him."[42] Using images that Marx would later use in turn, returning again and again, as we'll see later on, to this metaphor of negritude, Bauer has sometimes and rightly been presented as one of the inventors of a racist anti-Semitism that essentializes the Jews in an unchanging and a-historic identity. If however one examines this crucial text of his that gave rise to such polemics, one is surprised by its historical quality, by the author's constant wish to take into account the comparative dimension, his extreme attention to concrete situations that reveal contradictions. Let us first of all recall the general argument. Bauer, as a Hegelian admirer of the French Revolution, presents himself at the outset as a defender of a rational state that puts an end to the selfishness of civil society based on the market; he defends a state that, accordingly, abolishes the opposition between the middle class and ordinary citizens and transforms subjects into citizens by rejecting their social but also cultural and religious identity, which henceforth was to be relegated solely to the private sphere. In Bauer's opinion, a state that has on the contrary remained Christian, like the Prussian state, could not emancipate Christians any more than it could Jews, since this indispensable process can only be implemented by a state that has become rational. But even when the Hegelian state had been born, the Jews still could not, according to Bauer, benefit from a political emancipation, since they remained too attached to their traditions and beliefs, and did not show themselves ready to abandon them in the name of a common citizenship. For Bauer, the Jews want in a contradictory way both to benefit from emancipation and also to preserve their collective personality, their culture, a "privilege" that Bauer challenges in the name of a concept of citizenship that must necessarily be identical for everyone.

In Bauer's opinion, the Jews have "deserved the oppression they have undergone because of their essence" in Spain as well as in Poland, and the only solution that would put an end to it consists in requiring "Jews as well as all other peoples to sacrifice their old-fashioned traditions." Bauer condemns the "a-historical nature of this people" rooted "in its Oriental essence" and accuses the Jewish people of wanting to remain, in its religion and customs, in its "misunderstood and arbitrary rituals," "eternally separated from others": henceforth, "Jews always wanted to stay the same . . . the Jew remains Jewish, a foreigner. He remains a foreigner just as the nation—the Law expressly recalls this circumstance—

was also a foreigner in Egypt."[43] Endlessly insistent on this term, Bauer states that "the Jewish people did not want to be a people like others, not a people in the proper sense, a people alongside other peoples. Well, it has become what it wanted to be: a people like no other . . . the people of miracle, the people of illusion and chimera."[44] The emancipation of the Jews will succeed only if they "are not emancipated as Jews, that is to say as beings who must always remain foreign to Christians, but if instead they become men who do not separate themselves behind any barrier. . . . The question of emancipation is a general question. . . . Not only the Jews, but we too want to be emancipated."[45] For Bauer, "the emancipation of the Jews is possible only on condition of a total change of this essence—if in fact the Jews themselves abandon their essence, and to the extent they abandon it; that is to say that the Jewish question is only part of the major universal question that our time is working to resolve."[46] The only imaginable solution, then, is the advent of an atheistic state that does not recognize any religion within a civic society free from alienation, that rejects all religions: if the Jews, as well as the Christians, finally reject their religion, they will become the emancipated citizens of a rational state. The proof of this is, according to Bauer, that even in a society like the France of the July monarchy, which put an end to state religion and emancipated the Jews, who became citizens with access to Parliament, the Jewish deputy was obliged to go to the Chamber of Deputies on Sabbath and not on Sunday, the Catholic holiday. The state, even separate from the church, hence remains part of the religion of the majority, and the Jews as a minority can only yield and adapt to this reality that violates their conscience. It is better to recognize "the end of religion" for all, the only thing capable of favoring true emancipation.[47]

Of course, Bauer adopts a vision of the Jews that is too essentialist, that transforms them into anachronistic "Orientals." He minimizes their oppression by comparing it to that of the Christians, who were just as repressed according to him; curiously, he thinks that the Germans are incapable of emancipating the Jews so long as they themselves are not emancipated. Succumbing to prevalent fantasies, Bauer also accuses the Jews of exercising a "demoniac, diabolical" influence, of waging a war against all of Humanity, of living on usury, of satisfying especially their "selfishness," of actually dominating Europe by their financial power, of revealing themselves as having been incapable of inventiveness or creativity for eighteen centuries, in the arts as well as in the sciences, of thus distancing themselves from History and Reason, of revealing themselves to be servile, fatalistic, and having no aptitude for freedom,[48] so many biased or simply questionable assertions that demonstrate the severity of the charge, its open hostility. Nonetheless, for a young Hegelian concerned with the world of ideas alone, he still shows a surprising sensitivity to the most concrete history: he continually uses the expression the "Jewish people," consequently attributing to the Jews, in an innovative way, a collective existence; he mentions precise examples of its oppression throughout time, and even seems briefly to envisage favorably the Zionist hypothesis. Above all, in search of a theory of citizenship where no one would serve "two masters," God and the rational state, he poses, concerning the Jews, the essential question of the basis of this citizenship, which must be separated from any identity. His remarks about France, from this standpoint, are shown to be of a great subtlety when he mocks Minister Fould, reproaching him for his politics of the "happy medium" that led him to agree, out of submission and pure compromise, that the Chamber of Deputies meet on Saturday, a proposition that went contrary to his beliefs. Bauer's humor often strikes home and raises real questions about the limits of secularization in a French-style state that at the time pushed this process as far as possible: it was indeed a matter of finding out how the citizens could, in fact, deny their beliefs so as to stop being separate from their fellow citizens, a fundamental issue that the Third Republic would in turn come up against later on. For Bauer, no doubt is entertained: the Jews, as well as "ethnicities whose fusion constituted the French people," must abandon their "independence" and dissolve into the whole,[49] into the nation of citizens to which they will bring their contribution.

Today we know that at that time regional identities were far from having disappeared from the French national community, as Bauer thought, and that this vision of things, even at the turn of the century, stems more from ideology, from visionary politics, than from reality.[50] We are aware that the republican state was, beyond its proclamations, actually able to reconcile attachment to local or religious identities with an active citizenship devoted to public life, that the French Jews at the time did preserve their ritual ceremonies, their memory—even if it was "fanciful"—by revealing themselves to be faithful servants of the Republic, outstanding "State Jews,"[51] and that Jews could thus challenge in advance the demand formulated by Bauer for collective self-dissolution, which replaced religious conversion as the new individual "ticket for admittance" into state modernity. The same is true, too, in a society as different as the United States, where, unlike Bauer's assertions, it is false to claim that the model of the melting pot had managed to reduce collective identities. Bauer writes, "Have ethnicities, the influx of which has formed the population of the great modern republic of North America, kept their previous particularities? No."[52] He thus overestimates the impact of assimilation to make it conform to his ideal model of the republican city with a homogeneous public space. He reveals himself also to be especially attached to this example, since he mentions it several times: in 1842 in a series of articles on France, Bauer thinks that "the United States represents the true model of the modern republic. The United States represents the true renaissance, an improved transplantation of the Greek State, the republic of great States, the republic of the federation, the republic founded prematurely by the Girondins in France."[53] He shows he is aware of the novelty that France and the United States represent, where the state is no longer Christian, thus opening itself to a public space of citizens capable of detaching themselves from their collective identities while still preserving them, in each case. Bauer does not, however, see what radically distinguishes these models. He is unaware that the Jews, as well as the Italian, German, Irish, and other immigrants, managed without great difficulty in the United States, although in a more collective way, to assume their obligations as citizens of a state that had become more rational, without however having to abandon their specific collective organization, their group loyalty, their own memory. Despite his prejudices, and his negative vision of Jewish history, Bauer the Hegelian raises real questions concerning the limits of citizenship, the immense distance that separates political theory from the realities that citizens confront who are anxious to preserve an essential part of their personality in the space of citizenry. In some respects, the questions that Bauer asks, not the way he means to resolve them, presage the contemporary debates on multiculturalism applied to societies that are founded on a demanding citizenship and that legitimize, tolerate, or, on the contrary, challenge the expression of cultural differences regarded as threatening by the adherents of a homogeneous, rational public space. Once stripped of their solid prejudices, Bauer's analyses foreshadow the controversies between liberals and identitarians, with which contemporary political theory is busy—but we will return to that later on.[54]

Karl Marx's book *On 'The Jewish Question'* claims to take the opposing view to Bruno Bauer's text. This work is described by some as incriminating evidence, unarguably demonstrating the extent of Marx's anti-Semitism; others think that, despite appearances, it strives to defend the cause of the Jews.[55] Whatever the case, this work—which is undeniably inspired by certain ideas of Bauer's—strays from them on the most interesting points, the ones that have just been mentioned. In this sense, far from seeming like a continuation of the writings of Ludwig Feuerbach on religion, far from paling in significance compared to the writings of the time by Moses Hess, contrary to what the dominant historiography had long advanced that, on this point, without even noticing the paradoxical nature of its argumentation, justifies Marx by thinking he meant "to emancipate the humanity of Judaism but not of the Jews,"[56] Marx's text above all aims to reverse Bauer's reasoning by challenging its emancipatory dimension, which despite everything does underlie all Bauer's analyses that are hostile to the Jews. Although, in fact, both men, in terms that are of course different, agree in saying that emancipation implies the end of Judaism, Bauer justifies this dissolution of Judaism by the necessity of the end of all religions when a rational state is established that confers on everyone a citizenship, one that necessarily includes the Jews, who have become citizens just like all other citizens, having even forgotten that they were Jewish. Marx, by contrast, through a more violent vocabulary, mocks an emancipation based on the separation of church and state that would still let religions subsist and even reinforce them within civic society by leaving Judaism intact, which he associates with money and the reign of the bourgeoisie. In Marx's opinion, the solution implies the calling into question of the bourgeoisie, of money, and the disappearance of those who symbolize all the faults they give rise to—the Jews. Of course, Bauer, like Feuerbach and others, also describes the supposed selfishness of the Jews,[57] their relationship to commerce, to money, that supposedly serves them as a means of dominating all of Europe; but, unlike Marx, that is not Bauer's main argument, since he is inspired by a more political logic. Marx means to free society from alienation by calling the power of money into question and by rejecting the Jews who embody it; Bauer wants to free society from alienation by making all religions, including Judaism, disappear from the public space.

That is why Marx uses all his irony to demolish the comparisons Bauer set out with a fine effort at a comparative historical sociology (before the term existed) between Prussia, France, and the United States.[58] For Marx, regardless of the country, and regardless of whether the state is Christian or not, things are the same: religions remain equally powerful and the Jews keep their special role; thus it is good that the real cause of alienation is elsewhere, in the persistence of the rule of money. Marx immediately ridicules the political method of emancipation proposed by Bauer: although he acknowledges that Bauer poses "audaciously, trenchantly, wittily, and with profundity,"[59] the question of the Christian state, he questions his conclusions, thinking his a "*one-sided* formulation of the Jewish question."[60] While retaining the comparative method used by Bauer, Marx takes up his historical examples one by one and, in the end, reverses their conclusions. For Marx, it is not "*only* . . . the Christian state" but "the state as such" that is revealed as incapable of emancipating itself from religions.[61] Each example is a proof of this. On Prussia, there is no disagreement; it is indeed a question of a Christian state. Marx reproaches Bauer only for confining himself to a theological critique. As to France, for Marx, things are almost unchanged since there "the religion of the majority" remains the only legitimate one; Marx underestimates the slow movement of secularization launched by the French Revolution, which of course remained unfinished, but which on the contrary caught Bauer's attention when he described "the fusion of ethnicities" and regretted that Fould accepted the choice of Saturday as a day for the National Assembly to meet. The disagreement increases with the

American example: for Bauer, we are finally in the presence of "a state as such," a state that comes close to the rational one by rejecting the religious from civil society, from which religion is supposed, in the short or long haul, to disappear, thus liberating men, including the Jews, from their alienation. On the contrary Marx thinks, in a very provocative way, that "the existence of religion is not in contradiction to the perfection of the state. . . . Indeed, the perfect Christian state is not the so-called *Christian* state—which acknowledges Christianity as its basis, as the state religion, and therefore, adopts an exclusive attitude toward other religions. On the contrary, the perfect Christian state is the *atheistic* state, the *democratic* state, the state that relegates religion to a place among the other elements of civil society. . . . The consummation of the Christian state is the state which acknowledges itself as a state and disregards the religion of its members."[62] It's easy for Marx now to make himself the defender of the emancipation of the Jews, which Bauer seems to reject; for Bauer, the Jews should not ask for their emancipation as Jews but only as citizens identical to everyone else, once they have renounced Judaism.

An unequalled dialectician, Marx recognizes in the Jews, in the name of the defense of human rights, the right to exercise their religion: for Marx, "the privilege of faith is a universal right of man" that also applies to the Jews.[63] Driving his point home, Marx writes, "Therefore, we do not say to the Jews, as Bauer does: You cannot be emancipated politically without emancipating yourselves radically from Judaism. On the contrary, we tell them: Because you can be emancipated politically without renouncing Judaism completely and incontrovertibly, *political emancipation* itself is not *human* emancipation."[64] Bauer refuses the Jews' political emancipation in order to call for their fusion with a community of citizens freed from alienation, of which they will finally become part by forgetting who they were in the past. Marx on the contrary grants them political emancipation as a fundamental human right, but he challenges the hypothesis of the rational state and also rejects the idea of a community of citizens possible once the fusion between state and church is abolished. The political emancipation he concedes to the Jews is thus stripped of any real significance since, in his eyes, the only emancipation that calls religion as well as the state in question is human emancipation, which implies that man is no longer separate from man: it involves the abolition of selfishness, of money which separates men from each other, and it consequently implies, inevitably, the calling into question of the existence of the Jews, who are represented as the special agent of money, a permanent obstacle to human emancipation that must be suppressed.

This relationship between Jews and money, present in Bauer in a marginal way, becomes central in Marx in the second part of his essay where he expresses himself in the most brutal way possible:

> Thus, Bauer here transforms the question of Jewish emancipation into a purely religious question. . . . We are trying to break with the theological formulation of the question. For us, the question of the Jew's capacity for emancipation becomes the question: What particular *social* element has to be overcome in order to abolish Judaism? . . . Let us consider the actual, worldly Jew—not the *Sabbath Jew*, as Bauer does, but the *everyday Jew*. . . . Let us not look for the secret of the Jew in his religion, but let us look for the secret of his religion in the real Jew. . . . What is the secular basis of Judaism? *Practical* need, *self-interest*. What is the worldly religion of the Jew? *Huckstering*. What is his worldly God? *Money*. . . . Very well then! Emancipation from *huckstering* and *money*, consequently from practical, real Judaism, would be the self-emancipation of our time. . . . An organization of society which would abolish the preconditions for huckstering, and therefore the possibility of huckstering, would make the Jew impossible. His religious consciousness would be dissipated like a thin haze in the real, vital air of society. . . . We recognize in Judaism, therefore, a general *antisocial* element of the *present time*. . . . In the final analysis, the *emancipation of the Jews* is the emancipation of mankind from *Judaism*. "The Jew, who may have no rights in the smallest German state, decides the fate of Europe." (Bauer) . . . The Jew has emancipated himself in a Jewish manner, not only because he has acquired financial power, but also because, through him and also apart from him, *money* has become a world power and the practical Jewish spirit has become the practical spirit of the Christian nations. . . . Indeed, in North America, the practical domination of Judaism over the Christian world has achieved  . . . its unambiguous and normal expression. . . . The Jew, who exists as a distinct member of civil society, is only a particular manifestation of the Judaism of civil society. . . . Judaism continues to

exist not in spite of history, but owing to history. . . . The Jew is per-
petually created by civil society from its own entrails. . . . The mono-
theism of the Jew, therefore, is in reality the polytheism of the many
needs, a polytheism which makes even the lavatory an object of divine
law. . . . Money is the jealous god of Israel, in face of which no other
god may exist. . . . The bill of exchange is the real god of the Jew. His
god is only an illusory bill of exchange. . . . The species-relation itself,
the relation between man and woman, etc., becomes an object of
trade! The woman is bought and sold. . . . The *chimerical* nationality
of the Jew is the nationality of the merchant, of the man of money in
general. . . . Judaism reaches its highest point with the perfection of
civil society. . . . Selling [*verausserung*] is the practical aspect of alienation [*Entausserung*]. . . . Consequently, not only in the Pentateuch
and the Talmud, but in present-day society we find the nature of the
modern Jew. . . . Once society has succeeded in abolishing the *empirical* essence of Judaism—huckstering and its preconditions—the Jew
will have become *impossible*, because his consciousness no longer has
an object. . . . The *social* emancipation of the Jew is the *emancipation of
society from Judaism*.[65]

Though Marx begins by separating the "Sabbath Jew" from the "real
Jew" and wants to direct the fire of his critique against the latter alone,
actually both quickly become confused in his mind, since for him "the
secret" of religion is to be found in the "real Jew": it is indeed Judaism
that "reaches its highest point" with civil society and the absolute rule
of money. No doubt is permitted: on one of the very rare occasions
that Marx mentions Israel, it is to say that money is "its jealous god,"
that "the bill of exchange is the real god of the Jew," that is to say the
essence of his religion. Gathering into one single transhistoric entity
the Jews of the Pentateuch and those of today, Marx doesn't have words
harsh enough to decry their religion of money, the source of humanity's alienation, both yesterday and today. He does not shrink from using the vilest metaphors and fantasies used constantly by traditional
anti-Semitism, pointing a vengeful finger at the commerce immanent
in their religion to which the Jews devote themselves, accusing them of
constituting a "world power," a phrase that evokes both socialist and
Christian anti-Semitism, which, from Fourier to Toussenel and including Barrès, would ineluctably end up with the *Protocols of the Elders of*

*Zion* and the insane vision of world domination supposedly cherished by the Jews. Marx rejects emancipation "in the Jewish manner," that is to say an emancipation based on financial power; he speaks of the "thin haze" represented by Jewish consciousness that must be dispelled "in the real, vital air of society"; he emphasizes the "antisocial" nature of Judaism, which corrupts even the "lavatories" and endlessly develops the generalized prostitution of relationships between men and women. He bemoans the fate of the "woman bought and sold," another traditional image of Jewish perversity that asserts itself even in the sexual domain. Note too that in Marx's vocabulary "The Jew" henceforth replaces "the Jewish people," an expression still used by Bauer, and note that Marx reserves the word "people" only for the "Christian people."

Reversing Bruno Bauer's logic to the very end, Marx, his friend-turned-determined-adversary, and a precursor in this case of another anti-Semitic tradition that is especially vivid in the present day, sees the United States not as the republic of all republics à la Bauer, the dream finally become reality of a quasi-rational state in which citizens renounce their religious identity to establish themselves in the common public space, but the place of absolute domination of the Jews throughout civil society that is identified with the market and with money, a conclusion radically opposite to Bauer's, but which also goes against the theses that Marx himself presents in other writings of the same period when he maintains that in the United States, the state has made itself independent of civil society and of the market.[66] The "Judaification" of society is the issue that wins out over any other consideration of a comparative nature, sweeping aside the distinctions offered by historical sociology of national construction. Actually, nothing can be used for comparison, since the infrastructure—here, Jewish money—is in any case always in control of superstructures, whatever their particularities may be, and of the state, citizenship, public space, emancipation, in one society as well as in the other, despite the difference in their historical construction and their method of secularization. In Marx's opinion, the power of the Jews has no limit at all, since the very object of their religion, money and the commerce to which it inevitably leads, imposes its law on everyone, everywhere. Sinking into demonology and mythology, "Marx the sociologist," as Nathan Rotenstreich emphasizes in an amusing way, "does not even show that he's aware of the fact that he has left the field of sociology" and that he is also turning his back on the most elementary rules of Marxism.[67] Nothing holds up in this reasoning: Judaism was born centuries before capitalism and has no relationship to the rule of money; the Jews actually occupied a very inferior position in the financial world of the nineteenth century and were almost nonexistent inside industrial capitalism; at the time, the great majority of them were still suffering from extreme poverty, which Marx doesn't breathe a word of. The violence of the attack against the Jews and Judaism is such that we need a lot of goodwill to turn a blind eye, or to have recourse to some dexterous editorial cuts, to lessen the breadth of the argument, to ignore it calmly.[68]

*On 'The Jewish Question,'* though, was not much noticed at first. Jewish scholars were devoting all their strength to fighting Bauer's analyses, which annihilated the hopes they had placed in their assimilation achievable by the reform of Judaism. Marx returned to the attack by cleverly trying to use the arguments against Bruno Bauer that had been formulated by rabbis and Jewish intellectuals. This work would be *The Holy Family*, a voluminous work in which Marx vehemently attacks the spiritualism of the young Hegelians gathered round Bauer, and time after time returns, in terms that are just as critical and reductive, to his interpretation of the Jewish question. It is difficult to understand how these pages have remained so unknown by most commentators on Marx's first pamphlet against Bauer, *On 'The Jewish Question,'* since once again a lively hostility to Judaism is displayed but also a somewhat fundamental change of reasoning. Marx's method of argumentation has not held the attention of interpreters of Marxist thought, little aware of the character of the Jewish scholars Marx was now taking inspiration from to construct his refutation of Bauer's theses. But Marx still uses the same argumentation and resorts to the same heavy-handed and prejudiced metaphors.

> Consequently Herr Bauer has no inkling that real *secular* Jewry, and hence *religious* Jewry *too*, is being continually produced by the *present-day civil life* and finds its final development in the *money system.* . . .
> He considers not the active *everyday Jew* but the hypocritical *Jew of the Sabbath* to be the real *Jew.* . . . The existence of the *present-day* Jew was

not explained by his religion—as though this religion were something apart, independently existing—but the tenacious survival of the Jewish religion was explained by practical features of civil society which are *fantastically* reflected in that religion. . . . It was proved that the task of abolishing the essence of Jewry is actually the task of abolishing the *Jewish character of civil society*, abolishing the inhumanity of the present-day practice of life, the most extreme expression of which is the *money system.*[69]

His feeling has not changed; the Jews embody the dominating money in the heart of bourgeois society, and Judaism has come to symbolize the ideology of the bourgeoisie that should be suppressed. For him, the "Sabbath Jew" remained a "hypocrite," and he should be "stripped of the Judaism of his religious travesty."[70] Thus it is still a matter of an all-out attack on Judaism itself, "weird reflection" of bourgeois society, an ideology produced mechanically by the capitalist mode of production, in strict conformity with the mechanistic theory of the reflection that Marx definitively theorizes in *The German Ideology*, a profoundly negative view of all values and beliefs reduced purely and simply to legitimization of an economic order. It is difficult to imagine a more radical condemnation, not only of the Jews but also of Judaism as a religion.

Marx goes on to attack Bauer more subtly, this time using the Jewish scholars and thinkers of the Reform who were nonetheless so attached to this perspective, even if it meant twisting their refutation of Bauer's arguments around to fit his own logic. To begin with, Marx seems to support the supporters of the Reform in their struggle toward a complete assimilation, social as well as cultural and political, which Bauer condemns, since he rejects the notion that Jews can fully enter German society and reform their ritual practices to this end, abandon certain prayers, and abandon the use of Hebrew while still wishing to preserve their identity and their faith. For Bauer, assimilation implies the end of Judaism, which the supporters of the Reform want merely to modernize. Marx on the contrary approves of their approach: political assimilation allows for the preservation of religion, as the supporters of the Reform want it. "Herr Bauer was shown," Marx writes, "that when the Jew demands freedom and nevertheless refuses to renounce his religion, he "is *engaging in politics*" and sets no condition that is contrary to *political* freedom. Herr Bauer was shown that it is by no means contrary to political emancipation to *divide* man into the non-religious citizen and the religious *private individual*."[71] In order to refute Bauer, Marx has taken the trouble for the first time to read closely the texts of the Jewish thinkers of his day, at least those he thinks he can use in order to construct his own refutation.

Specialists in Marx as well as those interested solely in Jewish history have neglected this surprising new confluence.[72] In *The Holy Family*, Marx surprisingly approves of Gustav Philippson's arguments and those of Rabbi Samuel Hirsch, who led the fight in favor of the political assimilation of Jews in the name of equality of all citizens.[73] In these few pages, unique in their genre in all of Marx's oeuvre, Marx writes that "Herr Hirsch justly recalls" that the Jews are far from having played no role in history, as Bauer states. This point is important, since it authorizes the supporters of Reform, for whom Samuel Hirsch is one of the most important thinkers, to imagine changes, to conceive of a Judaism that is not petrified, by anchoring Judaism in history, by turning it away from an a-temporal messianism in order to ensure its continuity within the various societies whose fate it shares. Even though Marx cannot pass up a mean play on words about Hirsch (*Hirsch* in German means stag), he flies to his aid to assert that in "a perfect state" the Jews should enjoy all civic rights while remaining faithful to their convictions, which Bauer denied. Although Marx emphasizes that "the criticism cited earlier reveals to Herr Bauer the importance of Judaism for the *formation* of modern times,"[74] still we should not think that "the approbation he gives to Hirsch's reply is equivalent to recognition of the historical importance of Judaism" unless we stress, as Marx does, the *formation* of modern times.[75] In effect, though Marx now recognizes the historicity of the Jews, which he had taken care not to in *On 'The Jewish Question,'* it seems to be no longer acceptable in the contemporary era, when Jews are asked to want to efface themselves from history, which is to say that Marx brings only a curious strategic support to the reformist Jewish scholars, whose struggle is not at all his own.

On this occasion Marx also defends Gabriel Riesser, one of the most famous supporters of assimilation, who fought to obtain civic equality and who would soon be elected during the 1848 revolution to the

National Assembly, of which he would become vice president. "Hence, the political emancipation of the Jews and the granting to them of the *'rights of man'* is an act the two sides of which are mutually dependent. Herr Riesser correctly expresses the meaning of the Jews' desire for recognition of their free humanity when he demands, among other things, the freedom of movement, sojourn, travel, earning one's living, etc."[76] Thus Marx approves of Riesser and the Jews of the Reform fighting for the emancipation that Bauer rejects. "The developed, modern state" must politically emancipate the Jews, a perspective that "under-developed states" reject. Reading these passages in *The Holy Family*, one notes that in order to refute Bauer on his own terrain Marx shows he is now favorable to the political emancipation of the Jews, about which he had said nothing in *On 'The Jewish Question.'* Certain commentators have concluded from this that Marx was making himself an advocate for the Jews and could not then, a fortiori, pretend to be combating them or scorning them. Actually, if Marx advocates a political emancipation that respects individual beliefs, it is finally the better to show the vanity of a political emancipation that, contrary to what Bauer proposes with his American examples, and unlike the hopes of reformist Jews, does not in the least change, according to him, the Christian nature of an ostensibly secularized state. Marx denounces the illusion of that constitutionalism the Jews of the Reform yearned to see created through the fulfillment of a liberalism favorable to them: for Marx, "The Jew has all the more right to the recognition of his 'free humanity' inasmuch as 'free civil society' is of a thoroughly commercial and Jewish nature, and the Jew is a necessary member of it."[77]

Now we are back, after a detour in favor of political emancipation, to the arguments of *On 'The Jewish Question'*; actually, Marx has not changed his point of view. Only social emancipation and the abolition of money can free humanity and offer the Jews the opportunity to join it by disappearing as Jews. One suspects that Riesser did not share this vision of things expounded by his unexpected ally—Riesser, who devoted all his strength to winning political emancipation in Germany compatible with the maintaining of a reformed Judaism, was obviously proud of his Jewish identity. He did not hesitate to become engaged in an active Jewish solidarity and was openly infuriated, like Samuel

Hirsch, Abraham Geiger, Moses Hess, Heinrich Graetz, and Adolphe Crémieux, by the accusation of ritual murder brought against the Jews in Damascus, which Marx preferred loftily to ignore.[78] While Heinrich Graetz condemned the assimilationist viewpoint defended by Riesser, which turns the Jews away from their national calling, his friend Marx approved of this plan, but only as a stage toward a true social assimilation synonymous this time with disappearance, a viewpoint that offended Graetz, for whom, though Riesser had unquestionably "aimed chiefly at defending the honor and dignity of the Jews. . . . His thoughts, feelings, and dreams were German, and only slight traces of his Jewish origin are perceptible. . . . His ideal was Lessing," whence his fundamental role in favor of the emancipation of the Jews whose cause he successfully pleaded to the liberals, along with his fight against anti-Semites.[79] By contrast, Treitschke, the nationalist anti-Semitic theoretician, congratulated Riesser, as well as Marx, on a policy from which he also expected the disappearance of the Jews.[80] Graetz and Marx (but also Treitschke) mock the illusions of the assimilationist project pursued by the German Jews of the Reform like Riesser but for radically opposite reasons: the former desires the Jews to continue as a nation, the latter hopes for their disappearance within a reconciled humanity that will definitively reject the illusions of both individual liberalism and nationalism.

After *On 'The Jewish Question'* and *The Holy Family*, Marx no longer privileged the Jews as essential vectors of a socioeconomic change that involved their liberation and/or disappearance: in the rest of his work, they no longer exercise this crucial function in the march toward human emancipation. Henceforth, it is the bourgeoisie, as controller of the means of production, that comes onstage as a protagonist and whose suppression will allow a progression to a reconciled world. Marx reserved his most biting and scornful sarcasm for the petit-bourgeois who, by their alienation, blocked the transformation of social relationships, without however explaining this fundamental transfer. Indeed, we sometimes find again the images from *On 'The Jewish Question'* in certain historical writings of Marx like *The Class Struggles in France, 1848–1850* or *The Eighteenth Brumaire of Louis Napoleon*. "The Jews of the stock exchange" are accused of having written on the national flag *"Rien pour la gloire! La paix partout et toujours!"* (Nothing for glory!

Peace everywhere and always!), provoking a series of humiliations for French national sentiment. Marx also notes that the petit-bourgeois who had brought about the February revolution against these same "stock-exchange Jews" are forced to bow before their power, especially before the "Jewish stockbroker Fould, now French finance minister," the "usurious moneychanger and Orléanist Fould."[81] Elsewhere, Marx again likens Moses and the prophets to the money market.[82] Most often, however, he is content to sprinkle his historical texts with brief stories or allusions drawn from the Old Testament stripped of any anti-Semitic quality, which only help to clarify his reasoning through the use of metaphors. In 1848 he describes the dilemma of the Constituent Assembly thus: "It sought the 'son of his mother' and found the 'nephew of his uncle.' Saul Cavaignac slew one million votes, but David Napoleon slew six million. Saul Cavaignac was beaten six times over."[83] Marx is partial to this comparison between Bonaparte and King David since he returns to it elsewhere.[84] He also speaks of "the Potiphars of the National Assembly [who] had to deal with just so many Josephs of the provinces."[85] He thinks that "the present generation is like the Jews whom Moses led through the wilderness,"[86] mentions the role of a minor Hebrew prophet like Habakkuk,[87] and to tell of Montagne's struggle against the Parlement in 1849, he observes that "the democrats believe in the trumpets before whose blasts the walls of Jericho fell down."[88] Once again, to describe an incident that occurs during the Paris Commune when "one volley dispersed into wild flight those silly coxcombs who expected that the mere exhibition of their 'respectability' would have the same effect upon the Revolution of Paris that Joshua's trumpets had upon the walls of Jericho."[89]

Aside from brief allusions, observations that are openly critical of the Jews henceforth are nonexistent in Marx's major texts. Not one word against them, or almost none, in *Das Kapital* aside from the metaphor, published only in the German version, "of Jews with circumcised souls," which, if he had read it, could only have surprised his friend Heinrich Graetz, unless he chanced upon this other passage where Marx compares merchant peoples to "Jews in the pores of Polish society," or else this parallel, stripped of any ambiguity, between the Jews and money: "It is the old story: Abraham begat Isaac, Isaac begat Jacob, and so on.

The original capital of £10,000 brings in a surplus-value of £2,000, which is capitalised. The new capital of £2000 brings in a surplus-value of £400, and this, too, is capitalised, converted into a second additional capital, and, in its turn, produces a further surplus-value of £80. And so the ball rolls on."[90] Just a few allusions, for instance, in *A Contribution to the Critique of Political Economy* where the Jews are described, among other things, as the symbols of money or the merchandise.[91] Not one word about them in *A Contribution to the Critique of Hegel's Philosophy of Right*, a work published in 1841–42, just before *On 'The Jewish Question,'* in which Marx develops his theory of the state, citizenship, and to a certain extent, secularism—issues that underlie his *Jewish Question*; not a word either in the *Economic and Philosophical Manuscripts of 1844* where Marx introduces his theory of alienation linked to private property, describes the estrangement of the worker separated from himself in the capitalist system, and foresees the end of alienation, where man, finally rich, will be reconciled with himself without any need now at least explicitly to make Judaism disappear. Not a word either in *The German Ideology* (1846), where Marx argues once again with Bauer: to break ideological illusions and struggle against alienation, there is no need now to bring about the end of Judaism. Not the shadow of a remark on this theme in 1847 in *The Poverty of Philosophy*, which deals with currency and economic exchange. Nothing about the Jews in the long chapter on money in *Contribution to the Critique of Political Economy*, or in the rest of that long study (1857).

As we see, aside from *On 'The Jewish Question,' The Holy Family*, and a few passages in texts of a historical nature, the Jews hardly appeared again in Marx's work as key actors in a history that derived all its meaning from their specific destiny. Marx ignored them; no role was given them in the accumulation of capital, the circulation of goods, the search for profit, the regulation of salaries, impoverishment, class conflict, change in the mode of production, the revolution, or the end of alienation. History could now do without them, unfold according to its own laws sustained solely by the circulation of goods and the conflict of the social classes, stripped of any religious connotation: it did not find its significance in the emancipation or suppression of the Jews, who completely lost all their privileged role in the ineluctable progress of history. Were they so clearly doomed to disappear that there was no longer even any point in talking about them? Since *On 'The Jewish Question'* and *The Holy Family* still belong to his so-called youthful period, which Marx himself wanted to "leave to the mice," do the works written during the years when he was still concerned with philosophy, from which he would distance himself,[92] also fade away from history as protagonists without importance now, facing the scientific laws of reality that only historical materialism can bring to light? Actually, it was the entire Marxist problematic that was transformed with this sudden silence about the Jews: thereafter, Marx was no longer interested in religion and treated ideologies only as a more or less mechanical reflection of the relationships of production.

Although in his work as a sociologist Marx seemed to have settled the Jewish question in his own way, and although he seemed to be no longer concerned with it when he constructed his general theory of capitalism, this was not true in his private correspondence.[93] Marx flew into a rage, used all the means at his disposal, and, more than twenty years after *On 'The Jewish Question,'* forcefully ridiculed the Jews, unkindly and relentlessly. In the case of Lassalle—the German Jewish Socialist leader with whom he had a close working relationship for a number of years, with whom he shared a number of political viewpoints, and who regularly gave him money and helped in resolving his financial difficulties, and whom he regularly proclaimed to whoever would listen his unfailing friend—Marx continually called him the following names: "Isaac," "Baron Isaac," a "little Jew," "Ephraim the clever," or "Braun Yid," an expression he was particularly fond of and used shamelessly, along with "Itzig,"[94] diminutives often used also by the anti-Semites of the period, but explicitly rejected by his friend Moses Hess who, provoked by the straying of his friend, writes, "I am only sorry my name is not Itzig."[95] Marx goes so far as to assert that "Lazarus, the leper, is the prototype of the Jew and so also of Lazare-Lassalle."[96] Marx often goes even further. He writes to Engels, "That Jewish nigger Lassalle who fortunately is leaving at the end of the week has again managed to lose 5,000 thalers. . . . That guy would rather throw his money down the drain than lend it to a 'friend.' . . . He has the idea that he has to live like a Jewish baron or like a Jew who was made a baron." Marx makes fun "of the way that parvenu caresses his money bag" and, endorsing all the most hackneyed prejudices of traditional anti-Semitism of yesterday and today, sees in Lassalle "a Don Juan" endowed "with an inexhaustible chatter along with a falsetto voice." He adds, in the same letter, poking fun at "the gluttony and lechery of this idealist": "I am now sure, especially since the shape of his head and his hair prove it, that he is descended from the negroes who followed Moses out of Egypt (unless his mother or grandmother fornicated with a nigger). My word, this mixture of a Jewish and Germanic type, with a negroid background, can only produce a weird result. There is something nigger-like, too, in the way he has of imposing himself on other people." In a postscript, after much thought, Marx adds, "One of the great discoveries of our negro is that the Pelasgians descended from the Semites. His main proof: in the book of the Maccabees, the Jews send emissaries to Greece to ask for help, invoking a kinship of race."[97] Even after Lassalle's death in a duel fought for sentimental reasons, Marx celebrates the memory and struggle of this courageous socialist activist who never stopped giving him aid, but similar pejorative expressions nonetheless quickly return under his pen. Once again we find the "late Isaac," "the baron Isaac has bequeathed to us. . . . We must decontaminate the atmosphere and free the party from the stench Lassalle has left it,"[98] "the slogans of Isaac,"[99] "the revolting boot-licking attitude" that Isaac has bequeathed to the Chartist movement,[100] which has become just like himself through "flatteries and kowtows," which explains why they continue, to Marx's fury, to celebrate in "Isaac God the Son."[101] Marx often criticizes Lassalle's "Talmudic wisdom" and sees him as "the Braun Yid . . . the little Braun Jew," phrases that Engels in turn doesn't fail to use.[102] Engels deplores, "Lassalle's brief success came from that fawning respect peculiar to the Jews, which made him such that he could not fail to have respect for Louis Bonaparte"; worse, in Engels's opinion, Lassalle "is a real Jew from the Slavic border, [a] filthy Jew from Breslau":[103] Marx's closest collaborator mocked their common friend, since "his curly-haired Jew head must be very charming above the red nightgown, and in the finery of a Marquis with our Polish Yid showing through at every movement."[104]

Lassalle is not the only one to suffer Marx's wrath and his mockery charged with xenophobia and prejudices. When Paul Lafargue wanted to marry Marx's daughter Laura without his consent, Marx let him know that, in his financial condition, he could have no aspirations: Lafargue was then perceived by the irascible and future father-in-law (who would end up yielding) as "the descendant of a gorilla . . . our poor gorilla,"[105] whose "Creole temperament . . . is not adapted to the London meridian."[106] Marx kept focusing on the Jewish identity of certain people by shortening their names, explicitly highlighting their Jewish quality, using only their Hebraic first name, sometimes giving them a Hebraic first name they no longer used, and so on. His friend Moses Hess is thus referred to as "Moses"; Marx waxes ironic on "that miserly Moses," ridicules "Moses and Mosette" or else the "Moseses"; he makes fun of "Moses' epistles to the social democrat."[107] Throughout the pages of this inexhaustible correspondence, we find the most inventive phrases, like "the Portuguese Jew Castello,"[108] "the Jew Stibel,"[109] "the Jew Pulszky,"[110] "the wretched Jew from Vienna,"[111] "Steinthal and other Yids,"[112] "Kinkel, that sanctimonious liberal aesthete, as a parasite, pays court to the German Jews,"[113] "the Jew Wolff,"[114] "Oppenheim, that Jew Süss from Egypt,"[115] "Tausenau is a schemer. . . . He is endowed with that scheming sense that little Jews have,"[116] "Zerffi is not a Magyar by birth but a 'Souab,' and not just a Souab but the son of a Jew from Hannover who was probably named Stag," he has "Magyarized his name into Zerffi,"[117] the lecture by Gottfried "was welcomed with applause but as time passed it was a horrible oven—so much that even the horde of Jewish crooks with the look of aesthetes that had come couldn't manage to get their breath,"[118] "Vladimir managed to lure a nice rich old Jewish lady to take him in kosher wedlock,"[119] "the Jew Fould,"[120] "the little Jew Bernstein,"[121] "the Jew Reinach,"[122] "the Jew Reuter,"[123] "Frankelche is the spitting image of the Yid . . . the little Jew Frankel,"[124] "the rabbi Ein-Horn, Moses' friend," "the rabbi Einhorn, unicorn,"[125] "the Jew Horn,"[126] Max Nordau, the "German-Hungarian Jew,"[127] "a Jew who was presiding over a gymnastics festival in Paris,"[128] "la Hatzfeldt speaks with a Jewish accent,"[129] "the Jewish lady took great pleasure in the discussion,"[130] "the Isaac of old Cohen,"[131] "a Yid, crafty-looking, carrying a little suitcase, hurried to London in our compartment . . . our Yid was in a rage,"[132] "here [in Ramsgate] there are a lot of Jews and fleas."[133] Marx also makes fun of the editor of a conservative newspaper, of his "winks aimed at appetizing Jewesses."[134]

On April 10, 1861, Marx addressed a very compassionate and thoughtful petition, in an unusually respectful tone, which seemed to clash with his revolutionary personality, to the Prussian authorities in the hope of being naturalized a Prussian and benefiting from the right to reside in Berlin: "I was born on May 5, 1818, in Trier, in the Prussian province of the Rhine; I profess the Protestant religion and have, in the terms of the laws of my country, the right to appear in court. . . . The naturalization document should be delivered to me, and I should be authorized to settle here, in Berlin."[135] Accepted by high society, respectful of the proprieties, he nonetheless didn't neglect his anti-Semitic sarcastic remarks. Almost on the same day, during this time in Berlin, he described the way an evening organized by "his friend" Lassalle went, who was trying with all the means at his disposal to help him recover his nationality: "I was seated at table between the countess and Fräulein Ludmilla Assing, niece of Varnhagen von Ense and editor of the correspondence between Varnhagen and Humboldt. This young lady, who literally overwhelmed me with her benevolence, is the ugliest creature I have ever seen in my life: a frightful Jewish head, a thin, prominent nose, an eternal smile or giggle on her lips. . . . Spluttering over her audience in the transports of her enthusiasm. I am going to have to visit this little monster today, whom I treated with coldness and reserve."[136] This observation inevitably evokes that other exposition, also of a physiological nature, that figures in his text *Herr Vogt*, where he attacks Levy, the director of the *Daily Telegraph*: "Among the 22,000 people of the Levi tribe, whom Moses counted during the journey from the wilderness, there wasn't one whose name was written Levy with a *y*. . . . What's the point in Mr. Levy attacking Mr. d'Israeli and making us take a *y* for an *i* since Mother Nature has written his genealogy, in very excellent Gothic writing, right in the middle of his face? . . . Levy's nose has been, for an entire year, the subject of conversation in the city of London. . . . The work of art of Levy's nose serves as an elephant trunk, an antenna, a lighthouse and a telegraph. One can thus say without exaggeration that Levy writes his paper with his nose." A little further on Marx mentions a person named Vincke and adds that "the nose he had was longer that Levy's."[137]

Since issues of money were endlessly present in Marx's life, his financial difficulties gave rise to remarks that were not very kind toward, for instance, Lassalle, and led him to other anti-Semitic notations about a number of his debtors. Speaking, for instance, about his financial problems with Bamberger father and son, who lent him money, Marx writes, "I was very sorry I couldn't box the ears of those two Jews for keeping me waiting in that shameless way."[138] Elsewhere he often mentions the banker Bamberger: "I touched the little Jew Bamberger for 2 pounds,"[139] an influential member of the "synagogue of the stock exchange";[140] he makes fun of bankers from whom he borrows money, like Bamberger or Spielmann: "Spielmann always turns me away, saying to me in his nasal Jewish whine: 'Didn't get a receipt.'"[141] Always violent toward his detractors, Marx attacks the author of a text that was strongly critical of him in the following words: "Its author . . . is a Yid by the name of Meier, a relative of the *City-Proprietor*, an English Yid by the name of Levy. That is why these two individuals have reason to reproach Heine for being a baptized Jew. Enclosed is the last letter from Isaac, which you should keep like a rare document. How objective the man is! We should meditate on the malleability of this Jew who is the least Greek of all the Wasserpolacks."[142] And, in a very solemn letter addressed, in Berlin, to the law councilor Weber, Marx once again denounces "a Jew by the name of Meier."[143] His friend Engels sometimes outdoes Marx in this kind of anti-Semitic vocabulary, derides the stock-exchange Jews, continually waxes ironic at the expense of the "Yids," the "Yuds," the "Isaacs," "Itzigs," "Ephraims," and other "Polish Schmuhls": he also speaks about the Schiller Institute in Manchester as "a purely Jewish institute where a hellish noise reigns. . . . It's always the same with the Jews: If in the beginning they thanked God for giving them a Schiller Institute, scarcely have they entered it when, how to say it, it's no longer enough for them, and they want to build a big house, a real temple of Moses where History can be relegated."[144] Even if, unlike Marx, Engels explicitly condemned anti-Semitism many times, he used the same number of unkind phrases and was silent, like his friend, on the poverty of the Jewish proletariat, about whom he didn't breathe a word.[145] The fact that such uncomplimentary remarks were in vogue at the time within the worker's movement doesn't change anything. Ruge, Marx's companion in arms and a longtime friend, sees in him "a very mean guy and a brazen Jew," nicknames him "the rabbi" and dares to write that the Jews are "the maggots in the cheese of Christianity, who feel so comfortable in their calculating, swindling skins that they don't believe in anything and, for exactly that reason, remain Jewish."[146] Marx constantly makes this anti-Semitic vocabulary and imagery his own.

This litany of cut-and-dried phrases ridiculing the supposed failings of the Jews, always presented with a capital J in order better to designate a collective identitarian membership that he denies as a people but that in his mind diminishes the very possibility of their individual emancipation within German society, cannot be received with indifference. Most of the official biographers, anxious to lessen the impact of one of these declarations, remain almost totally silent about this aspect of Marx's writings, or purely and simply deny any anti-Semitic element in them.[147] Considering the tonality of the accusations formulated by Marx, his permanent denigration of the ways of behavior or thought of Jewish theoreticians, socialist activists, or bankers reveals an impression of irritation that easily leads to indignation, any and all methods are used to minimize their significance, trying to see in these phrases merely a way of expressing himself against the Jews taken just as useful "scapegoats" and not having any consequence.[148] In France, this censorship is so strongly exercised that it eliminates from the official editions Marx's phrases about "the nigger-Jew Lassalle" or others in the same mould;[149] there is censorship too when the text of *Capital* was mutilated to avoid discrepancies that were too unbearable. When Marx writes that "the capitalist knows very well that all goods, whatever their appearance and smell, belong too in the faith and truth of money," he ends this observation by adding "of Jews with circumcised souls." This remark is in the German edition of *Capital* but not in the French edition, which probably judged this passage too shocking.[150] An attentive reading could find many instances of prudent censorship meant to avoid shocking a reader who is usually indulgent toward Marx's excesses, taking them with a certain good-humored tolerance, a reader the publisher is constantly careful, moreover, to reassure by minimizing, from the height of his authority, the occurrence of such statements.[151]

Though in Germany and the Anglo-Saxon world a number of biographies and articles dealing with Marx's work approach this surprising and uncharitable aspect of his writings head-on and don't hesitate to describe with care the vocabulary used by the great revolutionary, disciple of the Enlightenment, and emancipator of humanity,[152] in France, as a general rule, the most orthodox specialists on Marx's work are almost all silent on this aspect of his correspondence and devote barely a few passages to *On 'The Jewish Question'* passing lightly over the main points, quotes at the ready, on the mercantile spirit of Judaism, which simply symbolizes, in their opinion, the spirit of bourgeois society. They prudently abstain from any commentary, let alone any critique.[153] Some, however, heartily approve.[154] Others emphasize the "frankly Judeophobic tendency" of Marx, who "felt a certain resentment against the religion of his ancestors," but they still think, curiously, that the first part of *On 'The Jewish Question'* is "Judeophilic" since "Marx's anti-Judaism has nothing specifically Judeophobic about it."[155] While an Althusserian structuralism was triumphing in France that paid little attention to the will of protagonists and even less to their values, and that reduced history to determined contradictory positions taken in a mode of production, and while a Marxism hostile to humanism, to the protagonist, to his values, to religions, and to cultures was being enthusiastically received on the Parisian scene, the commentators of *On 'The Jewish Question'* no longer felt the embarrassment that Marx's strange locutions produce. In their eyes, the concept of Judaism that comes to light in Marx simply represents a convincing "metonymy" for bourgeois society, and they add that "the anti-Judaism that has to some extent become anti-Semitism, in Hess and Marx, is one of those fortunate effects that facilitate the transition to communism."[156] "The asceticism of historical materialism" advances here, as we see, in strange ways. But above all else, why in the world privilege the Jews to such an extent in the metonymical choice?[157] Wouldn't other people besides the Jews that arouse less anguish and prejudice have been a more suitable choice? In the growing anti-Semitic and reactionary context of German society of

the time, is this choice of a single metonymy that evokes so many prejudices among all sorts of Christian or socialist anti-Semites the simple
result of the "asceticism of historical materialism" and not the indisputable proof of a real resentment that all anti-Semites share?

Outside of France, fascination with this aspect of Marx's work has
never died out. To tell the truth, it would be difficult to imagine writings more liable to arouse argument, but also scholarly studies, right at
the junction of all the questions about the nature of capitalism and the
state, human emancipation and the issue of the conversion of the Jews,
their assimilation, the self-hatred that was sometimes theirs, their relationship to the state, and about socialism and the anti-Semitism of the
Left. Through all this, there is also the more general problem posed by
the status of a work tainted in this way by the violent expression of prejudices that are to say the least hostile to the Jews and that were expressed
not only in private correspondence but also in the scholarly texts themselves. No one, or almost no one, will deny the significance of Marx's
whole work solely under the pretext that it contains anti-Semitic judgments. Still, the persistent silence about their presence is all the more
surprising since his constant derision aimed at Jewish identity illustrates
all by itself the immense malaise Marx felt faced with the identitarian
question in general, his incomprehension faced with the persistence of
values, cultures, and memories, his refusal to allow a place in history to
factors that do not stem from citizenship alone or, even less, from membership in a given social class.

In this sense, Marx's keen hostility toward the Jews inevitably evokes
his diatribes charged with xenophobia against the Slavs, the Polish, and
so many other peoples doomed to disappear from history since they
themselves are "without history."[158] We have often observed "the Marxist underestimation of nationalism as an independent force." As Isaiah
Berlin too expressed it, "Marx could not explain the origins or nature
of nationalism; he did not make much of it, any more than he did of
the strength of religion as an independent factor within society."[159] To
stress his texts about the Jews amounts to emphasizing his inability to
recognize in them a history, a culture, a future. Presaging the theses of
Sartre, Marx thinks of the Jews as individuals whose contribution to
history is negligible and whose fate is settled already with the help of

their emancipation and/or disappearance. This point of view conforms to Marx's structural-functional logic proceeding by means of contradictions, between modes of production and productive forces, which eliminate values. Ideologies are apprehended other than in the form of reflections, religions, and imagination perceived simply as "phantasmagoria" destined to disappear, stripped of efficacy. In their turn, the new contemporary Marxists, who reintroduce rational choice into classical Marxist theory, nonetheless neglect these questions.[160]

Marx and the Jews, Marx and Judaism, Marx and his Jewish identity, Marx's conversion as well as his father's, estrangement, the inclusion of Marx the individual in the general laws of socioeconomic history, his exogamic marriage, Marx the anti-Hirsch but also anti-Graetz as well as later on the anti-Hess, a unique history suddenly cut short, broken off at the moment when, in Germany, so many Jews were also distancing themselves from their identity in order to assimilate with the bourgeoisie or, on the contrary, struggle against it. A Marx, then, who was more tossed about by history than he thought, a Marx turning his back, like others, on his immediate past in the name of Reason and the Progress of Humanity, indifferent to his personal *Bildung*. An assimilation by revolution nourished on regenerative utopias, dreams of a re-unified Humanity that rejected the individual way followed by so many German Jews. Marx went swiftly from one Chosen People to the other, from the mocked Jewish people to the adored, justified, sanctified proletariat. One can of course argue that "Marx was trying to realize social justice like the old prophets in Israel. But the contrast between Marx's language and the exalted language of Amos shows that Marx was not a great Jewish prophet."[161] Or we can conceive, like Isaac Deutscher, of the "non-Jewish Jew" of whom Marx was a perfect representative, like Rosa Luxemburg, Trotsky, and Freud, Jews who were "very Jewish" by their messianism but who "all found Judaism too narrow, too archaic, too restrictive," and who also thought that "Judaism was essentially a theoretical epitome of market relationships and the faith of merchants."[162] We find it easy to accept messianism, the emancipating social prophecy of an Ernst Bloch or Walter Benjamin, the hope for a world stripped of all forms of alienation. But why so much hatred toward the Jews taken as symbols of the alienation that hinders the

progress of emancipation? Wasn't it enough to distance himself without denigrating, constructing this historical (or utopian) materialism
prophesying the future, a historical logic with no connection to any
sort of religious or cultural fidelity, but without disparaging and mocking the victims of conventional prejudice?

We still have to try to understand the spiteful anger, the excessive-
ness of Marx's anti-Jewish attack, the systematic hunt for the failings,
weaknesses, supposed perversions of the Jews, the almost anti-Semitic
obsession that does not balk at using the most hackneyed clichés, its
persistence revealed by an abundant private correspondence during
many years with Engels, his closest friend, the one who had his complete confidence, the only one to whom he could speak his private convictions and reveal his true thoughts, which he outrageously disguises
when he writes to his other companions in arms. Can one simply find it
"wise to omit" these citations from Marx and Engels written "quickly in
the privacy of their correspondence"?[163] Can one agree that Marx tried
"to purge from his personality the last traces of his own Jewishness so
that he could become a non-Jew and manage to convince others of his
non-Jewishness . . . his aversion of the Jews . . . was profoundly rooted
in his heart until the end of his life"?[164] Has he done everything so that
"the world not perceive him as a Jew"?[165] Some commentators venture
to speak of self-hatred and unhesitatingly practice summary psychoanalysis, the results of which reveal that the son denies the shame of the
converted father by reinforcing, to justify their arguments, the vigor
of the attack waged in so much journalism against converted Jews.
Lewis Feuer, for instance, dwells at length on the attacks of uncommon
violence directed by Marx at Joseph Moses Levy, the very liberal and
committed director of the *Daily Telegraph* who refused to change his
name. Marx seems to attack this person all the more because he might
be jealous of his success; Feuer focuses on Marx's malicious and unfair
accusation that Levy trimmed his personality with the help of a *y* that
replaces a too-significant *i* whereas his face and the shape of his nose
clearly designate his true personality;[166] for Feuer, the *y* in place of the *i*
inevitably evokes the move from Heschel to Heinrich, an evasion all the
more vain since Heinrich Marx as well as his son Karl themselves presented, according to Eleanor, easily identifiable physical traits. Marx's

famously "swarthy" appearance evoked the image of the "Moor," a nickname given to Karl Marx by both Engels and Marx's daughters, and that directly emphasized his eastern, un-Christian origins. In the 1850s, his daughters Jenny, Laura, and Eleanor in fact often called their father "the Moor."[167] Although Engels for a long time used the phrase "My dear Marx," it was only later on, beginning at the end of the 1850s and until the time their correspondence ends, that he repeatedly addresses his comrade in a familiar way by calling him "Dear Moor."[168] Is this eastern identity so perceptible that Marx wanted to reject it as a sign of an incomplete assimilation, the persistence of a difference that limited his integration into the proletariat or else . . . into Germany? Is that what accounts for an intellectual, internal logic that led to the rejection of any identity other than a socioeconomic one, and that pushed Marx to break with his own memory?

Eleanor, who physically resembled her father but who, unlike him, would later on proclaim her "pride in being Jewish," gave lectures in Yiddish to the proletarian women of Whitechapel and during a conference of the Internationale told a delegate known for his contribution to Jewish literature, "We Jews must band together."[169] She emphasized that her father had a boundless love for his own father (Heinrich) whose photograph he carefully kept with him until he died; this beloved/rejected father looked like his son, who "distinctly [was the image of] a handsome Jewish type." The three Marx generations must have shown a very marked physical identity. Marx's "Jewish" aspect was well known. In 1842, a person who financially supported the publication of the *Rheinische Zeitung*, the Cologne paper edited by Marx, described him in the following way, in the year that preceded the appearance of *On 'The Jewish Question'*: "Karl Marx, from Trier, was a twenty-four-year old man of strong constitution whose black, thick hair sprang over his cheeks, his nose, his ears. . . . He had a feverish Jewish insight."[170] In the present day, a biographer like Otto Ruhle can still write, "No one could forget that Marx was born a Jew, since not only was his face of a very marked Hebraic type, but his entire silhouette presented an openly Semitic aspect. . . . The reader cannot escape the feeling that Marx conspicuously showed his opposition to Judaism . . . but someone who devoted so many efforts to showing that he himself was not

Jewish must have had reasons for being anxious lest he be thought of as such."[171] For some, it is because Marx was ashamed of this somber, dark, swarthy appearance, of the Jewish aspect of his features, that he projected onto Lassalle this image of blackness from which he felt he was protected by his conversion, his adherence to German society, and his marriage, invalidating at the same time any rapprochement, which he deemed improper, with his friend who had remained Jewish, whom he denigrated all the more since he was anxious to point out what distinguished him from *that* blackness, *that* Orientalism, and to keep silent about his own "nasal Jewish style that sustained, whatever the issue, his own rhetoric, even in his phraseology that attacked the Jews."[172]

A Marx who was ashamed of his past, of his father's conversion as well as his own, of his identity, of his very appearance? Some immediately endorse this point of view, which although not devoid of interest is still weak, open to all sorts of misconstructions and the most extreme interpretations. Others challenge this psychoanalytical point of view that probes depths not accessible to the biographer and instead link the self-hatred exhibited by Marx either to rejection of the father or to rejection of a mother who was more attached to Judaism and who kept control of the heritage her son coveted.[173] They confine themselves to a Marx who was considered as being too vulnerable to the prejudices of his time; thus Salomon Bloom refuses to sense in *Capital* "the righteous breath of the Hebraic mind" and thinks that "it is more loyal to think that Marx absorbed the dominant prejudices of his time without much independence of mind than to assert that he transformed the Jews into scapegoats for his own frustrations."[174] In a way, the dominant ideology of the time was so convinced of the total "Judaization" of German society, of the triumph of the Jews expressed by the absolute reign of money, that Marx himself made it the central principle of his analyses, to the point of hypostasizing an eternal Jewish spirit, from the Middle Ages to modernity, impervious to any historical transformation, which nothing could resist, emerging from the medieval ghetto and "infecting" all future society without resistance, without any barrier able to protect it as it did before, hence penetrating the innermost depths of society.[175] According to this theory, Marx, the theoretician of scientific socialism, was thus content to make himself the echo of the prejudices of his time, a paradoxical acknowledgment for a thinker so attached to dismantling the dominant ideologies, to seeing in them the reflection of social interests. From this stand-point at least, Marx, the destroyer of superstructures, actually shared the values of his contemporaries, was complicit in an identical disap-proval of Jews and Judaism,[176] both of which he considered similarly "repugnant"; even though he was a scholar hungry for any form of knowledge, greedy to stretch his bibliographical sources to deal ever further with the most diverse subjects, he ignored the slightest scraps of Judaism.[177]

Marx made his own the dominant classes' anti-Semitic prejudices, which reached even the socialist milieus, and was supremely uninter-ested, even though he himself was so attentive to the history of his time in its various aspects, in the calamity that struck the Jews of Damascus, caught in the torment of accusations of ritual murder, which were also directed at Jews from different regions in Germany, in 1810, 1834, and 1847–48.[178] The fact that Marx claimed that the persecution of the Jews in Moldavia "doesn't seem to be so terrible" shows the extent of his indifference.[179] Marx also revealed himself to be deaf to the poverty of the Jewish proletariat, to its sufferings, to the persecutions it endured; he loftily ignored the violent anti-Semitic demonstrations of his time that affected even the most assimilated German Jews, whether they were bourgeois or proletarian, and far from coming to their aid, never silenced his acrimony, his rejections of the Jews, which was frequently expressed in the language of the most physiological racist theories that were already spreading in this second half of the nineteenth century throughout Germany and France. The fact that Marx intended, in his youth, to write a petition in favor of the Jews of Cologne for whom he desired "the maximum accommodation in the Christian state";[180] that he wrote a few sympathetic lines on the miseries of the Jews of Jerusa-lem in an article for the *New York Tribune* on April 15, 1854;[181] that he had a few Jewish friends; that he in turn became the target of recur-rent anti-Semitic attacks stemming, both in the past and today, from re-actionary forces but also from the socialist movement; that Proudhon, Ruge, Eugen Dühring, or Bakunin saw in him a Jew laden with all the faults of a Jew—all that does not in the least change or diminish the amplitude of his attack, which advocates the indispensable and ineluctable end of the Jews.[182]

With Marx took shape the radicalism that is so often considered Jewish; he was unconsciously a bearer of prophecy that he himself rejected. With this messianic figure of the revolutionary perceived in any case as Jewish, this rebel who rose up in the name of universalism against all injustices and devoted himself to work for the liberation of humanity, with him and following Marx Leon Trotsky, Rosa Luxemburg, Victor Adler, Otto Bauer, and so many others,[183] a lineage of thinkers was established that, contrary to Moses Hess, deliberately ignored the Jewish dimension of their engagement with universal liberation. In this sense, just as it is paradoxical to argue that "the true Jewish Marxism is embodied in the Jewish religion that Marx abandoned in his youth,"[184] a religion concerned above all with social justice but nonetheless rejected by Marx and other revolutionaries after him as "repugnant," just as one could not see these radicals as modern representatives of Jewish messianism any more than one could see them as unwitting rabbis who in their own way practiced the art of midrash on texts of political economy, thus showing an "unconscious" Jewish piety. We would have to make an almost impossible effort of the imagination to see in Marx a distant reincarnation of Rabbi Isaac Luria, who, like him, traveled in search of the *Shekhinah* (the presence of God) exiled in a world from which every trace of alienation would finally disappear, a world from which the proletariat would in its turn have surmounted its situation of exile in the heart of capitalism. Marx as symbol of the Jews of the diaspora,[185] Marx as author of a new form of *Haggadah* transposed to the scale of the entire world![186] It's easy to explain everything by exile. But exile does not imply the renunciation, the transfigurations that would come to compensate for unconquerable "revulsions." Exile opens up to the Other, is enriched by the presence and culture of the Other.

Beliefs, but also the idea of a nation, lose all reality in this world that obeys mechanical laws determined solely by the logic of political economy, insensitive to the values of individuals other than that of their social belonging. Marxist materialism represents a positivism anxious for scientific analyses of the laws regulating the social system. Marx the individual has no more past, no more memory of a history that is his own. His incessant sarcasms are proof of this. We can leave the conclusion to Isaiah Berlin: "What does seem clear is that Marx was a man of strong will and decisive action, who decided once and for all to destroy within himself the source of the doubts, uneasiness and self-questioning which tended to torment men like Börne, Heine, Lassalle and a good many others, including the founders of reform Judaism, and—until he resolved the problem in a Zionist sense—the first German communist, Moses Hess, whose origins and intellectual formation resembled Marx's own. Marx contemptuously swept this question out of the way and decided to treat it as unreal."[187] Or rather, we might add, Marx decided that Humanity should no longer face "the Jewish Question."

*Two*   Émile David Durkheim:
The Memory of Masada


An attentive reading of the work of Émile Durkheim, one of the founding fathers of sociology who won acclaim for this discipline in France, can be surprising. In *Suicide*, an essential work that establishes the foundations of methodological reasoning in the social sciences, throughout his meticulous analysis, we encounter empirical examples that are surprising. For instance, to refute the general interpretation focusing on mimicry that was advanced by Gabriel Tarde, extremely popular in his time, Durkheim curiously uses the example of Masada. Following the text of Flavius Josephus, *The History of the War of the Jews Against the Romans*, which he quotes twice, he emphasizes that "during the assault on Jerusalem some of the besieged committed suicide with their own hands. More especially forty Jews, having taken refuge underground, decided to choose death and killed one another": he deduces from this that suicide does not always obey merely the "contagious" imitation of a psychological nature but that these "mass suicides" sprang from an "idea . . . developed by the whole group which, in a situation desperate for all, collectively decides upon death." Even if Durkheim also alludes, in a more cursory way, to similar cases that occur, for instance, among the Peruvians or the Mexicans, we remain struck by this reference to Masada that comes so naturally to his pen.[1] Raised in our day to the dimension of a historical event endowed with a strong symbolism to the point of becoming almost a sentimental icon, Masada represents a classic case of contemporary reinvention of a past that has become mythical:[2] it is all the more remarkable since Durkheim mentions it. It alone testifies to Durkheim's interest in Jewish history when we know that Masada was at the time a little-known event, not very present in the consciousness of his contemporaries, never celebrated or commemorated, absent from the classic texts of Jewish tradition. The Masada

Society, devoted to the study of its history, wasn't created in London until the 1920s, and we had to wait till almost the present day for the works of the archaeologist Yigal Yadin finally to raise this collective suicide to the rank of an event that ought to be remembered.

The presence of examples like Masada taken from Jewish history in the austere work of Durkheim the republican, the figure who embodies the virtues of the French Republic and the secular ideal, has unfortunately continued to remain in obscurity and has not attracted the attention of the numerous commentators who almost always neglect the Jewish dimension of the sociologist's work. Some even come to distort its significance by keeping silent about essential passages that are sometimes deliberately amputated, with a quotation cut off, if they happen to cite, in a fundamental text, an example that is nonetheless highly symbolic in Durkheim's mind, drawn from Jewish history and from Jewish thought.[3] Very rare are those who, concerning his book *Suicide*, conjecture that "it could have come from personal experience—from a remembered fragment of the Talmud, from an intuition born of personal loneliness and marginality, a scrap of experience in Paris. Who can be sure?,"[4] or who note the reality of this connection by wondering if *Suicide* "might also be a reflection, triggered and dramatized by the Dreyfus Affair, about the difference of the ethical aptitudes requisite in the soldier and in the academic, a way of convincing himself that Dreyfus is not a coward when he lets himself be accused . . . a reflection silently pursued for a long time about the Jews' means of integration in contemporary France," a remark that is all the more important since "a compilation and an index of examples (historical, literary) would be extremely enlightening, since they are an aid for reflection and reveal certain hidden sources of the problematic. The presence-absence of Masada especially should be stressed." Nothing leads us to suppose, however, that it is a question here of a "hidden" source of the general problematic, even if it is innovative and enriching to allow that *Suicide* "is one of the moments when Jewish culture and tradition return in Durkheim's consciousness."[5]

This original and welcome reading of Durkheim that deals with the Jewish dimension implicit in his work has the advantage of going against the most current interpretations of the thinking of the founder of French sociology. Thus, even in our day, some people argue that "during the Dreyfus Affair, Durkheim rushed into the battle in the name of moral, not political demands, not at all as a Jew."[6] That his moral demands led him to enter the controversy under the aegis of the League of the Rights of Man and the Citizen, of which he would become the secretary in Bordeaux, is unquestionable. Yet how can we be certain of the absence of any political consideration in this convinced republican who favored a form of reformist socialism while the nationalist leagues hostile to the ideals of '89 were threatening? And who will ever know if it wasn't, in his innermost being, as a Jew linked to the family of Captain Dreyfus that he so passionately joined the fray that there were demonstrations against him, of an open and virulent anti-Semitism, which he courageously confronted?[7] Why is there a similar affirmation unequivocally expressed? It seems incontestable that the sociologist of "social facts considered as things," the republican concerned with positivism and secularism, the scholar attached to a rigorously methodological approach stripped of any preconceived notions, could also be preoccupied with his own identity, his particular place in the history of France at the moment at the end of the century that saw nationalist and anti-Semitic forces unleashed, recruiting from the extreme Right as well as from the extreme Left, even among the republicans themselves.[8] In this sense, many commentators think that all of Durkheim's work constitutes a reflection on implementing an assimilation that implies the disappearance of previous identities. As proof of his impenitent "Jacobinism," they refer, for instance, to this phrase in *The Division of Labor in Society*: "It is always a laborious operation to uproot habits that time has fixed and organized in us. . . . One generation is not enough to undo the work of generations, to put a new man in place of the old one."[9] Durkheim, the intellectual guide for the academics of the Republic, the sociologist of education, would thus have struggled with all his might so that the school would hasten this republican assimilation and establish a new form of collective identity distinct from past traditions, habits, and ways of thinking. High priest of national education, he also settled the question of his own Jewish heritage, which had long been relegated to the past. Arnaldo Momigliano was in agreement with this and remained so attached in Italy to his Jewish identity: in his opinion, "in the French cultural and philosophical framework," Durkheim and Marcel Mauss "elaborated a concept of the individual completely distanced from biblical tradition, and preferred to consider the masks of primitive societies as the distant precursors of the Kantian conception of personal responsibility. Evidently, we cannot understand Durkheim's and Mauss's thinking without asking ourselves questions about the Jewish cultural context they came from."[10] From then on, Durkheimian sociology would omit any reference to particular allegiances and would be radically incapable of accounting for the forms of engagement and solidarity that pervade citizenship, even in modern society with its clear division of labor, including in the public space. Still, these days, some people do come to the point of seeing in Durkheim a precursor of an Anglo-Saxon style of multiculturalism, respectful of all forms of identitarian adherence, thus justifying the maintaining of a collective Jewish identity.[11]

Each to his own Durkheim, then. As if assimilation ineluctably implied the renunciation of all faith or, conversely, as if any memory of a recent past supposed absolute adherence to a communitarian multiculturalism. As if there were only one way, for all intellectuals, whatever the personality or their values, to be a Dreyfussard: the way of the Enlightenment and of 1789, of Reason and Humanism. So many deceptive contradictions! How can one cast doubt, in such a simplistic way, ignoring Durkheim's personal values, on the austerity of the scholar by discovering, with statistics at the ready, that he "made a good marriage" with Julie Dreyfus, whose father Henry, along with his two brothers Salomon and Moyse, had founded a small smelting works in copper and iron?[12] Isn't that common to all upper-class members of the Republic at the time, and why compare, from this standpoint, Durkheim only with Lucien Lévy-Bruhl, Henri Bergson, and Léon Brunschvicg? Why compare this good marriage only with that of Captain Dreyfus? Is it really this single element that brings them together? Does marrying a woman whose father was the head of a small foundry, does receiving a dowry of 100,000 francs, make one less of a positivist sociologist? How does this alliance sully the austerity of the scholar little prone to extravagance or ostentatious expenses? Can one convincingly argue that "these economic and social givens perceptibly modify the image of rigorousness of the founder of academic sociology" or even that "Durkheim is implicated in the economic interests of society"? Can one see in him the figure "of a small-time boss bent on increasing his capital" merely from the fact that he answered his wife, who was reproaching him for working too much: "You've got to do things properly"?[13] What do these people want to prove? That Durkheim became more Jewish by entering the Jewish petit-bourgeoisie as a way of social climbing? That he embraced the interests of capital by defending the reformist form of Saint-Simonian socialism contradictory to the class struggle, which might infringe upon his own inheritance, which had become consequential? That his entire body of work, from *The Division of Labor in Society* up through his lectures on *Socialism* or even perhaps his increasingly marked interest in religious matters that haunted the last period of his life, is only the transposition of his interests in class, his desire to defend a social order based on the inequality of classes? Greatly exaggerating such a point of view, isn't it like the proposition that some people advance when they think that Durkheim, the son of a rabbi, defender of Captain Dreyfus, friend of Jaurès, severe critic of the pathological division of labor, source of hereditary transmission of property as a source of unacceptable inequalities, nevertheless represented a precursor to the Vichy regime and its falling into step with class conflict through the intervention of an authoritarian corporatism?[14] Durkheim is a Jewish small-business boss, or even worse, in this view. For others, on the contrary, Durkheim perfectly illustrates the figure of the "Jewish statesman," of someone "mad about the Republic" devoted to building the Third Republic, a high-ranking civil servant, a passionate defender of the ideals of the French Revolution, of rationalism as bringer of universalist progress, but who still remains, within his private space, a Jew anxious to preserve his own identity.[15] A boss propagating tranquility in society, or a scrupulous civil servant of the meritocratic Republic?

Another simplistic and clichéd contrast—that of the assimilated, republican, scholarly Jew, versus the Jew as prophet, bearer of a religious mission. Thus, for Hubert Bourguin:

> The face emerged, pale, ascetic, broad domed forehead, short beard, large moustache, nose of a rabbi, but the entire dry, hard face magnificently lit up by two deep eyes, of an intense and gentle power, that imposed respect, attention, even submission, and, at the same time, required in others the same serious simplicity and naked sincerity they saw them before them, sovereign, imperious, inspiring confidence. . . .

His entire physical being, his entire moral person attested to it: he was a priest more than a scholar. He was a hieratic figure. His mission was religious.[16]

Durkheim as prophet, as his former student Georges Davy attests: "His ascetic profile, his emaciated face, his decisive gestures, his eloquence and his gaze were imposing, provoking the enthusiasm of fascinated listeners as well as the terror of desperate candidates. How can one fathom the tender heart and uneasy soul this inspired prophet hid?"[17] A Durkheim that Sylvain Lévi, professor at the Collège de France so close to Durkheimian milieus, also describes as "an ardent, passionate, generous soul, distinctly real at the same time. A true Jewish type, for, whether one regrets it or is thankful for it, one can't find a match for him today."[18] For his part, the philosopher René Maublanc mentions "his hooked nose like that of a Jew . . . he looked like a rabbi who was also a mystic."[19]

The many faces of Durkheim, the destroyer of all preconceptions, who nonetheless took care to remind his interlocutors, "Don't forget that I am the son of a rabbi."[20] Did this son of a rabbi turn away from the path of his father, Moïse Durkheim, rabbi of Épinal, to fulfill his father's implicit expectation and better realize his father's scientific ambitions, which had been disappointed? Did David Émile Durkheim, the youngest child in the family, transform into a Moïse of sociology, a supporter of social assimilation as a way toward modernity "without rejecting the values or personality of the father but only his profession"? Did he show that he was convinced that "the necessities of a modern world imply that the rabbi abandon his archaic and particularist habits in order to reappear in the form of the universalist scholar"?[21] Did his absence of "marginality" encourage him to make himself the spokesman for universalist positions like those endorsed by Spinoza, radically rejecting Judaism like his illustrious predecessor in order to imagine a sacralized society, not nature this time, in the form of a monistic totality?[22] Did he take on the traits of a secularized rabbi, intending to restore order and harmony to a society deprived of solidarity? Did he represent a new Moses reaching the promised land that is the sociological continent as place of reinvention of the Covenant between men and men,[23] a prophet also concerned with justice who in his turn wants to leave the Egypt of authoritarianism, and injustice, by this time denouncing the ano-

mie of a contemporary world that has become inhuman,[24] the author
par excellence who "encountered the Jewish perspective of modernity"
and symbolized "the modern Jew as an *insider*"?[25] Although it seems
an exaggeration to think that, implicitly or explicitly, despite the positivist aim of its author, "any work by Durkheim is essentially Jewish,"
letting a real "enigma" persist,[26] it probably won't resolve the problem
by arguing, in an equally absolute way, that "there is little to gain, in
terms of *historical* knowledge about Jews or Durkheim, from attempts
to attribute essentially Jewish traits either to Jews or to Durkheim. . . .
Durkheim was not in effect a modern marrano, a kind of secret Jew
hiding under the cloak of conversion to the values of Third Republic liberalism. He was not secretly trying to express his Jewish identity
under the guise of his seemingly secular sociology of religion." That
we should reject any essentialist concept seems a good solution. But to
add that "throughout nearly all of his life, Durkheim seemed to have
resisted identification of himself as Jewish" constitutes an assertion that
poses more problems than it resolves and that, formulated in that way,
is untrue; moreover, to compare Durkheim to Marc Bloch, considering
that the latter best embodies Durkheim's ideal, is scarcely convincing,
since Bloch, the great historian of *Feudal Society*, distanced himself so
fundamentally from Jewish history.[27] That the intellectual biography
of Émile Durkheim that is still the most reliable reference book, the
biography by Steven Lukes,[28] remains almost completely silent on the
Jewish dimension of his life and work also does nothing but emphasize the almost inextricable nature of this question, which leads to such
contrary evaluations. The Jewish issue seems iconoclastic to a number
of Durkheimians anxious to construct an objective science of society
necessarily detached from any simplifying preconceived notion, which
is unacceptable in that, for some commentators, "The Jewish origins of
Durkheim and of some of his associates did not have any consequence
for their academic careers."[29] In the same sense, Étienne Halphen,
Émile Durkheim's own grandson, thinks that his grandfather "was always a-religious with a capital A; all those people who wanted to see in
his work whiffs of Judaism are taking the wrong path."[30] Who should
we follow, then? Why not adopt the hypothesis of E. A. Tiryakian according to which "Durkheim, who was an assimilated Jew, was in that
ambiguous situation of being assimilated but at the same time *uprooted*,

like the characters in Barrès. So he rehabilitated 'primitive' forms as the fundamental forms of social life."[31]

The major Jewish newspapers of the time were also indecisive in their interpretation of Durkheim's life. When he was buried in the Jewish section of the Montparnasse cemetery, his tombstone bore an old inscription in Hebrew that has unfortunately become illegible. The *Archives israélites* wrote, "Although no longer practicing Judaism, he remained Jewish in his heart, and our oppressed brothers could count on his devoted assistance. Durkheim had lost a son on the field of honor. As a member of the Commission of Review for Residence Visas for Foreigners, he had recently accepted the presidency of the Historical Commission of Research on the Role of French Israelites During the War. His high patronage was assured for all projects intended to shed light on Jewish merit."[32] The *Archives israélites* was unquestionably proud of paying tribute to someone who constantly defended "Jewish merit," as it did. But it is difficult to know what it means by this, since, though Durkheim certainly made himself an advocate for republican meritocracy, he never explicitly defended "Jewish merit" in the sense of the *Archives*. On the same page, this paper also basks in the glory of the "merit" of the deputy Ignace, named undersecretary of state at the Ministry of War; of L. L. Klotz, who remained minister of finances in the new Clemenceau government; and, finally, of Georges Mandel, the faithful servant of Clemenceau, named private secretary to the president of the council—so many people who, "born in Judaism," as this paper writes, doubtless practiced their religion even less than Durkheim, who did still remain attached to a certain amount of ritual. Although the *Archives israélites* sees Durkheim as a Jew on the honor roll of both the Republic and of Franco-Judaism, that is not the opinion of *L'Univers israélite*, which devoted to him, at the time of his death, two full pages. In this article, Durkheim is no longer portrayed as being "Jewish in his heart," or as having honored "Jewish merit," but rather as a highly respectable scholar who served only "science and country." Unlike the *Archives*, *L'Univers israélite* does not close its eyes to Durkheim's lack of religious practice: it even draws conclusions from this that are strongly negative with regard to the final significance of his work. The article begins with a detailed description of Durkheim's career, mentions his connections with Louis Liard, director of higher education and a key person in republican politics at the university, recalls the titles of Durkheim's main works, emphasizes the interest of his journal *L'Année sociologique*, and thinks he "can be regarded as the leader of the French sociological school." Then *L'Univers israélite* goes on to describe Durkheim's contribution to propaganda during the war, mentions the death of his son, André Durkheim, and severely condemns the statements of Senator Gaudin de Villaine who denounced the father of French sociology, in the course of a Senate session, as "an agent of German Kriegsministerium," and criticized his role on the Commission of Review for Residence Visas for Foreigners. *L'Univers* notes, "We owed the memory of Durkheim a reminder of this outrage." After listing these public activities, the paper adds:

> Mr. Durkheim, who always kept away from Judaism, on this occasion learned about the existence of a Jewish question; he learned it better as he became interested in the fate of immigrant Jews faced with a campaign of ill-will, despite the number of volunteers the Jews provided at the beginning of the war. He wanted to bring about a rapprochement between these Jews and the French Israelites, and presided over a Committee that had undertaken to achieve this goal. At the Committee for Information and Action for Neutral Jews, of which he was also a member, he at times reproached himself publicly for his past indifference with regard to his ethnic brothers who suffered as Jews. He saw no other solution to the Jewish question than the emancipation and assimilation of Jews, and in a letter to a paper he declared that the Russian revolution had liquidated the Jewish question. Finally, Mr. Durkheim had taken an active interest in the foundation of the Historical Commission for Documentary Research Related to the History of the Israelites of France During the War.
>
> Those who knew Mr. Durkheim assure us that the man was equal to the scholar and the citizen: he was a firm, upright character, of a scrupulous strictness and an inflexible probity. It is painful to us to think that this son of a rabbi did not know the religion of his fathers, that this social scientist could not appreciate the social nature of Judaism, that this scholar and pedagogue of Jewish origin probably contributed to alienating more than one Jewish intellectual from Judaism.
>
> These regrets are added to those called forth by the death of a man who served and honored science and his country.[33]

This text, which has also remained curiously neglected, reveals a public awareness of the author of *Rules of Sociological Method* who, in front of all the members of the Committee of Information and Action for Neutral Jews, "reproached" himself for his past "indifference" with respect to "his ethnic brothers who were suffering as Jews." Does this observation contradict the statement of the *Archives israélites* according to which "he remained Jewish in his heart"? An indifferent Jew, or a Jew in his heart? To tell the truth, probably neither one nor the other, but a Jew nonetheless. Can one actually endorse the assertion of *L'Univers israélite* according to which the anti-Semitic remarks formulated against him by Gaudin de Villaine at last revealed to him "on this occasion the existence of a Jewish question"? That would ignore the fact that Durkheim declared how he remembered the anti-Semitic demonstrations which he witnessed in his early adolescence in Lorraine, during the Franco-German war; that would ignore the anti-Semitic campaigns led against him in Bordeaux during the Dreyfus Affair; finally that would disregard all the texts, all the letters that show Durkheim to be horrified by the persistence of anti-Semitism in republican France. His body of work remains: at what point can one state that "this son of a rabbi did not know the religion of his fathers, that this sociologist did not appreciate the social nature of Judaism"? As we shall see, an attentive reading of his work reveals that this is not at all the case, that Durkheim was far from ignoring Judaism, and that he also showed himself to be aware of its specific role in the organization of society. Finally the regret remains that, in the mind of *L'Univers israélite*, almost equals a condemnation of the Durkheimian project itself, judged by its results: "This scholar and pedagogue of Jewish origin probably contributed to alienating more than one Jewish intellectual from Judaism." Is Durkheim, heir to a lineage of eight generations of rabbis, whose mother and wife also came from traditional Jewish milieus, simply "of Jewish origin"? Do they mean to say that he was "born Jewish" before "alienating himself from Judaism" by undertaking to construct a discipline—sociology—whose success was such that he contributed to "alienating more than one Jewish intellectual from Judaism"? The conclusion seems obvious: his sociology was totally deprived of any Jewish dimension; his intellectual project was even eminently opposed to Judaism; he eroded beliefs and dealt a mortal blow to Jewish studies.

Some commentators think, in the same vein, that it is indeed "the failure of the science of Judaism that Durkheimian sociology establishes. . . . The central thesis of Durkheim's sociology, which makes religion the divinized form of society, reflects the transition of a large number of Jewish intellectuals, exposed to a neo-Kantian rationalism, from a concept of a world still imprinted with religiosity to a secularized vision of society. . . . This divinization of society at the end of Durkheim's theses on religion reflects the practice of the French Jewish community at the end of the nineteenth century. In the diminished place henceforth reserved for individual belief, which stems from a collective belief, we find in effect the expression of the privatization of Judaism, and its fusion with a republican moral code."[34] This once again makes Durkheimian sociology the grave of Judaism, the special moment when the triumph of republican ideals leads to the divinization of society alone, the triumph of the secular fatal to religion and to transcendence. That Durkheimism threatens the lasting quality of the Munks, the Darmesteters, and the Derenbourgs is unarguable: from Durkheim to Mauss, Lévy-Bruhl, Lévi-Strauss, or Raymond Aron, the great intellectuals "of Jewish origin" turned away from the science of Judaism to focus their attention on the social logic of primitive or modern societies, radically distancing Judaism from the field of their study or their teaching at the Collège de France or at the Sorbonne. Still, a number of them encountered Judaism in the course of their studies and also preserved links with the Jews of their time. Moreover, the privatization of Judaism that followed the triumph of the republican public space does not imply its disappearance. If many Jews of the Third Republic distanced themselves from the more orthodox religious aspects, the vast majority of them still remained Jewish, even if that meant giving to this identity multiple significations. It was actually the Republic, the framework within which Durkheim's sociology flourished, that made collective beliefs illegitimate and rejected their presence in the public space. Deprived of an institutionalized church, the Jews took refuge more than others in their innermost being and worked enthusiastically toward reinforcing a republican public space. In this sense, one could argue that it was not Durkheim but the Republic itself that brought an end, in its universalist and rationalist vision, to the "science of Judaism" that was flourishing in imperial Germany hostile to secularism, before being reborn later on in the United States in particular, a democracy with a heterogeneous public space and a nonsecular society open to the religious in its collective form as well as to collective identities of a communitarian kind. Still, the acknowledgment was there: the science of Judaism would largely vanish when Durkheim, heir to so many rabbis, came to the fore. The concomitance was demonstrated—but Durkheimian sociology was not the cause of this disappearance, which stemmed largely from the internal logic of French republican society.

As Perrine Simon-Nahum argues convincingly:

> The similarity of themes around which the defense of Judaism in the 1860s and the defense of the Republic at the end of the century were organized should not conceal the transformation that the values of the science of Judaism underwent in its transition to the political dimension. . . . The Dreyfus Affair—and more generally the defense of Republican Judaism—provides a rationale for the disappearance of Jewish studies as an intellectual trend, and explains the causes for it. . . . For the first time, the values defined for half a century as the essence of Judaism, namely universalism and rationalism, have become, with James Darmesteter and Bernard Lazare, justice and equality, and must be defended on a concrete level. It is this transition from the realm of abstraction and science to that of politics that, by defining a complete secularization of issues that used to be linked to the sacred, shows the disappearance of the science of Judaism as an intellectual trend, a victim of the [Dreyfus] Affair.[35]

For her, since Dreyfusism and Durkheimism have almost become "synonymous" with each other, it is indeed Durkheim and the new code of ethics that he advocated that seal the fate of the science of Judaism.[36] The hypothesis is attractive, but it takes on all its meaning only if we conceive of the relationships of Durkheim with Judaism solely in terms of "divorce."[37] However, if sociology unarguably reduces the field of the religious for the sake of the social, Durkheim, in his personal life as well as in his professional life, did not confine his Jewish identity merely to the private sphere; he remained concerned, even if only secondarily, with its significance. Although he did not share the erudition of the scholars specializing in the science of Judaism, he was still preoccupied by the questions they raised. As the theoretician of the Republic, a zealous propagandist of both secularization and secularism, having sociologized the indispensable fraternity between the citizens of the Republic, and having justified the domination of a strong government sheltered from the intemperate and passionate rage of groups within civil society, a government embodying the republican ideal—none of all that, however, transforms him into an avowed enemy, or even an involuntary one, of Judaism.[38] The Dreyfus Affair and the Durkheimian victory which is that of the camp of rationalist intellectuals certainly reduces the sphere of the religious in general and affects the legitimacy of the science of Judaism: in all senses of the word, it reinforces the assimilation of citizens into the Republic, including, among opponents of assimilation, the Catholics who, reluctantly, little by little had to rally round to it. The question of the sacred remains just as keen, compelling citizens of diverse faiths to express their preoccupations, their identity, and their beliefs in other ways.

Let's begin with social inheritance, the family of which Durkheim wanted to be a loyal member, taking charge of his share of responsibility. David Émile Durkheim was born in 1858 in Épinal, where there was a Jewish community whose size was attested by the presence of three synagogues. This region of strong Jewish density played a special role in the history of sociology, since "in the north, and on the same river where Épinal stands, the Moselle, is Trier where Karl Marx, also a Jew, was born forty years before Émile Durkheim."[39] His father Moïse had become the rabbi of Épinal and had married Mélanie Isidor, whose father was named Marx Isidore; his paternal grandfather, Israël David Durkheim, was himself a rabbi in Haguenau, married to Bella Simon: as Henri Durkheim stressed, "in this family they were rabbis from father to son for eight generations."[40] His maternal grandfather was named Joseph Marx Isidor and was the husband of Rosette Lazard. Endogamy is especially strong since over four generations all descendents married fellow Jews: the grandparents and parents of David Émile Durkheim married Jews, as did his two sisters, one marrying Mirtile Cahen, the other marrying Gerson Mauss, and his brother Félix remained single; Durkheim's daughter Marie married Eugène Halphen; André, his young son, died during the battles of the First World War in Bulgaria, while his nephew Marcel remained single. Through the Mausses or the Halphens, endogamy reinforced alliances with other Jewish circles that had ties with the world and affairs of graduates of the École Normale; through his daughter's marriage, Émile Durkheim was linked to Henri Berr, creator of the *Revue de synthèse historique*.[41] Note that endogamy seems also to reign on the side of Durkheim's wife, since the father of Louise Julie Dreyfus, Henry Dreyfus, married Rosalie Lévy; her grandfather, Aron Dreyfus, married Sara Lévy; her uncle Salomon remained single, while Moyse Dreyfus, her other uncle, married Jeanne Cerf.

The choice of first name also shows the desire to maintain an explicit filiation: in the family, we in fact find in the two most distant generations, the ones born before the French Revolution and at the very beginning of the nineteenth century, on the male side two Moïses with different spellings, one Aron, one Israël, one Joseph, and one Salomon. On the female side, we note one Sara and one Bella, but more French first names like Julie, Rosalie, or Mélanie. In Durkheim's generation, people had stopped using an explicitly Jewish first name, aside from Durkheim himself; the same was true in the following generation, which appeared around the end of the nineteenth century or a little before. Nevertheless, the middle name is sometimes far from being as anonymous; thus Émile Durkheim's wife, Louise Julie Dreyfus, had as her middle name that of her maternal grandmother; Émile Durkheim's daughter Marie also bore the name Bella, that of her paternal great-grandmother whose husband was Israël David Durkheim; Marcel Mauss's middle name was Israël, which was also the name of Émile Durkheim's paternal great-grandfather and that of Rosine Durkheim, Marcel's mother. The common ancestor of Émile Durkheim and of Marcel Mauss, of the uncle and nephew whom he regarded as his own son, was named Israël David Durkheim; this rabbi, father of Moïse, joined together in his given names the symbolic fate of the two founders of the social sciences who turned away from orthodoxy, Émile Durkheim having given, as we have said, the middle name of Bella to his daughter in memory of Bella Simon, wife of this common ancestor and herself the daughter of a rabbi.

Even more explicitly respecting the custom peculiar to Jewish families, David Émile Durkheim bore, as his first name, the middle name of his paternal grandfather, as if his own father, Moïse Durkheim, had wanted to insist on the place of his son in this lineage of rabbis, to entrust him with a role of mediation and reproduction of the person of the grandparent. When Durkheim chose to inverse the order of his given names, he took a decision of essential symbolic importance, the circumstances of which we unfortunately do not know. What was David thinking in his innermost being when he decided to call himself Émile? Why did he take this decision that radically changed his image as founder of French sociology by partially erasing his Jewish origin, a step that foretold the move of Mauss, who in turn stopped using his middle name, Israël, to the point of never referring to it,[42] although he showed he was aware of its symbolism since he wrote in the single article he published in the *Revue des études juives*: "It is rather generally recognized that Israël is an artificial name. . . . For my part, I see no linguistic difficulty in admitting the Is-Rahel etymology, and I see difficulty only in the fact that the children of Rachel are Joseph and Benjamin and not Israël. But these changes of names from phratry to tribe, tribe to nation, then nation to subsection of a nation are a normal thing, and even often the best signs of historical events. It is possible that all this hides very distant and very cloudy pasts."[43] Note that Marcel Israël Mauss's paternal great-grandfather, the uncle of David Émile Durkheim, had precisely the first name of Joseph. Durkheim and Mauss both relegate their adherence to Judaism to the background by erasing their openly Jewish first names from their public identity: their identitarian filiation, however, remains keen in their innermost being.

Émile Durkheim, who was himself supposed to become a rabbi, was surrounded by an extremely traditional atmosphere; his home was "a house where austerity [reigned] more than opulence, where observation of the Law was a precept and example, with nothing arising to divert one from one's duty."[44] He received a serious religious education, had his bar mitzvah, then seemed to turn away from his religious calling in the course of his years at the École Normale Supérieure, although during his first year he decided to write an essay on a subject of his own choosing, "The Jews in the Roman Empire." This period of intellectual foundation in the Republic made him aware of philosophical debates, encouraged him to study Kant, to read Renouvier who established a close link between law and morality, to study the theoreticians of socialism in order to reflect on the conflict between individualism and membership in a collective, to discover Comte and his reflections on the social order, the evolution of the logics of solidarity, the specificity of society that justifies the sociological aim to which Durkheim would devote his life. In this period agitated by so many social and cultural conflicts, when opposition between the republican state and the Catholic Church shaped intellectual confrontations and rival conceptions of secular public space or of the space formed by the religious, Durkheim constructed his personality as a positivist scholar. He engaged in discourse as a sociologist, as a pedagogue responsible for the education of future citizens of this Republic as teachers proclaiming the supremacy of Reason over Religion. Durkheim moved closer to Louis Liard, director of higher education, to whom Jules Ferry entrusted the task of creating the new university. The "eight generations of rabbis" seemed no longer to weigh heavily on him; his readings and preoccupations were henceforth quite distant from those of his father or grandfather. Thereafter they would be those of a scholar who devoured Anglo-Saxon and German works, devoted all his attention to the works of Spencer, Schaeffle, Wundt, Marx, and Gumplowicz, and supervised libraries that rabbis never visited. Appointed in 1887 to the University of Bordeaux, he devoted all his strength to preparing *The Division of Labor in Society*, his future doctoral thesis, a founding moment in modern sociology. Did he thus shift his center of interest from the religious to the social, replacing the religious order and its divine laws with the social order and its human laws? Can one argue that

> as a new Moses, Durkheim would substitute "scientific" revelation for religious revelation: becoming a founding prophet would mean for Durkheim discovering the law stemming from the group, for the group, by scientifically discerning the object in which one *has* to believe—that would constitute being a sociologist. The identification with Moïse (his father) would thus take place, according to Jean-Claude Filloux, in a shift of the object of prophecy and of the relationship of revealer to revealed. . . . The desire to found a sociology, to make a sociology exist that would reveal a representation of the Group and its relationships with Man, is thus rooted in profound investments where we find both the wish to be the rabbi father and also not to be that father, or rather the wish to be the father *in other ways*?

Should we go even further and use arguments drawn from psychoanalysis, linking themes of solidarity or suicide with the fear of conflict threatening the cohesion of the parental group, of the Durkheim "tribe," "the communion, fusion in the group, as with a mother, in the archaic relationship, and the fantasy of a return to this relationship, protecting one from the risk of death. . . . From this point of view, one would have to take into account the articulation of pre-Oedipal elements and Oedipal confusions in the formation of identifications with parental figures and of the rupture with Judaism"?[45]

We'll take care here not to stray into unknown territory. We simply want to read *The Division of Labor in Society* one more time, to look for an explicit presence of Judaism in it, to examine more closely the books used as reference, the obvious sources of inspiration. What strikes one immediately is the very large number of references to the Old Testament that Durkheim quotes specifically to describe examples of "mechanical solidarity." In the opening pages of the second chapter of *The Division* in which Durkheim defines mechanical solidarity, he writes, "We know however what an important place in the repressive code of a mass of people the regulation of ritual, etiquette, ceremonial, religious practices occupies. We have only to open the Pentateuch to be convinced of this."[46] Durkheim shows that the Pentateuch, for instance with the Ten Commandments, refers only rarely to repressive systems since in his opinion this text does not constitute a code:

> Sometimes, the Pentateuch does not prescribe punishments, although, as we will see, it contains almost nothing but penal stipulations. This is the case with the Ten Commandments, as they are formulated in Exodus XX and in Deuteronomy V. But the fact is that the Pentateuch . . . is above all a summary of traditions of all kinds by which the Jews explained themselves to themselves, and also, in their own way, the genesis of the world, of their society, and of their main social practices. . . . Since the book is only a mass of national legends, one can rest assured that everything it contains was inscribed on everyone's consciousness. But it was essentially a matter of reproducing, by fixing them in place, popular beliefs about the origin of these precepts, on the historical circumstances in which they were supposed to have been promulgated, or the sources of their authority; from this point of view, the determination of the punishment becomes secondary.[47]

As we can see, one cannot simply argue that Durkheim's sociology brought an end to the science of Judaism: his aim is radically different, but he still uses some of its formulations. Durkheim thus insists at once on the example of ancient Jewish society to define the role of a flexible penal code whose function was above all to protect collective sensibilities that are gathered in a "collective consciousness." In his eyes, the Hebrews of ancient times constituted "a primitive people" and had a particularly extensive concept of punishment that even affected the innocent people connected to the guilty person;[48] they belonged to "inferior societies" where respect for religion matters more than any other obligation. Durkheim read closely the writings of Salomon Munk, one of the best representatives of the science of Judaism, who was a professor at the Collège de France; several times he cites Munk's work on Palestine.[49] Moreover, the knowledge he had of the Pentateuch is remarkable: in his first work, *The Division of Labor in Society*, as well as in his last work, *The Elementary Forms of Religious Life*,[50] he draws a number of examples from it to enrich his arguments, find exceptions, reflect on unexpected cases such as offences for which no punishment was foreseen. In this sense he cites the example in Leviticus of a man who goes out to gather wood on the Sabbath day: he is brought before Moses and Aaron, who "put him in prison, since it hadn't yet been declared what should be done with him," or else the case "of a man who had blasphemed the name of God. The Levites arrested him but didn't know how he should be treated. Moses himself did not know and went to consult the Lord."[51] All these examples, often taken from the Bible, led him to the conclusion that has so often been commented upon by which "punishment essentially consists, then, in a passionate reaction, of graduated intensity, that society exercises through the intermediary of a constituent body over those of its members who violated certain rules of conduct."[52]

The model of the Old Testament represents for Durkheim the exact opposite of modern society where organic solidarity and restorative justice flourish while repressive justice is declining: in the Old Testament respect for society is at its maximum; society is the object of sacred faith, individualism remains unknown, and no risk of anomie threatens. Durkheim comes up with a clever calculation. He writes, "The last four books of Pentateuch—Exodus, Leviticus, Numbers, and Deuteronomy—represent the oldest monument of this genre that we have. Out of these four or five thousand verses, only a relatively small number of them express rules that could, possibly, pass for not being repressive"; over half a page, he presents very precise supporting details of this that reveals a surprisingly detailed knowledge of the sacred texts. He comments on some of them, from which he quotes explicitly, emphasizing the virtual absence of the restorative justice and cooperative justice that characterize modern societies with organic solidarity. Evincing a veritable mastery of these texts, Durkheim thinks that the nonrepressive verses amount to 135 and that most of them, cloaked in a religious aspect, are just as oppressive. Whence this conclusion, which by itself illustrates the general significance of mechanical solidarity at work in "inferior societies":

> To varying degrees, all Hebrew law, as the Pentateuch reveals it to us, is imprinted with an essentially repressive nature. This is more marked in certain areas, more latent in others, but one always feels its presence. Because all the precepts it contains are the commandments of God, placed, so to speak, under direct warrant, they all derive from this origin a prestige that makes them sacrosanct; thus, when they are violated, public consciousness is not content with a simple reparation, but demands an expiation to avenge it. Since what creates the nature unique to penal law is the extraordinary authority of the rules it sanctions, and since men have never known or imagined a higher authority than the one the believer attributes to his God, a law that is supposed to be the word of God Himself cannot fail to be essentially repressive. . . . There is virtually nothing in common between Hebraic law and our own.[53]

We are left confused by the extreme attention Durkheim brings to the sacred texts of Judaism, by his surprising knowledge, by his reading that is so detailed that he notes that "contractual law, testamentary law, guardianship, adoption, etc., are things that are unknown in the Pentateuch," by the quantity of pages he devotes to this question, by the absolute silence of the best commentators of Durkheim's work on these numerous pages that testify to his intimate knowledge of these religious texts. A little later on, Durkheim gives another very detailed list of attacks on customs that are repressed by Hebraic law but are no longer repressed in societies where organic solidarity reigns: the capital punishment that is the penalty for cursing or disobeying one's parents (Exodus 21:13 and 21:17), corruption of another's betrothed (Deuteronomy 22:23–27), prostitution (Leviticus 19:29), union with a slave (Leviticus 19:20), sodomy (Leviticus 18:22), bestiality (Exodus 22), incest (Durkheim emphasizes that Leviticus, in Chapter XIX, counts seventeen cases of incest), the fraud of the young deflowered woman who presents herself as a virgin in marriage (Deuteronomy 22:13–21).[54] Durkheim observes that "all these crimes are punished with severe penalties: for most of them, death," and finally he notes that "it would be impossible to enumerate all the religious crimes that Pentateuch distinguishes and represses. The Hebrew subject had to obey all the commandments of the Law under penalty of destruction. For this reason, he was not only forced not to do anything that was prohibited, but also to do everything that was ordered, to have himself and his sons circumcised, to celebrate the Sabbath, the holidays, etc."[55] For Durkheim, "There are a multitude of rules, either of conduct, or of thinking, that are certainly religious but that are applied to relationships of an entirely different kind. Religion forbids the Jew from eating certain meats, orders him to dress in a predetermined way; it imposes some sort of opinion on the nature of man and things, on the origins of the world; it often regulates juridical, moral, economic relationships. Its sphere of action extends well beyond the commerce of man with the divine."[56] Thus it is starting from the sole example of the Jews that he utters this interpretation of the religious as a form of collective consciousness structuring a social group gathering together the Jews, who are designated in the text once again with a capital J as a people [in French, "juif" is not usually capitalized—Trans.], which surprises us coming from this representative of Franco-Judaism who could have used the small J, following the accepted usage that restricts Jewishness to a simple religious practice deprived of any collective dimension, and according to the generally dominant usage of French Jews of the time.

We know that for Durkheim "if there is one truth that history has made a certainty, it is that religion embraces an increasingly small portion of life in society. In the beginning, it extended to everything; everything that is social was religious: the two words were synonymous. Then little by little, political, economic, scientific functions are freed from religious function, are set up apart from it, take on an increasingly pronounced temporal nature."[57] We could not conceive, following this general approach, of any greater opposition between this Judaism and the society to the service of which Durkheim invests all his energy, to make the differentiation between the religious and the political keep progressing by upholding the academic policy of secularization. Durkheim, the sociologist of the Republic of citizens supposedly concerned only with Reason, seems thus to be turning away, body and soul, from the Judaism of his ancestors which represents the "inferior" religion of an archaic time. Actually, when he pronounces his fundamental thesis on the normal decline of religion in developed societies, when he is wondering about the consequences of this social fact on the state of solidarity that connects men to each other, then he evokes, by contrast, the Jewish religion whose "sphere of action extends . . . beyond the commerce of man with the divine." Here he becomes involved, starting with this example, in another perspective on the continuity of the fact of religion, one that will lead to *The Elementary Forms of Religious Life* where he writes that "rituals are, above all, the ways by which the social group periodically reasserts itself": beyond religion, collective consciousness can maintain itself in modernity as a form of collective identity and give structure, "beyond the commerce of man with the divine," to collective representations, thanks to which society survives. Far from ignoring Judaism, Durkheim gives it a significance that goes beyond the religious, even within secularized modern societies. Moreover, a little later on, in 1899–1900, in his essay in *L'Année sociologique*, "Two Laws of Penal Evolution," he even calls into question the purely repressive nature of Judaism within societies that have mechanical solidarity. After describing the severity of repressive law among the Syrians and Egyptians, he adds, commenting on several passages from Deuteronomy and Numbers that he cites again in a precise way:

> The Hebrew people certainly did not belong to a type that was superior to previous types. . . . Yet the Mosaic law is much less severe than that of Manu or than the sacred books of Egypt. . . . Mutilation, so widely practiced by the other peoples of the Orient, figures only once in the Pentateuch. . . . Where does this relative leniency come from? It is because among the Hebrew people, absolute government was never able to establish itself in a lasting way. . . . The spirit of the people remained profoundly democratic.[58]

Noting that "in the Pentateuch, prison is not once at issue," he emphasizes again the extent to which the repressive law that characterizes the society of the Hebrews is actually limited by the democratic values of the people, even within this primitive society that generally is accepted as "inferior" but where the Jews, so concerned with the observation of religious rules, nonetheless preserved democracy.[59] As if Durkheim were qualifying his previous analyses to shed light on the relative compatibility between democracy and the strict observation of religious precepts in the particular case of Jewish society, of course described as "inferior," but nonetheless endowed already with a "relative leniency" that was summoned to spread later on into the very society that possesses organic solidarity.

While he likened the clan-based kind of social organization of the Hebrews where "there is only a rudimentary division of labor" to examples of other "inferior" societies, such as the Iroquois or the Kabyles,[60] Durkheim also formulated another observation, over which we now want to linger. Noting that "a certain number of families made up the tribe and the gathering of the twelve tribes formed the entirety of the Hebrew people" which he described as the "Jewish nation,"[61] as if he wanted to justify the use of the capital J to designate the Jews, he showed, taking his inspiration especially from the example of the Hebrews,[62] that "these social masses were formed from homogeneous elements, because the collective type was very developed in them, and, since individual types were rudimentary, it was inevitable that the entire psychic life of the society took on a religious characteristic. That is also where the communism comes from that we have so often noted among these peoples. Communism, in fact, is the necessary product of this special cohesion that absorbs the individual into the group, the part into the whole."[63] Several times in their correspondence, Durkheim and Mauss mention the "communism" that dominated their family clan, as a source of solidarity, warmth, tenderness, intimate union of the group which evoked the structure of so-called inferior societies like that of the Hebrews. Thus, Durkheim admonishes his nephew Mauss, "You must stop your perpetual criticisms of our family communism. You benefit from it, in fact, since it's thanks to this communism that you can devote yourself to your favorite studies without any material concerns. You are in no position to reject its burdens."[64] Within this "family communism" that Durkheim valued but that weighed so heavily on Marcel Mauss, social relationships remained of a communitarian kind; cohesion was strong within it and had difficulty supporting deviant behavior like that of Mauss who led his bachelor life as he pleased, having an affair with a non-Jewish woman outside the ties of marriage. In the name of this social cohesion, Durkheim urges his nephew to break up with her. "You have only to tell yourself this: that you are going to shorten your mother's days. Just think about it a little, if tomorrow these emotions made her have a stroke, what remorse you'd feel then." A few days later, Durkheim again writes to Mauss, "I am suffering from the state you find yourself in: I am suffering because you are suffering and because you are weak." Finally he adds, in another letter, "You are living in a false household, morally divorced, and in a family that you have disorganized and where you are certainly radiating coldness. And you're stuck there, incapable of action except to invent sophisms that cover your moral poverty." Durkheim cast doubt on Mauss's "virility," his moral strength that should allow him to bring an end to a situation of such great social dysfunction; he grew irritated at Mauss's reply, which complained of "these family objections" and emphasized the sadness of Mauss's mother, whom her brother Émile Durkheim tried to console.[65]

"Family communism," an inferior type of social formation, suddenly became a panacea for the isolation and competition that occupied subjects in society. Breaking it meant radiating coldness, whereas society held together by mechanical solidarity, so disparaged before, was a source of warmth, emotion, interdependence. What if this image represented more—what if it testified, despite all the inferior characteristics such a civilization is burdened with, where repression is unrestrictedly expressed, to an attachment to a Jewish world where, according to the general example, the whole is independent of the parts, with the respected social structure preserving its sacred quality? When we know that Durkheim showed himself to be very pessimistic as to the future of the division of normal labor, that he insisted over and over on the dysfunctions linked to constraint or anomie, one suspects that, in his mind, the so-called normal evolution, which makes subjects truly autonomous by assigning them to functions equal to their competence, has very few chances to develop. With this image where he evokes for the last time, in *The Division of Labor in Society*, the Jewish people that sacralizes society and prefigures the communism of human solidarity, doesn't Durkheim confer a special distinction on this society that is "inferior" but nonetheless democratic, where pure repression is restrained—a society that bears so much warmth and solidarity, which he himself tries out on his own little "tribe"? Isn't it just this confidence that Mauss comes to miss when his uncle dies, on November 15, 1917? Mauss mourns his "deprivation of Durkheim's correspondence," which "leaves a void in the only moments when I could—still with prudence—open up my heart."[66] This term evokes the intimacy of a profound relationship born from the chrysalis of the original group, the clan, the "tribe," another way of realizing, according to the practices of long ago that come from "primitive" societies to which the Jewish world still bears witness, this "brotherhood" of the group that in modern society must base itself on a strong division of labor, an "ideal [that] is not about to be fully realized."[67]

In 1895, two years after *The Division of Labor in Society*, Durkheim published *The Rules of Sociological Method*, a work of methodology in which he lays the groundwork of positivist sociology, the only scientific method capable of explaining societal facts as the basis of other societal facts, rejecting all preconceptions, value judgments, and ideologies. For him, the aim of sociology is to give an objective account of the "ways of acting, thinking, and feeling, exterior to the individual, and endowed with a force of coercion by means of which they impose themselves on the individual."[68] From this basis, juridical or moral rules, aphorisms, and popular sayings, as well as "articles of faith in which religious or political sects condense their beliefs" all emanate from the group and impose themselves on the individual;[69] these societal facts constitute "things" that must be examined, setting aside "carefully all preconceptions," a difficult posture to take since "emotion often enters in. We feel passionately, in fact, about our political and religious beliefs. . . . The mere fact of submitting them, as well as the phenomena they express, to cold, dry analysis is revolting to certain sensibilities" that do not want to admit that these "feelings are a matter of science."[70] Now we are at the point where Durkheim elaborates the famous sociological method that will attract such a following, in France and throughout the world; in these few pages where he comments on his famous assertion, "social phenomena are things and must be treated as things," he breaks with the dominant spiritualizing positions at the university and courageously takes on his innovating role as "Moses," as a scholar who has rejected the ancient philosophical idols. Just after uttering this

other brief phrase, "We must systematically set aside all preconceptions," Durkheim quotes one single thinker against whom he fulmi-
nates, James Darmesteter and his book *Les prophètes d'Israël*! While he
is laying out the foundations for the positivist method, he rails against
Darmesteter, who was probably unknown to his sociology colleagues
then and now. He comments on the following long passage by this
eminent representative of the "science of Judaism" à la française:

> Woe betide the scholar who approaches the things of God without
> having in the back of his consciousness, in the indestructible crypt of
> his being, where the souls of his ancestors sleep, an unknown sanctu-
> ary whence the perfume of incense rises up from time to time, the line
> of a psalm, a sorrowful or triumphant cry that as a child he raised to
> heaven following the example of his brothers, and which places him
> once again in sudden communion with the prophets of long ago.[71]

At the same time that Durkheim utters the precepts that will make him
famous, in chapter One, a passage veering toward modernity, where
he establishes the "Rules relative to the observation of social facts," he
takes James Darmesteter severely to task, claiming that "it would be
difficult to reject strongly enough this mystical doctrine that—like all
mysticism—is at bottom nothing but a disguised empiricism, negating
all science. Feelings that have social things as their object have no more
privilege than other feelings, since they have no other origin. They too
are formed historically: they are a product of human experience, but
of a confused and disorganized experience. . . . Feeling is an object for
science, not the criterion of scientific truth."[72] The sole fundamentally
negative example that comes to his mind then, when he is distancing
himself from a traditionalist mode of thinking, is that of the scholar
who goes astray since he preserves in his heart the cry of the Jewish
child he had been. The condemnation of such an attachment as contrary to the scientific spirit is troubling in its vehemence. It is difficult
to imagine a stronger condemnation of all "mystical doctrine" in general and of Judaism in particular. Through the words of Darmesteter,
and by rejecting in such definitive terms "the cry of the Jewish child he
had been," a cry that must above all not perturb his own objective se-
renity as a sociologist, Durkheim publicly rejects such a preconception
that turns one away from science, but also at the same time confesses a
particular attachment that he must keep in check.

He has not, however, finished with Judaism in his work as a sociologist, since in an article published in the first issue of *L'Année sociologue* in 1896–97, "The Prohibition of Incest and Its Origins," Durkheim again quotes several times from Leviticus and Genesis. In his eyes, "It seems clear after abundant research that intermarriage increases the tendency for nervous disorders and deafness; but other statistics establish that it sometimes diminishes mortality. That is what Neuville established for the Jews. . . . Thus the unarguable tendency of the Jews for all kinds of neurasthenia is possibly due, in part, to too great a frequency of intermarriage; however, since it results in a more developed mentality, it has allowed them to resist the social causes of destruction that have assailed them for centuries."[73] He foreshadows the theses of *Suicide*, a work that would also be published in 1897, already emphasizing that the Jews can better "resist the social causes of destruction" by using whatever means are possible, including intermarriage, to reinforce their social ties, their intimacy—a source of confidence but also of internal constraint, expressed by the powerful "family communism" he spoke of before, a form of mutual aid and respect for social obligations. In *Suicide*, Durkheim notes that Jews commit suicide less than either Protestants or Catholics, even though Jews live more than those groups do in cities, an aggravating factor that increases the risk of suicide: "Since the rate for Judaism is so low, in spite of this aggravating circumstance, it may be assumed that other things being equal, their religion has the fewest suicides of all."[74] In pages that have become famous, Durkheim wonders about the different propensities of Protestants and Catholics for suicide and demonstrates superbly that "the greater concessions a confessional group makes to individual judgment, the less it dominates lives, the less its cohesion and vitality . . . the superiority of Protestantism with respect to suicide results from its being a less strongly integrated church than the Catholic church."[75]

Durkheim then turns to Judaism in two long passages, over which we would now like to linger. First he writes:

> This also explains the situation of Judaism. Indeed, the reproach to which the Jews have for so long been exposed by Christianity has created feelings of unusual solidarity among them. Their need of resisting a general hostility, the very impossibility of free communication with the rest of the population, has forced them to strict union

among themselves. Consequently, each community became a small, compact and coherent society with a strong feeling of self-consciousness and unity. Everyone thought and lived alike; individual divergences were made almost impossible by the community of existence and the close and constant surveillance of all over each. The Jewish church has thus been more strongly united than any other. . . . By analogy with what has just been observed apropos of Protestantism, the same cause must therefore be assumed for the slight tendency of the Jews to suicide. . . . Doubtless they owe this immunity in a sense to the hostility surrounding them. But if this is its influence, it is not because it imposes a higher morality but because it obliges them to live in greater union. They are immune to this degree because their religious society is of such solidarity. Besides, the ostracism to which they are subject is only one of the causes producing this result; the very nature of Jewish beliefs must contribute largely to it. Judaism, in fact, like all early religions, consists basically of a body of practices minutely governing all the details of life and leaving little free room to individual judgment.[76]

Here Durkheim is taking up the idea of inferior religion that he had to a large extent qualified, but now he develops two very different arguments to account for the low suicide rate among Jews. The first argument, already discussed, has to do with strong social cohesion, the "family communism" resulting from common beliefs controlled by the "Jewish church," an expression that seems more than strange coming from the pen of this son of a rabbi. Integration, then, protects them from suicide. Marriage too, which among the Jews takes on a "magical-religious quality. It is called *Kiddushin*, from the word *Kaddesh*, which is the Hebrew equivalent of the *sacer* of the Latins and implies the idea of consecration."[77] However, Durkheim summons another, quite different argument: this time, it is a question of taking account of the solidarity that binds the Jews together when faced with the "general animosity" with which they are confronted, in order to understand better their low rate of suicide, an act of individual behavior linked with disintegration of the community. In his opinion, education presents itself to them as "a means of offsetting the unfavorable position imposed on them by opinion and sometimes by law."[78] Moreover, he notes that when Catholics find themselves in a largely minority situation, they commit suicide less and come closer to the Jews, since "the less numerous confessions, facing the hostility of the surrounding populations, in order to maintain themselves are obliged to exercise severe control over themselves and subject themselves to an especially rigorous discipline."[79]

The cohesion that prevents suicide is now perceived as resulting primarily from strong external pressure, from "animosity," "hostility." Durkheim has trouble, though, clarifying the relationship between these two causes, internal and external, so much so that he writes about the Jews: "The ostracism that strikes them is only one of the causes that produce this result; the very nature of Jewish beliefs must contribute a large part to it." Odd commentary from the sociologist who devises in this same work the multivariate analysis intended to evaluate the specific weight of each variable as well as their relationships by distinguishing the independent variable, the intermediary variable, and the dependent variable! Does that mean that if ostracism were to disappear, "the Jewish church" would then be forced to abandon its preeminence, internal pressure would diminish, endogamy would lessen, collective values would lose their weight, individual behaviors would flourish, and suicides increase? Isn't that what Durkheim himself predicts in 1899, in his response to an investigation of anti-Semitism, when he thinks that "the Jews are losing their ethnic traits with extreme rapidity. In two more generations the change will be complete."[80] From this point of view, if the Dreyfus Affair had not relaunched anti-Semitic hatred with such force, assimilation would have reached its conclusion, and the Jews' protection from suicide would have been over: as he emphasizes in 1906, it seems "that the coefficient of preservation the Jews have enjoyed is tending more and more to diminish. . . . As the Jewish population grows more assimilated with the surrounding population, it loses its traditional virtues, without perhaps replacing them with other ones."[81] The values peculiar to the Jews do not seem to play a role in themselves; it is the social context that matters. Durkheim seems to share the point of view of Abbé Grégoire, and he curiously foreshadows that of Jean-Paul Sartre, spurning beliefs themselves, even when reduced to ritual alone, to which he does nonetheless submit independently of anti-Semitic pressure. We will have to return to this paradox later on. Let us briefly note here that such a devaluation of belief could only infuriate Zionist sociologists like Arthur Ruppin who, at the end of an analysis just as full of statistics of suicides of assimilated Jews in the West compared to those more traditional Jews from Eastern Europe, reproaches Durkheim for not having compared these distinct populations. For Ruppin, "suicides among Orthodox Jews of Eastern Europe are very rare compared to those of Western Europe. The Eastern Jew, despite the ordeals he has undergone, remains optimistic, he loves life. The religious rules that forbid him to commit suicide preserve their value for him. Pessimism strikes only the European Jew educated in the West."[82]

Durkheim then approaches another correlation, between education level and tendency to suicide, noting that "of all religions, Judaism counts the fewest suicides, yet in none other is education so general."[83] This time things seem clearer, since according to Durkheim education is not sought for its own sake by the people of the Book but simply as an instrumental means of self-protection:

> But if the Jew manages to be both well instructed and very disinclined to suicide, it is because of the special origin of his desire for knowledge. It is a general law that religious minorities, in order to protect themselves better against the hate to which they are exposed or merely through a sort of emulation, try to surpass in knowledge the populations surrounding them. . . . The Jew, therefore, seeks to learn, not in order to replace his collective prejudices by reflective thought, but merely to be better armed for the struggle. . . . This is the reason for the complexity he presents. Primitive in certain respects, in others he is an intellectual and man of culture. He thus combines the advantages of the severe discipline characteristic of small and ancient groups with the benefits of the intense culture enjoyed by our great societies. He has all the intelligence of modern man without sharing his despair . . . the religion with least inclination to suicide, Judaism, is the very one not formally proscribing it and also the one in which the idea of immortality plays the least role. Indeed, the Bible contains no law forbidding man to kill himself. . . . The beneficent influence of religion is therefore not due to the special nature of religious conceptions. If religion protects man against the desire for self-destruction, it is not that it preaches the respect for his own person to him with arguments *sui generis*; but because it is a society. . . . The more numerous and strong these collective states of mind are, the stronger the integration of the religious community, and also the greater its preservative value. The details of dogmas and rites are

secondary. The essential thing is that they be capable of supporting a sufficiently intense collective life.[84]

To summarize: the Jew, "cerebral and refined," nonetheless remains, as in *The Division of Labor in Society*, a "primitive" character rooted in his "collective prejudices," which are consolidated by external "hatred." It is not his values alone that propel him toward education but also the principle of collective survival, the need to maintain the unity of the group. Since the Bible seems to be indifferent on this point, hostility toward suicide cannot therefore be explained by beliefs; it is the result of an external pressure reinforced by surrounding hatred. The conclusion is self-evident and clear: if this hatred diminishes, the necessity of recourse to education will lessen, the solidity of the group will diminish, the Jews will become a less and less cerebral and refined people, and more of them will commit suicide. Durkheim firmly believed in this conclusion since, when he brought his famous work to a close, he emphasized again that it was "the most archaic religions," the ones that favor a unified community, that those who struggled against suicide should identify with: "Judaism, in spite of its great historic role, still clings to the most primitive religious forms in many respects. How true it is that moral and intellectual superiority of dogma counts for naught in its possible influence on suicide!"[85] Durkheim still noted the "great historic role" of Judaism, lending nuance once again to his appreciation of an ensemble of values that do not depend solely on principles capable of ensuring the coherence of primitive societies. Recalling his previous judgments he concluded, *in fine*, that the adjective "primitive" was not adequate, since the Jewish people were able to preserve their "democratic" character. Durkheim vacillated between reasoning by means of variables supposed to prove the strength of social causality and a basic appreciation of the nature of Judaism, since it was almost impossible for him to impugn completely a morality that led him to value the precious "family communism" to which he showed he was still so attached.

Few indeed are the commentators on *Suicide* who set out to clarify these ambiguities; almost all are silent about the pages devoted to the Jews, even though they might seem essential to the demonstration of the whole, underestimating once again the constant interest shown by Durkheim, in his very work, with respect to the behavior unique to the Jews. Thus, in his long analysis of *Suicide*, Maurice Halbwachs only briefly mentioned this point, simply thinking that "it's better to set aside the example of the Jews" since their religious values were being weakened due to an increasing exogamy, which brought an end to their immunity. We might think that he neglected the specific role attributed by Durkheim to education as a defense mechanism that can remain, even in an exogamic perspective, a privileged objective independent of religious beliefs because of its protective role.[86] In our day, the abundant literature on *Suicide* also remains silent on this aspect, and the authors are rare who take notice of this important dimension of Durkheim's work in their analyses, except to mention briefly his interpretation about the relative immunity the Jews enjoyed.[87]

Faced with so many ambivalences, Durkheim's work is silent on this point; it ceases almost completely to mention the Jewish dimension. When Durkheim grants the religious an essential place in his writings, when he considerably rearranges his centers of interest by placing the religious henceforth at the heart of his thinking, curiously Judaism seems to disappear. In 1912 he published his last great book, *The Elementary Forms of Religious Life*, in which he almost never took Judaism into consideration. What a supreme paradox! It was in Australia, in the Aruntas tribes, that Durkheim brought to light the structures underlying belief, ritual, and religious representations in order to demonstrate his iconoclastic thesis, that "religion is an eminently social thing,"[88] "a unified system of beliefs and practices relative to sacred things, that is to say, things set apart and forbidden—beliefs and practices which unite into one single moral community called a Church, all those who adhere to them."[89] Almost without exception he no longer chose to use any example drawn from the Jewish "church." Of course, through an attentive reading, one can still discover a few rare lines that evoke Jewish beliefs. Thus, to make the function of ritual understandable, Durkheim writes, "When the Jew stirred the air at the Feast of the Tabernacles by shaking willow branches in a certain rhythm, it was to make the wind blow and the rain fall; the belief was that the rite produced the desired result automatically, provided it was correctly performed."[90] It is true that Judaism is not, according to Durkheim, as "elementary" as animism or even totemism.

We know that Durkheim compares collective totemic beliefs to modern ways of thinking: "Although the country will not be lost if a solitary flag remains in the hands of the enemy or won if it is regained, the soldier is killed retaking it. . . . The totem is the flag of the clan. . . . A mere scrap of the flag represents the country as much as the flag itself; moreover, it is sacred in the same right and to the same degree."[91] Durkheim boldly likens religious ceremony to the idea of celebration by which "the group periodically revitalizes the sense it has of itself."[92] He concludes that religion represents "the image" of society, that mythologies and theologies only idealize reality, both in the most primitive religions and in "the most modern and most refined" religions, that they adapt society, "the only hearth at which we can warm ourselves morally."[93] When he returns once more to this "warmth" that is indispensable for the solidity of the social group, when he writes his "Conclusion," which is so often commented on, this is what he writes:

> Thus there is something eternal in religion that is destined to outlive the succession of particular symbols in which religious thought has clothed itself. There can be no society that does not experience the need at regular intervals to maintain and strengthen the collective feelings and the ideas that provide its coherence and its distinct individuality. This moral remaking can be achieved only through meetings, assemblies, and congregations in which the individuals, pressing close to one another, reaffirm in common their common sentiments. Such is the origin of ceremonies that, by their object, by their results, and by the techniques used, are not different in kind from ceremonies that are specifically religious. What basic difference is there between Christians' celebrating the principal dates of Christ's life, Jews' celebrating the exodus from Egypt or the promulgation of the Decalogue, and a citizens' meeting commemorating the advent of a new moral charter or some other great event of national life?[94]

As in *The Division of Labor in Society* or *Suicide*, Jewish society again represented one of the essential sources of "warmth," communion, community, that "family communism" so beneficial for mutual aid, for collective consciousness, and consequently, for strong collective beliefs that emanate from a close social bond. The fact that when he was bringing the work written at the prime of his life to an end, this book that preceded the death of his son as well as his own death by a few years, when he described sacrifices to country and the civil ceremonies that reaffirm the feelings of collective belonging, national identification, adherence to an almost "civil religion" capable of ensuring the moral communion of all citizens,[95] Durkheim evoked, using a small J, the "Jews' [les juifs] celebrating the exodus from Egypt or the promulgation of the Decalogue," confirming the place that Jewish history kept in his thinking. All the more so since, already in *L'Année sociologique* of 1897–98 in his article "On the Definition of Religious Phenomena," Durkheim argued that "the Jew must also believe that Yahweh saved his ancestors from slavery in Egypt." In this text, he then likened this collective belief that grounds the religious to the fact that, in our day, "the nation, the French Revolution, Joan of Arc, and so on are for us sacred things which we allow no one to touch."[96] That shows the similarity of argumentation, fourteen years apart. Following the example of "citizens" devoted to the secular Republic who thronged to festivals, for which he became the main theoretician, the Jews remembered collectively their exodus from the Egypt where violent tyranny reigned and thus their return to that democratic society whose virtues Durkheim once emphasized; they also remembered the promulgation of the Decalogue, the moral code par excellence that gave structure in a latent way to most contemporary societies. All at once, alongside Christians and citizens of the Third Republic, the Jews embodied the archetype of a merging society, of solidarity, of social "warmth" transformed into communal religion. They were no longer relegated to the past, to the side of primary, archaic religions. When this example came to Durkheim's pen, was he remembering Moses who led the Jews out of Egypt, or Moïse Durkheim, his father, whose role he assumed in a different way by leading citizens toward the secular Republic and scholars toward sociology?

Thereafter, Durkheim did not deal with this question, either in his propaganda written during the First World War,[97] or in the texts published posthumously, in the *Leçons de sociologie* particularly.[98] That it continued to gnaw at him is obvious, however, when we observe his political engagements, from the Dreyfus Affair to the First World War. Let's return briefly to the Dreyfus Affair. Durkheim was one of the first people to plunge into the fight in favor of rehabilitating the unfairly condemned captain, during the second stage of the affair, just after Zola's condemnation, when vigorous anti-Semitic demonstrations were breaking out everywhere. In the beginning of 1898, Durkheim, before many others, urged his collaborators on *L'Année sociologique* to become involved courageously in the struggle, to join the League of Rights of Man and the Citizen, of which he was the secretary for Bordeaux; he was himself at the origin of the creation of this league, which would play a considerable role in the birth of intellectuals and in the fight for revision. He sent a number of letters to solicit signatures, went to see Jean Jaurès and Émile Duclaux, the director of the Institut Pasteur, urged his nephew Marcel Mauss to join him in this action, and rose up against "the so-called nationalists," confessing, "It is true that our attitude is completely revolutionary. But whose fault is that? This revolt was so much in the nature of things."[99] The austere positivist scholar was transformed into a determined combatant, but one who was "morally weary," "isolated," one who complained about this "unbearable sensation of solitude" in which he found himself in the midst of his Bordeaux colleagues, who turned out to be timorous, indifferent, or even hostile.[100] The sensation of warmth, of solidarity characteristic of the society to which he was so attached, disappeared, to be replaced by a solitude stemming from a broken society. He still showed his concern for the preeminence of collective organization: "We will have to concern ourselves with the moral situation that this sad business, so minor in itself, has revealed. The group of intellectuals must not disband."[101] In Bordeaux, this "inner exile," as he now saw himself—paradoxically for this man attached to collective celebration of the country—had become the object of biting, personal anti-Semitic attacks, and, on this occasion, showed an undeniable personal physical courage.[102] He defended the senior professor Paul Stapfer, who had been dismissed for Dreyfusard opinions, debated at length with Ferdinand Brunetière, the anti-Dreyfusard Catholic theoretician, justifying in his famous article "Individualism and the Intellectuals" the compatibility of moral individualism directed toward the collective with the preservation of a social unity,[103] and responded to an investigation on anti-Semitism in terms that we would like to linger over now.

He did not hide anything: "We had seen it already in the regions in the East, during the War of 1870; since I myself am of Jewish origin, I was able to observe it up close. It was the Jews who were blamed for the defeats. In 1848, an outbreak of the same kind, but much more violent, had taken place in Alsace." This descendant of "eight generations" of rabbis who declared he was "of Jewish origin" offered a scapegoat theory of anti-Semitism: "When society suffers, it feels the need to find someone to whom it can impute its sickness, on whom it can avenge its disappointments . . . they are pariahs who serve as expiatory victims. What confirms me in this interpretation is the way the outcome of the Dreyfus trial was received, in 1894. There was an outburst of joy on the boulevards. People celebrated as a triumph something that should have been cause for public mourning. Then they knew who to blame. . . . It's from the Jews that the harm was coming." Durkheim refuted the accusations brought against the Jews as an explanation of this crisis: "The defects of the Jew are compensated for by unarguable qualities, and, if there are better races, there are also worse ones." This is curious language from the pen of a sociologist hostile to physiological determinisms, but an unmistakable taking sides that publicly reasserts his adherence to a community. An unquestionable shout of rage, too, from this scholar of the Republic who wants public authorities to repress "severely any incitement to hatred of citizens against each other" and who wants "the government to make it its business to enlighten the masses about the error in which they are caught, so that the authorities could not even be suspected of looking for allies in the party of intolerance." Profound disappointment of the sociologist of the Republic. Even the "men of good sense" aren't joining forces against "public madness." Durkheim in vain tries to reassure himself, to make the situation less tragic by comparing French anti-Semitism, "due to temporary circumstances," to German or Russian anti-Semitism, which he considers "chronic . . . of an aristocratic nature" and which "is inspired by violent, destructive passions";[104] his confusion was just as marked before the rise of this French-style anti-Semitism that threatened to sweep everything away with it, and which he had to confront in person.[105] All of a sudden, the assimilated French Jews, supposedly "citizens" like all the others, appear, according to the expression he uses and that can be found also in Max Weber or Hannah Arendt, as "pariahs," even in this triumphant Third Republic where science, progress, and fraternity reign! The shock was a rude one for someone who intended to be the theoretician of the secular, unified Republic, and who distanced himself from all the Moïses, Arons, and Sarahs of his childhood. Does Durkheim's Dreyfusard passion stem only from the universalist engagement of an intellectual, as some people think?[106] Can one really look into someone's heart and distinguish what stems from attachment to the Enlightenment from what expresses an identitarian feeling, a loyalty to a tradition with which he never broke, at least in the private sphere? In the intensity of his reaction, this sociologist from Bordeaux, how can one distinguish the affront to a citizen's honor from an anti-Semitic attack, how can one know it has to do with the former and not the latter? These distinctions are almost meaningless when we know that Durkheim remained immersed in this "family communism," his Jewish environment, whose virtues he knew, and that he worked, in the framework of *L'Année sociologique*, with a number of Jewish intellectuals, from Marcel Mauss to Emmanuel and Isidore Lévy, Jean Marx, Lucien Lévy-Bruhl, Albert Milhaud, and Robert Hertz,[107] and when we remember that Durkheim had close contact during the Dreyfus Affair with Salomon Reinach, who along with his brother was one of the most famous Jewish defenders of the captain,[108] that he was also in touch with the rabbinical council of Bordeaux who even invited him to lecture for them,[109] and that he was often, even during the most scholarly discussions among distinguished academics, thought of as being Jewish.[110]

If Durkheim did not show his communitarian adherence during the time of the Dreyfus Affair, even though he reacted to anti-Semitic accusations, he took fewer precautions during the First World War. He sat on the Special Commission created by the minister of the interior charged with examining the situation of foreigners residing in the *département* of the Seine, where he examined the fate of Russians in France, most of them Jewish. These Russians were the objects of a violent anti-Semitic campaign that found a favorable reception among the city's municipal council. In February 1916, Durkheim wrote a report to demonstrate the anti-Semitic mythomania; in turn, the report would make Durkheim the target of a virulent anti-Semitic attack from a member of the Senate who accused him of being a German spy. Adrien Gaudin de Villaine had denounced him in a public assembly on March 23, 1916, as "the representative of the Kriegsministerium," before Paul Painlevé, minister of public education, addressed the assembly on March 30 to protest indignantly such accusations, after having been alerted by the leading republican academics who had always been loyal to Durkheim—who were none other than Liard and Lavisse![111] Durkheim began his text by pointing out that since the beginning of the war, "the societies of emigrant Jews sent their fellow practitioners a warm appeal in which all that Judaism owes to France was recalled, a document that ends with the following words: 'Brothers, the time has come to pay our tribute of gratitude to the country where we found moral freedom and material well-being. Immigrant Jews, do your duty, and long live France.'" As a meticulous sociologist applying to this question the statistical tools he created for *Suicide*, proceeding in the same way in order to bring significant correlations to light, Durkheim shows the very powerful participation of Russian Jews fighting in the French army; since the very small proportion of them who benefited from reform was accounted for by the fact that they still came under the jurisdiction of Russian law (the case of only sons), Durkheim felt that "the conditions created for them among us could not be harsher than the one they legally have in their homeland. Otherwise, the same military requirements would have to be made of the Belgians and the English who live in France and who would be liable to being called up according to our recruiting law while still being exempt from it according to their own law." He also denounced the fact that Jewish volunteers had been incorporated into the Foreign Legion, where they underwent anti-Semitic hazing rituals: since many of them asked to serve in the regular army and refused to obey, they were condemned to death and shot, crying out as they died, "Long live France! Long live the army! Down with the Legion!" "We would not dream," Durkheim writes, "of absolving an obviously guilty act. But the fact remains that this tragic scene, which could have been foreseen and avoided, necessarily had the effect of chilling the enthusiasm that had been shown in the beginning." He finally emphasized to what point a "veritable panic" had taken hold of the Russian Jews, who left for America or Spain following the anti-Semitic campaign, bringing a harsh blow to France's prestige abroad, in world opinion as well as among the allied governments, for instance the Americans, whose role was essential in waging war against the Germans. Confronting such a disaster, Durkheim, emphasizing his own role, writes, "We have succeeded, not without difficulty, in calming this emotion. We have been able to let the interested parties know. . . . We have managed to secure the result that they have some confidence in us." He protested about these "very serious facts" and asked the minister to intervene quickly to bring an end to the campaign of anti-Semitic denigration that the Russian Jews were undergoing.[112] Devoting a large part of his time to coming to their aid, Durkheim writes to Mauss, "Never have I been so Jewified. If that continues, I will soon become the adviser and tutor of exotic Judaism. It must be admitted that there are great miseries there of all kinds. I have just now received a letter from an unfortunate Russian Jew who shows all the signs of being persecuted by the police, and whose existence they are trying to sabotage. What misery!"[113] Day after day, Durkheim showed he was concerned with "the Jewish question in Russia" and confessed: "I am not sorry that I know a little bit about the question, from methodical study."[114] Once again, on this occasion, he was confronted with the Zionist perspective from which he had wanted to distance himself, during a previous incident linked with the publication of a text by Georg Simmel in *L'Année sociologique*:[115] since the English decided to take measures against Russian refugees identical with those taken by the French government, Durkheim sent them "a note exposing the faults of these measures, suggesting procedures that would allow their application to be tempered. My note was submitted to the English Home Secretary and to the Minister for War. . . . It is the Zionists who have provoked this measure. Now, they are tearing their hair out."[116] In this text submitted to the British authorities, Durkheim argued against measures called for by the "anti-Semitic party" in France. He used the argumentation of his previous report, quoted testimony about the reactions it provoked in the United States, by Jews who wrote in "yüdisch" (*sic*) newspapers, and hoped that the English measures which "violate the right of asylum" would be rescinded, since "that would prevent French anti-Semitism from using the example given by the English government as a pretext."[117]

Concerned with Judaism in his work as well as in his commitments, Durkheim showed himself to be attentive, with humor, to the presence, in his hotel in the Swiss Alps, "of co-religionists in the house; one notices this from the [copies of] *Aurore* and *Siècle* that come in."[118] His prejudices about "exotic Judaism" are identical to those that show up in the writings of Hannah Arendt, Isaiah Berlin, or Raymond Aron. From the beach at Cabour, on August 12, 1916, Durkheim writes again to Mauss, the trusted nephew to whom he could confide everything,

"Have already met thirty-six Jews here (or Jewesses) I know to be so, not counting the names of unknown Semites heard around us. But not one Indo-European whom I know! Such a reversal of natural proportions distorts many judgments," and on August 19, "The beach is full of Jews. I know more than thirty Semites of both sexes at Cabourg, and not one Indo-European!"[119] Annoyance of the assimilated Jew who has almost come to make his own the racist vocabulary of the time, an observation that verges on self-hatred from this prophet of the rationalist Republic, embodiment of the severe Franco-Judaism sensitive nonetheless to the "sufferings" of the Russian Jews, his "co-religionists." Confusion of feelings, untenable stance?

All through these years, although devoid of any religious belief, Durkheim remained faithful to the rituals of the Jewish world, which had the advantage, beyond the religious sphere, of maintaining the cohesion of the group by celebrating the major holidays; he went to Épinal, to his family home, to participate scrupulously in the rituals. According to Marcel Mauss, Durkheim "comes here, travels for twenty hours, spends forty hours here, including twelve in formal dress";[120] he looked happy at the prospect of an upcoming bar mitzvah.[121] Let us mention in closing an incident that says a lot about Durkheim, about his aptitude for "sacrifice" to save his cherished "family communism," to reinvent in his own way a behavior he studied so much in primitive societies where "warmth" and indispensable social solidarity reign. A new crisis broke out in 1900 between Marcel Mauss and his mother, since Durkheim's nephew stubbornly refused to take his grandmother to synagogue for the services. Durkheim writes to him:

> Of course, you should not have let yourself be induced to going to temple under the pretext of accompanying grandmother. But what prevented you from saying to your mother: "I am quite ready, of course, to accompany Grandmother and to come pick her up when she wants to come home"? The fact that you might have spent a quarter of an hour or half an hour at the temple before it was time to leave would not have been interpreted by anyone as a demonstration of piety, since you did not come to Rosh Hashanah, and since you did not put in an appearance the rest of the day on Yom Kippur. They would have seen nothing more in it than a necessary step to allow you to fulfill your obligations to your grandmother. . . .

I'm sorry one other idea didn't come to me today. If I had been in your place, I would have gone to find my mother and I would have said to her:

"The refusal I am forced to make to you and which is so difficult for me arises only from the fact that for me it's a matter of conscience not to attend practices that contradict my private feelings, which would be hypocrisy on my part. But I don't want you to interpret my attitude as meaning that I don't have the feelings I should have for you, for my father, etc. For your sakes, I am quite ready to make the only sacrifice I can make, namely material sacrifice. If you like, I will agree not to eat all day, just to show you that I am quite ready to make physical sacrifices to do something that pleases you. Then you wouldn't be able to say in those conditions that my attitude is dictated by personal, selfish considerations."

Perhaps, or even definitely, I would have done the thing, without even asking any questions. And when night had come, when it was dinnertime, I would have said all that very seriously, indicating my reasons and their significance.[122]

This lesson from Durkheim to his nephew Marcel Mauss, although wordy and naïve, says a lot about his respect for family obligations as a form of solidarity between generations, as an approach that should be taken to ensure the permanence and "warmth" of the group in times of secularization, to try to maintain, even in the heart of modernity, the cohesion of a group that has lost faith.

## *Three*  Georg Simmel:
## The Stranger, from Berlin to Chicago

Émile Durkheim did not conceal his hostility to the sociological theory developed in Germany by Georg Simmel, so distant was it from his own conceptions. Hardly concerned with echoing in France the interactionist analyses coming from beyond the Rhine, he nonetheless decided to publish in *L'Année sociologique* of 1896–97, after many delays and deletions for which he himself was responsible, a text by the rival German sociologist he held at arm's length: "How Societal Forms Are Maintained."[1] Some time later, on April 3, 1898, at the height of the Dreyfus Affair, when a number of anti-Semitic demonstrations were breaking out, Durkheim wrote in a letter to Célestin Bouglé: "I seem to recall that you had told me Simmel was Jewish. But I am a little surprised that he didn't tell me that when I asked him to delete the passage in his article on Zionnism [*sic*], telling him I was of Jewish origin and that people would treat me as a Zionnist [*sic*]."[2] We will probably never know the source of the supposedly slanderous information preserved by Bouglé. The least we can say is that it hardly corresponds to reality, and that it testifies more to the Durkheim's own fears, as eulogist for the republican nation-state deeply hostile to an Eastern European perspective, than to the German sociologist's actual feelings, he who also wanted to bring the process of assimilation to fulfillment and who also showed he was not very friendly toward "so-called Eastern Jews." Not long before, in 1897 during the first Zionist congress in Basel, Simmel had been invited to offer his understanding of the nature of the Zionist movement. His two letters of reply, which have remained almost completely unknown, deserve to be carefully quoted, so thoroughly do they reduce Durkheim's anxieties and so close do they come on this very point of view—more than our two sociologists, otherwise so far apart, could imagine:

> The idea that European Jews could settle down in any non-
> European country and cut the ties that attach them to European

culture is utopian. That is necessarily the case of Western Jews: German, French, or English Jews will never have any desire to leave the country in which they are so deeply rooted. As for the so-called Eastern Jews, they will be afraid of letting the European that is in them die, which they have acquired with great difficulty: they could easily suppose that emigrating to Asiatic countries would make them Asiatic once again, just as young women sometimes think that taking a new name after marrying makes them new people, different in every way from the women they had been before. That is what Zionism resembles from the psychological point of view. It is even worse when one ponders what will happen if the ideas of Herzl and Nordau become reality.

A state is not constructed by the intentional aspirations of each of its citizens: it grows organically, and this gradual, slow growth depends on a whole series of factors that those whom we call the builders of a state usually perceive only a small part of. . . . To begin to build a state intentionally is like wanting to build a house that has no foundations by beginning with the roof; it means people are trying to replace a collective advantage that has developed over a long period of time, coming from several generations, through isolated efforts over a very brief period of time by individuals acting one by one . . . that is the greatest impudence, and can have no meaning. . . . From the historical point of view, such an impudence is called utopia; in real life, it would have to be called a crime, obviously not an intentional one since even among the most intentional people, a lot of nonintention remains. It is for this reason that I do not look favorably on the Zionist project: it is also for this reason that I do not believe in its success.

Faced with some objections made by his correspondents, Simmel writes later on:

The Jews can just as easily disappear without leaving a trace, just like any other people, whether they possess a culture of high quality. It is not a question of dissolution [*Aufgehen*] but of fusion [*Verschmelzung*] with the other, and in the course of such a fusion of two nations a third nation emerges in which neither of the two nations has disappeared without leaving a trace, a new nation that bears the elements of both nations alike. Haven't the Germans already acquired many Jewish elements, and isn't that because the Jews are participating in the cultural life of Germany? The Jews are also taking on numerous elements of the German spirit. . . . I am surprised by this fear of death that is currently seizing the Jews even while their influence is increasing among all European peoples. The risk of dissolution does not at all threaten the Jews; on the contrary, they are at the stage of the Judaization of Europe. From the psychological angle, one notes Jewish elements in the blood of all peoples endowed with a culture, and this Judaization of non-Jews is taking place at the same time as the Europeanization of the Jews. The more the Jews become assimilated, the more they assimilate themselves, and the moment of their utmost assimilation will correspond to that of their greatest psychic influence. It is for this reason that I do not think it is right to say that I am pessimistic: one who observes the permanent growth of the nation cannot be pessimistic. I think it is those who are of the opinion that Judaism can be saved only by isolating it, by shutting it up in a distant cage, located on the other side of the sea, against which no one can launch an attack and that would be brought from time to time to Europe as a rare and peculiar thing so that Europe would not forget its anti-Semitism—I think those are the ones who are most affected by pessimism. But all dreams are vain. The Europeans and the Jews are firmly held in a solid cultural embrace.[3]

It would be difficult to be any clearer. Simmel displayed strong anti-Zionism; he argued against this utopia, this dream with criminal consequences that threatened the Jews' assimilation in European societies. There should be no question, in his mind, of artificially locking the Jews up in a "distant cage" on the other side of the sea, far from Europe, with the sole aim of sheltering them from anti-Semitic threats. Europe was still their fate, the definitive place of their flourishing, one which they should never renounce. In both Western and Eastern Europe, none of them could imagine themselves as "Asiatics," letting "the European die" that was in them. No doubt crossed Simmel's mind at that time— none, not even the constant and distressing anti-Semitic machinations he had to confront almost all the time, could make him call into question his concept of assimilation by "fusion" that ensured "the constant growth of the nation." Assimilation implies not only the dissolution but the fusion of two "peoples," a fusion that ensures the Jews the "greatest possible psychic influence" over all the European nations. Simmel revealed himself to be the eulogist of this "cultural embrace" extolled by so many writers and philosophers, who all emotionally stressed the exceptional character of this fusion that had so long been fertile, and that had produced, as we will see, so many personalities like Simmel, with a "bifurcated, contradictory" soul.[4] The sociologist could never have imagined what came after: long after his death (1918), Simmel's son Hans, the doctor in charge of a hospital in Berlin, was declared a "half-Jew" in 1933 even though his grandparents had converted: sent to a concentration camp, he managed to escape before emigrating to the United States; Gertrud Kantorowicz, his lifelong companion with whom he had an illicit love affair, a writer and poet, close friend of Marianne Weber, died after being deported by the Nazis to Theresienstadt; while the daughter born from their union, whom he always refused to meet, Angela, emigrated to that "utopian" Palestine to escape the Nazi anti-Semitic persecutions organized in the heart of the Europe so adored by her father (she died accidentally in 1942). This final "dissolution" demonstrates unfortunately that the "pessimism" felt by certain people at the turn of the century was scarcely exaggerated, and that actually the "embrace" was very fragile.

Unlike Marx, Simmel did not see the definitive emancipation of society coinciding with the end of Judaism. The assimilation of the Jews magnified their own values by ensuring a Judaization of society, one though that was capable—and he showed he was aware of this—of giving rise in turn to a violent anti-Semitism against the "intrusion of a foreign body into the German organism." Simmel came, via his parents, from that legendary Breslau where the rabbinical Seminary was created, in 1854, where Zacharias Frankel taught, as well as so many other Wissenschaft scholars attached to Judaism, or straying from it, like Heinrich Graetz.[5] Foreign to Jewish culture and traditions which he never knew, Simmel wanted simply to be a European, but not the way of Marx in vogue in Triers, on the western border of Germany, where the Enlightenment was triumphing. Though opposed like Durkheim to Zionism, confronted with just as virulent an anti-Semitism, he was pleased with this Judaization that was so incompatible with the strictly positivist perspectives defended in *Rules of Sociological Method*. It is true that the Germany of that end of the century was scarcely comparable to republican France where, despite anti-Semitic initiatives often led by the supporters of an intransigent Catholicism that found some echoes even in republican ranks, the Jews in government, not forced to convert, as a general rule pursued their administrative careers without hindrance. Durkheim's loyalty to Judaism stems more from inner convictions, from a private sphere: it does not go counter to that positivist vision of the world drawn from the Enlightenment that also guided the Republic. Hostile to positivism in imperial, reactionary, and Christian Germany that imposed conversion and still fought the Enlightenment, Simmel on the contrary saw the solution in the Judaization of society, in an "embrace" that ensured the triumph of new values, new behaviors; he whose parents converted, he who saw his career continually hindered by anti-Semitism, imagined no other solution than in this "fusion" that would create shared values. In such a context, for him, it was these values that ensured the solidity of the "embrace," not positivist science. The solidarity that Durkheim expected from the functional division of labor in society was based, in Simmel's eyes, on social relationships formed from values that bore shared meanings.

A non-Jew who was nonetheless regarded as Jewish by his contemporaries, Simmel could only hope for the swift triumph of those values. Unlike Durkheim, who remained Jewish, and Marx who converted in his youth, Simmel was born to parents who had already converted.[6] His great-grandfather was named Isaac Israel. His grandfather, Simon Isaac Simmel, was still very religious; born around 1780 in Silesia, he had the name Simmel imposed on him when Jews were forced to adopt German patronymics: it was quite probably a kind of nickname for Samuel, an ironic way of publicly preserving the Jewish origin of all the Simmels. Simon Isaac Simmel became a small-time shopkeeper and settled in Breslau, where his son Edouard, Georg's father, was born in 1810. A shopkeeper in turn, Edouard, during a trip to Paris, had himself baptized Catholic and took the name of Edouard Maria Simmel. Fortunate in business, he founded a chocolate-making enterprise that brought him considerable income, and in 1838 he married Flora Bodstein, who was also born in Breslau to Jewish parents in trade but was baptized Protestant. Georg was their only son. Born in Berlin, he would remain Protestant until the end of his life, like his mother. Georg was a brilliant student in philosophy and little by little made his way up the academic ladder, without however managing easily to obtain a permanent, well-paid position; he married Gertrud Kindel, a young Catholic woman raised by her mother in the Protestant faith, who would herself become a philosopher and author of several distinguished books. During his first meeting with Simmel, the young woman's father, Albert Kinel, asked him, "Are you Jewish?" and Simmel laconically replied, "My nose unfailingly betrays me."[7] Beyond this slightly ironic reply, Simmel perceived in himself another testimony, not physical but mental, of his adherence to the Jewish world: during one of his lecture courses at Berlin, he noted that "a century is merely the length of time we can feel as being the intellectual present. We can only remember three generations at one time: what one's grandfather told one's father, etc."[8] The grandfathers he remembered, who ensured transmission, were precisely the relatives who remained profoundly Jewish.

Not a Jew according to Jewish tradition, Simmel was permanently perceived as Jewish by his enemies as well as by his friends. There are an infinite number of anecdotes that describe him as "typically" Jewish. His closest friends saw him through very marked clichés. Thus, his non-Jewish friend, the poet Paul Ernst, writes, "By birth the philosopher was Jewish and, in a curious way, he had integrated the particular traits of Jewish sensibility and thought." Sophie Rickert, the wife of Heinrich Rickert, who was a close friend of Gertrud Kindel, Simmel's wife, said in 1948 that "Simmel was a tall person, thin, a completely Jewish type. The features of his face could not claim any beauty. One might even say they were grotesque. This was particularly striking when his wife was next to him. She was at least as tall as he, a light blond, and of such an Aryan type that the Third Reich itself would not have been able to find anything to object to in her. And despite all that, he was absolutely elegant." Again in 1948, Marianne Weber in turn declared: "Gertrud Simmel was a beautiful woman, tall and thin, full of grace and dignity, of pleasant Nordic appearance, blond with blue eyes, gentle, impressive features that suggested a certain reserve. What a funny couple, she and her husband Georg. He was barely average height, smaller than she, typically Jewish, not handsome; but what importance can the outer aspect have in a man with such a rich mind!" In the same vein, we might also cite this observation by Sabine Lepsius. In 1935, fifty years after their first meeting, she describes her childhood friend who had been her lover for a time: "His movements were . . . awkward. They said he was ugly but if you took the time to look at him, he wasn't, since his skull had a fine shape, his forehead was also almost handsome, his eyes were small but incredibly expressive. His nose was of the Jewish type, his mouth very thin and his body well-proportioned. . . . Only his thin, veined hands were ugly, and he gesticulated much too much with them."[9]

Mockingly perceived as Jewish by those close to him, Simmel was also seen this way by those who succeeded in hindering his appointment under explicitly anti-Semitic pretexts. Simmel vainly presented his candidacy for a number of professorships and finally managed to be appointed at Strasbourg only at fifty-six years of age, after a debate in the Parliament of Alsace-Lorraine had concluded that he could not be considered Jewish. Aware of this fact, Simmel, just after his appointment, in a rare public reaction to anti-Semitism, wrote to a delegate, "I rejoice at your intention of using your mandate to ameliorate our academic situation. . . . But it would be very difficult to present things to you so that they could make an impression in Parliament. It is a question in many respects of pernicious tendencies on the part of the administration that everyone who is in the academic world is aware of, but against which one obviously cannot accumulate juridical proofs, and which the Government would quite simply deny—anti-Semitism, for instance."[10] He accepted this position without enthusiasm since it was so far from Berlin, from the city he loved, and from his enthusiastic audience that passionately followed the lectures he sometimes gave voluntarily, in temporary jobs that were paid for by the session. The failures that punctuated his career were many: he attributed them explicitly in his private correspondence to anti-Semitism. Thus, on December 13, 1915, he congratulated Heinrich Rickert on his appointment to Heidelberg and added, "Unfortunately, the issues of anti-Semitism and age hinder Husserl's chances as well as my own." And a few days later, on December 26, he confided again to Rickert, "I know there are rumors about me concerning everything and anything, what I am, what I am not, what I am capable of, what I am incapable of. . . . One minute I'm too specialized, the next too polyvalent, here 'in fact, too sociological,' there 'has only a Talmudic perspicacity,' most often 'is only a destructive spirit.'"[11]

We'll mention first of all his first accreditation, in February 1884. On this occasion, Count Yorck von Wartenburg sent a congratulatory letter to Wilhelm Dilthey, who was sometimes accused of sharing widespread anti-Semitic feelings: "I congratulate you every time you keep out of teaching posts the superficial Jewish habits that lack any sense of the responsible thinking that would come from an ethnic group that has a psychological and physical sense of the soil."[12] Later on in 1908 Simmel did not succeed at being elected professor of philosophy at Heidelberg, despite the support of Max Weber, Heinrich Rickert, and Georg Jellinek; a letter from Dietrich Schäfer, a student of Treitschke, the nationalist historian, suddenly cancelled the whole process at the last instant. For Schäfer:

> Whether or not Professor Simmel was baptized, I know nothing about that, and I have not asked. But he is completely Israelite in his external appearances, in his manner of self-presentation and of thinking. It is possible that that has prevented his being hired abroad and his coming here, but one has no need of making such explanations since his academic and literary merits and successes are scant and mediocre. He gloats over the large size of his audience. . . . He speaks very slowly, doling his words out one at a time, on limited subjects. Certain Berlin circles appreciate this behavior. He feeds his statements with points that his audience appreciates. The ladies represent a large proportion of this audience. What's more, the Eastern contingent that has settled in Berlin and comes in waves from countries in the East is very strongly represented there. His deportment corresponds to his orientation and his tastes. . . . The completely or partly philo-Semite teacher can find fertile ground in such circumstances. . . . I absolutely cannot believe that they are improving Heidelberg by offering an even larger space to the ideologies held by Simmel than the one they already enjoy within the teaching faculty, so far are they from our classical German Christian training. . . . I think those points of view that are more destructive than formative and constructive have only a limited legitimacy in an era that tends to undermine everything, not only in a spirit of investigation but also for the pleasure of shocking. . . . Because of this, a request of appointing to a permanent post as professor was submitted on

behalf of Schooners' engagement, who so wished for a renewal of his contract. But in my opinion, sociology still has to acquire its qualifications as a science. To want to posit "society" as the plane of reference for the coexistence of individuals, instead of considering the ties between church and state is, in my eyes, a fatal error. Nor do I think that one can gain much from Simmel's writings. One cannot treat the intellectual life of great cities with such mediocrity or with so much bias as he did with Dresden.[13]

Weber had seen precisely who it was, before the same appointment, who addressed this candid letter to the faculty: "Attached are two lists; the first one contains the names of three Jews, the second three other names; the Jew listed third is superior to the first one on the list of non-Jews; but all the same I know you will only choose a name on the second list."[14] A firm supporter of Simmel's candidacy, Weber emphasized the dominant anti-Semitism to explain his failure.[15]

His friends as well as his enemies thought that Simmel, deprived of any sense of the soil, remained irremediably foreign to the German race: thus, without masking his prejudices, Aloys Fisher published in 1918 an article in which he tried to understand by what paradox such a "man of non-Germanic blood . . . the Semitic thinker, at whom people like to look askance, was capable of circumscribing the German spirit in art and philosophy."[16] Just as Count Yorck von Wartenburg in his letter to Dilthey emphasized that Simmel symbolized a "thinking without attachment to the soil" (*Bodenlos*), which made him a foreigner (*Fremd*) adapted to large artificial cities and to "superficial Jewish routine," the poet Ernst, Simmel's friend, wrote a letter to Georg Lukács in 1916 in which he described him as an "intelligent man without instincts. He has no roots, so that in his early years he spread himself thin in a surprising way so that, in the years when he should have realized his full potential, his strength failed him. I don't know if he feels that way himself; nonetheless I perceive him as a tragic being, and I can think of him only with the greatest compassion."[17]

Presented as a Jew without any of that natural attachment to the soil that alone produces roots capable of ensuring complete participation in German society, Simmel was also perceived by benevolent contemporaneous commentators who knew him in Berlin such as Nicholas

Spykman (whose study would for a long time be the only systematic presentation of Simmel's work in the United States) as "a person in whom certain ways of thinking are typically Jewish. His gift for analysis and abstraction, the subtlety of his dialectics, his use of analogy and symbols can be attributed to his Jewish origin."[18] He thought too that "it is his Jewish origins that are mostly responsible" for his failures in the Berlin university with its "Prussian manners" unfavorable to "the rapid appointment of Jewish teachers."[19] In the same vein, later on René König thought in turn that "perhaps it isn't by chance that the first objective analysis of the phenomenon of the large city in the German language was produced not by a normal academic researcher but by the Jewish philosopher Georg Simmel, who came from Berlin." For König, large cities are more tolerant toward Jews than small provincial towns, "hence it is understandable that it is precisely a Jew like Simmel, and not a 'normal' sociologist, who developed a particular rapport with the large city, a rapport he would try to deepen in a more theoretical way."[20] David Frisby, by contrast, one of the best contemporary interpreters of Simmel's work, wrote, "The marginality of Simmel's position in German society has often been rightly interpreted as stemming from his Jewish origins; however, no particular Jewish dimension can be discerned in his thinking."[21] He agreed in this with Albert Salomon, who attended Simmel's lectures and declared he was incapable of finding "even a glimmer of uniquely Jewish style in his writings."[22] It is true that Simmel's position on this point was far from being always explicit, and that he preferred, for instance, to keep quiet when faced with the constant anti-Semitism he came up against, remaining a "silent spectator."[23] If Simmel showed he was aware of his de facto belonging to the Jewish people; if, in his private life, he didn't hesitate to tell Jewish jokes that revealed a surprising familiarity with a milieu he never frequented; if, in his book *Religion* published in 1906 in a series edited by Martin Buber, he relied extensively, in a somewhat surprising way, on the logic of Rabbi Meir, from Galicia, to demonstrate one of his arguments,[24] he still remained detached from any religious belief—religion in general representing for him simple social forms void of any transcendence.

Simmel adapted profoundly to his German environment by placing himself "at the periphery of Jewish history."[25] He very rarely mentioned publicly his attachment to an identity that had become very tenuous. Thus, in 1903, he was invited to the home of Count Kessler, who reports their conversations: "Simmel spoke about himself. . . . He had been an idiot until he was thirty-five years old. What's more, he had a lot of doubts about himself. For nothing is more fleeting or tragic than precocious Jewish talents. In young Jews, talent seems to be something external that could completely detach itself from the personality and often quickly disappear. If he had been talented and had precociously gone on to his actual experiences, as a Jew, he thinks he would have shot himself in the head."[26] The future sociologist Herman Schmalenbach, a Protestant, who was then his student, told how in 1906, during a meeting that took place at the Simmel's, as he was concluding a presentation on the metaphysics of the Jews, Simmel reacted by saying surprisingly, "With Judaism, you'll do just as badly as the rest of us."[27] This very rare use of the word "us" evokes another famous and even more surprising remark made by Simmel when he was addressing Martin Buber, the Jewish philosopher and another one of his Berlin students whose work would be profoundly influenced by his theories of society, to the point that during his appointment at the University of Jerusalem his course outline was almost an exact copy of Simmel's themes on the most various social forms.[28] Long before his departure for Palestine, since Buber gave Simmel a copy of his book on Hassidism, *The Tales of Rabbi Nachman*, in 1906, Simmel read the introduction and replied, "We are all the same a strange and wonderful people" (*merkwürdiges*). Buber added that that was the only time he heard Simmel use, in this context, the pronoun "we." He thought that Simmel "had a way of thinking, and hand movements, that were Jewish" and reported that he heard him once refer to his manner of thinking as "a Talmudic pilpul."[29]

Aware of his place in Jewish history, which conferred on him a particular status and shaped his destiny, but ignorant of its culture, Simmel was nonetheless, in Ernst Bloch's opinion, somewhat pejoratively, marked by "the Jewish habits of the East."[30] He was also severely condemned by Franz Rosenzweig as "a Mephisto of the Jewish world": for the author of *The Star of Redemption*, the most erudite work of messianic Jewish philosophy, "where there is a strange, truly strange, way of thinking, something Simmel-like, then it's no longer our concern";

in his opinion, what Simmel says "is smoke, not food"; his body language betrays "the soulless man" whose thinking comes only from his brain since his heart has "atrophied."[31] A diabolical "oriental" Jew with a physical appearance and movements foreign to German culture, for a long time rejected by the university because of intransigent anti-Semitism, Simmel, who wanted to be a European assimilated into the "ancient ethnic group" of Germany, eventually rallied round to the policy of limiting appointments of Jewish professors which so affected him, and in 1906, two years before his own failure in Heidelberg, he advised against the hiring of Friedländer in a letter addressed to Rickert:

> When he asked me for advice and support concerning his nomination, I immediately wrote to him that his Jewish origin would be an obstacle in Germany. . . . For the interested party, it is truly an injustice. However, if I had to make decisions in a department, I must confess that I too would not let the number of Jewish teachers increase indefinitely. The Jewish way of thinking is quite simply as a general rule very different from the Germanic style, and though it is desirable that the two occur side by side, precisely for that reason it does not seem good to me to let the Jewish style dominate. There is of course a whole series of Jews who no longer possess that specificity of Jewish thinking, like Laks. In Dr. Friedländer too, it is not much present, and he should not be affected by the argument according to which it is desirable to limit Jewish influence at the University.[32]

Simmel would in vain, to the astonishment of his friends, don nationalist garb in the beginning of the First World War—managing to arouse the irony of Ernst Bloch, who emphasized "the gestures and vocabulary of the Jew from Eastern Europe, the Jewish mannerisms" of Simmel,[33] who surprised people all the more since he "conducted himself like a Teutonic Zionist,"[34] and that though a "friend of Bergson, an admirer of French culture, of its wines, its cuisine, he could participate in this war then . . . as a Jew he was never able to obtain a post as professor at the University of Berlin . . . he eventually gave in,"[35] there was no way to avoid it. Even if he "suffered" from the sacrifices of "our people,"[36] that is to say from the sufferings of the German nation at war with France, he remained in many respects, despite his nationalism, "foreign" to that society, and he bore all its stigmata almost to the point of sharing, although in a more exceptional way, that feeling of self-hatred that appeared in the writings of the other non-Jew, Karl Marx, and in the context of republican France, in Durkheim on vacation on the beaches of Normandy. Simmel's conception of assimilation justified his thorough identification with European Germany, as well as his rejection of Zionism as an artificial utopia.[37]

Was this stance as a "stranger in the academy,"[38] as a marginal person who remained solitary and without disciples, unlike Durkheim who became the undisputed leader of an institutionalized sociological school of teaching,[39] his position as an *outsider*, his lack of being rooted in the land, what urged him to write in his *Sociology* (1907) about "the stranger":

> The classical example is the history of European Jews. The stranger is by nature no "owner of soil"—soil not only in the physical, but also in the figurative sense of a life-substance which is fixed, if not in a point in space, at least in an ideal point of the social environment. Although in more intimate relations, he may develop all kinds of charm and significance, as long as he is considered a stranger in the eyes of the other, he is not an "owner of the soil."[40]

Isn't it his own failure that Simmel speaks of who, despite the incredible "seduction" he exercised over his audiences, remained in the eyes of others, although he was neither a Jew nor a stranger, a foreign Jew without any ties to the soil? Even worse, this quality of being a stranger pursued him even in the "private relationships of person to person," in the very heart of this interaction to which he devoted the main part of his work as constituting social existence. This thesis of the Jew as symbol of the stranger appears as early as in his *Philosophy of Money*, published in 1900.

> There is no need to emphasize that the Jews are the best example of the correlation between the central role of money interests and social deprivation. . . . Because the wealth of the Jews consisted of money, they became a particularly sought-after and profitable object of exploitation, for no other possessions can be expropriated as easily, simply, and without loss. . . . If one deprives somebody of his land, it is impossible—except by turning it into cash—to realize the benefit right away, since time, effort and expenses are required. . . . The relationship of Jews to money in general is more evident in a sociological

constellation that gives expression to that character of money. The role that the stranger plays within a social group directs him, from the outset, towards relations with the group that are mediated by money, above all because of the transportability and the extensive usefulness of money outside the boundaries of the group. . . . There is another connection between the sociological importance of the stranger and of money . . . the basic interest of money expresses itself first and foremost in trade. . . . The fact that the Jews became a trading people is due not only to their suppression but also to their dispersal throughout all countries. The Jews became familiar with money business only during the last Babylonian exile, prior to which time it was unknown to them. This is emphasized by the fact that it was particularly the Jews of the Diaspora who followed this profession in large numbers. Dispersed peoples, crowded into more or less closed cultural circles, can hardly put down roots or find a free position in production. They are therefore dependent on immediate trade which is much more elastic than primary production, since the sphere of trade can be expanded almost limitlessly by merely formal combinations and can absorb people from outside whose roots do not lie in the group. The basic trait of Jewish mentality to be much more interested in logical-formal combinations than in substantive creative production must be understood in the light of their economic condition. The fact that the Jew was a stranger who was not organically connected with his economic group directed him to trade and its sublimation in pure monetary transactions. . . . It was of particular importance that the Jew was a stranger not only with regard to the local people, but also with regard to religion. . . . The high interest rate charged by Jews was the result of their being excluded from land ownership.[41]

Unlike Marx, Simmel explained the role of the Jews in their use of money as a means of exchange and their function in negotiation through historical reasons: far from being inscribed in their nature, from being at the heart of their culture, this special relationship with money is shown to be the consequence of their status as strangers without "attachment to the land," strangers "in their ethnicity but also in their religion." Simmel historicizes even better than Marx the function of the Jews in commerce through their dispersion after the time of the Babylonian exile, an exile that conferred on them the most formidable privilege of all, that of remaining the Other. As the Stranger par excellence, "rootless," the Jew was the only one capable of exercising that dangerous and unstable monetary function that in turn gave rise to retaliatory financial measures, confiscation, exorbitant financial requisitions, and the most unjust impositions. Also even better than Marx, Simmel explained in this way the anti-Semitic "hatred," provoked involuntarily by the Jews who assumed a function because of their status as Stranger, their "pariah" condition, which facilitated sudden and frequent expulsions. The "hatred of the people" was also directed against the big financial firms whose local representatives were most often foreigners and, against the Rothschilds, the Médicis, and the Grimaldis: "Tales of horror spread about the origin of the Grinaldi, the Medici and the Rothschild fortunes, not only in the sense of moral duplicity but in a superstitious way as if a demonic spirit was at work."[42] All the same, the hostility of the church toward Jews would concern their monotheistic beliefs, which would predispose them to the handling of the abstract symbol represented by money as the general and absolute equivalent of all values.[43] Again unlike Karl Marx, Simmel emphasized how much the persecutions provoked by their involuntary identification with money hurt rich Jews as well as poor Jews, with the latter, so numerous, affected by the same pitiless measures of repression and expulsion. Rich or poor, they both were perceived as foreigners without territorial attachments, lacking any organic link with their society.

In *The Philosophy of Money*, Simmel established a very close link between the status of stranger and the Jews who had "come from outside, and did not belong to the group." In these few pages devoted to the Jews of the diaspora who "represented the finest example" of his more general sociology of various social groups in charge of money,[44] Simmel continually described them as strangers and, mainly through them, constructed a veritable theory of the function the stranger performs. Simmel ended his study, writing that "today, there are no more strangers according to the old acceptation of the term; commercial liaisons, with their rights and uses, have made countries that are very far apart from each other one single organism becoming more and more unified. . . . The contradiction that . . . existed between natives and strangers has disappeared for the good reason that the monetary form of circulation, once carried by it, has now taken over the totality of the economic sphere."[45] Using this remark as an argument, some people conclude from it that "it would not be the exclusion of the Jew as stranger that constitutes modernity. The stranger, even in the case where the Jew was regarded as foreign, should always be understood as being the product of a form of interaction."[46] One tends thus to defend a more general theory of the stranger within the framework of the purely interactional approach unique to Simmel "analytically" separated from its content. In this sense, we can imagine that if Simmel regarded himself as a stranger, it was more from the geographic than from the sociological point of view; when he was teaching at Strasbourg, far from Berlin, in semiexile, he became a stranger who had nothing in common with the figure of the Jew as "the finest example" of a stranger within society.[47]

Such an interpretation, common to a number of commentators who downplay Jewish exemplarity in the Simmelian theory of the stranger, does not really seem based on a reading of *Sociology*, the other fundamental work by Simmel, published in 1907.

> The stranger is thus being discussed here, not in the sense often touched upon in the past, as the wanderer who comes today and goes tomorrow, but rather as the person who comes today and stays tomorrow. . . . He is fixed within a particular spatial group, or within a group whose boundaries are similar to spatial boundaries. But his position in this group is determined, essentially, by the fact that he has not belonged to it from the beginning, that he imports qualities into it, which do not and cannot stem from the group itself.
>
> The unity of nearness and remoteness involved in every human relation is organized, in the phenomenon of the stranger, in a way which may be most briefly formulated by saying that in the relationships to him, distance means that the near is far, while strangeness means that the far is actually near. For, to be a stranger is naturally a very positive relation; it is a specific form of interaction. . . . The stranger, like the poor and like sundry "inner enemies," is an element of the group itself. His position as a full-fledged member involves both being outside it and confronting it. . . .
>
> Throughout the history of economics the stranger everywhere appears as the trader, or the trader as stranger. . . . The classical example is the history of European Jews. The stranger is by nature no "owner

of soil"—soil not only in the physical, but also in the figurative sense of a life-substance which is fixed, if not in a point in space, at least in an ideal point of the social environment.[48]

The single empirical example of the stranger given by Simmel is indeed that of the European Jews who, as in *The Philosophy of Money*, assure, from the fact of their exteriority to the group, the financial and commercial function that has settled upon them all the more readily since they lack any link with the soil, in the physical as well as the metaphorical sense—an example used again almost identically in these two fundamental works.[49] The stranger differs also from the stateless person, the exile, the émigré, and even more from the nomad since he is the one who "comes today and stays tomorrow." He is an integral part of a group for which he definitively remains, like "the sundry inner enemies," a stranger preserving his "exteriority" despite a particularly intimate "specific form of interaction" since, unlike the nomad or the vagabond, he mingles in the normal social relationships of the group. Indeed, the figure of the stranger represents in a more general way "human relations," a social form that stems from an interactionist sociology that is applicable as such,[50] as we will see later on, in the most varied empirical contexts. Nevertheless, Simmel constructed it starting from the sole historical example of the European Jews, even though he did briefly mention the case of lovers who became strangers to each other, and the example of the relationship of the Greeks with the "barbarians" that he finally ended up excluding,[51] since it lacked any positive dimension and remained "a nonrelationship." In this sense, one can say that "the stranger in Simmel is, from a cognitive point of view, an *insider*, but, from a social and normative point of view, an *outsider*. . . . Simmel thinks that the Jews of Europe are the prototype of the stranger. They are not only visitors come from afar but they participate in an intimate way in the *Lebenswelt* of Europe while still remaining apart."[52] We can reflect that the foreignness of the Jew is above all the reflection of a phenomenological condition that, as Michael Walzer remarks in criticizing the image constructed by Simmel, is sometimes consciously used to make use of this distance and exercise a specific isolated role, protected from any involvement in the "local" framework in which Walzer wants to immerse completely.[53]

When he was concluding these classic pages, Simmel, despite every-thing, distinguished the situation of the stranger, emphasizing that "in the case of the stranger to the country, the city, or the race," what is not common does not stem from the individual but from the collective, that is to say from a like foreign origin.

> For this reason, strangers are not really conceived as individuals, but as strangers of a particular type: the element of distance is no less general in regard to them than the element of nearness.
> This form is the basis of such a special case, for instance, as the tax levied in Frankfurt and elsewhere upon medieval Jews. Whereas the *Beede* [tax] paid by the Christian citizen changed with the changes of his fortune, it was fixed once for all for every single Jew. This fixity rested on the fact that the Jew had his social position as a *Jew*, not as the individual bearer of certain objective contents. Every other citizen was the owner of a particular amount of property, and his tax followed its fluctuations. But the Jew as a taxpayer was, in the first place, a Jew, and thus his tax situation had an invariable element. . . .
> In spite of being inorganically appended to it, the stranger is yet an organic member of the group. Its uniform life includes the specific conditions of this element.[54]

The reification of the stranger, which almost makes him lose in the eyes of the other his dimension as singular social protagonist, is thus especially verified, in Simmel's opinion, in the example of the Jew who is liable to taxation first of all as a Jew. If he is nonetheless an "organic member of the group" despite his status as "being inorganically ap-pended to it," if he is doomed to be thought of, unlike the traveler, as a vagabond or an exile, as "someone who comes today and stays to-morrow," the Jew, who best symbolizes the close and distant situation of the stranger, arouses violent reactions of rejection. Such feelings are directed at a "close" person who has still remained distant, a man of "objectivity" in whom people have agreed to confide since he always re-mains different from those who are too close;[55] even if he is "an organic member of the group," he is a collective and not an individual figure that it is now a matter of rejecting with all the more force since that fig-ure has been too much integrated into the normal functioning of soci-ety. Thereafter, "although in more intimate relations, he may develop all kinds of charm and significance, as long as he is considered a stranger in the eyes of the other, he is not an 'owner of the soil.'"[56] Simmel offers us here an original interpretation of anti-Semitism as a form of rejection of the Stranger-Jew profoundly assimilated into society, who has even become, as in the Germany of the time, an organic element provoking the violent rejection of his now familiar presence. The particularly emphatic symbiosis between German society and its Jews is here alluded to, one which did not prevent the steady rejection of Simmel himself, who remained despite all the "seductions" he could exercise over his audiences a stranger to the academy but also, finally, to German identity itself, a "man without qualities" other than Judaism, an individual denied in his particularities, linked indissolubly to an unchanging collective entity devoid of any link to the soil, irremediably foreign.

Simmel's stranger can thus not be considered simply as a crystallized sociological form "analytically separate from the possible contexts that could be assigned to it," an Other who "is not just someone who lives in or comes from a foreign country but virtually any other, that is, all others outside of me."[57] Of course Simmel's distinctions between proximity and distance of the stranger, which confer on him a distant and thus more objective position, allowing him to become a privileged interlocutor precisely because he does not belong to the group himself, and thus ensuring a positive function and not being pure negativity, have led to a more general theory of social distance within the interactional relationship, valid as social form for all conceivable classes of figures, regardless of their context. As Simmel emphasizes, "in the relationship to him, distance means that he, who is close by, is far, and strangeness means that he, who also is far, is actually near." This fertile distinction has been the object of a considerable number of applications quite removed from the particular case of the Jews. Nevertheless, from one work to the other, Simmel sees above all in the Jew the exemplary figure of the stranger; he thus historicizes the quality that affected him throughout his own life. Although it has become one crystallized social form among others, applicable to every imaginable social context, one would be wrong, as many commentators propose, to evoke this dimension of the stranger only for the record, to make it the characteristic of an individual who is directly concerned in modern life by being profoundly integrated into the social interactions characteristic of great cities, and to see only the positive side of the situation of the stranger before anything else, passing quickly over the violent rejections the stranger provoked. Indeed, Simmel himself notes that "to be a stranger is naturally a very positive relation; it is a specific form of interaction." Simmel does not, however, disregard the "repulsion" the stranger arouses of an intimacy that has become too weighty,[58] which above all affected the Jews who left the ghettos and went straight into modern societies, within which they became assimilated, but from which they were often rejected, especially in the role that has settled on them, the handling of money or commerce. Like Siegfried Kracauer, who had been his student, and like Walter Benjamin, Simmel offers an early description of the immense metropolises, of those places of temporary residence where the Jews, under the gaze of other city-dwellers, symbolize the stranger, the nomad, the uprooted migrant come from elsewhere, the permanent exile.[59]

In his various writings, but especially in *Sociology*, Simmel shows a lively concern with Jewish history as well as with the nature of the solidarity that unites Jews despite their situation of great dispersion. Already, in "How Social Forms Are Maintained," he sets out to show "in the personal plasticity of the Jew, in his remarkable aptitude for getting used to the most diverse tasks, for adapting to the most adverse conditions of existence, like an individual reflection of the general characteristics of the group."[60] In this article, he asserts that "the social unity of the Jews, despite their physiological and denominational unity, has become singularly relaxed since their dispersion: it has never been solidly renewed except where one of their groups has remained solidly fixed in place, over a relatively long period, on one single territory."[61] The very place, consequently, where they are perceived as strangers destined, according to Simmel's phrase, to remain beyond the next day. In *Sociology*, almost ten years later, Simmel offers these considerations again, almost word for word, wonders about "the self-preservation of a social unit," its permanence which "can rest precisely on its plasticity," and on this plasticity that the Jews demonstrate in the "suppleness" of their relationships with their adopted society.[62] He shows how the destruction of the Temple of Jerusalem by Titus "attained its goal, to annihilate the Jewish theocratic state, which was a contradiction and a danger for the political unity of the Roman Empire—in the eyes of many Jews, for whom this centralization had almost no importance,"[63] and adds that "as long as the Temple existed in Jerusalem, an invisible thread tied it to each of the Jews scattered throughout many places with their diversity of nationalities, interests, languages, religious differences." From then on, "the true factor of the cohesion of the Jews was less and less religion and more and more race,"[64] which fixed them in a permanent and different entirety. Beyond the figure of the stranger, Simmel uses elements drawn from Jewish history to construct certain elements of his general sociology. Thus, when he looks for examples of the nature of the group being determined from the quantitative point of view, he shows that the decimal principle served in the distribution of the Jews in their return from the second exile, and he also emphasizes that "there must always be at least ten Jews present to pray."[65] He returns briefly to their specific case when he approaches the social forms of domination and subordination,[66] mentions several times their spatial form of organization,[67] and in this context shows real knowledge of the foundations of Jewish thought, even discussing the philosophy of Maimonides.[68]

Simmel could never have imagined that the German Jews would, not long after his death, become strangers pursued and exterminated in their own country, that the foreignness of the Jews, despite their organic belonging to the German nation, would trigger a hatred that would lead to the almost complete disappearance of German Judaism, to the deportation of his own people. A chasm would open between the German Jews who managed to survive by emigrating to the United States and their old country; the metaphors of proximity and distance no longer meant anything: the stranger had lost his function, his objectivity didn't make sense, confidence in him was no longer appropriate. The figure of the stranger in human relations was suddenly overtaken by History; tragedy stripped him of his normality, which was made of a subtle play of intimacy and distance, of attentiveness and withdrawal. Suddenly, the stranger no longer had his place in society; he lost any role other than that of victim for a people desperate for a scapegoat. From then on, Simmelian sociology would be without heirs in Germany. Aside from Max Weber and others who took inspiration from it at the turn of the century, Simmel's sociological perspective would be reborn, almost omnipresent, on the other side of the Atlantic, to such a point that one can argue that "Simmel occupies a unique position: he is the only European academic whose strong influence on American sociology was exercised throughout the entire twentieth century."[69]

The figure of the stranger, for the Jews of German culture who had emigrated to the United States because of the rise of Nazism, elicited contrasting interpretations: Alfred Schütz gave an optimistic version of it while Albert Salomon approached it in a decidedly more pessimistic way. Alfred Schütz, who had to leave his native Austria for lasting exile in America, in 1944 wrote his essay on the stranger, inspired by, among other things, the reflections presented by Simmel, although he refers only once to the example of immigrant Jews.[70] In his opinion, the stranger represents an individual "who tries to be accepted permanently or at least tolerated by the group which he approaches," while he is completely excluded from his past, from his memories, and he can share only his future; from the point of view of the group he is headed toward, "he is a man without history"; the stranger is thus "external" to this group and finds himself forced to "translate" his own values in order to adapt them to his host group. According to Schütz, "If we succeed in this endeavor, then that which formerly was a strange fact and a puzzling problem to our mind is transformed into an additional element of our warranted knowledge. We have enlarged and adjusted our stock of experiences. What is commonly called the process of social adjustment which the newcomer has to undergo is but a special case of this general principle . . . the stranger is no stranger any more, and his specific problems have been solved."[71] For Schütz, when the stranger refuses or shows he is incapable of carrying through this process, when he can't manage to "translate" his values to make them agree with those of the host group, if he doesn't succeed at "adjusting" by traversing the "labyrinth" that leads him to this group, then "the stranger remains what Park and Stonequist have aptly called a 'marginal man,' a cultural hybrid on the verge of two different patterns of group life, not knowing to which of them he belongs."[72] Setting aside this pessimistic hypothesis, which we will examine later on, Schütz is especially interested in the "newcomer" who manages to enter the in-group, to merge with the primary group. In this spirit, the stranger is transformed into an immigrant who succeeds at assimilating with the group and ultimately dissolving into it, losing all distance from it: the Simmelian figure of the stranger here undergoes a profound transformation. While in Simmel the stranger is part of society simply by being different and by preserving this difference, like the Jews in Germany, the "newcomer" corresponds to the immigrant who, having come from abroad, abandons his cultural models and disappears into the primary group. Schütz is inspired by Charles Cooley and Ellsworth Faris, classical authors of the American theory of primary groups, to justify this turning away from Simmel's work, which he nonetheless quotes favorably several times.[73] The United States is not Germany: the American assimilationist model feeds on a continuous emigration that the machine of the "melting pot" is supposed to transform effectively. Even if the "newcomer" is distinguished from the "homecomer,"[74] from the one who, like Ulysses, returns home, like American veterans coming home from the war, if he has more difficulties adapting to a new environment which requires only a swift readaptation in the "homecomer," both finally want to adjust, whereas the stranger wants to preserve his distance with relation to the host group and means to stay faithful to his own history while still being close, integrated, with the host group. Simmel's figure has changed its nature: the stranger has become an immigrant, like Schütz himself, who knows how to adapt to his new environment. In the United States, Jewish immigrants are thus no longer, like Simmel earlier in Germany, strangers to the academic system: no institutional barrier hinders their entrance into the different spheres of society.

This optimistic vision of the stranger was rejected by another Jew who left Germany, Albert Salomon. A native of Berlin, this former student of Simmel, who had belonged to Max Weber's circle, became a specialist in the philosophy of Weber. Fearing for his life, he left Hitler's Germany, and like many specialists in the social sciences who were Jewish, he joined as an exile the New School for Social Research, where he gave a number of seminars on Simmel's work.[75] Not only did Salomon write the article "Simmel" in the *Universal Jewish Encyclopedia* in 1943, but twenty years later, in January 1963, he gave another lecture on Simmel's work at the Leo Baeck Institute, a prestigious institution that has devoted itself especially to the study of German Judaism.[76] In the presence of Siegfried Kracauer, a Jewish philosopher and essayist who knew Simmel, Salomon discussed Simmel's career, emphasized the harshness of the anti-Semitism he had to confront, and then spoke at some length about the question of the stranger, first taking a stand against the interpretation he called too "optimistic" that Alfred Schütz gave of him, who regarded the stranger above all as a more or less conformist immigrant.[77] He then attacked Simmel's figure of the stranger, distinguishing it radically from the poor man who, unlike the perspective given in *Sociology*, was a member of the host group. He questioned the idea that the stranger receives a legitimate place among those who accept him. He lamented, too, that Simmel included the stranger in a supposedly positive process of reciprocity with the host group, concluding finally persuasively that "the situation of the stranger constitutes a veritable hell. Shakespeare, who knew everything, was better informed than Simmel. . . . The Simmelian definition of the stranger is, consequently, hardly satisfying, from either a sociological or ontological point of view."[78] Unlike the optimistic view of Schütz, Salomon attacked Simmel's definition, which he criticizes in the end for an identical all too irenic interpretation of the stranger, as if the two men—one in Germany, the other in the United states—thought they could finally be recognized and accepted by the host group, underestimating the "eternal malady" that anti-Semitism constitutes in both societies. This hopeless vision of the fate of the Jewish immigrant gives the status of the stranger its tragedy, its historic density; it could not simply be dealt with in terms of adaptation, of a subtle distance that might portend an often illusory intimacy. In this open and tolerant New York, in the presence of some survivors of German Jewry who had not long before been so prestigious, Salomon said simply that the Jewish stranger remained a stranger everywhere, that he lived "a hell." During this lecture, his last words were: "We are all living in the communion of suffering."[79] Facing his Jewish audience at the Leo Baeck Institute, this distant heir of those scholars of Wissenschaft who felt certain about their exceptional fruitfulness within the German society of long ago, Salomon did not share any of Simmel's or Schütz's illusions. His desperate gaze directed at the figure of the stranger was no less exceptional, especially in the context of America.

An adaptation that was more faithful to a less tragic and less charged vision of historicity would mark American social sciences, relegating Salomon's anxieties to the background. Elaborated long before the Shoah, it was imported to the United States by a non-Jew, the sociologist Robert Ezra Park, who in 1899–1900 attended Simmel's lectures in Berlin; from Simmel, Park writes, "I received my only formal instruction in sociology."[80] In this sense, "if one single person could be considered by Park as being *the* sociologist, it could only be Simmel."[81] It was through Park's work that Simmel would cross the Atlantic Ocean to be born again in Chicago. Park grew up in Minnesota, in America's heartland; he studied at the University of Baltimore, then at the University of Michigan, where he met John Dewey, who urged him to analyze journalism as an activity that was close to everyday life; he became a journalist in Baltimore, a profession he exercised for a long time also in New York and Chicago. He then returned to the university, to Harvard, where William James was teaching. It was then that he went to Germany and discovered Simmel and his phenomenology of everyday life, which he immediately felt close to as a journalist concerned with the small actions of life, with attentiveness to the people who performed them, analyzing their values. Once he had returned to Chicago, Park would devote himself to making Simmel's perspectives known, which the sociologist Albion Small, who had known Simmel when he was a student in Berlin before he founded the sociology department at Chicago in 1895, had begun to convey first. Park, a sociologist of primary groups, who succeeded Small as head of the department, was joined there by Ernest Burgess, with whom he would work closely: together they published a monumental *Introduction to the Science of Sociology* in 1921, which would for a long time influence the teaching of the discipline in the United States. This essential book gives a considerable place to Simmel, who is cited, as indicated by the index, more than sixty times.[82] Simmel's influence is perceptible; a number of his texts were presented here for the first time, such as the one that, in *Sociology*, deals with the stranger: introducing these pages, the authors also conceived of the stranger with the features of the immigrant confronted with adaptation (*accommodation*) or with "assimilation" into the society of welcome. Here Park constructs a theory of assimilation that would be discussed again later on to compare it with Simmel's perspectives, but the influence of Simmel can be gauged especially in the questions offered for students to discuss. Following the chapter devoted to the stranger, the questions are presented as a clarification of Simmel's opinions on the "near" and the "far," the prestige of the stranger, his intimacy with the people in the group; many of the questions, here as well as elsewhere in the book, concern the Jews in general, the wandering Jew, respect for the Sabbath, or else the relationships between the Jews and the Americans from the point of view of isolation and contact.[83]

A few years later on, in May 1928, Park published in the *American Journal of Sociology* his famous article "Human Migration and the Marginal Man," in which he presented this notion of the marginal man, which would be frequently used by many American sociologists.

> When the walls of the medieval ghettos were torn down and the Jew was permitted to participate in the cultural life of the peoples among whom he lived, there appeared a new type of personality, namely, a cultural hybrid, a man living and sharing intimately in the cultural life and traditions of two distinct peoples; never quite willing to break, even if he were permitted to do so, with his past and his traditions, and not quite accepted, because of racial prejudice, in the new society in which he now sought to find a place. He was a man on the margin of two cultures and two societies, which never completely interpenetrated and fused. The emancipated Jew was, and is, historically and typically, the marginal man, the first cosmopolite and citizen of the world. He is, par excellence, "the stranger," whom Simmel, himself a Jew, has described with such profound insight and understanding in his *Sociologie*. Most if not all the characteristics of the Jew, certainly his preeminence as a trader and his keen intellectual interest, his sophistication, his idealism, and lack of historic sense, are the characteristics of the city man.[84]

Park gave birth to the Chicago School, which placed the urban environment in the heart of its researches, and drew explicitly from the work of Simmel as a sociologist of large cities, but also as a theoretician of the stranger: the German sociologist that Park curiously thought of as Jewish and, consequently, from this point of view, as a stranger, was also perceived as being between two cultures, as were all marginal men whose position he tried to theorize as between "two peoples."

All of a sudden, the Jew as "perfect type" of the marginal man, as the best example of the stranger according to Simmel, played a considerable role in his work, insofar as he symbolized the inhabitants of large, open, modern cities, of which they themselves were the best analysts. Although Park spent more of his work studying black Americans, although he conducted empirical investigations on the black populations of the United states, although he was connected with black individuals who were anxious, like him, to bring an end to their intolerable racial situation, although this reformer who was supposedly favorable to a gradual development of black Americans did not hide the fact that he thought their violent rebellion both normal and productive of more justice,[85] though he constructed his work by reflecting above all on the status of blacks in large cities,[86] he never forgot, following Simmel's example, the example of the Jews when he came to describe the particularly delicate process of acculturation the stranger was confronted with because of his accent, his manner of expressing himself,[87] or when he described their racial status as a foreign and stigmatized cultural community, comparable from this point of view with the blacks,[88] with both perceived as "racial Hybrids,"[89] going on to contrast them nevertheless with the blacks as a particularly "sophisticated" people who readily acquired idealistic and revolutionary perspectives whereas the blacks, of whom he would be a great defender, were considered, since they were closer to nature and to the local, as "the woman among the races," an expression for which he would often be criticized.[90]

Thus Park constructed the notion of an "immigrant community" beginning with the example of the Jews, who "were more at home [in the United States] than in almost any other place in the world. The Jew is more at home in New York than in Jerusalem." More than any other group that immigrated to the United States, the Jews, as strangers/immigrants, illustrate a form of multiple identities, a "hyphenated American."[91] Park, who lived in Chicago in a Jewish neighborhood that had several Yiddish theaters, became a remarkable analyst of the Yiddish-language Jewish press, which started in the United States, and emphasized that "in America, the most interesting foreign-language newspapers are the Yiddish ones," since, through them, just as to a lesser degree through the other newspapers of the various minorities, both internal traditions and an openness to the world that allowed assimilation were expressed.[92] Comparing the Jews to the Italians and Mexicans in a very detailed way, describing their communitarian organization, their synagogues, their philanthropic and territorial organization, and so on, Park thought that "from the standpoint of organization the Jews are the most interesting of the immigrant groups."[93] Haunted by this subject, which he had certainly discovered almost half a century earlier through Simmel, as late as 1944, not long before his death, Park wrote the article "Jews in a Gentile World, The Problem of Anti-Semitism," in which he pursued his investigation of Jews as "strangers" in a society of gentiles.[94]

Still, Park seemed to hesitate. Though in his fundamental article "Human Migration and the Marginal Man" Park defined the Jew as a marginal man par excellence "who even if given a chance never wants to break with his past and his traditions"; though in much of his research he highlighted the Jew's desire for collective resistance to the host society, as well as the Jew's rejection of total assimilation; though he even seemed to admire this identitarian persistence that allowed the Jew to preserve a certain "distance"; though he consequently remained more faithful than was usually admitted to Simmel's definition of the Jew as stranger, the fact is that when Park constructed his general theory of assimilation into American society, he came to consider the Jew as the typical example of the immigrant marginal man on his way to rapid assimilation.[95] The stranger par excellence, a marginal being, the immigrant Jew seems henceforth to adapt perfectly to the process of entering American society that takes place, according to Park, in four stages that the various immigrant populations follow in turn, a process that takes them from competition to conflict, then to compromise, and finally, to assimilation.[96] Marginal men of large cities par excellence, the Jews are thus distinguished from the blacks, whom Park spent so long studying: by their adaptability and their mobility, Jews can rapidly climb the social ladder, leave their spatial ghetto, and through their own communitarian institutions, complete the process of assimilation. Park modified the definition Simmel gave of the stranger by identifying him now only with the immigrant come from elsewhere, who dissolves into the welcoming society by means of an assimilation that

Simmel's stranger doesn't seek. In this sense, Park adapted Simmel's figure to the American situation as an open society. For Park, the Jews "are losing the marks of [their] identity" as prejudices in the United States disappear: the Italians too should follow this example, according to Park, since their communitarian structure predisposes them "to identify [their] interests with America. Because Jewish organizations make the Jew efficient they prepare him to use all the American institutions. . . . Assimilation is thus as inevitable as it is desirable; it is impossible for the immigrants we receive to remain permanently in separate groups. . . . If we give the immigrants a favorable milieu, if we tolerate their strangeness during their period of adjustment, if we give them freedom to make their own connections between old and new experiences . . . then we hasten their assimilation."[97] Thus the example of immigrant Jews is from then on paradigmatic for the process of assimilation that all immigrant groups experience, a process "of interpenetration and fusion in which persons and groups acquire the memories, sentiments, and attitudes of other persons or groups, and, by sharing their experience and history, are incorporated with them in a common cultural life."[98] Having become a marginal man, the stranger is less and less a stranger to American society. In this sense, one could with reason show how much this assimilationist vision of the marginal immigrant who aspires to become assimilated even if he is sometimes rejected, of the marginal man torn apart and traumatized by such an experience, differs fundamentally from Simmel's stranger who remains distanced, arouses confidence thanks to his supposed objectivity, and keeps his identity, thus not suffering a rupture of personality. This interpretation of the marginal man is precisely the one that was preserved by Park's heirs, who wrongly liken it to the figure of the stranger constructed by Simmel. But this reproach so often made of Park himself is not always well founded.

Through the figure of the marginal man, Simmel's metaphor for the stranger, modified where necessary for the more open context of the United States, is introduced to American sociology. Chicago, the metropolis of the New World, thus takes over from Berlin, one of the great capitals of that Europe where the giant contemporary cities were born. In Chicago, Park's students would try to get a better understanding of the thinking as well as the social strategies of this marginal man, this "hybrid individual" in the process of assimilation. Some, like the black sociologist Edward Franklin Frazier, who were faithful to Park's studies concerning American blacks as tragic exceptions to the general process of assimilation, devoted their lives to enriching this sociology of a group that remained excluded from open society.[99] Others, less numerous and often Jewish, in the lineage of Simmel and Park, turned their attention to the future of American Jews. In 1925, when YIVO in Vilnius institutionalized the studies of the social sciences concerned with Jews, at the conference of the American Sociological Society presided over by Park, a number of students of the Chicago School presented papers: among them was Louis Wirth, whose lecture was entitled "Some Jewish Types of Personality."[100] This lecture was published in 1926 in the very official *Publication of the American Sociological Society*. It might be said to mark a turning point in the institutionalization of Jewish studies in the United States in a secularized profession like sociology; it preceded by one year the article that Wirth published in the *American Journal of Sociology*, "The Ghetto," which also dealt with the way of life of Jews in Chicago. From then on, Wirth gave an official status to Jewish studies by publishing his research work frequently, for instance in the *American Journal of Sociology* where he published an article in May 1943 entitled "Education for Survival: The Jews," while a few months earlier he had published in *Jewish Social Studies* a review of a work concerning the Jewish family.[101] Wirth was certainly the first sociologist to write simultaneously in the most prestigious journals both in the sociological profession and in the domain of scholarly Jewish studies. Following Park and thanks to Wirth, research was probably for the first time devoted to Jews in the contemporary world through prestigious academic institutions. At the same time, in New York, the other metropolis to which so many European Jews also immigrated, at Columbia University, Salo Baron, an immigrant from Galicia, the distant heir of Heinrich Graetz who was the unexpected friend of Marx, held the chair of Jewish studies in the history department.[102] Sociologists and Jewish historians combined their efforts, at the same time, to professionalize Jewish studies of contemporary societies at the most renowned universities.

Born in 1893 in a little village in the Rhine Valley, Louis Wirth spent his early years in the family home that had belonged to Wirths for at least four centuries. His parents were livestock dealers who lived in relative ease; his father, Joseph Wirth, very tolerant, went to synagogue as an Orthodox Jew; his mother came from a family of rabbis from the Sarre and was very attached to the faith. Louis Wirth went to an Evangelical school but also studied with a rabbi on Sundays. In 1911, his uncle Isaac, who had emigrated to the United States, offered to take him there to facilitate his studies. He lived in Omaha, Nebraska, and managed to get a scholarship to the University of Chicago at the beginning of the First World War, where he became a student of Park and also of Burgess, Thomas, Small, and G. H. Mead. Although he rejected all religious beliefs, he remained close to Jewish circles and became head of one of the divisions of a Jewish philanthropic institution for the aid of delinquent children (Jewish Charities of Chicago). In Chicago in 1923, he married Mary Bolton, whom he met when she was a student and who had become a social worker; she belonged to the Baptist Church, so Wirth became the first person in his family to marry a non-Jewish woman. After completing his doctoral thesis, *The Ghetto*, Wirth traveled to Germany in 1930–31, met L. von Wiese and Karl Mannheim, followed the rise of Nazism, and then returned to Chicago where, thanks to Park's help, he became a teacher in 1931. He then surrounded himself with several students who took part in his research, such as Herbert Goldhamer and Edward Shils, who would write several classic articles on the future of the Chicago School.[103] Having become one of the heads of the sociology department at the University of Chicago, Wirth not only later became president of the American Sociological Society but also was elected first president of the International Association of Sociology, after the Second World War; his professional expertise, based on studies on cities, on blacks, but also and perhaps above all on the Jews, is unarguable; his fame is great since he was named, during Roosevelt's presidency, member of a national committee on urbanism, became director of the planning committee of Illinois, president of the American Council on Race Relations, and prepared several reports for the Supreme Court to help it fight against all forms of racist policies in the United States, which, like Park, he courageously opposed.[104]

Influenced by Max Weber's sociology of values but also by Durkheim's reflections on social organization and anomie, Wirth, through Park (whose student he was and with whom he would always remain very close), continued the Simmelian tradition above all.[105] Like Simmel, Wirth questioned positivist and casual interpretations, emphasized the process of interaction based on values, sought what links individuals to each other, and analyzed changing social forms according to the number of individuals involved, particularly in large cities. A specialist in urban sociology, he emphasized in the bibliography he prepared for the famous book by Robert Park, Ernest Burgess, and Roderick McKenzie, *The City*, that Simmel's article "Metropolises and Mentalities" is "the most important single article on the city from the sociological standpoint."[106] In Wirth's own essential article concerning the urban,[107] he continues to grant Simmel a fundamental role when he writes that

> the heterogeneity of the urban population is highlighted by divisions between race and ethnic groups. Immigrants and their children constitute almost two thirds of all the inhabitants of cities with more than a million inhabitants. . . . If you remember that age, sex, race, and ethnic origin are associated with other factors like occupation or interest, it becomes clear that a major feature of the city-dweller is to be different from other people. . . . Generally speaking, and especially in America, cities include a colorful mix of people and cultures, and highly differentiated modes of life between which there is often an extremely thin line of communication, a great amount of indifference, and broad tolerance; there are sometimes bitter fights; always the contrasts are extreme.[108]

This statement refers back to his own research on the coexistence of multiple collective identities in large American metropolises.

Wirth's doctoral thesis, *The Ghetto*, is probably the most inarguable proof of the continued influence Simmel exercised over his approach to sociology. In return, it should be noted that Park was often inspired in his writings by Wirth's studies of the Jews. He also wrote a preface to *The Ghetto*, a work in which he found the faithful echo of his own preoccupations: "It is the interaction of this culture of the ghetto and that of the larger gentile community outside, involving the more or less complete participation of Jews in both worlds, that is the source of most that is problematic and enigmatic in the situation of the Jew of today, as of yesterday. . . . This attempt to investigate . . . one of the typical local areas of the Chicago urban community has led to the exploration of one of the most fundamental problems in sociology."[109] Just as Park saw in Simmel's stranger, and especially in the personality of the Jew analyzed by Simmel, the source figure of his marginal man of great cities, Wirth explicitly observed that "the Jews were, as Simmel has pointed out, the typical stranger, and in that role they acquired the objectivity and built up the relationship of the confidant, which served them well as counselors and diagnosticians."[110] In *The Ghetto*, only Simmel is cited among the great sociologists, aside from his masters Park, Burgess, and Ellsworth Faris, that is, the big names in the Chicago School. By contrast, strikingly, Wirth refers a number of times to the greatest historians of the Jewish people, such as Heinrich Graetz, Arthur Ruppin, and Simon Dubnow, the latter two having been at the origin of a more specifically sociological vision. Through this work that is emblematic of the Chicago School, one of the most well known of the series of books directed by Park, classical sociology meets scholarly historiography with a sociological focus on the Jewish people, probably for the first time; we will return to this later on. When we learn that Wirth also attentively followed the research of Salo Baron, heir to Graetz and Dubnow, and that he wrote reviews of some of Baron's books in *Historia Judaica*, thinking, for instance, that his book *The Jewish Community: Its History and Structure to the American Revolution* confirms "the very high level of Jewish studies in the United States,"[111] we become aware of his crucial role—at the border between two kinds of knowledge that only rarely meet—in the future standardization of Jewish studies in the contemporary era. At the junction of two worlds, through the quality of his own research investigations, Wirth facilitated the recognition of such a discipline in academic circles. Yet unlike Simmel who was in a hostile German context, but also especially unlike Salo Baron in the more open American context, Wirth revealed himself to be favorable, in sociology, to the development of Jewish studies as a scholarly discipline, while still foreseeing the decline of the Jewish world through its assimilation into American society. Salo Baron, by contrast, also a supporter of a scientific approach, remained firmly attached to the Jewish community as productive of a culture called on to flourish in this new "center" that American society constituted. The sociologist and the historian of the Jewish world diverged profoundly, then, in their interpretation of the future of the individual Jew in the New World.

*The Ghetto* marked an important moment. In this scholarly work, Wirth, as a sociologist who knew Yiddish, used empirical German, English, and French sources to analyze the population and relied especially on Park's theories to come to an understanding of it. Right away, he showed that "from the standpoint of the sociologist the ghetto as an institution" could be regarded as "a form of accommodation between divergent population groups . . . while the ghetto is, strictly speaking, a Jewish institution, there are forms of ghettos that concern not merely Jews. There are Little Sicilies, Little Polands, Chinatowns, and Black belts in our large cities . . . that bear a close resemblance to the Jewish ghetto. These forms of community life are likely to become more intelligible to us if we have before us the natural history of the Jewish ghetto. The ghetto may therefore be regarded as typical of a number of other forms of community life that sociologists are attempting to explore."[112] Faithful to Robert Park's thematic and continuing the theory of forms developed by Simmel, Wirth, beyond the Jewish ghetto, tried to shed light on the social form as an institution whose function favors contact between distinct populations. "The Jew as a stranger" first of all experienced the seclusion of the ghettos,[113] as in Frankfurt, which imposed his isolation; Wirth described the dissolution of these ghettos—in the nineteenth century, along with emancipation—but thought, like Simmel in his time or Karl Kautsky whom he quoted, that the Zionist solution would lead to a new form of "international ghetto" that he condemned.[114] He then undertook the description of "voluntary ghettos" by which the Jews reestablished, especially in the United States, a "distance" from their neighbors by placing the essential role played by the synagogue in the heart of his analysis. As a sociologist of large cities, he thus carried out a detailed study of the ghetto of Chicago, with a minute analysis of its topography; he showed that with its growth "the typical communal organization of the European ghetto gradually emerges" before the Jews once again try to leave this ghetto to scatter into different neighborhoods,[115] nonetheless involuntarily regrouping, after an identical but unconscious strategy of territorial mobility, in new, less visible ghettos ("the return to the ghetto") but still ones that are quite real, as a form of resistance to the strong anti-Semitic prejudices of the society into which they have come. A "separateness" is thus reconstructed that nevertheless facilitates, this time, the boldness of "the occasional adventurer into the camp of the enemy or the stranger who is finally the agent bringing about the fusion of the two."[116]

In the end, Wirth seemed to be confident in the final success of Park's assimilation process, since "the transition from one culture to another, from one personality to another, is a process that requires time, but also cooperation between the two groups"; explicitly following the passages in the *Introduction to the Science of Sociology* devoted to the future of the Jews, Wirth thought that "by leaving the ghetto, the Jew experienced once and for all a profound transformation. He not only changed his clothes, his expressions, and his beard, but also his consciousness"; the "taste for external life" first produced "hybrid" individuals who "oscillate" between two worlds but, after several generations, the children finally become assimilated or else experience the classic problems of social disorganization linked to large cities (delinquency, criminality, and so on).[117] Like Park, Wirth in turn modified Simmel's figure of the stranger who, in a host society, preserved his identity: in the United States, an open and democratic society, immigrants are strangers who, through the new form of the ghetto without walls, finally manage to become assimilated, to enter into "fusion" with the Other. This is its melting-pot function, eroding collective identities. Chicago is not Berlin: the Jew as stranger now has access both to normal science and to normal existence. From this Wirth draws a general interpretation of the transitory function of the ghetto, which gives rise to hope for the end of "the Jewish question" but also the end of the black question through an assimilation that has long been thwarted. In this sense, we can understand why, for the *Encyclopedia Judaica*, "Wirth's passionate interest in a sociology of Jews is part of his more general thinking concerning the incorporation of minorities within the democratic state."[118]

Insofar as Wirth seemed finally to have felt positively about the idea of the Jews' assimilation so that he then went on to prefer, like many others, to work more extensively on the blacks, we can see in him the example of the Jewish sociologist who, as Seymour M. Lipset argued, wanted to appear more as an American intellectual preoccupied by universalism and the fate of other ethnic groups than as a Jewish sociologist, from fear of being perceived as a "Jewish Jew."[119] Regarded from then on severely as "an assimilationist intellectual" who quickly set aside the study of American Jews, Wirth was harshly reproached, for that as well as for his exogamic marriage.[120] It is difficult to understand such critiques, which neglect Wirth's real, sustained interest in Jewish studies, as well as his decidedly more ambivalent appreciation of assimilation. Wirth, like Park, seemed actually to hesitate: he observed that despite the assimilation process, the Jew always "oscillates" between two worlds, the external world where "he metamorphoses into a new being" and the world of the "familiar primary group" where life remains "rich and deep and warm."[121] Thus, in the overview published in the scholarly *American Journal of Sociology*, he used a number of passages from his book *The Ghetto,* which would be published a year later, but he found in this particularly professionalized framework even stronger expressions to designate the phenomenon of voluntary return to the ghetto that follows upon the "disillusions and disappointments" encountered outside. In his eyes, the Jews sometimes return to "the intimacy and warmth of the ghetto" and leave the world that is "cold and so disregardful of their expectations."[122] As if Wirth was finally doubtful of the disappearance of the ghetto in which the Jews protect each other, but also in which other immigrant communities group together in order to preserve a form of identity in an open society like the United States, where the immigrant stranger has the possibility of not remaining a stranger forever. In the end, Wirth rediscovered the inspiration of Simmel and took back into consideration the analyses of Park and of Salo Baron about the decisive role of the Jewish community within American society as a structure of cultural transmission that ensures the permanence of a collective identity. Finally, like Baron, Wirth became actively involved in specifically Jewish institutions, like the American Jewish Committee.

Wirth is undoubtedly the first American sociologist who, in the lineage of Simmel, so openly approached the specific case of the Jews. It was probably the first time his colleagues discovered in their particularly demanding journal such detailed research on the primary groups unique to the Jews, their forms of socialization, the functions assumed by certain individuals whom Wirth designated by name and whose forms of interaction linking them to the other members of the group he traced, but he proceeded as his colleagues at the University of Chicago who specialized in remote societies (like Lyod Warner analyzing Melanesian societies in ethnology) or in examining nearby microsocieties (like Nels Anderson studying the "hobos") did.[123] This anthropology of the Jewish world carried out by Wirth and by others later on, even in the profession's major journals,[124] rarely attracted the attention of historians of sociology. The ones who were interested in the Chicago School take into consideration only its more general studies concerning the city, just as the commentators of Park's work were not very eloquent on his analyses (which however were repeated) concerning the Jews. Such a selective memory of Wirth's studies is regrettable, since Wirth had real virtuosity in describing the individual types in the ghetto, designated by their Hebrew or Yiddish name, who animated Jewish life and formed a veritable "topography of the Jewish community": the zaddik, the groberjung, the chazan, the schlemiel, the yeshiva bocher. . . . Wirth, like Simmel before him, analyzed the networks, the constellations that were woven around them and that were continually transformed.[125] Throughout his entire career he examined, as a sociologist endowed with a solid Jewish culture, the forms of sociability peculiar to the Jews; he often cited the Torah and the Talmud; he referred, like Simmel, to Maimonides, and to support his demonstration he quoted from well-known books by Salo Baron and from articles taken from scholarly, specialized Jewish journals like the Menorah Journal. In 1943, he published a text in the American Journal of Sociology, in which, after describing the tragedy the Jews experienced because of Nazism, he evoked the culture they had so long been endowed with as proof of a will to live, to transmit, to consolidate a community of values; in his opinion, this awareness of a separate identity could only bring them closer to American blacks, who were different from them in many respects but who had to rely on their experience of resistance to prejudices but also to assimilation.[126] This veritable manifesto in favor of a common agenda was surprising in such a journal. Wirth meant to remain faithful to this uncommon mixture of genres, to this open engagement in favor of all minorities, elaborated in proper academic contexts. Thus, in 1945, in a book edited by Ralph Linton, he wrote the chapter "The Problem of Minority Groups," which describes the subordinate position of racial minorities in the United States, like the Indians or the blacks, which he distinguished from ethnic minorities like the Jews or the Mormons: Wirth shed light on the extent of prejudices toward these groups. In this text, he shows that the assimilationist ideology of the melting pot can scarcely be applied to the blacks, and he thinks that ethnic minorities found before them "a way to assimilation that is not without serious obstacles"; he concludes by emphasizing how much anti-Semitism, in Hitler Germany and elsewhere, including in the United States, reinforces, even if only temporarily, the solidarity of the Jews.[127]

The figure of the Jew as stranger constructed by Simmel, preserved in the United States by Robert Park and Louis Wirth (who did sometimes yield to the myth of easy Americanization by transforming the stranger into a provisional marginal man, into an immigrant with a divided personality), gave rise to a large number of empirical studies carried out by Jewish or non-Jewish sociologists whom I would like to mention briefly in conclusion. The book by Everett Stonequist, *The Marginal Man*, is unquestionably the most accomplished. It begins, like Wirth's book, with a preface by Park, who emphasizes that the marginal man is condemned to live "in two worlds"; as a cosmopolitan and a stranger, he becomes, in relation to his cultural environment, "the individual with the wider horizon, the keener intelligence, the more detached and rational viewpoint. The marginal man is always relatively the more civilized human being. He occupies the position which has been, historically, that of the Jew in the Diaspora."[128] Simmel's heritage is continued more than is usually recognized, culminating in this classic book of contemporary sociology that starts directly with the example of the Jew as a special case of the stranger identified, too quickly perhaps, with the marginal man. In his introduction, Stonequist also makes the Jew one of the emblematic figures of the marginal man with a "dual personality," caught "in a conflict," of one who through immigration, education, or marriage is plunged into two universes.[129] Although he extends this figure to include the uprooted man, the parvenu, to all the cases of voluntary or involuntary marginalization, to all "hybrid" personalities who leave "one social group or culture without making a satisfactory adjustment to another" and "finds himself on the margin of each but a member of neither,"[130] although he applies this definition of the marginal man to all cases where "adjustment and conformity" are impossible to attain for the modern man who has become so mobile, he continually returns to the example of the Jews who, in his eyes, "illustrate many if not all of the problems discussed in this volume. . . . The modern Jew is likewise a cultural hybrid: half he is derived from the traditional Hebrew culture, half he is molded by Western culture in one of its national forms. Always on the move he appears in each country as an immigrant. . . . His group life is organized upon a marginal basis."[131] Stonequist, at first, seems to make the globally assimilationist vision of Park his own and thinks that in an open society like the United States the Jews can do nothing but adjust to their environment; while in Germany they remain, in Simmel's mind, strangers, for Stonequist, the Jews are assimilated into American society and will survive perhaps only in "certain Soviet districts" or in Palestine, where as a community they have a territorial basis.[132] His book continually evokes the case of the Jews who, like all immigrants, and unlike the blacks, can easily merge with the American nation.[133]

Stonequist, though, distances himself from the assimilationist perspectives attributed to his master Park and emphasizes (in a way that is actually close to Park's) how much the Jew in the United States has to confront an anti-Semitism that has "crossed the Atlantic" and hinders the process of assimilation: in his eyes, "the marginal Jew tends to remain persistently in the psychological centre of the cultural conflict." This reminds him of Heinrich Heine. This marginality is conveyed by feelings of inferiority, complexes, an exacerbated sensitivity that leads to aggressive or ostentatious behavior, a marked tendency toward neurasthenia that also expresses the state of profound social disorganization in large cities described by Louis Wirth.[134] Stonequist goes on to write, "The Jews' position of social isolation in the Christian world really made them strangers. The sociologist Georg Simmel, himself a Jew, has made an acute analysis of the role and psychology of the stranger."

This "stranger" is both near and far; his objective stance transforms him, however, into a confidant: "His relative detachment," Stonequist adds, "frees him from the self-consciousness, the concern for status, and the divided loyalties of the marginal man. When the stranger seeks to identify himself integrally with the group into which he has moved, but is held at arm's length, he has evolved into the marginal position" and is henceforth incapable of detachment or objectivity, since his personality is so affected by this rejection.[135] The marginal man differs from the stranger, who wants to preserve a certain distance from the host group: the stranger becomes the marginal man only when he wants to become completely assimilated and when he finds he is prevented from doing so by xenophobia or anti-Semitism.

Many commentators have emphasized this difference between Simmel and Stonequist, with Stonequist seeming at the same time to be moving away from Park's viewpoint. Actually, their interpretations scarcely differ from each other when we take into account the variable of the nation. The stranger can only remain a stranger in imperial Germany, even if he tries to become assimilated by agreeing to think of himself as a marginal man; in the United States, however, the open society par excellence, the stranger has several strategies at his disposal and can choose to preserve a collective identity or to become assimilated as an individual within a new reference group. In conformity with the predominant national logic, he will almost always be tempted to prefer the second way to the first, thus frequently risking being transformed into a marginal man. Stonequist's work, which continues Robert Park's perspective, also ends up with anti-assimilationist conclusions, both concerning the blacks and the Jews, definitively marginal men who, unlike other immigrants or groups without roots, both remain marked by this status that places them always, despite their social success—especially the Jews—in a position of strangeness.[136]

After Stonequist, a large number of empirical studies have been written on the behavior of American Jews: they confirm Simmel's concept of the stranger as well as the nonassimilationist considerations of Park, which of course were not predominant in his work. They also verify Wirth's final predictions and the descriptions of the author of *The Marginal Man*. Thus, Peter Rose offers a sociological analysis of the values of Jews who live in several small towns outside of New York; they remain, according to him, deliberately faithful to their own values, while still being accepted by the local communities. In his opinion, "Stonequist, Park and others were wrong to characterize the Jew as a disturbed marginal man, an eternal stranger incapable of reconciling his own traditions with those of the outer world." Using the conclusions of his research, he thinks he can oppose the interpretations of Park and Stonequist, which he thinks of as assimilationist whereas actually they verify Simmel's concept of the Jew as stranger, or at least as the rejected individual, whose "amalgamation," as it finally appears in their writings, he rejects.[137] Conceived of as an empirical study supposed to challenge the theories of the marginal man interpreted wrongly through an assimilationist prism, this investigation into American Jews verifies, actually, the permanence of Simmel's figure of the stranger and confirms the permanence of the particularism of American Jews attached to their identity. Far from imperial Germany that rejected them institutionally, broke their character, and endlessly ostracized them, this study emphasizes that the Jews want to preserve their position as strangers even in the most open American society. Paradoxically, the supposedly assimilationist perspective outlined by Park and Wirth does not differ fundamentally from the pessimistic approach of Horace Kallen, himself a Jew, the theoretician of pluralism whose main book *Culture and Democracy in the United States* was published in 1924, a crucial period when everything seems to come together.[138] Indeed, the ancestor of contemporary American multiculturalism justifies maintaining the collective identity peculiar to the Jews, who will come to play their music in "the orchestra" that is global American society. Kallen finally reveals himself to be close to the sociologists at Chicago who record the persistence of Jewish identity and applaud its communitarian strength. In this sense, these two traditions, independent of each other, developed in the same era and animated by Jewish thinkers, both rediscover the spirit of Simmel in the United States, which emphasized the resistance of the stranger to the host group. They foretell the positions favorable to multiculturalism adopted these days by a large number of scholars who explicitly assume their Judaism and who will be mentioned later on.[139]

Whether Jewish or not, there were many American sociologists linked at various times with the Chicago School who were inspired by Simmel's figure of the stranger and who kept the Jew as an exemplary case. Among the Jewish sociologists, there were, in the first generation, Louis Wirth, and later on Edward Shils, who in 1936 translated some texts by Simmel. Erving Goffman also claimed to be a follower of this school: after the Second World War he studied at the sociology department at Chicago, where he defended his doctoral thesis and remained profoundly influenced by Simmel's interactionism. In the beginning of his dissertation, he explicitly paid homage to Simmel's method of analyzing the daily social relations that are woven between individuals.[140] Apart from Chicago, in the 1930s, at Columbia, alongside Robert Merton who gave a large place to Simmel in his teaching, Lewis Coser, one of Simmel's students, devoted himself to a sociological analysis of Simmel's career as a stranger to the German academic institution.[141] Coser then wrote a long chapter on the work of Simmel, who entered his pantheon of great masters of sociological thinking along with Auguste Comte, Karl Marx, Émile Durkheim, Max Weber, Vilfredo Pareto, Robert Park, and George Herbert Mead.[142] Moreover, in a scholarly article published by the *American Sociological Review* that made remarkable use of the literature specializing in Jewish history, especially the classic book by Selma Stern, *The Court Jew*, Coser applied the perspective of the Jew as stranger to the characters of the Court Jews who, as strangers, effectively served the princes. In this fine article of historical sociology, Coser was inspired as much by Simmel as by Park in his account of the loyalty of these court Jews who nonetheless remained distant from power, strangers in whom people still willingly confided.[143] Not long before the Second World War, also in New York, Simmel's influence was being felt in other places. In the framework of the university in exile at the New School for Social Research, immigrant Jews, many of them from German-speaking countries, were often inspired by it: that is the case for Alfred Schütz, Albert Salomon, Hans Gerth, Kurt Lewin, and also Reinhard Bendix and Kurt Wolff, who together translated several essential chapters from *Sociology*, Simmel's master work. Later on, the appointment of Lewis Coser and Kurt Wolff to Brandeis University, an institution very sensitive to Jewish subjects because of its own beginnings, transformed this place into a new temple of Simmel studies.[144]

In the end, aside from the Jewish sociologists who, faithful to the figure of the stranger, emphasized the resistance of American Jews to radical assimilation, and also aside from those who attribute an essential place in their writing to the stranger, the main Jewish continuators of Simmels' work in the United States focused more on his general interactionist sociology, based on forms of socialization between subjects, between individuals in large cities who manage, in the urban setting, to escape a collective identity and new ghettos. This other Simmelian heritage remains almost intact through interactionist sociology, which is inspired by its researches into social forms, into the way subjects in large cities preserve a distance toward each other that lets various strategies be expressed, forms of civility able to ensure one-on-one social relations. In all its aspects, microsociology follows in a straight line from the works of Simmel.[145] A number of American Jewish sociologists contributed to this renewal of the study of social forms through which the freedom of individuals is expressed in a more open public space, far from the fixed systems of the past when Jews were faced with so many prohibitions and unconquerable barriers. From Alfred Schütz, Jacob Moreno, and Kurt Lewin, all three of whom took refuge in the United States to escape Nazi persecutions, to Erving Goffman, Howard Saul Becker, Aaron Cicourel, and Harold Garfinkel, there were many who continued this interactionist sociology, where the emphasis is placed on the mobility of subjects with respect to one another, on change and interplay as a substitute for a strategy of exile now become outdated. Simmel's perspective joins in with that of other American sociologists such as Charles Horton Cooley and George Herbert Mead to retrace the web of multiple forms through which the social game is realized for all individuals. From then on they seem to cease questioning the history-laden figure of the stranger bearing collective identity and to distance themselves from this question that is still crucial today in the United States, as we will see later on, to reflect instead in what is, though, a very Simmelian way but now one indifferent to the Jewish dimension, on tact, avoidance, the gaze, labeling, and language, and also on numbers, as so many factors of human interaction. If they evoke their

Jewish identity, most of these sociologists, unlike Simmel at the end of the nineteenth century or Wirth in the 1930s, no longer assign it any role in their professional activity: it does not guide them in the choice of their empirical research, or in the way they approach social exchange. Eliot Freidson, for example, recalled "the politely condescending version of anti-Semitism" he had to experience during his adolescence in an upper-class suburb of Boston, and he simply thought that "as a member of a minority," he "felt detached from conventional society" at which he could direct a critical gaze without, however, retaining that identitarian dimension in the choice of his sociological researches, like the study of professions.[146] Similarly, Howard Saul Becker, author of *Outsiders*, emotionally described his adolescence in a Jewish family; his grandfather came from Lithuania, and the fights between his father, born in the Jewish ghetto in Chicago, who was indifferent to religion but who spoke Yiddish, and his mother, who wanted him to have his bar mitzvah, his religious education, his Jewish friends. Although he felt "culturally" Jewish through his social adherence, his networks of friends, and the nature of the jokes told between friends, and although he still today knows a little Hebrew, his work centers on subjects that are far from any identitarian question of that kind: his attention focused solely on jazz musicians and marijuana smokers as deviants, since from his adolescence on his identity was defined as a jazz musician.[147]

Erving Goffman also symbolized this other current of Simmelian sociology indifferent to collective identities, unconcerned with the question of assimilation of ethnic minorities, less sensitive to history and to the fate of the stranger. The sociologist of *The Presentation of Self in Everyday Life* was born in Canada to a family of immigrant Ukrainian Jews. He grew up in a little town in Alberta where an explicit anti-Semitism reigned,[148] which he would always remember: "You forget that I spent my childhood [in Yiddish] in a town where expressing yourself in another language made people suspect you of being homosexual."[149] Goffman, who, like Wirth and Becker, had an exogamic marriage and married a Protestant woman of upper-class Boston society, only rarely, in his writings, approached uniquely Jewish themes, even if some people have found the presence of biblical references in his work.[150] In essential books like *Asylums*, he often returned to the example of the concentration camps and described cases of moral contamination or depersonalization that affect Jews especially;[151] in *Stigma*, he mentioned several times, in a more than biased way, the way the Jews display symbols of stigmatization to "cut themselves off from a society of normal people": thus, "hard of hearing persons who wear a batteryless hearing aid; the partly blind who affect a collapsible white cane; Jewesses who wear a Star of David as a necklace." Goffman compared the Jews to homosexuals, emphasizing that they "may also flaunt some stereotypical attributes which [they] could easily cover."[152] Despite this presentation of the personality of the Jews linked to a simple play of roles around a deliberate self-stigmatization, Goffman, from his years as a student at Chicago on, found himself surrounded by Jewish friends, many of whom would become big names in American sociology, like William Kornhauser or Howard S. Becker, with whom he argued "like a rabbi."[153] Thereafter, despite this relative silence, one could say that his work presented itself as "an autobiography," so much did it manifest "a continual caution in self-expression," the feeling of a profound malaise that Freud also shared. "Everything happens," he observed, "as if their experience as emancipated Jews were reinjected into their work, either, in Freud, in the form of a medicalization of the traces of the former Jewish identity that turn into psychic symptoms, or, in Goffman, in the form of taking control of the social dimension of these traces which are then mastered within a system of continual bluff. In the lives of both men, one finds the same social climbing and the same malaise. In the work of both men, one finds traces of strategies of adaptation. In Freud, it's the burying of his Jewishness in a project that transcends the usual categories of religion, politics and history. In Goffman, it's the objectification of social climbing in a work devoted—to a degree—to the study of the 'code of civility,' to paraphrase Cuddihy."[154]

The extreme difficulties of the great journey to the West of European Jews, of emergence from the ghettos, to which the figure of the stranger conceptualized by Simmel testifies, continue to weigh heavily on certain American Jewish sociologists who spent time in Chicago, as different from each other as Wirth and Goffman, who scarcely agreed with each other, despite their swift and brilliant careers in the highest positions of the academic profession. In Germany, an imperial and authoritarian society, as well as in the United States, a democratic and open society, it was decidedly suitable to remain "on one's guard almost all the time."[155] Still, times have definitely changed: American Jewish sociologists can, to varying degrees, preserve a more or less present Jewish memory, but most of them examine the complex network of social relationships in open modern societies more as sociologists not concerned with the collective identitarian question. They are especially numerous among the contemporary heirs of Simmel in post-World War II Chicago (Edward Shils, Harold Finestone, Fred Davies, Anselme Strauss, Erving Goffman, David Riesman, David Salomon, Howard Becker, and Eliot Freidson) and also in New York. But it is not the question of the stranger symbolized, for Simmel, by the Jews that preoccupies them. "The Jewish question" has suddenly lost its historicity.[156]

Jean-Paul Sartre thought that the Jews "cannot take pride in any collective work that is specifically Jewish, or in a civilization properly Jewish,
or in a common mysticism"; to do that, "they must indeed end up by
exalting racial qualities."[1] He set out to create a physical and psychological overview, at the two extremes of the social hierarchy: on the one
hand, the poor Jew on the Rue des Rosiers, and, on the other, without
any forewarning, his "little comrade" Raymond Aron, the assimilated
Jew, the elegant tennis player from the Parisian western suburbs. Here,
first of all, was the Jew encountered by the author of *Anti-Semite and
Jew* on the Rue des Rosiers, with his "murky cup of coffee opposite an
open-air rag peddler":

> Here is a Jew seated on his doorstep in the Rue des Rosiers. I recognize
> him immediately as a Jew: he has a black and curly beard, a slightly
> hooked nose, protruding ears, steel-rimmed glasses, a derby pulled
> down over his eyes, black clothes, quick and nervous gestures, and a
> smile of strange and dolorous goodness. How am I to disentangle the
> physical from the moral? His beard is black and curly; that is a somatic
> characteristic. But what strikes me above all is that he lets it grow; by
> that he expresses his attachment to the traditions of the Jewish com-
> munity; he indicates that he has come from Poland, that he belongs
> to emigrants of the first generation. Is his son any less a Jew for being
> clean-shaven? Other traits, like the form of his nose and the position of
> his ears, are purely anatomical, while others, like the choice of clothing
> and glasses, expression and mimicry, are purely psychical and social.[2]

At the other extreme of the social hierarchy, Sartre evoked either a
French Jew who "had the typical characteristics of the French Jew—a
hooked nose, protruding ears,"[3] and so on, or one of his Jewish friends
who was in Berlin at the same time as Sartre: he "was of a 'marked

169

Semitic type': he had a hooked nose, protruding ears, and thick lips. A Frenchman would have recognized him as a Jew without hesitation. But since he was blond, lean, and phlegmatic, the Germans were completely taken in."[4] Whether he was an immigrant, a traditional Polish Jew of the Rue des Rosiers, or an assimilated French Jew from a good neighborhood, both kinds could be "recognized" right away; or rather, a Frenchman from France "recognizes" them without any difficulty, even if the second kind, completely assimilated, was "blond and phlegmatic." Aron, the "authentic French Jew" of whom Sartre spoke in *Anti-Semite and Jew*,[5] no doubt served as a model. Thus, when Sartre evoked "one 'authentic' French Jew who, after fighting in 1940, directed a French propaganda review in London during the Occupation,"[6] without signing his articles from fear of compromising his wife and daughter who had remained in France, it was obvious that it was still a question of his little comrade Raymond Aron, who was perceived as a "masterpiece of assimilation."[7] Sartre referred to him explicitly only once, twenty years later, exclaiming, when he referred to that book, "The Jews I knew were atheist intellectuals, with no special knowledge of Jewish traditions— Arons, we'll say."[8] The surprising representation of Raymond Aron by his École Normale friend has, however, almost always escaped the notice of the respective biographers of the two comrades, who had been so close when they were at the École Normale Supérieure; nor does it appear in the books that detail the intersecting lives of these two essential actors in contemporary political and cultural life. Strangely, the many biographers devoted to the two men almost always remain silent on this point, which is nonetheless so essential in the perception each had of the other for many years. In the voluminous Sartrean bibliography,[9] there is no trace of the presence of the Raymond Aron of *Anti-Semite and Jew*, even though he was ever-present in the author's awareness; not a word, beyond their ideological and political disagreements, on the identification of Raymond Aron with the character of the French Jew for which he served curiously as a model in this book that marked a key but debatable moment in the twentieth century of the "Jewish question" in the style of Bauer or even Marx, centered on whether the Jews' indispensable emancipation or their disappearance was the factor for the liberation of all humanity. Nor is there a word about this in the less numerous biographies or studies devoted to Raymond Aron.[10] One can only note an identical semisilence even in the rare works devoted exclusively to the intersecting lives of the two little comrades who were so close and so different.[11]

Aron, by contrast, showed he was aware of the strange honor conferred on him by referring often to *Anti-Semite and Jew* and to the role that was unintentionally granted him. He remembered this book so well that, long afterward, he repeated Sartre's description almost word for word to sketch the physical characteristics of the young man he was. In his *Memoirs*, almost forty years later, Aron returned to his stay in the German capital: "Demonstrations of anti-Semitism never touched me directly. With my blond hair and blue eyes, I did not present to the Nazis an image in conformity with their representation of the Jew. My friend Susini, Corsican, dark, Mediterranean, was sometimes insulted in the street; I never was."[12] After the lapse of such a long time, Aron spontaneously used, without even referring to Sartre's text, the comparison formulated by Sartre between the French Jew protected by his blond hair and blue eyes and his Corsican companion perceived as Jewish because of his Mediterranean features; thus Sartre contrasted his "blond, lean, phlegmatic" Jewish friend whom the Germans didn't recognize with his other friend, "a Corsican and a Catholic, the son and grandson of Catholics, [who] had hair that was black and a bit curly, a Bourbon nose, a sallow complexion, and he was short and fat. The children in the street threw stones at him and called him 'Jude.'"[13]

There is no doubt that in his youth, Aron, the brilliant sportsman who lived in a fine house in Versailles, represented the assimilated Jew, unrecognizable from the anti-Semitic caricatures. Since the eighteenth century, his ancestors had lived in the Lorraine: they followed the assimilation process of the Jews of France, becoming integrated into the bourgeoisie, acceding to intellectual functions through the university. Thus, on both sides, Aron came from families of well-off small businessmen from the east and the north of France, while on his father's side, he was related to Émile Durkheim and to Marcel Mauss, whom he met frequently. Raymond Aron's ancestor, Abraham Aron, was born in Blénod-lès-Toul in 1760; his son Moïse, who would become a butcher, married Julie Isidor in Toul, who gave him three sons, including Isidor, called Ferdinand, Raymond's grandfather; on her side, a sister of Julie Isidor married Moyse Durkheim, rabbi of Épinal, the father of Émile Durkheim and the grandfather of Marcel Mauss.[14] His father, Gustave Aron, decided to leave the family textile business, but failed the teacher's exam in Roman law in the history of law: throughout his life he taught with a feeling of failure that his son Raymond would spend all his life mending. The Arons and the Lévys (Aron's mother was born Suzanne Lévy and also came from the textile world) abandoned almost all religious practice: Raymond Aron remembers that they "stopped practicing almost completely, except for observing Yom Kippur. Only a small number of rituals, practices, or symbols remained in my family."[15] During this turn of the century, this "solid French Jewish bourgeoisie,"[16] as Aron himself calls it in his *Memoirs*, seems to have distanced itself from its Jewish identity, even though the young Aron, after hasty training, had his bar mitzvah. An atheist even though late in life he read "fragments, from time to time,"[17] of the Old Testament, Aron refused to "think of himself as a soldier in a Judaic army" and added, "I do not accept the idea of myself as 'traitor' if I have a wife who is not Jewish."[18] Aron was fascinated, for example, by the many different aspects of the Dreyfus Affair, which he discovered when he was ten; he learned all the details of the affair by heart after reading documents he had discovered in his father's library: he came to know it so well that, later on when he was a junior in high school, he calmly objected to his history professor's demonstrations by stating a more precise version of the facts; however, it was patriotism more than Judaism that seemed to animate Aron when he sang the praises of his country, which eventually recognized the injustice committed toward one of its citizens: he remembered that "the Dreyfus Affair had no effect on my feelings as a little Frenchman"; moreover, "in this dialogue with my teacher, neither one of us, as far as I remember, had mentioned or, in any case emphasized, the fact that Dreyfus was a Jew, and that I was too."[19]

In search of himself, throughout his life Aron evoked Sartre's *Anti-Semite and Jew* like a leitmotif that allowed him to question himself on his own identity, assessing the attempt, reevaluating it, evoking it in a demonstration, tirelessly returning to it as if it had disturbed him, as if it still affected him, almost conveying uncertainty about his own identity. Even more, and perhaps without realizing it, he appropriated some of Sartre's observations, though briefly stated. Thus, in his lecture given in February 1951 to B'nai B'rith, he declared that "Sartre, in his study On 'The Jewish Question,' perfectly clarified [what] the banker Jew and the Communist Jew have in common. . . . Each is a man of abstraction and rationalism." He quotes Sartre several times and, inspired by Sartre's reflections, he notes, "Many of the professions exercised by the Jews, being professions of communication and exchange, are professions that are linked to relationships between men. We Jews live much more often in human-relation professions than in professions that place us in relation with matter, or, as has been said, we occupy functions of 'civility.'"[20] There is no doubt that this "as has been said" clearly refers to Sartre's analyses in *Anti-Semite and Jew*. Aron shows he is so sensitive to Sartre's interpretations that he almost seems to make them his own by taking up, identically, the same ideas, the same words (matter, civility, and so on), the same problematics: "I have often said in conversations with Christian friends that those who can do the most against anti-Semitism are non-Jews," a phrase one can find almost word for word in *Anti-Semite and Jew*, whose author sometimes surprisingly presents himself as a Christian. As late as 1972, Aron acknowledged that certain French Jews "will always risk remaining Jewish in the Sartrean sense of the word."[21]

Aron hesitated, however, and often questioned Sartre's reasoning, which he kept coming back to. In 1962, he wrote, "Sometimes the Jew from France or England who no longer takes part in uniquely Jewish culture receives his Judaism from the surrounding world and from anti-Semitism. It is to the de-Judaized Jew, so to speak, that Sartre's *Anti-Semite and Jew* applies. But, as assimilated as he may be or thinks he is, the Jew keeps a feeling of solidarity, both for his ancestors, and for the other communities in Diaspora."[22] Similarly, in *History and the Dialectic of Violence*, he notes:

> Two examples hold Sartre's attention: workers and Jews. The former because of their political impact, the latter because of their exemplary value, as a borderline case. Do we have to say that being a Jew and being a worker is the same thing? Yes and no. There is no radical difference unless you reduce Jewishness to the vision others have of it. . . .

But while the status of worker or bourgeois is determined objectively, the Jewish situation is exclusively the result of the opinion of non-Jews. The only way of being a member of the Jewish community is to be considered as such by others. In fact, Sartre's analysis, in *Anti-Semite and Jew*, has to do essentially with de-Judaized Jews.[23]

Aron does not subscribe, then, to Sartre's arguments and even questions the portrayal that his former comrade made of him. Several times, he remarks:

It is a fine book but Sartre does not know the Jews. He imagines that the Jews are all like his little comrade Raymond Aron, who was completely de-Judaized, essentially French, largely ignorant of Jewish tradition and who, because of this, was Jewish only because others called him Jewish. Sartre wrote a text that sets aside the reality of the Jews, of those who are authentically Jewish.[24]

Aron consistently challenges Sartre's judgment, thinking of himself as an inauthentic Jew while he is represented, in *Anti-Semite and Jew*, as the model for the authentic Jew. Here we touch on the surprising Sartrean proposition concerning the authenticity of the Jew, which simply consists in accepting being a Jew in the eye of the other, to "derive his pride" from his humiliation. Authenticity consists, then, in "having a true and lucid consciousness of the situation, in assuming the responsibilities and risks it involves, in accepting it in pride or humiliation, sometimes in horror and hate." Faced with such a behavior, which requires so much "courage," the Jews often prefer to be inauthentic, that is wishing only for universalism and rationalism—thus sometimes manifesting an anti-Semitism of a "masochistic" kind that leads them to "the voluntary and passionate negation of the traits of his race"; "in a word," Sartre adds, "the inauthentic Jews are men whom other men take for Jews and who have decided to run away from this insupportable situation."[25] In Sartre's eyes, the inauthentic Jew is a creature emptied of meaning, of culture, of values, stripped of all choices other than the choice imposed on him by the Anti-Semite. As Harold Rosenberg forcefully observes, "The only choice left to the Jew is *to be* 'authentic,' that is, to accept himself as the creature of the anti-Semite and nothing more. . . . He proudly becomes what the anti-Semite says he is. . . . The Sartrean categories of the authentic and the inauthentic are only applied to concentration camp victims. . . . Sartre's Jew personifies the camp individual."[26] Strangely and almost contradictorily, then, to show oneself as authentic is simply to endorse this established fact, not to flee from it. So Sartre did not understand much about his little comrade: though he remembered certain physical characteristics of his, he was not aware of his profound convictions and understood nothing of the convictions of the Jew sitting on his doorstep on the Rue des Rosiers. In both examples, he was reduced to lingering over appearances, to describing the shape of the nose and the ears, reifying individuals who were so remote from each other, but also denying them the choice of their own values which were found to be shaped each time by determinisms of distinct situations. Finally, what distinguished one from the other was simply the curly beard, the low derby hat, the black clothing. After all, didn't his little comrade also have "a smile of strange and dolorous goodness"?

Thinking of himself as a de-Judaized Jew, Aron does not recognize himself either in the character of the authentic Jew or in that of the inauthentic Jew in the Sartrean sense. Continually emphasizing the qualities of this "fine book" *Anti-Semite and Jew*, he thinks its author "is quite the opposite of an anti-Semite and . . . is on the contrary philo-Semitic,"[27] but challenges several times his concept of a determination of the purely external Jew perceived through the gaze of the other. In 1951, Aron writes:

> Considering the moment when the Jew no longer feels either religiously Jewish or nationally Jewish, Sartre is tempted to say: who is the Jew? He is simply one whom the surrounding world calls Jewish. Unfortunately, the Jewish question is not entirely resolved by such a formula. Some of us in fact do fall into this example. I myself was brought up in a family that wasn't religious, where the ties with the community were weak, and, in the end, I discovered I was Jewish the day a friend at school called me by that name, at a time when, in all sincerity, I barely knew what it was to be Jewish, when I thought of myself in all naiveté as a French high school student, like all the others, when truly my Judaism was thrown back at me by someone else's word. . . . The problem was revealed to me by my German experience.[28]

Admitting his "naivety," Aron does not, however, content himself with emphasizing this determination by the Other that shatters the life of the Jew who is unaware of himself as such; he adds, countering Sartre's general argument, "There is something we cannot deny, which is an exceptional history of a community that is both national and religious, scattered, and which has lived for centuries in surrounding environments without intermingling with the national community."[29] This analysis radically contradicts the Sartrean perspective and also damages the idea of the increasing assimilation of Jews in France, for which Aron is the best example: to this de-Judaized Jew who nonetheless thinks of himself as Jewish, this "community" did not "intermingle with the national community"; he shows he is aware of the tragic consequences of the events of Vichy. Although it could be argued that Aron was not "on the way to being assimilated, but was completely assimilated,"[30] he still thought that "the notion of total assimilation that seemed to be an obvious fact not too long ago no longer seems as obvious to me now, because of the irreparable events that have simply taught us that in the community to which one thought one was most profoundly attached, where it didn't even occur to one to make a distinction between oneself and another who was not of the Jewish religion, events can occur that cause the problem to take on an extreme intensity."[31] This means that a total adherence to French society did not make questions of identity disappear, questions that unexpectedly rearose in the wake of Vichy and that transformed in a lasting way the issue of the relationship between the Jews and France.

Aron always vacillated between external determination of Jewishness (by the gaze of the Other, by Vichy, and so on) and internal determination by adherence to a community that did not try to disappear into the national community. In 1960, long before the shock of 1967, he again took up this balance between successive explanations in an almost identical way as he had before, without really being able to make clear the nature of this Jewish community in which he recognized himself:

> I received French culture without any visible imprint of Jewish tradition. And even more, Christianity was the religion for me, the one that revealed to me philosophers whom I read with passion, the one to which I referred to define the rights and requirements of reason. So I

belong to those Jews that Sartre, in his essay, regards as typical, Jewish because the external world declares them such, who assume their Judaism out of dignity but who do not spontaneously experience it. But let us think. To the extent that I came from the Jewish community and feel "French like the others," without attachments to my "coreligionists," I could challenge this judgment by which the social milieu decrees me Jewish. I would be wrong, since the community to which my grandparents belonged remains quite close to me.[32]

At the end of his life, Aron returned several times to Sartre's essay, questioning more and more strongly its logic, if not its imagery: "It is true that in *On 'The Jewish Question,'* [Sartre] did not know whether or not the destiny of the Jews was metaphysical."[33] When he concluded his *Memoirs*, which were published the year of his death, Aron, in the last chapter entitled "The End of a Generation," then in the "Epilogue," continued to wonder about his Judaism, reverting to Sartre's definitions, which he accepted as a de-Judaized Jew while still wondering to the end, in the very final pages, "how can I reconcile in practice my belonging to the nation of which I am a citizen and my loyalty to my Jewish ancestors,"[34] an approach that involves action and carefully thought-out choice, which is not part of the Sartrean theme.

Wanting to understand the sources of his Judaism while challenging Sartre's simplistic propositions, Aron does not escape the clichés that Sartre's analysis conveys; this analysis seems to obsess him so much that he continually returns to it, to the point of reusing, as has already been noted, the vocabulary and representations that testify to his incomprehension, despite his good will.

I had read Sartre's *La Question juive,* and I had spoken with him about it. I raised objections on two fundamental points. The first had to do with the very basis of his analysis: the Jew was claimed to be designated as such only in the eyes of the other. It was a rather facile remark that could be applied to any interpersonal relation. For example, I am arrogant only in the eyes of others; it remains to be seen whether or not I behave in a way to deserve such a characterization. If one takes as a model a Jew like me, de-Judaized, an unbeliever, nonpracticing, of French culture, with no Jewish culture, it is true to state that the Jew is a Jew for and through others and not for himself. But the Jew with earlocks, rocking back and forth as he says his prayers before the Wailing Wall, belongs to a historic group that is appropriately called Jewish, Jewish in itself and for itself.

My second objection had to do with the portrait of the anti-Semite. Sartre dissolved the being of the Jew, reducing him to a phantasm of non-Jews. On the other hand, he hardened the being of the anti-Semite to the point of attributing an essence to him.[35]

Aron, curiously, here accepts Sartre's analyses, which he had so often challenged, acknowledging himself as Sartre portrayed him, as a model French assimilated Jew, without seeming to be aware that he does not correspond at all to the authentic Jew or to the inauthentic Jew. He abandons his reservations, recognizing himself as Jewish through the gaze of the other, whereas he had so often called for a Jewish community—vague, imagined, but made at least of loyalty and solidarity anchored in time. Renouncing this minimal form of claimed identity, here he oversimplifies, à la Sartre, taking his inspiration almost half a century later from Sartre's vocabulary and caricature figures. In order the better to mark the distance that separates him from the real Jew, independent of the gaze of the other, who actually does not correspond to any of the Sartrean categories, isn't it the figure of the Jew on the Rue des Rosiers who reappears now under Aron's pen when he describes "Jews, genuine Jews,"[36] the Jews with side-curls who rock back and forth saying their prayers in front of the Wailing Wall, apprehended as unique Jews, in themselves and for themselves? Is it so mysterious, then, to want to be Jewish in a different way than in the name of a mysterious fidelity that leads Aron to designate simplistically those who wear side-curls as the only "genuine" Jews? Why Raymond Aron's incomprehension when "a young man—I can still see him, about twenty-five, as unlike the conventional image of the Jew as possible, with carefully pressed trousers, a light-colored jacket, an open face,"[37] takes the stage during a meeting Aron was chairing, organized by Rabbi Feuerweker, to justify, as a Jew, Israel's intervention during the war of 1956. What does it mean to look "as unlike the conventional image of the Jew as possible"? Is it to have "carefully pressed trousers, a light-colored jacket, an open face" or, like Aron himself, "blond hair and blue eyes"? What is there in common between the atypical, assimilated Jew, unrecognizable, but who assumes his Jewishness, and the Jew, instantly recognizable by the other, with a "curly, black beard" who snoozes on the Rue des Rosiers or one who wears side-curls and rocks back and forth in front of the Wailing Wall, or else the one who displays an obvious "Jewish anxiety" with which Aron had "deep sympathy"?[38]

Raymond Aron, wanting the truth, gnawed by a wish to understand the feeling that animated him in his innermost being, hesitated between clichéd images that testify to his distance from "genuine Jews," whether they wear caftans or light-colored jackets; between proclaimed de-Judaization, and loyalty to a history, to a community, to a family heritage; tirelessly, he applied Sartre's vision to himself, even if it meant, in the same sentence, letting an interior, incomprehensible feeling come to expression. In his summing up at the end of his *Memoirs*, he writes, "Enough regrets. Assuming that someone takes the trouble to read me in the future, he will discover the analyses, aspirations, and doubts that filled the consciousness of a man who was impregnated by history: a French citizen, but a Jew whom a semi-free French government had excluded from his country through a statute based on racial criteria."[39] Like a man profoundly wounded by the arrival of Vichy and the exclusion of the Jews from the public space, Aron confesses the suffering felt in seeing himself rejected, through the action of the other, that is to say of the state itself, from the national community. This obsession, which has not lessened with time, does not keep him from writing harshly, "I encounter Jews, old and young, who, so to speak, have not forgiven France, or the French, for the Jewish law and the roundup of the Vélodrome d'Hiver by the French police (under the orders of Vichy or the occupation authorities). If they have not forgiven France, it is no longer their nation, but only the country where they live pleasantly. This is a normal attitude for the old. . . . But why do the young who have become indifferent to the fate of their 'adopted country,' their nation, not choose Israel?"[40]—a suggestion that is difficult to accept, and that illustrates Aron's dilemma, wounded until the end of his life by the status that designated him as Jewish, but still wanting to proclaim his loyalty to the French nation, to the point of dispatching to Israel those who didn't want to forget . . . who, moreover, are like him.[41] From insults heard at school to his stay in Berlin, where he was confronted with the rise of anti-Semitism,[42] from the Vichy laws to the speech of General

de Gaulle, the gaze of the other has continually been shown to be reifying, shutting him up in his Jewish condition despite all the honors
given him: admission to the École Normale Supérieure; appointment
to the Collège de France; the company of the leading figures in society;
the national influence he exercised through *Le Figaro* and *L'Express*; his
intellectual prestige; his international renown; his functions as elder
statesman.

In this epilogue, it was Aron's condition as a French citizen excluded
as a Jew on racial criteria that he wanted his future reader to remember.
This statute that rejected him, turned him into a thing despite himself,
and imposed on him an identity from without, forever broke his faith
in the Republic of citizens—Aron had not mentioned this since London, when, in *La France Libre*, he commented on the events that were
taking place in France. What's more, he restrained himself from too
severely condemning the Maréchal's Vichy and imposed on himself an
obligation of reserve, as a Jew who didn't want others to think he took
sides because of this identity. Later on, Aron regretted this silence, emphasizing the contradictions the French Jewish Resistants of London
found themselves entangled in:

> It's true, I should have spoken about it. The anti-Jewish laws were
> promulgated on October 30, 1940, before the Germans demanded
> it. It was an initiative taken by Vichy. And then there was the exhibi-
> tion: *The Jews and France*. And above all there was the roundup of
> the Vélodrome d'Hiver in 1942. Why didn't I comment on these
> events? . . . The first reason is that we were French Resistants in
> London. As French citizens, we were obviously against all these anti-
> Semitic measures. But there was a kind of convention to talk about
> it as little as possible. Probably because I myself was Jewish, I talked
> about it as little as possible. There is probably another, deeper reason,
> which is not to my credit, but which is understandable: all the mea-
> sures the French could take against the Jews deeply affected me pre-
> cisely because I am French, if I can say so, before I am Jewish. It was a
> kind of emotional precaution for myself to think as little as possible of
> what certain French people were doing to the Jews.[43]

And, in a confidential remark Aron shared with Daniel Cordier who
visited him in 1981, when Aron mentioned his regret at not having

fought as he wanted in 1940 and having remained in London editing a paper, when Cordier insisted on the importance of this intellectual combat, Aron immediately replied, "You may be right, but you forget that I am Jewish."[44]

An assimilated, de-Judaized Jew, Aron wanted first of all to be French and explained his London reserve as one he imposed on himself all his life, faced with the vicissitudes of Israeli history that he commented on while trying to preserve distance and coolness, keeping his role as an analyst of international relations between states pursuing their respective interests confronting each other, "monsters" whose strategies defy all friendships, even those that seem the most lasting, like the friendship that for many years linked France with Israel. A French citizen, Aron expressed himself above all as such. In "De Gaulle, Israël et les Juifs," as well as in innumerable articles, he opposed the war of 1956 started by Israel, quivered with emotion during the war of 1967, and examined as a strategist the Yom Kippur War, wondering about the "possible defeat of the conqueror,"[45] condemned without hesitation the invasion of Lebanon and the massacres of the Palestinians.[46] It was above all the war of 1967, when Israel was threatened and suddenly deprived of French armament, that troubled him profoundly, even though later on he regreted having let himself be carried away by an emotion that diverted him from a rational, cool strategic analysis.[47] During those days when the fate of Israel seemed in doubt, he gave vent to a "burst of Jewishness,"[48] which urged him to break with the De Gaulle who spoke of the "elite people, sure of itself and overbearing." Since this phrase was accepted without any perceptible reaction, and the great voices, those for instance of Malraux or Mauriac, were not making themselves heard, Aron publicly took the stage as he had never done before, in a strong and particularly dramatic way:

> To call "sure of itself and overbearing" the people of the ghettos seems to me, even today, as laughable as it is odious. . . . No Western statesman had spoken of the Jews in this style, nor has anyone characterized them as a "people" with two adjectives. We all know this style, and these adjectives; they belong to Drumont, to Maurras, not to Hitler and his people. After all, Georges Bernanos never admitted any link whatsoever between his old master Drumont, to whom he remained

faithful to the end, and Hitler, who inspired a profound horror in him. . . . I will say that General De Gaulle has, knowingly, willfully, opened a new period in Jewish history and perhaps in anti-Semitism. Everything is now possible again. Everything is now beginning again. There's no question, of course, of persecution: just "malevolence." This isn't the time of scorn, but the time of suspicion.[49]

Returning once again explicitly to the Sartrean perspective, at this time when he accused, in front of everyone, the head of the state of making himself the spokesperson for French-style anti-Semitism, he knew that, whatever his detachment with regard to Israel, "the Jewish Frenchman, in the eyes of others, belongs also 'to this elite people, sure of itself and overbearing,'" and he adds, "I also know, more clearly than I did yesterday, that the very possibility of the destruction of the state of Israel that the massacre of a part of the population would bring with it wounds me to the bottom of my soul. In this sense, I have confessed that a Jew can never attain perfect objectivity when it's a question of Israel," and he serenely notes: "I cannot achieve this kind of detachment, and I don't want to achieve it."[50] Objectivity, then, is impossible to find in this domain: "When it's a question of Jews and their fate, I cannot without hypocrisy feign the objectivity of the pure spectator."[51] Once again, he sways between the Sartrean position that imposes on detached, inauthentic Jews their identity, regarded as overbearing, and the reality of his "inner experience" of someone who has "never been a Zionist, first and foremost because [he] doesn't feel Jewish" and who still thinks that "we Jews, whether we want to or not, will live dangerously, in Israel or elsewhere."[52] This danger can also appear in France, from the very fact of this sudden collective solidarity toward Israel, which is scarcely compatible with French-style centralization which makes almost comprehensible the reaction of the government faced with "the emotionalism of the French Jewish community." "We can say, then, that the Six Days' War was the moment of extreme emotional solidarity, that it's also the time when there was a beginning of a reaction . . . from the French government: a reaction with regard to a minority that expressed itself and asserted itself the way American ethnic groups did, and that is not in the French, Jacobin tradition."[53] This emotionalism that he shared led to dysfunctional communitarian behavior, compared to the logic of the

French public space with its citizens revolving around the state; Aron, who shows himself on other occasions favorable to a multinational citizenship open to differences, cannot admit the birth of internal counter-societies that urge people toward emotive mobilization, even though as an individual he can feel such emotion and doesn't hesitate to show it publicly, or openly break profound ties.

His dialogue on this occasion with Claude Lévi-Strauss reveals the originality of his stance on De Gaulle's discourse. On April 9, 1968, Lévi-Strauss sent Aron a long letter in which he thinks that "the chosen epithets corresponded to reality." He thinks that "certain Jewish elements in France, taking advantage of their power over the written and spoken media and of the positions they had acquired, and arrogating to themselves the right to express themselves in the name of all the others, did reveal themselves as being 'sure of themselves and overbearing.'" He adds, "That smacked of conspiracy, and I would almost say of treason. As a Jew, I was ashamed of it."[54] Using the phrase of General De Gaulle's (writing, however, "one could, however, say it to them, without answering the mix they wanted to produce by another mix just as outrageous as the first, which was seriously so, and of their own doing") and applying it more explicitly only to the Jews of France, whereas the General was especially aiming at Israel by including it in "the Jewish people," Lévi-Strauss took a position that was diametrically opposed to Aron's, who rejected with all his strength De Gaulle's accusation and denied any idea of conspiracy. Aron vindicated emotionalism and concern for the security of Israel; he proclaimed it; he hammered out a vehement rejection of the accusatory Gaullist vocabulary, seeing in it only the indicator of the resurgence of anti-Semitism. Aron felt no "shame," saw no "conspiracy." In his still unpublished reply dated April 15, he went so far as to refute point by point Claude Lévi-Strauss's accusation and stressed how Lévi-Strauss's arguments "surprise" him: "The radio and television are closely controlled by the government. *Le Monde* has published articles of all tendencies, including the opinions of an anti-Semitic rabbi and of Rodinson. At *Le Figaro*, I am the only Jew. . . . Jews seem to me to be participating with a surplus of passion in a collective movement."[55] All to no avail, since in his reply dated April 19, Lévi-Strauss doesn't concede anything: "The people I am thinking of [the

Jews] . . . have committed an extremely grave sin against us all. . . . You think it moving and excusable that French Jews have enthusiastically seized the occasion that was offered to them to proclaim themselves both French and Jewish. I think, on the contrary, that they should not have done so; even less should they contribute to fomenting this enthusiasm secretly."[56] On this essential point, the "many parallelisms" that Lévi-Strauss traced, in a letter dated September 11, 1983, between his own life and Aron's since their shared childhood spent in Versailles where their mothers waited together for their sons as they left the Lycée Hoche, came to an end and gave way to a radical divergence.[57] During a journey to Israel, Lévi-Strauss does not at all have the impression of touching his "roots,"[58] and he forcefully writes, "I feel totally, wholly, and exclusively French, even if it matters to me to know that my roots plunge into a multicellular past, rich in culture and historical events. But the idea that my political choices or my votes could be influenced by other considerations than my citizenship is, for me, unthinkable."[59] As to Aron, while still proclaiming himself essentially French, he is still in search of another citizenship more open to personal identity.

Raymond Aron's hesitations come to light in his very writing. He declares, from one text to the other, that he is a Jewish Frenchman, a French citizen who has been de-Judaized but is Jewish nonetheless; he continually presents himself as a Jewish Frenchman to assert the preeminence of the national bond, of his inclusion within the French Republican tradition, to proclaim his single and complete adherence to the history of the nation that leads him to "mourn the misfortunes of France at Waterloo or at Sedan, not when listening to the story of the destruction of the Temple."[60] He writes without hesitation: "The question 'Jewish or French first' has hardly any meaning for me."[61] And yet often his pen seems to falter; in his text read in Jerusalem, where he received an honorary degree, he thanks the Hebrew University and its president for the choice "that they made for this Frenchman" who is thus honored, and he adds:

> The one to whom you have, on this day, given this mark of esteem is a French Jew, or a French citizen of Jewish origin. I say "of origin" because I am not religious, not a believer in the conventional sense of the term. . . . I am French, I have been so since the beginning, I will be

so to the end. . . . Having come from a Jewish community in Lorraine, I received from my parents an easily offended patriotism that I would like to cherish without any vanity or xenophobia, a demanding and severe patriotism. . . . The fact that the Collège de France welcomed me would, I know, have fulfilled my father's wishes. The tribute of the University of Jerusalem would have touched him no less.[62]

As a French Jew or French citizen of Jewish origin, or even a de-Judaized one, recognized as an eminent Frenchman by the Collège de France, but also received as a Frenchman and a Jew by the University of Jerusalem, a twofold symbolic bond is formed. On other occasions, Aron even mentions the pangs of the "French, English, American Jew," those of the "French Jew" who questions himself about his identity,[63] of the "French Jew who warned his compatriots against the German peril."[64] He now thinks, however, that "most French Jews have become Jewish Frenchmen,"[65] and he strongly challenges any accusation of a dual allegiance that could, in the name of an openly proclaimed emotion and attachment, impeach the primacy of the national bond. "As an unbeliever, I will not equivocate about my sympathy with Israel, but I refuse it a national loyalty that goes to my homeland. . . . The choice lies, on one hand, in French citizenship and, on the other, the desire not to break the link with the other Jews in the world and, at the same time, with the Israelis."[66] He does not hesitate to confess "a special love" for Israel, and writes, "I plead for a patriotism that should not be exclusive or totalitarian. A national adherence does not exclude elective or traditional affinities with other nations and other peoples."[67] Far from Sartre, it is indeed a question this time of will, choice, personal involvement, emotions, and values, and not of the gaze of the other. Even Pierre Goldman, author of *Souvenirs obscurs d'un Juif polonais né en France*, admits he is convinced and "admired Aron, his rigor of thought, his absence of moralizing and sentimentalism, his Jewish loyalty without Messianism."[68]

This predominance of the Frenchman over the Jew is logical so long as Aron constantly presents himself as a de-Judaized Jew who nonetheless "suffers" with French Jews, "like them, with them," when Israel is threatened; he goes so far as to say that the destruction of this state would "take the strength to live away from him,"[69] a very strong phrase

that demonstrates an existential attachment to the Jews and to Israel.
Actually, rereading all the texts by Raymond Aron that concern in one
way or another the Jews in Germany, in France, in Israel, or elsewhere,
one is struck by the repetitive use of "we" with its strongly identitarian
resonance. It is surprising, coming as it does from the pen of one who
presents himself as a de-Judaized Jewish Frenchman, in its recognition
of the existence of a Jewish "community" within French society. In his
1951 lecture to B'nai B'rith, the phrase "We others, we Jews" is continually repeated, with variations;[70] similarly, in 1981, mentioning Vichy, he
thinks that "for the Jews who lived through this period, there remains
the memory of a government that was popular at the time, but that
practically excluded Jews from the French community. That was a blow
to us."[71] When Aron distanced himself from a carefully posited ana-
lytic approach, faced for instance with a Jewish audience or a journalist
who was just as explicitly Jewish by the nature of his commitments, he
sometimes endorsed a collective dimension that he rejected elsewhere
in a number of declarations where he tried to clarify his attachments as
a "de-Judaized Jew" remote from any communitarian affiliation. His
1951 lecture is particularly surprising from this point of view since, having been given not long after the end of the war and the publication of
Sartre's *Anti-Semite and Jew*, it shows a strong feeling of collective belonging. The "We others, we Jews" of the beginning of the text returns
like a leitmotif. One loses count of all the phrases like "we live," "we
occupy," "we have lived," "the notion of Jewishness projected onto us,"
"when they don't reproach us," "we are the ones," "if we were all aware
of it," "they do us too much honor since we cannot be both agents of
capitalism and agents of the revolution," "some of us," "there is something we cannot deny," "I don't personally think that we Jews could
have done much against anti-Semitism," "it is quite obvious that we
are against anti-Semitism, we Jews," "we have a good proportion of
Nobel Prizes."[72] In 1960, he declares in the same vein, "It is not up to
us to brag about our merits or denounce those who do not love us."[73]
In 1980, he writes again, "François Mitterand made some remarks to
which all of us Jews are sensitive."[74]

    This claimed inclusion in a "we Jews" appears in other texts, which,
although written in a number of different circumstances, almost all

refer to events that affected the Jews of France or Israel. In 1960, Aron writes about the future of Israel: "I understand this aspiration to a nation that can no longer be denied to us," "what degree of sympathy is permitted to us without accusing us of a dual allegiance. I ask it of all my compatriots." He goes on: "The state of Israel represents a great event for all Jews. It can only awaken strong feelings in us all"; "This outcome is closed to us since Israel and the Jewish communities of the Diaspora will live side by side"; "Many different ways are opened to each of us"; "We other Jews, whether we like it or not, will live dangerously, in Israel or elsewhere"; "It is not up to us Jews to brag about our merits or denounce those who do not love us. . . . The rest does not depend on me, the rest does not depend on us."[75] In 1973, during the Yom Kippur War, at a conference of French-speaking Jewish intellectuals, he fires, "What can we do, we Jewish Frenchmen, or simply Frenchmen who are friends of Israel?"[76] In 1980, after the attack on the Rue Copernic, he thinks that "François Mitterand has made some remarks to which all of us Jews are sensitive."[77] For more than thirty years, while he acquired an undeniable national reputation, and while he knows that the stances he takes, in *Le Figaro* or elsewhere, will certainly benefit from a lot of attention, Aron doesn't hesitate to include himself in a flaunted "we Jews" that owes nothing to Sartrean perspectives, and that refutes the pure and simple assimilation of the Jews, as French citizens, into the national community.[78] What's more, even though Aron often criticizes the Jewish "community," though he doesn't identify with it, he notes its existence within the national community, refuting, almost two centuries later, the predictions of the Abbé Grégoire about the disappearance through assimilation of the Jews of France. Though, following his own logic, Aron is careful to emphasize that "this community does not exist as such; it has no organization, it should not have any,"[79] one can nevertheless find many passages that refer to this community, often positively, such as the following: "Born to a Jewish family, I owed it to myself not to deny belonging to a community, a distant one and for a long time almost an abstract one, my own";[80] "I would be wrong, since the community to which my grandparents still belonged is still quite close";[81] "As assimilated as he is or thinks he is, the Jew keeps a feeling of solidarity with

the other communities of the Diaspora";[82] "having come from a Jewish community in Lorraine";[83] "I accept a certain solidarity with the
Jewish community, with the Diaspora, while still ranking my French
citizenship above everything in the political order";[84] "the many Jews
who do not believe in God while preserving the community's way
of life";[85] "The Jewish community of France is divided into several
groups";[86] "In 1967, the General's statements provoked conflict with
the Jewish community";[87] during the War of 1967, "The Jews of France
have for the first time given the impression that they form some kind
of community";[88] "Since the Algerian War, the Jewish community has
swollen and been transformed by the Sephardic Jews of North Africa";[89] B.-H. Lévy "should appear to be the interpreter of the Jewish
community";[90] "the hatred unleashed against the Jewish community"
in Nazi Germany,[91] and so on.

This constant use of the idea of community to designate French Jewish milieus not only radically refutes the Sartrean argument but, by
posing the question of the nature and reality of assimilation, reveals
that Raymond Aron adheres to an open concept of citizenship that is
not very Jacobin, since he doesn't hide his desire to remain close to his
"ancestors" and to preserve his "roots," words that he uses on many
occasions.[92] Thus, he offers his assistance to the Unified Jewish Social
Fund and agrees, like Marcel Mauss before him, to sit on the Central
Committee of the Universal Israelite Alliance, not simply as a formality
but sometimes taking the time to go in person to the Rue La Bruyère.[93]
The publication, in 1991, of his previously unpublished lecture given at
the New School of Social Research in April 1974, entitled "Is Multinational Citizenship Possible?" lets us understand this shift. Aron gave
himself the theoretical means to make the notion of citizenship evolve
beyond the model of the nation-state with its vision of citizenship revolving solely around public space, ignoring any communitarian bond
that would hinder its realization. Very much ahead of the contemporary
multiculturalist trend, which justified inclusion in more or less "dense"
communitarian identities, Aron writes:

> What the experiment of the United Kingdom teaches us is the compat-
> ibility of linguistic and ethnic plurality with political unity . . . while
> the French state, for historical reasons that we are aware of, without

necessarily approving of them, barely tolerates and certainly does not favor the survival of the Celt (and of the Breton), of Basque and Occitan. The tendency of certain monolithic governments toward homogeneity of culture, not without recourse to pressure or constraint, would become inconceivable in a federal state like a country in Western Europe. Because of this, certain cultural minorities could more easily obtain full and complete recognition. With this reservation, I maintain that enlarging the political entity leads to a transfer rather than a mutation of citizenship.[94]

This "transfer" within a future European federal state nonetheless profoundly calls into question French-style militant citizenship hostile to all forms of cultural adherence imagined by the French Revolution and also justifies identitarian allegiances that the Jacobin or Republican state did not tolerate, at least officially. This contrast between Great Britain and France is particularly interesting, since it brings into play the comparative sociology of states, which describes these distinct kinds of state-based logic leading to very different concepts of citizenship.[95] Aron clearly for the first time attacks the politics of unitary states that, through "pressure" or "constraint," tend "toward homogeneity of the culture."

This little-known lecture bears witness to an important turning point in the thinking of Aron, who continually lays claim to an "easily offended patriotism" which was shown to be not easily compatible with maintaining strong cultural identifications, even if, in reality, many compromises were found, for instance in the course of the nineteenth century, between loyalty to one's "region" and republican public space.[96] Aron is explicit on this point:

> I mean by mini-nationalism the claim for cultural or linguistic autonomy of close communities of Bretons, Basques, even Occitans. Insofar as the act of accusation attacks the rejection the nation-state would make of cultural pluralism, I readily subscribe to it, provided, however, that I am not asked to subscribe to the independence, as a state, of Corsica or Brittany. The fact that even nation-states bear a certain diversity of culture does not constitute an argument in favor of empires. Individuals become citizens of the same state only provided they experience a certain community of fate.[97]

Several times Aron exhibits such ideas, taking the examples of France, Great Britain, or Spain, where there were legitimate "desires for re-rooting."[98] Although he attacks the compulsion exercised by the nation-state to the detriment of internal "cultural pluralism," Aron remained attached to a strong citizenship that ties the individual, despite his iden-titarian and linguistic allegiances, to the nation-state experienced as a "community of fate" identical for everyone, a state where "the citizen has the calling of soldier" and doesn't hesitate to take part "in defense of the country."[99] This general interpretation corresponds perfectly, more-over, to his defense of "us Jews" in the framework of France. In this same lecture, Aron briefly evokes this point, in a personal way, charged with the emotion he acknowledges when he speaks of the Jewish ques-tion: "Whoever has known the experience of the loss of his own politi-cal collectivity has felt the existential anguish (even if only temporary) of solitude. . . . The Jews of my generation cannot forget the precari-ousness of human rights, in the world as it is, when they do not coin-cide with the rights of citizens. But the rights of the citizen also imply duties, in the continental tradition of Europe, the duty of serving the flag, if the state or circumstances require it."[100] There is thus no con-tradiction, in Aron's opinion, between proud patriotism and inclusion among "us Jews."[101] This lecture given in the United States remains the sole text Aron devoted to the question of the degree of compat-ibility between citizenship and identities. French logic would lead him to confine himself to a citizenship revolving solely around the State, indifferent to multiple identities, leading to the perfect assimilation he so often calls for, which justifies his condition as a de-Judaized Jew. But Aron here, not long after the Six Days' War and in the American context so favorable to him, becomes involved in another perspective, one of a multiculturalism that is thought to be incompatible with the model of the nation-state embodied by his French homeland. In this crucial text, Aron justifies his attachment to his Jewish identity, evoked in an unexpected way during the lecture, in the framework of the na-tion-state to which he remains profoundly attached as the privileged public space of citizens.

In 1960, Aron writes, "The Frenchman of Jewish origin seems to me legitimately to have the right to keep his faith and the elements of traditional culture to which he remains attached. Why should a Jew be a good Frenchman or a good Englishman only if he loses, through assimilation, the beliefs and practices of his ancestors? Only the doctrines, avowed or covert, of totalitarianism require such alienation as the price of citizenship."[102] Seven years later, in response to General De Gaulle's speech on "the elite people, sure of itself and overbearing," in the tragic context where the Jews' membership in the French nation seems called into question, when the implicit reproach of dual nationality comes to light, and when Aron was finishing his essay written in one stretch under the pressure of profound emotion, Aron returns once again to the equivalence of assimilation to totalitarianism. With De Gaulle in mind, he writes this passage, where the echo resounds of his New York lecture in support of mininationalisms, so long as they respect, following the example of the Jews, the preeminence of the state:

> Will they require [of the Jews], as certain exegetes of Élysée policies suggest, not only a choice they have already made, but a total choice? No state accepts dual allegiance (even though French laws have allowed a number of Jews to become Israeli without losing their French nationality); only the totalitarian state imposes an allegiance exclusive of any other attachment. . . . The Fifth Republic will not become either theocratic or ideocratic, but France, Gallican or Jacobin, willingly or not, eliminates both religious separatism and linguistic particularism. The Bretons don't learn their language at school any more than the Basques do their native language. The French school "de-Judaizes" the Jews with an impressive efficiency. . . . Is [De Gaulle] acting as a descendant of Louis XIV, who didn't tolerate the Protestants? Or as an heir to the Jacobins who loved liberty so much that they forbade citizens to feel any other emotion? I don't know. I only know that all nationalism, pushed beyond a certain limit, ends up driving some Jews (of whom I am not one, but whom I do not want to desert) to the alternative of rejection and denial.[103]

This perspective is particularly striking since it identifies assimilation with totalitarianism, likens Jacobinism to totalitarianism, France's exceptional status [*l'exception française*], and its repression of all legitimate "cultural diversity." It also implies, on the part of its author, a rejection of assimilation, which distances Aron so much from Marx's views, as

well as from those of his little comrade Sartre, driving him to link himself, out of a refusal to "desert" their fight, with these Jews driven "to the
alternative of rejection and denial." While Aron continually proclaims
his desire to take up arms and serve his country, and while he identifies
citizenship with military service, now he uses the term "desertion" to
indicate his will to stay by the side of the Jews who do not want to deny
their identity within the nation. Love of one's country and the will to
serve it do not imply the necessity of denying one's "roots," of turning
one's back on the values of one's "ancestors," even if it does imply the
determined rejection of a dual citizenship joining a French citizen to
both France and Israel: "Modern citizenship implies, by its very nature,
obedience to the orders of the state and above all to military obligations.
I can be a Frenchman of Jewish religion and yet cannot be both French
and Israeli."[104] If he clearly challenges dual allegiance, he still claims his
own "twofold loyalty" to France and to his Jewish identity.[105]

In a number of texts, Aron returns to this point, sometimes slightly
changing his position, as he often does when he approaches the question of Jewish identity, taking pains to examine its basis. While he
compared it to that of the Basques or the Bretons in the name of the
legitimate "cultural diversity" of a nonoppressive French society, now
he calls this idea into question. In his eyes, "The resurgence of Occitan,
of the religion of the Albigensians, and the return of Basque traditions"
or of Alsatian ones do not pose any problem, and do not imply

> rediscovering the warmth of close communities; the case of the Jewish
> community is different from that of the Bretons or the Basques because
> it is not a community that has territorial roots. It is a community of a
> special kind. . . . As sound and legitimate as it is to claim responsibility
> for safeguarding the survival of regional specificities, the Jewish case is
> not part of this general phenomenon, since it is not the same thing; it is
> always the special case. . . . From the moment they [the Jews] chose to
> live in France, they had to realize that it is the nature of French culture
> both to tolerate and to try to erase differences; it tries to erase them by
> its power of absorption and by the implicitly authoritarian side of ratio-
> nalism, or so-called rationalism.[106]

From then on, what is understandable for the Basques or the Bretons
is no longer valid for the Jews of France, who this time are expected to

become assimilated with French culture, while Aron himself explicitly asserts that since the statute governing the Jews in 1940, this assimilation, which had seemed so natural, has been called into question for a long time to come. Two years later, in 1983, in his *Memoirs*, Aron nevertheless confirms this restriction, which places French Jewish identity in an almost impossible situation, beyond vague loyalty to roots, remote too from the side-curls of the "genuine Jews" with practices foreign to rationalism or to "so-called" French rationalism.

> It may be that in France now the Jews are profiting from the fashion for the cult of difference. Why should Jewish difference not be tolerated or even proclaimed like that of other ethnic groups—Basque, Celtic, or Occitan—that have revolted against the straitjacket of Jacobinism? But the Jews, genuine Jews, do not place themselves on the same level as the micronationalists or the ethnic groups for which French culture has not erased particular characteristics. They believe in one God, who has imposed exceptional obligations on the Jews, but who rules over all mankind. The many Jews who do not believe in God while preserving the community's way of life are inclined, consciously or not, to associate their Judaism with any group—Breton or Corsican—that has demanded a separate "cultural" identity. Is this identity enough to form the basis for a people? . . . Objectively, according to the criteria customarily used to identify a people, the Jews of the diaspora are not a people. . . . Assuming that they accepted their belonging to a Jewish people, this belonging imposes almost nothing on them.

And Aron goes on to evoke once again his awareness that he is "a Jew, of French nationality and culture, concerned not to uproot himself, respectful of the beliefs of his coreligionists—beliefs that he does not share,"[107] and to express clearly his quality as a "Jewish intellectual."[108]

From then on, it's the notion of "roots" that wins out to justify an irrational attachment to the past. This notion, actually void of any spiritual foundation, even less of a religious one, replaces culture with a vague loyalty to the past, a Jewish past that Aron never really studied, any more than his little comrade Sartre. In fact, he has never devoted the slightest bibliographical research to it; he is as ignorant of Joseph Salvador as of the scholars of the French-style Wissenschaft or of the great modern panoramas having to do with the history of the Jews by

Heinrich Graetz, Jacob Katz, or Salo Baron—not to mention all the historians and sociologists who, in the second half of the twentieth century, considerably enriched "Jewish Studies," so many authors that he never quotes in his observations about Jewish history, while a number of scholars of yesterday and today are evoked to support his vast syntheses of international relations, his portraits of industrial society, his reflections on contemporary sociology, and so on. In a footnote, in the Jewish context, only the writings of Léon Poliakof, to whom Aron was close, are sometimes mentioned, even though they are usually more of a literary than a scholarly nature. It gets to the point where, to evoke ancient Jewish history, Aron comes to quote copiously none other than Arnold Toynbee![109] The "roots" send the Jews back to a distant, imaginary, unknown past, not to a contemporary cultural project in which one could try to participate: it is just a question of not betraying this distant past in order to preserve the esteem of one's ancestors by showing at least a duty of solidarity. As he expresses it in 1962, this "solidarity" is vital: "Especially in our era, after Hitler's persecutions, a Jew cannot flee his destiny and ignore those who, elsewhere, believed or believe in the same God as Isaac's or Jacob's, the God of his ancestors."[110] Aron goes on, "Today, I justify in a way my attachment to Judaism by loyalty to my roots. If, by some miracle, I were to appear before my grandfather, who lived in Rambervillers, and who was close to the ghetto, I would like not to be ashamed before him; I would like to give him the feeling that though no longer Jewish as he was, I have remained in a way faithful. As I have written many times: I do not like to tear up my roots."[111] He returns often to this metaphor: "For reasons that might be emotional, or that could also be rational, I do not like to cut off my roots. I am animated by the sense of continuity and tradition."[112] In this sense, Aron remains faithful to the precept he uttered in his *Introduction to the Philosophy of History*: "At every instant, we should recreate our self by attaching the past to the present. Thus are joined, in a continually renewed dialectic, retrospective knowledge and choice, acceptance of the given and striving to surpass it."[113] Jewish "roots" are thus part of a distant "given" that one can only accept, but that consciousness is free to reinterpret without submitting to it.

Aware of not being a "real" Jew, and refusing now to liken Jewish identity to the identity of the legitimate micronationalities that are re-emerging in France, Aron tirelessly seeks to discover what drives him to affirm his Jewish solidarity despite "beliefs that I do not share." Although he means to preserve his roots, to maintain a scrupulous fidelity to his ancestors, a solidarity with the Jews of France and also of Israel, often he does not conceal the fact that he nonetheless feels closer, because of his culture, to a virulent anti-Semite than to a Moroccan Jew:

> You know who was Drumont's disciple? Bernanos, who wrote a book to the glory of Drumont. So if I tell you that there are more points in common between Bernanos, even when he was an anti-Semite, and me, than between me and a Jew from southern Morocco, is that wrong, or paradoxical? One can hold forth indefinitely on that statement. But it signifies quite simply this: a Frenchman, Jewish by origin, who is not religious, who does not believe in God and who, through reflection or through affectation, decides on a certain solidarity with Jewry, can at the same time say: "The fact is that I have more common traits, more shared ideas and experiences, let's say, with Bernanos or a respectable anti-Semite—there are some who aren't respectable—than with a Southern Moroccan with whom I share neither language, nor experience, nor belief."[114]

How can Raymond Aron, profoundly disturbed till the end of his life by the situation of the Jews, wounded by General De Gaulle's remarks on "the elite people, sure of itself and overbearing," the anti-Semitic nature of which he courageously denounced when he wrote "This style, these adjectives—we all know them, they belong to Drumont, to Maurras, not to Hitler,"[115] emphasizing the difference between French-style anti-Semitism and Nazism—how can Aron at the same time declare himself close to Bernanos? How can he, even in 1983, think that in "my view, there are many ways of being an anti-Semite, and Georges Bernanos who was one in his way, like his master Édouard Drumont, bears no resemblance to the portrait sketched by Sartre; Bernanos has never possessed anything"?[116] How can he declare he is closer to a "respectable" anti-Semite like Bernanos—whose incredible violence aimed at the Jews, from whom he expected conversion as proof of the salvation of humanity (like Marx before him, on a different register?), a violence inspired by the absolute adoration he had for his master Drumont, is well known—than to a Jew from the Moroccan South? How can Aron almost succeed at clearing the name of this anti-Judaism that is more of a Christian than a racist inspiration, which greatly facilitated the acceptance of the statute governing the Jews imposed by Vichy, which to Aron was the undeniable proof of the rupture of the national contract to which he was so attached? How can he come to argue that "no one will accuse André Siegfried of anti-Semitism" while he himself quotes an extract from Siegfried's *Voies d'Israël* in which Siegfried writes, "Pessimistic, the Jew is also singularly so in matters concerning societies where his fate makes him live. Thanks to a kind of intellectual dissociation, he can judge this fate with the cold lucidity of a foreigner"? How can he prove Siegfried innocent while Siegfried takes excerpts from Barrès, from the ideas and political practices so often close to those of Drumont, in which he thinks that the Jews "manipulate ideas with the same thumb that a banker does shares"?[117] In view of the ensemble of texts by Siegfried published at the time, it is difficult to ignore the xenophobic and racist nature of a number of his writings and his lectures.[118]

Although Aron immediately attacked Hitlerian anti-Semitism, carefully dismantling its lunatic mode of thinking, in the face of which "the effort at objectivity must yield to necessary indignation,"[119] one can argue that, out of a concern for his own integration with the nation, Aron tended to underestimate the influence of French-style anti-Semitism, as well as the reality in France of the temptation to extreme nationalism, in some respects close to the Fascist movement in 1930s France.[120] We can also think that, while he was confronted with his own Jewish condition in London, Aron downplayed the deep-rootedness of the Vichy regime, whose leaders, according to Aron, followed only the "will of the conqueror, and not the sentiment of the nation"; and, optimistic, Aron asserted that in an occupied zone the population "resists anti-Semitism just as it resists everything imposed on it by Germany."[121] Why is it that Aron doesn't hesitate to exonerate the Vichy regime, even writing, "For me, the date of the essential, radical, final rupture was November 1942"?[122] Isn't it a wish to minimize the responsibilities of the French people that makes him write later on, "I have sometimes been severe to French writers close to the Collaboration, in some cases too severe"?[123] We can win a better understanding of the strange context of Aron's sudden death when he publicly flew to the aid of his friend Bertrand de Jouvenel to help him in his legal proceedings brought against the Israeli historian Zeev Sternhell, who had accused him of seeming to be sympathetic to collaborationist ideas during this era, and did not indicate that he had later on become a Resistant.[124] In this sense, when Aron was writing the first draft of his *Memoirs*, the title that figures in its manuscript version is "Living in History: Memories of a Jewish Frenchman." As Pierre Manent observes, not only did Aron remove from the final version of the book this "Living in History" but, above all, "he took out the 'Jewish Frenchman' that indeed faithfully conveyed what had been the preoccupation of his life, but that no doubt risked making the reader focus on the adjective, and thus unbalance the equilibrium that Aron had chosen to maintain throughout his life."[125]

Even though his loyalty to Jewish identity was never denied, and though it seems to be accentuated in the final texts where Aron claims his adherence to this long, distinct history of that identity in his French country, the foundation of this identity nonetheless remains foreign to him. Aron did not think of himself as a "genuine Jew" and happily rubbed shoulders with upholders of a "respectable" anti-Semitism, who were scarcely offended by the statute governing the Jews, which struck him a harsh blow in 1940. Wanting above all to affirm his full and complete adherence to France, his desire to construct a body of work with universalist and "normal" dimensions, Raymond Aron lived like a scholar confronted with Weber-like choices, having to do with one's relationship to values, to the question of relativism. He was able to track errors of reasoning, challenge ideological procedures, fight scientistic temptations, engage in the battles of the twentieth century in the name of an ethics of conviction that does not forget the ethics of responsibility. A product of French-style emancipation, Aron sought the sources of his liberal inspiration in Montesquieu, Tocqueville, and Alain; in Weber, Simmel, and Dilthey he sought the principles of an effective sociological approach; all his life he maintained a special relationship with Marx as an economist and sociologist; he neglected none of the Anglo-Saxon authors of social stratification; read attentively the elitist Italian theoreticians like Pareto and Mosca; knew the importance of

Clausewitz. As a sociologist, Aron devoted his life to the analysis of social action, to the values that form its basis, to the relationships between ends and means. As a philosopher, a sociologist, and a political theorist, a scholar who drew crowds to the Sorbonne and to the Collège de France, he approached Jewish reality only rarely, as a question having to do with the "motherland," whether in its historical, identitarian, or political dimension. Even when he presented the works of Marx, Durkheim, or Simmel in long expositions, he purely and simply ignored this Jewish dimension. Although Aron devoted hundreds of pages to analyzing Marx's work in detail, he only mentioned his book *On 'The Jewish Question'* twice. In one lecture and in one journalistic essay, little-known texts without any academic status, he refers to it in the vaguest way: in *L'Express* in February 1981 he writes *"On 'The Jewish Question,'* Marx's most anti-Semitic text, illustrates this willful confusion."[126] In his lectures where he dissected Marx's thinking, when he was examining the writings of Marx and briefly mentioned *The Holy Family*, nowhere did he discuss the way Marx approached the Jewish question, which however was central to this work.[127] In the same sense, Aron wrote, from 1931 onward, a number of reviews of scholarly books in academic journals: none of them have to do with Jewish history in its many aspects. Actually, it seems that the texts—which in the end are numerous—where he examines Jewish identity are essentially journalistic writings, more or less heated reactions to political events that concerned the Jews of France or Israel, speeches given in Israel during official ceremonies organized in his honor, articles or interviews of an autobiographical nature, and so on. These circumstantial writings do not in any way form part of his profession as a sociologist. We should remember, however, that when he came to publish *Main Currents in Sociological Thought*, Aron, in an interview with *Le Monde*, openly explained his "sympathy" toward Tocqueville and the constant attention he gives to that writer's work: "Perhaps there is also another kinship. Tocqueville was descended from a great family of Norman aristocrats. And I am a Jewish intellectual. But throughout his entire life, Tocqueville was marked by the memories his parents had kept of the Terror; his father and mother were almost sent to the guillotine. There was a trauma at the beginning of his life that explains why he declared,

'I am not sure I love our world, but that is how it is.' The trauma I knew is that of Hitlerian anti-Semitism."[128]

In studies of an academic nature written later on in life, aside from his Sorbonne lectures or his seminars conducted at various other academic institutions, Aron often evoked recent Jewish history. He often returned to the subject of the gas chambers, making a strong distinction between Nazism and Stalinism; he steadily referred to the Nazi extermination of the Jews when he discussed Clausewitz or the future of industrial societies, when he analyzed the future of secular religions or the consequences of industrial progress on the organization of modern societies. In his *Dimensions de la conscience historique*, Aron emphasizes that "the Jews were exterminated"; later, examining the exportation of a nationalist standpoint by Europeans when the collapse of empires was occurring, he mentions the "extraordinary" Zionist adventure of reconstructing a nation-state. Aron prefigured the contemporary theses on nationalism formulated by Anthony Smith, who stressed the imagined aspect of nationalism as opposed to its perennial dimension which implies continuity through the centuries of one single people with a unique ethnic identity, thus foreshadowing the ideas of E. Gellner on the role of the state in the creation of a culture favorable to the birth of a nation. Aron thought that they had witnessed

> the creation of the State of Israel growing from the national idea, characteristic of modern Europe, mythically confused with the biblical notion of the Jewish people. . . . They are creating a nation building on a nationalism that is half-religious, half-mythological. They are expressing themselves as if the Israelis were the descendants of the people of Solomon and David—which, for most of them, is false. . . . They are giving all immigrants, all children, one language—Hebrew; one past—that of the Bible; one State—that of Israel, which they learn to know and serve.[129]

Ample pages are devoted to Israel in his general reflections on war and military strategy in the twentieth century.[130] Similarly, in an article on Clausewitz published by the *Zeitschrift für Politik*, Aron emphasizes that "what wasn't implied either by the magnitude of what was at stake, or by the weapons, or by the hatred brought to a white heat by the war itself, is the extermination of millions of Jews," and he adds, "I am not very sensitive to anti-Semitism (at my age, I have become hardened); the vague anti-Semitism and the Francophobia of Clausewitz leave me indifferent."[131] In 1971, in his opening lecture at the Collège de France, Aron emphasized the "pre-established harmony or, in more modest terms, the concord of sensibility" that reigned between the sociology of Max Weber, "a sociology of war between classes, parties, gods, and the lived experience of a doctor in philosophy, French, Jewish, living in Berlin during the first months of the Third Reich." To describe the consequences of socialization, Aron writes, "How many children from Catholic families were raised from their infancy by Jews; how many children of Jewish families were raised by Catholics; and these same children will become Jewish or Christian. Even if they rebel against the faith of their environment, they will still remain marked by what they have received and rejected."[132] Similarly, in *Progress and Disillusion; The Dialectics of Modern Society*, while Aron wants to evoke the persistence of the Tönnies sort of *gemeinschaft* in modern societies where a rapid disintegration of the family is occurring, he takes the example of the "gathering in the same neighborhoods of families of similar status, each one withdrawn into itself . . . in Jerusalem in the state of Israel as well as in Paris or New York."[133] In this work of unarguable academic status, he describes how, in Hitler's Germany where the Jews had been very much integrated, "a community became an object of hatred," analyzes anti-Semitism at length as a violent social prejudice, and outlines an interesting parallel between the anti-Semite and the anti-anti-Semite, both of whom essentialize their target: "The anti-anti-Semites . . . outline a portrait of the colonist, of the anti-Semite or of the Southern white that is as coherent, as global, as the stereotypes of the Jew, of natives, or of Blacks."[134] In *History and the Dialectic of Violence*, as he rereads Sartre, Aron questions the phenomenological project that reifies subjects to the point of caricature: "Nothing struck me more, reading *Anti-Semite and Jew*, than the progressive resemblance between the anti-Semite, observed by Sartre, and the Jew, observed by the anti-Semite. The anti-Semite, as well as the colonist and the bourgeois, defined by their aim or their objective spirit even in their innermost being, finally offer as contorted a face as their antagonists do to them."[135] In *Three Essays on the Industrial Age*, in the introduction to this "general" work, Aron

presents himself as "Jewish, surviving the biggest massacre of the in-
nocents that modern times have ever known"; later on, he republishes
a text that appeared in a scholarly study concerning the consequences
of industrialization, in which, wanting to analyze the crimes of scientific and technical rationalization, he thinks that "the organization of
the transports of Jews was just as rational as the arrangement of traffic
in Paris or New York . . . to the extent that scientific, technical, economic, administrative rationality is strictly instrumental, it lends itself
to any kind of use, productive or destructive, human unification or
extermination."[136] And, at the most solemn of all instances, when Aron
received the first Tocqueville Prize, in December 1979, while he was retracing the career of the author of *Democracy in America*, to which he so
often proclaimed his closeness, Aron wonders, "Why this commerce,
this amity, between the Comte de Tocqueville and the academic intellectual, the grandson of a tradesman in a Lorraine village, of Jewish
religion? I can see at least one reason: I feel a kind of elective affinity
with complex, divided personalities, firm on principles but wracked by
doubt, who do not confuse the desirable with the probable, their tastes
with reality, aware both of the constraints history imposes on us and
the margin of liberty it leaves us."[137] To accentuate the differences and
emphasize more the unforeseen character of the encounter between
these two philosophers of liberalism, Aron presents himself here, in
front of all his university colleagues, as the "grandson of a tradesman
in a Lorraine village, of Jewish religion" and not, as he usually does,
as the son of a de-Judaized teacher who was well-off socially and who
just barely failed the law exam. Ancestors and roots seem to give more
meaning to his existence, and Raymond Aron publicly includes himself
in the "we Jews" that he often uses, joining a process of transmission,
to say the least. Aron, at the height of fame and honors, shows this
identification that drives him, for once in an almost holistic way, to
write almost systematically *juifs* with a capital J, a way of recognizing
the collective and historic dimension of Jewish existence, the reality of
a Jewish people. One last time rejecting, in an academic work, the conclusions of *Anti-Semite and Jew* by his little comrade, about which he
so often said they could scarcely be applied to him, he thinks that they
take on meaning only for "de-Judaized Jews," while "the pious Jews,

or the Jews who are attached to traditions, bear within themselves an entity as a semination, comparable to a class-entity. I use this term 'semination' for lack of a concept that can adequately designate the condition of the Jews, whose religion is not separate from nation, and who have lived for centuries in diaspora, that is to say political, non-Jewish entities."[138] "De-Judaized" but firmly attached to his past, to his roots, to respect for his ancestors, "animated by the sense of continuity and tradition,"[139] displaying his "solidarity" with his "coreligionists" and his ancestors, "those who believe or have believed in the God of Isaac and Jacob," attached, as he repeats, to Jewish traditions and culture, including himself many times firmly in "the diaspora" that he refuses to see as a "second-class entity":[140] isn't it definitively to claim his adherence to this "semination" that he describes with a capital J? Isn't it this latent self-affiliation that the Alliance Israélite Universelle means to celebrate by including in its 1986 calendar the day of the death of Raymond Aron, who sat on its Central Committee, with several quotations from him on various other dates throughout the year?[141] This alone allows us to understand that this self-proclaimed "de-Judaized" Jew is nonetheless paradoxically perceived, by the president of the Alliance Israélite Universelle, Ady Steg, during a eulogy delivered at the Central Committee of the alliance at the time of Aron's death, as "a fully fledged Jew, a wise man, a just man among Jews." In the eyes of the president of the alliance, "it was the Jew who was involved as soon as it was a question of guiding our decisions."[142]

## Five

Hannah Arendt:
Hannah and Rahel,
"Fugitives from Palestine"

Rahel's last words: "What a history! . . . With real rapture I think of these origins of mine. . . . The thing which all my life seemed to me the greatest shame, which was the misery and misfortune of my life—having been born a Jewess—this I should on no account now wish to have missed."[1] A little more than a century later, in February 1950, Hannah met Heidegger again, her former lover, her teacher who had been compromised by a surprising adherence to Hitler's regime, and in one breath, far from Rahel, her double, her image, she says, stripped now of any collective identity, "I never felt I was a German woman, and I've stopped feeling for a long time now that I was a Jewish woman. I feel simply what I am: namely, someone who comes from elsewhere."[2] Two years passed: from the United States, Hannah Arendt was getting ready to publish her "autobiography" of Rahel, her "own confession" constructed by "shaping Rahel's life," by "taking the life of Rahel as if it were her own," by making "[Rahel's] letters her own" as a German Jew, by "identifying" with her.[3] Begun in Germany at the end of the 1920s, this book, which Arendt carried within her for so long, which, lost and then found, almost never saw the light of day—now all of a sudden Arendt seemed to break loose from it. In September 1952, she writes to Karl Jaspers, longtime friend and mentor, with whom she has conducted for almost her whole lifetime a dialogue based in reason: "The book is alien to me in many ways. . . . This whole project has not been very important to me for a long time, actually not since 1933. . . . I feel this whole so-called problem isn't so very important or at least is no longer important to me."[4]

The Jewish individual, caught between two shores, two adherences, "Egypt or Palestine" on one hand, and Germany on the other, "the person come from elsewhere" as Arendt called Rahel, designating

203

herself that way also, is no longer present to the historical world but takes refuge rather in Humanity: foreign to her people, Arendt also distanced herself from her other people, the German people. Then only the German language remains, detached from any particular national inscription, "the language in which I think and in which the poems I love best were written. I won't lay false claims to either a Jewish or an American past."[5] Did Arendt really "renounce" her Jewish past, to which Rahel on the contrary turned, suddenly abandoning the mirages and contortions of assimilation? Did she definitively distance herself from Rahel, whose life she carried within her at the very instant when she finally, in 1957, brought to light her convoluted history, by transforming herself, beyond the generations, into Rahel's spokesperson, and by telling, in English and translated from "her" language, German, Rahel's life as "as she herself might have told it"?[6] Everything seems to indicate just this, since in 1959 in Hamburg, in her speech on Lessing, Arendt clearly says

> If I so explicitly emphasize my adherence to the group of Jews chased out of Germany, it's because I want to prevent certain misunderstandings that arise only too easily as soon as one talks about humanity. In this context, I cannot remain silent about the fact that, for a number of years, I thought that the only fitting reply to the question "Who are you?" was: a Jew. Only that reply took into account the reality of the persecution. . . . By saying "a Jew," I wasn't even referring to a reality that was foregrounded or charged with history. I was only recognizing a political present, in which my adherence to that group had decided the question of personal identity based on anonymity. Today, when such an attitude can be perceived as an affectation, one could easily note that those who react thus, far from taking a step toward "humanity," have fallen into the trap held out by Hitler and have thus succumbed in their own way to the spirit of Hitlerism.

Arendt theorizes the rejection of this "affectation," which to her eyes has become useless and even inadmissible in the present, finally liberated, world, where action based on Reason is offered to everyone as the only means of asserting one's freedom, one's creativity—in a word, a deliberate *vita activa*, not hindered by particularist bonds; in her eyes, if one can feel attracted "in dark times" by "the warmth that for pariahs is the substitute for light," if one can admit their "flight" into "invisibility," into an "acosmia" that makes them absent from the world, everything changes when the public space is finally opened up. The "pariah peoples" undergo

> such a radical loss of world, such a terrifying atrophy of all the organs by means of which we correspond with it—from common sense, thanks to which we orient ourselves in a common world in relation to ourselves and to others, all the way to the sense of beauty, or taste, thanks to which we love the world—that, in extreme cases, when the character of pariah has persisted for entire centuries, one can speak of a veritable acosmia. And acosmia, alas, is always a form of barbarism.

The Jews, a pariah people par excellence, did indeed preserve the privilege of the "warmth" of the group from which a real "vitality" emanates; they are familiar with that "fraternity of people closely linked to each other," "a substitute for light" that protects their "invisibility": the price of this is still considerable, since it implies a radical "absence to the world." Her conclusion is intended to be unanswerable: "The humanity of the humiliated and the offended has never survived the hour of liberation, even for a minute."[7] Now plunged into history, the Jews must not adopt the "pose" of a necessarily innocent collective pariah: they must separate themselves from a "warmth," from an intimacy that has become artificial in a world where they now find themselves on equal ground, in dialogue, with others, and they must reject all the "spirit of Hitlerism" that would encourage them to preserve this "pose" from barbaric times. The break seems complete in the name of the advent of liberating Reason, of involvement in a public citizenship that cannot retain the identitarian "warmth" of the closed group.

On July 24, 1964, however, just after the trial of Eichmann, after Gershom Scholem harshly accused Arendt of lacking a "love of the Jewish people," she spontaneously rediscovers this "pose" and replies, all in one breath, "The truth is I have never pretended to be anything else or to be in any way other than I am, and I have never even felt tempted in that direction. It would have been like saying that I was a man and not a woman—that is to say, kind of insane. . . . To be a Jew belongs for me to the indisputable facts of my life, and I have never had the wish to change or disclaim facts of this kind."[8] Now describing herself as a Jew, even though she is subjected to vehement reproaches from a large number of Jewish circles shocked by her provocative presentation of the Eichmann trial, cut off once again from her identity, misrepresented, rejected, she still appears, to the eyes of Jaspers, as a modern Rahel, a *"Mädchen aus der Fremde"* [young woman from elsewhere],[9] an involuntary reincarnation henceforth of her "friend" from long ago: sympathetic, Jaspers approved of her fundamental letter addressed to Gershom Scholem, in which Arendt proclaims her nature, her Jewish essence, loud and clear, even if no one wants to hear her.

Three months later, on a German television show during a public appearance that was exceptional in its autobiographical dimension, Arendt expressed herself in her *muttersprache*, the German language, facing a German audience. When the journalist returned to this sentence sent by Arendt to Scholem where she gave an unarguable dimension to her "Jewishness," she began by discussing her reactions as a Jewish woman faced with the Hitlerism of the "dark times," then, explicitly mentioning her "Speech on Lessing" and quoting from memory, modifying it slightly, her own affirmation, namely that "This humanity cannot survive the day of liberation, cannot survive liberty by five minutes," a sentence she had uttered five years ago already and that she repeats almost word for word, she adds, rediscovering the "warmth" of the humiliated: "The Jewish religion is a national religion. But the concept of politics was valid, however, only with major restrictions. This loss of world that the Jewish people underwent in dispersion and that, as with all pariah peoples, engendered a very particular warmth among all its members—all that was changed during the foundation of the state of Israel." When the journalist asks her, "Was something lost by that, something whose loss you deplore?" Arendt replies, "Yes, freedom costs dearly. Specific Jewish humanity, under the sign of the loss of world, was something that was very beautiful. . . . It was very beautiful to be able to remain outside of any social bond. . . . All that has naturally undergone extremely serious damage. We pay for liberation,"[10] that liberation by the nation-state which, according to Arendt, nothing can resist, in any case not Jewish identity, not for one or even five minutes.

Does Arendt the Jew, who gave all her support to the Zionist movement, finally turn her back on Rahel Varnhagen the parvenu, who imagined herself definitively as a pariah, the famous hostess of *salons* finally received in the world who, completely lacking any sense of shame, when all cards have been played, doesn't hesitate for an instant to place herself in the long lineage of those who long ago fled from Egypt, not "seventeen hundred years before her birth" as Arendt curiously says in the beginning of her biography,[11] but several centuries before Christ? The older she gets, the more indifferent Arendt seems to Judaism. Even if she can still get upset when Israel suddenly seems threatened with annihilation, for instance during the Six Days' War, the "Jewish question" visibly no longer interests her; it's humanity with which she is preoccupied, it's Greek democracy she admires, it's the human condition she wonders about, it's *amor mundi*, love of the world, that now animates her thoughts, a love of the world not without a religious dimension since Arendt declares, before the American Society for Christian Ethics, in 1973, "I don't feel any loyalty toward Christ, but I can feel loyalty toward Jesus, since he truly is an example; what Jesus did, his entire life, his *logoi*, are truly an example,"[12] a disconcerting observation that reminds us of Rahel's final thought, which Hannah Arendt is careful not to quote: "I thought of Jesus and mourned his Passion; I felt for the first time that he is my brother. And Mary, how she suffered! She saw her beloved son suffering but did not succumb. She stayed by the cross. I couldn't have done that. I wouldn't have been strong enough. God forgive my weakness, I confess my weakness."[13] One can always argue that the adult themes elaborated by Arendt are only the transposition of the preoccupations of her youth, a way of rethinking, in a more universalist way, the pangs, the dilemmas of the Jewish question.[14] This hypothesis is attractive, but it seems forced.

A certain break with the past did take place: faced with the aporias of "the human condition," identitarian adherence no longer makes sense. The vita activa of the citizen concerned with public "happiness" is henceforth the sole source of action.[15] In New York, at the New School for Social Research, far from old Europe and its identitarian and cultural clashes, as a pure philosopher coming from the tradition of Kant, Arendt finally resumes in her scholarly works the dialogue she had begun in Germany in the 1920s with Jaspers and Heidegger, her teacher and then her friend and lover, who remained, despite everything, dear to her heart, whom she often visited in that distant but still close, familiar Germany, where one can hear that native language that almost all by itself now structures her identity. Challenging any philosemitic interpretation of Arendt's work, Ernest Gellner finds it easy to mock harshly an Arendt suddenly attracted, in Manhattan, to the romanticism of a Heidegger, the "last of the romantics" as she admiringly described him, to whom she remained passionately loyal, an identitarian romanticism worthy of a community from which she now finds herself excluded, which breaks with the universalism she calls her own, with that same universalism that once justified Rahel's passion for emancipation: "The circle that began with the Enlightenment during Rahel's time is now almost closed," she notes. Pitilessly, Gellner goes so far as to write, "She loved [Heidegger] not despite the leanings that led him to Nazism but rather because of them. And to condemn romanticism would have been to condemn him." The British sociologist is determined to be deaf to the reality of an exceptional passion that shows through in poems exchanged, in letters of an immense reciprocal tenderness. Arendt writes to Heidegger in 1929, "Don't forget me, and don't forget how keenly and profoundly I know that our love has become the blessing of my life." Gellner wants to understand none of this and doesn't hide his fierce irony worthy of Woody Allen before an Arendt always fascinated, through Heidegger, with a *gemeinschaft* stripped of all meaning in the "post-Enlightenment, born modern" America.[16] In the same spirit, George Steiner wants to see in the Arendt-Heidegger couple only "one of the most macabre stories in the history of philosophy" where the relationships of domination and submission between the Master and his Jewish student are exacerbated.[17]

Despite more normative trends in her work, Arendt did not give up. Until the end, she increased the signs of her adherence to the Jewish world: at the very time of her sudden death, on December 4, 1975, she had Salo Baron over for dinner, the first professor to occupy a chair of Jewish studies at Columbia University, one of the principal contemporary historians of Judaism, whom she met in the 1940s and continued to see again, with whom she had just had a last working session—Baron was the director of the monumental thesis on the Marranos by Yosef Yerushalmi. Despite her denials, her loyalty to Judaism was such that

Arendt remained an active member of the journal created by Salo Baron, the *Jewish Social Studies*, in which to her great pride she published soon after her arrival in the United States, "From the Dreyfus Affair to France Today." Through the years, a thousand different signs bear witness to this loyalty that was never really abandoned; thus, in the winter of 1934, she decided to take private Hebrew classes, declaring, "I want to know my people";[18] thus, the letter she writes to Jaspers on January 20, 1946, where she shows only too clearly, "I would gladly write something if I can write as a Jew on some aspect of the Jewish question";[19] thus, she wanted *kaddish* to be said on November 4, 1970, over the grave of her husband, Heinrich Blücher, a non-Jewish former communist proletarian, the love of her life, her faithful soulmate.[20] In Manhattan, Arendt the philosopher of democracy, the world-renowned theoretician of the public space where the vita activa would not be hindered by any kind of social determinism, she who could "arrive" without paying the price of the mutilating assimilation that she condemns, she who is neither a pariah nor a parvenu, still thinks of herself as Jewish. During the last *Pesach* she took part in at the end of 1974, she was happy, surrounded by her friends, listening to the recitation of the *Haggadah*, "singing the traditional songs of that celebration," a few months before returning, one more time, in February 1975, to Germany to see Heidegger. At her funeral, which took place on December 8 of that same year, one of her nieces from Israel recited some psalms in Hebrew.[21]

Surprising phrases that convey the imprecision of her identitarian claim that, to varying degrees, supports her entire existence, are no less abundant. Take, for example, this remark made by Arendt in a letter to Jaspers, when the debate born from her Eichmann book finally seems to be calming down: "I think the war between me and the Jews is over."[22] In the beginning, almost nothing but appearance seems decisive. In the 1930s, in reply to Jaspers, who says, "Of course you are German!" Arendt replies, "Not at all, as you can see!"; in October 1964, in discussing her childhood, she notes, "I seemed Jewish, that is, I seemed different from the others. I was entirely aware of this. However, that was not in the least concealing a kind of inferiority: it was just like that, that's all." This appearance, which distinguishes her from others, cannot be forgotten when she arouses anti-Semitic statements: "The word 'Jew,'" Arendt remembers, "was never uttered among us when I was a little girl. It was through the anti-Semitic remarks uttered by children—which are not worth repeating—that this word was revealed to me for the first time. It was from that instant that I was so to speak 'enlightened.'" Arendt in this way discusses the incidents that made her confront anti-Semitic children. Following the will of her mother, who exclaimed, "You must not lower your head! You must defend yourself," Arendt learns to cope: "One can," she writes, "defend oneself all alone against children."[23] This uniquely external definition of Judaism seems so significant in Arendt that some have hastily compared it to the Sartrean definition of the Jew, as a pure creation of the anti-Semite. But it is not at all the same, and Arendt did not hide the keen reservations she felt in 1946 about Sartre's *Anti-Semite and Jew*. A little later on, she explicitly challenges, in *Origins of Totalitarianism*, his vision of the Jew who became so under the gaze of the Other, the anti-Semite. For her, "Even a cursory knowledge of Jewish history, whose central concern since the Babylonian exile has always been the survival of the people against the overwhelming odds of dispersion, should be enough to dispel this latest myth in these matters, a myth that has become somewhat fashionable in intellectual circles after Sartre's 'existentialist' interpretation of *the* Jew as someone who is regarded and defined as a Jew by others."[24] Arendt many times opposes this external definition that, according to her, justifies the strategies of parvenu Jews, fixed in an imposed identity that they often try all their lives to escape. However, things are not so simple, since, as she herself acknowledges, it was indeed the anti-Semitic statements of her schoolfellows that made her aware of her identity; it was indeed the features of her face that made her be "seen" as Jewish; it was indeed Hitler's rise to power that pushed her to become involved in the Zionist movement to fight as a Jew and not as a simple human being. Finally, her hero, Bernard Lazare, also returned to Judaism when he was confronted with anti-Semitism.[25] Similarly, Arendt says that Rahel "was so little mistress of her inner self that even her consciousness of reality was dependent upon confirmation by others."[26] Arendt's position is thus far from being clear, since as we will see later on, it is her own definition of Judaism that remains more than vague, like a veritable impasse.[27]

Arendt's determined, courageous action in favor of the Jews was, however, constant, and in her mind, it was indeed as a Jew that she helped the Zionist groups in Berlin and got arrested by the Gestapo; it was always in the name of this identity that she brought aid in Vichy France to Jewish children threatened by the Nazis, facilitating their journey to Palestine. By then a Jew who had taken refuge in the United States, she called, in 1941, for the creation of a "Jewish army" to fight next to the Allies and finally get beyond the pariah/parvenu antinomy. Identification is inarguable: "We must still be patient . . . for the first time our fate is not an exceptional fate, for the first time our fight is identical with the fight for freedom that Europe is waging. As Jews, we want to fight for the freedom of the Jewish people."[28] A few months later, she calls Moses "our hero" and notes with bitterness that "as long as the Passover story does not teach the difference between freedom and slavery, as long as the Moses legend does not call to mind the eternal rebellion of the heart and mind against slavery, the 'oldest document of human history' will remain dead and mute to no one more than the very people who once wrote it."[29] In January 1943, in a tragic text where she notes, in the manner of Durkheim, that Jews usually have the lowest suicide rates, she now evokes the suicide of the Jews in Berlin or Paris, Budapest or New York, or Buenos Aires, the suicides in the ghettos, and she writes, "We are the first nonreligious Jews persecuted—and we are the first ones who, not only *in extremis*, answer with suicide," even if pious Jews condemn such an act by the phrase that Arendt cites, *Adonai nathan veadonai lakach* ("The Lord hath given and the Lord hath taken away").[30] Arendt then attacks the attitude of French or other Jews who rejected the new arrivals from Eastern Europe, makes fun of the "Mr. Cohn" from Berlin who "had always been a 150 percent German" before becoming, once they were expelled, superpatriotic Czechs or Frenchmen, guided by the wish for total assimilation: "In 1933 that Mr. Cohn found refuge in Prague and very quickly became a convinced Czech patriot. . . . Time went on and about 1937 . . . Mr. Cohn went to Vienna; to adjust oneself there a definite Austrian patriotism was required. The German invasion forced Mr. Cohn out of that country. He arrived in Paris . . . he prepared his adjustment to the French nation by identifying himself with 'our' ancestor Vercingétorix." And Arendt concludes, "As long as Mr. Cohn can't make up his mind to be what he actually is, a Jew, nobody can foretell all the mad changes he will still have to go through. . . . We are willing to become loyal Hottentots, only to hide the fact that we are Jews."[31] The Jews must remain themselves in order to join all the other émigrés, to associate with non-Jewish pariahs in a common struggle: "For the first time Jewish history is not separate but tied up with that of all other nations."[32]

In all these texts written during the Second World War in New York, Arendt wishes for the rebirth of a Jewish nation fully entering history and political involvement, definitively turning away from the eternal assimilationist temptation of so many Jews who try individually to "escape" their condition. Following the conscious pariah Bernard Lazare, who in her opinion is almost alone by the strength of his involvement as a Jew during the Dreyfus Affair, she constructs an anti-assimilationist theory that goes against that of most European Jews. For her, Lazare alone "tried to elaborate a new political category starting from a fundamental situation of the political existence of the Jewish people"; in his example, the Jewish people must turn away from illusions of assimilation but also from those of the "schlemihl," and also avoid those of the "lord of the dreamworld." The conclusion is strong and straight to the point, advocating a collective form of action capable of connecting again with humanity, presaging contemporary communitarian theses, yet opposing, in advance, any identitarian self-isolation: she thus distanced herself radically, as we will see, from contemporary communitarian perspectives that are often identified with her by her rejection of any form of Jewish nationalism.[33] For her, in effect, "it is only within a people that a man can live as a man among men, if he does not want to die of exhaustion. And only a people living in a community with other peoples can contribute to establishing on the earth we inhabit a world of men created and controlled in common by us all."[34] A grave, almost contradictory task: to invest oneself in the heart of the Jewish people but "by living in a community with other peoples." Jewish existence involves a particularly difficult challenge. All the more so since Arendt means to maintain the complete freedom of individuals in the heart of their "community" that is also directed outward, toward all of humanity: in Palenville, a little country town where she was far from New York, "people know, naturally, that I am Jewish, which, the first summer, produced the result that they didn't want to include me wherever there were barbecues with pork. But, after some explanations, I got the right to eat whatever I like."[35]

In a word, unlike Sartrean perspectives, Arendt came out resolutely in favor of a politically active Jewish people faithful to its identity. Only this voluntary mode of action would be capable of breaking the erring ways and humiliations of an assimilation that was so harmful that, for Arendt's part, she had always rejected it: thus she thought that "it would have had no sense for me to get involved with those who were on the point of becoming assimilated, and moreover I have never had anything to do with them."[36] What, then, does entering politics mean for the Jewish "people" or "nation"? First of all, unquestionably, the Zionist movement that Arendt participated in in 1933 in Berlin, without being really Zionist herself. "The only group I belonged to," Arendt remembers, "was the Zionist organization. That was only because of Hitler, obviously, between 1933 and 1943. Afterward, I broke with them. That represented the only possibility to answer, to fight, as a Jew and not as a human individual, for if they attack you as a Jew, you have to respond as a Jew, you cannot reply, 'Excuse me, I'm not a Jew; I am a human being.' That makes no sense."[37] During the summer, Kurt Blumenfeld and the German Zionist Organization asked her to organize documentation on Nazi anti-Semitism, which led to her arrest by the police. Freed soon afterward, she left with her mother for Geneva, where she worked briefly for the Jewish Agency, then went to Paris, where she volunteered her help for a Zionist youth organization, the Kadimah; in 1935, she accompanied a group of children from Paris to Marseille and then, by boat, to Haifa; upon her return, she gave a lecture on kibbutzes, whose experimental capability she appreciated, even if, in private, she conceded that "one could not live there. 'Rule by your neighbors,' that is of course what it finally amounts to."[38]

Let us return to that decisive meeting with Kurt Blumenfeld. Their dialogue, which continued from 1933 to 1963, can almost be compared to that of Gershom Scholem with Walter Benjamin, so similar were the great questions that often came to light in it. Scholem had left Germany for Palestine without any difficulty, like Blumenfeld; Walter Benjamin, on the contrary, hesitated for a long time, intersected with Arendt's fate as a refugee in France, and killed himself in the Pyrenees after failing to cross the border to Spain; Arendt never imagined living in Palestine, even if she was active for Zionist organizations, and once she had miraculously escaped the internment camp in Gurs in that same southwestern France that was fatal to Benjamin, she managed to leave for the United States. Her dialogue with Blumenfeld would never be interrupted. It is rich in teachings. Promptly, to her friend's utter confusion, Arendt has doubts about whether the Zionist solution as she has adopted it could allow other peoples to live "in a community." She still passionately follows the events affecting Palestine, to such an extent that she writes to Blumenfeld, on July 19, 1947, "It has become a habit to open the *Times* every morning with anxiety, beginning with the page on Palestine."[39] That shows how far Arendt, without being a convinced Zionist, reveals herself concerned about the difficult future of the Settlement; she writes a number of texts on this point whose accuracy might be questionable.[40] Her article "Zionism Reconsidered" appeared in 1944, as the expression of a distancing that would only increase. In her eyes, the Jews no longer individually commit suicide as an extreme reaction to the difficulties of assimilation, but now threaten to do so as a nation by giving free rein to a bellicose nationalism that justifies the exclusion of the Arabs and can only give rise to endless wars fuelled by an unlimited anti-Semitism. In this same text she denounces the plan to construct a uniquely Jewish state that rejects a more cultural vision of Zionism, which she calls her own; she bluntly attacks Ben Gurion, whom she accuses of having recourse to a policy of "insane isolationism" in the name of a nationalist vision like that of German nationalism in having a biological and organic foundation. For her, Palestinocentrism is unacceptable, for "it will not be easy either to save the Jews or to save Palestine in this twentieth century."[41] Profoundly pessimistic, Arendt returns a little later, in May 1946, to what is in her opinion the suicidal tendency of Zionism, which aims to construct a state in a hostile environment, building from a vision of anti-Semitism wrongly interpreted as a doctrine that eternally threatens the Jewish people, rejecting, like her friend Baron, a sentimental concept of history. For Arendt, a new secularized messianism parallel to the one once developed by Sabbatai

Zevi threatens the Jews of Palestine with a similar fatal decline through its failure to understand the reality principle that is once again pushing them outside the sphere of political action: it can lead only to another "catastrophe."[42] She perseveres in this very negative judgment about the plan to create a specifically Jewish state that implies the separation of Jews from other peoples: without mincing her words, she goes so far as to assert in May 1948, in the midst of a euphoric period of the creation of the state of Israel, that a "completely chauvinistic and racist" strategy is involved, doomed to failure faced with the superiority of the Arab world, a plan similar to others that justify the domination of master races that can lead only to the collective suicide of Israel, which people should rather be trying to "save" as a "Homeland." She also attacks the "fanaticism and hysteria" that produce a unanimous nationalism throughout the entire Jewish world, so extensive that the supporters of the creation of a federal state who want to reconcile Jews and Arabs cannot make themselves heard. Things are clear, then: for Arendt, it is indispensable "to sacrifice the pseudo-sovereignty of a Jewish state."[43] In January 1950, Arendt was less vehement, but she did not renounce asking for the formation of a Confederation of Palestine that would gather together Jews and Arabs for the greater profit of a common development and which would have Jerusalem as its capital. She was pleased, however, with the rise of a nonnationalist pole in Israel, one supported by the Hebrew University in Jerusalem and the kibbutz movement in the spirit of Ahad Ha'am, which she prefered to that of Herzl. This later text on Israel still ends with a warning: if it is not given such a cultural and social environment, "Tel Aviv could become a Levantine city overnight. Chauvinism of the Balkan type could use the religious concept of the chosen people and allow its meaning to degenerate into hopeless vulgarity."[44] Arendt seems decidedly hostile to this nationalist form of political action that Israel represents.

She does not pay attention to the words of her friend Kurt Blumenfeld when he speaks of the fulfillment of living in Israel, of the fact that he feels there "in a profound relationship with this nature: with nature, trees, and some people,"[45] words that are somewhat like those used by Rahel Varnhagen and repeated exactly by Arendt herself in a letter to Jaspers in September 1952.[46] What does nature matter, "the land" where Blumenfeld is so happy to live, knowing Arendt's indifference. He writes to her, "Being without a land is what counts for you; for me, it's having a ground to set my feet on. I don't hold the place where we are finding our fulfillment as of no account. This is how we can govern ourselves, how we can see that humanity isn't a mere word, that it is put into practice."[47] Blumenfeld guesses that, together with political criticism, this indifference to the land of Israel will distance Arendt more and more. He says to her, "For you, Israel will certainly have less and less importance."[48] All the more so since the woman who always wanted to be "bohemian" vehemently rejected "the nationalist verbiage" that she thought she heard coming from Israel.[49] In her opinion, "What has been done in Palestine itself is extraordinary: not merely colonization but a serious attempt at a new social order. . . . But hand in hand with that—and this is truly dangerous--goes a basic mistrust of all other nations."[50]

There remains the cruel episode of the Eichmann trial, over which we do not want to linger here. From all sides came reactions of outrage and total incomprehension. Arendt's theses on the banality of evil are misconstrued, for they do not necessarily make the Shoah banal, even if Arendt surprisingly neglects the specificity of the gas chambers and somewhat relativizes the scale of the genocide.[51] Criticizing the Jewish councils that collaborated with the Nazis, she places emphasis on the behavior of certain Jewish notables, but overlooks the courage and self-denial of other leaders who sought an impossible way in an inextricable situation. Her speculative and unverifiable calculations about the smaller number of Jewish victims that would have resulted from rejecting any relationship with German authorities, as well as her considerations, logical in the framework of her general system of thinking, about the responsibility of the Jews in their unconscious path toward the Shoah, their lack of comprehension of History, can lead to inadmissible and shocking conclusions. Her deliberate rejection, finally, of any "emotion," her unnecessarily cold and sometimes sarcastic tone, her biting irony, are despite everything pointlessly irritating, whence Gershom Scholem's terrible reaction:

> It is that heartless, frequently almost sneering and malicious tone
> with which these matters, touching the very quick of our life, are

treated in your book to which I take exception. In the Jewish tradition there is a concept, hard to define and yet concrete enough, which we know as *Ahavat Yisrael*: "Love of the Jewish people. . . ." In you, dear Hannah, as in so many intellectuals who come from the German left, I find little trace of this. . . . I regard you wholly as a daughter of our people, and as nothing else. Thus I have little sympathy with that tone—well expressed by the English word *flippancy*—which you employ so often in the course of your book.[52]

Everything, or almost everything, has been said on the chasm that was created on this occasion between Israel and Hannah Arendt, on the harshness of the criticisms that overwhelm Arendt—some even compare the "Arendt Affair" to the Dreyfus Affair,[53] and the author of *Eichmann in Jerusalem* says in her deadpan way that despite everything she still doesn't risk . . . being assassinated by the Mossad![54] The wound was so keen that as late as December 1998, during a conference on the Shoah organized in Jerusalem by the Yad Vashem Institute, Arendt's name was immediately booed by a good portion of the numerous audience, while the mention of the first Hebrew translation of her controversial work caused a stir. What I would like to remember here is only the way Arendt once again approaches the Zionist question, the nature of this Israeli society to which she has never felt very close despite the absolute solidarity she shows throughout her life toward Israel itself. Before writing her book, when the trial was only beginning, when she had just arrived in Israel, a journey she so often delayed under every possible pretext, the tone of her first letter written to Jaspers reveals her absolute lack of empathy, the vigor of her prejudices about all the oriental features of Israeli Judaism, whether they were Polish or Arab:

All three of the judges are German Jews. The comedy of speaking Hebrew when everyone involved knows German and thinks in German. Landau speaks very good Hebrew (people tell me). The prosecutor, on the other hand, a typical Galician Jew, very unsympathetic, is constantly making mistakes. Probably one of those people who don't know any language. . . . The country's interest in the trial has been artificially whetted. An oriental mob that would hang around anyplace where something is going on is hanging around in front of the courthouse. . . . My first impression: On top, the judges, the best of

German Jewry. Below them, the prosecuting attorneys, Galicians, but still Europeans. Everything is organized by a police force that gives me the creeps, speaks only Hebrew, and looks Arabic. Some downright brutal types among them. They would obey any order. And outside the doors, the oriental mob, as if one were in Istanbul or some other half-Asiatic country. In addition, and very visible in Jerusalem, the peies and caftan Jews, who make life impossible for all the reasonable people here. The major impression, though, is of very great poverty.[55]

Two days later, Arendt sent from her residence in Beit Hakerem, in Jerusalem, another letter to her husband, Heinrich Blücher:

I have moved—out of the city, which is loud and horrible, filled with the oriental mob typical of the Near East, the European element very much pushed into the background, the balkanization highly developed in every sense . . . the trial itself . . . the public prosecutor . . . a Galician Jew, who talks a blue streak . . . the defense lawyer, an oily, adroit, and without a doubt thoroughly corrupt fellow. . . . And, towering high, the three judges, all of them German Jews, and in the middle the *presiding judge*, Moshe Landau, who is really and truly marvelous—ironic and sarcastic in his forbearing friendliness. Kurt [Blumenfeld] told me I would meet him at his place. . . . In front of the courthouse, a mob of oriental Jewish children and Peies Jews.[56]

Everything is said and repeated many times. The famous "Levantine night" mentioned earlier has become a reality according to Arendt's prediction. Beyond the discussion of the arguments about *Eichmann in Jerusalem*, unprecedented polemics unleashed by this book in Israel and throughout the world, it is Arendt's view of Israeli society, the severity of her criticisms, but above all the extent of her prejudices, full of scorn for that Orient in which, unlike Martin Buber, she does not in the least recognize herself, that are striking. Her solidarity with the Zionism of her youth, the undeniable emotion she felt when danger threatened Israel at various times, give way, when she is faced with the reality of Israeli society finally encountered a little closer up, to an ensemble of clichés that recall the scorn of German Jews toward the *Ostjuden* from "the Orient," that is, at that time, from Poland, negative impressions close to the xenophobia that curiously her friend Blumenfeld shared, who however had lived for a long time in Israel, but who always felt as if he were a thousand times removed from the "oriental Jews" and their "Levantism."[57] Arendt still thinks of Israel "with terror," and she still has only one wish, that of rediscovering, in Zurich or Basel, "civilized regions" once she in turn has, as her friend Rahel Varnhagen says, "escaped from Palestine" which she describes to her husband with the following definitive equation:[58] "Climate + language (Hebrew, of course unlearnable!) + poverty = fanaticism."[59] As Walter Laqueur politely notes, teasing Arendt, "You can't argue with the fact that Zurich is a more civilized city than Tel Aviv, that the Rhine is a more impressive river than the Yarmuck, and that the Black Forest is more impressive than most of the hills of Israel."[60]

While Arendt was so often amused by the prejudices of French or German Jews toward immigrant Jews, now her "brothers" are also revealed to be "foreigners" with disturbing physical aspects. Far from Rahel's *salons* or from Manhattan coffeehouses, the Jewish, "semi-Asiatic" "populace," the "crowd" that is manipulated and ignorant of the real issues at stake, all the more so since it is "oriental," do not seem to her to share the preoccupations of Goethe, let alone those of Heidegger; moreover, aren't they "oriental" just like the "oriental Jewish high-school students" of her adolescence who were subjected, even more than Arendt herself, to the anti-Semitic insults of their non-Jewish schoolfellows in the 1920s without Arendt intervening?[61] As for the "Peies Jews in caftans" that she denigrates from one letter to another, the "people of good sense," like Arendt, have nothing in common with them, so much do the East European Jews bear the public marks of an identity that dictates a practice, even a language, Yiddish, that she does not know, even if she knows that through it this identity is shaped which makes sense but which escapes her. The mockery of Hebrew, of the rebirth of this language that had however once been glimpsed, is now complete, as well as the condemnation of orthodoxy, of the Jewish presence visible in the public space through its traditional religious attributes, those that break most distinctly with the assimilation that Arendt however continuously denounces. Be Jewish, yes, but without the use of Hebrew, without knowledge of the rabbinic tradition, without a land. Is Woody Allen's Jew unexpectedly resurfacing? Without representing the purely negative Jew defined by the gaze of the other in Sartre's definition, what is this Jew, a conscious pariah, but conscious of what?

It has often been thought that the writing of *Eichmann in Jerusalem* by its coldness and its distance shows the effects of this question; by contrast, the prejudices formulated in this work about Israeli society, although not as pronounced as those in the letters to her confidant Jaspers, have rarely been picked out and compared to similar expressions that appear in her private correspondence. Thus, in the opening pages of the book, we find these disconcerting "oriental Jews" who are always supposed to be without any of their own intentionality and without the most basic historical knowledge since they "have never heard of" the history of the Jews during the Second World War. Similarly, in a letter sent from Tel Aviv to Blücher in April 1961, Arendt doesn't hesitate bluntly to compare the infamous Nuremberg Laws of 1935, which prohibited and punished marriage and relationships between Germans and Jews, with the rabbinical laws that were applied in Israel. These merely prevented the registering of a marriage between a Jew and a non-Jew, but Arendt takes the comparison up again in the first chapter of *Eichmann in Jerusalem*![62]

What, then, does the outrage at the publication of *Eichmann* matter, the attempts to boycott the work by American Jews, the insults, the cheap shots, the bad faith. Arendt's somewhat haughty apparent indifference, her lack of sensitivity faced with the tragic issues in those times of extermination, intensify an indifference toward her "people," her "community," from which she is now separating herself, she who used to think that the individual flourishes only within a community, open to the world and to others. Once again, and more than ever, as her teacher and friend Karl Jaspers writes to her at the height of the debate,[63] Arendt is *das Mädchen aus der Fremde*, the cursed one in the eyes of the entire Jewish people, whom Jaspers compares to Spinoza. This distance presages the almost complete silence that, aside from exceptional events, will henceforth be the rule. Arendt intellectually turns away from Israel, from that Jewish nation that she hasn't taken the trouble to learn to know, that she does not want to know, everything about which she is ignorant. Thus, in her thinking, the project of a national destiny comes to an end, one of the main uniquely political forms of Jewish history, the formation of a "community" favorable to socialization, to the transmission of a language and a culture, capable of politically defending its interests, and of recognizing its friends and its enemies. During the last twelve years of her life, aside from dealing with controversies born from *Eichmann in Jerusalem* that will come up again, for instance in 1965, with the publication of the very critical work by Jacob Robinson, aside from these polemics that scarcely have to do with Jewish history or with Zionism as such, even if certain aspects of the debate about the decisive role played by Ben Gurion in the organization and finalities of the trial are mentioned, the silence slowly takes over, while Arendt acquires her status as a political philosopher. She no longer seems concerned with the question of the Jews' entering politics in a collective form, an issue she used to advocate during the Second World War.

The Israeli-Arab war of 1967, however, provoked in Arendt a brief but real anguish before the menace that weighed all of a sudden on the very existence of Israel. Beyond the emotion that to a greater or lesser degree overwhelmed Jews all over the world, this sudden metamorphosis was inexplicable, and Arendt went straight from a critical state of mind to semienthusiasm. She went to Israel for the last time, and everything there turned out to be "very encouraging." Even better, great news, "the oriental, Arabic-speaking Jews . . . performed admirably in the war." That conveys the extent of the change, which affected even "oriental Jews." The conclusion of the letter that an almost happy Hannah Arendt writes to Jaspers is striking: "I felt very much at ease. And as far as the country itself is concerned, one can see clearly from what great fear it has suddenly been freed. That contributes significantly to improving the national character."[64] The nationalist impasse that Israel represented not long ago suddenly fades away: Arendt's emotion is visible, the era of her *Eichmann* is miraculously relegated to a distant past. She writes to her friend Mary McCarthy, "Any real catastrophe in Israel would affect me more deeply than almost anything else."[65] When the danger is past, Arendt can leave reassured, to devote herself again to world affairs. The Zionist issue and the Jewish question in general seem to depart from her preoccupations, even if a certain psychological alertness remains. Thus, during the Israeli-Arab war of 1973, she fears that Israel might be destroyed: in her eyes, "the Jewish people are united in Israel."[66] She took part in protest demonstrations at Columbia University, gave money to the United Jewish Appeal as she had already done in 1967, and showed she was deeply moved by the war. Her profound personal preoccupations were quite remote from the problems linked to Jewish identity, and by the end of the conflict, she took up her manuscript on Will again. Arendt preferred henceforth to devote her strength to the great philosophical issues. She traveled the world and the major capitals, but never returned to Israel. Arendt was wholly devoted to her seminars on Plato, Kant, or Nietzsche; she began to reread Max Weber attentively, devoted herself especially to her work *The Life of the Mind*.[67] When she showed herself attentive to current events, she was above all interested in the future of China, in the rapid transformations the Soviet society was experiencing, in the civil rights question in the United States, in the Vietnam War, in the agitation of the students on the American campuses, which make her exclaim, "Rosa has returned." Her identity as a Jew was no longer in the forefront.

The fact, however, that she remained till the end very close to the Jewish historian Salo Baron, that she was anxious to remain a member of the *Jewish Social Journal*, proves that though she was careful not to intervene in the collective future of the Jews, she still remained concerned with the history of the Jews, with the meaning of Jewishness. As Steven Ashheim observes, "Scholem was interested in Judaism; Arendt, who knew very little about the body of Judaism itself, was the great explicator of 'Jewishness' and its psychological machinations. She highlighted its ambivalences, multiple loyalties, fissures, breakdowns, and partial reconstitutions."[68] From then on we understand better why the character of Rahel Varnhagen, that *Mädchen aus der Fremde* who remained to the end, despite her almost complete social integration, a pariah, could haunt Arendt's life and correspondence so pervasively. Begun in 1928, Arendt's research on Rahel never leaves her mind: the one whom Arendt calls "my closest friend, though she has been dead for some one hundred years,"[69] finally returns to life through Arendt's manuscript completed in 1933 while Hitler was coming to power. That same year, Arendt published, in German, her first article on Rahel Varnhagen in commemoration of the hundredth anniversary of her death.[70] The manuscript, lost and then found during Arendt's peregrinations, was published discreetly in 1958, a year when that completely different work *The Human Condition* appeared and seven years after *The Origins of Totalitarianism*. In the latter book, which made Arendt so famous, Rahel, along with for instance Disraeli or Captain Dreyfus, already occupies a considerable place: after having noted that "France was the land of political glory for Jews, the first to recognize them as citizens. Prussia seemed on the way to becoming the country of social splendor,"[71] Arendt sketches the portrait of Rahel's salon whose apogee corresponds to the emancipating consequences of the Napoleonic conquest and whose ineluctable decline immediately follows the rout. At the height of their glory:

> Most representative of these salons, and the genuinely mixed society they brought together in Germany, was that of Rahel Varnhagen. Her original, unspoiled, and unconventional intelligence, combined with an absorbing interest in people and a truly passionate nature, made her the most brilliant and the most interesting of these Jewish women. . . . [But this] came to an end in 1806 when, according to their hostess, this unique meeting place "foundered like a ship containing the highest enjoyment of life." Along with the aristocrats, the romantic intellectuals became antisemitic, and although this by no means meant that either group gave up all its Jewish friends, the innocence and splendor were gone.[72]

Without being explicitly designated in *The Human Condition*, Rahel's salon remains in the background of the original analysis Arendt gives of the function of the public space in modernity. Rahel does indeed disappear from the great theoretical works that would henceforth succeed each other. But she appears recurrently in Arendt's abundant private correspondence: Rahel has haunted her life to such a point that her book, strongly titled in its German version after many discussions between Arendt and her publisher, *Rahel Varnhagen: The Life of a German Jewess During the Romantic Era*, and not merely *Rahel Varnhagen: The Life of a Jewess*, as in its first publication in the United States, could be considered as her true "New Testament,"[73] the testament of Arendt but perhaps also that of the Jews who had died in Germany following the final failure of the assimilation process of all the Rahels. As late as 1973, or two years before her own death, Arendt writes several letters in order to find certain texts by Rahel that had gone astray: it shows the constancy of her attachment, her loyalty to her "friend" who has accompanied her throughout her entire life.

Curiously, this book, *Rahel Varnhagen: The Life of a German Jewess During the Romantic Era*, fundamental for whoever wants to understand Arendt's life and thought, remained for a long time intentionally ignored, regarded as a minor work compared to the *Origins of Totalitarianism*, *The Human Condition*, *On Revolution*, *Eichmann in Jerusalem*, or the treatise *The Life of the Mind*. A number of authors say almost nothing about it since, to them, Arendt the philosopher doesn't have much to do with Arendt the Jewess; Arendt the historian doesn't have much in common with Arendt the theoretician. At best, in recent publications, an introductory chapter is hastily devoted to it, and it is not referred to again. This work, however, is at the center of Arendt's life. Thus, in 1966, she waged a long fight, one that in her opinion was essential and of a strong symbolic significance, with the help of Jaspers, to compel the German government to recognize her work on Rahel as a doctoral thesis that she was not permitted to defend; whence, when she was not a candidate, her surprising attempts to win financial reparation for a university career that had become impossible under the Nazi regime. She asked Jaspers, who had been reserved about this work on Rahel, for a letter certifying that the manuscript on Rahel Varnhagen was excellent and should have been accepted as accreditation, which would have allowed her quickly to climb the levels of the German university. After an initial failure in 1967, Arendt renewed her request, which was accepted by the German government in November 1971, taking into account this "exceptional" case. In this sense, formally, she retrospectively obtained a university appointment opening the way to an academic career with this book devoted to the history of a German Jew, not with her *Saint Augustine* or her *Human Condition*.[74] It was as if, once and for all, she were determined to enter the public space par excellence that the university scene represents with a work explicitly having to do with a Jewish theme, contributing more than is thought, following the example of her friend Salo Baron, to the "standardization" of Jewish studies in the Western academic world.[75]

One can moreover see in *The Human Condition*, a work that establishes Arendt in the position of a theoretician of public space comparable in many respects to Jürgen Habermas by their shared rejection of the explicit presence of cultural identities,[76] an echo of her *Rahel Varnhagen*. That is where she elaborates for the first time her interpretation of the salon as constituting the public space, as a privileged space of the exercise of citizenship, and as a form of microsociability where personality takes root. Arendt, who has read *Remembrance of Things Past*, gives us an original analysis of salons as a place of social mobility for Jews but also as a means of defending a status threatened by the bourgeoisie, one that allows "all paths to be confused,"[77] all social strategies to be attempted that can ensure "escape." "Excluded" from society, a "pariah," "marginal" and "petrified,"[78] Rahel used this singular space to animate, thanks "to her unique talent," a brilliant salon in her studio on Jägerstrasse to which come, on the margins of society, the Humboldt brothers, Friedrich Schlegel, Schleiermarcher, and Jean Paul, but also princes and sovereigns, ministers, and diplomats: Rahel, according to Prince Louis-Ferdinand, her friend, is "a moral midwife."[79] For Arendt, the Jewish salon, an always dreamed-of idyll of a composite social life,

> was the product of a chance constellation in an era of social transition. The Jews became stop-gaps between a declining and an as yet unstabilized social group: the nobility and the actors; both stood outside of bourgeois society—like the Jews . . . in the Jewish houses of homeless middle-class intellectuals they found solid ground and an echo which they could not hope to find anywhere else. . . . Precisely because the Jews stood outside of society they became, for a short time, a kind of neutral zone.[80]

This sociohistorical analysis of Jewish salons is superb: Arendt shows how, by a coming together of circumstances due to the victories of Napoleon, an artificial, distorted public space was temporarily opened to Jews like Rahel, who could leave the "silence" in which to her great despair she found herself confined. Outside as they were of the social game, they were accessible as "a neutral ground" to all ambitions, a space that would be swept away by the triumph of the reactionary bourgeoisie after the Napoleonic defeats, which undertook to "exclude" them once again, to render them silent as before. As Rahel writes to her friend Rebecca Friedländer, all that was left was to "stand still, breathless, out of fear of the whole living world and of the beating of your own pulse."[81] Silence, then "nothing. I let life rain on me."[82] From now on, "officialdom now came to the fore," a noble and patriotic world where a virulent anti-Semitism explodes, an extreme chauvinism as a reaction to the French Enlightenment. Circles are created, like the *Christlich-Deutsche Tischgesellschaft*, or German-Christian Company, which exclude women, Frenchmen, philistines, and Jews.[83] Rahel "rebels," "stands her ground," "revolts"; she now has only one way to escape the silence again, the "shame," "this burden": to marry "the beggar by the wayside," August Varnhagen, "her last chance" who will allow her, through conversion and changing her name—she will henceforth be called Friederike Varnhagen von Ense—to "get into" the new reactionary salons.[84] "The only way out was Varnhagen,"[85] who in turn has become patriotic and conservative. Rahel finally "arrives,"[86] giving rise to the sarcastic commentary of her friend Wilhelm von Humboldt: "I hear . . . that Varnhagen has now married the little Levy [*sic*; it should be 'Levine'] woman. So now at last she can become an Excellency and Ambassador's wife. There is nothing the Jews cannot achieve."[87] However, she remains a pariah, she is "sick" of it, expects nothing more of these salons, and regrets having left aside "green things, children, love, weather."[88] It is as if she has fought for nothing, as if she never became "a veritable parvenu," as if in her innermost being, in her great solitude, she has remained Rahel. In *The Human Condition* published in the same year as *Rahel Varnhagen* but written much latter, Arendt argues that "a life without speech and without action . . . is literally dead to the world. . . . Action, as distinguished from fabrication, is never possible in isolation; to be isolated is to be deprived of the capacity to act."[89] Without any reference to Rahel, Arendt thus implicitly marks the final failure of her heroine forever kept apart from the domain of action that is the property of the human condition, forced back to her personal psychological torments that came from a confused identity that no longer has its place in public space. That is why Arendt considers things from the hypothesis of a veritable public space, which remains stuttering and perverted in that Prussia where Jews are not even citizens.

Despite the critical appreciation of the fate of Rahel, "her closest friend," Rahel seems to obsess Hannah Arendt, whose life however unfolds in another society, from Weimar to New York; it is also her own existence that is at stake, torn between identity and action. Can we, for all that, agree with Elzbieta Ettinger when she argues that Arendt "shared the insecurity of many assimilated Jews who were still uncertain about their place, still harboring doubts about themselves. By choosing her as his beloved, Heidegger fulfilled for Hannah the dream of generations of German Jews, going back to such pioneers of assimilation as Rahel Varnhagen." [90] Hannah's passion bursts forth in this dedication, never sent, to the German translation of *The Human Condition*, written in October 1960, twenty-five years after the beginning of their affair:

> Re *Vita Activa*
> The dedication of this book is left out.
> How could I dedicate it to you,
> my trusted friend,
> to whom I remained faithful
> and unfaithful,
> And both in love. [91]

Until her death, Arendt traveled to Germany to see Heidegger though she was aware of his activities during the Nazi regime and knew of how as vice chancellor he ousted all Jewish teachers from their positions, as well as the scorn with which he treated her dear Gertrud Jaspers, Karl Jaspers's Jewish wife in whose company, along with Heidegger, they all formed a brilliant "ménage à trois": [92] nonetheless, she, the Jewess so anxious to assert her identity, defended him to the end, used her boundless energy with American publishers and translators to further his recognition in the United States and throughout the world. What link can one establish between Rahel, Hannah, and Heidegger? Did Arendt borrow the "mask" of Rahel's history to let her own emotion show through, to speak of her own suffering, and to express her attachment to the condition of pariah, at the very moment when her status risked transforming her into a parvenu? [93] Did the wish for assimilation of a German Jewish woman lead her to a kind of inevitable blinding, a negation of self, whether at the beginning of the nineteenth century or in the middle of the twentieth? On the contrary, Arendt strongly rejects all assimilation as a way of escaping from Judaism, all the more so since "this country is not a nation-state . . . it is not necessary to assimilate into it,"[94] she reproaches "her friend" Rahel for having given in too much to this solution to resolve the contradictions inherent in her identity as a Jew in a Christian world; she never regarded the Jewish condition, as Rahel did, as a "disgrace," an "infamy of birth" that inspires "disgust" and "nausea";[95] she unequivocally rejects all compromises to which parvenu Jews subject themselves. Such a comparison is inapt when Arendt, unlike the "poor Rahel," became a cult figure in Germany and, thanks to her intellectual notoriety,[96] from Marburg to Princeton and Chicago, benefited from so many eminent positions that she readily contrasted to those occupied by the "exceptional Jews" who were socially assimilated, whom, as a self-proclaimed and scarcely credible pariah,[97] she fiercely mocked. Arendt never changed her name as Rahel Lewin who became von Ense did; she never thought of converting as so many German Jews and Rahel herself did in the nineteenth century, in another era, it's true, one that was infinitely more constraining, and in a closed, rigid, oppressive society, completely unlike the United States and even unlike the Weimar Republic, which by comparison seem like a haven of free thought. She can avoid, in Rahel's words, living "her own existence almost completely secretly" by entering the American public space on the same level as everyone else,[98] by constructing a body of work that assures her an international reputation, while Rahel must be content with feverishly setting down her thoughts, unaware that they will penetrate, but not until our own time, the public space and become an object of admiration and almost of worship, the subject of conferences and scholarly publications, to the point of being compared to the writings of Goethe, whom she admired above all else; Rahel, at last, will escape the attentive gaze of her friend Hannah and win her own autonomy and impose herself, in the world of letters, as Arendt's equal. Identification between the two heroines can quickly be found, then, to have its limits.

Heidegger, Arendt's mentor and lover, and Blücher, her husband and her confidant throughout her life, are both different in every respect from Karl August Varnhagen, Rahel's husband. They have nothing in common with Rahel's disappointed love affairs in her youth with Count von Finckenstein, Don Raphael d'Urquijo, or Alexender von der Marvitz. At varying degrees, Rahel's love affairs involved conservative men, nobles who must open the doors of society to her, a society which she would finally, once she herself had become a countess thanks to Varnhagen's promotions, be able to enter almost legitimately. Arendt loved first an unrivalled philosopher who intellectually dominated his era, a mind that nothing, not even his anti-Semitism, could diminish, by whom she despaired of being recognized. Until the end, as in her speech for the German philosopher's eightieth birthday, she claimed her admiration for Heidegger, whose anti-Semitism was in her opinion only a "mistake," the "escapade" of a man "still quite young"; she compared his proximity to the dictator to Plato's and underplayed its significance, since "it hardly matters where the storms of their century can toss them."[99] Arendt had only one wish, that of being regarded as an equal by the theoretician of technology, whereas Rahel, faithful to the emancipating dreams of German Jews, was desperate to be recognized by Goethe, the theoretician of human fraternity. One, Arendt, openly and tirelessly pursued her aim, whose visibility she assumed; the other, Rahel, trembled with emotion at the idea of meeting Goethe and, far from trying to seduce him, didn't pay any attention to her clothes when such an event occurred unexpectedly.

Their lovers were completely different. Their husbands too. After a first marriage with a young Jew whom she didn't love but who got along well with her mother, Arendt quickly married a former communist proletarian for whom she would be a contented wife, and who would be her faithful companion throughout a life of dialogue and real mutual comprehension, an example of German-Jewish symbiosis that Scholem regarded as impossible.[100] Rahel, far from this symbiosis, married Varnhagen, whose ambition she guided toward aristocratic circles that would give her once again access to the salons, to public space. Customs change with the times: both women marry non-Jewish men who help them construct and preserve their work. They both embody the central class of the society of their time, the aristocracy or the proletariat, forces through which they become present to the world. But, with this aim, Rahel must convert and keep her nighttime dreams to herself, her intimate thoughts that she could not share with her faithful and inattentive husband, to whom she did not confide her torments; pariah and parvenu, she hid her despair from him, while Arendt, far from all obscurities, from all forms of acosmia, constructed an egalitarian loving relationship, stripped of any ambiguity, with her husband, her companion, her lover; their loving correspondence reveals the intensity of a physical passion that was certainly unknown to Rahel, who also remained "foreign" to the world, in her mind as well as in her body, which she thought lacked grace. Distance in one woman, confidence in the other: Varnhagen weakened the Jewish dimension of Rahel's letters which might lead others to doubt her assimilation by transforming the names of some of her correspondents, while Blücher, whom Arendt tenderly calls her "miraculous rabbi," shows a real knowledge of Jewish history and culture and doesn't hesitate to fight for Israel and for the Jews in general, sometimes beyond Arendt's own political stances. In a word, everything brings close and everything separates these two brilliant, ambitious women of independent spirit, who more than a century apart conceive of writings that mark their era: some compare the essentially epistolary work of Rahel to that of Goethe whom she met several times.[101] One of them went into exile of her own accord; the other, fighting, left Germany not to distance herself temporarily like Rahel who went to Paris or Prague, but forever, as a carefully planned break endowed with historical significance. She joined the American public space where she could, in front of everyone, speak out, instead of confiding her thoughts like Rahel only to her private correspondence in the unlikely hope of being heard, but only much later.

Everything contrasts these two heroines, yet both answer the call of Goethe's *Bildung*, the construction of a way of life made of culture and education, these two hostesses of salons who, in the Prussian and aristocratic Berlin of the 1800s or in cosmopolitan and modern New York, gather the finest minds around them. One feverishly dreams in the silence of her interiority of another life that would get her out of the shadow, of submission to dominant and conformist milieus. The other, cigar in her mouth, "self-proclaimed pariah,"[102] triumphs in the heart of public space, imposes her work, her judgments, her moods, successfully wages war in a world of men that she seeks out and that once annihilated Rahel's expectations, the misunderstood, the scorned, the dominated, Rahel the feminist before her time, now recognized as such by a movement that at the same time has scarcely any sympathy

for Hannah.[103] Everything distinguishes and everything brings close
these two German Jewish rebels, then, who know how to reserve their
critical mind while they reached the summits of society and notoriety,
these two secularized Jewish women, indifferent to religion, who think
condescendingly of the traditionalist Jews from the East, those "Orientals" (Hannah), those "Bohemians" (Rahel) so remote from them.[104]
Everything separates these headstrong women who, breaking with their
native milieus, both marry non-Jews by whom they will not have any
children, thus both breaking the essential generational link that ensures
the transmission of Jewish culture, these two heroines who hesitate between accepting themselves as "a conscious parvenu" or passing themselves off, more nobly, as a "conscious pariah."[105]

What, then, is the mystery of Arendt's fascination with "her friend"
Rahel, so different in many respects from herself, who haunts her youth
as well as her adult years? She doesn't hesitate to mention it when she describes the "schlemiehl, the dream prince" of whom Heine, with whom
Rahel maintained a correspondence and whose faithfulness to Judaism she admired, remains for Arendt the revered prototype.[106] She also
compares her to the superlative figures of "conscious pariah" Jews that
for her are Heine, Shalom Aleichem, Bernard Lazare, Franz Kafka, and
Charlie Chaplin, to all those who naturally possess "all vaunted Jewish qualities—the 'Jewish heart,' humanity, humor, disinterested intelligence."[107] That conveys the esteem Hannah has for Rahel, even if she
reproaches her a little facilely for having sought an individual solution
for her torments by eluding any kind of collective solution, any engagement that would have led her to join the fight of other oppressed people. In her pantheon of Great Men, Rahel is still the only woman to be
hauled up to that level by the magic of her writing, scattered throughout so many often unpublished letters. But what is Arendt looking for
in Rahel? The answer is obvious: a soulmate who experienced similar
pangs when identitarian or religious adherence becomes remote, before the vertigo of the necessarily individual *Bildung*, a being who is at
once identical and different also confronted with the anguishes of the
*muttersprache*, who like her invents an open public space for discussion,
who creates a form of Jewish politics necessarily doomed to failure and
who still leads Hannah Arendt to an impasse when she abandons any

plan to carry out a collective Jewish politics in one form or another. From then on, beyond loyalty, what is this Jewish identity that Arendt so strongly claims? Not much, really; to describe it in a few words, though, to her friend Jaspers, Arendt quotes vague, almost inconsistent words by Rahel:

> Judaism doesn't exist outside orthodoxy on the one hand or outside the Yiddish-speaking, folklore-producing Jewish people on the other. There are also people of Jewish background who are unaware of any Jewish substance in their lives in the sense of a tradition and who for certain social reasons and because they found themselves constituting a clique within society produced something like a "Jewish type." This type has nothing to do with what we understand under Judaism historically or with its genuine content. Here there is much that is positive, namely, all those things that I classify as pariah qualities and what Rahel called the "true realities of life"—"love, trees, children, music." In this type there is an extraordinary awareness of injustices; there is great generosity and a lack of prejudice; and there is—more questionably but nonetheless demonstrably present—respect for the "life of the mind." Of all these things only the last one can still be shown to have a link with originally and specifically Jewish substance. The element of Judaism that has persisted longest simply in the way people live is family loyalty. That is not an intellectual quality, however, but, rather, a sociological and political phenomenon.[108]

It could not be clearer: it is as good as saying that Judaism, for Rahel as well as for Hannah, has lost all its original spiritual significance and has been reduced to a vague humanism lined with a keen sense of family. Neither Rahel nor Hannah have anything in common with Orthodox Jews; they both are ignorant of the Yiddish of "oriental" Jews; the "sociological and political" side remains, the pariah side, that Arendt so appreciates but that is not by any means unique to the Jews: the *outsider* who can preserve a social distance capable of engendering and maintaining a critical mind, the rebel who mocks respectable society, the marginal who refuses any form of social control, all have nothing specifically Jewish about them. Goethe's ideal, love of the arts, of nature, of family, could not pass for the essential principles of Judaism any more than secularization could. How can Arendt acknowledge that "many Jews such as myself are religiously completely independent of Judaism yet are still Jews nonetheless," adding "that may lead to the disappearance of the Jewish people; there's nothing anyone can do about that." [109] Anxious for intellectual coherence, Arendt finds herself here before a real aporia, a crucial question, one that concerns the meaning of her existence and which she doesn't know how to grasp. [110]

If one abandons the religious, if one also distances oneself from a Zionist type of collective politics, can the humanist Jewish individual, enemy of dominant norms, imagine another political way of a more individual nature while, even if he feels only ridicule for it, he still makes his way toward total assimilation and fully enters, at least in our time, the public space? Arendt is severely critical of a sociological Jewishness, a way of maintaining a mythical originality in terms of election or special aptitude, which comes to be substituted for Judaism.

> Judaism became a psychological quality and the Jewish question became an involved personal problem for every individual Jew. . . . Since Rahel Varnhagen's unique attempt to establish a social life outside of official society had failed, the way of the pariah and the parvenu were equally ways of extreme solitude, and the way of conformism one of constant regret. The so-called complex psychology of the average Jew, which in a few favored cases developed into a very modern sensitiveness, was based on an ambiguous situation. . . . Wherever Jews were educated, secularized, and assimilated . . . they lost that measure of political responsibility which their origin implied . . . Jewish origin, without religious and political connotation, became everywhere a psychological quality, was changed into "Jewishness." . . . The result was that their private lives, their decisions and sentiments, became the very center of their "Jewishness." And the more the fact of Jewish birth lost its religious, national, and socioeconomic significance, the more obsessive Jewishness became. . . . Both believed their difference to be a natural fact acquired by birth. . . . [They] always wavered between such apologetic attitudes and sudden, provocative claims that they were an elite. [111]

The analysis is biting in its truth: sarcastic, mocking, Arendt touches on an essential point here. More effectively than anyone else, she asserts that Jewishness cannot replace Judaism without involuntarily entraining tragic consequences for all those who adopt such a "pose," one that she herself rejects, the anti-Semites taking aim at the assimilated Jews, so that their difference is now innate or natural, stripped of all religious or national dimension, reduced solely to the private domain. Her demonstration remains luminous, original, overwhelming, even today. But does she herself manage to escape this irrevocable judgment?

Arendt often defines herself as Jewish. In her letter to Gershom Scholem already mentioned, she writes, "The truth is I have never pretended to be anything else or to be in any way other than I am, and I have never even felt tempted in that direction. It would have been like saying that I was a man and not a woman—that is to say, kind of insane. . . . There is such a thing as a basic gratitude for everything that is as it is; for what has been *given* and not *made*; for what is *physei* and not *nomo*."[112] Arendt, in this response, almost returns to the naturalist argument that she condemns. She indeed stays away from any kind of elitist claim and makes fun of "exceptional" Jews, but hasn't she become one herself through her brilliant career, and doesn't she congratulate herself on this many times? Arendt cannot resolve these paradoxes. She wants to be Jewish without professing any kind of Judaism, while rejecting an obsessive Jewishness as foundation of a henceforth imagined identity; she rejects the Sartrean vision of the Jew defined by the gaze of the Other but, in the end, how is she Jewish? Once she has distanced herself from Zionist, essentially secularized, nationalist politics, no other option is open to her apart from a kind of almost pathetic self-proclamation, so much does she herself correspond to this "pose" that she abhors and from which she wants to keep her distance. The paths of Arendt and Scholem, who both condemn assimilation, irremediably diverge here, since Scholem makes a return to Judaism stem from a rejection marked by his "climb" to Palestine, whereas Arendt tries to maintain a fragile Jewishness within open American society.[113] How can she, however, challenge all at the same time religious orthodoxy, Zionism, assimilation, the definition of oneself through the gaze of the Other, but also semibiological Jewishness, yet have only an approximate knowledge of a culture and a language, and still conceive of her life as essentially Jewish, a quality that "goes without saying, beyond any controversy or discussion"?[114]

The range of choices for her "friend" Rahel was more limited: the Zionist solution did not exist, the openly critical posture of the pariah in the style of Bernard Lazare was unimaginable and suicidal, assimilation compatible with maintaining a Jewish identity resting on unique values in the style of Mendelssohn was still threatened; as to political action alongside other secularized Jews, wasn't that a mirage, at the time? When Arendt writes, "After Heinrich Heine and Ludwig Börne, the best among the assimilated Jews never lost their awareness of necessary solidarity with the underprivileged in general; they inevitably shared the fate of certain movements, took part in certain revolts. But to Rahel, with her still unblemished Enlightened concept of the certainty of progress from which would come reform and a reshaping of society, all struggle was alien,"[115] how does she really trace the outlines of a Jewish politics as distinct from a politics conducted in the name of humanist or social considerations? What is to be done when the religion of the ancestors has lost all meaning? Deny oneself, disappear, erase oneself, change your name, your identity, your society, and even your God. Rahel tried everything, desperate with the "shame," the "misfortune," the "disgrace" of having been born Jewish. "I wish for nothing more now," writes Rahel Varnhagen, "than to transform myself, externally as well as internally. . . . I am disgusted with myself." And Arendt: "Rahel's struggle against the facts, above all against the fact of having been born a Jew, very rapidly became a struggle against herself. She herself refused to consent to herself; she, born to so many disadvantages, had to deny, change, reshape by lies this self of hers. . . . Rahel wanted to escape from Judaism."[116] If, in the context of an open society, Hannah assumes, almost without reason, this Jewishness stripped of all Judaism while mocking the mirages of assimilation, no similar choice is offered to Rahel, and Hannah Arendt, the theoretician of action, notes, a shade coldly, that "she can neither choose nor act."

Isn't she a little too scathing toward her "friend," crushed by her time, with scarcely the resources to act or show herself responsible, in the Arendtian sense of the word, for her future, unlike her Catholic friend Pauline Wisel whose boldness and capacity to assume her life publicly Rahel admires?[117] Arendt does not, however, want to see in Rahel a pure victim; she reproaches Rahel for her passivity, her alienation, as she will do later on with respect to the Jews confronted with the Shoah; she resents her "friend" for not speaking for herself, for not being capable of taking charge of her life, for lying to herself, for not being more courageous in adversity. From experience Arendt knows that, suddenly reduced by Nazism to the state of a pariah, although in a radically different political context where the temptation of assimilation has become null and void and when the "way out" that Rahel dreads has become inevitable, no lie is possible: the way out is imposed as a choice that must be made.[118] She retrospectively judges her "friend's" hesitations on the basis of her own history. Hannah's "empathy" for Rahel is inarguable; she truly haunts her "parallel" life.[119] When she thinks that she wrote her book about Rahel from the perspective of a critique of assimilation,[120] she does not seem to take into account the extent of the tragedy that "petrified" Rahel's life.[121] Rahel saw herself being forced to assimilate, to abolish herself in order to integrate into this new community "by way of Fichte's *Addresses to the German Nation*" to such a point that she writes to her brother, "The Jew must be extirpated from us," a terrible phrase that seems to stay in her mind, since she repeats it when she declares, "The Jew must be extirpated from us, that is the sacred truth, and it must be done even if life were uprooted in the process." Rahel shows herself determined to want to make "the infamy of her birth" disappear.[122] As she complains in a letter to her friend David Veit, to be Jewish is to have one's heart "stabbed," to wait for death.[123] Faced with an overt anti-Semitism, is Rahel attracted by self-hatred?[124]

In reality, Rahel does not try to assimilate, preserving, like so many women, an internal Judaism capable of disappearing into a Germanness that Arendt can more easily reject,[125] but that in turn tempts Arendt in a romantic way, through Heidegger. To tell the truth, we see Arendt, profoundly integrated into the United States while still proclaiming her imaginary Jewishness, as lacking all consistency. Hannah wants to be a pariah while still being a professor at Princeton or Chicago, invited by the most prestigious institutions in the Western world; Rahel, the frustrated salon hostess, haunted by the daily anti-Semitism she comes up against, ashamed of her Judaism, has no way out but the negation of herself, changing her name and her religion. The way of assimilation that Arendt thinks of criticizing is actually closed to her. Lucid, Rahel cries out, "I feel despair over being nothing . . . not a sister, not a sweetheart, not a wife, not even a citizen."[126] What a statement!

What an exclusion from the public space, where on the contrary Hannah Arendt parades, theoretician of the *polis* where citizens agitate! In Marburg, but even more in Manhattan, all strategies are possible, even unbounded passion for Heidegger, whose letter of recommendation, along with Jasper's, allowed her to win a scholarship to undertake her research on Rahel.[127] Arendt forgives Heidegger, her lover throughout her life, for his "mistake"; her passion for him coexists without any apparent difficulty with her involvement with Zionism, or with her self-proclaimed adherence to the Jewish people. Rahel Varnhagen also loves non-Jews but rejects her own Jewishness to the point of converting, as so many secularized Jewish women of the time did, who, without any alternative solution, having left the ghetto once and for all, "arrive" in society by formally losing their identity. Rahel remains lucid about the friendship the great have for her: in 1819, after the "Hep Hep" massacres, she writes to her brother, Ludwig Robert, "I am overwhelmed, as I have never been, by the story of the events concerning the Jews. If their identity is preserved, it is only in order to torture them, insult them, brutalize them. The new love of Christianity (may God forgive me) for the Middle Ages and its art, poetry, and horror, only urges the people on to abomination. They teach people to shout 'Hep! Hep!' . . . The great professors, 'our relatives,' like Arnim or Brentano, are full of prejudices."[128]

Arendt gives us a superb analysis of the "arrivals" and "exits" Rahel finds herself forced to make. As Arendt left Germany to enter the American public scene, of which she became a full-fledged citizen, Rahel in her time was forced to "leave" her Judaism by marrying Varnhagen in order to enter, this time as a Prussian citizen, the Berlin salons. The French version of *Rahel Varnhagen*, translated from the German text, sometimes erases the significance of the concepts used by Arendt to retrace Rahel's "exits" and her arrivals not only among the bourgeoisie but into citizenship itself, which conferred a recognized public existence on her.[129] To be a Jewish woman is an impossible condition. As Rahel exclaims, "I can, if you will, derive every evil, every misfortune, every vexation from *that* [my Jewishness]."[130] The only solution offered to her is to "leave" this condition: this image of "leaving" or "exit" returns in Arendt's work as a leitmotif. Actually, where the French translations uses *sortir*, the English text prefers the verb "to escape," to accentuate the idea of flight, of escape from a social state that keeps Rahel prisoner and prevents her from arriving "into the world" (the title of the second chapter). The French translation entitles the last basic chapter of the book *On n'échappe pas à sa judéité* (One cannot escape one's Jewishness), this time abandoning the less dramatic notion of Arendt's "leaving." Rahel, she writes, like her friend David Friedlander, "did not want to be emancipated collectively. All they wanted was to escape their Judaism, as individuals," "Rahel wanted to escape Judaism," "she had wanted to escape from Judaism . . . all her friends who came from the same milieu had wanted to escape from Judaism and had managed to do so."[131] The constant desire to "escape," not just to "leave," is also conveyed by the idea of "fleeing" from Judaism, which is rendered as such in the French version: Rahel "flees" abroad, she "flees" to Berlin, she "flees" far from her family, "a distant flight from her entire previous existence, a flight in short in the direction of Varnhagen," "the flight far away is the desperate attempt to be reborn . . . unfortunately, such attempts at flight were only an ephemeral recourse. . . . One cannot be reborn a second time."[132] Rahel tries in vain to "wend her way in secret." In the end, when her life is ending, Rahel acknowledges, "Can one entirely get away from what one truly is; away, far away, like a feeble little ship driven far off on a vast ocean by wind and tempest! The one thing that in truth still concerns me personally, that has sunk deep into my heart and lies down at the bottom, dark and heavy as granite—that far down, I cannot see; I let it lie. . . . All my life, I considered myself Rahel and nothing else."[133] This is Rahel's final faithfulness to a Jewish identity she so often wanted to escape so as finally to be recognized by society, her final return to the secret condition of "pariah" despite a now brilliant position as a "parvenu" in high Berlin society.

What was Hannah looking for, then, in this long hunt for Rahel who had to, who was able to, remain a pariah? "It was never my intention to write a book *about* Rahel. . . . What interested me solely was to narrate the story of Rahel's life as she herself might have told it."[134] Does this biography push the identification of one woman with another so far that one might think of it as "an autobiography," a "mimetic act" that "makes the difference between author and subject disappear," a "theatrical play" during which Hannah gives her voice to Rahel, a meeting between two women at a similar moment in their lives, Hannah having left Heidegger to marry Günther Stern who does not share her intimate thoughts as Rahel protects herself from her husband, Karl August Varnhagen, Stern whom Arendt dominates and who will faithfully serve her work, since the writing of the book was finished before Arendt meets the man of her life, Heinrich Blücher?[135] That is Jaspers's feeling, who writes to Arendt, "You wrote this book before Heinrich Blücher came into your life. Perhaps your work on Rahel made it possible for you to keep your heart and eye open for the new direction of your life, which in no way resembles Rahel's."[136] In fact, what Arendt reproaches Rahel for was not having been able to go, like Arendt, to meet the Other, the non-Jew, not having known how to create with him any bonds of confidence, of intimacy,[137] of having made this German-Jewish symbiosis impossible that Arendt herself was able to construct with her husband Blücher. Jaspers finds Arendt's book too obsessed with Rahel's Jewish dimension and thinks that it thus neglects Rahel's qualities as a human being: "This work still seems to me to be your own working through of the basic questions of Jewish existence, and in it you use Rahel's reality as a guide to help you achieve clarity and liberation for yourself. . . . I think it likely that you could do Rahel greater justice today, mainly because you would see her not just in the context of the Jewish question. . . . Your book can make one feel that if a person is a Jew he cannot really live his life to the full."[138]

To the probable surprise of Jaspers, Arendt makes his assertion her own: "You're absolutely right when you say this book 'can make one feel that if a person is a Jew he cannot really live his life to the full.' And that is of course a central point. I still believe today that under the conditions of social assimilation and political emancipation the Jews could not 'live.' Rahel's life seems to me a proof of that."[139] This is also what Rahel herself notes in her own time, when she writes, "I've had enough of being taken in":[140] she decides suddenly, without calling her conversion into question (at the end of her "testament" deliberately cut off by Arendt, she still claims her love for Mary), nonetheless to rehabilitate her Jewish being, to write in Hebrew to her brother, to urge Heine to assert their common Jewish identity in the eyes of everyone, for, as

Arendt writes, "there was no escape, unless it were to the moon."[141] For Arendt, definitively, "Judaism was as innate in Rahel as the lame man's too-short leg."[142] Assimilation is a delusion that leads straight to anti-Semitism, which she rejects with all her strength. Rahel knows this now and writes these words to Heine: "No philanthropic list, no cheers, no condescension, no mixed society, no new hymn book, no bourgeois star, nothing, nothing could ever placate me. . . . *You* will say this gloriously."[143] In this sense, Heinrich Graetz is mistaken about his account just as, for opposite reasons, Heinrich von Trietschke is: both admire Rahel's subtle work, but Treitschke thinks that despite her wish for assimilation, it is still "Talmudic blood" that is expressed through her, while Graetz on the contrary condemns her as a romantic Christian admiring Goethe, who could "seduce" her by turning her away from Judaism.[144] Close to Graetz on this point, Dubnow thinks in too simplistic a way that as "a faithful disciple of the literary prophets of Germany, Rahel was completely foreign to the spirit of the ancient prophets of her people. The social milieu from which Rahel and other 'new men' of that type drew their ideals was profoundly penetrated with antipathy for the Jewish people and for its spiritual values . . . thus Goethe was hostile to ethical Judaism."[145] Actually, Rahel's character is more complex, and she claims her final and irrevocable attachment to Judaism, from which even Goethe and the temptation of assimilation could not distance her for long.[146]

Arendt is aware of the impasses of assimilation, but, unlike Rahel, thinks the failure of any Jewish politics, individual or collective, is inevitable, as she refuses any form of inner exile but also all valorization in herself of exile, of *Galut* as a lasting condition of the Jews, which distances them from indispensable participation in the public sphere.[147] Isn't that Arendt's very thesis, according to which Jews have found themselves, until almost the twentieth century, in a situation of "acosmia" and have "the great privilege of being discharged from the world's care,"[148] of finding themselves alongside reality, outside of history? Isn't it Arendt herself who then turned away from the Zionist collective or internal paths toward an open society, forms of entry into history, in order to imagine a Jewish politics of another kind, actually a non-Jewish, simply humanist politics? Her *Rahel*, as Jaspers sees it and as Hannah herself emphasizes, was indeed written from a standpoint that was hostile to assimilation, compatible with a Zionist critique of the path of individual liberation that leads, according to Arendt, to another impasse. In reply to Jaspers's pertinent observation, Arendt confesses, as we remember, that "this whole project has not been very important to me for a long time, actually not since 1933."[149] Rahel remains simply "her friend" till the end, an assertion that signifies that despite her constant interest in Jewish destiny, Arendt has finished with Jewish politics and is turning more toward the human condition, toward the politics of citizens stripped of any particular identity, entering public space with only their Reason. Arendt thus distances herself from "her friend" Rahel. Rahel, however, chose late in life, while reasserting her Christian faith (to the great displeasure of Arendt, who cuts out a passage of Rahel's testament, just as Varnhagen makes the Jewish dimension disappear from his wife's correspondence), to return to a Judaism about which she was probably better informed, as her letters written once again in Hebrew attest, than they had been when she was little, when she hadn't yet undertaken her journey, her unfruitful "escape" toward assimilation into a society that continued to remain closed. In the end, Arendt admits that "Rahel had remained a Jew and a pariah."[150] Like Arendt, or even more than Arendt?

In the opinion of Virginia Woolf, there was no doubt that Isaiah Berlin represented the quintessence of the "violent," "over-intelligent" Jew.[1] This brutal assertion is surprising in its simplistic quality, even if it comes from a writer who did not hide her anti-Semitic feelings. How could this eminent philosopher, this specialist in Herder and Vico, the author of the famous comparison between negative freedom and positive freedom, this polemicist who understood the logic of the de Maistre position and who rehabilitated thinkers deep within Russia confronted with French universalist claims, this brilliant British knight, member of the Establishment, who surprised people with his renderings of Verdi, this much-honored president of Covent Garden, friend of the poet Anna Akhmatova and of Stravinsky, this unpredictable, caustic thinker who, as proof of his absolute liberalism, liked to quote Kant's observation "Out of the crooked timber of humanity no straight thing was ever made," a liberal and pluralist vision par excellence, be summed up as a "violent Jew" who was masking his true personality?

That would mean the man was twofold: behind "the man who knew too much" (according to Mario Vargas Llosa's affectionate description),[2] the Oxford philosopher from All Souls, "the free thinker . . . hostile to all -isms,"[3] the brilliant speaker on the BBC who could fascinate hundreds of thousands of British listeners with his mastery of the history of ideas, was there a flagrantly aggressive Jewish zealot hiding? Woolf's venomous remark is all the more surprising since the specialists on Berlin almost all ignore his Jewish connection in their writings, or, at best, reduce it to a few paragraphs, or even to a chapter that annoys the reader who is almost surprised by such an implication.[4] In France, for example, as another proof of such a stance, the two chapters on Judaism were removed from the edition of *Against the Current*, as if a strict separation had to be maintained at all costs between the two Berlins: the official, presentable one, and the other one, the Jew, even worse, the Zionist. These two chapters were banished, removed from the original work and added to a different text in order to form a little uniquely "Jewish" volume that, although remarkably edited, still emphasized the aspect regarded as marginal to this nonconformist Berlin: he meant to remain a faithful heir of Jewish history and went so far as to declare, "We are a people."[5]

Let us listen, in order to be persuaded of this, to the oration by the chief rabbi of Great Britain, Jonathan Sacks, during the funeral of the famous knight of Her Majesty who was Isaiah Berlin, on November 7, 1997. In the beginning of his long discourse, the chief rabbi emphasizes that Berlin's existence "allows us to believe in the crooked timber humanity is made from." Aware of the central nature of this metaphor in Berlin's work, the rabbi once again mentions it, even allowing himself to correct, according to him, a mistake made by Berlin who attributed this judgment to Kant, in a translation by Collingwood. The chief rabbi thinks that actually it comes from Ecclesiastes (7:13), that is, unknown to Berlin, from the most profound source of Jewish thought.[6] As he made this final homage, the chief rabbi mentioned several times this phrase of Kant's that fascinated Berlin throughout his life almost to the point of making it, starting from a rereading of Vico and Herder, the foundation of his thinking; he applied it here subtly to the future of the Jewish people to emphasize its particularity. This recurrent theme in Berlin's work, used as a title of his most famous book,[7] appeared for the first time in 1952, in a little-known text entitled "Jewish Slavery and Emancipation," about the fate of the Jews.[8] That conveys how much this insistence on the indispensable cultural diversity of humankind that obsessed Berlin and urged him endlessly to assert his rejection of all determinism, of any monistic vision of history, destructive in the name of Reason of infinite cultural pluralism, is from the beginning inspired by a reflection on the permanence of the Jewish people, who deny any standardization of the world. In this sense, the chief rabbi of Great Britain remarkably perceived the consubstantial link between Berlin's writings and his Jewish adherence. Following biblical tradition, he added, "Today we mourn the loss of a prince and of a great man of the Jewish people." The chief rabbi was aware of the fact that Berlin "was not religious": one day, Berlin even supposedly said to him, "Chief rabbi, don't talk to me about religion. When it's a question of God, I become completely deaf." Still he thinks that he "was Jewish, not only from the ethnic point of view, but also through a profound moral conviction," and ends with the essential point by recalling that Berlin himself led the Passover seder every year, commenting on the Hebrew text that tells of the flight from Egypt, the slavery, the bitterness; that Berlin read this text remembering that he himself had once tasted this *maror* of bitterness as a child, when the Bolsheviks seized power, and that he had experienced it again with the deportation by the Nazis of a part of his family from Riga. The chief rabbi finally concludes his impressive speech with the following strong observation: "If I had to summarize his fundamental work from the point of view of a Jewish perspective, I would say that it constitutes a prolonged commentary on the *Haggadah*, thus applying the lessons of Pesach to our time."[9]

With finesse, the chief rabbi gives voice perhaps better than the scholarly academic commentaries, which neglect the Jewish dimension of Berlin's personality, to the logic that underpins all Berlin's writings and that connects the indispensable fidelity to a specific culture with the defense of freedom. This Oxford graduate who received honorific titles, from knighthood to the presidency of Covent Garden, of Wolfson College and of the British Academy, was also president of the Association of Friends of the Hebrew University of Jerusalem and—little-known among commentators who above all remember his public roles—sat as a judge on the arbitration council for the chief rabbi. This latter function gives us a superb anecdote told by the chief rabbi who compares, point-blank, the Oxford spirit that penetrates Berlin with the pilpul that Jews have always practiced, a way of maintaining a dialogue by splitting hairs for the pleasure of it. He remembers that not long before, when he was sitting next to Berlin and awaiting the decision of the judges, he warned Berlin, "Isaiah, don't tell me your verdict before the day of the ceremony." Berlin immediately tells him the result of the vote. When the chief rabbi reproaches him for not knowing how to keep a secret, Berlin retorts humorously, "I am applying the Oxford method of keeping a secret. You tell it to only one person at a time."[10] In the opinion of the chief rabbi as well as in that of his friends, Berlin's fidelity to the intricate history of the Jews can never be doubted. Thus, a little later, Avishai Margalit, Berlin's friend, pays homage to him by writing almost in the same words, "If the Jews embodied the family to Berlin, what did Isaiah represent for the Jews? For many of them, he was *Resh Galuta*, the Prince of the Exiles, who knew better than anyone else what the absence of *home* means; his childhood was shaped by an uncertain immigration."[11] That Berlin was above all a Jew "attached until his deathbed to the idea of a *home* in Israel," that is a fact uttered solemnly once again during a funeral service in his honor held at the synagogue in Hampstead.[12]

Berlin's life in fact intermingles to the point of fusion the impregnation of Oxonian customs with fidelity to Jewish culture: in his opinion, nothing can set these two adherences that exist naturally in the heart of his identity in opposition to each other. When he is asked why, as a conclusion to his involvement on behalf of the Zionist movement, he did not go to live in Israel, Berlin replies:

> Too late for me, because I don't speak Hebrew freely: I am too old to cut myself off from my present way of life. When I go to Israel I do feel free, I do not feel that I am in a foreign country. In Israel I don't particularly feel a Jew, but in England I do. I am neither proud nor ashamed of being a Jew. I am as I am, good or bad. Some people have dark hair, others have blond hair, some people are Jews as some people are Welsh. For me being a Jew is like having two hands, two feet, to be what one is. Israel is a country where I have a natural affinity with the inhabitants. I remain totally loyal to Britain, to Oxford, to Liberalism, to Israel, to a number of other institutions with which I feel identified.[13]

This naturalist, essentialist conception of Judaism, Herder-like to an extreme that almost seems to fall into the category of the biological (which we will return to later on), seems to him compatible, paradoxically, with the multiplicity of allegiances that are quite remote from this form of "thick" identitarian claim, determinist, scarcely favorable to the individual choice that Berlin advocates, herald as he is of freedom and of free decision of individuals. This strong identitarian implication did not however lead him, as he is sometimes reproached for, to a "realism of a tribal nature" from which everything sets him apart despite these surprising naturalist declarations.[14]

This descendant of the famous lineage of the Lubavitchers was the first Jewish academic appointed to the prestigious All Souls college, as Hannah Arendt was the first woman to be named professor at Princeton. Born on June 6, 1909, in Riga, capital of Lithuania (which was then a Russian province), Berlin's great-grandmother was a Schneerson; thus he descended directly from the founder of the Hassidic movement. Berlin's mother was the daughter of Zemach Zadeck, then the head of the Lubavitchers. His first name, Isaiah, was given to him to honor the memory of his great-grandfather, who was also a member of the Lubavitch movement. If Berlin showed throughout his life an antipathy to the Lubavitchers, whom he regarded as "fanatics," in Hebron as well as in Brooklyn, if he deplores their customs and mocks their black clothes,[15] he jests no less significantly with the chief rabbi of Great Britain. Aware of the marked sympathy of the latter for this movement, Berlin teases, "You are an adept, but I am a *mishpahrah*, a member of the family."[16] His mother however received a modern education and became a singer. Isaiah's father, a businessman, came from an Orthodox Jewish milieu but entered the gymnasium in his youth and then turned toward German culture, no longer kept kosher, neglected the synagogue, little by little forgot his Yiddish. Isaiah however received a religious education at the Hebrew school where he was a student, in Andreapol, then in St. Petersburg where his family moved in 1916. In St. Petersburg Berlin continued his Talmudic studies and was present at the start of the Bolshevik Revolution, at scenes of violence that marked him for life. The family villa was searched from top to bottom by the Cheka. The Berlins then decided to emigrate and after careful thought decided against the Palestine option, also rejecting the idea to go to a France that was regarded as anti-Semitic after the Dreyfus Affair; on October 5, 1920, they headed for Lithuania, abandoning to Isaiah's great regret a precious copy of the *Jewish Encyclopedia*. In February 1921, after having lived through some anti-Semitic experiences, the young Berlin accompanied his parents who left Riga for good to go to an unknown Great Britain, where the prodigy son would soon find glory.[17]

There, Isaiah Berlin confronted the old question of assimilation. An *outsider*, exiled, he nonetheless easily entered English society, soon mastered the language, and accumulated scholarly successes without however renouncing his identity. His family often went to a synagogue in the West End; his mother became a firm believer in Zionism, became involved in Zionist associations, made sure she cooked kosher, prepared the celebration of Passover, fasted on Yom Kippur. Skeptical and unbelieving, Isaiah, who had his bar mitzvah, nonetheless went to certain synagogues in working-class neighborhoods, became interested for a little while in Hassidic ritual, respected, as he would throughout his life, the chief Jewish holidays as forms of identitarian adherence. Then there's the great leap: having been admitted to Corpus Christi College, in 1928 he entered Oxford, in the holy of holies that he would never leave. After a position at New College, which he obtained in October 1932, came his apotheosis; to his great astonishment, he was in 1932 the first Jew appointed to All Souls, and the third ever appointed to a college in Oxford, a city that became his true home, to which he devoted his life with unfailing loyalty. Congratulated by the chief rabbi of Great Britian of the time, welcomed by Baron Rothschild, celebrated by the *Jewish Chronicle*, the famous Jewish weekly to which Berlin would regularly contribute, he was admitted into the narrow circle of the British "establishment," became friendly with the upper crust of the nation, met stars and celebrities, became involved in philosophical controversies, exhibited an ease that gave him an increasing notoriety, and pushed social assimilation to the point of embracing the smallest details of British customs—clothing, for example.

Fame, involvement in the great debates of the time on truth and positivist logic, did not however turn him away from his keen interest aroused in St. Petersburg during the Balfour declaration in the Zionist movement, of which he would throughout his life be a fervent defender. On November 9, 1917, he experienced the excitement that overcame a number of Jews during the publication of the essential text that was the Balfour declaration, which promised them for the first time a home in Palestine: Berlin remembered the blue-and-white flags that children waved at that time in synagogue. In 1988 he says:

> I was a Zionist even as a schoolboy. My parents were not Zionists in
> Russia. I drifted into it as something quite natural. I thought it was

right. . . . It seemed to me that there was no Jew in the world who was
not, in some degree, socially uneasy. . . . There must be somewhere, I
felt, where Jews were not forced to be self-conscious,—where they did
not feel the need for total integration, for stressing their contribution
to the native culture—where they simply could live normal, unob-
served lives. The purpose of Zionism is normalization; the creation of
conditions in which the Jews could live as a nation, like the others. . . .
When I go to Israel I do feel free, I do not feel that I am in a foreign
country. In Israel I don't particularly feel a Jew, but in England I do.[18]

In Great Britain he reached the height of renown, became a knight of
the realm, and presided over the destinies of Covent Garden, but nothing could erase a difference from his consciousness: it is impossible to
lead a "normal life," "not supervised" by others, no matter how close or
free of prejudice they are. "Just as Greeks have Greece, Germans have
Germany so Jews have a homeland in Palestine, in Jerusalem. . . . If
Jews don't have real geographical roots, they are made happy by imagining ones—by an enormous act of psychological self-transformation,
by being decolonized."[19] Spontaneously using the metaphors of Bene-
dict Anderson, Berlin sees in Israel an "imaginary community" that
gives, for example, to British Jews like himself, who are deprived of
"roots" however brilliant their assimilation in society may be, a substitute adherence that is purely imaginary but whose centrality is revealed to be the only one capable of "decolonizing" them. This term
seems particularly strong: it takes into account the confusion of those
Jews most assimilated into the dominant values of society. But there's
nothing for it: these people colonized from within, endlessly forced to
negotiate their place, must in turn be liberated, decolonized from the
gaze directed at them even in the places supposedly most stripped of
prejudice. This wound will never be erased, despite all the honors received, and Berlin confides again, in the twilight of his life, "I am still
a Russian Jew from Riga and all my years in England cannot change
that. I love England, it has become my home, I have even been treated
well here and I feel close to most of the aspects of the British way of life,
but I remain a Russian Jew: that is how I was born and I will remain
so until the end of my life."[20] This confession recalls the regard he has
for his colleague and friend, also a specialist in nationalism, the Jew-

ish sociologist John Plamenatz, who, a native of Montenegro which he had to flee, also earned all honors during his career at Oxford: when Berlin gives his eulogy, after his death, identifying himself with his fate marked by emigration, he notes straightforwardly that "he remained all his life in exile."[21]

Let us go back to the seemingly commonplace observation by Berlin according to which "the Greeks have Greece and the Germans Germany," a statement that probably implies, *a contrario*, that the Greek Jews and German Jews who find imaginary roots far from their adopted country "have" neither Greece nor Germany despite their long assimilation into these societies. Under one form or another, in the name of Herder, his mentor, Berlin hammers out the same proclamation, namely that

> Greek culture is uniquely and inexhaustibly Greek; India, Persia, France are what they are, not something else. Our culture is our own; cultures are incommensurable. . . . If you exile a German and plant him in America, he will be unhappy; he will suffer because people can be happy, can function freely, only among those who understand them. To be lonely is to be among men who do not know what you mean. Exile, solitude, is to find yourself among people whose words, gestures, handwriting are alien to your own, whose behaviour, reactions, feelings, instinctive responses, and thoughts and pleasures and pains, are too remote from yours. . . . The idea of a single, perfect society of all mankind must be internally self-contradictory, because the Valhalla of the Germans is necessarily different from the ideal of future life of the French, because the paradise of the Muslims is not that of Jews or Christians, because a society in which a Frenchman would attain to harmonious fulfillment is a society which to a German might prove suffocating.[22]

"Suffering," "solitude," risk of "suffocating": living in "exile" in a cultural space that is not one's own is perilous; one cannot play with impunity with the incommensurability of cultures: what's more, if the suffering of a German exiled to the United States is great, what can one say of that of a German Jew who finds himself confronted with such an exile? Evidently, however, as things are, such is not the case; Germans, whether they are Jewish, are hardly suffering in the United States, any more than the Greeks are in France or the French in Germany. Exile can be a source of emancipation and liberation and not necessarily of solitude. It is true that adaptation to the other is not without a price, without misunderstanding, so great is the distance that separates cultural codes and ways of living, expressing oneself. Here Berlin touches on the limits of the "exit" strategy dear to Albert Hirschman: one cannot leave a nation as one changes products, car makes, or televisions; assimilation into another nation often has a high cost, implies immense suffering from all the signs of incomprehension that are often followed by rejection, and, sometimes, by signs of intolerance. One cannot emerge unscathed from this: Berlin himself, late in life, still feels profoundly Jewish, or different, in Great Britain.

A similar expression of suffering and solitude recurs in the writings of another Jew who had immigrated to Great Britain, Ernest Gellner. His life was almost parallel with Berlin's: although a little younger, he left not St. Petersburg threatened by the Bolsheviks but Prague occupied by the Nazis to go to Great Britain and join not New College but the famous Balliol College at Oxford before becoming a professor at Cambridge, the rival university. In turn he attained an intellectual fame comparable to Berlin's through the breadth of his exceptional body of work; his career was crowned by the presidency of the Royal Anthropological Institute and by election to the British Academy. His family came from the Sudeten Mountains in Germany and went to Prague after the fall of the Austro-Hungarian Empire: it became resolutely involved in a profound process of assimilation with Czech society, following the example of thousands of Jewish immigrants drawn to the great modern city. Although Gellner's mother was interested in Zionism, his father, who had a law degree, adhered to universalist values. A veritable "puritan of the Enlightenment" as he calls himself, Gellner fought every form of relativist perspective and severely criticized Wittgenstein's later thought.[23] He admired Descartes and Kant, however, and supported a secularized vision of history, hostile to any form of "local" knowledge, privileging methodological individualism over holism, individualism over any form of community. Anxious not to isolate himself in one particular culture, Gellner saw himself, more than Berlin, as a European intellectual straight out of the rationalist tradition that Berlin, who presented himself as heir to Herder's culturalism, rejected. To Berlin, modernity superimposes cultural identifications and condemns religious fundamentalists: Gellner seems like a "fundamentalist of the Enlightenment" and continued the positivist heritage of Marx or Durkheim, to whom he devoted numerous studies.[24]

Starting from such an optimistic and somewhat mechanistic interpretation of the decline of cultural traditions, Gellner breaks the link between nationalism and identitiarian adherence. He thinks that nationalism linked to the expansion of industrial society represents "the organization of human groups into large, centrally educated, culturally homogenous units."[25] Far from Berlin and faithful to Renan, Gellner argues that adherence to the nation implies forgetting: "Anonymity, amnesia are essential; it is important not merely that each citizen learn the centralized, standardized and literate idiom in his primary school but also that he should forget or at least devaluate the dialect that is not taught at school."[26] Like Berlin, about whom he never speaks in his writings,[27] Gellner advocates saturation in the cultural logic unique to each nation, rejecting however the romantic dimension, the semi-ethnographic point of view supposed to depend on a given language, religion, or geography, which so influenced Berlin's nationalism, modeled on Herder. To Gellner, the nationalism he regards as functional and normal stems from modernity, and all the rest is only the product of the imagination, of the invention of a disappeared past, an outdated folklore. For him, repeating Renan's famous phrase, it is indeed "the everyday plebiscite" that justifies the existence of a nation and founds the nationalism of the state that embodies it.[28] Our two heroes diverge here, then, irremediably: one looks to Herder and a distant past for the source of common contemporary culture that feeds a legitimate nationalism; the other turns away from these romantic daydreams, can't speak harshly enough about them, and retains only the homogenizing action of the nation-state that implements from above a nationalist sentiment indispensable to solidarity in a society that has become, Durkheim-fashion, anomic. Reexamining even the period of the beginnings of the nineteenth century and the nationalistic reactions that are commonly supposed to come into existence in Germany or in Italy as a form of resistance to France, some people, in the vein of Gellner, think that the appearance of nationalist ideologies, for example in Fichte, does not by any means imply the birth of nationalist movements: they in fact constitute strategies for constructing a state, with the lure of nationalism less powerful in nonunified societies. Already at that time, consequently, unlike Berlin's constant vision, it is not nationalism that gives meaning to national identity, for the state assures this role by pursuing its task of control of the territory; moreover, Stein and other high Prussian functionaries who built the state turned out to be indifferent to nationalist ideologies.[29] Ignoring the identitarian nationalist trends that also appeared in Western Europe, in the industrialized regions, Gellner thought that dysfunctional nationalism occurs only in the East, with, for example, the collapse of the Soviet regimes.[30] A deep gulf separates him, then, from Berlin's approach: while Gellner mocked the ethnic or perennialist theories of the nation that are widespread these days throughout political theory, while he firmly rejected even the more nuanced positions of Anthony Smith, one of his former students who wrote his thesis under his guidance,[31] Berlin, like Herder, came over somewhat implicitly to the side of the supporters of these theories, ignoring the invented, reshaped, and often artificial aspect of contemporary nationalisms, whose existence he justified in light of a vague cultural, almost ethnic logic.

On one point, however, which concerns the identity of the two men, their opinion is identical. Assimilation in this national culture, whether it originates in a distant past or results from an artificial construction brought about by the state, does not occur without giving rise, for both men, to intolerable sufferings that long affect the immigrant who has come from outside and who is trying to settle down in his new nation. Though himself benefiting from substantial public recognition, like Berlin, Gellner nonetheless writes, in almost similar terms:

> Modern life *is* contact with bureaucrats. . . . It is this which pushes people into nationalism, into the need for the congruence between their own "culture" (the idiom in which they can express themselves and understand others) and that of the extensive and inter-connected bureaucracies which constitute their social environment. Non-congruence is not merely an inconvenience or a disadvantage: it means perpetual humiliation. . . . Nationalism is not explained by the use it

has in legitimizing modernization but by the fact that individuals find themselves in very stressful situations, unless the nationalist requirement of congruence between a man's culture and that of his environment is satisfied.[32]

Was the humiliation so great, despite his intellectual fame recognized by all, that Gellner left Great Britain and returned, in 1991, near the end of his life, to Prague, which he had left long ago in order to construct his life? Unlike Berlin, challenging even the most intimate cultural identifications, Gellner never, or almost never, mentioned his adherence to Judaism to account for this suffering:[33] Gellner was indifferent to Zionism and to his own Jewish identity even when, as an undeniable expert on the Muslim world, he underestimated the anti-Semitism present more often than he thought within Moroccan society.[34] Gellner went back to Prague, returned to the Czech nation from which Hitler's armies had once expelled him, and henceforth found himself confronted with other nationalist trends that were equally unsettling. He recognized in Vaclav Havel the heir of the good Masaryk preoccupied with morality, who professed a "liberal" nationalism opposed to "aggressive and romantic nationalism,"[35] and who knew enough to reject the accusations of ritual murder made against the Jews.[36]

Is it the radicality of his existence that rebels at identifications that are empty of meaning, like his adherence to Judaism, that turns Gellner, unlike Berlin, away from such a personal part of his own fate? Gellner debates fiercely with Hannah Arendt, who is active on all fronts, from successful assimilation in American society, to an articulated rejection of all assimilation that could affect a Jewish identity of the sort that Gellner deems largely imaginary, or even to a Zionism of pure convenience, since it does not imply a desire on her part to merge with a cultural logic unique to another nation. In the midst of so many contradictory attitudes, Arendt, who in Gellner's opinion had remained under the profound influence of a romanticism he abhors, is according to him transformed into a female Woody Allen, pitiful, dragging behind her a folklore stripped of meaning in modern Manhattan, in the heart of an American nation whose culture she does not share. "New York, like Königsberg, is a treacherous port," he notes. "But there the resemblance ends. America is a post-Enlightenment society: it was born modern. . . . America has no Goethe, and its intellectuals have no bitter-sweet love affair with the local folk culture or a nostalgia for its *Gemeinschaft*, whether real or illusory."[37] Gellner assassinated Hannah Arendt, whose work he deems hollow and lacking in rigor: "The verbosity, logical untidiness, impressionism and imprecision of her style make her contribution of dubious value."[38] On this point at least, he joins Isaiah Berlin, who does not hide his profound scorn for Arendt. Are these the vain screeches of strong personalities who are working in finally similar fields, between Enlightenment and romanticism, assimilation and Zionism, private space of negative freedom and public space of positive freedom? We don't really know. But for Berlin, who has nothing to say about Gellner, who in turn ignores his talented rival despite their shared interest in nationalism, Arendt "produces no arguments, no evidence of serious philosophical or historical thought. It is all a stream of metaphysical free association. She moves from one sentence to another, without logical connection, without either rational or imaginative links between them."[39] How kindly he expresses the matter! Berlin and Gellner do not think of themselves as "pariahs": they assume and call for assimilation into British culture despite the "sufferings" it occasions. For them, it is unthinkable to want to assume a position as pariah, voluntarily to assert a distance, to be or not to be a member of a society in the full sense of the word; society moreover would not tolerate it. Even though Berlin displays his Jewishness and his active solidarity with Israel, his inclusion in British society remains complete; the knight he became does not at all seem an English-style Woody Allen, even if the wound remains in his innermost being. Whence his reflections on the normality of nationalism that Arendt could not make her own, desirous as she is to merge with a space of pure citizens stripped of collective or particular national identities or else detached from specific cultural or religious groups to which she denies all legitimacy—so many dimensions that would mutilate citizenship in action.

Despite their profound differences, not the least of which is Berlin's unfailing loyalty for Great Britain, Berlin and Gellner, these two great Jewish intellectuals, British by adoption, emphasize the inevitable and desirable cultural homogenization unique to each society, the foundation of a normal, nonaggressive nationalism, indispensable to the socialization of citizens, to their recognition in a national space of mutual comprehension. A universe, however, separates the two thinkers as to the meaning of this nationalism. Explicitly challenging ethnic interpretations of nationalism, Gellner writes, "Nationalism is *not* the awakening of an old, latent, dormant force, though that is how it does indeed present itself. It is in reality the consequence of a new form of social organization based on a deeply internalized culture protected by its own state" that thus breaks the links with supposed roots that had remained unchanging throughout the centuries.[40] Berlin, however, thinks, for example, that the Dreyfus Affair "through the violent shock it produced awakened a dormant feeling of Jewish identity"; inverting Gellner's statement, he readily uses this metaphor that has become fashionable in those days in certain theoreticians of nationalism of the awakening of a dormant identity that has been preserved intact throughout time despite everything. Curiously, Berlin finds in the writings of Moses Hess, whom he so admires, this same metaphor of dormant identity: the Jews, Hess writes, have "slept a deep sleep under gravestones upon which various preachers have inscribed their soporific formulas."[41] In this sense, Berlin has nothing to say against the interpretation of Jewish history formulated by Zionist theoreticians: "Without accepting the consequences of a false racial theory, they thought and stressed that the Jews formed a worldwide community bound together by ties that would be qualified today as ethnic: a unified whole through a common origin, a memory, customs, loyalties, values and shared social and especially religious attitudes." While Gellner insists on the assimilation inherent in modern nationalism, with the Jews, about whom he doesn't say a word, being supposed according to this logic to merge like all their fellow citizens into the nation-state, Berlin irrevocably condemns the "grotesque contortions of assimilation"; his fanatical attachment to "Britishness" does not presuppose a rupture with the "ethnic" ties unique to the Jewish nation, of which Israel simply expresses the rebirth within public space.[42] In Berlin's opinion, in a liberal democracy, one can feel several loyalties: toward one's country and toward Israel. It's the famous question of the "dual allegiance": "I think that the Jews of the diaspora generally have the feeling that Israel is the center of their Jewish existence . . . without that in any way affecting the 'calm loyalty' they feel for their country of residence and of birth."[43]

To understand such a stance, surprising and complex on the part of a respectable member of society, one must consult the writings of Herder, who for a long time inspired Isaiah Berlin's view of the world. Herder is truly his mentor. In a repetitive, almost tiresome way, Berlin reveals his ideas, validates his rejection of the principles of the Enlightenment—incapable, according to him, of accounting for the extreme diversity of human societies by dint of proclaiming the unicity of humankind based on a universalist Reason: "According to this doctrine, to every well-formed question, there existed, in principle, one single reply: truth is one, error is multiple. Correct answers must, necessarily, be universal and fixed, that is to say true in every case, at all times, and for all men. One can find them thanks to a judicious use of reason, thanks to appropriate experiments, to observation, to experimental method, to logic, to calculation."[44] Such a claim seems to him unacceptable, all the more so since it comprises a closed vision of the world, a systematic explicative system that leaves little room for the imagination of individuals, for the pluralism of values; he also rejects it because it leads, in the end, to the temptation to impose a unique, restrictive political order based on the possession of Truth. For him, there is no worse monster than Utopia in its various guises, the unifying and simplifying image of a world actually plunged into an enriching diversity.[45]

Berlin stands unconditionally alongside Herder who "is indeed the first person to emphasize that the need to belong to a community is a basic human need, just as strong as that for eating, drinking, warmth, security. . . . Herder, so far as I know, was the first person who said that to belong to a community was an essential need. . . . Herder thinks that it is language, habits, gestures, instinctive reactions, that create unity and solidarity."[46] As he says again in his work *The Roots of Romanticism*, "The whole notion of being at home, or being cut off from one's natural roots, the whole idea of roots . . . was largely invented by Herder. . . . Herder does not use the criterion of blood or of race. Roughly speaking his argument is this: That which people who belong to the same group have in common is more directly responsible for their being as they are than that which they have in common with others in other places."[47] Herder expresses the humiliation of peoples dominated by a France that exports its universalist ideas by also imposing its political order: father of nationalism, he justifies the awakening of nations that are losing their identity when confronted with a dominating French society, which reigns as master during the entire seventeenth century in both spiritual and military sectors. Through Herder is expressed this "nationalist self-assertion" of nations denied in their identity. Against their standardization allegedly justified in the name of the Enlightenment, identical for everyone, he means to defend the necessary diversity of cultures in opposition to all homogenization, "the uniqueness of national cultures, above all their incommensurability, the differences in the criteria by which they could be understood and judged."[48] From one text to another, Berlin exonerates him from any vagrant impulse toward an aggressive nationalism: although Herder's writings were used by a number of nationalist ideologists until the present day, and although the triumph of the Nazis was brought about in the name of the return to the natural culture of a *Volk* whose cultural and social unity was for a long time denied by the Enlightenment, Berlin thinks that "Herder was no nationalist: he supposed that different cultures could and should flourish fruitfully side by side like so many peaceful flowers in the great human garden. . . . [In Herder's opinion] the world was like a garden, where each tree, each flower, grows in its own way. . . . This cut athwart the dominant *philosophia perennis*, the belief in the generality, uniformity, universality, timeless validity of objective and eternal laws and rules that apply everywhere, at all times, to all men and things."[49] Unlike Voltaire, Diderot, Holbach, and Condorcet, Herder is the first to advocate the romantic rebellion that rejects the aim of a universal civilization, the notion of progress that inevitably leads all nations, one after the other, toward a similar form of organization based on Reason.

In this sense, prudently, Berlin advances an iconoclastic thesis, namely that the anti-Enlightenment people tap into a part of truth that it would be pointless not to understand, all the more so since their principles have attracted the attention of a number of great thinkers in Eastern Europe, from Herder to Herzen, another hero of Berlin's whom, apparently, he physically resembled,[50] and who also spread this particularist message, this time in Russia. Herzen is a scholar with solid peasant roots whom Berlin admires so much that in a reply to a German newspaper that asked him about the person he would have liked to be, he unhesitatingly replied "Herzen": "For him, England was England, France was France, and Russia was Russia."[51] Like Herzen, Herder seems like the father of the romantic reaction: Berlin does not see him as a nationalist because his rejection of the violence a nation uses to serve its pretension to omnipotence, to preeminence, is constant. He thinks rather that Herder embodies the populist rejection of the standardization of cultures, of the rediscovery of traditional forms of existence: Herder "is the father, the ancestor, of all those travelers, all those amateurs, who go round the world ferreting out all kinds of forgotten forms of life . . . he feeds the streams of human sentimentality to a very high degree."[52] Romanticism thus rightly rediscovers, according to him, nations in their ancient particular cultural logic: Herder's message must, consequently, always be listened to, for it constitutes an appeal to revolt against established order in the name of a return to the autonomy of nations, to their cultural independence that liberates men and allows them to flourish within the cultural logics that alone recognize them.

Berlin likes to quote this sentence by Herder: "Every nation has its own inner center of happiness, as every sphere has its own center of gravity."[53] The feeling of "belonging" to a "home" is so vital that it renders ineffective any cosmopolitan factor of uprooting and rejects in advance any claim to the domination of another people, any form of colonization: "Every group has a right to be happy in its own way. It is a terrible arrogance to affirm that, to be happy, everyone should become European."[54] The pain Berlin felt throughout his life as a Jew perceived as such by British society, the distance that despite everything persisted in the home to which he gave his whole life, the subtle fissure in the feeling of "belonging," all say a lot about the implicit way he turned his attention to the writings of Herder. He saw in him a distant spokesman capable of explaining his own dissatisfaction, which left a shade of distance, of irremediable exteriority, to this man celebrated by everyone, this president of the British Academy listened to by the queen and by successive prime ministers, complimented by Churchill for the effectiveness of his work during the Second World War in the service of Her Majesty. "Is this nationalism?" Berlin wonders. "In an obvious sense it is. . . . A wounded national feeling breeds nationalism but it is important to realize that Herder's nationalism was never political."[55] This point is vital, for it authorizes Berlin to consider himself as "a moderate populist" who rejects aggressive, violent nationalism, one that seeks to negate differences and the Other.[56] He always remained faithful to this interpretation: when in February 1996 a Chinese professor from the University of Wuhan asked him to write an introductory text about his thinking for a Chinese audience, he once again mentions this distinction. In this text, published for the first time in May 1998 in English, he argues, courageously condemning the nationalist trends that an omnipotent party embodying a supposedly unique cultural identity are necessarily guilty of, that "Herder is the father of cultural nationalism. He is not a supporter of political nationalism (that kind of nationalism did not exist at that time), but he believes in the independence of cultures and in the necessity of preserving them in their unique dimension. . . . Herder was not a relativist theoretician."[57]

From that, how can one reconcile the universalism of the Enlightenment to which Herder and Berlin remained faithful with that insistence on the plurality of cultures and values, on their incommensurability? That is one of the great questions that Berlin asks himself throughout his life and that he resolves, seemingly, with difficulty. He means to preserve the lessons of the Enlightenment without toppling over to the side of romanticism, pessimism, and relativism, while still paying attention to the counterrevolutionary message: "Fundamentally, I am a liberal rationalist. The values of the Enlightenment, what people like Voltaire, Helvétius, Holbach, Condorcet preached, are deeply sympathetic to me. . . . They liberated people from horrors, obscurantism, fanaticism, monstrous views. . . . But they are dogmatic and too simplistic. I am interested in the views of the opposition. . . . I do not share, or even greatly admire, the views of these enemies of enlightenment, but I have learnt a good deal from them."[58] It should be said that Berlin pushes his admiration for Herder far, and for the counterrevolutionary trend humiliated by the French Revolution; he does not hide his attraction for the emotion that the romantics expressed, desirous of finding meaning in cultural identity. To such a point that, in a superb chapter devoted to Joseph de Maistre, he notes that "Maistre is our contemporary, too, in denouncing the impotence of abstract ideas and deductive methods. . . . Maistre was among the earliest thinkers to perceive the very great social and philosophical importance of such 'natural' institutions as linguistic habits, modes of speech, prejudices and national idiosyncrasies in moulding the character and beliefs of men."[59] For Berlin, Maistre's intuitions are close to those of Vico and Herder; he shares their rejection of a humanity that is disembodied so as to retain only the existence of peoples. What makes Maistre distasteful, however, is his proximity to Jacobin ways of thinking, which he execrates: Berlin admirably describes the parallel between Jacobin excesses and those of Maistre, both intoxicated by total visions of society. Berlin's conclusion, arguable in itself, but from this point of view close to the remarks formulated by J. Talmon, is that the fascism and totalitarianism engendered by Maistre's work, as well as his limitless taste for bloodshed, result partly in his upside-down Jacobinism: "Temperamentally he resembled his enemies . . . like them he was a total believer, a violent hater, a *jusqu'au boutiste* in all things. . . . Maistre was the polar opposite of this."[60] Berlin, who swims "against the current," following the example of nationalists who are possibly more acceptable like Herder, this time wound up with this unacceptable model. This prolonged and admiring study of counterrevolutionary thought poses some problems.

Desirous too of avoiding any accusation of relativism that would place him in a difficult position from the point of view of morality, human rights, and, simply, of his relationship with truth, Berlin sees in Herder a relativist in the acceptable sense of a pluralism compatible with the idea of one single human race. Given in 1964 as a lecture at Johns Hopkins University, his study on "Herder and the Enlightenment," published in 1965 and reprinted in 1976 in *Vico and Herder: Two Studies in the History of Ideas*, is again included in *The Proper Study of Mankind*, the English edition of which was published in February 1997, a few months before Berlin's death. As proof that until the end of his life Berlin continued to settle his accounts with the question of relativism, in this edition of a text that was more than thirty years old, he adds one single long note, written in 1996, in which he defends himself, just as he did in 1988 in his Agnelli lecture, from the accusation of relativism which was often made of him, especially by his friend Arnaldo Momigliano who saw himself forced to conclude that Berlin "must admit his defeat: one cannot reconcile, in the works of Vico and Herder, cultural pluralism with relativism. . . . Berlin leaves us alone faced with the question of the inevitability of moral relativism."[61] Repeating almost word for word his reply to Momigliano dated 1988, Berlin claims once again that "in the present study of Herder, I sometimes use 'relativism' not to mean a species of ethical or epistemological subjectivism but to refer to what I have elsewhere identified, I hope more perspicaciously as objective pluralism, free from any taint of subjectivism."[62] In his final text, written for a Chinese audience, Berlin returns to this one last time and takes up this distinction to which he is so partial: "I can enter a system of values that is not my own but that nevertheless represents a way followed by other human beings with whom I can communicate. . . . That is why pluralism is not relativism."[63]

Still, the crucial question is far from being settled in that way. Berlin himself admits it and spontaneously discusses the fluctuations of his own thinking: "Vico's and Herder's opposition to the central tenets of the French Enlightenment have commonly been described as a form of relativism. This *idée reçue* seems to me now to be a widespread error . . . an error which, I must admit, I have in the past perpetrated myself. . . . But I now believe this to be a mistaken interpretation of Vico and Herder, although I have, in my time, inadvertently contributed to it myself."[64] This veritable mea culpa repeated in a tone of contrition and regret indicates the importance of the issue from the point of the view of the meeting with or opposition between universalism and nationalism, between Enlightenment and nationalism, between liberalism and counterrevolution. Can one see in Berlin a "liberal hostile to the Enlightenment" who, faithful to the message of the Enlightenment,[65] wants only to rehabilitate pluralism, make compatible a pluralism of beliefs, maintaining a negative freedom that protects them, as opposed to positive freedom that threatens them by its public dimension, and unicity of mankind regarded as a space of communication between various cultures all sharing a similar ethics? Does he manage, in a coherent way, to avoid sinking into detestable relativism by proclaiming his simple attachment to a pluralist vision of the world acceptable by all supporters of liberalism? Alan Ryan is convinced of this and stresses this particularity of Berlin's thinking: "He was a liberal because he hated cruelty and a nationalist because he thought that each culture needs to flourish in the shelter of its own political system. These preoccupations are rare in American political philosophy."[66] This is what John Gray also seems to think, who asserts that Berlin is "almost alone among liberal theoreticians of the twentieth century" in continuing the perspective of Tocqueville or Stuart Mill by anchoring freedom in a national framework,[67] a common national culture, by turning away from the dominant tradition inspired by John Rawls focused on rights and justice, an equally strong point of view remote from all contractualist interpretations or, a fortiori, from the use about which Berlin doesn't say a word, the theory of rational choices as foundation of a democratic order; Berlin "seems to find in Romantic criticism hostile to liberalism a more vital support for liberal ideas than he could find in the Enlightenment";[68] paradoxically, in his opinion, tolerance, that essential value, would thus be hand in glove with the counterrevolution.

That is also what Michael Walzer thinks, who writes, "Pluralism can be revered as a necessary product of human liberty and creativity. But this celebration of pluralism does not imply relativism, for two reasons: first of all, because the discovery of a pluralist universe is a real discovery, one effectively observes the existence of many different visions of the world, of different legitimate and incompatible ways of conceiving of it; and then, because the freedom that gives birth to these visions is authentically precious."[69] Once again coming to the aid of Berlin, Walzer, in 1995, drives the point home and silences all his detractors: "Berlin is not a relativist. Certain beliefs, attitudes, practices, and ways of life—most obviously those associated with the Nazi and Communist dictatorships—he firmly rules out as inconsistent with our common humanity. But however this humanity is conceived, it doesn't entail political liberalism. There are (some) illiberal or not-liberal values, among them values associated with traditional religious belief, that are—here too he is no relativist—genuinely valuable." For Walzer, theoretician of a liberal communitarianism, the pluralism defended by Berlin differs completely, then, from the relativism of which his opponents, or even his friends, accuse him; he recalls, in approving of it, that, according to the author of *The Crooked Timber of Humanity*, pluralism does not only mean that "people hold many different, sometimes incommensurable, sometimes incompatible ideas about what is valuable, but that there actually are different, incommensurable, and incompatible values. Now, I know quite a few liberals who don't believe this."[70]

Faced with such positions endorsing theses that can still seem contradictory, Steven Lukes, on the contrary, fiercely attacks, with humor but also with vehemence, an attitude that finally consists, according to him, of an attack on universalism, a denial of a truth that is finally identical for everyone. In the *Times Literary Supplement*, a periodical that, like the *New York Review of Books*, serves as a veritable digest of the Berlin saga, so numerous are the articles in it devoted to Berlin, Lukes, although an admirer of the Oxford philosopher whom he often visited, lends his support to the criticism formulated by Momigliano and writes, "Can a pluralist, who holds that values can be plural, conflicting and even incommensurable, take them to be capable of being true or false, in a sense that does not collapse into 'true for us' or 'true for the Trobrianders' (and thus into relativism). At this crucial point, Berlin leaves us, as Momigliano observed, with an open question."[71] Berlin does not manage to decide between two equally legitimate but still almost contradictory points of view.[72] Caustic and ironic, Lukes wonders how pluralisms of this kind can defend themselves from a relativist attitude that consists of proclaiming, while respecting the values of each person and without ending up in judgments that necessarily stem from a reactionary philosophy, "liberalism for the liberals; cannibalism for the cannibals." For Lukes, Berlin's pluralism must, consequently, be defended against any possible deviation toward relativism, a point of view that may be acceptable when one considers the past but is insupportable when it is a matter of taking a stand in today's debates concerning, for example, the intervention of Amnesty International "or what to do in the face of the imminent threat to the Albanian inhabitants of Kosovo from a dominant, rabidly anti-pluralist nationalism; and if 'cannibalism' stands for an extinct and exotic way of life, from the study of which much value can be learned, then the case to be argued had better be: 'pluralism for the liberals; relativism for the cannibals'."[73]

This discussion takes a semitragic turn when one evokes examples of bloody nationalisms that openly reject pluralism. To avoid this dangerous rapprochement, Berlin tries to mark the distance that separates him from the major figures of nationalism who at first sight share so many similar ideas by comparing, for example, the discourse of Herder to that of Maistre. To do this, he tries to distinguish liberal nationalism from the bloody nationalism that he finds hateful. Faced with the desire of the Enlightenment to make the world uniform in the name of Reason, the rehabilitation of cultures—the sources of distinct nations—seems to him all the more legitimate since it does not imply, according to Herder himself, the often violent negation of other nations: in his opinion, this nationalism compatible with the pluralism of cultures does not at all imply a totalitarian nationalism, à la Joseph de Maistre with his limitless radicalism, his recourse to terror inspired by Jacobin practices. This point is essential, for under threat of falling in turn into an ideology from which everything distances him, Berlin must set the limits of this "soft" nationalism by clearing the name of Herder of the excesses committed in his name by his successors. Anxious to clear him of all suspicion, Berlin hesitates: at one point he argued that Herder, wrongly regarded as the father of German nationalism, was actually "anti-nationalist";[74] at another he sees him as the founder of a "nonaggressive nationalism" that is infinitely more acceptable;[75] at yet another he sounds an alarm against the "dangerous" nature of the nationalist claim in general, against "cultural relativism" that this nationalism "in theory" can serve as a vehicle for "opening the door to war of all against all"; he waxes ironic on the "florid and emotive prose," on "this kind of value-laden language" that appears in Herder, whom he then strangely places alongside Burke and Fichte, whose names are however associated, in Berlin's own writings, with Maistre, the sanguinary precursor of modern fascism; finally he wanted to see Herder only as the precursor of a nationalism "not tainted by aggressive nationalism" that is embodied in Mazzini's Young Italy, in Young Poland, in Young Russia, in the revolutionary movements of 1848, in the operas of Verdi—not in the writings of Treitschke or Barrès.[76]

After some hesitations, Berlin's religion is definitively decided: for him, Herder's writings on the *Volksgeist* and *Nationalgeist* express only

a nationalism that wants to preserve the rehabilitation of the awareness of belonging to a group that was denied by French universalism.
Berlin thinks that "under the impact of the French revolutionary and
Napoleonic invasions, cultural or spiritual autonomy, for which Herder
had originally pleaded, turned into embittered and aggressive nationalist self-assertion."[77] "Pathological form of self-defense" engendered
by "a wounded national consciousness," this nationalism takes, in this
perspective, extreme forms in societies that experience a Durkheimian
anomie, the "vacuum" produced by destruction, under the impact of
industrialization and bureaucratization, of traditional hierarchies, the
old social order in which people's feelings of loyalty were profoundly
invested. Anomie and alienation provoke a call to a "real or imaginary"
past, a desire to go back to the lost *Gemeinschaft*.[78] We will not linger
here over the rather summary nature of the interpretation offered by
Berlin on Durkheimian anomie, a concept that is however more rigorous and does not necessarily lend itself to such extrapolations. It is still
used by Berlin, accompanied by the sempiternal "bureaucratization of
the world" of Weber, to apprehend, with the help of a sociological vocabulary from which he often unhesitatingly deviates, the rise of radical
nationalism, which he condemns, this time attributing it to causes that
are scarcely different from those that motivated Maistre's, Herder's, or
Fichte's revolt. This extreme form of nationalism arises, according to
him, in Germany or Russia before spreading throughout the world as
a remedy for the humiliations imposed by a rationalism that scorns the
various cultural identities and replaces them with an "alienating" social
and political order. Unlike Italian nationalism à la Garibaldi, whose
attachment to liberalism Berlin praises, these movements of reaction
to the French Revolution and, later on, to the Versailles Treaty which
writes off as a total loss artificially reshaped national identities, to colo-
nizing imperialism disdainful of the cultures of the conquered populations, or, finally, to the Soviet attempts at imposing a unique order by
relegating dominated nations to the margins of history, all take root in
a determined rejection of a sociopolitical order that brings "emptiness"
and negates all cultures. From modernity associated with industrialization and bureaucratization stems the violence of their rejection.

Starting from a constant logic animated by a wish to rehabilitate the diversity of cultures, to found a moral, fundamentally pluralistic order, Berlin many times modifies the variables taken into account to understand nationalism. Sometimes it is the French-style Enlightenment, then the French Revolution and Napoleon that, through their suddenly imposed universalist dreams, justify the reaction, regarded as nonaggressive, of Herder, whose name is nevertheless linked at times with Fichte or, by association, with Maistre; sometimes, it is, reluctantly, Kant—who detested Herder's traditionalist emotions, who was the man of the Enlightenment, the zealot of Reason, the cosmopolitan opposed to nationalism—who, through his insistence on the freedom of the subject and on free will, unintentionally justified the nationalist romanticism of Fichte, who would have horrified him;[79] sometimes, it is the sociological variables that, in a context of reaction to universalism regarded as crippling, more directly provoke the emergence of openly aggressive nationalisms; sometimes, finally, it's the Soviet version of French-style rationalism with the implementation of a sociopolitical order that is just as alienating and conducive to the "vacuum" that logically leads to these extreme forms of contemporary nationalism. In every case, Berlin's "Britishness," associated with respect for cultures and traditions, fortunately serves as bulwark against all these nationalist temptations. And his anti-French charge can on the contrary be a source of great enjoyment. *Cherchez la femme, cherchez le Français*: Rousseau or Diderot, Robespierre, Napoleon Bonaparte or de Maistre, even Louis XIV himself will do, who was already pursuing, according to Berlin, a rationalizing aim of assimilationist standardization fundamentally foreign to the customs of Her Majesty's kingdom. Berlin found a permanent explanation for the nationalisms that bubbled up throughout the course of history: from the seventeenth century to the present day, it is always a question of French expansionist arrogance that imposes, under cover of universalism and through various masks and ideologies, its rationalist, state-based vision that wants to unify the world, a vision Berlin wholeheartedly rejects and which he accuses of all evils.[80]

Nevertheless, faced with so many competing explanations of the rise of nationalisms, their rise seems to rest on highly dissimilar historical facts that all justify the legitimate return to identitarian consciousness.

One cannot deny the presence, in the writings of Berlin, of preoccupations comparable to those that the more orthodox communitarian thinkers of today share, who however are scarcely concerned with liberalism or even universalism. The fact that Charles Taylor, the theoretician of the politics of recognition that was the source, in large part, of the American multiculturalist trend, pays homage to Herder in a recent work written in honor of Isaiah Berlin stresses the close proximity of these approaches. A student of Berlin's at Oxford, Taylor continues his inspiration by transposing his lesson onto complex societies, not unified ones as in Herder. He shows how, in the United States and in Canada, the claiming of particular identities leads, here, to multiculturalism, there, to a toned-down version of nationalism, to the demand for autonomy and even, for some, for political independence, which, still in the perspective of Herder and Berlin, is alone capable of protecting a collective cultural identity thanks to which the profound sense of self can finally flourish. In Taylor's opinion, "Herder's notion that the primary locus of a language was the *Volk* which carried it. Humboldt takes up the same insight. Language is shaped by speech, and so can grow up only in a speech community. . . . We can say that it is not just the speech community which shapes and creates language, but language which constitutes and sustains the speech community."[81] Intervening recently in a purely imaginary meeting between Isaiah Berlin, with whom he was close, and Ernest Gellner, Taylor, faithful to the logic of Herder that inspired Berlin, challenges the idea put forward by Gellner according to which it is the state that invents nationalism and imposes a cultural homogenization that is indispensable for solidarity among citizens of the same national community. For Taylor, nationalism emerges, on the contrary, from the legitimate "emotion" shared by individuals whose language is not recognized by the state: he discusses the desire for recognition, and for political secession if necessary, the constitution of another political order capable of identifying with this denied language, with this culture refused by the state. The perspectives of Herder, Berlin, or Taylor are here at opposite poles from those of Gellner. If, for Gellner, nationalism can fade away once the modern nation-state is solidly constructed around a homogeneous culture, Taylor thinks on the contrary that nationalism, far from being an atavistic reaction or even a purely modern and temporary phenomenon implemented by the state, that is to say the almost artificial creation of a common consciousness imposed from above, consists of "a call to difference." For Taylor, "in the modern world, identities are more and more formed in this direct relation to others, in a space of recognition. . . . Modern nationalist politics is a species of identity politics. . . . Understanding nationalism in terms of a 'call to difference' allows for a great variety of different responses." As we see, Taylor's position strays from Herder's and Berlin's, which presuppose the continuity of a culture, the awakening of "dormant identities," while Taylor thinks that national communities, in order to be legitimate, are also to a large extent "imagined."[82] His interpretation also diverges from theirs by opening the way to nonnational forms of recognition that imply considerable rearrangements of the national space of the state that loses its unity, as in the case of Canada, a hypothesis that Berlin can only condemn, for instance when he writes, in a little-known and surprising text, "I must confess my pro-British inclination. . . . Everything I have done and thought remains unquestionably British. I cannot judge British values impartially, for they are a part of myself. . . . All this is profoundly and uniquely British, and I freely admit that I am marked by it, I believe in these values, and I could breathe freely only in a society where these values are regarded as more or less obvious."[83] Immersed in his "Britishness," a subject of Her Gracious Majesty down to his bones, Berlin cannot conceive of coming over to the side of separatist values, of the emergence of a cultural nationalism that is internal, in the vein of Herder, but that also bears with it a demand that breaks the unity of the nation made of longstanding shared traditions, not imposed by the state, à la Gellner, but immanent and natural. The teacher, raised with a love for *Britannia*, for a common cultural code, for a way of life that draws its logic from a distant past, separates himself from Charles Taylor, his student, who foresees cultural or political secession in the name of a nationalism that may be ridiculed, but that emanates this time from within the nation itself. Whence the somewhat scornful condemnation by Berlin of the American multiculturalism that nonetheless finds an attentive ear in two of his closest followers, Charles Taylor and, to a lesser degree, Michael Walzer. Questioned about his appreciation of multi-culturalism, Berlin, in a curious synthesis of his irreducibly Herderian vision of the world not without prejudices, answers with this surprising text, which openly endorses a vision of a "normal" nationalism, alone capable of serving as vehicle for an innovative culture:

> Yes, I know. Black studies, Puerto Rican studies, and the rest. I suppose this too is a bent-twig revolt of minorities which feel at a disadvantage in the context of American polyethnicity. But I believe that the common culture which all societies deeply need can only be disrupted by more than a moderate degree of self-assertion on the part of ethnic or other minorities conscious of a common identity. Polyethnicity was not Herder's idea. He didn't urge the Germans to study Dutch or German students to study the culture of the Portuguese. . . . Herder, I think, would have looked unkindly on the cultural friction generated in Vienna, where many nationalities were crammed into the same narrow space. It produced men of genius, but with a deeply neurotic element in a good many of them—one need only think of Gustav Mahler, Ludwig Wittgenstein, Karl Kraus, Arnold Schoenberg, Stefan Zweig, and the birth of psychoanalysis in this largely Jewish—particularly defenseless—society. All that tremendous collision of not very compatible cultures—Slavs, Italians, Germans, Jews—unleashed a great deal of creativity. This was a different kind of cultural expression from that of an earlier Vienna, that of Mozart or Haydn or Schubert.[84]

We can sense immediately what side his heart is leaning toward, where his preferences as a former president of Covent Garden lie, sensitive to the music coming from a homogeneous culture, according to the good precepts of Dr. Herder, resistant to the innovations of a Schoenberg or a Mahler who on the contrary found their sources in a mosaic of distinct cultures artificially gathered together under the aegis of a bureaucratic state, a state which was close, it is true, in its administrative institutions and the values of its high functionaries attached above all to defending the supremacy of a supranational state, to the French example, so harshly rejected. What an incredible condemnation, without any nuance, of fin-de-siècle Vienna, of its creativity regarded as "neurotic" and stemming from a shared and contradictory identity, from the anxiety and uncertainty of a Wittgenstein or a Freud! At bottom, Berlin cannot bear either the culture stemming from a strongly heterogeneous society like that of the Austro-Hungarian Empire, or the culture emanating from a society homogenized around universalism, not starting from a specific cultural code. In the first case, he condemns all the "neurotic" Jewish creators of Vienna; in the other, he wages war against the French-style intellectuals, mocks their pretensions, their pedantic manners, their airs of brilliant drawing-room conversationalists, their often high social status; he doesn't have words harsh enough for Condorcet or Mably, for d'Holbach or d'Alembert, Rousseau or Diderot, Rameau or Couperin, no one finds favor with him. Following the provincial and pietistic Herder, Berlin feels on the contrary close to Bach or Mozart, Haydn or Lessing, Hegel, Schelling, or Hölderlin, all creators from more modest social origins, more concerned with their inner lives, anxious about their cultural and religious place in provincial life that makes them allergic to French-style drawing-room intellectuals. Berlin shows he is sensitive to the romantic aspect of these men wounded in their allegiance to the particular mutilated culture that surrounds them.[85]

What scorn on the part of Her Majesty's knight, close to Saul Bellow's scorn for American-style "cultural studies"! Formulated in caustic terms, of an extravagant relativism in favor of the survival of all cultures provided each of them remains homogeneous, the strict Herderian position, which recognizes different cultures, their right to mark their specificity, can also lead to justification of their separation, for, in order to remain fertile, each must preserve its own language, the source of its imagination. While understanding the logic of such a culturalist interpretation of knowledge, doesn't one risk falling into the differentialist visions advocated, for example, in France, by the extreme right? Modifying the phrase by Steven Lukes, we could then write, "relativism for the liberals as well as for the cannibals." In top form and Herderian to the core, Berlin ends this subversive interview with a surprising lamentation about the mass culture exemplified by the singer Madonna, a lamentation that is easily justified but that is still phrased in terms too compatible with preservation of a salvationist relativism: if this sort of artificial culture prevails to the point of the extinction of local cultures, in Polynesia or in the Caucasus, then, he confides, "that would be the death of culture. I am glad to be as old as I am."[86]

The fact remains that Berlin, who means to appear faithful to Judaism, is gnawed by a private contradiction that he affects elegantly to master, without any apparent crisis of conscience: How can one seem Herderian "from within," favoring a distinct culture, and Herderian "from without," by acting in favor of a homogeneous national culture? This problem is not unique to Berlin, for the multiculturalist theory confronts a similar difficulty by falling smoothly into an internal nationalism that almost inevitably calls into question external nationalism.[87] All of a sudden, even if Berlin cannot be perceived as an internal communitarian insofar as he means to remain faithful to Jewish culture and its practices, even if he doesn't ask, like Taylor, for communitarian recognition within the public space, he necessarily distances himself, reluctantly, from the strict Herderian position that supports a national, homogeneous culture. These hesitations bring him closer, whatever he may think of them, to his student, Charles Taylor. Embodiment of the Oxford-style intellectual, enjoying national prestige, representing to everyone the British mind, hostile to any shade of multiculturalism, Berlin knows that he remains Jewish, different from his fellow citizens, a "Russian Jew," and that he will die thus. Indeed, he does not advocate a form of communitarianism in Great Britain that could bring him closer to Taylor and distance him from Herder; if he actively participates in the life of English Jewish institutions, it is not in the name of a communitarian demand for collective recognition. He even warns the Jews who live in Great Britain that it is not a question of "producing a version, even a toned-down one, of the State within the State."[88] Berlin would have been surprised that one could compare his thinking to the "ethnic" rights that "colored people," as he calls them, claimed in Great Britain. Still, he wants to maintain a Jewish tradition with its ways of thinking; he wants to continue a Jewish history. Moreover, he does not hide his long-standing support for Zionism, a nationalist movement of rupture from the common cultural code whose aim is to create, elsewhere, a homogeneous nation, by calling into question the assimilation of Jews in societies that have emancipated them, from Great Britain to France. This spirit of secession, which remains virtual in his mind, still represents an attack on homogeneous culture of national adherence in the Herderian mode: it unexpectedly brings closer the nationalist aims of rearrangement of national unity pursued by Charles Taylor, even if Berlin challenged any strictly communitarian identitarian vision.

As if to reassure himself before his a priori unliberal choice of a hero, Berlin delights in stressing Herder's philo-Semitism, thereby justifying his own identification with Jewish culture. In his seminal text, "Herder and the Enlightenment," Berlin notes, "Herder was fascinated by the survival of the Jews; he looked upon them as a most excellent example of a *Volk* with its own distinct character."[89] Still, this way is strewn with hazards, since Herder's unquestionable philo-Semitism, his recognition of a living Jewish culture issuing from the dawn of time, is accompanied by a wish to see the Jews reconstruct a particular nation, shaped by its distinct culture: in Herder's eyes, such a return to collective existence must necessarily go through establishment on a particular territory that serves as an indispensable foundation for cultural rebirth. He implies leaving the nation of residency, which breaks allegiance with the original national culture, isolating from his fellow-citizens whoever adheres to this original form of decolonization brought to a distant territory. Berlin congratulates Herder on his Zionist philo-Semitism without realizing that this perspective, which favors a return to Zion, is shared by the most violent and most determined supporters of anti-Semitism who have only one wish: to see the Jews break all ties with a nation that is supposed to be foreign to them in order to settle, among themselves, in Palestine where they will be free to celebrate their own culture, to which they are so attached.[90] "The Jews," Berlin observes,

> are typical for Herder of a remarkably fertile native culture which managed to survive. That's why he says that we have to understand how these Judaens lived and felt and thought, to understand the Bible which was their national epic. . . . That is why Herder is interested in the Jews, and he wants every little cultural entity to survive and develop and not be crushed. . . . If you replant the Jews in Palestine there will be a nation again. This is not sympathy of German Jews like Mendelssohn who believed in some form of integration, but it's the belief that the Jews have their own contribution, which they cannot make if they are absorbed by other cultures. . . . [Herder] blames the Jews for not going back to Palestine.[91]

The condemnation of the project for reform of Judaism led by Mendelssohn is complete: his translation of the Old Testament into German, his search for integration into the German nation that limits Judaism to a religion of the soul compatible with immersion in Germanic *Volk*, a project acclaimed by generations of German Jews who identified with Goethe's *Bildung*, is, in the opinion of Herder and Berlin, invalid from the beginning. In these conditions, what harsher words could they both have against the "regeneration" of French Jews pursued by the French Revolution and the Third Republic, against the Reinachs and even the Durkheims who identify with this search for integration into the nation and who both severely condemn the Zionist renaissance! In this vein, Berlin mentions several times, mockingly, the phrase of Lord Edwin Samuel Montagu who, a brilliant minister of Her Majesty, faced with the horror of such a Zionist perspective that he rejected with all his strength, declared to his colleagues that he flatly refused to be sent to a ghetto![92]

Berlin, however, finds himself in an awkward position, between the British identity that he preserves in his innermost being and his desire, always publicly asserted, to maintain his fidelity to Judaism. Here, without recognizing it, he distances himself from Herder and comes closer to the multiculturalist Charles Taylor: "So long as they don't fight each other and are not aggressive," he writes, "why shouldn't you allow people to develop their own culture in their own way? Let us take the Black problem in America: integration and autonomy for the Blacks are terrible problems. It is the same thing with coloured people in England. I mean in theory we ought to have peaceful, well-integrated, multi-cultural societies, but clearly it's not something that is easily achieved."[93] In "theory" the multiculturalism dear to Charles Taylor or to Michael Walzer is finally imaginable, and Berlin, curiously, sees nothing more to say about it.[94] But what is to be done if these demands for cultural recognition end up in aggression and the war of all cultural identities against all the others? Does cultural pluralism, legitimate in itself, lead to relativism, to some peoples being closed to others in the name of different cultures that are valued as such? Is the war that nations wage with each other in the name of their superiority of culture coupled with a latent internal war between communities anxious to mark their differences but also, potentially, their superiorities? Berlin does not want to envisage this perspective, either within or without: he has a believer's faith that, as Herder said, nationalisms do not necessarily adopt an aggressive form. They are even compatible with each other to such a point that Berlin expresses his profound "Britishness" as well as his Judaism, which is undeniable and, what is more, ever-sensitive to the siren calls of Zionism.

Berlin's writings on Judaism and Zionism are countless and widely spread out; they have never been the subject for a collection of essays, so many of which have been published by gathering together his "noblest" articles, to the point that some are repeated from one book to another. The link between "normal" science and Jewish identitarian preoccupations is however so close in his work that aside from a few writings on logic or epistemology, one can't really dissociate these two dimensions. Very logically, when Berlin approaches the Jewish condition throughout time, he endlessly refers, as is his habit, to his favorite philosophers, to those who justify attachment to traditions and timeless fidelity to values, like Herder or Burke or even Fichte. Thus, in the opening pages of his remarkable text "Disraeli and Marx," Berlin invokes Herder's way of thinking to analyze the way these thinkers are situated in relation to a "need to belong to a particular group, united by some common links—especially language, collective memories, continuous life upon the same soil, to which some added characteristics of which we have heard much in our time—race, blood, religion, a sense of common mission, and the like."[95] In Berlin's opinion, Disraeli and Marx, both converts, project this need of belonging onto the nobility for one of them or onto the proletariat for the other; at the same time, the former evinces a boundless Jewish pride, while the latter—and Berlin often emphasizes this dimension of Marx's personality—does not hesitate to use the most hackneyed anti-Semitic expressions, thus displaying a kind of radical self-hatred that Berlin frequently condemns. For the Oxford philosopher, "His origin obviously constituted a stigmatization that he didn't manage to hide from others; his rejection of the importance of national and religious ties, his insistence on the international nature of the proletariat, was cloaked in a very particular harshness of tone."[96]

In the same sense, when Berlin devotes a long study to Moses Hess, the friend of Heinrich Graetz, Berlin's second hero, the one who best symbolizes the desire to favor the rebirth of a Jewish nation faithful to its past, Berlin stresses the similarity of Hess's views to those of Herder and even argues that Hess "believed deeply in the faithful preservation of historical tradition. He spoke about this in language scarcely less fervent, but a good deal less biased and irrational, than Burke or Fichte."[97] When Berlin tirelessly and enthusiastically describes the Zionist adventure and merits of his third hero, Chaim Weizmann, he again writes, "Jewish Palestine [is in] profound continuity with the immediate Jewish past. You might well ask, how can a state be constructed artificially? Is it really feasible to put up a pre-fabricated society? Even if one does not fully accept the traditionalist views of Burke and his brand of conservatives, one is liable to be told that states cannot be made, they must grow. . . . There must be roots, growth, soil. There must be an imperceptible traditional accumulation, a sort of precipitate of tradition throughout the ages."[98]

In a very Herderian spirit, and in conformity with his own general theory, Berlin stresses how his "Jewish roots [are] so profound, so natural." He then writes the following text, which continues, this time from the point of view of the history of the Jews, his reflections hostile to cosmopolitanism and to the Enlightenment:

> I have never been tempted, despite my long defence of individual liberty which you have been good enough to speak about, to march with those who, in the name of such liberty, reject adherence to a particular nation, community, culture, tradition, language, the "myriad impalpable strands," subtle but real, that bind me into identifiable groups. This rejection of natural ties seems to me noble but misguided. When men complain of loneliness, what they mean is that nobody understand what they are saying: to be understood is to share a common past, common feelings and language, common assumptions, possibility of intimate communications—in short, to share common forms of life. This is an essential human need: to deny it is a dangerous fallacy. To be cut off from one's familiar environment is to be condemned to wither. Two thousand years of Jewish history have been nothing but a single longing to return, to cease being strangers everywhere; morning and evening, the exiles have prayed for a

renewal of the days of old—to be one people again, living normal lives
on their own soil—the only condition in which individuals can live
unbowed and realise their potential fully; no men can do that if they
are a permanent minority—worse still, a minority everywhere, without a national base. . . . Such criticisms as I have made of the doctrines
of the French Enlightenment and of its lack of sympathy for emotional
bonds between members of races and cultures, and its idealistic but
hollow doctrinaire internationalism, spring, in my case, from this almost instinctive sense of one's own roots—Jewish roots, in my case—
of the brotherhood of a common predicament—utterly different from
a quest for national glory—from a sense of fraternity—perhaps most
real among the masses of the poor and socially depressed, especially
my ancestors, the poor but literate and socially cohesive Jews of Eastern Europe—something that has grown thin and abstract in the West
where I have lived my life.[99]

All the themes of political theory having to do with recognition
find their intellectual origin here, in this Herderian cultural tradition
critical of the crippling abstraction of the Enlightenment, in a desire
to proclaim the natural characteristic of a self "molded" in culture, a
"thick" self and not a "thin," inconsistent one, reduced to solitude, to
the impossibility of communicating with others, a position that, despite his fundamental liberalism and his limited acceptance of a plurality of identities, inevitably brings Berlin closer to Charles Taylor and
distances him from Michael Walzer. Perhaps it also prevents him from
glimpsing, like the author of *The Politics of Recognition*, the conditions,
difficult as they are to implement, of a civic multiculturalism neither
"primordialist" nor ethnic.[100] As we see, the great debates of contemporary political theory are linked directly by Berlin to his considerations
on Jewish destiny, on his own need for recognition. Witness this text
in which he invites the Jews to go, at least as tourists, to Israel in order
to discover for themselves the origin of their identity: "The first thing
a man should know, if he wants to be free and not remain under the
influence of illusions and ignorance, if he wants to know who he is and
what his place is, is not to forget where he comes from, the history of
the group to which he belongs, why his family and himself, his community and his people think and feel and act as they do."[101] To do this,
it is imperative for every Jew to go to Israel.

Berlin's approach to Jewish history is, like all his work, widely influenced by a primordialism supposedly compatible with the birth, always according to Herderian logic, of a nonaggressive nationalism. Berlin often evokes, in this sense, the hypothesis of a "dormant" identity that, once awakened, justifies nationalist rebirth. He likes to play, on this subject, with the metaphor of the glacier that symbolizes the profound identity of the Jewish people capable of crossing the ages unchanged even if it sees some of its members stray from it who leave it by assimilation with the environment: in fact, the crust of the glacier, exposed to the sun, decomposes and flows into countless streams that end up disappearing into nature. In an inspired text, "Jewish Slavery and Emancipation," Berlin uses at length, following his historian friend Sir Lewis Namier, himself a Jew who to everyone's surprise ended up converting, this image of the glacier representing the Jewish mass in its entirety whose most exposed part, under the influence of the Enlightenment, had "disappeared by evaporation," by assimilation into global society, while "the heart of the glacier remained hard and frozen." Optimistic, Berlin thinks that "the evaporation" only affects a "negligible proportion" and thinks that "as a radical solution . . . it was a failure." He maintains, however, that "there is no future in the heart of this lifeless glacier, in this forever frozen mass," and he thinks that historical transformations finally impose a general thaw, a radical modification of this Jewish people from Eastern Europe who remained sheltered from the Enlightenment but fixed in their traditions and their culture, transformations that can only push it toward the Zionist solution, which he himself advocates as a substitute for assimilation.[102]

These Jews "frozen" in their identity—a bit like how these days people commonly talk about peoples from Eastern Europe who managed to preserve their identity "in the icebox" during the era of the Soviet glaciation, a parallel that makes sense to the extent that Bolshevism also invoked the name of the Enlightenment and, although it toyed with it, also revealed itself to be hostile to nationalism—were able to avoid the assimilationist temptations of Jews placed close to the "crust." They also differ, for Berlin, from those "who couldn't manage either to evaporate or to remain frozen": they lived through "a history of anxiety and unawareness," "of suffering," "they lowered their voices below a whisper. They imitated others with a confounding skill. . . . And all that served no purpose whatsoever." Despite everything, they do not "form an organic part" of the people into which they are trying to merge, who end up "turning against them." "This parable," Berlin adds, "illustrates the fate of the Jews in Europe and in America."[103] Berlin on the contrary takes a stand in favor of Jews who, in such a context, according to a nicely imagined formulation, "remained betwixt and between, unmoored from one bank without reaching the other, tantalized by incapable of yielding, complicated, somewhat tormented figures, floating in midstream";[104] while they sought to distance themselves in the name of universalism, of the great human fraternity, they return to Judaism, resume their Jewish surnames or first names, turn away from "empty and artificial cosmopolitanism," and like Moses Hess, the former companion of Marx and for a long time a delegate of the First Internationale, henceforth turn their attention to Jerusalem and stray away from an internationalist socialism that denies nations and deliberately ignores the Jewish destiny.[105] For Berlin, Moses Hess's book, *Rome and Jerusalem*, is a "masterpiece" in which "the morbid condition that Hess seeks to diagnose and cure has not vanished. . . . The conscientious internationalism of his young Hegelian days was replaced by the realization (it seems destined to come, late or soon, to almost every Jewish social thinker, whatever his views) that the Jewish problem is something *sui generis*, and seems to need a specific solution of its own, since it resists the solvent of even the most powerful universal panaceas."[106] As we have noted, Berlin overdid himself in showing himself convinced that every Jewish thinker cannot help but arrive at conclusions identical to those of Moses Hess, whose "simple and moving book . . . still contains more truth about the Jews, both in the nineteenth century and in our own, than any comparable work."[107]

Berlin shows his Zionist convictions in his early youth and always stands by them. Forcefully, in very poetic language, he writes that the Jews "pray for rain or dew at the seasons at which their forefathers did so in the Holy Land. . . . Everything that comes from Palestine, everything that reminds them of it, moves them and is dear to them as nothing else."[108] Berlin does not recoil from the repeated use of a certain vocabulary ("my forefathers," "my ancestors"), which inscribes him in the long biblical tradition; he is moved by Hess's return to Judaism, who firmly announces, "Here I am again, after twenty years of separation, in the midst of my own people,"[109] without fearing the mockeries of Marx or Engels, who wax ironic about "Rabbi Hess" or "Rabbi Moses." Berlin knows the price of this return to "normality": though he scarcely has any consideration for Mahler or Freud, deeming their historical context and their relationship to culture both neurotic and cosmopolitan, though he condemns, nevertheless, the rationalist and assimilationist efforts of Mendelssohn and Hermann Cohen, he knows that the state of a "nation among nations" will certainly entrain, to his delight, the end of the assimilationist "evaporation" that perverted German Judaism, and the end of a "pathological" creativity which struck the intellectuals and artists of the Austro-Hungarian Empire. That the fate of the Jews is to constitute, according to the ironic expression of Alexandre Kojève, another "Albania," that is to say simply a little country among others, supposedly without any particular history, Berlin accepts fully in a strange dialogue with the Hegelian philosopher who does not hide his pained surprise.[110] The standardization implemented by Zionism hardly alarms him: Berlin strays from traditional Jewish messianic visions for which Ernst Bloch made himself a spokesman by deploring, for his part, the idea that the Jews could tomorrow constitute an "Asiatic state of a Balkan nature."[111]

The flamboyant Oxford philosopher shows he is ready to do everything to help the birth of this banal "Albania." His implication in the creation of Israel is impressive, to such a point that Chaim Weizmann, the man he admires most for his moderate Zionist leanings, faithful despite the vicissitudes and denials to British politics, from which they each expect everything, asked Berlin to come join him in Israel to serve as his right-hand man within the Jewish Agency, an offer that Berlin nonetheless declines. Berlin continually sings the praises of his friend who, to his mind, seems to him to continue Herderian logic: in this sense, he compares him to Garibaldi or to Kossuth, to Moses or to Nehru, or even to Cavour. Weizmann could, according to Berlin, express the values of his "community":

> His language, his images, his turns of phrase were rooted in Jewish tradition and piety and learning. . . . He was not a religiously orthodox

Jew, but he lived the full life of a Jew. He had no love for clericalism, but he possessed an affectionate familiarity with every detail of the rich, traditional life of the devout and observant Jewish communities, as it was lived in his childhood, in the villages and small towns of eastern Europe. . . . I was present on more than one occasion, towards the end of his life, when he celebrated the *Seder* service of the Passover with a moving dignity and nobility, like the Jewish patriarch that he had become. In this sense he had always lived in close contact with the life of the Jewish masses.[112]

Berlin's activity on behalf of the Zionist engagement is revealed to be tireless and determined, public, visible to everyone. In 1934, he went for the first time to Palestine, visited the kibbutzes, walked around Tel-Aviv, wove his way between British officials with whom he was so close in culture and values and Zionist friends firmly opposed to British politics. A little later he met Chaim Weizmann in New York, at the same time that Great Britain was taking steps to favor the Arabs and limit Jewish emigration. From Berlin's official post in Washington where, from January 1941, his mission was to facilitate America's entering the war and to inform British authorities about the development of American opinion as well as the state of mind of the country's leaders, he also worked with Jewish organizations that risked becoming hostile to Great Britain because of its policies favoring the Arabs; in the American capital, he found his friend Weizmann, also sent by the English government to influence American Jews in its favor. Berlin then played a decisive role between Weizmann and the British government, between Weizmann and Ben Gurion, going from one to the other to pacify conflicts, to the point that the British secret services began to wonder about Berlin's loyalty to the Crown.[113] His dispatches very often show the influence acquired by American Zionists, who "represent five million voters," with the American government, with the political elite, and with American journalists, whom Great Britain urgently needed for its war effort. Berlin particularly insisted on the Zionist sympathies of President Truman, on the essential role of Zionist groups in the reelection of the mayor of New York, La Guardia, and on the dependence on the "Zionist battalions" of Senators Taft and Wagner, thus sounding the alarm to the British leaders about the consequences of their policies in the Middle East.[114]

During the entire war, Berlin sent the best information possible to his government, to the great satisfaction of Winston Churchill. He tried at the same time to limit the anger of American Jews, supported as best he cound Weizmann's moderate policies, facilitated the creation of a Palestinian Regiment, and tried to reduce the strongly pro-Arab influence of the Foreign Office. Having learned that the American and British governments, out of fear of losing Arab support, were getting ready to make a declaration hostile to Zionism, he let the American Zionist leaders know before turning to Lord Halifax to warn him that this declaration, which had mysteriously become known to everyone, would provoke wrath against Great Britain; this bold move brought a sudden end to the plan. Troubled by his own behavior between two loyalties to nations that oppose each other, Berlin henceforth never held himself apart, even though he did try to convince the British to raise the ban against all Jewish immigration to Palestine, an urgent decision that could perhaps save a million people. Still active after the war, a defender of the Zionist cause but also of Her Majesty's interests, he wrote part of the speech given by Weizmann in 1946 in Basel before the Zionist Congress, in which Weizmann firmly condemned the terrorist actions against the British. In July 1947, he went to Palestine at Weizmann's request, when the British had just prevented the Exodus from occurring, when war was being waged between the English army and the Zionist militants of Palestine. There he met his uncle by marriage, Yitzhak Sadeh, one of the leaders of the Palmach, a clandestine elite group that confronted the British armed with weapons. Before such an imbroglio, faced with the complexity of his own feelings, he little by little renounced all direct involvement in a cause that was too openly hostile to the British world, nonetheless congratulating Weizmann on his election as head of Israel.[115] In 1952, however, he published "The Jews: From Servitude to Emancipation," an article that ends with a general attack on Arthur Koestler, who holds that the Jews had no choice but to assimilate and disappear or else emigrate to Israel. Berlin on the contrary argues that one could remain Jewish in diaspora, without becoming assimilated or falling into a communitarian politics leading to the creation of a "State within a State":

> The old servitude came from the fact that the Jews were told that there was at least some doubt about their right to their plenary liberty as individuals and citizens as long as they insisted on remaining fully Jewish. . . . Today, assimilation is nothing but the sad phantom of what it was. But another danger exists . . . that attempts are made to impose new chains on backs that are only too used to irons, even if it's a matter of completely different chains: it is seemingly being hammered into the heads of the ignorant and those who can't see their way clearly that they have only half a right, as Jews, to live outside the borders of Israel. . . . The future of the Jews as a community is in Israel. The Jewish religion will survive in the hearts of those who believe in it, wherever they are.[116]

Pious hope, difficult exercise between noncommunitarian loyalty and assimilation without "evaporation," with identitarian recognition being projected toward Israel, a vision that either goes against today's multiculturalist arguments, or joins them in their nationalist perspective, by secession.

As devoted as he may be to Israel, Berlin also knows that "Zionism has unfortunately been transformed into a nationalist movement. In the beginning, Zionist was civilized and Herderian."[117] He rejects its ultranationalist and aggressive tendencies that divide it from the *Risorgimento*,[118] doesn't turn away when faced with problems born from the failing integration of Eastern Jews, does not ignore the fact that the question of the place of Arabs, inside and outside Israel, is "the most considerable moral and political problem, the resolution of which is not in sight." He conceals none of the "injustice" done to the Arabs; he condemns the murders committed in *Deir Yassin* and even belongs to Peace Now.[119] Still, in his eyes, "what clearly predominates is, despite everything, the good side of the things that have been accomplished": for Berlin, the creation of Israel "constitutes a prodigious human realization, the resolution of the oldest, most cruel, most permanent and most systematic evil that has ever afflicted a human group within the memory of history."[120]

The rebirth of Israel is more important than any other consideration,

even if it involves consequences—unavoidable ones in Berlin's opinion—to the future of Jewish culture in this normal national context
that he perceives, seeming to delight in it, in radically negative terms
that are fundamentally incorrect, and, in his anxiety for normalization,
more than arguable:

> There are in Israel very few eminent bankers, very few eminent
> lawyers, not many scientists of genius, there are very few persons
> principally occupied with the accumulation of wealth. Again, there
> are few professional critics (I say nothing of the amateurs); there are
> few sophisticated, chess-playing, café intellectuals—late-night figures,
> dispensers of a peculiar compound of Freud, Marx, Sartre, or whatever
> else is at once shocking and fashionable; seekers after strong sensations,
> partly genuine, partly fraudulent, sometimes interesting, at other times
> deliberately sordid and obscene, amusing, destructive, superficial,
> and liable to exhibitionism and vulgarity; with a tendency to flourish
> within declining or insecure cultures—in the Weimar Republic of Ger-
> many, or in certain sections of the United States today. . . . That may
> be a cause for regret, or it may not. . . . There are no great Israeli novel-
> ists; there are some good short-story writers, but they are older men
> who perfected their genius before they went to Palestine. There are on
> the whole no great thinkers, poets, painters, sculptors, composers. . . .
> Israel, consequently, has a chance of continuing to grow, under condi-
> tions which may be described as almost normal.[121]

Or else this text from 1973, very close in tone and content to that
one from 1958, and which many Israelis would probably not appreciate
either, despite their concern to recreate a "normal" life:

> The citizens of Israel are not tortured by questions of self-awareness,
> they do not ponder with perplexity the opinion that "others" have of
> them, they are not anxious to please their fellow citizens and, on the
> other hand, do not give in to an arrogant self-defense provoked by the
> humiliating spectacle of the anguish of their father or mother, their
> brothers or sisters. The citizens of Israel constitute a nation among na-
> tions and their vices as well as their virtues do not result from a patho-
> logical social derangement.
>
> Those who hope for an explosion of intellectuals of genius, an un-
> precedented rebirth of creative imagination on the part of writers and
> poets, painters and composers, scholars and philosophers, historians

and critics born in the country, those who are looking forward to the presence of a sublime morality incomparably greater than the one that reigns in other societies, risk being disappointed.

The Zionist movement has expressly undertaken to restore the health of the social organization that, for well-known historical reasons, had been formed in an abnormal way; the society was mutilated and afflicted with diseases whose presence was stressed, still not without malice, as much by its friends as by its enemies, be they Jewish or non-Jewish. That agriculture more than finance, technology and the applied sciences more than abstract thought, chess, or avant-garde literature characterize the Israel of today certainly constitutes a sign not of spiritual poverty but rather a proof of cure or convalescence, exactly the opposite of neurosis and decadence.[122]

Berlin endorses the fundamental elements of Zionist discourse, close in certain points to anti-Semitic arguments that denounce the pathological and neurotic nature of Jewish presence in non-Jewish societies, which also propose as a solution . . . the return to Zion as a guarantee of a normality regained. Desirous of cultural anchorage in the Herderian way, Berlin unreservedly adheres to the Zionist perspective that, since the nineteenth century, has been devoted to the aim of normalizing the Jews, transforming the old man in them, giving them back their language, Hebrew, but also a land that they must learn to cultivate, the aim of removing Jews from the neurotic world of the big cities so that they can flourish close to nature, content with the treasures of their own culture instead of giving the world their genius in some denatured, pathological form that arises from the hybrid status they occupy in the diaspora, from the distance—desired or imposed—that decisively separates them from their host society. Close in this point of view to the theses of Max Nordau on the "muscular Jews" who reshape their bodies by gymnastics and sport in order to free their soul from fantasies of cosmopolitanism, Berlin even comes to use curious biological metaphors that say a lot about the complexity of his own Judaism. Thus, using implied images that have been circulating since the dawn of time among anti-Semites, Berlin launches into a story of the hump in the back that all Jews allegedly have. According to him, they either purely and simply deny this physical disgrace, or they glory in it and exhibit it, or at least mask it by wearing ample clothing:

> But then came those who said: a hump is a hump, an undesirable appendage that one cannot disguise, and that one cannot lessen by applying mild palliatives; it is, in the meantime, a cause of great distress for those who are afflicted with it. They recommended—and people saw in this a boldness close to mental alienation—that the hump be surgically removed. . . . If all one wished for above all else was to make the humps disappear en masse, in short if anything were preferable to a hump, then there were no other solutions; only an operation of this kind would guarantee the desired results. In fact, this is what the Zionist solution offered in its completed form. One fact shows its triumph: that the Jews of Israel, especially those born there recently, find that they are, whatever their qualities and defects might otherwise be, people with a straight spine . . . the three attitudes cited above are historically discredited by the creation of the state of Israel.[123]

Having become aware of the implications of such a physiological vocabulary heavy with prejudices and anti-Semitic fantasies, which evokes surgical operations of normalization of the nose or the de-circumcisions practiced by American Jews described recently by Sander Gilman,[124] Berlin, anxious to avoid any ambiguity provoked by such metaphors as he had imagined to justify his normalizing perspective, decides to forbid republication of this text, which figures in an obscure collection of contributions and which, in fact, is never mentioned again in any of the numerous anthologies of his work.

Without using similar physiological images, most theorists of Zionism, whether they belong to the governmental, culturalist, socialist, or nationalist wing of the movement, have also made this observation: in their opinion, the pathologies of Jewish existence in diaspora imply that a normalization in a national framework is indispensable. Formed by a nineteenth century increasingly obsessed with the supposedly unhealthy nature of big cities, alert to the dangers of industrial civilization purveying innumerable mental pathologies, such an ideology appears pretty much everywhere in Europe at that time in political thought, as well as in literature, with its procession of commonplaces endorsing all the nationalist, biological, and identitarian blunders. It leads straight

to the radical protest of Barrès against "uprooting," or to the grandilo-
quence of Wagner and Spengler. Like most national movements that
were flourishing at the time as reactions to the supposedly alienating
modernism that resulted from the rationalism of the Enlightenment,
Zionism appears as an identitarian protest, the will to refound the natural "community" broken by "society." Though it is also inspired, as
Berlin stresses, by the liberal nationalism embodied by Mazzini, though
it sometimes shows itself hostile to a governmental recourse to violence
by preferring the long-term logic of cultural rebirth, according to the
precepts of Ahad Ha'am which will soon be forgotten, though it does
not give itself the aim, as in France or later on in Germany, of destroying a democracy or a republic regarded as foreign to the fundamental
values of society, and though it does not start a war, in order to justify
itself in its own eyes, against other nations, almost completely ignoring
the Arab question, the Zionist plan still shares some of the prejudices
of the identitarian nationalisms of the end of that century.

Berlin's Zionism leads him here to a sociology of knowledge that is
both artificial and formidable, with unquestionable "normal" nationalist traces: after all, if the Greeks could create only in Greece, the Romans in Rome and the pietistic Germans in Germany, why couldn't
the Israelis create in Israel, whether this culture prolongs their Jewish
anguish of the past or whether it rests now on other native foundations? Berlin almost becomes the echo of the prejudices of the nationalist extreme Right, actually similar, from this point of view, to those
of Herder, which deplore the artificial nature of Jewish creativity in
the Western world. Unfair to writers of the Enlightenment as well as
to the inventors of modern culture in fin-de-siècle Vienna, Berlin is
also unfair in the end to Israeli artists who, in order henceforth to be
"normal," are nonetheless bearers of questions and creativity. By seeing
only the rebirth of a homogeneous, holistic, atemporal Jewish culture
in the Israel of today, he also underestimates the irruption of an Israeli
form of multiculturalism from which cultural shocks emanate that penetrate a Jewish culture that has become, to varying degrees, Israeli and
strongly diversified in terms of traditions but also of genres.[125] Berlin
does not want to hear about this multiculturalism from within, whether
in Great Britain or in Israel, Herderian in logic but turned away from

its national application, unless he is constrained and forced to hear it. If need be, with an unconcealed scorn, he accepts it in the United States. Doesn't he thus justify, without admitting it, his own status as creator, faithful to Jewish history more than to his own specific values, having remained "between two shores," where allegiance to the nation, to "Britishness,"[126] turns out to be compatible, outside of any communitarianism, with an assumed loyalty? Berlin's internal "suffering," which never stops gnawing at him, is at the source of an unquestionable body of work; it has no relation, though, to the identitarian doubts from which, according to Berlin, the troubled fin-de-siècle culture of Viennese Jews emanates, and it is also foreign to the rationalist temptations shaped by the Enlightenment that inspired the Königsberg Jews and all those who these days mean to remain faithful to them.

## Seven

Michael Walzer:
The End of Whispering

Theoretician of war, of justice, of pluralism, Michael Walzer often takes hold of these great subjects of political theory from a single starting point, the question of identity. For Walzer, oriented toward universalism and indifferent to innumerable particularisms, "the left has never understood the tribes,"[1] the Left has never known what place it should grant to collective identity, to the national question, to memory transmitted and shared, to deep-rootedness in a specific culture, to the weight of the local. Walzer intends to rehabilitate adherence to "tribes" while at the same time laying claim loud and strong to his involvement in the American Left. For many years head of *Dissent*, the famous journal involved in various progressive fights in the United States over several generations, he does not propose to compromise on the legitimate maintaining of cultural diversity; this must be taken charge of by the Left and not abandoned as is most often the case to the ideologies of the Right. Does this constant concern to stress an anchorage in the past, in culture, in tradition, this affirmed desire to found a liberal and pluralist politics not on transcendental perspectives but on "local" realities, as Walzer continually calls them, make him into a new "left-wing Burke,"[2] wanting to reconcile the Enlightenment with an indispensable adherence to a specific community? The image is attractive, since it reveals Walzer's keen hostility toward the homogenizing and rationalist universalism of certain members of the Enlightenment, his definitive rejection of any process of change based on revolutionary ruptures rejecting the past and guiding from above, imposed in the name of Reason on a people that could do nothing about it. Walzer's attention is to the history particular to each society with its passions, its prejudices, its values, its attachment to the concrete; the image is however simplistic, since Michael Walzer cannot be considered as a man attached to a tra-

288

ditionalist order, to an immobile past, who depends this time on left-ist ideals that have become static, uniform, exclusive. What is striking in his engagements is on the contrary his attachment to "cacophony,"[3] to disorder, to "dissidence," to the multiplicity of allegiances, so many qualities that are unacceptable even for a "left-wing Burke" who wants to be the herald of Reason.

Walzer recounts with emotion the fear felt by Jewish immigrants at the turn of the century who had to be content with "whispering" and feared making "noise," showing themselves, being noticed; they saw themselves merely as "guests" of their adopted country. As Isaiah Berlin noted before him that in such a context the Jews "lowered their voices below a whisper,"[4] Walzer writes:

> I remember that in the 1930s and 1940s, every sign of affirmation of the Jewish community—including the appearance of "too many" Jewish names among the New Deal Democrats or among socialist or communist intellectuals—was greeted with a shudder in the community. The old people in the community recommended not making noise, not attracting attention, not pushing yourself forward, saying nothing that might be taken as a provocation. They regarded themselves as guests in this country long after they acquired their citizenship. Today, all that is a thing of the past. . . . No one imposes silence on us anymore: no one is intimidated anymore. . . . All the voices are loud, the intonations are varied, and the result is not a harmonious music but a cacophony.[5]

Walzer often mentions this "noise," which bears witness to the democratic dimension of public space where the most antagonistic opinions clash with each other, where a dialogue is constructed based on distinct points of view, a "noise that forces people to pay attention to others,"[6] to their values, their culture. Like Hannah Arendt in *The Human Condition*, Walzer fears silence, withdrawal into the private, the end of public engagement, of confrontation. Noise is the possibility of talking loudly, without shame, of being heard even if one is an immigrant, different. This healthy noise is for Walzer the expression of a specific identitarian adherence expressed at the top of one's voice, while in Hannah Arendt's view, noise results from the force of a purely rational argumentation. The claim of a particular cultural adherence such as Judaism, regarded as legitimate, distances Walzer from the diehard rationalism of Arendt, who proposes to speak more in the name of universalism, of Truth, of the Spirit, of Man and not of Man situated, linked to a social or cultural identity. In Walzer's mind, noise makes a particular history audible, a demand uttered publicly by an ensemble of individuals who share a memory, a culture, an engagement in the community. If one takes this noise seriously, this way of existing together openly, in the view of all, one almost logically comes to defend, like Walzer, a communitarian theory that inserts the individual within a particular "we" in the framework of which he constructs his personality. Walzer even to this day thinks of himself as a "guest" in the United States, a temporary situation that was supposed to be, a few years before, that of his parents and no longer his own. "I have certainly always had," he writes, "the profound feeling of being a Jew in America—and also the feeling, which my children do not have, of being a guest in America; a guest in what is probably the best host nation in all history for the Jewish diaspora, but which is not 'our own.' My children for their part have the feeling of simply being American."[7] Theoretician of the "local," who reactualizes without explicitly saying so the tradition of Tocquevillean America or even the America of Thoreau, Walzer, born in the United States to parents who were already American by birth, becomes the eulogist for a nation where he considers himself simply a "guest," so attached is he to the Jewish diaspora as culture, as a way of thinking. All of a sudden, it is in this privileged framework that the following question takes on the most cogency: "Can Jewish distinctiveness be preserved under conditions of democratic mutuality?"[8]

As proud of being American as Isaiah Berlin was of being English or Raymond Aron of being French, Walzer asserts, probably even more than they, his adherence to Judaism, his unfailing support of Israel. His familiarity with a biblical culture, which underlies most of his work, his constant effort to penetrate, with the help of the best specialists in Torah and Talmud, its profound meaning, is unrivalled by Berlin's attitude or that of Hannah Arendt who, in her famous epistolary exchange with Gershom Scholem, boasts about not belonging to any nation, no more to the Jewish than to any other. If Berlin's choices are often linked to his Jewishness, the "local" he claims is that of Vico and

Herder, of Herzen and Schubert or of Mozart; he has only scorn for the uniquely Jewish "local" in its Viennese cosmopolitan version or in its Israeli version. Walzer speaks directly in the name of a Jewish "local," from which he intends to argue against universalism. Like all the social critics to whom he feels close, from Martin Buber to Ignazio Silone or Albert Camus, he chooses to speak from within the "cave,"⁹ not to try to see things from above, in an abstract way. It could be said that his entire thinking rests on the following judgment: "A little to the side, but not on the side." "Now the critical enterprise," he asserts, "was said to require that one leave the city, imagined for the sake of the departure as a darkened cave, find one's way, alone, outside, to the illumination of Truth. . . . Critical distance makes a new sort of criticism possible. But the possibility is hard won, for it requires a willful break with the fellowship of the city."¹⁰ Invoking the names, on the contrary, of Socrates and the prophet Amos, from whom he often takes his inspiration, Walzer questions any such break with the "local" and rejects all purely normative thought. "My argument is radically particularist. . . . I mean," he firmly declares, "to stand in the cave, in the city, on the ground."¹¹ Can one say that, for his part, his "cave" is Jewish, that he constructs his oeuvre wholly in accord with his deep-rootedness in Jewish culture? As he notes elsewhere, "Moses indeed climbed the mountain, but no one need do that again. There is no longer any special role for mediators between the people and God."¹² And he adds, "The concern of the prophets is for *this* people, their own people, the 'family,' as Amos says, that came up out of Egypt. . . . They are rooted, for all their anger, in their own societies. . . . Each nation can have its own prophecy, just as it has its own history, its own deliverance, its own quarrel with God: 'Have I not brought up Israel out of the land of Egypt, / And the Philistines from Caphtor, / And Aram from Kir?'"¹³

Walzer openly claims his Jewish identity, which is spread throughout his entire work.¹⁴ That makes it hard to see why the few books that are devoted to him, in France for example, ignore this essential dimension of his life.¹⁵ His grandparents were Ostjuden, immigrants from Eastern Europe. His grandfather, Moses Walzer, came from Galicia; his grandmother, Rachel Hochman, was a Litvak born near Brest-Litovsk: like so many immigrants from Eastern Europe, both left just before the twentieth century for the United States, where they knew all the people on Hester Street, the same society described by Irving Howe. His father, Joseph Walzer, was born in 1906 in New York, in the ghetto of the Lower East Side, while his mother came from a farm in Connecticut subsidized by Baron Rothschild, who wanted to encourage Jews throughout the world to return to the land. A businessman ruined by the Great Depression of 1929, Joseph Walzer became a worker before he opened a small jewelry store in a little mining and steelworks town in Pennsylvania. His mother looked after the nursery in the synagogue and became secretary to the rabbi. Throughout her life, she remained active in community affairs, continuing in Chicago where the family settled later on. At home, they lit candles on Sabbath and often went to synagogue on Friday evening. The young Michael Walzer received a religious education and had his bar mitzvah in 1948, the year of the creation of Israel, which delighted his family; he himself remained throughout his life faithful to Israel as a confirmed Zionist, and he went there in 1957, the beginning of a series of visits for regular study that allowed him to establish profound ties with the Israeli academic milieu.

In his hometown, Jonestown, Walzer witnessed hard struggles waged by the local unions, which played an important role in his political formation; he took part in Jewish community activities and was active in the local life of unions and associations, which he defended throughout his life as an indispensable form of social relations. Faithful to maintaining a collective identity, he attended Brandeis University, where almost all the students, at the time, were Jewish. There he met his wife, Judith, and with her constructed the life of a traditional family (lighting candles, Hebrew courses outside of public school, Jewish scout camps for the children, visits to Israel); his daughters remain faithful to their identity, with one of them, a lawyer, becoming a veritable pillar of the synagogue. At Brandeis, a large number of professors were Jewish, often leftist and immigrant, like Herbert Marcuse, Kurt Wolff, Frank Manuel, Max Lerner, Lewis Coser, Irving Howe, and Mary Sirkin. Walzer obtained his first teaching position in the political science department at Harvard, where he joined a prestigious teaching staff made up of Carl Friedrich, Judith Shklar to whom he would long remain close, Sam Beer, and V. O. Key; then he headed a social studies department to which Barrington Moore, Alexandre Gerschenkron, and Stanley Hoffman belonged. Immersed in a Jewish milieu since birth, Walzer nonetheless undertook studies of classical political science, knew all the classical works—by David Truman or Robert Dahl for example—acquired a solid culture in political theory, and taught Locke regularly as well as Rousseau. His career was light years away from "Jewish studies," which had not yet taken off, chairs of Jewish studies being still almost nonexistent. His doctoral thesis and his first important books have only a symbolic link with his "local," with his affirmed deep-rootedness in Jewish culture. When he began his dissertation at Harvard, which he finished in 1965, Jewish studies were scarcely recognized within the academic world aside from rare personalities who embodied them individually. Thus the Association for Jewish Studies wasn't created until 1969. The explosion would come later on.

In the hushed, WASP ambiance of Harvard, Walzer temporarily distanced himself from the prophets of Israel and embarked on a vast study of the Calvinist prophets responsible for the Puritan revolution that disrupted England in the seventeenth century. It is not the Weber of *Ancient Judaism* who is consulted, as he will be later on, but the Weber of Protestant ethics that allows for the radical modernization of English society through a revolutionary moment unique in its history. Walzer set out to demonstrate that "it was the Calvinists who first switched the emphasis of political thought from the prince to the saint (or the band of saints) and then constructed a theoretical justification for independent political action. What Calvinists said of the saint, other men would later say of the citizen. . . . The saints saw themselves as divine *instruments* and theirs was the politics of wreckers, architects, and builders—hard at work upon the political world."[16] It is a matter of understanding what motivates these men, these "exiles" motivated by "resentment," these people "detached from feudal bonds and obligations," these political entrepreneurs who decided to "experiment politically and ignore, whenever necessary, the age-old customs, the trained passivity, and the traditional loyalties of their fellows" to become involved in this revolutionary process of rupture with the values and beliefs of their contemporaries.[17] Here we find the origin of all Walzer's hostility to explanatory claims, to the methods of rupture that consist of importing truth from outside the social bond, to the brutality of Puritan, Jacobin, or Bolshevik radicalism advocated by the "saints," hard-line heroes who impose on the people a disciplinary order able to put into play their evasion of the world. If their political enterprise does certainly hasten political transformations, they still fail, in Walzer's opinion, in their aim of establishing a new utopia alien to the customs of society, and these Puritans of all kinds end up by abandoning this war waged in the name of Truth. The saint then wears the clothing of the respectable man. "I am tempted to say," Walzer writes, "of Lenin and his friends . . . that they were bad social critics, looking at Russia from a great distance and merely disliking what they saw." On the contrary, he adds, "The prophets try to work up a picture of the tradition that will make sense to, and connect with the experience of, their own contemporaries. They are parasitic upon the past, but they also give shape to the past upon which they are parasitic."[18] As we have noted, it is still the "left-wing Burke" who expresses himself through these remarks on the cultural anchorage of prophets, much to be preferred over Puritans of all kinds.

This almost cyclical interpretation of history, which evokes the theme of the circulation of the elite in the theory of Vilfredo Pareto, is presented here as a sociology of ideologies that, far from traditional Marxist interpretation, stresses, in the manner of Karl Mannheim, the importance of the uprooting of these intellectuals "in exile" undertaking, from without, "outside,"[19] their enterprise of sudden political transformation. Here the real contribution of this book can be found: to place oneself in the position of a "foreigner" to the people, to the masses, to the community, is heavy with consequences from the point of view of the future of democracy. Walzer, without explicitly indicating it, follows in the footsteps of a Jacob Talmon, critic of Jacobinism, or of a François Furet debating with the supporters of the Communist Party, and through his study of Puritanism foreshadows the analyses made later on by Mona Ozouf or Lynn Hunt concerning the new man, the regenerated man who separates himself from his compatriots still bogged down in their traditions. He undertakes, however, an approach that is unique to him by insisting especially on the status of the exile, the foreigner, which is that of the Puritans and which will moreover be that of Lenin. Here the real common thread can be found that runs through all his writing, denouncing the prophetic attitudes of saints who impose, from above, their truth, their discipline, their Puritanism and who, far from favoring primitive accumulation as Max Weber argued, turn away from all economic liberalism and, even more, distance themselves from the political liberalism that conduces to the development of the market. As Walzer notes, "Liberalism and capitalism appear fully developed only in a secular form, that is, only after Puritanism is spent as a creative force. . . . The holy commonwealth would have been neither liberal nor capitalist—no more, indeed, than would the Jacobin Republic of Virtue. The spread of the capitalist and liberal spirits parallels the decline of radical enthusiasm."[20]

Unlike most Jewish prophets, unlike Amos, with whom Walzer is literally obsessed and to whom he will devote the main part of his work, Puritan prophets (the study of whom seems more legitimate in the conventional framework of a doctoral thesis in political science at Harvard) sin by their exteriority, by their distance from the "local." The distance kept by these prophets from the people they try to lead from without, by preserving their foreign status having direct access to Truth, is at the origin of their attacks on liberalism that as a man of the Left Walzer means to safeguard for the zeal of all political apparatuses. At bottom, *The Revolution of the Saints* reinforces the search for pluralism that haunted American political science of his time; it dominates the thinking of Barrington Moore and continually returns as an imperative among Jewish thinkers who immigrated from Germany, hostile to all forms of totalitarianism established by a single disciplined party. Walzer will remain faithful throughout his life to the defense of internal pluralism that, according to him, is consubstantial with every society. In the first part of his academic life, this defense of pluralism is elaborated from within classical or contemporary political theory, from Rousseau to Locke, from John Stuart Mill to John Rawls; the references to the Old Testament or to the Talmud are timid, almost nonexistent, and remain in the background. In *Obligations*, it is also starting from Hobbes, Locke, or Rousseau that he undertakes a classical exercise in defending the refusal of obedience. With this intention, in harmony with the spirit of the end of the 1960s, Walzer questions the conclusions of more classical contemporary theoreticians who too easily take the side of depoliticization and political apathy, of electoral abstention in the name of the pluralism of the elite and of groups, like J. P. Plamenatz, Bernard Berelson, Charles Lindblom, and Robert Dahl, while still taking his inspiration from other classical texts of political science of his time, such as those by Grant McConnel, Charles Tilly, Gabriel Almond, and Sidney Verba.[21]

Even more than in *The Revolution of the Saints*, here Walzer joins the liberal trend of Anglo-Saxon political science; he earns his exalted status as a political theorist, which justifies his brilliant career within the American academic world. Actually, he does not simply defend liberalism, contractualism, or participatory democracy as so many others do: faithful to his first intuition, which informs all his books, including those concerning communitarianism and multiculturalism, he means to proclaim an obligation of fidelity to one's own people. He repeats the same message, his refusal to delegate to others, to saints or political professionals or even holders of governmental power, the concern to watch over the defense of those lower down. He thus considerably changes the direction of dominant American liberalism by bringing to the forefront the inclusion of individuals within networks of solidarity that they have an obligation to defend, even against the state.[22] In his eyes, the monad-individual of classical liberalism, who only soliloquizes, isolated as he is in his own individuality, is not capable of fraternity with those who are in the same "cave," with all those who constitute the "local," the basis of a common cultural and historical demand. In this sense, the polyarchic pluralism dear to Robert Dahl changes its nature to the extent that the action of groups dons a more cultural dimension rather than a strictly socioeconomic one. The Walzerian theme also calls into question traditional American political science oriented toward a pure contractualism by reintroducing the question of cultural pluralism—all the more so since when political science turns away from this, it is to invoke the name, in the style of Arendt, of a "strong democracy," a public space of citizens, directed by a transcendental Reason that also deliberately ignores the diversity of adherences. A liberal, Walzer does not share the principles of individualist liberalism that he continues to fight, mocking, these days, the supporters of rational choice whose triumph marks, according to him, the end of political science departments, so pluralistic in their centers of interest, to which he is attached.[23] He is just as remote from the academic Left that gives itself a holistic image of public space that is regarded as a conveyor of truth and that ignores the adherence of individuals to those very social groups whose strong pluralism alone assures, for Walzer, the democratic foundation of multiple society. From then on, his condemnation of Jacobinism as an adept movement of endless terror hostile to pluralism is complete; Walzer cannot accept the Jacobin position, which refused to put Louis XVI on trial; Walzer is against their being able to condemn the king a priori as an enemy of the people by claiming that he had actually remained outside of it, foreign to it. Here again, Walzer argues that the trial of the king must take place starting from the community to which he belongs, according to its values.[24] "Killing Louis because of what kingship is sounds frighteningly like killing $X$ (an aristocrat) because of what aristocracy is or $Y$ (a Jew) because of what Judaism is."[25]

As we can tell, Walzer fights on multiple fronts. Against reactionary and racist conservative populisms, but also, within the Left, against the various individualisms or theories of participative democracy or against the theories of public space, from Hannah Arendt to Jürgen Habermas, that undervalue the fraternity stemming from within the social bond as source of creation of identity. "I can imagine," he says,

> quantities of little old men whispering things to their grandchildren, telling them stories. I am not a supporter of fighting against those people. Let them tell their stories in public. The positive side of the stories will be reinforced; the negative, the fanatical, the part that is only resentment, will be exposed to criticism. So long as they do not imply any injustice toward those who tell different stories, these stories must be allowed to be aired. For that a lot of creativity and political savoir-faire will be necessary, as well as a great variety of institutional arrangements—decentralization, local autonomy, federalism, etc.[26]

In the name of Reason, Arendt and Habermas banish from public space these stories told by so many little old men attached to their own culture and have to do only with those "institutional arrangements" that divide up public space and threaten its unity. Without discussing here the polemics that opposed Habermas to Ernst Nolte, the former refusing in the name of constitutional patriotism based on reason to continue a German past, a cultural way unique to Germany that on the contrary justifies in Nolte many revisionist readings of history, we can measure the originality of Walzer's position, who for his part wants to reconcile universalism with particularism, Reason and anchorage in the local. This perspective is logically contested by Habermas, in whose opinion Walzer thus joins the conservative camp in the name of respect for cultures, a position that encourages him for example to approve only with many reservations of external military intervention in a country that is violating human rights, whereas "interventions of this sort are probably best carried out by neighbors since neighbors will have some understanding of the local culture."[27] For Habermas, "Walzer who is light years away from a militant ethno-nationalism in the style of Schmitt nonetheless defends a similar position. Without suggesting false analogies, I would like to cite his identitarian-inspired reservations against humanitarian intervention," with such intervention being legitimate only if the citizens themselves rise up against a government "that threatens the integrity of the community."[28] Walzer concedes that one cannot imagine, à la Habermas, a postnational world, but he cannot accept that it be comprised simply of friends, voluntary casual acquaintances, to the exclusion of all collective adherence based on particular memories and traditions.[29] In the books of his youth that belong to more classical political theory, Walzer continually stresses, unlike many others: "The citizen is safer, it seems to me, in his groups, safer from bureaucratic neglect or abuse, safer also, as the example of the working class suggests, from social oppression."[30] For him, the "pluralist citizen,"[31] loyal to his political community, to his state which he agrees to serve and for which he does not hesitate to die, at least in the just wars it decides to wage, belongs, outside of the state, to a number of groups whose presence is indispensable to the development of his own action.

The intuitions of *The Revolution of the Saints* can be found again in Walzer's study on citizenship and on the refusal to serve blindly a state or a party, such as the Communist Party,[32] led by an elite of militants who claim to know the meaning of history. This attachment to the pluralism of "locals" of fraternity, this mistrust of power, are clearly expressed in *Spheres of Justice*, a book published in 1983, which establishes Walzer's reputation as a great political theorist, in reply to *A Theory of Justice*, the famous book by John Rawls. *Spheres of Justice* is the crowning point in Walzer's career as political theorist. It is the crucial work that establishes his reputation as a thinker of pluralism, that raises it to the rank of a classical work of political theory, transforms Walzer into one of the contemporary protagonists of democracy, and gives him a definitive status in the academic world, without the Jewish aspect of his oeuvre being in the foreground. His colleagues, as well as his students, upon reading his first books, might even not have perceived this dimension. Professionalism is realized in the domain of political theory, discourse focuses almost exclusively, in appearance, on the dominant political science. In *Spheres of Justice*, Walzer expresses once again his rejection of all forms of domination exercised by an elite or an avant-garde in the name of equality; it is an attack of egalitarianism that tends to eliminate differences. In a word, Walzer advocates the separation of spheres within which a kind of specific power is exercised, starting from the control of particular goods: "The principles of justice are themselves pluralistic in form; different social goods ought to be distributed for different reasons, in accordance with different procedures, by different agents; and all these differences derive from different understandings of the social goods themselves—the inevitable product of historical and cultural particularism."[33]

Steadily repeated, this assertion aims to stress the importance of differences of concepts of justice rooted in historical and cultural particularisms that are specific to each human group, according to their particular values. For Walzer, there can be no transcendental justice valid for all societies, normative, identical to the one defended by John Rawls as an abstract contractualism. To place a "veil of ignorance" over the adherences of individuals with the aim of constructing a general theory of justice comes down to rejecting the fundamental "localism" according to which each individual conceives of justice differently, rejecting the "cave" from which they form their images of the just and the unjust; it does not pay any attention to the representations unique to each social group. "Rational men and women in the original position, deprived of all particular knowledge of their social standing and cultural understanding, would probably opt, as Rawls has argued, for an equal distribution of whatever goods they were told they needed. But this formula doesn't help very much in determining what choices people will make, or what choices they should make, once they know who and where they are. In a world of particular cultures, competing conceptions of the good, scarce resources, elusive and expansive needs, there isn't going to be a single formula, universally applicable."[34] Proponent of a radical pluralism and not of a systematic egalitarianism, even an abstract one, Walzer thinks that "good fences make just societies."[35] They must delimit autonomous spheres where distinct principles of justice prevail, on the basis of which the internal distribution of each property unique to each sphere can be organized; such a distribution, respectful of the diversity of predominant concepts within each sphere, alone avoids the establishment of any monopoly, any unique power reigning over the totality of the spheres. It is a matter, then, of preventing any conversion of one good into another good that would allow its possessor to invade neighboring spheres, the owners of capital trying for example to control political power, or to appropriate charisma for themselves, or to obtain meritocratic positions or even to influence love life in their favor. It is a matter of refusing to let political power control the economic management of society, or obtain positions that should be merit-based, and so on, unlike all the unitary projects formulated by the Left, since "the art of separation has never been particularly highly regarded by the left, especially not by the Marxist left."[36]

Walzer readily acknowledges, "My argumentation is radically particularist. I do not claim to have managed to take much distance from the world in which I live." Refusing to "walk out of the cave, leave the city, climb the mountain" in order to fashion "an objective and universal standpoint," he wants rather "to interpret to one's fellow citizens the world of meanings that we share."[37] Walzer the American refuses to see "from afar," like the Puritan prophets, from without, from exile, but also like Rawls and all those who think of justice in an abstract way, according to general principles; he elaborates on his thinking in conformity with a feeling of belonging. Arguing with Rawls, Walzer writes with humor but also with a sense of the necessity of belonging to history:

> It is as if we were to take a hotel room or an accommodation apartment or a safe house as the ideal model of a human home. Away from home, we are grateful for the shelter and convenience of a hotel room. Deprived of all knowledge of what our own home was like, talking with people similarly deprived, required to design rooms that any one of us might live in, we would probably come up with something like, but not quite so culturally specific as, the Hilton Hotel. . . . We might still long for the homes we knew we once had but could no longer remember. . . . I have been assuming that my own view of hotels is widely shared, and so I should note one telling dissent—a line from Franz Kafka's journal: "I like hotel rooms. I always feel immediately at home in hotel rooms, more than at home, really." Note the irony: there is no other way to convey the sense of being in one's own place except to say "at home."[38]

Walzer thus joins, on this point at least, the communitarian critique of the theory elaborated by Rawls by making his own interpretation of justice rest on a collective feeling of belonging to a particular social ensemble.[39] For Walzer, "the theory of distributive justice begins, then, with an account of membership rights,"[40] with the formation of an ensemble of individuals who share similar values and refuse to establish an internal discrimination between foreigners, immigrant workers who must not be transformed into modern "metics" ["guest workers"], and themselves. Though the choice of accepting or refusing the presence of refugees or foreigners is our duty, "we who are already members," though this choice can legitimately favor the "national or ethnic 'relatives'" with whom there is "an ideological and ethnic affinity," though "our benevolence goes spontaneously out to our relatives and our parents," to those who have "a more direct link with our own way of life," the nation being regarded as an extended "family," borders are still indispensable in the foreseeable future since "the right to restrain the flow remains a feature of communal self-determination."[41] Unlike Jürgen Habermas, Hannah Arendt, and especially John Rawls, Walzer does not believe that "every victim of authoritarianism and bigotry is the moral comrade of a liberal citizen . . . that would press affinity too hard";[42] he consequently justifies the permanence of the national fact as the place of solidarity, of a shared feeling of belonging, and he joins authors like David Miller who, from a leftist perspective, justify the nation as place of redistribution of common property.[43] "Communitarian self-determination" thus is regarded as a founding principle so long as the hosts offer an identical status to nationals, an equal access to citizenship, to property, to jobs, so long as they make "local" values their own. For Walzer, "people who do share a common life have much stronger duties" than Rawls admits.[44]

*Spheres of Justice* was the object of many critiques. It was rightly pointed out that Walzer too easily accommodated himself to the inequalities within each sphere, which can be quite profound and unfair. Walzer was also criticized for not perceiving that the isolation of spheres can turn out to be prone to prejudice (for example, in access to care), for not paying enough attention to principles of justice shared by different spheres (such as loyalty, fairness, equal citizenship, the dignity of the individual), for granting a hybrid status to politics presented sometimes as an autonomous sphere and sometimes as a place of autonomous regulation, and finally for the fact that by refusing to subscribe simply to a universal morality he reintroduces questionable criteria of ideological and ethnic affinities, setting up a politics of admission of refugees to a nation whose particular culture must be preserved.[45] The weakness of Walzer's theory of the state is patent, to the same extent, perhaps, as the weakness of the American government itself. We will particularly stress this dimension, since it reveals how preoccupied Walzer is especially with the common man, with the feeling of adherence, with the community that citizens claim as their own, neglecting the state as vector of national integration. Like the American pluralists such as Robert Dahl or David Truman, whose classical books on political science he read (and some of whose conclusions he even subscribes to, such as the inevitable professionalization of politics), Walzer implements a pluralist theory that is indifferent to the function of the state. The pluralism of groups (Truman) or that of the elite (Dahl) is transposed here to the domain of spheres and here again expresses a culture unique to Anglo-Saxon liberalism hostile to the state and to any form of republic of citizens mobilized for carrying out the public good. Thus we can understand the difficulty of the author of *Spheres of Justice* in conceiving the action of the state, which however he often wishes for, since it alone is capable of implementing a social-democratic politics.[46] Recently, Walzer wrote, ambiguously, "Only a very strong government could be capable of collecting and distributing the necessary funds. . . . To bring civil society to save the state would require a large-scale governmental action. This is a paradox, but it is solvable, at least in theory."[47] This appeal to a strong state goes against cultural identity constructed by "those below." By privileging identitarian adherence and maintaining traditions, by asserting his Burke side, so sensitive to cultural anchorage, Walzer shows himself indifferent to calling the state into question, to internal violence justified by adhesion either to contrary cultures or to an idea of common citizenship closer to the procedural universalism of Habermas. He is scarcely inclined to imagine a violent rupture, a brutal internal conflict, a revolution that sweeps aside the separation of spheres in the name of a different idea of community and its cultural code.[48]

This stance then poses a fundamental question, which arises afresh upon reading a number of Walzer's writings: What justice are we talking about when one privileges a particular cultural code, when one wants it to agree with local values, when one desires it to be in harmony with the values unique to the cave? Can't we legitimately fear that certain values, such as significant religious beliefs, might try to impose themselves on society as a whole, and thus might break the desirable separation of spheres? Isn't Walzer also close to a rigid communitarianism, with the risk of subjecting the state itself to a particular culture, by taking from it all universalist dimension à la Weber, by imposing on it values that are incompatible with its rules of bureaucratic functioning? Doesn't he call into question, as Charles Taylor explicitly wishes,[49] the separation between private and public space, by favoring at all costs a feeling of identitarian adherence that cannot bear their autonomy? Here we touch on the question of culturalism that underlies all of Walzer's oeuvre at the risk of relativism, against which he defends himself. If we set aside the more general discussion about justice that opposes, based on *Spheres of Justice*, the contractualists and the communitarians, we come back to the question of the "local," of the "cave," of cultural particularism according to which a theory of justice is developed.

A number of commentators have stressed how much the example of the separation of spheres evokes American society and its pluralism; certainly, Walzer speaks from within the American "cave" and does not want to leave it, does not try to impose on it abstract ideals drawn from the Enlightenment. It is the American experience that shapes his thoughts: in his eyes, every universalist theory can only "reiterate" particularist experiences. Walzer constantly denounces abstract universalism, imposed from above, in the name of Truth, universalism "from above": "There is only one single God, thus one single law, one single justice, one single exact concept of the right life or the right government, one salvation, one messiah, one *millennium* for all humanity. I will call this the 'from above' version of universalism." According to the second type of universalism, by contrast,

> each people receives its own liberation from the hands of a single God. . . . I propose calling this position reiterative universalism. . . . I thus show a particular care for my own children, my friends, my comrades, my fellow citizens. As do you. . . . We all do that by ourselves, in a particular here and now, with the help of a local ensemble of concepts and values. Which is just another way of repeating that reiteration is a true story. Reiterative universalism operates rather within the limits of ours and theirs—not Reason with a capital R but our or their reason.[50]

In this spirit, it is not a question, then, of waiting for the flight of Minerva's Owl but rather of replying to precise and urgent requirements.[51]

Walzer tries to go beyond the universalism/particularism opposition and to avoid the trap of relativism by showing that universal morality can be apprehended simply through the prism of specific cultures. Confronting the same dilemmas as Isaiah Berlin, he too hopes to find in the pluralism of cultures a way out of unacceptable relativism. Coming to the aid of Berlin when he was accused of relativism,[52] Walzer explicitly refers in his Tanner Lectures to his hostile attitude to universalism and draws inspiration from the heroes of the author of *The Crooked Timber of Humanity*, Herder and Mazzini, to defend the idea of a reiterative universalism that respects the local.[53] Nationalism seems to him legitimate insofar as it does not claim to embody an absolute truth preferable to all others. If absolute evil can come out of nationalism, "national self-determination as the paradigmatic form of moral reiteration."[54] Adherence to the nation constitutes the essential form of defense of particularism so long as it does not imply the domination of another nation in the name of a privileged access to the meaning of history, to universalism, which would give this nation the unique mission of bringing Truth to the world and would justify its domination of the world, its desire to encroach upon other cultures. The opposition between relativism and universalism would thus be overcome, since through each particularism a "thin" morality shared by all is expressed. Taking issue in turn with Rawls and even more with Habermas, Walzer thinks that the rules of public space, of engagement, are themselves rooted in a "thick" culture unique to a specific culture, in a nonuniversalist "local": we all know what tyranny means but

> At the same time, the same words have further meanings for the marchers, which they will argue about among themselves and which we, looking on from far away, may well miss. They resonate differently than their translations resonate in, say, Paris or New York. . . . So we march together, and then we return to our own parades. The idea of a moral minimum . . . explains how it is that we come together; it warrants our separation. By its very thinness, it justifies us in returning to the thickness that is our own.[55]

For Walzer, if we sympathize with the demonstrators in Prague who march in 1989, if we share their ideals, their culture remains foreign to us, based as it is on an experience of history that is not familiar to us: "We cannot conscript people to march in our parade."[56]

Unlike so many prophets or critics who, from afar as well as "from above," try to enounce a universally valid Truth, or culturalist theorists who follow a basic relativism that isolates men inside their traditions regarded as immutable and incommensurable with other traditions, Walzer seeks another way. For him, provocatively, "watching from abroad," one can only explain the rules of democracy to the Chinese, but "Chinese democracy [must] be defined by the Chinese themselves in terms of their own history and culture. . . . I do defend the minimal rights of Chinese, as of Czech, demonstrators. . . . They must make their own claims, their own codifications (a Chinese bill of rights?), and their own interpretative arguments. I support the dissident students, encouraging them to make their own way, without worrying about whether their way will also be mine."[57] These distinctions may not be convincing to everyone. It is possible to argue that one is still sacrificing too much to local traditions, that if we demand respect for each "cave," or call for the "loyalty" of inhabitants to their cultural code, we fail to justify calling into question certain local customs that are unjust in terms of "thin" morality—in China as well as in caste India, in societies that practice slavery, in the South Africa of apartheid or even in a Germany that still is inspired by the jus sanguini. For many commentators, Walzer leaves little room for internal conflict, to theorists who are inspired by universalist considerations and who object, from within, to norms deemed legitimate by the community.[58] By overvaluing "internalism,"[59] because of a rejection of external universalism uttered by any of the Hercules of criticism,[60] we fail to see how individuals, deprived of any external criterion of justice, alienated and subject to unfair norms that they however consider legitimate, could rebel, if by chance "thin" morality were completely eliminated by an unjust "thick" morality. In the same sense, some people criticize Walzer when he questions the right to self-determination of national minorities in the United States, seeing them as forms of unacceptable dissent that exceed a pluralism of identities proper for a nation, as an extended community that accepts hyphenated identities.[61]

Logically, Walzer does not dignify the status of the foreigner, of someone who magnifies the exile in himself as a strategy of distance, of distancing, someone who no longer has any anchorage in a local place and who poses as a prophet of the absolute, of the "from-above" universal. Walzer continually returns to Ulysses and Penelope, seeming to admire Penelope more, who looked after the house while Ulysses wandered, knowing that when he returned to his house, his "local" would still be alive. For Walzer, there is no question of "intellectual or emotional detachment" procured by the journeys; at best, one can feign a detachment, like Montesquieu through the eyes of Usbek.[62] Walzer even attacks Simmel's figure of the stranger, distinguishing it, however, from the "outsider," who is truly foreign to society:

> Marginality has often been a condition that motivates criticism and determines the critic's characteristic tone and appearance. It is not,

however, a condition that makes for disinterest, dispassion, open-mindedness, or objectivity. Nor is it an external condition. Marginal men and women are like George Simmel's stranger, in but not wholly of their society. The difficulties they experience are not the difficulties of detachment but of ambiguous connection. Free them from those difficulties, and they may well lose the reasons they have for joining the critical enterprise.[63]

In this sense, Walzer questions the permanence of the position of the stranger presented by Simmel, since it implies a distance within the local asserted by an individual who is no longer actually foreign to society but who seeks to maintain a distance toward it, an almost affected marginality that seems like a "deforming prism." Walzer does not disclose that this figure of the stranger remaining outside was identified by Simmel with the Jew, eternally both inside and outside. He has only scorn for one who goes to Oxford or to Paris and who returns to criticize local practices; on the contrary, Walzer wants the critic to be "connected" to society. "This critic is one of us. Perhaps he has traveled and studied abroad, but his appeal is to local or localized principles; if he has picked up new ideas on his travels, he tries to connect them to local culture."[64] In the United States, Simmel's stranger would thus have no reason consciously to maintain his marginality.

The Burke side of Walzer continually resurfaces, so attentive does he seem to the diversity of human societies, to their pluralism, their internal unity. He does not conceal his loyalty toward the United States and openly subscribes to "the specifically American version" of morality, with his work on pluralism or justice developing according to the particular "thickness" that has formed in America.[65] We could take his article "What Does It Mean to Be an American?" as representing almost the quintessence of his thinking. Published for the first time in 1974, it gives a key to the works that would appear ten or twelve years later, such as *Spheres of Justice*, *The Company of Critics*, *Thick and Thin*, and *On Toleration*. Walzer begins by noting in this text that the United States does not "constitute a country but a multitude of countries," that this appellation does not designate a nation like Germany or Brazil but an anonymous union of undefined states: "It is a name that doesn't even pretend to tell us who lives here."[66] The United States is not, in

Walzer's eyes, a nation-state; it differs from most European societies that give themselves a single aim whereas the United States magnifies the multiplicity of adherences, the diversity of allegiances. The "oneness" of nation-states is thus contrasted with the "many-ness" of the United States, a nation of immigrants loyal to their past, to their traditions, to their respective "locals."[67] In this essential article, Walzer utters the great themes to which he will continually return, probably ignoring the existence of an American politics that is violently hostile to the arrival and assimilation of a number of immigrants, including the Jews from Eastern Europe, according to a restrictive concept of culture that, far from being neutral, is also unique to it.[68] Doubting that one might someday be able to talk about an American state that would result from an unacceptable Americanization of an imaginary collective, he makes this fundamental pluralism depend on the heterogeneous composition of its inhabitants who come from the four corners of the world. To describe this fact, essential to his pluralistic vision, he draws his inspiration in the opening pages of this founding essay from the book by Horace Kallen, *Culture and Democracy in the United States*, published in 1924.

Kallen's work is mentioned in most of Walzer's writings and interviews; Walzer constantly bases his pluralism on the writings of this first theoretician of American multiculturalism: "Perhaps my attachment to cultural pluralism as Horace Kallen defined it is the reflection of this personal experience as a Jewish child having the feeling of being 'a guest in the United States.'"[69] Kallen is a Jewish thinker who was attentive to the consequences of immigration. Thanks to a recent republication of his seminal book,[70] we have a better knowledge of this thinker, son of an Orthodox rabbi born in 1882 in Silesia, who immigrated to Boston with his father and family when he was five years old. Studying at Harvard, he was the student of William James, who defended a "pluralist universe": he obtained his doctorate in philosophy, taught there, but spent the main part of his academic career at the New School for Social Research in New York, which he helped found and to which a number of Jewish academics fleeing Nazism came. Kallen married a non-Jewish woman, Rachel Oatman Van Arsdale, daughter of a Methodist minister, who subsequently devoted herself to mastering Jewish rituals and raised their son with respect for the traditions. Kallen was actively involved in Jewish community life, founding for example the Menorah Society at Harvard, and he became vice president of the American Jewish Congress. Hostile to the Orthodox world but also to reformed Judaism, he showed himself from 1903 onward to be an ardent supporter of Zionism as a substitute for religious beliefs and also revealed himself to be resolutely hostile to assimilation, to the "melting-pot" theory proposed by the English Jewish thinker Israel Zangwill, whose ideas were imported to the United States at the turn of the century by a Jewish immigrant, Mary Antin. For Kallen, loyalty to Judaism was on the contrary fundamentally compatible with complete adherence to citizenship, and there is no contradiction between maintaining identitarian allegiances and participating in the public sphere in the United States, regarded as a giant orchestra within which each ethnic group plays its own part. Starting with the Jewish example, Kallen constructed a new philosophical interpretation of American society.[71]

An opponent of homogenization—which means, in effect, the triumph of Anglo-Saxon particularism—Kallen sets himself up as defender of a "democracy of nationalities," apprehended in an ethnic sense rather than a "racial" one, thus above all according to Kallen concerning immigrants of European origin: it's important to think of the United States as a "nation of nationalities" rather than an assemblage of states. In this context, the Jews symbolize the compatibility between pluralism and citizenship. Lacking the political aspirations that pit them against other states, unlike the Irish or the Polish, "they come to the United States with a desire to incorporate themselves completely in the body politic the state comprises" while still self-organizing themselves as Jews in countless individual organizations. In this sense, the Jews are "the most deliberately American of immigrants, are also the most autonomous and the most aware of themselves from the spiritual and cultural point of view."[72] They thus embody this hyphenated identity that multiplies adherences without any contradiction arising between them, with complete legitimacy giving this identity an almost official quality, which is also claimed by the Mexican-Americans, the Irish-Americans, the Italian-Americans, the African-Americans, or the Asian-Americans. Unlike the unitary concepts of citizenship that unitary nation-states impose (Kallen mentions France, Germany, England, and Russia), hyphenated identity suits the United States admirably, since it allows the multiplication of identities that unites instead of divides, and that at the same time furthers a democratic cultural pluralism.[73] Many times stressing what distinguishes France from the United States, Kallen also uses the Swiss example as an exemplary case where the multiplicity of collective allegiances turns out to be compatible both with a democratic order and with a citizenry that is particularly loyal to the country.[74] Even today, in Michael Walzer as in Will Kymlicka, Switzerland is seen as a privileged place where a multiculturalism reached through the model of constitutional democracy can flourish.

Hostile to assimilation, Kallen emerges as a theoretician of hyphenated identity and goes on to inspire a number of American thinkers of ethnicity; he can be found in the heart of the work of Walzer who, as we will discuss later on, uses the same examples as Kallen did fifty years earlier. Moreover it is often Jewish theoreticians who draw inspiration from Kallen's work to justify American ethnic and cultural pluralism: thus Milton Gordon invokes Kallen's work to describe the structural ethnic pluralism of American society, which according to him persists independently of the decline of cultural pluralism that so held Kallen's attention.[75] Nathan Glazer first declares he is more in favor of a weak ethnic pluralism inasmuch as considerable socioeconomic inequalities separate ethnic groups and, for example, give education a very variable importance. To reduce these disparities, which especially affect American blacks, in whom Kallen was only moderately interested, Glazer, like John Higham, wants a stronger common social integration that would limit this kind of pluralistic but unfair distribution of advantages.[76] He admits today, however, the semi-impossibility of a weak pluralism and, faced with the unjust socioeconomic situation in which American blacks are trapped, he also proclaims, "We are all multiculturalists now,"[77] still hoping to preserve affirmative action policies for African Americans. In the end, the perspective outlined by Kallen—which, to a lesser degree, could also be found almost at the same time in someone like Louis Wirth, rehabilitating adherence to the ghetto—which calls into question the more assimilationist views held by Robert Park and some of the Chicago School, carries the day. It foreshadows contemporary studies on the place of the Jews in a society that has legitimately become multiculturalist, studies which offer assessments of a more evolutionist nature according to which modern societies leave little room for identitarian allegiances, which come to be erased when faced with the rise of individualism or the "lonely crowd" imagined by David Riesman.[78] We also stray from the general perspectives outlined by Talcott Parsons (who however was aware of the difficulties posed by the black question in the United States), and we reject a modernizing, functionalist if simplistic vision of identitarian adherences that for a long time responded to the desire of certain Jewish thinkers to integrate into the American "golden medina." This liberal interpretation, compatible with Zangwill's vision to which so many Jewish sociologists anxious for assimilation wanted to adhere, was already not accepted, as we have noted, by Louis Wirth. Even less so was it by the successors of Horace Kallen, who also conferred a vital role on the Jews in the development of American-style multiculturalism, although the "affirmative action" that resulted from this, and that aimed at promoting positive discrimination in order to struggle against glaring inequalities, had undeniable negative consequences on their own mobility, especially in elite universities that, in the period between the two world wars, put in place for the first time mechanisms to preserve diversity with formidable barriers against negative discrimination.[79]

As we have recently noted, a number of Jewish authors figure among the rare "white" sociologists who were quick to extol the merits of multiculturalism while still fearing its consequences: they try to justify it intellectually while still vowing their loyalty to the universalist ideals of the Enlightenment and of emancipation. This is because they seem to occupy a strange and rather unique status, that of "insiders who are outsiders and outsiders who are insiders. . . . They probably form the group that is most used to living an identity that itself is multicultural in a multicultural context. . . . As insiders who are also outsiders, they seek to rescue the virtues of the Enlightenment from the shards of its failures and salvage an inclusive vision from multiculturalism, where fragmentation and divisiveness reign. . . . [They] are emblematic of the postmodern condition."[80] Actually, through their own examples, these sociologists gave American society a particular way of conceiving of pluralism. Horace Kallen emerged in the opinion of everyone as the creator of this pluralism that he thought of in too ethnic a way; once presented as a cultural pluralism, it can take on more malleable forms, more open ones, more sensitive to change, to the choice of individuals. Zangwill's melting-pot theory and Kallen's cultural pluralism are both seen as having "a certain instructive commonality: in both the Jews are paradigmatic for the future of America."[81] Formulated in the beginning of the twentieth century, Kallen's prognosis, however, imposes itself, in its cultural version, at the end of the 1960s, through the explosion of "ethnic studies" but also of "Jewish studies," which flourish at the same time. Jewish studies develop at the time when Jews, such as Michael Walzer himself, felt fully integrated into American society; they saw in Jewish studies a kind of confirmation of the recognition of their identity, while ethnic studies became an instrument to question order and the Enlightenment. Thus one was judiciously able to observe that unlike Jewish studies in the nineteenth century in Germany, which sought to stress a specifically Jewish contribution to Western philosophy, "Jewish studies typically subscribed to an Enlightenment vision of the university while ethnic studies often challenged this vision."[82]

Walzer in turn joins this learned assembly of Jewish sociologists and philosophers who, following Kallen, theorize about pluralism or multiculturalism and celebrate them in a number of ways, imagining a post-ethnic identity that would be even more radical than hybridity, to such a point that "the slogan of the Enlightenment, 'to be a human being outside and a Jew at home,' is now being realized in an unusual form: it is possible to have many identities, both outside and at home."[83] Like Michael Sandel, a Jewish philosopher, Walzer is one of the supporters of communitarianism, in its weakest, most open, most liberal version: "Sometimes," he writes, "I describe myself as a 'liberal communitarian'; sometimes I label myself as a communitarian-liberal. In fact, I do not want to identify myself with either of these two groups."[84] Fearing all forms of constraint that affect the individual in his choices, in his freedom of leaving the group that shaped him, in his right to modify his identities, Walzer distances himself from strict communitarian models: "I do not feel at ease with communitarian warmth and with the slightly stifling idea that one single community can suffice for all our needs.

I know my inner divisions and I can perceive the same signs of division in my friends."[85] The Jewish example immediately comes up when he undertakes to justify his adhesion to American-style cultural pluralism, which makes adherence to communities compatible with the citizenship of the individual. For Walzer, the case that must at all costs be avoided is that of the French Jews emancipated by a French Revolution that requires them to disappear as a nation. Walzer is almost obsessed with the French-style nation-state that in his eyes embodies, from the mode of emancipation of the Jews forward, the rejection of all identitarian presence in public space.

From one text to the other, the famous sentence by the Comte de Clermont-Tonnerre, "We must refuse everything to the Jews as a nation and grant them everything as citizens," represents for Walzer absolute evil. Already in "What Does It Mean to Be an American?" Walzer sings the praises of the United States, which is not "a jealous nation" since it rests on cultural pluralism: he directs a more severe gaze at the French concept of citizenship, which is symbolized by the principle uttered by Clermont-Tonnerre. What a contrast with the contemporary preferences of Kallen in favor of a pluralism that protects Jewish identity! Walzer stresses the Jacobin concept of regeneration, which implies the construction of a new man; applied to the Jews, as Brissot and the Abbé Grégoire intended, this view, for Walzer, implies that the Jews "could be good citizens only insofar as they became French."[86] Walzer is not wrong, even if he underestimates the resistance of French Jews and does not see that in the private domain, according to this Jacobin tradition, they managed to remain faithful to their identity. His lack of understanding of the comparative history of the various states, the little importance he grants in general to the state in his works, both prevent him from taking into account a tradition that results from a long particular history, that of the construction of the state unique to France, which differs radically from an American state that knew nothing of feudalism. Distinct historical forms of logic led to different states and to contrasting modes of emancipation of the Jews; legitimate in one case, their cultural particularism is not so in the other. We could not, however, think that the debate on the emancipation of the Jews led during the French Revolution represents a high point "in the ethnic history of France."[87] That would be to set aside the long movement of secularization that not only distances the state from Catholicism but also separates it from all ethnic collective adherence. One cannot argue so simply that the United States, open to a multiplicity of ethnicities and cultural groups, is the opposite of a France that is regarded as ethnically unified. Walzer, the American, adheres to a schematic representation of an adversary who has the audacity, in his eyes, to transform the Jews into citizens of one specific ethnicity, the French. He demonstrates moreover that he is faithful to this oversimplistic opposition since, in *On Toleration*, he returns twenty years later to similarly simplified imagery. For him, France, "a classic nation-state . . . exercises ever stronger pressure over minorities and immigrants: 'Assimilate or leave!' it proclaims, following the example of other nation-states, in the name of its own 'ethnic identity.'"[88] Once again, Walzer justifies this very biased vision of French society by citing the imperatives uttered by the Comte de Clermont-Tonnerre during the debate on the emancipation of the Jews.[89] In Walzer's opinion, in such a nation-state, even civil religion separate from the state remains shaped by the majority group and offers no possibility of expression to minority groups; in the end, "in order to become French, you must be able to imagine that your ancestors took the Bastille."[90]

On the contrary, in more tolerant societies like empires, constitutional societies like Switzerland, or societies of immigration like the United States, a hyphenated identity that legitimizes plural identitarian adherences can easily be developed. Drawing his inspiration explicitly from Horace Kallen, Walzer even thinks that in the United States, "it little matters which of the two terms of this hyphenated identity carries the day . . . , an American has the opportunity in principle to choose one side or another of his double identity." Mocking patriotic fervors as "symptoms of a republican pathology," Walzer defends twofold loyalty:

> Hence Kallen's program: assimilation "in matters economic and political," dissimilation "in cultural consciousness." The hyphen joined these two processes in one person, so that a Jewish-American (like Kallen) was similar to other Americans in his economic and political activity, but similar only to other Jews at the deeper level of culture.

It is clear that Kallen's "hyphenates," whose spiritual life is located so emphatically to the left of the hyphen, cannot derive the greater part of their happiness from their citizenship. . . . So Horace Kallen is best described as a Jewish (-American) communitarian and a (Jewish-) American liberal.[91]

It is this immense diversity of changing cultural allegiances that persuades Walzer that the United States will never become a nation-state with one single American identity, exactly insofar as Americanization does not presuppose calling hyphenated identity into question. Walzer takes the stand of a determined defender of a "meat and potatoes multiculturalism" inspired by the kind of action led by Jewish Americans who seem to him "transposable to other groups," a multiculturalism based on a local collective search for the resources capable of nourishing the functioning of local institutions of mutual aid (daycare centers, synagogues, homes for the aged, institutions to care for the sick, hospices for the terminally ill). The example of the Jewish collective mode of action that requires the participation of the individual leads him to oppose the dominant multiculturalism that is above all expressed by litigation meant to obtain the intervention of governmental authorities. Faithful to the optimistic outlook of someone like Kallen, who supported a cultural life active in associations and organizations in search of its own validation, Walzer regrets the aggressive side of contemporary political multiculturalism that seeks to obtain recognition via the authorities, a politics of quotas, an affirmative action redistributing collective property, all actions from above that fix individuals in identitarian adherences defined by the state outside of any shared citizenship.[92] We might think that his reserve toward affirmative action, which benefits African Americans especially, reveals a certain minimizing of the black question, yet paradoxically, Walzer had been involved since his youth with the black protests in the American South. Too confident in the virtues of American society as a society of immigration capable of promoting the social progress of all minorities, following the example of the Jewish minority, Walzer, like Michael Sandel,[93] neglects the specificity of the black question whose severity makes illegitimate the irenic concept of a citizenry equal for all being compatible with a cultural pluralism benefiting everyone.

So what being an American means is also this devaluing of citizenship and of a pluralism that benefits everyone, as Judith Schklar, the faithful and respected friend of Michael Walzer, has shown.[94] The fact remains that major changes seem to prove him right, since contemporary immigrants anxious to maintain their culture remain equally loyal to shared American values, unwilling to isolate themselves in the communitarianism indispensable for affirmative action.[95]

Unlike *The Revolution of the Saints* or even *Spheres of Justice*, Walzer now builds his work by bringing to the foreground his own "local," his own hyphenated identity, his twofold loyalty to the United States and to Judaism. He indeed remains a political theorist, but the problems he approaches now, those of multiculturalism or universalism, are presented through the prism of Judaism. In an ever more accentuated way, as we will note, his Jewish identity, as it is experienced in this American society regarded as so tolerant, comes to the forefront. Thus, in the opening lines of *On Toleration*, we read, "As an American Jew, I grew up thinking of myself as an object of toleration. . . . My dawning sense of the United States as a country where everyone had to tolerate everyone else was the starting point of this essay."[96] "I like to talk," he says, "about what I am, perhaps a little too much: American, Jewish, intellectual, democratic socialist, etc."[97] From *Exodus and Revolution* (1985) to the coeditorship of *Jewish Political Theory* (2000), Walzer approaches Jewish themes more and more openly. A "secular Jew,"[98] who declares "I am not a believer,"[99] he thinks of himself as an "amateur" and a "novice" in the realm of Jewish studies.[100] Nonetheless he has collaborated actively every year for more than twenty years with American colleagues such as Hilary Putnam, Michael Sandel, and Allen Silver, and also eminent Israeli professors of Jewish philosophy who are often practicing Jews, like Moshe Halberthal or Moshe Idel and Menahem Loberbaum, on rigorous collective studies conducted by the Shalom Hartman Institute of Jerusalem.[101] In this particularly fruitful framework founded on the strict collective study of the most arduous texts, Walzer tries to reinterpret political theory from Jewish "premises" while also reexamining its tradition according to a conceptualization drawn from political theory.

With this aim in mind, Walzer seems to show a boundless predilection for the prophet Amos, who literally haunts his most recent work. In his essential article, "The Two Universalisms," Walzer begins by contrasting two concepts within Jewish thought. One is posited by the prophet Isaiah, who designates Israel as "light of the nations," with the election of the Jewish people having a universal significance—it brings, "from above" as it were, truth to the whole world. This kind of universalism appears in different versions, the chief of which is Christianity. According to the other concept, uttered by the prophet Amos, a veritable alternative doctrine of Judaism, "liberation is a particular experience that is repeated for each oppressed nation." Thus it is said, "I took Israel out of Egypt. But didn't I also take the Philistines out of Cappadocia, and the Syrians out of Cyrene?" For Amos, Israel is not the only chosen nation, and exodus takes on a universal, reiterative dimension by occurring in conformity with multiple local histories: "The Philistines and the Syrians had claims that were similar (although not identical) with those of Israel: they also lamented, although their lamentations were different in their themes and idioms from those of the Jews."[102] Walzer devotes all of chapter 3 of *Interpretation and Social Criticism* to the prophecies of Amos: "And how better to prove," he exclaims, "that the connected critic is flesh of our flesh than to give him the name of Amos, the first and possibly the most radical of Israel's literary prophets?" While Jonah is presented as a prophet "who appears to know nothing about and take no interest in" the religion of the inhabitants of Nineveh whose end he predicted, while his conversation with them was centered only on notions of morality that "does not depend upon a particular moral or religious history," "the concern of the prophets is for *this* people, their own people, the 'family,' as Amos says, that came up out of Egypt."[103] Indeed Amos also is preoccupied with respect for a universal law, the implementing of a kind of international law aiming at supervising the treatment of enemies, "but alongside this universalism there is a more particularist message, delivered only . . . to the children of Israel," which concerns the rejection (uttered in the name of an exodus from Egypt the spirit of which is preserved even in contemporary Israel) of social inequalities internal to society. Amos "evokes the core values of his audience in a powerful and plausible way. He suggests an identification of the poor in Israel with the Israelite slaves in Egypt and so makes justice the primary religious demand. Why else did God deliver the people, *this people*, from the house of bondage?" While Jonah appeals to a minimal code and seems to be a "minimalist critic" capable of calling for the implementation of a uniquely "thin" morality, Amos's criticism "goes deeper than Jonah's because he knows the fundamental values of the men and women he criticizes. . . . And since he in turn is recognized as one of them, he can call them back to their 'true' path. . . . In a strange country, Amos would resemble Samson in Gaza. Not eyeless, but tongueless: he might indeed see the oppression, but he would not be able to give it a name or speak about it to the hearts of the people."[104] This is the basis of Walzer's boundless admiration for the prophet Amos, who represents more a spokesman for a "thick" ethics: though he might wonder about the elaboration of universalist rules against violence between nations, though he intones in favor of international relations that respect human rights, he also protests against a particular social oppression, the one that remains internal to Israel, whose rules he seeks to transform. What Amos invites us to do, Walzer concludes, "is not application but reiteration. Each nation can have its own prophecy, just as it has its own history, its own deliverance, its own quarrel with God."[105]

Formulated differently, it is still this idea of reiteration that can be found in Walzer's work as a means of going beyond the opposition between universalism and particularism and of avoiding falling into the trap of relativism. The detached prophet launches himself into universalist struggles directed from far away, valid for all of Humanity: like Amos, "by contrast, the national-popular intellectual seeks the common language. . . . The biblical prophet was a national-popular intellectual: he spoke to the hearts of his people even when he was most harshly critical of their behavior, reminding them of Egypt, Sinai, the covenant—the sacred events, ritually celebrated, that made them a *people*. . . . And, for all his rage, he maintained his own connection too."[106] Walzer is glad that "critical distance is not much in evidence in Amos' prophecy,"[107] who did not detach himself from his people like a distant Hercules. Amos declares, "You only have I known of all the families of the earth, therefore I will visit upon you all your iniquities." Walzer comments on this sentence in the following way: "These are examples, I suppose, of ancient parochialism. Some combination of kinship and consent ties the critic to the people he criticizes; he has a special interest in their virtue or well-being."[108] If Walzer can be presented as a leftist Burke, it is precisely because of his identification with Amos, reformist prophet blaming above all his own people, his family, whose values he shares and whom he lambastes from within, while a right-wing Burke would easily accommodate himself to all internal injustices provided they do not affect the natural order of things. Amos is the anti-Lenin "looking at Russia from a great distance,"[109] the anti-Sartre, and we might add, the anti-Rawls in his first version, that of *A Theory of Justice*.

Walzer shows a rare antagonism toward Jean-Paul Sartre, theoretician of universalism who denies humanity to his adversaries and has only scorn for a local regarded as alienating, crippling; to Walzer, Sartre exemplifies the attitude of the detached intellectual.[110] Walzer harshly criticizes *Anti-Semite and Jew*, written without any knowledge of Judaism, which Sartre understands according to a universality to which the Jew must, once liberated, be able to conform.[111] If the state of mind of the prophet Amos can be found more, according to Walzer, in Albert Camus or Ignazio Silone, it also inaugurates, from within the Jewish tradition, a long lineage of thinkers that extends from Ahad Ha'am to Martin Buber.[112] The latter reveals himself to be, in Palestine, a constant critic of the politics advocated by David Ben Gurion; he wants to remain faithful to the spirit of the Exodus, to recognize the Other (that is, in this context, the Palestinians) in order to understand "that the others have experiences and ideas similar to ours. . . . It is," Buber writes, "the prophet Amos's achievement when he tells his people that the God who brought them out of Egypt also brought the Philistines out of Caphtor and Aram out of Kir. Instead of imagining a universal exodus, Amos imagines a series; and the fact that he can specify the details of only one of the series does not deter him from acknowledging the moral value of the others."[113] Walzer notes again with emphasis that, for Buber, "hell is not the cave; it is someplace far worse. . . . Buber's claim is not that the philosopher must leave the cave but that he must leave the concentration camps," he must avoid denouncing the entire world and remain close to his people, as Buber did when, in 1948, in the new state of Israel, he rejected external criticism while still declaring himself in favor of a confederation with the Arabs, for "Were we not refugees in the diaspora?"[114] These Jewish thinkers are not the only ones to implement the reiterative universalism concerned with the fate of others and desired by Amos: Walzer stresses how much Camus, unlike Sartre, or even unlike the detached Michel Foucault,[115] "resembled Martin Buber," Camus as the "pied-noir [Algerian] writer," "*solitaire et solidaire*," who operates from within by knowing the texts and "the tender places of [his] own culture. . . . [His universalism] was constructed out of repeated particularities; it worked by what I have called reiteration, not by abstraction."[116]

Thus we must turn to Exodus, which justifies this reiterative universalism and henceforth serves as a foundation for the general thinking of Michael Walzer, fascinated by the interpretation given of it in the Old Testament, in those few exceptional lines, by the prophet Amos. Two years after *Spheres of Justice*, a work of political theory where Walzer refers, by the way, to Jewish history in order to construct his general model of spheres (to give an example of simple equality, he cites the agrarian laws of the Hebrews; to describe a striking example of assistance and an assumption of responsibility by the community, he describes at length the example of medieval Jewish communities; to illustrate his suggestion for the distribution of manual labor, he evokes the kibbutz, and so on),[117] Walzer publishes *Exodus and Revolution*.[118] This is his first book that belongs explicitly to the domain of Jewish studies. Actually, he seems to have been obsessed by this theme ever since his bar mitzvah, and although preparing his works of political theory, he thinks about it constantly, as in the 1960s when, as a young activist taking part in the struggle for the emancipation of American blacks, he listened with emotion in Montgomery, Alabama, to sermons drawn from the Book of Exodus, which in his eyes symbolizes the paradigm of revolutionary politics. Beginning with a thorough reading of the biblical text, of the Midrash, and of the commentaries of medieval Jewish thought, Walzer undertakes a study based on a certain mastery of Hebrew that, at first glance, may surprise the reader of *The Revolution of the Saints* or of *Spheres of Justice*. He describes the servitude of the Hebrews in Egypt; while they were never reduced to slavery, the process of national liberation that occurred there is paradigmatic for modern history in the rejection of submission and of extreme assimilation. He also stresses divine intervention as a way of starting off this national liberation while the acceptance of slavery was still pronounced, the fruit of long habit that cripples a desire for liberation. Walzer nevertheless opposes the Leninist interpretations of the Exodus from Egypt that attribute a decisive role to the elite or to leaders like Moses in charge of guiding the people toward a truth that they are incapable of desiring for themselves. Walzer in effect emphasizes that, in the desert, another generation of Hebrews, which did not know slavery in Egypt, would rise up to give this exodus a more deliberate aspect. For Walzer, "if there is a Leninist reading" of the Exodus from Egypt with Moses acting from outside to lead his people, there also exists a "social-democratic" version according to which Moses is only a "pedagogue" who teaches the Israelites to "fight their own battles."[119]

Walzer sees the Exodus from Egypt as the model that anticipates the modern theory of consent, with the Covenant announcing the contract entered into by the people themselves: "At Sinai, in any case, the people decide, and that implies that they have what they seemed to lack in Egypt, the capacity for decision."[120] The first movement of national liberation, the Exodus from Egypt also announced the birth of a democratic mode of government that rejects the model of liberation imagined by Cromwell or Robespierre and that depends on an elite of virtuous citizens. Moses received the divine order to associate a council of elders with his decisions; according to the calculations of Rashi, the council included about 82,600 leaders, or about 15 percent of male Israelites. This first constitutional text, drawn both from Exodus XVIII and Numbers XI, invented a new method of government distinct from charismatic power such as the traditional tribe-based power, a more democratic government conceived for passing through the ordeal of the desert and reaching the Promised Land. American society could, according to Walzer, identify with this democratic experience if it weren't sinking today into political apathy and didn't prefer in turn to go back, like the first Israel, to the practices current in Egypt, thus annulling all hope for exodus: once the Jordan was crossed, the Israelites found themselves again suddenly in Egypt because of their failure to keep the Commandments; they forgot they had been slaves in Egypt and so abandoned the terms of the Covenant.[121] We can comprehend that, in order to maintain the state of affairs on the basis of which we sustain our liberty, it is essential for each generation in its turn to remember, by reviving this crucial episode, for example at the particularly "decentralized" moment and democratic moment of the family-wide, collective reading of the *Haggadah*.[122] It must show a similar determination for the sake of the goals that are henceforth its own. Without respect for the injunction to remember the Exodus from Egypt and the Covenant that alone made this exodus possible, the return to slavery is inevitable, even after one had reached Israel, transformed, for this very reason, into Canaan.

Some commentators draw from the Exodus out of Egypt a messianic vision of history, a hope for the end of history, a promise of a utopia finally realized beyond the failure of the Hebrews' Exodus from Egypt, the transformation of human nature with final divine redemption in sight—interpretations lacking any historical or geographical dimension, whether Jewish or Christian, which illuminates just as much utopian thought, even when it is hostile to the religious. Walzer questions this messianic program, especially in contemporary Zionist versions of it defended by the Israeli revisionist right yearning for apocalypse. He claims rather to follow Ahad Ha'am and Gershom Scholem, and the revolution led through the desert that must be pursued well beyond it. Against messianism with its universalist claim, he finds his favorite hypothesis in the anchorage of a liberation movement in multiple histories that reiterate a similar message:

> Compared with political messianism, Exodus makes for a cautious and moderate politics. . . . The Exodus story is open to interpretation, and one can imagine social democrats and (some) Bolsheviks at home within it. The biblical text tells a tale of argument and contention, and the commentators read the text in the same spirit; there is always "another interpretation." . . . So pharaonic oppression, deliverance, Sinai, and Canaan are still with us, powerful memories shaping our perceptions of the political world. The "door of hope" is still open; things are not what they might be—even when what they might be isn't totally different from what they are. This is a central

theme in Western thought. . . . Wherever you live, it is probably Egypt; . . . there is a better place. . . . "The way to the land is through the wilderness." There is no way to get from here to there except by joining together and marching.[123]

Thus, "the centrality of the Bible in Western thought" explains the endless repetition of this same story between liberation and slavery, a self-interested search for "milk and honey" or the rigorous accomplishment of the divine message, the Covenant, by strict respect for the Sabbath, for the law, between the democratic government and recourse to power of the leaders: "[These] are *our* alternatives. In other cultures, men and women read other books, tell different stories, confront different choices."[124] The Western world is presented as an immense "local," a giant "cave" in which the biblical tale of the Exodus from Egypt is retold indefinitely. This tale in which Western thought recognizes itself seems, according to Walzer, to find no echo in the country of the Enlightenment, in revolutionary France "whose leading actors were as resolutely hostile to Jewish as they were to Christian conceptions of history."[125] In this spirit, revolutionary France is once again opposed to America, which is moved by the biblical story, endlessly inspired by it, and permanently places the Exodus from Egypt in the heart of its own tale of national or social liberation. Aside from almost the sole example of the French, in Walzer's view, Western history repeats this archetypal process of liberation based on the Exodus in a number of ways, whereas elsewhere other stories serve as identically founding myths.

The Old Testament serves as a pattern for modern revolutionary political history. Aside from the story of the Exodus, one can also find in it a theory of exile symbolized by the wandering of the Hebrews after the fall of the Temple, for which Babylon is the founding moment. After studying the Exodus from Egypt and its ethical consequences down through contemporary societies, including Israel, Walzer turns to the exile to which the Hebrews were forced, when they became Jews at the fall of their own state. Unlike Exodus, which is reiterated throughout all of Western history, the exile into which the Jews have found themselves plunged ever since their diaspora, following the fall of the Temple and the loss of all political sovereignty, is not endowed with such a universal dimension. Throughout history it only concerns the Jews in relation to the nations. Along with a study of exile, Walzer pushes the radical transformation of his centers of interest to an extreme: this time, light years away from the political theory to which he devoted most of his previous works, only Jewish history is dealt with, a history that goes from Babylon to the birth of Israel in 1948, a history that is reinterpreted solely through traditional texts. Actually, in Walzer's opinion, "the birth of a truly liberal and pluralistic society in the United States as well as the birth of the Jewish state in the country of Israel mark the end of exile. They make possible, but do not guarantee, our liberation from the politics of exile."[126] For Walzer the American, Jewish exile reaches its end as much in the United States as in Israel, since in both these societies, Jews can live in harmony with their culture, either because they benefit, like all other minorities, from a hyphenated identity whose first word on the left (Jewish) carries the day over that on the right (American), or because they have a "thick" Israeli nationality that is compatible with a "thin" universalist adherence.

Michael Walzer's most recent books, then, explicitly concern Israel ancient and modern in its relations with politics, power, and the state. Lacking a state for almost two millennia, reduced to exile and to dispersion after the destruction of the Temple, the Jewish people, deprived of sovereign power, set in place strategies of accommodation with the aim of maintaining its identity. Following in the footsteps of a number of commentators,[127] Walzer in turn tries to annihilate the thesis of radical absence of political power of the Jews in exile and to show that for them the absence of state does not necessarily imply an absolute political incapacity, absolute subjection, resignation, servitude. The Jews preserve the possibility of making choices, of putting into place educative or philanthropic institutions, of protecting their community, the *kahal* that is presented as "the polis of exilic Jewry . . . one of the most compelling features of their political tradition,"[128] of establishing various relationships with the authorities of the country of exile; even in such an unfavorable context, politics is thus not reserved to Gentiles, as a certain interpretation of exile argues.[129] Walzer stresses, for example, the role of the court Jews, the strategy adopted in a number of historical contexts that consists in seeking out a privileged alliance with the prince, the king or the emperor as a defense mechanism faced with the hatred and prejudice of the masses. Walzer however restricts himself to reading only the traditional texts in order to decipher these defensive strategies; he does not try to bring to light new archives or new documents and does not adopt the stance of today's "Jewish studies"; rather, Walzer remains faithful to political theory.[130] He confines himself strictly to a reading of the Old Testament along with its scholarly commentaries and refers only to books that have to do with one episode or another of the Bible. Starting with the example of Esther, Walzer closely examines the texts and uses the most recent scholarly bibliography: deprived of all power in their situation of exile, the Jews are miraculously saved by the decisive intervention of Esther with Ahasuerus to whom, when seduced by her beauty, he deigned to choose her as queen, she did not reveal her adherence to the Jewish nation. As a figure of exile, Esther does not represent the Jews and was not chosen by them, but rather by the will of the king alone, proof of the radical absence among the Jews during the time of exile of any mastery over their fate. Walzer is compelled to present Mordecai, Esther's tutor who became an important and feared personage of the court, as a court Jew, and even compares him to Joseph. He considers them both as ambiguous characters, not very charming, scarcely honorable, who do not take responsibility for a passive and dependent people; in Walzer's opinion, they ensure the survival of the Jews through their political cleverness, the sole strategy for this situation of exile where the coming of redemption remains illusory.[131] In Babylon a "radically new" relationship to politics is invented, then, which foreshadows the method of survival adopted by the Jews during their long exile when they found themselves in a situation of extreme fragility: the search for "compromises" supported by communitarian institutions that manage, in the best case, in the absence of any actual state power, to defend their autonomy.[132] It is in Babylon that the Jews detach themselves from their monarchic institutions and, having lost their sovereignty, put their faith in rabbis, wise men, and judges, and it is then that the Book itself replaces the state.[133] This new situation arouses an unprecedented reaction that will accompany the Jews throughout their entire exile. Walzer, in a very original way, sees in fact Haman as the first of the anti-Semites,[134] his hatred of the Jews resting on personal feelings, on the rejection of the presence of these foreigners scattered throughout the world whom he accuses of preserving their traditions and not respecting the laws of the kingdom. In the tale of Esther, one can read this sentence of Haman's, addressed to Ahasuerus: "There is a certain people scattered abroad and dispersed among the people in all the provinces of thy kingdom; and their laws are diverse from all people; neither keep they the king's laws: therefore it is not for the king's profit to suffer them. If it please the king, let it be written that they may be destroyed" (Esther 3:8–9). The war that once set Israel as a nation endowed with a state against its enemies is followed, then, in exile, by an anti-Semitism destined to last in identical historical contexts throughout the ages.

Walzer luminously describes this new situation that historians find in other eras: the trust reposed by the Jews in king or emperor, the economic or even political services the Jews rendered in exchange for the protection of state institutions. This is the single bulwark against popular prejudices and hatreds, but also against the various jealousies that their status as foreigners arouses, made obvious by their observance of the rules of the Covenant (celebration of the Sabbath, practice of Kashrut, endogamous marriages, and so on). To defend themselves from such an accusation that makes them into outcasts, the Jews, from the time of their experience in Babylon, tried on the contrary to make the laws of the kingdom their own in order to demonstrate their loyalty. From Babylon to Alexandria or Madrid, from Berlin to Paris, everywhere the Jews proclaimed their adherence to the laws of their host nation and fervently carried out their duty as citizens, giving their lives for their country of exile. Close to the texts and rather indifferent to sociohistorical realities, Walzer, following in the footsteps of other commentators, sees in a letter sent from Jerusalem by the prophet Jeremiah to the exiles of Babylon the origin of the conduct to uphold in exile: "Thus saith the LORD of hosts, the God of Israel, unto all that are carried away captives, whom I have caused to be carried away from Jerusalem unto Babylon; Build ye houses, and dwell in them; and plant gardens, and eat the fruit of them; Take ye wives, and beget sons and daughters; and take wives for your sons, and give your daughters to husbands, that they may bear sons and daughters; that ye may be increased there, and not diminished. And seek the peace of the city whither I have caused you to be carried away captives, and pray unto the LORD for it: for in the peace thereof shall ye have peace." (Jeremiah 29:4–7).[135] The prophet suggests a real material and political coming to terms with the city of exile, with any city where Jews live, whatever its regime or its dominant religion: what matters is to integrate into that society, to settle there, to live there fully by showing that one is loyal. This essential compromise without any political ambition seems, for Walzer, easier in an empire or a city of a cosmopolitan nature:[136] in fact, it is logical that a French-style nation-state sets about to limit this compromise by imposing its norms on each of its citizens.[137]

What remains is to find a solution to make complete integration in the city of exile compatible with maintaining Jewish identity. Walzer stresses that it is precisely in Babylon that the maxim is formulated by Samuel that regulates the bonds between Jews and their city of adherence, *dina de malkhuta dina*: "the law of the country is the law," a phrase that gives a Halachic justification to obey non-Halachic laws, provided however that they do not concern religious laws, which cannot be subordinated to the law of the kingdom, especially for anything concerning marriage, divorce, conversion, and so on.[138] Do we really think that any law, even one that contradicts the Torah, must be accepted by the Jews? As Menachem Lorberbaum shows in *The Jewish Political Tradition*, only the civil law of the kingdom (concerning for example the levying of taxes), which is applied uniformly to all citizens and which all have tacitly accepted, must also be respected by the Jews; an unjust law that treats Jews differently cannot be regarded as legitimate.[139] Walzer has recently become involved in a remarkable commentary on this precept, which suddenly gives his entire body of work a very striking coherence. He begins by stressing that through the putting into practice of dina de malkhuta dina, the Jews integrate non-Jewish laws into the Jewish law and thus respect their own law. Faced with an unjust law, they do not rebel, but simply try to avoid its consequences, for, in Walzer's eyes, in these times of pre-emancipation, the Jews have no confidence in the possible justice of the political system in which they

live, "emancipation being revealed thus as a precondition for any politics of a revolutionary kind."[140]

Thus the Jews invent a kind of "universalism of the weak," accepting
a foreign law, making it their own insofar as it is legitimate, equal for
all. Thus dina de malkhuta dina symbolizes the "universalism of the
weak" that regulates the life of Jews in exile and requires that the law
that is applied to foreigners responds to universalist criteria. Walzer invents, at this point on his intellectual journey, a formula with a strong
ethical charge that concerns all foreigners in exile and that questions all
states as to how they treat foreigners. Already in *Spheres of Justice*, Walzer stressed the necessity of thus considering the foreigner who is not
passing through, like the immigrant laborer who wants to return to his
country of origin, in order to avoid recreating modern "metics."[141] The
universalism of the weak appears as much in international relations and
laws of war as it does within each nation, as the prophet Amos shows.
Each time, it implies respect for fair rules shared by the strong and
weak alike, by the citizen and by the foreigner. In this sense, the Bible
says that "One law shall be to him that is home-born, and unto the
stranger that sojourneth among you" (Exodus 12:49).

In a very subtle way, Walzer sets out to construct a Jewish interpretation of universalism whose appearance he hopes for, a little like Isaiah
Berlin, by separating it from the universalism of the philosophers of the
French-style Enlightenment or from their Jewish proponents who give
voice to a kind of universalism of a cultivated elite, a universalism from
above. Unlike the *maskilim*, the enlightened Jewish elite who drew inspiration from the Enlightenment of the emancipation, Walzer wants
to validate a Jewish universalism previous to emancipation, one that is
seen, on the contrary, as a "universalism of the weak."[142] In agreement
with Michael Wyschogrod who thinks, provocatively, that a Judaism
concerned solely with ethics and reason only represents the Judaism of
assimilated Jews,[143] Walzer, who claims the heritage of the Enlightenment, means however to found a universalism conceived by Jews on the
basis of their traditions, which "could not be abandoned to those who
defend them as conservatives."[144] Here again, Walzer shows he is close
to Isaiah Berlin and to his extreme reservations about the Enlightenment that he accused, following Herder, of being indifferent to mul-

tiple cultural codes. Like Herder and Berlin, Walzer thinks in turn that they standardize, in the name of a reason from above, cultures that take on their meaning only when anchored in the long continuity of their traditions. To go beyond the universalism-particularism opposition and to avoid the relativism that threatens Herder and Berlin, Walzer tries to demonstrate, on the basis of his reading of the oldest texts, of writings previous to rationalism in the style of Mendelssohn, that from the oldest Judaism, not yet affected by the Enlightenment, there can arise another universalism that is all the more legitimate since it rests this time on beliefs "from below."

The code of Noah proclaimed by the Lord before the Covenant of Sinai and the gift of the Torah (which includes the code of Noah) through the intervention of Moses, represents in this first perspective, for a number of rabbis quoted by Walzer, "a kind of international law . . . a Jewish law for Gentiles. It is 'our' universal law for 'them.' . . . It only makes sense when the Jews exercise political power, take responsibility for the seventh commandment, and establish a system of law capable of applying the first six to their non-Jewish subjects. . . . The rabbis conceived of a minimal array of legislations that can be applied to non-Jewish residents, and that all human beings must respect."[145] Walzer relies on the recent interpretations of David Novack to decide that the code of Noah does not at all constitute the responsibility of the Jews: in the exile where they find themselves later on, it will be implemented by the Gentiles.[146] It is a matter of a body of commandments revealed to humanity during the time of Adam and of Noah, which henceforth governs all nations and founds the normativity of the Other. From then on, and this is the main point:

> The code of Noah gives a new foundation to the *dina de malkhuta dina* rule which can no longer be interpreted simply as a way for the Jews to accommodate themselves in exile to the power of the Gentiles: it actually implies the recognition of the validity of the content of the law of the Gentiles. . . . It is possible to recognize a minimalist version of the code that all nations must respect and apply. And from this point of view, 'we' can learn 'their' laws.[147]

The Jews accept the law of the country all the more easily when this law conforms to the code of Noah. Their accommodation to the law of the country is thus not purely for the moment. As a philosopher of politics, Walzer does not enter into a discussion of examples that contradict this optimistic interpretation; he does not linger over historical examples where dina de malkhuta dina legitimizes on the contrary the implementation of laws that are profoundly discriminatory against the Jews, laws they are nonetheless forced to accept under pressure from a strong or authoritarian state that seeks to bring an end to their particularism.

Faithful to the general perspective posed in his first works, Walzer tries to link this universalism, which owes nothing to the Greeks or to the Christians, and even less to Kant or to the Jewish reformers who are inspired by them, to a particularism based on the most fundamental Jewish tradition, to demonstrate that it is indeed a matter of a putting into practice of a reiterative universalism from "below," a Jewish "local," which is illustrated through the words of the prophet Amos by his definitive refusal of any possibility of "exiling and reducing to slavery an entire population." Tirelessly, Walzer takes up the statements of Amos from one book to another, quoting them in the texts to the point of making it the main unifying thread essential to his own general interpretation. Aware of the iconoclastic nature of his positive appreciation of Amos's reasoning, which is hardly ever accepted by Jewish tradition, Walzer even suggests that it can also be applied to the Israel of today, this time for the benefit of the Other, of the non-Jew living according to the laws of the Jewish state that marks the end of exile.[148] In his turn, the non-Jew, in a fragile and marginal position, could accept the *dina de malkhuta dina* formula only on condition that the law of the country, namely that of the Jewish state, is just and is applied identically to all citizens in conformity with the code of Noah, which applies to all of humanity.

Imagined during the depths of exile, in that Babylon that announced the time of a long dispersion, by rabbis anxious to maintain the identity of the nation while still accepting the law of the country (hoping also to be able to count on the support of its king), this formula takes on an entirely different meaning with the end of exile. For Walzer, Israel must preserve its Jewish character, but in the "minimal" sense of the term, without being transformed into a Catholic Ireland or, on the contrary, into a fiercely secularized France as during the time of the Third

Republic. The state of Israel can thus remain in harmony with its Jewish culture, and those who want to can study the Talmud and celebrate Hanukkah while still being able to read Plato, without the state having any possibility of intervening in an authoritarian way in the application of the halacha. From then on, unlike the United States, a country where Jewish exile has also reached its end, the state that has become Jewish must remain fundamentally liberal by including minorities that it does not oppress. A "liberal nationalism" that is both imaginable and indispensable in Israel will thus be protected from any propensity toward ethnic nationalism.[149] Hence Walzer's determined condemnation of a Great Israel conducive to the establishment of a "horrible and cruel local": "The Jews who are aware of their own diasporic history should identify more with the Arabs than with the Jews of Great Israel. And if it should happen that the policies of ethnic transfer are implemented, wouldn't we say that the exile of the Arabs would resemble the exile of the Jews from Spain in 1492, with the Jews perceived this time as the Spaniards?"[150] As a true friend of Israel, which he profoundly associates with his own life, Walzer calls for a particular Jewish ethics in order to ensure, in the framework of the Jewish state, universalism that prevents any discrimination and allows, in public space, the flourishing of this pluralism to which he shows himself so passionately attached.[151]

## Eight

Yosef Hayim Yerushalmi:
A Home for "Fallen Jews"

The first chapter of *From Spanish Court to Italian Ghetto*, Yosef Hayim Yerushalmi's masterwork, opens with a quotation by Salomon Ibn Verga, from the *Shebet Yehudah* (The scepter of Yehuda) that has fascinated him throughout his life: "And what will it profit our lord and king," Solomon ibn Verga wonders, "to pour holy water on the Jews, calling them by our names, 'Pedro' or 'Pablo,' while they keep their faith like Akiba or Tarfon? . . . Know, Sire, that Judaism is one of the incurable diseases."[1] In 1991, twenty-five years after writing this masterwork that formed his doctoral thesis devoted to that other, Nearer East that is the Sephardic continent, Yerushalmi published his *Freud's Moses*. At a crucial passage in this book, which sheds light on Freud's psycho-Lamarckism, which favors the "interminable" transmission of Jewishness from one generation to the next while Judaism itself is "terminable," we again find this citation, translated in almost the same way. This time it introduces the following statement by a Spanish monarch being imagined by Ibn Verga, a Spanish Jew who took refuge in Portugal and was forced to convert in 1497: "I am far from the opinion of the kings who preceded me, who sought to force the Jews to believe in Jesus. . . . My reason is as follows: The Jews who, *when their religion was given to them*, witnessed those awesome and holy assemblies and those marvels and fires from heaven, *had the image of all that so strongly impressed upon them that it remains with them naturally*."[2]

From one book to another, the question remains the same: how to account for the persistence of Jewish identity through the centuries when it comes up against so many constraints, so much violence and hatred, when it experiences the temptations of assimilation, of full-fledged entrance into open societies that offer it the opportunity to disappear? Does identity stem from individual choice, or is it rather expressed

through "incurable diseases" by a Lamarckism "deconstructed into Jewish terms" that illustrates "the powerful feeling that, for better or worse,
one cannot really cease being Jewish, not merely because of current anti-
Semitism or discrimination, and certainly not because of the Chain of
Tradition, but because one's fate in being Jewish was determined long
ago by the Fathers, and that often what one feels most deeply and ob-
scurely is a trilling wire in the blood"?[3] Felt as "a point of anchorage or,
on the contrary, as a ball and chain," the Jewish past as "subjective dimension" could not be rejected by modern Jews like Freud, Spinoza, or
Marx, who are seen, in the eyes of Yosef H. Yerushalmi, as "Psychological Jews" for whom "content is replaced by character."[4] Freud, however,
is not portrayed solely as a "Psychological Jew," and despite his latent
Lamarckism, his Jewish identity also has to do with intentional choice,
is based on an assumed culture, whose undeniable reality Yerushalmi
has shown, along with its essential place in his education, its constant
presence through numerous personal objects to which Freud was especially attached.[5] Throughout history, from Spanish and Portuguese
Marranos to Jews in Berlin or Vienna, all confronted with different issues, and despite forced or voluntary conversions, or multiple methods
of escape toward assimilation, Jewish identity persists and imposes itself
as a fitting subject for a historian not as a particular culture that could
be distinguished from a "universal" vision, "that canard of the Enlightenment which became and remains a major neurosis of modern Jewish
intellectuals,"[6] but simply as the culture of the Jewish people, which
does not, for Yerushalmi, imply any kind of relativism.

Like Freud, whom Yerushalmi presents as a "Jewish historian,"[7]
Yosef H. Yerushalmi continually claims this unique quality. A "Lithuanian rationalist," as he calls himself,[8] he plainly assumes this self-
designation that forcefully links identity to professional competence,
without any contradiction arising from the combination. Even as a
young student, Yerushalmi decided to "become a Jewish historian," a
phrase that is often repeated in his work:[9] "I am a historian of the Jews"
for "as a contemporary Jewish historian I chose to project myself on
Jewish history itself."[10] As a Jewish historian, Yerushalmi stressed for
example that throughout the four lectures that form *Zakhor*, he always
spoke "unabashedly in inner Jewish terms."[11] Aware of the fact that

non-Jews can acquire the competence that will make them historians of the Jews, he writes, "If I continue to limit myself to the Jewish case that is not only because, as an historian of the Jews, I fancy that I know it best, but also because, as a Jewish historian, I find myself personally involved."[12] This openly assumed identity appears in the very beginning of his "Monologue with Freud"; addressing the latter, he declares right away, "We both have, as Jews, an equal stake. Therefore in speaking of the Jews I shall not say 'they.' I shall say 'we.' The distinction is familiar to you."[13] In *Zakhor* as well, Yerushalmi does not try to mask the empathy he feels as a Jewish historian for his people, toward which he tries to construct "a bridge."[14] The same is true when he evokes, more recently, *Galut*, the book by Yitzak Baer concerning the tragic fate of the Jews of Spain, written in urgency as if to warn his German Jewish compatriots of the new threat looming over them, a work that has constantly been present in Yerushalmi's mind ever since *From Spanish Court to Italian Ghetto*. In Yerushalmi's opinion, this "work was not only written by a historian of Judaism but by a Jewish historian implicated existentially in his subject, considering Jewish history from within, and addressing his people while it was going through its hours of crisis."[15] "As a Jew," Yerushalmi thinks that Jewish history above all else "for my people, now as in the past, is in grave peril of its life."[16] This claimed identity is expressed in similar terms in Freud, his hero, that other "Jewish historian" who wrote, "I have always had a strong feeling of belonging together with my people and have always nurtured it in my children as well."[17]

Jewish historians should try to reduce the weight of the myths that turn them away from the sense of a history that remains perilous, in order to help the Jews grasp the significance of possible analogies that are just as devastating but that utopias and messianic beliefs nonetheless minimize. Secularized, the history implemented by Jewish historians means to be secular, scientific, capable of detecting and warning the Jewish people of the possible, logical occurrence of events that bring disaster. We can thus take a better measure of the implication, the involvement of the author of *Zakhor*: the Jewish historian devotes all his strength to deciphering the lineaments of the history of the Jews in order to enlighten "his people" on the dangers but also the hope borne by a history that also carries him along with it. Not hiding his "empathy" for his object of study, the Jewish historian must nevertheless maintain, even more than his precursors in the Wissenschaft, a "distance" that can ensure the objectivity of his research, a "detachment" thanks to which he can calmly "stand guard" against all those who set about shredding documents, inventing myths, "raping memory."[18] For Yerushalmi, that is not at all specific to Jewish historians who devote their work to Jewish history, for "the problem of objectivity is the same for all historians; it is not by any means unique to historians of the Jews who are themselves Jewish. Why should my anxiety be greater than that of the French or Russian historian working on the Napoleonic wars? My own concept of historical research and writing oscillates between empathy and distance" for it is through "the particular" that we can reach "the universal."[19]

When, in June 1970, he approached this question before students at the Hebrew College during a public lecture on the occasion of his appointment to Harvard University as a professor of Hebrew and Jewish history, Yosef H. Yerushalmi showed he was firm in his convictions and spoke out loud and clear about the certainties he would continually defend:

> Amnesia is not a goal but a disorder. And historical amnesia can be no less grave than that of the individual . . . we must consciously carry a Jewish past within us. The first *zakhor*—remember—was uttered in the Torah. The amnesia of a Frenchman or an Italian or a Spaniard is more easily cured than that of a Jew, being only partial to begin with . . . their history surrounds them physically. . . . With us it is different. Our physical monuments in the diaspora almost all vanished. Even in Eretz Ysrael, even with the remarkable achievements of the archaeologist's pick, only sparse remnants come to view of what once was. . . . In the past, history as a subject was of little concern to Jews, for history was present in the organic complex of Jewish learning, law, and practice. Today, after the Aquarian shocks of the last two hundred years, that unity has been rent asunder and as a consequence history itself becomes vital.[20]

Thus a vast program of research supported by a certain number of principles is drawn up: the Jews have up to modern times constituted a people, like the French or the Italians; knowledge of one's own past is almost inaccessible to them, since their history is deprived of all the physical continuity thanks to which a national symbolism is constructed. With the hindsight of liturgy and Jewish education, which was the only thing to preserve the collective identity in diaspora, Jewish history becomes essential to the struggle against the amnesia that threatens identity all the more so when assimilation (or conversion) is eroding the collective imagination.

We remember how Renan, in his famous speech on the nation, advised the French deliberately to forget the tragic events that once divided them; he boasted of the virtues of amnesia as a definitive way to institutionalize an ancient nation capable henceforth of founding its unity on "a daily plebiscite." Yerushalmi, by contrast, means to fight with all his strength against amnesia by giving his people the knowledge of their own historic past, by helping them remember past despair but also the hope that punctuated the desire to ensure a Jewish continuity to a scattered people still menaced in the exile that weakens them. While old, firmly established nations must forget what might divide them, the Jewish people in diaspora must endlessly remember; the role of the Jewish historian is thus plainly outlined: like the archaeologist, by distancing himself from the atemporal logic peculiar to liturgical time, he must rediscover the traces of a buried past. His function in the construction of a scattered nation is undeniable. By attributing such a role to the Jewish historian, like that of the archaeologist, Yerushalmi anticipates and foreshadows the theoreticians of nationalism who will also grant a fundamental influence to archaeology as a method of reconstitution of a past indispensable to the collective imagination of the nation. Thus, following the example of Émile Durkheim, a specialist in nationalism like Anthony Smith is inspired by excavations like those led by the Israeli archaeologist Yigal Yadin to reject both the perennialist visions of the nation as an intangible organic reality and the modernist conceptions that on the contrary conceive of the nation as stemming from a modern invention of artificial nature under control of the state. Israel is seen here as an exemplary case of the rebirth of a nation reimagined through myths and legends, then rooted once again in historical reality thanks to the efforts of archaeologists who discover the traces of a buried and forgotten past of religious liturgy and tradition: Masada, a tragic and forgotten event, forgotten for centuries, once it was rediscovered, legitimizes the continuity of the nation.[21] The archaeologist as historian manages thus to construct this "bridge" toward "his people."

As a continuation of his 1970 lecture, Yerushalmi also shows, in his text "Clio and the Jews" published in 1980, that for the first time the Jews are "obsessed" with history: "In the measure that we have become modern Western men and women, the historical outlook is now part of our innermost selves."[22] In *Zakhor*, a key work published two years earlier, he again accentuates this interpretation and emphasizes that the Jewish historian is involved in "a radically new venture" since his method of studying the past leads him to "a decisive break with that past." From then on, "the contemporary effort to reconstruct the Jewish past begins at a time that witnesses a sharp break in the continuity of Jewish life and hence also an ever-growing decay of Jewish group memory. In this sense, if for no other, history becomes what it had never been before—the faith of fallen Jews. For the first time history, not a sacred text, becomes the arbiter of Judaism."[23] The thirst for history comes, then, from this fall of the "ahistorical past."[24] The Jews have now tasted the forbidden fruit of knowledge; they have become historicized. Yerushalmi insists on this by using strong expressions that emphasize the extent of the "break" between yesterday and today: in his opinion—and this point, which is of secondary importance in our own perspective, has been keenly disputed[25]—"Only in the modern era do we really find, for the first time, a Jewish historiography divorced from Jewish collective memory and, in crucial respects, thoroughly at odds with it."[26] Faced with the decline of Jewish memory linked to the erosion of the sacred, to the calling into question of faith in an era when secularization is triumphing, the historian serves as a "pathologist" even if his work "represents . . . a new kind of recollection" that cannot entertain the ambition of giving back life to the atemporal memory of before resting solely on knowledge of traditional texts.[27] Product of this "revolution," of this incredible "break" that affects "the fallen Jews," the historian all of a sudden "himself is the product of rupture,"[28] responsible for "the burden of building a bridge to his people." Yerushalmi adds, "I do not know for certain that this will be possible."[29]

Yosef H. Yerushalmi's career illustrates his refined ambition since he occupies, at Columbia, a chair bearing the name of his master Salo Baron, whom he himself calls "foremost of Jewish historians in our time" and who presided over his thesis board.[30] Yerushalmi shows he is aware of the innovative quality of his academic position:

> As a professional Jewish historian I am a new creature in Jewish history. My lineage does not extend beyond the second decade of the nineteenth century, which makes me, if not illegitimate, at least a *parvenu* within the long history of the Jews. It is not merely that I teach Jewish history at a university, though that is new enough. Such a position only goes back to 1930 when my own teacher, Salo Wittmayer Baron, received the Miller professorship at Columbia, the first chair in Jewish history at a secular university in the Western world. More than that, it is the very nature of what and how I study, how I teach and what I write . . . the very mode in which I delve into the Jewish past represents a decisive break with that past.[31]

Curiously using the same somewhat pejorative terminology as Hannah Arendt, Yerushalmi sees himself as "a parvenu." However, he does not present any of the defects described by Arendt when she speaks of the parvenu Jews of the last century, and we note too that he does not at all seem like a pariah, according to the terminology proposed in Arendt's *The Origins of Totalitarianism*, a work to which he refers many times. He is not a pariah simply because his professional competence assures him a prestigious position within the institution of the university. To his surprise even now, he had "the privilege of teaching in both institutions—Harvard and Columbia—that were the first secular universities to integrate postbiblical Jewish studies into the patrimony of global civilization."[32] If Yerushalmi is a "parvenu," it is because he cannot rely on an already institutionalized tradition.

By following his teacher Salo Baron, although he does not occupy the same chair, Yerushalmi symbolizes the culmination point of the efforts of the scholars of *Wissenschaft des Judentums* at the beginning of the nineteenth century; his books also illustrate his profound transformation in how he can "sniff out connections hidden beneath the surface," like a veritable "historical detective,"[33] with the help of the most sophisticated methods of contemporary historians who reject the philosophical idealism that the Jewish scholars of the nineteenth century shared, or by distancing himself from the big pictures they were partial to, so as to confine himself to a more limited but profoundly researched domain. With Yerushalmi, probably for the first time in the diaspora, a Jew, a historian of Judaism, approaches the Jewish past in the framework of one of the most prestigious universities in the Western world that, like most of them, has for a long time remained inaccessible to the scholars of the Jewish Wissenschaft and their heirs, despite their doctorates that recognized their professional competence.[34] Neither Leopold Zunz, nor Abraham Geiger, nor Zacharias Frankel, nor, later on, Heinrich Graetz could pursue their erudite studies, despite their diplomas, in a university: they were forced to teach in the framework of rabbinic seminaries, without any hope of having a career in academic institutions that, in Germany and Russia but also in the United States and Great Britain, remained closed to Jewish professors even sometimes in the middle of the twentieth century. Thus, Zunz directed a teachers' seminary in Berlin; Geiger earned his living as a rabbi in Breslau and then in Frankfurt and Berlin; Frankel, appointed grand rabbi of Dresden, founded in 1854 the famous seminary of Jewish theology in Breslau where Graetz and the philologist Jacob Bernays—who was also disappointed at not being able to get into a university—joined him. Confronted with such requests, the minister of education thought in effect that the German university had to preserve its Christian character. All these scholars tried to obtain a position as university professors to which their title of "doctor" entitled them; none succeeded, despite urgent and numerous attempts. King Friedrich II intervened in person to prevent Eduard Gans, the famous disciple of Hegel, from obtaining a position as professor at the University of Jena. In 1848, Zunz, who "offered a new type of religious leadership, the historian,"[35] failed in his attempt, the Prussian government retorting that "a professorship that would be established with the ulterior motive of supporting and strengthening the Jewish organism in its particularity, in its alienating laws and customs, would contradict the purpose of the new freedom that levels stubborn differences. It would mean a special concession to the Jews, an abuse of the university."[36] Dubnow, finally, taught only briefly, beginning in 1907, at St. Petersburg, in a private Jewish school of higher learning, the Institute of Eastern Studies, and later on, during the 1917 revolution, in the public Jewish university, or else in his own apartment.[37]

We thus gain a better understanding of the radical novelty of the chair created at Columbia for Salo Baron, Yerushalmi's teacher and Arendt's faithful friend. In many respects, far from Europe, this appointment illustrates or even foreshadows the moment of "standardization" of Jewish studies in the United States,[38] which led to the contemporary explosion of Jewish studies. The appointment of Yosef H. Yerushalmi to the history department at Harvard in 1970 expresses the consecration of Jewish history, which was distancing itself from its parochial dimension, confined as it was before almost always to restricted seminaries, to colleges or departments devoted to Middle Eastern studies. Until then, it was the *Jewish Publication Society* that, almost exclusively, published works written by Jewish historians on Jewish history.[39] In the 1970s, things changed at the same time as, in a more general way, social history was replacing diplomatic or intellectual history in the large Western universities; from then on new paths opened up for those who were interested in the history of labor, poverty, class, peasants, or the marginal. Far from intellectual history or the history of the elite, ordinary Jews became in turn objects of legitimate history in their migratory undertaking, their involvement in revolutionary movements, or their mode of life in the suburbs of large cities.[40] Even if it deliberately distances itself from the great panoramas dear to Leopold Zunz, Heinrich Graetz, and Salo Baron, vast panoramas that had become unrealizable, remote from contemporary methodological preoccupations, the work of Yosef H. Yerushalmi represents the culmination of the Wissenschaft of the nineteenth century by joining these profound transformations that were affecting History as a discipline. It is innovative in its method of profoundly "excavating" a specific domain following the example of today's best historians concerned with non-Jewish areas. It appears as an essential turning point, a crucial moment when great questions are making themselves heard again even if the professional historian now approaches them by the book.

While Leopold Zunz remained, in Germany, in a profoundly hostile context, at the "periphery,"[41] Yerushalmi, in the United States, unquestionably took his place in the center, an unexpected situation when we recall the way Wissenschaft scholars like Frankel and Graetz looked down in their time on American Jews, whom they regarded as deprived of all historicity because of their lack of acquaintance with suffering.[42] Following the example of Yerushalmi, and often under his direction, the distant heirs of the Wissenschaft prospered henceforth in most large American universities.[43] Though it is true that Yosef H. Yerushalmi doesn't regularly study "ordinary" Jews as is often done today, drawing inspiration from the new historiography that is more attentive to the common people or to those who are unknown, we can't restrict his enterprise only to the history of ideas or of high culture.[44] Actually, Yerushalmi's project continues that of the scholars of the nineteenth century, since he also strives in his own way to apprehend the Jewish fate in all its scope through a few exceptional people, often Marrano emigrants, since they "stand out as perhaps the first modern Jews."[45] "If I began by studying the Marranos, it is because one dimension of Marranism seems to draw our attention, existentially, shall I say. This was the duality, the profound tearing-apart, that divided their life, and which I continue to think is a contemporary dimension. The Marranos were perhaps the first Jews who had to live in two radically different universes at once, with all the inner tensions and conflicts that resulted from this."[46] From the Jew Baruch, tried in July 1320 in the name of the Catholic Inquisition by the tribunal of Pamiers, the study of whom constitutes the first text published by Yerushalmi,[47] to Ibn Verga, Isaac Cardoso, Spinoza, Schoenberg, or Freud, it is indeed the fate of "modern Jews" as a whole that can be found in the heart of the long-term work undertaken by the author of *Zakhor*. He retraces the history of the Jews whose soul is "bifurcated" into antagonistic parts, between myth and history.[48]

When he undertakes his various investigations, Yerushalmi readily heeds the stern warning according to which "in the private sphere, there are limits that should not be crossed":[49] a number of items of personal information seem to him as not apt to enlighten us on the intellectual or imaginative logic of a person, whether it's Joyce or Freud himself. The historian still delves into history, and without venturing too far into the private sphere, it is important, by drawing especially from sources whose publication he has authorized, to return to his personal history to the extent that, as Yerushalmi observes, "he himself is a product of rupture."[50] Born in May 1932 in New York, Yerushalmi was raised in the East Bronx by his parents Leon and Eva (née Kaplan). Just after the Russian Revolution, his father had gone to Palestine, where he remained until 1928, when, sick from malaria, he was invited by an uncle in America (as in a legend) to move to the United States, where he met his wife. His parents were not Orthodox but were still profoundly attached to Jewish traditions and culture, to the extent that Yosef H. Yerushalmi learned first, in the family circle, Hebrew and Yiddish, which he spoke before English. When he was eight, he studied in a yeshiva and, throughout his primary and secondary schooling, became familiar with the canonical Jewish texts. After he received his BA, he entered the Jewish Theological Seminary, where a large number of renowned scholars taught, with whom he studied for four years.[51] Active during his youth in Zionist movements, he remained faithful to Israel; his wife, the pianist Ofra Yerushalmi, was born there.

> Diaspora today is no more Babylon than it is Alexandria. . . . Interesting and creative developments can be seen among Jews in the United States and elsewhere, but the heart of all Jewish life beats in Israel. . . . It is the place of our spiritual birth that is existentially decisive. In that, I can almost say that I am an "Israeli." . . . It is not for ideological motives that I decided to remain in America. It was the circumstances that decided it.[52]

"Israeli" in an existential way, according to his own definition, Yerushalmi still regards himself as a historian of exile and of the survival of Jewish identity in the diaspora, as the discoverer of a thousand of the most unexpected methods of rebirth of the Jewish soul in exile, in the most untoward, unforeseeable circumstances, while everything presses onward to strict assimilation, toward pure and simple disappearance within various cultural continents. In America, he elaborates his work in a new context where, according to Salo Baron's observation, the "dialectics between the homeland and exile has become a purely theoretical exercise for American Jews."[53]

Yerushalmi embodies a moment in time when the historiographical ambition of the nineteenth century sustained by scholars excluded from the academic world who were moved by global visions of Jewish history, by rabbis involved with science, is joined to the explosion of contemporary Jewish research professionalized in a myriad fragmented, sophisticated studies undertaken from within the university, respectful of the rules of historical research but often without any message that could be heard by the Jewish people. With all his strength, Yerushalmi gives himself the task of constructing this "bridge" toward the people even though he knows that "the contemporary Jewish historian often accomplishes prodigies of scholarship even as, concomitantly, he is able to remove himself thereby from the 'large' issues that only the whole can pose with any urgency. . . . The enterprise has become self-generating, the quest—Faustian."[54] He shows he is determined to keep hold of both extremes of professional research and almost messianic questioning. He went to Columbia to begin his doctoral studies under the direction of Salo Baron, whose teachings he studied at the Jewish Theological Seminary. Defended in 1966, his dissertation would allow him to participate fully, like Marc Bloch, historian of feudal society, or E. P. Thompson of the working class, in the most prestigious academic institutions. If he devoted himself less than Baron to matters of the community, he still gave lectures in various synagogues and played an important role at the helm of essential institutions like the Jewish Publication Society,[55] which published a large number of scholarly books including those of Graetz, Baron, and Baer, or the Leo Baeck Institute, which promoted researches and publications devoted to German Judaism.

In Yerushalmi's work is realized the aim of the Wissenschaft reviewed and corrected by Heinrich Graetz or Salo Baron: to step back from strict rabbinic culture, but to give its due place to the religious in sketching the outlines of a specifically Jewish history, and by relying on the most varied sources of a socioeconomic or political nature, to "rummage" with an immense talent through the archives in search of a general interpretation of Jewish history, an aim that the new generation of Jewish historians does not always share, since it often seems to be less fond of the big questions. It is a matter, then, following the example of the Wissenschaft scholars, of making a rich and veritable "subculture" be reborn, whose sustaining turns out to be compatible with the ineluctable entrance into society, and thus to pursue the process of "decolonization" of Jewish history to which, in his time, Abraham Geiger devoted himself when he rehabilitated Judaism within the Western world, and by questioning, as Geiger tried to do at the time, the dominant ideology shaped by Christianity.[56] We know that, in this same end, certain thinkers have been inspired by the visions of Herder to stress the genius unique to each nation. This culturalist posture is not without risk—it could even be argued that Heinrich Graetz in turn played "the role of Edmund Burke," that of an ideologue who means to preserve the traditions of each nation by mistrusting universalist visions based on reason alone. It is true that Graetz, the historian of the emancipation, is anxious to present Judaism as a form of rationality and thus shares the lively reservations of most historians of the Wissenschaft about French-style rationalism that, in the name of universalism, ignores specific cultural traditions often nourished by the religious life. In this sense, some have even thought that "in its heart, the *Verein* represents a rupture with the Haskala" and the Enlightenment as a whole.[57] Adopting such an ironic vision about the "old slogans of the Enlightenment," not hesitating to use multiple biological metaphors to account for the organic unity of the social body that the Jews, not yet historicized, constituted,[58] Yerushalmi stays away from any cultural relativism with conservative accents. He uses non-Jewish sources, adapts the usual methods of general historiography, and gives due importance to time, to which the religious remains indifferent. He knows how to "translate Judaism into Western categories,"[59] to catch hold of a general history of the Jewish people throughout history in order to spot its outlines, its constants, but also its variations according to endlessly, prodigiously distinct national histories, to set out what is at stake in it as so many paths capable of reactivating memory, finally to complete a new cycle of historiography begun within the German universities to confer on it a definitive legitimacy and recognition in the most prestigious American academic scene by institutionalizing it within secularized university structures—history departments and not religion departments, capable of promoting researches that take Jewish history as a subject approached using the methods of general history.

If Yosef Yerushalmi recognizes himself as an heir of Jewish Wissenschaft, he is still, even more directly, the student of Salo Baron. Baron preferred to take on the directorship of the Jewish Institute of Religion and then to occupy a position as professor at Columbia University, a secular institution, than to pursue a position offered him in 1928 as the head of the Breslau seminary, even if, actually, it was certainly a less prestigious position than the one that Graetz once occupied there. With Salo Baron, German Wissenschaft enters fully onto the American academic scene, its profound mutation in a more open historical context now less marked by anti-Semitism and exclusion from the public space, its reorientation toward more socioeconomic and political circumstances. Born in 1895, after the death of the leading names of the Wissenschaft, in then-Austrian Galicia, into an Orthodox but enlightened Jewish milieu, Baron as a child wore the traditional caftan, studied the Talmud from the age of five, and went to heder. As a student, he attended the University of Vienna where he obtained three doctorates—in history, political science, and law; his thesis in political science on Ferdinand Lassalle was written under the direction of Hans Kelsen. At the same time he pursued rabbinic studies, taught Jewish history, then emigrated to the United States, where Stephen Wise appointed him in 1928 to the Jewish Institute of Religion, the rabbinic school of New York.[60] In December 1929, Baron was given the first American chair of Jewish history, at Columbia University (the Miller Chair), and became in 1930 the first tenured Jewish professor at Columbia, an appointment that, along with that of the philosopher Harry Wolfson at Harvard, marked a fundamental turning point in the institutionalization of Jewish studies in the diaspora, all the more so since it occurred in a history department and not in a department of Jewish studies or religious sciences, as is still sometimes the case these days in service of an almost identitarian vision of cultural studies. At the same time, fleeing Europe, a large number of Jewish intellectuals had left for the United States or Palestine. In New York as well as in Jerusalem, the competition was stiff: candidates vied with each other, attracted by Columbia's prestige, like Louis Ginzberg who taught at the Jewish Theological Seminary, or Ismar Elbogen from Berlin. Finally winning out over his rivals despite various maneuvers, Baron was appointed to Columbia and, after many hesitations, was assigned to the history department, while still maintaining his functions at the Jewish Institute of Religion.

Baron's wife, Jeannette Meisel, was an American Jewish student who studied Jewish bankers; throughout his life, Baron closely associated her with the construction of his own work. Their daughters, whom they named Shoshanna and Tobey, received a solid Jewish education. Working together in their professional and family lives, the couple spent part of their year in their house in Connecticut that they named after their two Hebrew names; their home in New York was carefully kept kosher. Baron led a double life as university professor, president of the American Jewish Historical Society, but also and especially the organizer of Jewish community organizations for which he became an eminent personality through his constant activities, his lectures, and his prestige. He thus enjoyed a twofold fame, as professor at Columbia who exercised a strong influence over the American academic milieu and as a true leader of community associations.[61] Active in the Jewish Welfare Board and in Bnai-Brith, he organized various commissions that had the aim of coming to the aid of European Jews; in 1945 he even led a delegation that met with the American general in charge of the occupation in Germany to try to preserve anything having to do with Jewish culture, a commission that he presided over while Hannah Arendt became its executive secretary. He played an essential role in contributing to saving more than half a million books. Attentive to her friend's ambition, Arendt, on the occasion of his seventieth birthday, praised him in the following terms: "Even before I met you in this country, about twenty-five years ago, I knew that the Jewish people had at last found its historian. You became the first Professor of Jewish History in this country because you have been indeed the first to establish the history of your own people as an academic discipline."[62] We know that the two friends disagreed on a number of points in their vision of Jewish history, with Arendt for example emphasizing more the passivity of the Jews and their absence of political strategy in the course of their recent history: nevertheless, she recognized the crucial role played by Baron, which Yerushalmi has now inherited.

Baron thus becomes one of the most visible personalities in the American Jewish community, since, in keeping with his general concepts of Jewish history, he seeks to reevaluate the importance of the Jewish community, from the Middle Ages until the present day, as a locus for creation, for resistance, and also for survival, as a collective mechanism in which religious values and social solidarity are closely linked, capable of preserving and maintaining a certain autonomy even in situations of duress. Close to Dubnow's perspective celebrating the capacity of the Jews to protect their social and community ties in exile, Baron's book *The Jewish Community: Its History and Structure to the American Revolution* represents a turning point in his oeuvre;[63] it constitutes a rehabilitation of even nondemocratic community ties based on religion and on ethnic specificity as well as a stirring appeal to the rebirth of such communities living within an American society directed toward individualism and free choice. Referring explicitly to classic sociological texts such as Ferdinand Tönnies's *Community and Society*, or the more recent book by Robert McIver, *Community*, Baron's contribution in this domain is obvious. It is moreover noted by Horace Kallen, the Jewish theoretician of ethnicity, the ancestor of multiculturalism whose influence, as we have seen, was acknowledged by Michael Walzer. In the *American Journal of Sociology* in which Louis Wirth analyzes the ghetto during the same period, Kallen strongly emphasizes, in his review, the quality of this book,[64] which makes its author a precursor of ethnic minority rights in the United States.[65] In a letter to a colleague in April 1940, Baron thinks he will title his book "The Ghetto Community: A History of the Jewish Community from the Babylonian Exile to the Emancipation."[66] This title, which was abandoned, does however touch on the essential point: to retrace, in exile, the protective function of the ghetto community. It is also a way of continuing the controversy begun by his famous article on the ghetto as a living form of Judaism called anew into question by emancipation and the Enlightenment, a crucial moment of historiography that went against all the received ideas about the ghetto as a structure of imprisonment, poverty, and ignorance.

It is impossible to analyze Baron's work here as an indispensable link to approach Yosef Yerushalmi's work, but it seems important to examine his famous thesis, hostile to the lachrymose concept of history, an argument that was directed against, among others, Heinrich Graetz, and that remains an essential element in contemporary debates. Published in 1928, Baron's article "Ghetto and Emancipation: Shall We Revise the

Traditional View?" had the effect of a bomb, and its repercussions are still being felt today. Graetz, however, symbolizes to Baron the historian of the Jewish people par excellence, the one whom he hopes to succeed, but while going beyond a perspective that isolates that history too much from those of different civilizations within which it unfolds, since it is conceived of in terms of a unique spirituality, whether it be religious or secular, a history whose particularity, which distinguishes it from all others, is that it is not just one long series of sufferings and misfortunes. This question turns out to be crucial, for the answer that it gets also depends on the standardization of Jewish history to which Baron is attached and which is also welcomed by most contemporary American Jewish historians. In Baron's opinion, "Emancipation, in the judgment of Graetz, Philippson, Dubnow and other historians, was the dawn of a new day after a nightmare of the deepest horror, and this view has been accepted as completely true by Jews, rabbis, scholars and laymen, throughout the Western world. It is in terms of this complete contrast between the black of the Jewish Middle Ages and the white of the post-Emancipation period that most generalizations about the progress of the Jews in modern times are made."[67] As far as Baron is concerned, he "lives between the two worlds. . . . He is a man both of the ghetto and of the emancipation"[68]; he refuses to prefer one over the other since he argues that, through contradictory eras, the Jews have still managed to live, to prosper, to create; they haven't simply suffered passively since the beginning of time. Reevaluating the era of the Middle Ages, Baron sees it not as a moment of tragic exploitation or unspeakable sufferings, according to traditional historiography, but on the contrary a period during which the lot of the Jews is infinitely more favorable than that of the peasants. He shows that the tortures of the Inquisition afflicted just as many non-Jewish heretics or witches, downplays the anti-Judaism of the Catholic Church, stresses the remarkable demographic progression of the Jews, and argues that, in the time of the emancipation, supporters of assimilation, with the theoreticians of the Wissenschaft leading the way, had an interest in denigrating the Middle Ages in order, by contrast, to celebrate modern times, while the supporters of Zionism denounced the medieval period as well as that of the emancipation in order to demonstrate the impossibility of a normal Jewish life in the diaspora.[69]

Above all, and this is a point often neglected to which we will return at length, Baron is perhaps one of the first to stress so strongly an essential characteristic of the Jews of the Middle Ages, that of being "serfs of the State from the point of view of public law," and thus of benefiting from the protection of the state embodied by the king or emperor who often comes to their aid and guarantees their legal privileges, indispensable for the self-regulation of the community, "privileges that the modern State no longer grants them." This in fact reduces particular collective institutions and imposes a new kind of citizenship, equal for everyone, which encourages assimilation as a form of adaptation to the homogenizing logic of a state turned toward nationalism.[70] Critical of the emancipating nation-state that favors the standardization of values, Baron is close in this point of view to Dubnow or Ahad Ha'am without sharing the latter's Zionist convictions as passionately, even though those convictions foreground spiritual qualities and culture as opposed to the state-based logic of Herzl. Baron is considerably innovative and opens the way to a veritable political sociology of the Jewish condition in the diaspora, a "historical sociology,"[71] as he himself calls it without really controlling this designation.

Salo Baron remained faithful throughout his life to this iconoclastic thesis, echoes of which can be found in Hannah Arendt and in Yosef H. Yerushalmi. Baron steadfastly defended it in a number of writings, even though he recognizes the inventiveness and intellectual richness of the Jews of modern times who contribute greatly in the present day to creativity, an observation that also reinforces his globally positive evaluation of life in the diaspora.[72] This calling into question of the status of the Jews in the Middle Ages allows him to distinguish himself from most of the historians of the Wissenschaft, such as Zunz, Geiger, or Graetz, who stress the weight of the suffering that has rained down on the Jews since the beginning of time.[73] Baron especially takes issue with Heinrich Graetz, whose work he admires, but thinks that the "excessive subjectivity" he continually shows constitutes "his major weakness as a historian,"[74] a subjectivity and emotion that lead him, in Baron's opinion, to become the spokesman of this lachrymose concept that Baron for his part is trying systematically to reverse. With this purpose, Baron exaggerates the importance that Graetz attributes to suffering compared to his many observations on the creativity of the Jews in exile, on "the miracle" of their survival, with Graetz even arguing that "thinking characterizes the Jewish people just as much as suffering."[75] The Nazi danger and the massacres that annihilated European Jews, including his own parents and his sister, do not lead Baron to modify completely his optimistic vision of Jewish history.[76] As to the Shoah, however, the sufferings of the Jewish people are without precedent: Baron notes this and is active in trying to save a number of Jews during the Second World War, but does not abandon his general thesis, arguing more for happiness than despair. Can one argue that Baron "failed" in his refutation of the lachrymose theory of history, in his rehabilitation of Jewish happiness in exile elaborated in the context of Columbia even while the Nazi danger was carrying away the Jewish people, thus confirming—all too strongly—the constancy of its sufferings?[77] Such a judgment of Baron's attempt scarcely pays tribute to the project of a man who means, despite everything to the contrary, to restore hope and to have done with fatalist concepts based on infinite despair as a token of an absolute exclusion from history.

Salo Baron, the Jewish historian, heir to the Wissenschaft, that Yosef Yerushalmi professes to follow, focuses on a history that normally unfolds in the diaspora and does not find its finality either in the messianic or the nationalist return to Zion, unlike other great Jewish historians of the twentieth century like Fritz Baer, Gershom Scholem, or Ben Zion Dinaburg, who decided to immigrate to Palestine. The normal history of the Jewish people remains confined, in this spirit, to the question of the future of Jewish identity in the framework of non-Jewish societies; it is in no way shaped, imagined, induced by the Zionist ideal, since, for Baron, "the history of the Jewish people offers a supreme example of a group attempting (and to a certain extent succeeding) to live despite nature: a nationality gradually divorced from state and territory which has consequently become somehow immune from the influence emanating from the soil and its derivative."[78] He comes close to Dubnow not by adhering to his autonomist positions in the form of political self-organization for obtaining a form of representation in central organs of government, but rather by defending the idea of a cultural loyalty in the diaspora that is independent of any form of sovereignty.[79] Despite certain stances favorable to the Zionist project (which he defended very clearly while still doubting its realization), Baron can be viewed more as a hero of American Judaism, for which he is a spokesman and which he considers as being henceforth in the "center" of Jewish history, according to the themes of centers proposed by Dubnow who, outside of the limited center in Palestine, foresaw the birth of an imposing American center as the inevitable and desirable result of the immigration of Russian Jews.[80] In 1946, Baron argues in this sense that "the destruction of European Jewry had not only shifted the center of gravity of the entire Jewish people to the United States. . . . The American Jewish community center has long combined some of the best features of the traditional community with the needs of a community integrated into a Western nation."[81] Moreover, as Dubnow already foresaw, who delighted in Jewish immigration to the land of freedom, the United States, the lachrymose theory of history, which reflects "the sufferings that, for example, the transferal of the historic centers of the Diaspora engendered" seems,[82] for the first time, to become inadequate, given the nature of the American political system and its tolerance of cultural differences. Baron has thus remained generally resistant "to the Zionist return to history," which on the contrary motivates a number of great researchers who have become Israeli and who have tried to continue the effort toward objectivity and the science of the German Jewish Wissenschaft scholars, but have produced a second generation of historians more inspired by Palestine-centered values.[83]

The parallels and divergences between the two contemporary processes of institutionalization of Jewish history that unfold simultaneously in Jerusalem and in New York are still striking, while at the same time, in 1925 in Vilna, a third center is born with YIVO, the Institute for Jewish Research, in the heart of the European diaspora. Overlooking the symbolic importance of the creation of the chair at Columbia and keeping in mind only the parallelism between Vilna and Jerusalem, Dubnow notes that "it is probably not a coincidence, but rather a profound symbol that, in the Jerusalem of Palestine and the Jerusalem of the Diaspora, two institutions were founded in the same year."[84] In Jerusalem, the inaugural lecture, given by Fritz Baer, dates back to winter 1930: it marks the beginning of the teaching of

Jewish history at the Institute of Jewish Studies in modern Palestine, inaugurated in 1924. It was during that academic year that Salo Baron taught for the first time at Columbia University in New York. At the same moment, in Vilna the third process of institutionalization of these studies was being put into place in another even more brilliant center, even though its brilliance would unfortunately be suddenly tarnished by the German invasion. The creation of YIVO took place exactly at the same time as if to mark the competition to which these three centers take part, which result either in Zionism (Baer), or in emigration to the United States (Baron), or in the autonomist perspective defended in the European diaspora by Dubnow, with YIVO being re-created in New York, in the American diaspora, after the swallowing up of the East European diaspora and the tragic disappearance of the center in Vilna. Unlike Dubnow who, in the even more ungrateful conditions of Russian Judaism, could not teach in a university, Baer and Baron, the two great historians of the Jewish people, both completed their doctoral theses, as the Wissenschaft scholars did before them, in the universities of the Germanic cultural realm, Baer in Fribourg and Baron in Vienna. They became involved, however, in divergent interpretations of Jewish history in the diaspora, so much so that Baer (who changed his first name from Fritz to Yitzak) came in 1938 to criticize Baron's presentation of the life of Jews in Spain under Muslim domination. In order better to justify the Zionist perspective hostile to the *galut* (perceiving it exclusively as the source of innumerable sufferings) and reverse his own interpretation of the Spain of that era that had previously been fundamentally positive, Baer from then on supported the traditional lachrymose concept of history, which was in part that of Graetz, and which Salo Baron tried rightly to refute. For Baer, "the fact that medieval Jewish history represented one unending line of persecution."[85] In this sense, these Jewish historians become involved at the same time in using similar objective methods applied to an original and complex material of archives, but in ways that gradually distance them from each other even if they both are opposed to the perspectives of most of the Wissenschaft scholars, anxious to erase the national aspect of Jewish history while still preserving its cultural dimension. We understand why Yerushalmi, the author of *From Span-*

*ish Court to Italian Ghetto*, had his heart set on reexamining the ideas of the bold critique of his master, while at the same time also directing a less somber gaze at exile and life in the galut, for which he becomes the most convincing theoretician.

That in fact is one of the constants of Yerushalmi's work: tirelessly to bring to light the Jews' aptitude for happiness, their will to survive, their creativity in exile, although their status for so long a time has been that of a minority often confronted with anti-Semitic hatred. What better example of their basic optimism than the saying of Jeremiah, who in 587 BCE from the prisons of the king and when Jerusalem was besieged by the Babylonians, thus just before the exile of the Jewish people, paradoxically advises, in the name of God, buying a field in Anathoth and writing, in front of witnesses, a deed of sale for the future! Yerushalmi remembers Jeremiah's advice, which has haunted him since his adolescence, and when he approaches it again in the present day, it is to write strongly that "if the history of hope is important for the history of humanity, it is essential for the intelligence of Jewish history. . . . The prodigious energy expended in reconstructing the social, economic, and intellectual history of the Jews has not had, as a counterpart, an equal passion in researching in depth how the Jews lived, felt, perceived this same history."[86] It is a matter, then, of taking an inventory of all the forms of hope that have coexisted or followed despairs faced with so many sufferings undergone, so many prospects blocked, so many temptations to escape Jewish identity by converting, defecting, leaving; it is also a matter of paying attention to messianic forms of hope and redemption, without neglecting "average Jewish hopes." Yerushalmi knows how these average hopes inhere in Jewish history, in its everyday life: through the "historian's sieve," he seeks to gather the elements by which "ordinary Jews" could "raise themselves up," hope again for the future, undertake to rebuild here or to go into exile again not for solely economic or political reasons stemming from oppression but in order to follow that "geography of hope" that leads toward so many promised lands, yesterday and today, either in exile where assimilation can nonetheless preserve a messianic dimension of hope, or in the return to Zion. He sets out to bring to light this "dynamic of Jewish hope thanks to the prayers recited three times a day by all those of our people"; he goes back to the rituals most firmly rooted in tradition, even if it means setting aside messianic writings alone; he apprehends the hope that emerges from reading the *Haggadah*, which, in its coming into being, illustrates the "the changing patterns of Jewish migrations, and the rise and decline of major Jewish centers"; he reexamines the sacred texts scattered through time and space that illustrate "the 'hyphenated' Jewish languages," which they were able in the course of their successive exiles to construct alongside their non-Jewish neighbors and in symbiosis with them.[87] The historian bases the quest for social meaning, the comprehension of individual values focused on hope despite everything, on a kind of sociology of daily life; these values alone save the "fallen Jews" from the despair that overwhelms them, the ones immersed in unhappiness, the ones who renounce their identity since "they despair of a Jewish future."[88]

In many respects, Yerushalmi also assumes the continuity of Heinrich Graetz's perspective, since he willingly concentrates on the darkest periods of Jewish history, from the Lisbon massacre to the cruelties of the Inquisition down to the Shoah, which often figures in the background of a number of his writings. He takes the measure of the despair that pushes people to renouncing, abandoning their Jewish identity. By focusing on the resistance of communities, by his choice to emphasize the decisions of individuals who persist in not passively undergoing their fate but who take their lives in hand in the aim of remaining faithful to their values, by his scrupulous attention to the forms of Jewish hope that can be sustained both by the religious and by secular orientations, he also becomes part of Salo Baron's heritage. With this sociohistory of individual choices, he foregrounds the intention, the hope of individuals. From then on, he can only reject the criticisms that Baer made of his teacher Salo Baron and strongly assert that "the rejection of the exile of the Jews in Baer is altogether excessive, leaving a feeling of distress in the reader"; he particularly rejects this phrase of Baer's, fundamentally opposite to his own vision of Jewish identity in exile: "Everything we have accomplished in foreign lands was *treason* to our own spirit."[89] In Yerushalmi's opinion, such an assertion is contradicted by so many examples that, "in agreement with Salo Baron,"

Yerushalmi rejects "this distortion of history," which ignores the fact that whose who remained in their country also underwent severe calamities, while on the contrary, in exile, the Jews often managed to defend their national identity as well as their religious identity creatively and keenly. For him, consequently, "aside from the eras when severe persecutions took place," it is not at all proven that exile inevitably represents an intolerable situation.

Taking the precaution of advancing such a proposition without, however, presenting himself as "a defender of assimilation," Yerushalmi thinks that "it is simultaneously possible to be ideologically in exile and existentially at home."[90] Exile does not, then, imply either persecution or disappearance, vanishing into the host society. Completely unlike the lachrymose vision of history, which is once again explicitly condemned, the author of *Zakhor* comes to argue that the Jews can legitimately be "feeling at home within exile itself." In a number of societies, including Spain, France, and the regions of Eastern Europe, the Jews have "homes" that are reimagined in biblical contexts and compared to ancient Israel to such a point that "the Judaization of exile" transforms in their eyes the European realities into places of redemption that are now realizable, so much so that the society of exile suddenly seems like a Zion that has come here and now. Yerushalmi stresses the importance of these transpositions in exile of biblical images that inflect the perception of time and space within coherent microneighborhoods where a protected community life unfolds organized around synagogues, in those Jewries, those *judería* or *Judengassen* that delimit closed zones, cut off from the rest of the population, so many places perceived as Jewish by their inhabitants, "homes" that protect identity and community, suitable for an atemporal, normal life immunized against any feeling of radical danger emanating from the situation of being minority exiles. Thus, Toledo symbolizes Toledos or Toletula, from the Hebrew *tiltul*, "migration" or "wandering"; Yepes represents Jaffa; Bohemia, Canaan; and Nîmes is also called Kyriat Ye'arim, "the city of the forests," as it is mentioned by Joshua or in other books of the Bible, while Montpellier, Lunel, Bari, Amsterdam, and Vilna are seen as new Jerusalems endowed with an irrefutable, concrete existence, where the life of Jews can peacefully unfold, to such a point that the threat of expulsion from one of these cities is felt as an exile: exile then represents the exclusion from a "home" that is felt to be definitive and is no longer experienced in the eschatological way as biblical exile; the loss of Zion disappears into the far recesses of time, even though ritual continually recalls its memory. In this sense, one can argue that "the Jewish quarter or street—juderia, juiverie, Judengasse—a Jewish territory in microcosm where, even in times of alienation from the gentile population, one could always feel Jewishly 'at home.'"[91]

Nonetheless the Jews did undergo a tragic series of exiles that culminated with the expulsion from Spain, leaving Western Europe almost without any Jewish life, which was transferred from the West to the East. Yerushalmi retraces this long series of expulsions, which began in France (1182) when Philippe Auguste ordered the Jews to leave the kingdom, was followed by England (1290), then by the new exile that this time struck all the Jews of France (1394) before the catastrophe of the expulsion from Spain occurred (1492), then from Sicily and Sardinia, from Provence (1501) and from the Kingdom of Naples (1510), and finally from all of southern Italy. Despite all the "Judaization of exile," despite their seeming durability and normality as "homes," the irremediable can still rain down in the diaspora; the suffering the Jews endured in these exiles, lived as so many normal, rich, atemporal situations, takes on a permanence and well-nigh gives life to the lachrymose conception of history. By a strange paradox that demands an explanation, while he doesn't even approach the Shoah, it is more the spirit of Graetz than that of Baron that finally shows through in this laudatory vision of exile. Many times quoting in various texts the exclamation of the Portuguese Marrano Samuel Usque, dated 1553, "Europe, oh Europe, my hell on earth!" Yerushalmi thinks that it could have been uttered after the Shoah, whereas it was uttered after the forced conversions and expulsions from Spain, Portugal, or the Kingdom of Naples, since "the trauma of all these catastrophes that occurred as an inexorable chain would turn out to be *subjectively* comparable":[92] in one era as well as in another, the silence of God is similar, the abandonment unbearable that redoubles the sufferings that punctuate the long term of Jewish history. We can understand why, faced with Auschwitz, Yerushalmi in turn exclaims, "My people, now as in the past, is in grave peril of its life."[93] Hence this "fruitful comparison" between the Spain and Portugal of the end of the Middle Ages and contemporary Germany, although the situations are not "identical." And the question, "How is it that the Iberian society and German society, so radically different in their nature and culture and so far from each other in time, experienced such similar reactions to what they perceived as an intrusion of Jews into their midst?" is not very remote from the one Baer asked in just as anguished a way; in order to answer it, he found himself forced, according to Yerushalmi, to make the situation of the Jews in Spain blacker than it was in order to warn his German Jewish ex-compatriots. But these analogies could not hide obvious differences: "The Inquisition, for all its excesses, was not the Gestapo; Spanish and Portuguese anti-Semites were not the Nazis. There is no genocide there. The most virulent theoreticians of *limpieza* never called for the physical extermination of the New Christians, only, at the most extreme, for their expulsion—an essential medieval solution—and the state did not comply even with that."[94] Even more explicitly, Yerushalmi writes, "The student of modern German Jewry who turns to the history of Spanish New Christians will find characteristics that are familiar to him, and may feel almost an inverted sense of *déjà-vu*. The ambiguity and insecurity of the assimilated Jew, the anxiety of hovering between acceptance and rejection, integration and marginality, *jüdischer Selbsthass*—all are present there, albeit expressed in the vocabulary and under the conditions of another age and culture."[95] Yerushalmi more than once uses this comparison, which indicates that it is for him a constant synonym for catastrophes.[96]

Isn't this admitting that in each of these so-different societies, one at the dawn of modernity and the other in the heart of it, Jews can find themselves confronted with sufferings that are "subjectively" comparable, even though the Jews are confident, happy within their homes in which they were able, every time, to implement that "Judaization of exile" that protects their identity and is offered as the favorite framework of expression of their hope in a Jewish future of which they might, in such a favorable context, despair? Isn't that implicitly to go back, to a certain extent, to the lachrymose vision of history that Salo Baron set out to reject despite the Shoah? Following the tragedies of the

Inquisition and the expulsion, the cruelty of Hitler's genocide comes almost to break the idea of a possible happy dwelling in the diaspora and probably makes Jeremiah's command, so often quoted throughout the ages as well as by Yerushalmi himself, pointless—namely to cultivate the gardens, make the cities prosper, build families, ensure the conditions of a realizable happiness in successive exiles, from Babylon down to Spain or Germany. Many times, Yerushalmi quotes the letter from Jeremiah to the exiles of Babylon:

> Thus saith the LORD of hosts, the God of Israel, unto all that are carried away captives, whom I have caused to be carried away from Jerusalem unto Babylon; Build ye houses, and dwell in them; and plant gardens, and eat the fruit of them; Take ye wives, and beget sons and daughters; . . . that ye may be increased there, and not diminished. And seek the peace of the city whither I have caused you to be carried away captives, and pray unto the LORD for it: for in the peace thereof shall ye have peace. . . . Let not your prophets and your diviners, that be in the midst of you, deceive you, neither hearken to your dreams which ye cause to be dreamed. For they prophesy falsely unto you in my name: I have not sent them, saith the LORD. (Jeremiah, 29:4–9).[97]

This letter has always been interpreted as an encouragement to live fully in successive diasporas, to participate unreservedly in the life of the host city, to have children, to flourish even far from Zion and to turn away from prophecies, false messiahs who urge departure and return, in order to hasten redemption. It also gives a foundation to the rule dina de malkhuta dina, "the law of the country is the law," which justifies accommodating to the laws of the country provided they do not infringe upon the rules that regulate family life or marriage. In this sense, the letter from Jeremiah, valid for all the Jews' exiles, serves as a charter for happiness in the diaspora and supports the hope of a fully Jewish life far from Zion in "homes" favorable to maintaining collective identity in a minority context. Mentioned explicitly, we remember, by the supporters of contemporary multiculturalism, such as Michael Walzer,[98] isn't this hope-filled letter once and for all contradicted by the terrible sufferings experienced by the Jews in Spain in the Middle Ages or in the Russia of the pogroms, by Auschwitz and the Shoah, by the persecutions undergone in the Soviet Union?

Yosef Yerushalmi seems finally to hesitate between these perspectives that, without being contradictory, stem from distinct visions of Jewish life in exile. Can home, the Judaization of exile, the happiness it procures, be preserved beyond the short term, beyond a period that nonetheless can be stretched out over several centuries, as in the cases of Spain and Germany? In the long run, does suffering inevitably follow happiness, or desertification follow flourishing, or negation of identity its complete recognition, or expulsion integration? What average period of time separates these radically opposite periods? Can one envisage a society of exile where, even after many centuries of happy domiciliation, the moment of suffering and hurried departure would never occur? Can't one argue that assimilation, independently of discrimination, expulsion, and suffering, is itself not "a reversed messianism" but a kind of servitude stripped of hope, a way of renouncing collective identity, without recourse to repressive force, to negation of self? In the spirit of Ahad Ha'am or of Dubnow, who lambasted supporters of assimilation, or more recently of Amos Funkestein who quotes the rabbi Moses of Pressburg according to whom, in exile, assimilated German or French Jews are "like prisoners of war" to the point that they have lost the sense of exile, that they no longer have "any history but just a past,"[99] does a home actually authorize collective happiness, does it give meaning to a Jewish history? Far from Europe and its troubled relationships with Jewish identity which Samuel Usque pointed out before, can the United States, as an open society traditionally favorable to all immigrations—but which did not hesitate to establish a severe and dramatic policy of quotas in the time between the two world wars, excluding especially those of the *yiddishkeit* who were the last to arrive—be seen as a haven of peace that nothing could come to disturb, today or tomorrow, in the most distant future?[100] Can the Europe of tomorrow, having become a semiconfederation of states where free circulation of people and merchandise reigns, ensure Jewish happiness in the long term and lastingly guarantee a citizenship that immediately eliminates any idea of expulsion? Can these two immense ensembles of integrated states be, on the contrary, joined by a tragic history that could result in intercommunity clashes influenced as much by internal rivalries as by the fallouts from the conflict in the Middle East?

Finally, isn't it indispensable to reflect more about what kind of states are more susceptible than others to welcoming such protective homes? The "strong" state is capable of better protecting the Jews while still imposing on them a standardized public space that is not very compatible with keeping specific collective domiciles; the "weak" state is shown to be more favorable to self-organization of particular communities but risks, in the event of a populist and xenophobic upsurge, to turn out to be ineffective in the defense of Jews confronted with the mobs.[101] Hence the fundamental nature of the American example as a "weak" state compatible with recognition of domiciles where the hope of a Jewish life can flourish, in comparison to French-style strong states hostile by nature to such forms of identitarian organization. The question of the state is thus essential.

Such vital questions about Jewish destiny can be approached working from the themes outlined by Yosef H. Yerushalmi. To try to confront them and also to attempt to foresee the future, we should return to Salo Baron's intuition about the protective links that join Jews to the state. Baron, we remember, stresses the fact that for a long time the Jews were "serfs of the State from the point of view of public law"; they remained under the protection of the king or the emperor until the modern era, when the state became the embodiment of the nation, calling back into question any privileged link with identitarian structures and, in particular, with the Jews. Yerushalmi forges this innovative perspective, which makes the nature of the state the key to the future of the Jews, to its happiness or its suffering. From *From Spanish Court to Italian Ghetto* down to his recent text "Servants of Kings and Not Servants of Servants: On Some Aspects of the Political History of the Jews," he sheds light on this fundamental relationship on which, for many, Jewish happiness depends. We can better understand the major role the Ibn Verga's book, the *Shebet Yehudah*, which concerns precisely this "covenant," plays in Yerushalmi's thinking. Yerushalmi translates a key passage from this text, concerning the massacre of the newly converted Christians, in April 1506, in Lisbon:

> On Passover Eve the Christians found Marranos seated before unleavened bread and bitter herbs, according to all the rites of Passover. . . . At that time there was a famine and drought in the land, and

the Christians gathered and said: "Why did the Lord do this unto us and unto our land, if not because of the guilt of these Jews?" And as their words were heard by the Order of Preachers who are called *Predicadores*, they concentrated on seeking a device with which to help the Christians. So one of them arose in their house of worship and preached extremely harsh and bitter things against the seed of Israel. . . . Then there arose men from among the mob with swords in their hands, and in three days they slaughtered three thousand souls. They would drag and bring them to the street and burn them. They would throw pregnant women from windows and receive them on their spears, the foetus falling several feet away . . . The magistrates of Lisbon are not at all to blame, nor are its nobles and leaders, for all this was done in spite of them. They themselves went forth to save them, but because of the size of the mob they could not . . . And the king of Portugal was a gracious king . . . He wept and cried out against the evil event . . . He intended to execute all the murderers . . . The king commanded that the friars be arrested, and he decreed that they be burned.[102]

This "gracious king" was none other than Dom Manuel, who ordered the sudden mass conversion of all the Jews of Portugal; Yerushalmi interprets this text as a perfect example of glorification of the public authorities from whom the Jews had always expected their salvation, even though they were aware of the fact that, in this case and in many others, they were no help whatsoever.[103] This deliberate heroization of the king despite proofs of his passivity is indispensable: Ibn Verga and Samuel Usque embellish the action of the monarch, asserting that, by his swift return to the city, he saved many Marranos. Yosef Yerushalmi quotes Samuel Usque: "Then the king who returned speedily from his quarters in the town of Abrantes, aided them,"[104] and he notes that actually Dom Manuel did nothing of the sort, since he was afraid of an epidemic that was raging in Lisbon. To give an account of this wish to exonerate the king of all responsibility in the massacre of the Jews, Yerushalmi stresses:

Throughout medieval Christian Europe the Jews inevitably, yet willingly, allied themselves to the Crown as the best and, ultimately, the only guarantor of stability and security. . . . [The relationship was] regarded by Jews as a firm anchor through all vicissitudes. Again, though there were "court-Jews" and lobbyist (*shtadlanim*) in other countries, nowhere else did conditions favor the rise of so large and powerful a class of Jewish aristocrats, servants of the king and rulers of the community. . . . It was this courtier class which forged the royal alliance into a central ideology. Conceived of in ultimate terms, Spain was of course *galut*, exile, and the advent of the Messiah was awaited and entreated. But until that time should arrive, the Jews of Spain placed their trust in temporal monarchy. . . . What makes Ibn Verga's panegyric of kingship especially instructive is that it comes *after* the Expulsion and that it is generalized to *all* kings, even those of other countries. The benevolence of kings to their Jews becomes, in the *Shebet Yehudah*, a universal principle.[105]

To such a point that the kings of the Visigoths, who suddenly converted the Jews, along with the kings of France, such as Louis X and Charles IV who expelled the Jews from France in 1322, are showered with praise.

Faithful to the view proposed by Salo Baron, Yerushalmi is involved in a remarkable sociology of the state through bringing to light its fundamental role in the defense of Jewish happiness, its essential function in the protection of the Jews. He shows that the "quest for vertical alliances" has been, ever since the Roman era, a major strategy to protect them "from the goodwill of their kind neighbors [and] from the whim of local authorities."[106] This approach is constant in his work; it can be found in his first article, written in 1964, in which he stresses the role of the pope in the creation of Spanish and French inquisitions and the extent of royal intervention in the protection of the "juifs du roi," a source of substantial income.[107] He already attributes a large importance to court Jews, Jews of the king, elite Jews who attained the neighborhood of monarchic power by their competence, who had access to the court and played an important role in internal and external politics—these subjects were very visible, wealthy, and knowledgeable, and their talents were put to good use by kings or emperors, from Dom Manuel to Bismarck, for their own considerable benefit. Yerushalmi brings an essential contribution to the historiography of the court Jews by continuing the perspective of Salo Baron,[108] who examined the decisive influence they exercised in the indispensable protection of the community. Through numerous societies in the Middle

Ages where "the royal Covenant" was observed in its "fullness," from Austria to Hungary, from Poland to Lithuania, but also and especially Spain, England, and France, Yerushalmi stresses these charters that regulated relations between the state and the Jews. These were seen as the "King's Jews," or, for the Emperor Frederick I (Barbarossa), Jews who "belong to our treasury,"[109] a privileged status that assures them, as Baron notes, aiming to refute the lachrymose thesis of history applied to this period, a much better situation than that of serfs, peasants, and other social groups who had more advantages on other levels. At this stage of his demonstration, Yerushalmi again evokes the *Shevet Yehudah*, the "first precious attempt at a sociopolitical analysis of the Jewish condition in exile," this time insisting on this passage: "When the Jews learned this, they went to one of the ministers of the king, for he loved them greatly, as they had been loved in Spain by the king, the nobles and all the scholars and sages, and were very honored by them all. The expulsions were only decided on because a few members of the lower classes claimed that because of the Jews and since their arrival in the kingdom food had become dearer. . . . The expulsions were also provoked by the priests. . . . They had the daily habit of preaching venomous sermons against the Jews."[110] In both excerpts from the *Shevet Yehudah* quoted here, the gracious king as well as his ministers and nobles as a whole are shown to be firmly bent on protecting the Jews whom they openly "love." These Jews are threatened above all by the "crowd," the "lower classes" jealous of the situation of the Jews and stirred up by the clergy. It is from their ranks that those who commit the massacres come, although the king and his governors vainly try to stop them. The state can, at worst, expel the Jews or in rare cases convert them, but not massacre them: "When there was a massacre, it did not come from above."[111]

We can understand better, in this sense, the essential place assigned to the person of Isaac Cardoso in the long research carried out by Yosef Yerushalmi. Cardoso embodies the king's Jew, so exceptional is his professional success in Christian Spain. It is in this narrative, organized around the history of one particular life, that the "historian of the Jews" brings the history of the Jews to its full maturity. It is here that Yosef Yerushalmi, the explicitly "Jewish historian," professionalizes this discipline by including "Jewish studies" in history as the great ones practiced it, to the point perhaps of diluting specificity by stripping it of any messianic, teleological, or lachrymose dimension. *From Spanish Court to Italian Ghetto* gives the history of the Jews its definitive legitimacy and marks in the diaspora a veritable historiographical turning point of which we have not yet taken the measure; nothing is comparable to it. A distant heir of Zunz, Graetz, and even more of Baron, Yerushalmi strikes us as one of the masters of a historical sociology attentive to the fates of individuals caught in various fields of constraint but who remain capable of taking their life in hand in the name of their specific values. Starting with a dazzling abundance of unpublished archives and uncovered manuscripts (without having, he humorously remarks, to wear the yellow hat that Jews in those regions wore),[112] thanks to these collections scattered from Portugal to Italy or Spain, Yerushalmi gives all due respectability and authenticity to the history of the Jews, which he does not approach as a national narrative through time, or one based on geographical, demographic, or economic facts, concerning a particular period. He follows to their conclusion the strongest intuitions of Salo Baron concerning the place of politics and the state; like Ibn Verga, he places the state at the heart of the history of the Jews by fastening onto the vertical alliances but, in conformity with the most stimulating contemporary historical (or sociological) perspectives, he approaches those alliances with royal power as initiated by the decisions of the subjects who, even in this privileged context, alone remain largely responsible for the management of their identity, whatever the eminence of the function may be.

The story of Isaac Cardoso is emblematic of the search for vertical alliances. However, unlike the deliberately optimistic, even purblind view of things that underlies the *Shevet Yehudah*, it reveals, in Yerushalmi's treatment of it, the possibility of a deliberate break of the alliance, the choice made by one of the most exceptional of the king's Jews in calling it into question in the name of a return to the community. It opens the way to the search for a new alliance with coreligionists only, to a radical isolation that once and for all cuts off the splendors and glories of the public space where the court Jews shone, a return to the private space of the ghetto, implying the rejection of any modernization that includes assimilation with the state. The exemplary history of Isaac Cardoso bears witness to the fidelity of the Marranos to an identity preserved in their innermost being in a context of extreme peril; it is the story of a doctor, a scholar whose reputation lifted him to the height of the Spanish state. Making his own the definition of the Marrano religion proposed by the French Jewish historian I. S. Révah, namely "a potential Judaism that entrance into a Jewish community most often transformed into actual Judaism," Yerushalmi wants to demonstrate that "even before he began to Judaize, every New Christian was a potential Marrano, whom any of a variety of circumstances could transform into an active Marrano. . . . The Marrano potential existed in any New Christian of the seventeenth century, so long as he was even barely aware that he was of Jewish extraction,"[113] an awareness capable of producing "a syncretism that still preserved his Jewish essence,"[114] despite all the borrowings from Christianity. Isaac Cardoso is the perfect example of one who succeeded to the most prestigious of royal functions and who, while still an "active Marrano," became involved at the risk of his life in a strategy of breaking away from integration, one that led him to exile. Can one argue that it is precisely the impossibility of "a Judaization of exile" in this context of forced expulsions and conversions that prevents any establishment of a "home" and thus pushes people either to the disappearance of their identity or to exile? Since the Portugal and Spain of the Inquisition made vain any form of vertical alliance arranged with the authorities, an active Marrano as prestigious as Isaac Cardoso can only break with them and distance himself, exile himself into a milieu of his own people, to Italy where a viable "home" awaited him.

Born in 1603–4 in Portugal to a family of New Christians, Isaac Cardoso then accompanied his family to Spain. The lack of reliable facts concerning Cardoso's life makes Yerushalmi, as well as other particularly innovative contemporary historians,[115] resort to bold guesses. One statement allows him to "suppose," another "suggests"; thus it seems "most likely," it is "practically certain" that Cardoso "very probably" knew a certain person, it is "possible" that Cardoso met another, it is "reasonable to suppose" that he witnessed the auto-da-fés that took place at the Plaza Mayor in Madrid in July 1632, but "we do not know if he was among the huge crowd . . . or if he witnessed" the lighting of the pyres on which so many people accused of "Judaizing" perished.[116] It is certain, however, that Cardoso, after the tragic events of 1632, remained in Madrid for fifteen years, hiding "his real thoughts . . . beneath a smile" of one aware of a special destiny.[117] Although he was interrogated as a witness by the Inquisition, he frequented the circle that had gathered around Lope de Vega, who did not conceal his hostile feelings to the Jews and, in agreement with the logic of vertical alliance, placed himself under the protection of the Count of Olivares, the powerful prime minister of Spain who devoted his life to constructing a strong state in this aim and did not scruple to use the New Christians and the Marranos. Cardoso dedicated one of his books to him: "Whoever once chooses such a good patron knows that the choice itself involves also constancy, for it would be frivolous to exchange a master toward whom one's affection has not changed. . . . Much happiness was in store for the monarchy when it found such a counselor."[118] Cardoso conforms to the logic advocated by Ibn Verga: he does it all the more easily since Olivares embodies the powerful protector of the Jews capable of facilitating an exceptional ascent for them. In fact, not long afterward, in 1640, Cardoso was named physician to the King. Nonetheless, a few years later, probably in 1648, he left Spain without any intention of returning; "the Peninsula now lost another gifted son, soon to be reclaimed by the Jewish people."[119] Everything leads one to believe, as testimony in 1659 before the Inquisition confirms, that Cardoso persuaded many people to follow the law of Moses, to practice Judaism, thus that he was, long before he went into exile, an active Marrano while still being officially a high personage of the state, following the example of the biblical Joseph who remained loyal to his faith while still serving the Pharaoh, the first unquestionable model of the Jew who, in exile, placed his competence at the service of the state.[120]

Indeed, notes Yosef H. Yerushalmi, "We possess no open window to Cardoso's soul," we cannot "trace his inner thoughts,"[121] since, before his exile to Italy, he constantly wore a mask and took care not to let his real identity show through. Nevertheless we realize, Yerushalmi adds, that, like so many others who decided to leave or who, on the contrary, tried to continue living their double identity dangerously in Spain, Cardoso maintained a fidelity that could not be explained merely by the hatred encountered or by the discriminatory statutes concerning *limpieza de sangre* that stigmatized and rejected even converted Jews. At the peak of restrictions and danger, Jews, like Cardoso, thus decided to remain loyal to their faith, to their culture, to their traditions. It is also to recognize the fact that, even without a home and outside of all "Judaization of exile," in the worst conditions where a particularly severe control was exercised, Jewish identity could be preserved in the galut. Still, the departure, the deliberate break from the vertical alliance with a state that had become openly repressive but that Ibn Verga almost absolved, whatever its breaches of the alliance, from the protection due to Jewish subjects, must be explained. Every day danger threatened Cardoso even more, but we may choose instead to think that it was more the desire to live a Jewish life fully by returning to the community that suddenly caused him to break (in a way that Ibn Verga could not have foreseen) the traditional bond with the state in order to go in anonymity to the Verona ghetto where his fame as a devoted doctor and eminent scholar no longer passed outside the narrow borders of the ghetto and was confined solely to erudite Jewish milieus scattered throughout the diaspora. As if history did not inevitably obey an evolutionist logic that led from the ghetto to modernity, from the community to public space, from the civil to the civic, as if the way of emancipation that Cardoso could more easily have found in Holland, England, or France were less attractive than the opposite path, the one leading to the ghetto, the place of complete separation from non-Jews, of voluntary segregation regarded as indispensable for the observation of the Law. For the doctor from the Verona ghetto, the former king's Jew used to celebrations of the court, to civilized conversations with the intellectual circles of the Madrid capital, the fact that the Jews were henceforth "marked and distinct, as well in their dwellings as in their dress, is not so much due to the deprecation of the nations as it is the particular providence of their separation."[122] Cardoso came to appropriate biological vocabulary, this time turned to the favor of the Jews:[123] in his apologetic book *Las excelencias de los Hebreos* published in Amsterdam in 1679, he defends the ethnic purity of Israel, a claimed form of limpieza that now confers value on the Jews; he delights in the indispensable separation that the Jews now seek as a people "separate and distinct, its Law diverse from others."[124]

Other Jews will come to experience later on, in France for example, after emancipation at the revolution, but especially in Germany and Austria, the temptation to set aside emancipation and the Enlightenment and return to a private life and faith whose flourishing the "eastern" ghetto would permit thanks to a chosen separation.[125] Still others, like the supporters of state or cultural Zionism, will instead become involved in the project of return to Zion as a new form of community that has once again become a nation separate from others. All of these will willingly break the vertical alliance with the state, whether it is Spanish, French, German, Austrian, or Russian and will prefer a return to identitarian ties confined or enlarged to the nation envisioned as Jewish. All will want to reconstruct, in exile, that "nation within a nation," that "Republic apart, which lives and governs itself by its laws and precepts which God gave them at Sinai, and which He commanded them to keep forever in all their generations,"[126] or in Zion, a Jewish nation that has once again become capable of endowing itself with its own state within which the vertical alliance radically changes its meaning. What is especially useful to remember is that Cardoso justifies separation in exile by an all-out attack on states and princes, accusing them of deliberately seeking to increase the sufferings of the Jews. Though he repeatedly quotes Jeremiah's letter to justify the complete loyalty of the Jews to their host city—by showing that in Persia as in Rome, in Spain as in Prague or Venice, the Jews continually defended the authorities and the state—it is to be even more shocked at the way the state and princes have so often betrayed them.[127] Cardoso denounces the Spanish Inquisition, the pogroms of Chmielnicki, stresses the harshness of monarchs punished by God for having attacked the Jews, from Pharaoh to Nebuchadnezzar, from Pompey to Philip IV of France, from Ferdinand and Isabelle to John II of Portugal, notes with anguish (agreeing with Ibn Verga on this point) that "the populace does not listen to the wise men or obey the princes when hatred dominates reason," and denounces at length the sufferings inflicted throughout all times on the

Jews.[128] Does he already foreshadow the lachrymose vision of history to which Graetz in part subscribes and that Baron—as well as to a lesser degree Yerushalmi—rejects in the modern era? By insisting so much on the sufferings endured by the Jews, on the Ashkenazi martyrology, and on the misfortunes that rained down on the Sephardim despite the constant search for a vertical alliance, on the extreme violence of the anti-Semitic literature that raged endlessly in Spain, as well as in Germanic countries or in France where accusations of ritual murder were regularly made against them, Cardoso seems to abandon all hope in nations in which Jews live their exile and make the lands prosper, according to Jeremiah's letter, but also while respecting their laws, according to the precept *dina de malkhuta dina*.

The so much sought-after vertical alliance seems to be in vain, because of the strategy of the powerful, or due to the transports of the "populace" that managed to convince them to join in their anti-Semitic hatred; the "home" is temporary so long as the "Judaization of exile" is only, in the end, every time and in even the most favorable historical contexts, a tragic illusion that is soon dissipated by the permanence of the hatred, by traditional anti-Semitic violence and rejection; the abrupt judgment of Baer on the basic misfortunes that have always, everywhere struck Jews in exile, that Yerushalmi strongly rejects, turns out to be, seen close-up, often correct: Is it better, then, to prefer a return to the ghetto, for Cardoso, or immigration to Israel, for Baer, over the glory of the public space of the various societies of exile? The author of *Zakhor* almost, despite his optimistic theses on the possibility of constructing a protective home rich in potentialities in the situation of exile, comes to doubt its durability, its solidity in the face of so many ordeals. We realize this when we turn our attention to the comparison between the two great catastrophes to which, like Baer and in a similar spirit,[129] he repeatedly returns: the one that occurred in 1492 (the expulsion of the Jews from Spain) and 1497 (the forced conversion of the Jews of Portugal) and the one that began in 1933 (the triumph of Hitler's Germany). If these societies, "radically different in their character and culture and so remote from each other in time," reacted in an "analogous" way to "what they perceived as an intrusion of Jews into their midst,"[130] it is because once converted, that is to say "emancipated by baptism" (in Spain and in Portugal) or assimilated (in Germany),[131] having become invisible, they appear to be all the more formidable. This invisibility facilitated their entrance in large numbers into all spheres of society, sometimes assigning them a brilliant role: hence legislation of statutes of blood purity (*estatutos de limpieza de sangre*), of a racial anti-Semitism capable of once again provoking a separation that conversion or assimilation had caused to disappear. In this sense, weren't both Cardoso and Freud confronted with a similar form of rejection on the part of their respective societies, a rejection that was perhaps made more intense by their shared role as doctors, evoking a particularly feared Jewish perversity, which biological, racial anti-Semitism tries to banish?[132]

Both times, suddenly, and in an unforeseeable way for those who believe in the solidity of a vertical alliance that prevents kings and states from extreme measures attacking, in a deliberate way and from above, Jewish existence in exile, we see in each of these societies, so distanced from each other in history, an unimaginable violence rain down precisely from above on loyal Jewish populations, reducing protective homes to ashes, destroying identitarian bonds, putting an end to the Judaization of exile. Until the very end, or almost, in Spain as well as in Germany, a number of Jews, however, remained confident in their government, from which they expected protection. Not many German Jews would repeat the phrase of certain Castellan Jews who, even in 1487, celebrated their "just and charitable" sovereign and neither foresaw nor suspected the decision that would end their presence on Spanish soil.[133] Still, for both groups, such a decision (that of expelling the Jews from Spain or that, taken in January 1942 at the Wannsee Conference, to annihilate them) was not imaginable. For Yerushalmi, despite the tragic events of 1492 and 1497, until the contemporary era that saw the triumph of the modern state, "that a monarch could deliberately rule in favor of the physical annihilation of the Jews remained inconceivable."[134] In the modern period as well as before, even to protect themselves against being abandoned, the Jews showed themselves incapable of forming horizontal alliances, for example with elements of the people or, later on, with the socialist movement, which tended to adhere in turn to anti-Semitic prejudices: they did not manage to find allies within civil society and were all the more subject to the irrationality of the "mob," of crowds. Arendt, cited here by Yerushalmi, writes in the same sense that "authority, and especially higher authority, was favorable to them while subordinate authorities and the mob were dangerous,"[135] thinking at the same time that the Jews were partially responsible for the misfortunes that rained down on them, since they remained so isolated and blindly submitted themselves to the state. This idea also appears in Ibn Verga, the defender of vertical alliance: "What gain is there in the benevolence of the king and the judges of the land, if the will of the peoples is not with us and they constantly seek our ruin?"[136] Oblivious of the necessity of a horizontal alliance and incapable of finding allies among the "populace," the Jews in the modern era threw themselves as they did before into the arms of the authorities, which now had the face of the omnipotent centralized state. This state, in the name of its standardizing logic, can indeed harm Jewish identity more than before; indeed, as the German example has shown, it can even go as far as the Nuremberg Laws or imprisonment in ghettos, terrible but well-known practices. Genocide, in its extreme dimension, was however unforeseeable: "It is not merely the fact that a state sought willfully to destroy the Jews that made the phenomenon unprecedented and thus impossible to anticipate; added to this was the fact that the destruction was carried out by Germany, which made the thing even more incredible."[137] In fact, confidence in the Judeo-German osmosis, thanks to which the Jews could brilliantly build their "subculture" while still fully participating in national culture, was complete. Yerushalmi, though, challenges the criticisms made by Hannah Arendt of the Jewish Councils, which maintained dialogue with the Nazis; according to Yerushalmi, Arendt does not see that "those who went every day to negotiate with the SS or the Gestapo did not essentially differ, in the conception they had of their role, from a Philo meeting Gaius Caligula." But, as he notes, "Caligula had not prepared the Jews for Hitler": in this sense, the royal alliance "stopped being a myth. Henceforth the Jews know one thing that they did not know before: they know that even the highest authorities of a government can deliberately decide to destroy them,"[138] with the more or less acknowledged indifference of all other governments.

The Shoah, consequently, was a tragic moment of a final calling into question of the protective vertical alliance in so many homes that were thought to have been permanent. How ironic it is to note that it is the modern and secular state that implements genocide while in the Middle Ages Christianity could be the source of discrimination and expulsions, massacres under pressure from crowds, but not of radical physical extermination coming deliberately from above! Unlike the Christian kings of long ago who preserved Jewish presence in their own interests, "the Holocaust was the work of a thoroughly modern, neopagan state."[139] Here the analogies with Christian Spain and its anti-Semitism based on blood stop: whence Yerushalmi's "J'accuse," when he stresses that the Holocaust took place in an era when secularization ruled, genocide occurring "on the initiative of the state" and thanks to the silence of a pope who for the first time broke with the protective practices of a number of his predecessors. Is it because the Jews can now never again trust in the state, or is it because "the Jewish state can itself be destroyed" that Yosef H. Yerushalmi utters this warning:[140] "My people, now as in the past, is in grave peril of its life,"[141] adding, "Could the horror be repeated? In 1945, I thought the thing impossible. Today, I have lost that certainty."[142] One might indeed reflect, unlike Yerushalmi, that it was more the deliberate destruction of the Prussian state by the Nazis, who hated that rational public power remote from the fundamental values of the *Volk*, as well as the birth of an extreme power in the service of one man and his party elected by the "populace," supported by various allies in working-class society, both blue- and white-collar workers, that made the extreme decision the Shoah represents possible; with that in mind one might qualify the responsibility of a state that often could do nothing about it.[143] Still, today, at this turning point of the twenty-first century, the fundamental uncertainty of the vertical alliance considerably weakens the places of habitation throughout exile, and other threats weigh on the state of Israel, as well as on the survival of Jewish identity, here or there, so that now the question must be asked: Is exile as home once and for all giving way to exile as "hell"?[144] Is hope dying out, even in American society, so protective of all homes, tolerant of multiculturalism, where it is inconceivable that such suffering could ever occur?[145] Must one be deaf and blind to respect even today

Jeremiah's command, "plant gardens," "seek the peace of the city" of exile, buy, despite all your fears, "a field in Anathoth"? Does scholarly knowledge of Jewish history brought to its highest point paradoxically bring a fatal blow to all forms of hope? Even if "simple historians" cannot "claim to be prophets,"[146] aren't Jews once again forced to despair of their future?

# Conclusion:
# Exile, the Enlightenment, Disassimilation

What a paradox! That Karl Marx the revolutionary attacks, precisely in *On 'The Jewish Question,'* the human rights that separate "the egoistic man" from his "community" in terms that an Edmund Burke would not have challenged![1] That by proclaiming his new Zionist fervor, Moses Hess, Marx's faithful companion, is supposed to feel the same enthusiasm as Burke about the past![2] That Émile Durkheim, friend of Jean Jaurès, the positivist Dreyfusard sociologist who became the mentor for generations of teachers in the Third Republic during the time of emancipation and rationalism, could for some people have the traits of a Burke, with his theses on the nature of social activity sometimes considered "similar" to those advanced by the author of *Reflections on the Revolution in France!*[3] That Heinrich Graetz, the first historian of the Jewish past, from a Wissenschaft fed by the Enlightenment, could be seen as a "Burke of the Jewish people" who doubts the rationalist way in which the philosophers of that movement were engaged![4] That Isaiah Berlin, who however "recognizes" himself in the Enlightenment, the contemporary scholar who embodies pluralism, also proclaims his admiration for Burke to the point of seeing, in the present day, the creation of Israel as the logical outcome of a Burkean interpretation of nations![5] That the world vision of Max Horkheimer and Theodor Adorno, the founders of the Frankfurt School, the authors of *Dialectic of Enlightenment*, is supposed to present "more than

The idea of a "geography of hope" is imagined by Yosef H. Yerushalmi in his article "Un champ à Anathoth: vers une histoire de l'espoir juif" [A Field in Anathoth: Toward a History of Jewish Hope], *Mémoire et histoire*, Paris: Denoël, 1986, p. 102. I would like here to thank Jean Baumgarten, Richie Cohen, and Aron Rodrigue for their admirable patience and their boundless knowledge that they were so generously willing to share. I also thank Éric Vigne for his exacting reading of the manuscript. —P.B.

one resemblance with Burke's"![6] That Michael Walzer, the social-democrat thinker anxious to rehabilitate the local, the cave, reiterative universalism molded by a "thick" identity fostering the transmission of histories that little old men tell out loud, is described as "a leftist Burke"![7] That Daniel Bell, the ex-Trotskyite turned theoretician of the end of ideologies and postindustrial society, has come to be compared, like the Raymond Aron of *The Opium of the Intellectuals*, with Burke who was hostile to the eighteenth-century French Philosophers, and that both are presented as the heroes of the conservative trend that is carrying the day among contemporary democracies![8] That Jacob Leib Talmon, author of *The Origins of Totalitarian Democracy*, which denounces the various contemporary authoritarianisms, can argue that "the bonds that join Jews to each other, in Edmund Burke's sense, are as invisible as the air and as solid as the heaviest chains"![9] That Hannah Arendt, finally, the philosopher of the vita activa and of public space, plainly confesses that she shares a number of assessments formulated by Edmund Burke!

These comparisons are debatable, iconoclastic, and unsettling, since they call into question so many received ideas. They do, however, encourage a reexamination of the relationships the Jews had with the Enlightenment, but also with those who were against the Enlightenment, all the more so since from Jacob Talmon to Jacob Katz or Arthur Herzberg, from Max Horkheimer and Theodor Adorno to Zygmunt Bauman, many are the contemporary Jewish thinkers who, following the example of Leo Strauss or Emmanuel Lévinas, sharply attack the proponents of the Enlightenment.[10] In an often simplistic way, they accuse them, like certain sociologists attached to the preeminence of traditional organic social bonds,[11] of being the source of all evils, of individualism and totalitarianism, of the unmitigated reign of alienating technology in the service of irrational capitalism with the limitless domination of a Reason that is radically hostile to every form of religious sentiment, of the fanatical negation of every cultural identity or genre, and even of the invention of a new type of secular anti-Semitism even more radical than the Christian anti-Semitism of which Voltaire made himself champion,[12] and that led straight to Auschwitz where "the clean-shaven" were exterminated as well as "the bearded,"[13] the final stage of the destruction of Reason. In this sense, and whatever they felt about it, these thinkers of various intellectual origins unintentionally offer arguments to all those who resolutely fight the ideals of the Enlightenment in the name of attachment to the Volk, to the community, but also, on the contrary, to pluralistic democracy, to the point of taking on the traits of determined enemies of the government of the people who, like Leo Strauss and Hannah Arendt, provide grist for the mill of the most reactionary conservatives in the United States of today.[14]

The enigma that the unexpected connection between Arendt's and Burke's thinking poses deserves some attention, all the more so since Arendt also joins the chorus of theoreticians hostile to the French-style state model understood in a very simplistic way, like a useful foil, accused by the supporters of pluralism, in the vein of Isaiah Berlin or Michael Walzer, of eroding all differences within the public space.[15] In Arendt's *The Origins of Totalitarianism* as she is concluding the section devoted to imperialism with a description of the decline, in her opinion inevitable, of the nation-state, Arendt argues that the Rights of Man offer no protection to all those who lose their citizenship. As she nicely phrases it, "We became aware of the existence of a right to have rights . . . and a right to belong to some kind of organized community, only when millions of people emerged who had lost and could not regain these rights."[16] Questioning the natural character of the Rights of Man proclaimed in too abstract a way, she adds:

> These facts and reflections offer what seems an ironical, bitter, and belated confirmation of the famous arguments with which Edmund Burke opposed the French Revolution's Declaration of the Rights of Man. They appear to buttress his assertion that human rights were an "abstraction," that it was much wiser to rely on an "entailed inheritance" of rights which one transmits to one's children . . . and to claim one's rights to be the "rights of an Englishman" rather than the inalienable rights of man. . . . The pragmatic soundness of Burke's concept seems to be beyond doubt in the light of our manifold experiences. Not only did loss of national rights in all instances entail the loss of human rights; the restoration of human rights, as the recent example of the State of Israel proves, has been achieved so far only through the restoration or the establishment of national rights. . . . The survivors of the extermination camps, the inmates of concentration and internment camps, and even the comparatively happy stateless

people could see without Burke's arguments that the abstract naked-
ness of being nothing but human was their greatest danger. . . . Burke's
arguments therefore gain an added significance if we look only at the
general human condition of those who have been forced out of all political communities.[17]

Linked body and soul with the future of the nation-state, European
Jews suddenly found themselves plunged into uttermost abandonment
at the moment when its existence was threatened. The acknowledgment of the radical destitution of the Jews, the vast majority of whom
came from East European *yiddishkeit*, which had once been the source
of community life and unique cultural creations, encourages Arendt
to return to Burke to attack the abstract vision of rights issuing from
the revolution, which preferred to speak of the inalienable rights of
man as against the "right of Englishmen," individuals integrated into a
national community capable of offering them the protection of which
the Jews, yet again sent wandering, have henceforth been stripped.
Even if Arendt admits that this acknowledgment is "ironic and bitter," it acquires a formidable significance at the very time when the
Jews, throughout all of Europe, are losing the privileges of integration
within a nation. The limits of assimilation of the Jews in the West,
their sudden disassimilation and, even more radically, their abandonment in the East, where the Jewish masses were suddenly deprived of
every right, becomes clearly manifest in the period between the two
wars before it leads to general annihilation during the Second World
War. Strangely, Burke is cited to justify the necessity for the Jews to belong to a state and the creation of the state of Israel, for which the new
wandering Jews who escaped from the camps have a vital need in order
to become, like the English, citizens and thus human.

We know, however, that Arendt turned away from the Zionist solution, despite her constant attachment to the existence of the Jewish state,
in order to validate the American way, the only society, in her opinion,
whose exceptionalism ensures the Jews, as well as the other minorities,
the protection of their rights without requiring total assimilation. After
repeating, in *On Revolution*, that "Burke was right,"[18] she contrasts the
projects of the men of the French Revolution with those of the Americans, who endowed themselves with a nonabstract constitution; Arendt
wants to establish restraints capable of ensuring freedoms and adds that

"the perplexities of the Rights of Man are manifold, and Burke's famous argument against them is neither obsolete nor 'reactionary.'"[19] By challenging in advance the reactionary conceptions, sometimes verging on racism, that some people have sought to draw from the historicist perspectives outlined by Burke, she continually associates his name with that of Montesquieu, a thinker whose reflections are sometimes rejected as aristocratic and conservative, to emphasize their common preoccupation with maintaining public freedoms. She knowingly risks this comparison, which can seem, especially in France,[20] iconoclastic, stating that the English theoretician can be regarded as the "best British disciple" of Montesquieu: it has been argued that Burke saw in him "a genius, a Herculean mind" that admired the English Constitution, from which he drew inspiration to oppose the abstract rationalism of the French Revolution. From then on, "Burke's enemies would also be Montesquieu's," since "the similarity of their thinking is obvious."[21]

The Montesquieu of *The Spirit of Laws*, who originates this current of thought, is seen as a thinker respectful of the diversity of cultures; he dares to write, "Let them leave us as we are."[22] He portrays himself as the protector of the values of the Jews, whom, however, he deems "intolerant," since they show "an invincible obstinacy in their religion which borders on madness."[23] Still, Montesquieu thinks that "the laws of Moses were perfectly wise,"[24] denounces the "most severe regulations against the Jews," and notes in passing "how this nation has been sported with from one age to another: at one time, their effects were confiscated when they were willing to become Christians; and at another, if they refused to turn Christians, they were ordered to be burned"; in his opinion, "the policy of enclosing the Jews in a neighborhood where they cannot spread out and where they are packed in pell-mell is barbaric."[25] He attacks the Inquisitors of Lisbon through the "most humble remonstrance" of an unknown Jew who exclaims, "You put us to death who believe only what you believe, because we do not believe all that you believe. We follow a religion which you yourselves know to have been formerly dear to God. We think that God loves it still. . . . If you are cruel to us, you are much more so to our children. . . . You would have us become Christians, and you will not be so yourselves."[26] In a more general way, for Montesquieu, "In China the Chinese are governed by the Chinese ceremonial and the Tartars by theirs; and yet there is no nation in the world that aims so much at tranquility. If the people observe the laws, what signifies it whether these laws are the same?"[27] This is a basically pluralistic vision that announces the stances favorable to cultural minorities of a Condorcet, a Mirabeau, or even a Burke who, without pomposity, simply notes, "We have in London some very respectable members of the Jewish nation whom we quite gladly keep here."[28]

Initiator of a kind of nonrelativist reiterative universalism à la Walzer, Montesquieu opens another way than the one defended strongly by Voltaire, in the name of a Reason resolutely hostile to all forms of beliefs. He justifies in advance those Jews "obstinately determined" on remaining faithful to their values during the French Revolution.[29] In his rejection of the Old Testament, Voltaire draws his inspiration, on the contrary, from Spinoza, the "Messiah of the Enlightenment," the inventor of the "radical philosophers of the Enlightenment" who also radically turns his back on Judaism as if the Enlightenment, through the personality of their precursor, implied precisely the negation of Judaism.[30] The Montesquieu tradition thus feeds, within the French model, other members of the Enlightenment who were less flamboyant, more respectful of liberalism, of the pluralism of values, and who were also concerned to assure a Jewish future. Isaiah Berlin thinks in this sense that "Montesquieu abhors the concept of man in general, no less than do later thinkers like Burke or Herder, or the cultural anthropologists of our own time. . . . [Montesquieu's] opposition to the enforcement of any orthodoxy . . . inaugurates the struggle within the camp of Enlightenment between democrats and liberals. . . . [His] dry sense of historical reality [is] as concrete as Burke's [but] free from his violent prejudices and romantic distortions."[31]

Arendt also frequently invokes the name, in this line of thinking, of Tocqueville, who sang the praises of American democracy and did not conceal his anxieties about the abstract approach of the French philosophers: she refers to the author of *Democracy in America* to present her defense of the pluralistic American model, averse to any temptation to totalitarianism, whose federal system, along with its Constitution, its system of balance of power, permanently, according to Arendt, protects the human rights of all Americans, including the Jews.[32] Within this nonhomogenizing political system whose logic differs from that of nation-states, in this society which, as Tocqueville noted, rests on the local and respects the customs of individuals, Arendt finds her place and feels free. In a remarkable letter to Karl Jaspers that seems to paraphrase the author of *Democracy in America*, she writes:

> There is much I could say about America. There really is such a thing as freedom here and a strong feeling among many people that one cannot live without freedom. The republic is not a vapid illusion, and the fact that there is no national state and no truly national tradition creates an atmosphere of freedom or at least one not pervaded by fanaticism. (Because of the strong need the various immigrant groups feel to maintain their identity, the melting pot is in large part not even an ideal, much less a reality.) Then, too, people here feel themselves responsible for public life to an extent I have never seen in any European country. . . . In conditions of freedom every individual should be able to decide what he would like to be, German or Jew or whatever. In an a-national republic like the United States, in which nationality and state are not identical, this becomes more or less a question with only social and cultural meaning but no political meaning. (For example, so-called anti-Semitism here is purely social, and the same people who wouldn't dream of sharing the same hotel with Jews would be astonished and outraged if their fellow citizens who happened to be Jews were disenfranchised. That may change, but for now that's the way things are.) In the European system of nation-states it is all much more complicated.[33]

Indeed, Hannah Arendt underestimates the emancipating power of the nation-state and excessively magnifies, on the contrary, the atmosphere of tolerance, freedom, and shared responsibility that animates American political life, strangely paying little attention to the extent of racism and anti-Semitism that threatens to reduce the sweetness of the rediscovered "home" to nothing.[34] Still, she perceives a relationship connected with the defense of political and social pluralism,[35] with respect for the diverse values that flourish in an "atmosphere of freedom," a statement that is surprising in this expert on the public space of citizens supposed to give voice according to the model of the ancient polis curiously identified henceforth with the American democracy.[36] Arguing that "No doubt, wherever public life and its law of equality are completely victorious, wherever a civilization succeeds in eliminating or reducing to a minimum the dark background of difference, it will end in complete petrifaction and be punished,"[37] she traces the outlines of a liberal, nonabstract tradition of the Enlightenment, whose founder is Montesquieu, the admirer of the English model, a more liberal or conservative tradition than a reactionary or counterrevolutionary one, distinct, however, in the spirit of Rousseau, from the ambition of participatory democracy that Tocqueville also rejects. This way of Montesquieu's reconciles, in Arendt's opinion, the egalitarian tradition of the Enlightenment with freedom-guaranteeing pluralism and is embodied in American constitutionalism, which protects a real right to difference. For Arendt, the American way imposes itself on its own, for, as she writes to Jaspers, "Today, the Jews are no longer an important and integral component in the European nations. Will they become one again? I don't know, but I don't think so."[38] She offers the Jews, and other minorities, a "home" that the nation-state would refuse them in the name of its standardizing concept of public space.

Arendt's confidence in American society curiously brings her closer to the theses formed in the same era by Mordecai Kaplan who, with the help of an Americanization of the concepts of Simon Dubnow on the essential nature of the community, sees in American democracy the possible framework for a cultural flourishing of the Jews. Rejecting the assimilationist way, cautious about the future of a unitary national way, they both think that only the "nation of nations" offers the Jews a legitimate home that can put an end to exile and abolish the condition of pariah in the diaspora.[39] In the perspective of Louis Wirth, Horace Kallen, Daniel Bell, Michael Walzer, and also Salo Baron and Yosef H. Yerushalmi, the American model is presented as the framework favorable to expression of an autonomous Jewish socialization, to the reincarnation of the yiddishkeit of long ago, to the reconstruction of a community, a dwelling-place, a home where loyalties and beliefs can be sheltered that are capable of putting an end to the posture of Simmel's Stranger, fertile in other more tragic contexts. Thus this "estrangement" of the creative soul familiar to Jews "on the tightrope" between antagonistic mental universes would be reduced, if not completely abolished. The New World, although sensitive to conservative and antiegalitarian ideas, to prejudices, to religious fundamentalisms as well as to rivalries engendered by an invading and often intolerant multiculturalism, in turn is seen as a center capable of replacing the old center that once existed in Eastern Europe, land of authoritarianisms and pogroms, land of desolation where Jewish life is moribund today.

The Montesquieu relationship, which Raymond Aron also discovered when he ranked him first among the founders of the sociological tradition,[40] leads straight to Max Weber, to the "Montesquieu of the twentieth century,"[41] anxious in his turn to privilege a comparative historical approach. It thus leads to the author of *Ancient Judaism*,[42] to the thinker from whom Simon Dubnow tries clumsily to draw inspiration to construct his stammering but fertile sociology of the Jews. It challenges in advance the fundamentally simplistic projects of values led in the name of the Reason or truth of History, which encouraged Karl Marx to imagine a humanity without Jews into which he would manage to merge, whereas his daughter Eleanor, faithful to her father, still did not hesitate to harangue English workers in the Yiddish he strongly rejected. It tragically sheds light on Simmel's desire for assimilation, who was perceived, against his will, as a Jew of Eastern Europe, an unstable situation he theorizes through his reflections on the Stranger. It announces the slow arrival of a relative Girondization of contemporary French society, the awakening of community life, the recognition of multiple, changing, and sometime rival identities, which makes the unitary model appear in a bad light but does not change the republican, egalitarian logic from which a strong vision of shared citizenship comes. The pluralistic tradition lets us glimpse the possibility of more specific conceivable homes, still threatened by exclusive logics that are particularly threatening when the alliance with the state withdraws and when the most virulent prejudices and populisms rearise.[43] When Émile Durkheim, the prophet of republican assimilation, continually invoked the warmth of "family communism" to justify maintaining a Jewish fidelity, when Raymond Aron, in search of his roots, finally called assimilation into question and advocated the coming of a multinational citizenship compatible with an extreme loyalty toward one's country, were they announcing, in an unexpected way among those "crazy about the Republic," that form of contemporary public recognition compatible with the maintaining of a republican, militant citizenship within a public space emerging from the distant dream of the philosophers, of whom Jürgen Habermas emerges as the principal heir, anxious to preserve attachment to various cultures, even in postnational space?[44]

Freed by the Enlightenment, we cannot conceive that the Jews could dissociate themselves from it. Paradox would have it that it is especially the Montesquieu connection, both liberal and conservative, with sometimes culturalist trends but which also inspired the men of 1789, that plainly legitimizes a home for the Jews. This connection rejects the notion that their hopes, their happiness, are solely the result of the regenerating emancipation of humanity. All of a sudden, it gives meaning to the astounding approach of Isaac Cardoso who, from the deepest part of Sepharad, the continent of the Western Jews, rejected the rifts of assimilation, openly assumed a fidelity that did not however imply isolation, and showed a complete adhesion to rationalism by maintaining a bridge between Judaism and Western heritage that distanced him from his brother, who had become a devotee of the messianism of Sabbatai Zevi. Finally, it favors, in the spirit of *The Persian Letters*, a comparative sociology of Jewish worlds in distinct historical contexts by going to meet another, more fragile sociological imagination implemented by the precursors of contemporary Jewish studies anxious to preserve the world of yesterday or today. By a final paradox, from their recent flourishing there suddenly rearise ways of thinking, forgotten or denied dreams and loyalties, with such a strong acuity that they henceforth make precarious the adherence, once so enthusiastic, solely to salvation through assimilation. As if, coming from the deepest part of history, reconstructed, reinterpreted, transposed, the values and modes of social life of that distant East European space and, to a lesser extent, those of that other East that is the Sephardic world, still haunted the imagination of assimilated, uncertain diasporas even more, weakening their perception of themselves and of their existence, making them doubt once again the solidity of their wind-battered homes.

# Notes

## Introduction: Toward a Counterhistory

1. Charles Kadushin, *The American Intellectual Elite* (Boston: Little Brown, 1974).

2. *Lire*, April 1981.

3. Claude Lévi-Strauss, *Tristes Tropiques* (Paris: Plon, 1955), pp. 21–22.

4. Claude Lévi-Strauss, Didier Éribon, *De près et de loin* (Odile Jacob, 1990), pp. 215 and 217.

5. David Damrosch, "The Ethnic Ethnographer: Judaism in *Tristes Tropiques*," *Representations* (spring 1995).

6. Emmanuel Lévinas, *Difficile liberté* (Éditions de Minuit, 1976), p. 69.

7. Stanley Diamond, "The Myth of Structuralism," in Ino Rossi, ed., *The Unconscious in Culture* (New York: E. P. Hutton, 1974). Thomas Shaley, *Claude Lévi-Strauss: Social Psychotherapy and the Collective Unconscious* (Amherst: University of Massachusetts Press, 1979). On this point, the recent biography by Denis Bertholet adds nothing new: *Claude Lévi-Strauss* (Paris: Plon, 2003).

8. George Steiner, "Some Meta-Rabbis," in Douglas Villiers, ed., *Next Year in Jerusalem: Jews in the Twentieth Century* (London, 1976), p. 75. Paul Mendes-Flohr includes Claude Lévi-Strauss in that long lineage of thinkers in *Divided Passions: Jewish Intellectuals and the Experience of Modernity* (Detroit, MI: Wayne State University Press, 1991), p. 428.

9. Isaac Deutscher, *Essai sur le problème juif* (Paris: Payot, 1969).

10. Rachel Ertel, *Brasier de mots* (Liana Levi, 2003), p. 159.

11. See Howard Simon, *Jewish Times: Voices of the American Jewish Experience* (Boston: Houghton Mifflin, 1988), p. 70.

12. Daniel Bell, *The Winding Passage* (Cambridge, MA: ABT Books), pp. 131–35. *Yichus* refers to a distinguished family lineage.

13. Bell, *Winding Passage*, pp. 316ff. See Malcolm Waters, *Daniel Bell* (London: Routledge and Kegan, 1996).

14. Joseph Dorman, *Arguing the World: The New York Intellectuals in Their Own Words* (Chicago: University of Chicago Press, 2001), pp. 11, 35, 110, and 148. See also Alexander Bloom, *Prodigal Sons: The New York Intellectuals and Their World* (New York: Oxford University Press, 1986). Terry Cooney, *The Rise of the New York Intellectuals: Partisan Review and Its Circle* (Madison: University of Wisconsin

Press, 1986). Deborah Dash Moore, *At Home in America: Second Generation New York Jews* (New York: Columbia University Press, 1981).

15. Daniel Blatman, *Notre liberté et la vôtre. Le mouvement ouvrier juif Bund en Pologne, 1939–1949* (Paris: Le Cerf, 2002), p. 287.

16. See, for instance, Daniel Bell, "Parable of Alienation," *Jewish Frontier* (November 1946).

17. Jürgen Habermas, *Profils philosophiques et politiques* (Paris: Gallimard, 1974), p. 77.

18. Alain Touraine, *Un désir d'histoire* (Paris: Stock, 1977), p. 76.

19. Thorstein Veblen, "The Intellectual Pre-Eminence of Jews in Modern Europe," *Political Science Quarterly* (March 1919): 35–37. On the place of Jews in sociology, see René König, "Die Juden und die Soziologie," in René König, ed., *Studien zur Soziologie* (Frankfurt: Fisher, 1971); and Dirk Kaesler, "Jewishness as a Central Formation-Milieu of Early German Society," *History of Sociology* no. 1 (1985).

20. Raymond Aron, *Sur la condition juive contemporaine* (Paris: Éditions de Fallois), p. 272.

21. Claude Lévi-Strauss, *Le Nouvel Observateur*, July 5, 1980.

22. Ibid.

23. David Biale, Michael Galchinsky, and Susannah Heschel, eds., *Jews and Multiculturalism* (Berkeley: University of California Press, 1998).

24. Werner Cahnman, "Scholar and Visionary: The Correspondence Between Herzl and Ludwig Gumplowicz," in *German Jewry: Its History and Sociology*, Selected Essays by Werner Cahnman, Joseph Maier, Judith Marcus, and Zoltan Tarr, eds. (New Brunswick, NJ: Transaction Publishers, 1989), p. 163.

25. See Chapter 2.

26. Letter from Émile Durkheim to Marcel Mauss, July 26, 1916, in Émile Durkheim, *Lettres à Marcel Mauss* (Paris: PUF), pp. 537–38. See Chapter 3.

27. Georg Lukács, *Record of Life: An Autobiographical Sketch*, Istvan Eörsi, ed. (London: Verso, 1983), p. 29.

28. See David Kettler and Voker Meja, *Karl Mannheim and the Crisis of Liberalism* (1995), p. 287. By contrast, during the same period, Franz Oppenheimer in Germany devotes a part of his research to the Jewish domain and becomes co-director of the *Neue Jüdische Monatshefte*. Dirk Kaesler, "La sociologie: Une secte juive? Le judaïsme comme milieu d'émergence de la sociologie allemande," *Revue germanique internationale* no. 17 (2002): 102.

29. On Talcott Parsons, whose father was a minister, see Uta Gerhartd's recent biography, *Talcott Parsons: An Intellectual Biography* (Cambridge: Cambridge University Press, 2002).

30. Dan A. Oren, *Joining the Club: A History of Jews and Yale* (New Haven, CT: Yale University Press, 1985), pp. 261–68 and 326. See also Susanne Klingenstein, *Jews in the American Academy, 1900–1940: The Dynamics of Intellectual Assimilation* (New Haven, CT: Yale University Press, 1991); and Paul Ritterband and Harold

Wechsler, *Jewish Learning in American Universities* (Bloomington: University of Indiana Press, 1995).

31. See the interesting book by David Hollinger, *Science, Jews and Secular Culture: Studies in Mid-Twentieth Century American Intellectual History* (Princeton, NJ: Princeton University Press, 1996), ch. 2.

32. Marcia Graham Synott, *The Half-Open Door: Discriminations and Admissions at Harvard, Yale and Princeton, 1900–1970* (Westport, CT: 1979).

33. See Seymour Martin Lipset and Everett Carl Ladd Jr., "Jewish Academics in the United States: Their Achievements, Culture and Politics," *American Jewish Yearbook* (1972).

34. See Seymour Martin Lipset, "The Study of Jewish Communities in a Comparative Context," *The Jewish Journal of Sociology* (December 1963): 163.

35. Seymour Martin Lipset, "Jewish Sociologists and Sociologists of the Jews," *Jewish Social Studies* (July 1955): 7–8. During the same period, Salo Baron asked the question in similar terms, during a 1958 lecture: "These days, the most important question," he writes, "is whether Jews can prove themselves creative in the context of the Emancipation. . . . The Jews will unarguably contribute to the culture of their environment . . . but will they also have enough energy to devote to their own Jewish heritage? We have no answer to this question, since Jewish emancipation is without precedent in history." *Steeled by Adversity: Essays and Addresses on American Jewish Life*, Jeannette Meisel Baron, ed. (Philadelphia, PA: Jewish Publications Society of America, 1971), p. 548.

36. John Murray Cuddihy, *The Ordeal of Civility: Freud, Marx, Lévi-Strauss and the Jewish Struggle with Modernity* (Boston: Beacon Press, 1974). See W. Rabi, "L'intellectuel juif dans la société contemporaine," *Les Nouveaux Cahiers* (spring 1977): 11.

37. Simon Dubnow, *Histoire moderne du peuple juif* (Paris: Le Cerf, 1994), pp. 1604–5.

38. On the presence of the many Jewish sociologists in the Second Chicago School, see Gary Alan Fine, ed., *A Second Chicago School? The Development of a Postwar American Sociology* (Chicago: University of Chicago Press, 1995). On the First Chicago School, see Chapter 2.

39. John Murray Cuddihy describes the predominance of the Parsonian paradigm based on differentiation and, in a more than cursory way, sees Parsons as the heir of Calvin, in *Ordeal of Civility*, pp. 9–11.

40. See the fine article by Marshall Sklare, "The Jews in American Sociological Thought," *Ethnicity* (1974): 1.

41. Lucien Goldmann and Serge Moscovici should be added to this list, both of them from Eastern Europe. About Lucien Goldmann, see Mitchell Cohen, *The Wager of Lucien Goldmann: Tragedy, Dialectics and a Hidden God* (Princeton, NJ: Princeton University Press, 1994). See also Serge Moscovici, *Chronique des années égarées: Récit autobiographique* (Paris: Stock, 1997).

42. Of course, Georges Friedmann, a sociologist specializing in labor, became

interested later on in the fate of Israel in his book *Fin du peuple juif?* (Paris: Gallimard, "Idées," 1965). See also *La puissance et la sagesse* (Paris: Gallimard, 1970), p. 387. On Raymond Aron, see Chapter 4. These days, however, Dominique Schnapper has carried out "generalized" studies on unemployment, high-ranking civil servants, or citizenship, in his book *Juifs et israélites* (Paris: Gallimard, "Idées," 1980), as well as a number of articles in the same vein.

43. As well as Melville Herskovits and Alexander Goldenweiser.

44. We can also cite Philip Selznick, Ernest Nagel, Irving Louis Horowitz, Albert Salomon, Elihu Katz, Abraham Garfinkel, Aaron Cicourel, Erik Erikson, Leonard Reissman, Georges Lichteim, Sydney Hook, Hans Gerth, Samuel Stouffer, Herbert Hyman, Marion Levy Jr., Gary Marx, Joseph Gusfield, Joseph Blau, Herbert Goldhamer, Melvin Tumin, Immanuel Wallerstein, Anselme Strauss, Arthur Vidich, and Hans Rosenberg.

45. Also David Glass, John Plamenatz, and Zygmunt Bauman.

46. Also Gabriel Almond, David Apter, Daniel Lerner, and Nathan Leites.

47. Kohn, after publishing a work in Germany on the political dimension unique to Jewish history, nonetheless devoted long passages to Jewish nationalism focused specifically on time and universalism, though with little attention paid to territory, quoting the Prophets as well as the Talmud in his classic work *The Idea of Nationalism*. See *Die politische Idee des Judentums* (Munich: Meyer and Jessen, 1924), as well as *Idea of Nationalism* (New York: Collier Books, 1944).

48. On Gabriel Almond, see, for instance, his autobiography in Hans Daalder, *Comparative European Politics: The Story of a Profession* (London: Pinter, 1997). On Marion Levy Jr., see *Modernization: Latecomers and Survivors* (New York: Basic Books, 1976). On Lewis Coser, see Walter Powell and Richard Robbins, eds., *Conflict and Consensus: A Festschrift in Honor of Lewis Coser* (New York: Free Press, Macmillan, 1984). On Alvin Gouldner, see *Sociological Quarterly* no. 1 (winter 2002). On Gary Marx, see his autobiography "Reflections on Academic Success and Failure," in Bennett Berger, ed., *Authors of Their Own Lives: Intellectual Autobiographies by Twenty American Sociologists* (Berkeley: University of California Press, 1990). On Herbert Marcuse, see Bertram Katz, *Herbert Marcuse and the Art of Liberation: An Intellectual Biography* (London: Verso, 1982). On Anselme Strauss, see Isabelle Baszanger, "Les chantiers d'un interactionniste américain," in A. Strauss, *La trame de la négociation* (L'Harmattan, 1992), p. 15. On E. Goffman, see Chapter 2.

49. Franz Boas, *Race, Language, and Culture* (New York: Free Press, 1966), pp. 121–23. Franz Boas, *Race and Democratic Society* (New York: Augustine Publishers, 1946), pp. 40–42. On Boas, see Julia Liss, "German Culture and German Science in the Bildung of Franz Boas," in George Stocking Jr., ed., *Volksgeist as Method and Ethic: Essays on Boasian Ethnography and the German Anthropological Tradition* (Madison: University of Wisconsin Press, 1996). George Stocking Jr., "Anthropology as Kulturkampf: Science and Politics in the Career of Franz Boas," in Walter Goldschmidt, ed., *The Uses of Anthropology*, American Anthropological Association, no. 11 (1978). Leonard Glick, "Types Distinct from Our Own: Franz Boas

on Jewish Identity and Assimilation," *American Anthropologist* (1982): 82. Ellen Messer, "Franz Boas and Kaufmann Kohler: Anthropology and Reform Judaism," *Jewish Social Studies* (spring 1986). For Michel Espagne, "one can try to approach Boas's work as an attempt to relegate conflicts to which his situation as a German Jew immediately confronted him on a theoretical and political level. The Indian populations threatened with disappearance, and especially the Black Americans or immigrants, are a kind of substitute field that allowed Boas to think about his own situation as a German Jew." In "La question des imbrications culturelles chez Franz Boas," *Revue Germanique Internationale* 17 (2002): 150.

50. There are also brief allusions to Robert Lowie in *Social Organization* (New York: Rinehart and Co.), pp. 159ff., 275ff., and 380ff. See Robert Murphy, *Robert Lowie* (New York: Columbia University Press, 1972).

51. On Marcel Mauss, see Marcel Fournier, *Marcel Mauss* (Paris: Fayard, 1994). On Robert Hertz, see Alexandre Riley, "Whence Durkheim's Nietzschean Grand-children? A Closer Look at Robert Hertz's Place in the Durkheimian Genealogy," *Archives européennes de sociologie* (1999): 2. The author quotes a letter from Robert Hertz to Alice Hertz that is dated December 1914, when he was taking part in the "epic" of the First World War, in which he speaks of France as a place of the "chosen people," p. 325. See also his letter of November 3, 1914, in which he writes, "Darling, as a Jew, I feel the time has come for me to give a little more than what I owe. If I can get bonafide, real letters of naturalization for my son, it seems to me that that is the greatest gift I can give him." In Alexandre Riley and Philippe Besnard, *Un ethnologue dans les tranchées. Lettres de Robert Hertz à sa femme Alice, août 14, avril 15* (Paris: CNRS-Editions, 2002).

52. Personal conversation with his son. Note however that at the end of his life, Max Gluckman became an adviser in anthropological studies at the University of Jerusalem. His most famous book is still *Custom and Conflict in Africa* (Oxford: Blackwell, 1955).

53. Virginia Dominguez, "Questioning Jews," *American Ethnologist* 20 (1993): 618 and 622.

54. Paul Lazarsfeld, "An Episode in the History of Social Research: A Memoir," in Donald Fleming and Bernard Bailyn, *The Intellectual Migration: Europe and America, 1930–1960* (Cambridge, MA: Harvard University Press, 1969), p. 302. For Anton Pelinka, "according to Paul Lazarsfeld, Austria seems like a country that imposed an identity on him, with or without his consent: Judaism," "Paul Lazarsfeld As a Pioneer of Social Science in Austria," in Jacques Lautman and Bernard-Pierre Lécuyer, eds., *Paul Lazarsfeld, 1901–1976. La sociologie de Vienne à New York* (Paris: L'Harmattan, 1998), p. 31.

55. David Morrison, "Paul Lazarsfeld: The Biography of an Institutional Innovator" (PhD diss., Leicester University, 1976), p. 127. Quoted by Lewis Coser, *Refugee Scholars in America* (New Haven, CT: Yale University Press, 1984), pp. 119–20.

56. See Richard Merritt and Bruce Russet, eds., *From National Development*

*to Global Community: Essays in Honor of Karl Deutsch* (London: George Allen and Unwin, 1982), pp. 2–3.

57. Malachi Hacohen, *Karl Popper: The Formative Years, 1902–1945* (Cambridge: Cambridge University Press, 2000), p. 200.

58. Thomas Kuhn, *The Road Since Structure: Philosophical Essays, 1970–1993, with an Autobiographical Interview,* James Conant and John Haugeland, eds. (Chicago: University of Chicago Press, 2000), p. 266.

59. Karl Polanyi also completely distanced himself from Judaism, to such a point that the biography devoted to him does not mention his origin. Kari Polanyi-Lewitt, *The Life and Work of Karl Polanyi* (Montreal: Black Rose Books, 1990).

60. Karl Popper, *Unended Quest: An Intellectual Biography* (London: Routledge and Kegan Paul, 1993), p. 107. See also David Edmonds and John Eidinov, *Wittgenstein's Poker: The Story of a Ten-Minute Argument Between Two Great Philosophers* (New York: Harper Collins Publishers, 2001), chs. 9 to 13.

61. Ibid.

62. Quoted by Hacohen, *Karl Popper,* pp. 25 and 305.

63. Reinhard Bendix, *From Berlin to Berkeley: German-Jewish Identities* (New Brunswick, NJ: Transaction Publishers, 1990), p. 81.

64. Ibid., p. 198.

65. Reinhard Bendix, "How I Became an American Sociologist," in Berger, *Authors of Their Own Lives,* p. 464.

66. Bendix, *From Berlin to Berkeley,* pp. 291 and 298.

67. *New York Times,* May 19, 2002.

68. David Riesman, "A Personal Memoir: My Political Journey," in Walter Powell and Richard Robbin, eds., *Conflict and Consensus: A Festschrift in Honor of Lewis Coser* (Glencoe, IL: Free Press, 1984), p. 357. See also the long autobiographical text "Becoming an Academic Man," in Berger, *Authors of Their Own Lives,* Riesman, in one of his very rare texts devoted to the Jews, emphasizes that "they react too strongly to anti-Semitism" and "waste their time" in this struggle, *Individualism Reconsidered and Other Essays* (New York: Free Press), pp. 143 and 147.

69. Kingsley Martin, *Harold Laski: A Biographical Memoir* (New York: Viking Press, 1953), p. 3.

70. Albert Hirschman, *Défection et prise de parole* (Paris: Fayard, 1995). *Deux siècles de rhétorique réactionnaire* (Paris: Fayard, 1991). See his autobiography, *Un certain penchant à l'autosubversion* (Paris: Fayard, 1995). See also Coser, *Refugee Scholars in America,* pp. 163ff., as well as the numerous collective works published in homage to him.

71. Alfred Schütz's cultural origins are not even mentioned in his biography of reference: Helmut Wagner, *Alfred Schütz: An Intellectual Biography* (Chicago: University of Chicago Press, 1983). See, however, Coser, *Refugee Scholars in America,* p. 121.

72. Howard Becker, *Outsiders* (Paris: Métaillié, 1985). Private conversation with the author.

73. Herbert Gans, "The Origin of the Jews of Park Forest," in Marshall Sklare, ed., *The Jews: Social Patterns of an American Ethnic Group* (Glencoe, IL: Free Press, 1958). See his autobiography in Berger, *Authors of Their Own Lives*; Gans discusses his involvement in sociology as a way to "sublimate" his ties to Judaism and realize them in other ways, p. 447.

74. This little-known episode was brought to light in recent studies by David Gordon, who criticizes, among others, the numerous French admirers of Elias who often interpret his work through the logic of Pierre Bourdieu. See David Gordon, "The Canonization of Norbert Elias in France: A Critical Perspective," in *French Politics and Culture, and Society* (spring 2002). On Elias's involvement in Zionist movements in Breslau, see especially Hermann Korte, "Norbert Elias in Breslau. Ein Biographisches Fragment," *Zeitschrift für Soziologie* (February 1991). I thank David Gordon for bringing these texts to my attention, as well as several articles from Elias's youth. For a severe critique of *The Germans*, see Jeffrey Herf, "The Uncivilizing Process," *The New Republic*, April 21, 1997.

75. Zygmunt Bauman criticizes Elias's vision on this point: *Modernité et Holocauste* (Paris: La Fabrique, 1989), pp. 39 and 180. One of Elias's most admiring followers curiously writes, to justify Elias's almost complete silence about the Shoah in his consideration of the future of violence: "The Holocaust refutes the theory of the process of civilization in Europe in pretty much the same way that the Black Plague led people to have doubts about the population of the continent increasing over a long period of time," Stephen Mennell, "L'envers de la médaille: Les processus de décivilsation," in Alain Garrigou and Bernard Lacroix, eds., *Norbert Elias. La politique et l'histoire* (Paris: La Découverte, 1997), p. 225. In the same sense, ignoring what this absence might symbolize, see the defense of Elias by Nathalie Heinich who strangely addresses Z. Bauman in the following words: "Without mentioning the fact that one wonders what 'recent history' signifies for Bauman: is he aware of the fact that Elias' theoretics rests on phenomena that have occurred five to ten centuries ago?" in "De quelques malentendus concernant la pensée d'Elias," *Tumultes* (October 2000): 164. For a presentation more open to criticism, see Robert van Krieken, *Norbert Elias* (London: Routledge and Kegan Paul, 1998).

76. *Norbert Elias par lui-même* (Paris: Fayard, 1991), pp. 151 and 159. See also the interview with Elias where several times he calls himself "a German Jew, a Jewish sociologist," in Herlinde Koelbl, *Jüdische Portraits* (S. Fischer, 1989), p. 60. There is also a portrait of Karl Popper in this book, p. 189.

77. Some commentators interpret Elias's brief text on the expulsion of the Protestants from France, published in October 1933 after his emigration to Great Britain, as an implicit reference to the expulsion of the Jews from Germany. In this text, no allusion is made to the Jews, and the author remains truly within absolute implicitness. See "The Expulsion of the Huguenots from France," in Johan Goudsblom and Stephen Mennell, eds., *The Norbert Elias Reader* (Oxford: Blackwell, 1998).

78. Quoted by Alain Boureau, "Histoires d'un historien, Kantorowicz,"

in *Ernst Kantorowicz. Oeuvres* (Paris: Gallimard, "Quarto," 2000), p. 1254. See Thomas Serrier, "D'où sortira Kantorowicz? Historiens juifs à Posen avant 1914: Figures et milieu," in *Les Cahiers du Judaïsme* (winter 2001–2002).

79. Marc Bloch, *L'étrange défaite* (Paris: Gallimard, "Folio," 1990), pp. 32–33 and 314. See Hartmut Astma and André Burguière, eds., *Marc Bloch aujourd'hui. Histoire comparée et sciences sociales* (Paris: Éditions de l'École des hautes etudes en sciences sociales, 1990). See also Carole Fink, *Marc Bloch. Une vie au service de l'histoire* (Lyon: Presses universitaires de Lyon, 1997), as well as, by the same author, "Marc Bloch at Narbonne," *Contemporary French Civilization* (spring 1996). On the UGIF (General Union of Israelites in France) episode, see Adam Rayski, *Le choix des Juifs sous Vichy* (Paris: La Découverte, 1992), pp. 75–77. See also Claude Singer, "Des universitaires juifs dans la Résistance," in RHICOJ, *Les Juifs dans la Résistance et la Libération* (Paris: Éditions du Scribe, 1985).

80. Personal letter from Étienne Bloch to the author, January 20, 1996.

81. Saul Friedlander, "Marc Bloch et Ernst Kantorowicz," in Elie Barnavi and Saul Friedlander, eds., *Les Juifs et le XXe siècle* (Paris: Calmann-Lévy, 2000), pp. 525 and 531.

82. Felix Gilbert, *A European Past: Memoirs, 1905–1945* (New York: W. W. Norton and Company, 1988). We note that Gilbert is the distant descendant of the philosopher Mendelssohn; he is also the heir of the Oppenheim bankers. See also Peter Gay, whose family is partly from Breslau, *My German Question: Growing up in Nazi Berlin* (New Haven, CT: Yale University Press, 1998). More generally, as a tool for scholarship, see Catherine Epstein, *A Past Renewed: A Catalogue of German-Speaking Refugee Historians in the United States After 1933* (Cambridge: Cambridge University Press, 1993). On the difficulties encountered by American Jewish historians, see Peter Novick, *That Noble Dream: The "Objectivity Question" and the American Historical Association* (Cambridge: Cambridge University Press, 1988), pp. 172–73.

83. Arnaldo Momigliano, *Essays on Ancient and Modern Judaism,* Silvia Berti, ed. (Chicago: University of Chicago Press, 1994), preface, pp. xxv–xxvi.

84. Ibid., p. xxvi.

85. Quoted by Joanna Weinberg, "Where Three Civilizations Meet," in *The Presence of the Historian: Essays in Memory of Arnaldo Momigliano* (Middletown, MA: Wesleyan University Press), p. 17. A slightly different version of this article can be found in *The Kaufmann Memorial Lecture* (Leo Baeck College, which published Joanna Weinberg's lecture, given April 27, 1988).

86. Silvia Berti, in Momigliano, *Essays on Ancient and Modern Judaism*, intro., p. viii.

87. Quoted by Weinberg, "Where Three Civilizations Meet," pp. 15–16.

88. Peter Burke, "Arnaldo Momigliano, 1908–1987," *Proceedings of the British Academy* 74 (1988): 435–38.

89. Momigliano, *Essays on Ancient and Modern Judaism*, preface, p. xxviii.

90. Quoted by Burke, "Arnaldo Momigliano, 1908–1987," p. 433.

91. The recent discovery of a letter written by Momigliano, on November 3,

1938, to the minister of national education, in which he expressed the desire to remain at his post despite new racist legislation, provoked intense debates in Italy, all the more so when the press also revealed that Norberto Bobbio and Alberto Moravia also tried to come to an accommodation with the fascist authorities. I thank Silvia Berti for sending me these documents. We know that Marc Bloch also sent a similar request to the Vichy authorities and that he obtained a special dispensation in January 1941, when Pétain agreed to sign ten dispensations for professors in higher education.

92. Note that when Silvia Berti asked Momigliano to comment on Yosef Yerushalmi's analyses of the relationships between Jewish history and memory, Momigliano replied, "Historical research that seriously studies these questions necessarily implies a religious dimension." Quoted by Silvia Berti, "Autobiografia, Storicismo e Verità Storica in Arnaldo Momigliano," *Rivista Storica Italiana* 2 (1988): 306.

93. Momigliano, *Essays on Ancient and Modern Judaism*. See also his book *Alien Wisdom: The Limits of Hellenization* (Cambridge: Cambridge University Press, 1975). On Momigliano, see E. Gabba, ed., *Tria Corda. Scitti in onore di Arnaldo Momigliano* (Cuomo, Italy: New Press, 1983); and Edward Shils, *Portraits: A Gallery of Intellectuals* (Chicago: University of Chicago Press, 1997), ch. 9. Aside from Momigliano, the example of the historian Carlo Ginzburg also shows, in Italy, this attachment to the Jewish world in the heart of scientific research: see *Le sabbat des sorcières* (Paris: Gallimard); and *À distance* (Paris: Gallimard, 2001).

94. The manuscript of this book had already been sent to press when Pierre Bourtez's work was published, *Témoins du futur* (Paris: Gallimard, 2003).

95. See Rainer Funk, *Erich Fromm: The Courage to Be Human* (New York: Continuum, 1982). See also Svante Lundgreen, *Fights Against Idols: Erich Fromm on Religion, Judaism and the Bible* (Peter Lang, 1998). Paul Zawadzki, "Liberté de l'homme et paradoxes de l'espoir chez Erich Fromm," *Diasporiques* (October 2002). See the texts of Erich Fromm, *Beyond the Chains of Illusion* (New York: Simon and Schuster, 1962); and *You Shall Be as Gods: A Radical Interpretation of the Old Testament and Its Tradition* (New York: Henry Holt & Co., 1991).

96. Max Weber, *Ancient Judaism* (New York: Free Press, 1967); and Max Weber, *The Sociology of Religion*, Ephraim Fischoff, trans. (Boston: Beacon Press, 1993), p. 314 of the French edition. The literature dealing with the first of these two works is considerable. Salo Baron challenges the use of the "pariah" notion by emphasizing that Jews can gain access to the heart of society: *A Social and Religious History of the Jews* (New York: Columbia University Press, 1952), vol. 1, p. 24. See the classic article by Hans Liebeschütz, "Max Weber's Historical Interpretation of Judaism," *Leo Baeck Year Book* (1964), pp. 41ff. Jay Holstein, "Max Weber and Biblical Scholarship," in *Hebrew Union College Annual* (Cincinnati, 1975), vol. 6. See also Gary Abraham, *Max Weber and the Jewish Question* (Urbana: University of Illinois Press, 1992).

97. On Louis Wirth, see Chapter 2.

98. Aaron Wildawsky, one of the best specialists in public policy, published, late in life, his *Assimilation Versus Separation: Joseph the Administrator and the Politics of Religion in Biblical Israel* (New Brunswick, NJ: Transaction Publishers, 1993).

99. Pierre Birnbaum, *The Jews of the Republic: A Political History of State Jews in France from Gambetta to Vichy*, Jane Todd, trans. (Stanford: Stanford University Press, 1996).

100. Perrine Nahum-Simon, *La Cité investie. La "Science du judaïsme" française et la République* (Paris: Le Cerf, 1991). The author states strongly that "at the end of the nineteenth century, Jewish studies would progressively disappear, to become the sole domain of religious instruction"; in the 1920s, "the distribution of professorships constituted the best indicator, if not of the abandonment of exclusively Jewish fields by the Jews, at least of the shift that occurred toward disciplines where Judaism began to seem merely secondary, or even disappeared from scientific studies. Judaism stopped being the central interest of that generation, with nothing to distinguish one people from another," pp. 268–69. According to Jay Berkowitz, the rationalist perspective imported from Germany to France and applied, for instance, by Samuel Cahen to his translation of the Bible aroused a severe reaction from traditionalist rabbinic milieus: "Jewish Scholarship and Identity in Nineteenth-Century France," *Modern Judaism* 18 (1998): 18–20. See also Aron Rodrigue, who brought to light that unique moment when "a radical universalism" came to the fore: "Les totems, les tabous et les Juifs: Salomon Reinach et la politique universitaire dans la France fin-de-siècle," *Les Cahiers du Judaïsme* (spring 2004). Aron Rodrigue emphasizes the specificity of Jewish studies of that time inserted into universalist and republican logic in relation to those of German Jewish scholars. These days, Léon Poliakov, born in St. Petersburg, was one of the rare people to have come from East European Judaism (see his autobiography, *L'auberge des musiciens* [Mazarine, 1981]), as well as Georges Vajda, come from the Hebrew seminary in Budapest, from which so many students emigrated either to the United States or to Israel. By contrast, Bernard Blumenkranz came from the assimilated German emigration.

101. Since its creation in 1880, the erudite and remarkable *Revue des études juives* has proved to be more concerned with philological and paleographical studies, the history of the Jews of Antiquity and of the Middle Ages, discussion of the lives of rabbis, as well as haggadic studies.

102. See Ezra Mendelsohn, *The Jews of East Central Europe Between the Wars, 1915–1926* (New Haven, CT: Yale University Press, 1981). Rachel Ertel, *Le shtetl. La bourgade juive de la Pologne: de la tradition à la modernité* (Paris: Payot, 1982). Mark Zborowski and Elisabeth Herzog, *Olam. Dans le shtetl d'Europe centrale avant la Shoah* (Paris: Plon, 1992). Jean Baumgarten, "Les études juives en Europe orientale," in Jean Baumgarten, Rachel Ertel, Itzok Niborski, and Annette Wieviorka, eds., *Mille ans de cultures ashkénazes* (Liana Levi, 1994). Jean Baumgarten, *Le Yiddish. Langue, culture, société* (Paris: Presses du CNRS, 1999); and *Récits hagiographiques juifs* (Paris: Le Cerf, 2003). Sylvie-Anne Goldberg, "Histoire juive, Histoire des Juifs: D'autres approches," *Annales* (September–October 1994):

1022ff.; and *Les deux rives du Yabbok* (Paris: Le Cerf, 1989). Delphine Bechtel, *La renaissance culturelle en Europe centrale et orientale. 1897–1930* (Paris: Belin, 2002).

103. Joseph Lichten, "Notes on the Assimilation and the Acculturation of Jews in Poland, 1863–1943," in Chimen Abramsky et al., eds., *The Jews of Poland* (Oxford: Blackwell, 1986). Elie Lederhendler, *The Road to Modern Jewish Politics: Political Tradition and Political Reconstruction in the Jewish Community of Tsarist Russia* (New York: Oxford University Press, 1989). Gershon Bacon, "La société juive dans le royaume de la Pologne du Congrès (1860–1914)," in S. Trigano, *La société juive à travers l'histoire* (Paris: Fayard, 1992), vol. 1.

104. Steven Zipperstein, *The Jews of Odessa: A Cultural History, 1794–1881* (Stanford: Stanford University Press, 1985). See also David Myers who emphasizes this "continuity," "History, Memory and Jerusalem Scholars," in David Myers and David Ruderman, eds., *The Jewish Past Revisited: Reflections on Modern Jewish Historians* (New Haven, CT: Yale University Press, 1998), p. 95. See also the same author's *Re-Inventing the Jewish Past: European Jewish Intellectuals and the Zionist Return to History* (New York: Oxford University Press, 1995).

105. See David Vital, *The Origins of Zionism* (Oxford: Oxford University Press, 1975). Jonathan Frankel, *Prophecy and Politics: Socialism, Nationalism and the Russian Jews, 1862–1917* (Cambridge: Cambridge University Press, 1981). Michael Stanislawski, *For Whom Do I Toil? Judah Leib Gordon and the Crisis of Russian Jewry* (Oxford: Oxford University Press, 1988). The author also emphasizes the strong influence exercised by David Gordon on American Jewish life, p. 228. See also Steven Zipperstein, *Elusive Prophet: Ahad Ha-am and the Origins of Zionism* (Berkeley: University of California Press, 1993).

106. Haim Nachman Bialik, "Le livre hébreu," in Denis Charbit, *Sionismes. Textes fondamentaux* (Paris: Albin Michel, 1998), p. 305. In the same sense, for Rachel Katznelson, "although Yiddish is a living language, the language of the people and of democracy, the currents of thought, which for us could only be revolutionary, were expressed in Hebrew; Yiddish literature was dominated by a limited thinking, generally inert, and frankly reactionary in our opinion; even in the best case, it was only a pale reflection of the revelations of Hebrew": "Errance des langues," in Charbit, *Sionismes*, p. 265.

107. See Jeffrey Chandler, "Beyond the Mother Tongue: Learning the Meaning of Yiddish in America," *Jewish Social Studies* (spring–summer 2000).

108. Here we can quickly point out that in Israel too Jewish studies are almost always institutionally separated from the departments of sociology and even of history. Thus, S. Eisenstadt, a "general" sociologist of great renown who, moreover, conducted work having to do with Jewish studies, taught in a sociology department at the University of Jerusalem of which he had long been the director, after Martin Buber, who was its founder. The British sociologist Morris Ginsberg acted as consultant during the creation of this department. Buber as well as Ginsberg both came from the Yiddish-speaking milieu of Eastern Europe.

109. Quoted by Mendes-Flohr, *Divided Passions*, p. 194.

110. See the remarkable book by Mitchell Hart, *Social Science and the Politics of Modern Jewish Identity* (Stanford: Stanford University Press, 2000), pp. 34, 36, and 61. See also Paul Mendes-Flohr, "Fin-de-Siècle Orientalism, the Ostjuden and the Aesthetics of Jewish Self-Affirmation," in Mendes-Flohr, *Divided Passions*, ch. 4.

111. S. Ansky, *The Enemy at His Pleasure: A Journey Through the Jewish Pale of Settlement During World War I* (New York: Metropolitan Books, Henry Holt and Company, 2002). See David Roskies, *Against the Apocalypse* (Cambridge, MA: Harvard University Press, 1985).

112. Enzo Traverso also analyzes this rejection of Judeo-Germanic symbiosis, *Les Juifs et l'Allemagne* (Paris: La Découverte, 1992), pp. 46ff.

113. *Isidor Kaufmann* (Vienna: Judisches Museum der Stadt Wien, 1995). Samuel-Joseph Agnon, *La dot des fiancées*, French translation by Michel Landau and Charles Leben (Paris: Les Belles Lettres, 2003).

114. Barbara Kirshenblatt-Gimblett, "Coming of Age in the Thirties: Max Weinreich, Edward Sapir and Jewish Social Science," *YIVO Annual* 23: especially pp. 80–82.

115. David Mandelbaum, "Edward Sapir," *Jewish Social Studies* 3 (1941): 140. See Regna Darnell, *Edward Sapir, Linguist, Anthropologist, Humanist* (Berkeley: University of California Press, 1990). By Edward Sapir, see his main book, *The Psychology of Culture* (The Hague: Mouton de Gruyter, 1993).

116. Gelya Frank, "Jews, Multiculturalism and Boasian Anthropology," *American Anthropologist* 99 (1997). On Louis Wirth, see Chapter 3. On Salo Baron, see Chapter 8.

117. Mel Scult, *Judaism Faces the Twentieth Century: A Biography of Mordecai M. Kaplan* (Detroit, MI: Wayne State University Press, 1993), pp. 55, 87, 143ff., and 312–13.

118. David Sorkin, *The Transformation of German Jewry* (New York: Oxford University Press, 1987). See also Jacques Ehrenfreund, *Mémoire juive et nationalité allemande. Les Juifs berlinois à la Belle Époque* (Paris: PUF, 2000).

119. Kurt Lewin, *Resolving Social Conflicts* (New York: Harper and Brothers, 1948), chs. 9, 10, 11, and 12. See Martin Gold, ed., *The Complete Social Scientist: A Kurt Lewin Reader*, American Psychological Association, 1999, especially the biographical presentation, p. 7ff.

120. Seymour Martin Lipset, *Political Man: The Social Bases of Politics* (Baltimore, MD: Johns Hopkins University Press, 1981); and Seymour Martin Lipset, *The First New Nation* (New York: Doubleday, 1967). S. M. Lipset and S. Rokkan, *Party System and Voter Alignments* (New York: Free Press, 1967). Seymour Martin Lipset, ed., *American Pluralism and the Jewish Community*; Seymour Martin Lipset and Earl Raab, *Jews and the New American Scene* (Cambridge, MA: Harvard University Press, 1995). "The Socialism of Fools: The Left, the Jews and Israel," *Encounter Magazine*, December 1969. See also the various articles by Lipset already cited. On Lipset, see Jesús Velasco, "Seymour Martin Lipset: Reflexiones en torno de una vida intelectual," *Istor* no. 8 (March 2002).

121. Personal conversation with Nathan Glazer. See Nathan Glazer, *American Judaism* (Chicago: Chicago University Press, 1989). Nathan Glazer, "The Beginnings of Modern Jewish Studies," in Alexander Altmann, ed., *Studies in Nineteenth-Century Jewish Intellectual History* (Cambridge, MA: Harvard University Press, 1964). Nathan Glazer and Daniel Moynihan, *Beyond the Melting-Pot* (Cambridge, MA: MIT Press, 1963). Nathan Glazer, *Affirmative Discrimination: Ethnic Inequality and Public Policy, We Are All Multiculturalists Now* (Cambridge, MA: Harvard University Press, 1997). We can also cite the example of Sidney Hook, author of *From Hegel to Marx*, friend of Daniel Bell, Horace Kallen, and John Dewey, who urged him to give pluralism all its importance.

122. Lewis Coser, *The Functions of Social Conflict* (New York: Free Press, 1964); Lewis Coser, "The Alien as a Servant of Power," *American Sociological Review* no. 5 (1972). This article is criticized by Werner Cahnman, "Pariahs, Strangers and Court Jews," in *German Jewry: Its History and Sociology*, pp. 21–134. Lewis Coser, *A Handful of Thistles: Collected Papers in Moral Convictions* (New Brunswick, NJ: Transaction Books, 1988); see the introduction in the form of an autobiography. Coser, *Refugee Scholars in America*. Bernard Rosenberg, "An Interview with Lewis Coser," in Walter Powell and Richard Robbins, eds., *Conflict and Consensus: A Festschrift in Honor of Lewis Coser*. The book on refugees is dedicated to Irving Howe, a leader of the group of New York Jewish intellectuals who also taught at Brandeis, and one who kept the memory of the people of Yiddish alive more than anyone else in America, and also the director, along with the Daniel Bell, Nathan Glazer, and Lewis Coser, of the critical journal *Dissent* edited today by Michael Walzer who was a student at Brandeis at the time where he studied with Lewis Coser. We can also add to these names that of Irving Louis Horowitz, sociologist of modernization and development, who published "The Jewish Community of Buenos Aires," *Jewish Social Studies* (1962): 24.

123. Robert Putnam, *Bowling Alone: The Collapse and Revival of American Community* (New York: Simon and Schuster, 2000), ch. 6.

124. Edward Shils, *Portraits: A Gallery of Intellectuals*, intro. by Joseph Epstein, "My Friend Edward" (Chicago: University of Chicago Press, 1997).

125. This term is proposed by Shulamit Volkov, "The Dynamics of Dissimilation," in Reinharz and Schatzberg, eds., *Jewish Response to German Culture* (Hanover, NH: University Press of New England, 1985). Salo Baron uses the same notion but to designate, on the contrary, the process of dis-assimilation, of exclusion brought about authoritatively to reject the Jews. See Salo W. Baron, *Steeled by Adversity: Essays Addressed on American Jewish Life* (Philadelphia, PA: Jewish Publication Society of America, 1971), p. 500.

126. Hannah Arendt and Karl Jaspers, *Correspondance. 1926–1969* (Paris: Payot, 1995), p. 286.

127. Personal conversation with Daniel Bell, July 2003. All the more so since contemporary sociologists and political theorists are increasingly abandoning the purely political kind of involvement in the management of social questions

familiar to New York intellectuals, between socialism, liberalism, and public policies.

128. A similar and unusual joining did in fact take place, almost at the same time, in Great Britain. This time it formed around Morris Ginsberg, born in Lithuania, for whom Yiddish was the native language; it was a more fragile milieu, though, more limited than in the United States since it was less enriched by Eastern European emigration. Ginsberg, who also spoke perfect classical Hebrew, became, in 1929, professor of sociology at the London School of Economics thanks to his work on industrial society and, through this work, one of the most eminent British sociologists, so that T. H. Marshall emphasizes that "his fame as a sociologist is universally recognized." While Aron became more integrated in the French nation by following the logic peculiar to its kind of state emancipation, Ginsberg was closer to Bell, with whom he shared his Eastern European origin and Yiddish culture. He managed to have, in this other Anglo-Saxon society, two parallel careers, one devoted to general sociology, the other to Jewish research. In 1958, he created, unknown to most of his sociology colleagues, *The Jewish Journal of Sociology*, an erudite journal of the social sciences that has no equivalent in France, where the scholarly *Revue des Études juives* deals only with the premodern era. Ginsberg remained the director of *The Jewish Journal of Sociology* until his death in 1970. This publication is comparable to the American *Jewish Social Studies*, but in *The Jewish Journal of Sociology* mostly sociologists or political theorists are involved, rather than specialists in Jewish studies, since the latter were much less numerous in Great Britain. On its editorial board were Nathan Glazer as well as Shmuel Eisenstadt, and one can find articles and essays written by eminent Jewish specialists in the social sciences like Samuel Finer, Seymour Lipset, Elie Kedourie, Joseph Ben-David, Leonard Reissman, Nathan Glazer, Marshall Sklare, Ernest Gellner, and Georges Friedman, as well as non-Jews like T. H. Marshall, Donald MacRae, or Robin William Jr.

129. The situation is, from this point of view, very different depending on the university in question. At Yale or Indiana, for instance, appointments are shared by the department of Jewish studies and the department of history, whereas at Harvard, New York University, or Brandeis there are no connections between the departments, with Jewish history not being taught in the history department; at Columbia, however, or at Stanford, appointments are made directly in history, even if several teachers have a double affiliation, with Jewish studies constituting an interdisciplinary program that integrates teachers from separate departments. I thank Steven Zipperstein and Aron Rodrigue for this information.

130. Sara Horowitz, "The Paradox of Jewish Studies in the New Academy," in David Biale, Michael Galchinsky, and Susannah Heschel, eds., *Insider/Outsider: American Jews and Multiculturalism* (Berkeley: University of California Press, 1998), p. 122. See also Frank, "Jews, Multiculturalism and Boasian Anthropology," p. 741.

131. A number of sociologists, like Daniel Bell and even Nathan Glazer (despite a brief period during his youth in a Zionist movement), have nonetheless shown

themselves hostile to the idea of a Jewish State. See Nathan Glazer, "From Social-ism to Sociology," in Berger, ed., *Authors of Their Own Lives*, pp. 194ff. Dorman, *Arguing the World*, p. 109ff.

132. Lévinas, *Difficile Liberté*, pp. 69, 294, and 355.

133. On the notion of a counterhistory, see Amos Funkenstein, *Perceptions of Jewish History* (Berkeley: University of California Press, 1993), pp. 36ff. See also the innovative work by Susannah Heschel, *Abraham Geiger and the Jewish Jesus* (Chicago: University of Chicago Press, 1998). "Jewish Studies as Counterhis-tory," in D. Biale, M. Galchinsky, and S. Heschel, eds., *Insider/Outsider*; "Revolt of the Colonized: Abraham Geiger's Wissenschaft des Judentums as a Challenge to Christian Hegemony in the Academy," *New German Critique* (spring–summer 1999). Finally, see Jonathan Hess, *Germans, Jews and the Claims of Modernity* (New Haven, CT: Yale University Press, 2002), pp. 11ff. Personal conversation with Su-sannah Heschel.

134. Sylvie Anne Goldberg thinks that the birth of YIVO in 1925, with its at-tention to yiddishland, "marks the definitive break that occurred between the first generations of the science of German Judaism—contemporary with the emancipa-tion movement (the Haskala)—and the generations that would replace it with a scientific ensemble of 'Judaica.'" She quotes an editorial by Nohem Schtif, who wrote, "The famous science of Judaism founded by scholars from Western Europe, by German Jews, could serve us neither as a model nor as a point of departure. . . . In Eastern Europe, we have to do with a living Judaism that continues to produce a material and spiritual culture," "L'étude du judaïsme: science historique ou reli-gieuse?" *Préfaces* (June–September 1990): 93.

135. Karl Polanyi, *The Great Transformation: The Political and Economic Origins of Our Time* (Boston: Beacon Press, 2001).

136. Pierre Birnbaum and Ira Katznelson, *Paths of Emancipation: Jews, States and Citizenship* (Princeton, NJ: Princeton University Press, 1995).

137. Vicky Caron, *Between France and Germany: The Jews of Alsace-Lorraine, 1871–1914* (Stanford: Stanford University Press, 1988). Paula Hyman, *The Eman-cipation of the Jews of Alsace: Acculturation and Tradition in the Nineteenth Century* (New Haven, CT: Yale University Press, 1991). As Paula Hyman notes, in 1848 the Strasbourg Consistory published the *Prières d'un coeur israélite* to replace the prayers in "corrupted Yiddish," p. 61. She also shows that "insofar as the govern-ment guaranteed their equality, Alsatian Jews were pushed to acquire French cul-ture as a symbol of their civic status," pp. 158–59. See also Pierre-André Meyer who analyzes the decline of the Judeo-German, *La communauté juive de Metz au XVIIIe siècle* (Nancy: Presses universitaires de Nancy, Éditions Serpenoise, 1993), pp. 85–86. See also Claude Rosenfeld and Jean-Bernard Lang, *Histoire des Juifs de Moselle* (Metz: Éditions serpenoise, 2001), pp. 130ff.

138. Simon Dubnow, *Lettres sur le judaïsme ancien et nouveau*, intro. by Renée Poznanski (Paris: Le Cerf, 1989), p. 467. Robert Seltzer elaborates on this oppo-sition between the Slavophile and the Westerner, "Ahad Ha'am and Doubnow:

Friends and Adversaries," in Jacques Kornberg, ed., *At the Crossroads: Essays on Ahad Ha-am* (Albany: State University of New York Press, 1983), p. 70. By the same author, "Affirmation of the Diaspora: America and Palestine in Dubnow's Thought," in B. W. Korn, ed., *A Bicentennial Festschrift for Jacobs Rader Marcus* (New York, 1976). See also L. Kochan, "Graetz and Dubnow: Two Jewish Historians in an Alien World," in C. Abramsky, ed., *Essays in Honour of E. H. Carr* (London, 1974). Michael Stanislawsi emphasizes the distance that separates Ahad Ha'am from the visions of a Max Nordau or a Vladimir Jabotinsky, who were little concerned with the religious and the worship of Hebrew, and who joined the Zionist movement from outside the Jewish world, *Zionism and the Fin-de-Siècle: Cosmopolitanism and Nationalism from Nordau to Jabotinsky* (Berkeley: University of California Press, 2001).

139. Dubnow, *Lettres sur le judaïsme ancien et nouveau*, pp. 118, 133, 138–39, and 180.

140. Two texts are quoted here by Ahad Ha'am, "Servitude dans la liberté" and "Degrés de la conscience nationale," in Charbit, *Sionismes*. We know that Ahad Ha'am exercised a strong influence over Martin Buber who, after he emigrated to Palestine, created the first department of sociology at the University of Jerusalem. Chaim Weizmann considers himself his disciple; we have noted his role in the implementation of the first sociological researches sponsored by the Zionist organization.

141. Simon Dubnow, "The Sociological View of Jewish History," in Koppel Pinson, ed., *Nationalism and History: Essays on Old and New Judaism* (New York: Atheneum, 1970). Jacob Katz is very severe with regard to Dubnow's interpretation of the sociology of Weber, and accuses him of underestimating the factors of change that alone explain Jewish history. In Katz's opinion, "Dubnow has an erroneous interpretation of the aims of sociology." Jacob Katz, "The Concept of Social History and Its Possible Use in Jewish Historical Research," *Scripta Hierosolymitana* 3 (1956): 308–9. He also takes issue with the work of Salo Baron, which he considers "eclectic," emphasizing his "failure," his incapacity to construct concepts such as that of community. He also questions the idea of placing emphasis on successive centers to the detriment of the unity of the Jewish people, all the more so since in his opinion essential episodes did not occur in the center but at the periphery. Ibid., pp. 306, 310–11.

142. This preface by Salo Baron figures only in the original American edition of the book by Yosef H. Yerushalmi, *From Spanish Court to Italian Ghetto: A Study in Seventeenth-Century Marranism and Jewish Apologetics* (Seattle: University of Washington Press, 1971), p. xi. The work is published in French with a slightly different subtitle, *De la cour d'Espagne au ghetto italien. Isaac Cardaso et le marranisme au XVIIe siècle* (Paris: Fayard, 1987).

143. Jonathan Frankel retraces the history of this "reconfiguration" (*remapping*) of Jewish studies and notes the influence of the sociological concepts proposed by Dubnow about Salo Baron, in the United States, and Jacob Katz, in Israel, "Assimi-

lation and the Jews in Nineteenth-Century Europe: Toward a New Historiography?" in Jonathan Frankel and Steven Zipperstein, eds., *Assimilation and Community: The Jews in Nineteenth-Century Europe* (Cambridge: Cambridge University Press), pp. 1 and 18–19. On this subject, see also Shmuel Trigano, "Une sociologie historique du judaïsme," in Shmuel Trigano, ed., *La société juive à travers l'histoire* (Paris: Fayard, 1992), vol. 1. See also the extremely enlightening article by Robert Seltzer, "From Graetz to Dubnow: The Impact of the East European Milieu on the Writing of Jewish History," in *The Legacy of Jewish Migration: 1881 and Its Impact* (New York: Social Science Monographs, Brooklyn College Press, distributed by Columbia University Press, 1983). The author thinks that "America has become the place that is most open to the spirit of Dubnow, the place where his essential ideas are best applied to Jewish history," p. 58. The Hannah Arendt quotation is taken from her lecture given on the occasion of Salo Baron's seventieth birthday. This unpublished text is quoted by Robert Liberles, *Salo Wittmayer Baron: Architect of Jewish History* (New York: New York University Press, 1995), p. 10. Thus, when Salo Baron published his book *The Jewish Community*, not only did he base his analysis on the *kehiloth*, the Jewish communities of Eastern Europe, and on material coming from the *responsa* written by the rabbis, but he also quotes, in an entirely different tradition, from classics of general sociology like books by Ferdinand Tönnies or Robert McIver. When this book was published, Horace Kallen, in the *American Journal of Sociology*, praised it, considering this work was written "according to scientific methods," *American Journal of Sociology* 49 (1943–44): 95. See also Chapter 8 of this book.

## Chapter One. Karl Marx:
## Around a Surprising Encounter with Heinrich Graetz

1. This letter, discovered by Boris Nikolayevsky, was published for the first time in German with a commentary by A. Tcheikover in an article entitled "A Letter from Heinrich Graetz to Karl Marx," in *Yiwo Studies in History* (1937): vol. 2. It can also be found under the classmark D 2167 in the archives of the International Institute of Social History in Amsterdam. See the brief remarks by Arthur Prinz, "New Perspectives on Marx as a Jew," *Leo Baeck Year Book* (1970), pp. 119ff.

2. Marx several times evokes his stays at Karlsbad. See, for instance, "Letters from Marx to Engels, April 14 and July 5, 1870," in Marx-Engels, *Correspondance* (the French edition) (Paris: Editions Sociales, 1985), vol. 9, pp. 4 and 349. See also Egon Erwin Kisch, *Karl Marx in Karlsbad* (Berlin, 1953).

3. Thomas Servier, "D'où sortira Kantorowicz? Historiens juifs à Posen avant 1914: figures et milieu," *Les Cahiers du judaïsme* (winter 2001–2002): 93.

4. Shulamit Volkov, "The Dynamics of Dissimilation: *Ostjuden* and German Jews," in Jehuda Reinharz and Walter Schatzberg, eds., *The Jewish Response to German Culture* (Hanover, NH: University Press of New England, 1985), pp. 204ff. Georg Herlitz, "Three Jewish Historians: Jost, Graetz, Täubler," *Leo Baeck Year Book* (1964).

5. Steven Ashheim, *Brothers and Strangers: The East European Jew in German Jewish Consciousness, 1800–1923* (Madison: University of Wisconsin Press, 1982).

6. I thank Jean Baumgarten for the kindness of translating this long commentary, as well as the letter by H. Graetz quoted here.

7. Isaac Heinemann, "Samson Raphael Hirsch: The Formative Years of the Leader of Modern Orthodoxy," *Historia Judaica* XIII (1951): 40.

8. Henrich Graetz, "The Correspondence of an English Lady on Judaism and Semitism," in *The Structure of Jewish History and Other Essays* (New York: Jewish Theological Seminary of America, 1975), p. 220.

9. Ber Borochov, *Class Struggle and the Jewish Nation* (New Brunswick, NJ: Transaction Books, 1984).

10. Simon Dubnow, *Histoire moderne du peuple juif* (Paris: Le Cerf, 1994), pp. 542–43.

11. On this question in general, see Ezra Mendelsohn, ed., *Essential Papers on Jews and the Left* (New York: New York University Press, 1997).

12. On the whole of this debate, see the fine article by Nathan Rotenstreich, "For and Against Emancipation: The Bruno Bauer Controversy," *Leo Baeck Year Book* (1958), pp. 3–36.

13. Ibid., p. 12.

14. On the critique of Bauer by Hirsch, see Gershon Greenberg, "The Historical Origins of God and Man: Samuel Hirsch's Luxembourg Writing," *Leo Baeck Year Book* (1975).

15. Thus Ismar Schorsch names Graetz in the introduction to his work, *Structure of Jewish History*, p. 32. See also Ismar Schorsch, *From Text to Context: The Turn to History in Modern Judaism* (Hanover, NH: Brandeis University Press, 1994), pp. 278ff.

16. Richard Cohen, "Urban Visibility and Biblical Visions," in David Biale, ed., *Cultures of the Jews: A New History* (New York: Schocken Books, 2002), pp. 659–760.

17. See Edmund Silberner, "Moses Hess," *Historia Judaica* (April 1951). Ronald Sanders, "Moses Hess: The Hegelian Zionist," *Midstream* (winter 1962). Shlomo Avineri, *Moses Hess: Prophet of Communism and Zionism* (New York: New York University Press, 1985).

18. The correspondence between Graetz and Hess was published in *Annali dell'Instituto Giangiacomo* (Milan: Feltrinelli, 1961). See also some letters exchanged between Hess and Graetz in Edmund Silberner, ed., *Moses Hess Briefwechsel* (The Hague: Mouton, 1959). See also Reuven Michael, "Graetz and Hess," *Leo Baeck Year Book* (1964); and his preface to H. Graetz, *Geschichte Der Israeliten* (Berlin: Arani-Verlag, 1996).

19. Sidney Hook, *From Hegel to Marx* (Ann Arbor: University of Michigan Press, 1962), p. 186.

20. Moses Hess, *Rome and Jerusalem* (New York: Bloch Publishing Company, 1945), pp. 88–90 and 93.

21. Ibid. Samuel Hirsch replies to Hess in *Les Archives israélites*, March 15, 1864. We can also note that Hess approved of Riesser for calling his journal *Der Jude*, giving it a national dimension, while the writings of Riesser were given greater value by Marx to the extent that, like Hirsch but this time in the political realm, Riesser was favorable to the integration of Jews into German society and did not support maintaining a collective Jewish identity.

22. Quoted by Boyer in his introduction to *Rome and Jerusalem*.

23. Hess, *Rome and Jerusalem*, p. 65.

24. Ibid., pp. 50, 51, 55, and 66.

25. Letter from Heinrich Graetz to Sybille Hess on May 5, 1877, in *Moses Hess Briefwechsel*, pp. 638–39.

26. David Sorkin, *The Transformation of German Jewry* (New York: Oxford University Press, 1987), pp. 31ff.

27. There are very few writings on these demonstrations. See Eleanor Sterling, "Anti-Jewish Riots in Germany in 1819: A Displacement of Social Protest," *Historia Judaica* 12 (1950): 105–42.

28. This period is rarely studied. See Jacob Katz, *From Prejudice to Destruction: Anti-Semitism, 1700–1933* (Cambridge, MA: Harvard University Press, 1980), pp. 148ff.

29. Herbert Strauss, "Pre-Emancipation Prussian Politics toward the Jews, 1815–1847," *Leo Baeck Year Book* (1966), pp. 113ff.

30. Jonathan Frankel, *The Damascus Affair: "Ritual Murders," Politics and the Jews in 1840* (Cambridge: Cambridge University Press, 1997).

31. Shlomo Avineri, *Moses Hess: Prophet of Communism and Zionism* (New York: New York University Press, 1985), p. 178. As Dubnow notes, "The Damascus affair, which revealed an abyss of Judeophobia in modern civilized societies, was a terrible blow for Hess," *Histoire moderne du peuple juif*, p. 841.

32. Frankel, *Damascus Affair*, ch. 8 and pp. 425–26, 435ff.

33. Michael Mayer, "Reform Jewish Thinkers and Their German Context," in Reinharz and Schatzberg, eds., *Jewish Response to German Culture*, pp. 79ff.

34. See the remarkable article by Jacob Toury, "The Jewish Question: A Semantic Approach," *Leo Baeck Year Book* (1966), pp. 93ff. This article remains pivotal for an understanding of the intellectual context in which Marx's On 'The Jewish Question' was written. See also Peter Pulzer, "Why Was There a Jewish Question in Imperial Germany?" *Leo Baeck Year Book* (1980).

35. Yirmiyahu Yovel, *Les Juifs selon Hegel et Nietzsche* (Paris: Le Seuil, 2001), p. 59.

36. Eugene Kamenka, "The Baptism of Karl Marx," *The Hibbert Journal* (November 1956).

37. Richard Laufner and Albert Rauch, *Die Familie Marx und die Trierer Judenschaft*, Schriftem aus dem Karl-Marx-Haus Trier (1975), p. 16.

38. Lewis Feuer, "The Conversion of Karl Marx's Father," *Jewish Journal of Sociology* (December 1972).

39. On Karl Marx's family, see Fritz Raddatz, *Karl Marx: A Political Biography*

(Boston: Little, Brown and Co., 1978), ch. 1. See also Helmut Hirsch, *Marx und Moses. Karl Marx zur "Judenfrage" und zu Juden* (Frankfurt: Peter Lang Verlag, 1980), pp. 85ff.

40. Arnold Kunzli, *Karl Marx, Eine Psychographie* (Vienna: Europa Verlag, 1966).

41. H. F. Peters, *Red Jenny: A Life with Karl Marx*, (London: Allen and Unwin, 1986), pp. 41ff.

42. Simon Dubnow thinks that "the liberal Bauer thus promised the Jews emancipation in exchange for their religious suicide, which also included their national suicide," *Histoire moderne du peuple juif*, p. 541.

43. Bruno Bauer, *La question juive* 10/18 (1968): 62, 64, 71, 81, 95, and 102. See Rotenstreich, "For and Against Emancipation," pp. 4–10. See also David McLellan, *The Young Hegelians and Karl Marx* (New York: Macmillan, 1969), pp. 48ff. Zvi Rosen, *Bruno Bauer and Karl Marx: The Influence of Bruno Bauer on Marx's Thought* (The Hague: Martinus Nijhoff, 1977). Hook, *From Hegel to Marx*, ch. 3. On the historical context, see Reinhard Rürup, "Emancipation and Crisis: The 'Jewish Question' in Germany, 1850–1890," *Leo Baeck Year Book* (1975).

44. Bauer, *La question juive*, p. 107.

45. Ibid., p. 130.

46. Ibid., p. 61.

47. Ibid., pp. 136ff.

48. Ibid., pp. 69, 103, and 182.

49. Ibid., p. 71.

50. Jean-François Chanet, *L'école républicaine et les petites patries* (Paris: Aubier, 1996).

51. Pierre Birnbaum, *The Jews of the Republic: A Political History of State Jews in France from Gambetta to Vichy*, Jane Todd, trans. (Stanford: Stanford University Press, 1996).

52. Bauer, *La question juive*, p. 71.

53. Quoted by Rosen, *Bruno Bauer and Karl Marx*, p. 121.

54. Daniel Brudney even, from this point of view, compares Bauer's analyses to those of W. Kymlicka, comparing their approaches to multiculturalism. Daniel Brudney, *Marx's Attempt to Leave Philosophy* (Cambridge, MA: Harvard University Press, 1998), p. 138: "Besides being an extreme supporter of liberalism, Bauer is also an extreme communitarian."

55. This argument, seldom expressed in such an abrupt way, also appears in major works. See, for instance, Francis Wheen, *Karl Marx* (London: Fourth Estate, 1999), p. 57.

56. Julius Carlebach, *Karl Marx and the Radical Critique of Judaism* (London: Routledge and Kegan Paul, 1978), pp. 118ff.

57. Allan Arkush shows the recurrence of this theme of the selfishness of the Jews, from Spinoza to Feuerbach, but he emphasizes that only Marx gives it such a negative and aggressive dimension of a pursuit conducted solely in the name of

individual self-interest, an interpretation stemming from Marx's his own "prejudices": "Judaism as Egoism: From Spinoza to Feuerbach to Marx," *Modern Judaism* (May 1981): 218–22.

58. Dov Barnir also notes that Bauer shows himself to be more of a sociologist than Marx: "Le marxisme sioniste" (PhD diss., University of Strasbourg, 1972), p. 9.

59. Karl Marx, *On 'The Jewish Question,'* www.marxists.org

60. Ibid.

61. Ibid.

62. Ibid.

63. Ibid.

64. Ibid.

65. Ibid.

66. See Bertrand Badie and Pierre Birnbaum, *The Sociology of the State*, Arthur Goldhammer, trans. (Chicago: University of Chicago Press, 1983).

67. Rotenstreich, "For and Against Emancipation," p. 26.

68. Francis Kaplan gives a series of examples of authors who, from the nineteenth century to the present day, including, in France, Robert Mandrou and Henri Lefebvre, have either denied or completely erased this aspect of things: *Marx Anti-Semite?* (Paris: Editions Imago, 1990), pp. 50ff.

69. Marx, *The Holy Family*, www.marxists.org

70. Ibid.

71. Ibid.

72. Nonetheless one can still find a few brief remarks on this conjunction in Shlomo Avineri, "Marx and Jewish Emancipation," *Journal of the History of Ideas* (July 1964).

73. On Samuel Hirsch, see Jacob Katz, "Samuel Hirsch - Rabbi, Philosopher and Freemason," *Revue des Études juives* (January–September 1966): 1–3. Greenberg, " Historical Origins of God and Man," especially pp. 133–36. See also Michael Meyer, *Response to Modernity: A History of the Reform Movement in Judaism* (Oxford: Oxford University Press, 1988), pp. 72ff.

74. Marx, *The Holy Family*. Note that Samuel Hirsch, a Reform rabbi, criticizes the Zionist book by Moses Hess, Marx's friend who had become Graetz's friend, *Rome and Jerusalem*, since, for Hirsch, the Jews have only a "spiritual" identity. See Gershon Greenberg, "The Reformers' First Attack Upon Hess's *Rome and Jerusalem*," *Jewish Social Studies* XXXV, nos. 3 and 4 (1973).

75. Note written by Maximilien Rubel in the Pléiade edition of *La sainte famille*, p. 1609.

76. Marx, *The Holy Family*.

77. Ibid.

78. Moshe Rinott, "Gabriel Riesser: Fighter for Jewish Assimilation," *Leo Baeck Year Book* (1962), pp. 12 and 18–20. On Riesser's role during the 1848 revolution, Adolf Kober, "Jews in the Revolution of 1848 in Germany," *Jewish Social Studies* (April 1948): 142ff.

79. Heinrich Graetz, *History of the Jews* (Philadelphia, PA: The Jewish Publication of America, 1895), vol. 5, pp. 598–600.

80. See Hans Liebeschütz, "Treitschke and Mommsen on Jewry and Judaism," *Leo Baeck Year Book* (1962), pp. 172–73. Similarly, see Michael Meyer, *Judaism Within Modernity: Essays on Jewish History and Religion* (Detroit, MI: Wayne State University Press, 2001), pp. 68–69.

81. Karl Marx, *The Class Struggles in France, 1848–1850*, Part II, www.marxists.org
On "The Jewish Fould," see also Marx, *The Eighteenth Brumaire of Louis Bonaparte*, www.marxists.org

82. Ibid.

83. Marx, *The Class Struggles in France, 1848–1850*, Part II.

84. Marx, *The Eighteenth Brumaire of Louis Bonaparte*.

85. Marx, *The Class Struggles in France, 1848–1850*, Part III, www.marxists.org

86. Ibid.

87. Marx, *The Eighteenth Brumaire of Louis Bonaparte*.

88. Ibid.

89. Karl Marx, *The Civil War in France*, The Third Address, May 1871, www.marxists.org
Note that these reactionaries who think of themselves as Hebrews are described later on as "cosmopolitan swindlers."

90. Karl Marx, *Economic Manuscripts, Capital,* vol. 1, www.marxists.org
Marx also uses in his analysis passages from the Old Testament, such as "Thou shalt not, said Moses of Egypt, muzzle the ox that treads the corn."

91. Karl Marx, *Contribution à la critique de l'économie politique* (Paris: Éditions Sociales, 1957), p. 230.

92. See Daniel Brudney, *Marx's Attempt to Leave Philosophy* (Cambridge, MA: Harvard University Press, 1998).

93. Curiously, Murray Wolfson thinks that if *On 'The Jewish Question'* stems from self-hatred, starting from the instant Marx turned his attention to the economic system as producer of class struggle, his Jewish stereotypes no longer have their place, to the extent that the Jews did not take much part in industrialization, only in commerce. Thus he does not take into account either their persistence in Marx's economic works or their constant presence in the correspondence between Marx and Engels. Murray Wolfson, *Marx: Economist, Philosopher, Jew* (New York: St. Martin Press, 1982), p. 186.

94. Letters from Marx to Engels, February 25, May 25, 1859, *Correspondance,* vol. 5, pp. 273, 275, 276, 279, and 341; June 9, July 2, 1858, *Correspondance,* vol. 5, pp. 196 and 200; July 21, August 7, 9, 14, 20, 1862, *Correspondance,* vol. 7, pp. 55, 70, 74, 79, and 81; January 28, April 9, May 29, June 12 and 22, July 6, August 15, 1863, June 3, 1864, *Correspondance,* pp. 130, 161, 165, 169, 171, 178, and 233.

95. Hess, *Rome et Jérusalem,* p. 115.

96. Letter from Marx to Engels, May 10, 1861, *Correspondance,* vol. 6, p. 329.

97. Letter from Marx to Engels, July 30, 1862, vol. 8, pp. 58–61. For her part,

Jenny Marx writes to Engels: "I am going to write soon to the Jew from Berlin," that is, to Lassalle, Letter to Engels, *Correspondance*, vol. 5, p. 179.

98. Letter from Marx to Engels, February 3, 1865, *Correspondance*, vol. 8, pp. 33–35.

99. Letter from Marx to Engels, February 11, 1865, *Correspondance*, vol. 8, p. 48.

100. Letters from Marx to Engels, January 30, February 3, 10, 13, 1865, *Correspondance*, vol., 8, pp. 26, 34, 46, and 50. Letter from Engels to Marx, February 13, 1865, *Correspondance*, vol. 8, p. 50. Letter from Marx to Engels, December 10, 1869, *Correspondance*, vol. 10, p. 231.

101. Letter from Marx to Engels, March 14, 1868, *Correspondance*, vol. 9, p. 183. In the same letter, he repeats "our Braun Yid" several times.

102. See, for instance, Letter from Engels to Marx, January 31, 1860, *Correspondance*, vol. 6, p. 17.

103. Letter from Engels to Marx, March 7, 1856, *Correspondance*, vol. 4, p. 281.

104. Letter from Engels to Marx, April 14, 1856, *Correspondance*, p. 296.

105. Letter from Marx to his daughter Jenny, September 5, 1866, vol. 8, p. 315. On the view of Blacks in Marx's work, see the well-informed but very debatable book by Nathaniel Weyl, *Karl Marx: Racist* (New York: Arlington House, 1979), ch. 7.

106. Letter from Marx to Paul Lafargue, August 17, 1866, *Correspondance*, vol. 8, p. 308.

107. Letter from Engels to Marx, May 12, 1865, *Correspondance*, vol. 8. Letters from Marx to Engels, September 22, 1856, *Correspondance*, vol. 4, p. 331; December 26, 1865, vol. 8, p. 188; January 25, 1868, vol. 9, p. 161.

108. Letter from Marx to Engels, March 16, 1851, *Correspondance*, vol. 5, p. 288.

109. Letter from Marx to Engels, March 31, 1851, *Correspondance*, vol. 2, p. 179.

110. Letter from Marx to Adolf Cluss, March 25, 1853, *Correspondance*, vol. 3, p. 344.

111. Letter from Marx to Engels, May 25, 1859, *Correspondance*, vol. 5, p. 340. Max Friedlander is being discussed.

112. Letter from Marx to Engels, August 26, 1859, *Correspondance*, vol. 5, p. 375. See also, Letter from Marx to Engels, February 16, 1857, *Correspondance*, vol. 4, p. 365.

113. Letter from Marx to Adolf Cluss, December 7, 1852, *Correspondance*, vol. 3, p. 300.

114. Letter from Marx to Engels, May 10, 1861, *Correspondance*, vol. 6, pp. 330–31.

115. Letter from Marx to Engels, June 3, 1864, *Correspondance*, vol. 7, p. 234.

116. Letter from Marx to Engels, August 25, 1851, *Correspondance*, vol. 2, p. 304.

117. Letter from Marx to Engels, September 22, 1853, *Correspondance*, vol. 3, p. 341.

118. Letter from Marx to Adolf Cluss, April 17, 1853, *Correspondance*, vol. 3, p. 358.

119. Letter from Marx to Engels, September 22, 1856, *Correspondance*, vol. 4, p. 329.

120. Letter from Marx to Engels, September 28, 1852, *Correspondance*, vol. 3, p. 225. See also Letter from Marx to Engels, October 12, 1853, *Correspondance*, vol. 4, p. 41.

121. Letter from Marx to Engels, August 25, 1879, *Correspondance*, vol. 2, p. 243.

122. Letter from Marx to Jenny Marx, *Correspondance*, January 11, 1865, vol. 8, p. 6.

123. Letter from Marx to Engels, April 12, 1860, *Correspondance*, vol. 6, p. 142. This expression also figures in the Letter from Marx to Engels, June 1, 1860, *Correspondance*, vol. 6, p. 163.

124. Letter from Marx to Engels, April 15, 1870, *Correspondance*, vol. 10, p. 349; Letter from Marx to Engels, July 8, 1870, *Correspondance*, vol. 11, p. 12.

125. Letter from Marx to Engels, February 3, 1865, *Correspondance*, vol. 8, p. 34.

126. Letter from Marx to Engels, February 10, 1865, *Correspondance*, vol. 8, p. 46.

127. Quoted by Helmut Hirsch, *Marx und Moses. Karl Marx zur "Judenfrage" und zu Juden* (Frankfurt: Peter Lang Verlag, 1980), p. 113.

128. Letter from Marx to Engels, August 5, 1865, *Correspondance*, vol. 8, p. 153.

129. Letter from Marx to Engels, May 7, 1861, *Correspondance*, vol. 6, p. 324.

130. Letter from Marx to Engels, October 13, 1851, *Correspondance*, vol. 2, p. 324.

131. Letter from Marx to Engels, May 10, 1866, *Correspondance*, vol. 8, p. 270. Concerning Frederic Blind, father-in-law of Ferdinand Cohen, the student responsible for a failed attempt on Bismarck.

132. Letter from Marx to Engels, August 21, 1875, *Correspondance*, vol. 8, p. 32.

133. Letter from Marx to Engels, August 25, 1879, *Correspondance*, vol. 2, p. 243.

134. Letter from Marx to Lassalle, February 4, 1859, *Correspondance*, vol. 5, p. 265.

135. Letter from Marx to the Prussian authorities, April 10, 1866, *Correspondance*, vol. 6, p. 310.

136. Letter from Marx to Antoinette Philips, March 24, 1861, *Correspondance*, vol. 6, p. 290.

137. Karl Marx, *Herr Vogt* (Ed. Costes, 1927), vol. 2, pp. 206ff. See Kaplan, *Marx antisémite?* p. 103.

138. Letter from Marx to Engels, July 31, 1851, *Correspondance*, vol. 2, p. 259.

139. Letter from Marx to Engels, August 29, 1853, *Correspondance*, vol. 3, p. 399.

140. Quoted by Hirsch, *Marx und Moses*, p. 116.

141. Letter from Marx to Engels, August 19, 1853, *Correspondance*, vol. 4, p. 7.

142. Letter from Marx to Engels, February 8, 1860, *Correspondance*, vol. 6, p. 44.

143. Letter from Marx to the counsel Weber, February 24, 1860, *Correspondance*, vol. 6, p. 93. This observation stands out when one notes that, in his discussion with the attorney connected with his trial against the *National-Zeitung*, Marx adds, curiously for a revolutionary leader, "Since I myself am the son of a lawyer, the late Councilor Heinrich Marx, of Trier, who for a long time was President of the Bar of that city, and distinguished himself as much by the probity of

his character as by his talents as a lawyer," Letter from Marx to Councilor Weber, March 3, 1860, *Correspondance*, vol. 6, pp. 115–16.

144. Letter from Engels to Carl Siebel, *Correspondance*, vol. 8, p. 45. See other remarks by Engels on the Jews, as in his letter to Jenny Marx, November 5, 1859, *Correspondance*, vol. 5, p. 408. Unlike Marx, Engels still attacked anti-Semitism. He writes, "Anti-Semitism is nothing other than the reaction of medieval, declining social classes against modern society. . . . It is a kind of feudal socialism. . . . We owe too much to the Jews. Without speaking of Heine and Boerne, Marx was of pure Jewish blood. Lassalle was Jewish. . . . I myself have been treated as a Jew . . . and truly, if I had to choose, I would rather be Jewish than 'Herr von,'" quoted by Maximilien Rubel, *Karl Marx. Essai de biographie intellectuelle* (Marcel Rivière, 1957), p. 88.

145. Edmund Silberner, "Friederich Engels and the Jews," *Jewish Social Studies* (October 1949): 331, 333–34.

146. Hirsch, *Marx und Moses*, pp. 70 and 77.

147. See, for example, Franz Mehring, who practically never approaches this question: *Karl Marx: The Story of His Life* (New York: Covici, 1935). An author like David McLellan protests Marx's good faith: through the Jews, Marx meant, according to McLellan, simply to discuss commerce: *Marx Before Marxism* (London: Pelican, 1970). This point of view is very often adopted, especially in France.

148. This is the interpretation of Helmut Hirsch, who severely criticizes the analyses of E. Silberner, and who considerably plays down the significance of these quotations hostile to the Jews: Hirsch, *Marx und Moses*, p. 124.

149. As Francis Kaplan shows, this sentence is suppressed in his *Marx anti-sémite?* p. 113. Similarly, in their official edition of Marx's works, August Bebel and Eduard Bernstein expurgated Marx's texts of most of their anti-Jewish tone.

150. Karl Marx, *Oeuvres économiques* (Paris: Gallimard, "Bibliothèque de la Pléiade," vol. 1, 1963), p. 1646.

151. Thus, after publishing a letter from Marx in which Marx makes fun several times of the "little Braun Jew" and "his Talmudic wisdom" that he does not share, Gilbert Badia begins by recalling that Marx also gives Lassalle the surname of Itzig, "a German diminutive of Isaac, a pejorative term often given to the Jews," but then adds, "Is it necessary to add that the use of this surname—even if it shocks the reader—does not in the least imply in Marx—himself Jewish, moreover, and author of *On 'The Jewish Question'*—the least anti-Semitism?" I do not have the cruelty to comment on this observation. *Lettres sur "Le capital,"* intro. by Gilbert Badia (Paris: Éditions Sociales, 1964), p. 107.

152. Aside from the articles by S. Bloom, E. Silberner, and G. Meyer already quoted, see Leopold Schwarzschild, *The Red Prussian: The Life and Legend of Karl Marx* (New York: Charles Scribner's, 1947), pp. 259ff.; Raddatz, *Karl Marx: A Political Biography*, ch. 7. See also Albert Glotzer, "Marx and the Jews: A Paradox of Sorts," *Midstream* (May 1997). By contrast, an author of a more functionalist inspiration like G. A. Cohen devotes only a few lines to *On 'The Jewish Question,'*

contenting himself with mentioning the theory of the state that it presents: *Karl Marx's Theory of History: A Defense* (Princeton, NJ: Princeton University Press, 1978), p. 128. Similarly, Shlomo Avineri, starting from a more philosophical approach, is also completely silent about *On 'The Jewish Question,'* merely mentioning in a few lines that one can find in it a theory on the state that he recounts: *The Social and Political Thought of Karl Marx* (Cambridge: Cambridge University Press, 1968), p. 46.

153. See, for example, the benchmark works by Jean-Yves Calvez, *La pensée de Karl Marx* (Paris: Le Seuil, 1956), pp. 64ff., and by August Cornu, *Karl Marx et Friedrich Engels* (Paris: PUF, 1958), vol. 2, pp. 267–71.

154. See Maxime Rodinson, Preface to Abraham Léon, *Sur la conception matérialiste de l'Histoire* (EDI, 1968), p. 41.

155. Maximilien Rubel seems thus to have varied considerably in his interpretation of these tendentious images. In his introduction to the second part of *On 'The Jewish Question'* where there are more attacks against Lassalle, he emphasizes Marx's "frankly Judeophobic tendency. . . . It seems to us unarguable, however, that Marx felt a certain resentment against the religion of his ancestors," *Karl Marx. Essai de biographie intellectuelle*, pp. 87–88. By contrast, in his editing of Marx's work for the Pléiade edition, Rubel reveals himself to be more subtle and almost contradictory. Though he continually defends Marx from any accusation of anti-Semitism, finding even the first part of *On 'The Jewish Question'* "frankly Judeophilic," though he also argues that his "anti-Judaism has nothing specifically Judeophobic about it," though he doesn't disdain a strange argument, in commenting on a passage from *On 'The Jewish Question,'* that "the ghetto is not peculiar to the Jews, since we all live in a ghetto, like free monads authorized to enjoy the right to isolation. Jewish, Christian, atheist or believer, the monad individual is a self being," though he asserts without convincing us, "as to the Jewish proletariat, Marx is aware of pleading for his cause by pleading for that of the universal proletariat" whereas Marx does not devote a single paragraph in his immense work to the specifically Jewish proletariat, though he takes literally, without finding anything to say about it, Marx's expression of his "repugnance for the Jewish religion"; nevertheless, Rubel still finally confesses, "The fact remains that by reducing the Jewish religion to the morality of a sordid practice—like his master Feuerbach—Marx simplifies excessively, and lays open to criticism his superficial critique of a simplistic Manichaeism." Refusing, however, to compare the Marxist vision of the Jews with the point of view offered by Proudhon whose anti-Semitism is obvious, Rubel writes later on, without any other commentary, "The fact is that the phobia about money is such, in Marx, that his denunciation seems to stretch, beyond the rich minority of the Jewish community, to this entire religious minority, the majority of which lives on a modest, or even less than modest, income," Karl Marx, *Oeuvres philosophiques* (Paris: Gallimard, "Bibliothèque de la Pléiade," 1992), pp. 1574–77.

156. Openly drawing his inspiration from the works of Althusser, to whom she repeatedly refers very favorably, Élisabeth de Fontenay clears Marx's name of any

anti-Semitic attitude. In her opinion, once he had abandoned "the ambiguity of certain pages on the Jews . . . those accidents of birth" that *On 'The Jewish Question'* still symbolize, and that reveal an author "ill-informed indeed of the Jewish reality of his time, and anxious to transform an old and false question into an allegory," Marx gives "the only rejoinder possible: Judaism, metonymy for bourgeois society." "That's good work, they'll say, if people dared to have Marx talk not in order to prove him innocent but to laugh along with him, that's good ideological work: the old Jewish hag also deserves compliments," meaning, probably, in Marx's mind, digging one's own grave better by way of digging the grave of capitalism, the condition sina qua non for the emancipation of humanity. We can in fact laugh at it, in order the better to mask the huge tragedy that is hidden behind this mechanistic vision of history. Laugh at it or cry at it, before the small importance given to the Jewish destiny itself thus merrily abandoned to a historical logic that offers no place for it, since its disappearance alone is the irrefutable proof of human emancipation. Curious "apprenticeship," surprising dialectics: citing Althusser, according to whom Marx's rejection of Hegelianism had a retrograde quality on the theoretical level but nonetheless exercised fortunate progressive effects from the ideological point of view, one theorist has written, "We would dare to add that the anti-Judaism, which had become to a certain extent anti-Semitism, in Hess, in Marx, is one of those fortunate effects that facilitate the transition to communism." We understand that with such a concept of dialectics one can think shocking the procedure that consists of "hunting down" the anti-Semitic metaphors in Marx's works; they are made out to be, actually, only "ornamental," without any theoretical consequences, the only ones that count; the "snippets," the "confidential remarks" of the correspondence indeed demonstrate that "Marx verbally mistreated Judaism and the Jews, and even that he did not like them. . . . But those are opinions about the private man" that fortunately concern only "scholiasts" anxious about "practices that might undermine their reading." Curious way of evading the question, justifying the unacceptable, and diverting attention toward the putative guilt of some reader with perfidious intentions.

After the tainted language of structuralist Marxism made to serve the prosecution, psychoanalysis enters as a new mechanism of defense for Marx the individual. Now Marx is reproached just for letting feelings burst forth too volubly, albeit halfheartedly, "as if without his knowing it"; his subconscious is supposedly pushing him to reveal fantasies that the rigorous scholar that he is ought to be able to reject, or at least silence. This is when Élisabeth de Fontenay takes up a peculiar, extremely complex interpretation of these few words of *Capital* censored from the French edition, "Jews with circumcised souls": for her, this merely refers to "Jews who are internally circumcised" according to the translation she provides to make this metaphor acceptable, which would simply symbolize the abstract, monadic man, a "useful image" that concerns "one who, following a mutilation that marks him as the property of another, God or capital, is both disowned from himself and taken away from the community, locked up in the ghetto where he continually reinforces his separation." Becoming involved, as she herself admits, in a "so-called psychoanalysis" of Marx that is supposed to shed light on the role of abstraction in his way of thinking, she adopts Althusser's phrase of Marx's "rupture [*coupure*]," which she thinks too absolute in this work, which is in fact wholly marked by Jewish abstraction. So many "displacements," so many "metonymies" finally reduce the Jewish individual to nothing: he is only a mirror, a representation of another reality. Élisabeth de Fontenay, *Les figures juives de Marx* (Paris: Galilée, 1973), pp. 39–40, 77–79, 88–89, 96–97, and 107. In the same vein, François Chatelet thinks that these "metaphors" are revealed to be of "great political richness"; Introduction to Karl Marx, *La question juive* (Paris: Aubier, 1971), p. 42. Other commentators think, on the contrary, that these "metaphors" are "in bad taste, uncalled-for, unfortunate": Frédéric Vandenberg, *Une histoire critique de la sociologie allemande* (Paris: La Découverte, 1997), vol. 1, p. 73.

157. As Francis Kaplan rightly observes, "The metonymy is not innocent. If one chooses a part to stand for the whole, it is not just any part, it is what represents it best, what represents it most eminently. . . . Marx does not say that the Jew just represents the bourgeoisie, but that the Jew just represents the Judaism of bourgeois society. . . . Bourgeois society is made Jewish, as the Christian is made Jewish. There are no traces of metonymy in this," *Marx antisémite?* pp. 62–63.

158. See Georges Haupt, Michael Lowy, and Claudie Weill, *Les marxismes et la question nationale. 1848–1914* (Maspéro, 1974). Walker Connor, *The National Question in Marxist-Leninist Theory and Strategy* (Princeton, NJ: Princeton University Press, 1984). Roman Rosdolsky, *Engels and the "Nonhistorical" Peoples: The National Question of 1848* (Glasgow: Critique Books, 1986). Erica Benner, *Really Existing Nationalisms: A Post-Communist View from Marx and Engels* (Oxford: Clarendon Press, 1995).

159. Isaiah Berlin, *Karl Marx: His Life and Environment* (Oxford: Oxford University Press, 1996).

160. The methodological Marxist individualism that abstains from any prejudice unfortunately does not concern itself much with cultural or collective identification with a religious system in accounting for social facts and doesn't linger over this sort of problem that nonetheless does involve questions of ethics and responsibility. See John Roemer, ed., *Analytical Marxism* (Cambridge: Cambridge University Press, 1986).

161. Werner Dannhauser, "Marx and Judaism," *Jewish Journal of Sociology* (June 1981): 70–71.

162. Isaac Deutscher, *Essai sur le problème juif* (Paris: Payot, 1969), pp. 37 and 43.

163. Hook, *From Hegel to Marx*, p. 279.

164. Edmund Silberner, "Was Marx an Anti-Semite?" *Historia Judaica* (April 1949): 13 and 51. In a text that was published for the first time in Hebrew in 1936, in Tel Aviv, Moshe Glickson sets out to analyze "Marx's blind hatred toward the Jewish people," which seems all the more surprising to him since Marxism found, in the Palestine of the time, a great number of followers. He hopes that his study will turn Jewish children away from the errors of "this brilliant giant of Jewish

origin": *The Jewish Complex of Karl Marx* (New York: Herzl Press, 1961), pp. 7–8. W. Blumenberg speaks for his part of "typical self-hatred": *Marx* (Paris: Mercure de France, 1962), p. 87. Arnold Jünzli uses the expression "Jewish autophobia": *Karl Marx, eine Psychographie* (Europa Verlag, 1966), p. 195. On this discussion, see Boris Nicolaïevski and Otto Maenchen-Helfen, *La vie de Karl Marx* (Paris: La Table Ronde, 1997), append. 1. For Claude Vigée, "Marx's anti-Semitic rage" is such that "the water of the anti-Semitic bath has truly damaged the nerve centers of the 'bɔ'  y.' Where is the cure? Certainly not in the *Manuscripts of 1844*": "Les effets .ɛ l'antisémitisme de Karl Marx sur la structure théorique du marxisme," *Saisons d'Alsace* no. 55 (1976): 251 and 257. Robert Wistrich emphasizes that throughout his entire life Marx maintained this self-hatred, his "Judeophobia": *Revolutionary Jews: From Marx to Trotsky* (London: Harrap, 1976), pp. 36–37. In a curious and little-known article, Marcos Weinstein wonders by what mystery Marx, "the most genial of modern sociologists, so Jewish in his character," could "completely lose his mental equilibrium," since in *On 'The Jewish Question'* "everything is vulgar and puerile; these are pages written under the effects of unconscious impulses that cover its author with shame. It is a book written by one of the most terrible enemies of Israel": "Marx y la Cuestión Judía," *Judaica* no. 55 (summer 1938): 1 and 19. In our day, Amos Funkenstein thinks that *On 'The Jewish Question'* stems from "hatred of his Jewish self . . . [which] constitutes a dimension that forms part of his argumentation": *Perceptions of Jewish History*, pp. 229 and 231. See also Yuri Maltsev, *Requiem for Marx* (Montgomery: University of Alabama Press, 1993), pp. 117ff.

165. Otto Rühle, *Karl Marx* (New York, 1929), p. 377.

166. Feuer, "Conversion of Karl Marx's Father," pp. 157–58.

167. Letters from Jenny Marx to Engels, December 17, 1851, *Correspondance*, vol. 2, p. 389, and January 7, 1852, *Correspondance*, vol. 3, p. 298; January 17, 1870, *Correspondance*, vol. 10, p. 260. Letter from Jenny Marx to L. Kugelmann, November 19, 1870, *Correspondance*, vol. 11, p. 119. In this volume, unlike the preceding one where the expression "Moor" (p. 389) is simply glossed as "a nickname for Marx used by those close to him," the editor of the Éditions Sociales provides this letter with the following remark: "His thick black hair and his swarthy complexion earned Marx this nickname," p. 9. August 9, 1857, November 4, 1859, *Correspondance*, vol. 5, pp. 13 and 408; March 30, 1865, vol. 8, p. 109. Letter from Laura Marx to Engels, January 13, 1868, vol. 9, p. 155. Letter from Eleanor Marx to W. Liebknecht, December 29, 1871, *Correspondance*, vol. 11, p. 401.

168. See the countless letters from Engels to Marx in volumes 7 and 8 of the *Correspondance*.

169. Yvonne Kopp, *Eleanor Marx* (New York: Beekman Publishers), vol. 2, p. 510.

170. Quoted by David McLellan, *Karl Marx: His Life and Thought* (New York: Harper and Row, 1973), p. 53.

171. Ruhle, *Karl Marx: His Life and Work*, p. 377.

172. Sander Gilman, "Karl Marx and the Secret Language of Jews," *Modern Judaism* (October 1984): 286 and 292.

173. Lewis Feuer, in the article cited above, stresses the relationship with the father but, in another text, he ties the hatred of self to rejection of the mother: "Karl Marx and the Promethean Complex," *Encounter* (December 1968). Robert Misrahi in turn endorses an explanation of a psychoanalytic nature in terms of repression: *Marx et la question juive*, pp. 237ff.

174. Salomon Bloom, "Karl Marx and the Jews," *Jewish Social Studies* (January 1942): 15–16.

175. Steven Aschheim, "The Myth of 'Judaization Germany,'" in Reinharz and Schatzberg, eds., *Jewish Response to German Culture*, pp. 219–21.

176. Gustav Mayer, "Early German Socialism and Jewish Emancipation," *Jewish Social Studies* (October 1939): 418.

177. Silberner, "Was Marx an Anti-Semite?" p. 15.

178. Herbert Strauss, "Pre-Emancipation Prussian Policies Towards the Jews, 1815–1847," *Leo Baeck Year Book* (1966), p. 129.

179. Letter from Marx to Engels, May 6, 1868, *Correspondance*, vol. 9, p. 226.

180. On March 13, 1843, Marx wrote to Ruge: "I have just received a visit from the president of the local Israelite community [Cologne], who asks me to write a petition in favor of the Jews. I will do it. Whatever the disgust I feel for the Israelite faith, it seems to me that Bauer's opinions are nonetheless too abstract. We have to make the maximum number of breaches in the Christian state and fraudulently introduce the rational into it, as much as we can," quoted by Rubel, *Karl Marx*, p. 89.

181. Silberner, "Was Marx an Anti-Semite?" p. 42.

182. Edmund Silberner, "German Social Democracy and the Jewish Problem Prior to World War I," *Historia Judaica* (April 1953). Robert Wistrich, "Anti-Capitalism or Anti-Semitism? The Case of Franz Mehring," *Leo Baeck Year Book* (1977); and, by the same author, *Socialism and the Jews* (London: Associated University Press, 1982). More recently, Jack Jacobs, *On Socialists and the Jewish Question After Marx* (New York: New York University Press, 1992).

183. Robert Wistrich, "Marxism and Jewish Nationalism: The Theoretical Roots of Confrontation," *Jewish Journal of Sociology* (June 1975): 44.

184. See the curious forgotten text by Rabbi Raphael Breuer, "Marxism and Judaism," in Jacob Breuer, ed., *Fundamentals of Judaism* (New York: Harcourt, 1949), p. 239.

185. Dennis Fischman, *Political Discourse in Exile: Karl Marx and the Jewish Question* (Amherst: University of Massachusetts Press, 1991). For this author, "Marx does midrash on Hegel and other philosophical texts. . . . Marx rejected Judaism even if he studied philosophy and political economy as he would have analyzed the Torah. He shows a strange and unconscious piety" that is revealed in his manner of reading texts and evokes that of the rabbis, pp. 85–87 and ch. 5. "The Marxist theory of alienation shares the same feeling of exile that we can find in the narrative of exile and return in Rabbi Luria," p. 94. Let us emphasize

that Fischman, in these same pages, to justify his interpretation of Marx's body of work, is moreover completely opposed to the scientific perspective of Althusser. In this sense, for this author, Marxist theory bears fundamental witness to galut, the exile of man from himself.

186. Wolfson, *Marx: Economist*, p. 223.

187. Isaiah Berlin, "Benjamin Disraeli and Karl Marx," in Henry Hardy, ed., *Against the Current* (New York: Viking Press, 1980), p. 278.

## Chapter Two. Émile David Durkheim: The Memory of Masada

1. Émile Durkheim, *Suicide*, John A. Spaulding and George Simpson, trans. (New York: Free Press, 1951), pp. 131–32 and 170.

2. See Antony Smith, "Gastronomy or Geology? The Role of Nationalism in the Reconstruction of Nations," *Nations and Nationalism* (1995): 1. See Yarl Zerubavel, *Recovered Roots: Collective Memory and the Making of Israeli National Tradition* (Chicago: Chicago University Press, 1995). See also Barry Schwartz, Yael Zerubavel, and Bernie Barnett, "The Recovery of Masada: A Study in Collective Memory," *The Sociological Quarterly* 27, no. 2.

3. In his remarkable book, W. Watts Miller not only never mentions Durkheim's Judaism but also leaves out essential quotations in which Durkheim bases his analyses on examples taken from Jewish history; this fine specialist in Durkheim thus removes a long passage in which Durkheim compares the Jews celebrating the departure from Egypt or the promulgation of the Decalogue to a meeting of citizens of the Third Republic: *Durkheim, Morals and Modernity* (London: UCL Press, 1996), p. 236.

4. Robert A. Nisbet, *The Sociological Tradition* (New York: Basic Books, 1966), p. 19.

5. Jean-Claude Chamboredon, "Émile Durkheim, le social, objet de science. Du moral au politique?" *Critique* (June 1984): 497 and 531, n. 163. Such an approach is not written about, except of course in a footnote, in a learned discussion of the application in his work of the hypothesis of rupture traditionally applied to the works of Althusser (who allowed people to distinguish between a period of youth and a period of maturity): "Let us note one more difficulty with the thesis of epistemological 'rupture' (which, moreover, is decidedly heavy-handed in speaking of a rabbi's son)," pp. 523–24, n. 106. This out-of-place joke on the theme of circumcision is surprising, as are the strange comparisons between Durkheim's nose and that of Captain Dreyfus, p. 506, n. 44. Is this saying that the Jewish dimension of Durkheim's work always remains problematic, that we cannot approach it more calmly, aside from a few scarcely admissible allusions, through studying the work? We remember that this image of the "rupture" was also used, in a similar register that was even more surprising, about Karl Marx.

6. Émile Durkheim, *Lettres à Marcel Mauss*, intro. by Philippe Besnard and Marcel Fournier (Paris: PUF, 1998), p. 16.

7. Pierre Birnbaum, *Jewish Destinies: Ciitizenship, State, and Community in Modern France*, Arthur Goldhammer, trans. (New York: Hill and Wang, 2000).

8. Pierre Birnbaum, *The Anti-Semitic Moment: A Tour of France in 1898*, Jane Marie Todd, trans. (New York: Hill and Wang, 2002).

9. Émile Durkheim, *De la division du travail social* (Paris: PUF, 1960), p. 220. See the commentary by Stéphane Beaud and Gérard Noiriel, "L'assimilation, un concept en panne," *Revue internationale d'action communautaire* (spring 1983).

10. Arnaldo Momigliano, "Marcel Mauss e il problema della persona nella biografia greca," *Rivista storica italiana* 97 (1985): 255. On this point, see G. W. Bowersock, "Momigliano's Quest for the Person," in *The Presence of the Historian*, p. 32.

11. Mark Cladis, *A Communitarian Defense of Liberalism: Emile Durkheim and Contemporary Social Theory* (Stanford: Stanford University Press, 1992).

12. See Christophe Charle, "Le beau mariage d'Émile Durkheim," *Actes de la Recherche en sciences sociales* (November 1984).

13. Ibid., pp. 47–48.

14. This viewpoint comes to light in certain articles by Yvon Bourdet.

15. Alain Policar, "Destin du franco-judaïsme ou les illusions de l'universalisme abstrait," *Les Temps Modernes* (November 1993): 56. This author takes his inspiration explicitly from the thematic of the *fous de la République*, the zealots of the Republic.

16. Hubert Bourguin, *De Jaurès à Léon Blum* (Paris: Fayard, 1938), p. 219.

17. Georges Davy, "Allocution," Commemoration of the hundredth anniversary of Émile Durkheim's birth, *Annales de l'université de Paris* (January–March 1960).

18. Quoted by Marcel Fournier, *Marcel Mauss* (Paris: Fayard, 1994), p. 37.

19. René Maublanc, "Durkheim, prof de philo," *Europe* 22 (1930): 297.

20. Quoted by Jean-Claude Filloux, *Durkheim et le socialisme* (Droz, 1977), p. 34.

21. Louis Greenberg, "Bergson and Durkheim as Sons and Assimilators: The Early Years," *French Historical Studies* no. 4 (fall 1976): 630.

22. Donald Nielsen, *Three Faces of God: Society, Religion and the Categories of Totality in the Philosophy of Émile Durkheim* (Albany: State University of New York, 1999), pp. 240–42. See also Paula Hyman, *De Dreyfus à Vichy* (Paris: Fayard, 1985).

23. W. S. F. Pickering, *Durkheim's Sociology of Religion: Themes and Theories* (London: Routledge and Kegan Paul, 1984), p. 521.

24. Eugen Schoenfeld and Stjepan Mestrovic, "Durkheim's Concept of Justice and Its Relationship to Social Solidarity," *Sociological Analysis* 50–52 (1989): 125.

25. Deborah Dash Moore, "David Emile Durkheim and the Jewish Response to Modernity," *Modern Judaism* 6 (1980): 289 and 292. See also Jacob Jay Lindenthal, "Some Thoughts Regarding the Influence of Traditional Judaism on the Work of Emile Durkheim," *Tradition: A Journal of Orthodox Thought* 11 (1970).

26. W. S. F. Pickering, "The Enigma of Durkheim's Jewishness," in W. S. F. Pickering and H. Martins, *Debating Durkheim* (London: Kegan Paul, 1994), pp. 29 and 35.

27. Ivan Strenski, *Durkheim and the Jews of France* (Chicago: University of Chicago Press, 1997), pp. 2–6. Pondering the reality of any kind of Jewish influence on Durkheim, this author writes: "I have found none." "Durkheim, Judaism and the Afterlife," in Thomas Idinopulos and Brian Wilson, eds., *Reappraising Durkheim for the Study and Teaching of Religion Today* (Leyden: Brill, 1999), p. 118.

28. Steven Lukes, *Emile Durkheim. His Life and Work: A Historical and Critical Study* (London: Allen Lane, 1973). See the observations on pp. 39–41.

29. Terry Clark, *Prophets and Patrons: The French University and the Emergence of the Social Sciences* (Cambridge, MA: Harvard University Press, 1973), p. 166.

30. Étienne Halphen, Preface to *Durkheim, cent ans de sociologie à Bordeaux* (Bordeaux, 1987), p. 6.

31. E. A. Tiryakian, "L'École durkheimienne à la recherche de la société perdue: La sociologie naissante et son milieu culturel," *Cahiers internationaux de sociologie* 66 (1979): 112.

32. *Archives israélites*, November 22, 1917.

33. *L'Univers israélite*, November 30, 1917.

34. Perrine Simon-Nahum, *La Cité investie. La "science du judaïsme" français et la République* (Paris: Le Cerf, 1991), pp. 280–84.

35. Ibid., pp. 268, 272.

36. Ibid., p. 279.

37. Ibid., p. 278.

38. Pierre Birnbaum, "La conception durkheimmienne de l'État: l'apolitisme des fonctionnaires," *Revue française de sociologie* (April–June 1976).

39. W. S. F. Pickering, *Durkheim's Sociology of Religion: Themes and Theories* (London: Routledge and Kegan Paul, 1984), pp. 14–15.

40. Quoted by Filloux, *Durkheim et le socialisme*, p. 7. We are using here the family tree drawn up by Christophe Charle, "Le beau marriage d'Émile Durkheim," p. 46, as well as the one that figures in the introduction by Philippe Besnard and Marcel Fournier to *Lettres à Marcel Mauss*, p. 3. See also Greenberg, "Bergson and Durkheim"; Marcel Fournier, *Marcel Mauss* (Paris: Fayard, 1994); and Philippe Besnard, "A Durkheimian Approach to the Study of Fashion: The Sociology of Christian or First Names," in W. S. Pickering and H. Martins, *Debating Durkheim*.

41. G. Gemelli, "Communauté intellectuelle et stratégies institutionnelles: Henri Berr et la fondation du Centre international de synthèse," *Revue de synthèse* (April–June 1987): 233–36.

42. Fournier, *Marcel Mauss*, p. 38.

43. Marcel Mauss, "Critique interne de la légende d'Abraham," 1926, in Marcel Mauss, *Oeuvres* (Paris: Éditions de Minuit, 1969, vol. 2), p. 532 n. 13.

44. George Davy, "Durkheim, une voie nouvelle ouverte à la science de l'homme," 1960, in George Davy, *L'homme, le fait social et le fait politique* (Paris: Mouton, 1973), p. 18.

45. These reflections are drawn from Filloux, *Durkheim et le socialisme*, pp. 39–42.

46. Durkheim, *De la division du travail social*, p. 37.

47. Ibid., pp. 41–42.

48. Ibid., pp. 52–53. See also pp. 58–59.

49. Ibid. See, for example, pp. 60, 111, 154, 375, and so on.

50. Émile Durkheim, *Les formes élementaires de la vie religieuse* (Alcan, 1921). He also cites here Leviticus or Deuteronomy, for instance on p. 47.

51. Durkheim, *De la division du travail social*, pp. 62–63. Durkheim cites here Numbers 15 then Leviticus 24. John Cuddihy is one of the very few commentators to have emphasized these numerous references to the Pentateuch: John Murray Cuddihy, *The Ordeal of Civility: Freud, Marx, Lévi-Strauss and the Jewish Struggle with Modernity* (Boston: Beacon Press, 1974), p. 151.

52. Ibid., p. 64.

53. Ibid., pp. 109, 110, 111, and 113.

54. Ibid., pp. 129–31.

55. Ibid., p. 132. Later on, in 1906, Durkheim thinks that "as a whole, Jewish criminality is essentially less than that of other faiths," in E. Durkheim, review of Bruno Blau, *Die Kriminalitat der deutschen Juden*, in Émile Durkheim, *Journal sociologique* (Paris: PUF, 1969), p. 621.

56. Ibid., p. 142. Durkheim also mentions, in one line, the example of Buddhism.

57. Ibid., p. 143. This uniquely Jewish dimension of *The Division of Labor in Society* is always ignored by commentators who never point out its role, although of course not a decisive one, in Durkheim's reasoning. Thus in *Division du travail et lien social. Durkheim un siècle après*, there is no allusion to it anywhere: published under the direction of Philippe Besnard, Massimo Borlando, and Paul Vogt (Paris: PUF, 1993).

58. Émile Durkheim, *Les formes élémentaires de la vie religieuse* (Félix Alcan, 1925), p. 553.

59. Émile Durkheim, "Deux lois de l'évolution pénale," in Durkheim, *Journal sociologique*, pp. 251–52 and 257. Similarly, in a book review published by *L'Année sociologique* in 1897–98, he notes that rabbis have helped the Jewish law to evolve by making divorce possible for women. Émile Durkheim, review of David Werner Amram, *The Jewish Law of Divorce According to Bible and Talmud*, in *Journal sociologique*, p. 478.

60. Durkheim, *De la division du travail social*, pp. 152, 153, 157, 158, 159, 161, and 295. In his article in *L'Année sociologique* of 1897–98, "De la définition des phénomènes religieux" (On the definition of religious phenomena), Durkheim also likens the Hebrew people to the Iroquois or the Greeks, considering that "not only does the Jew believe that Yahweh is God, that he is the only God, creator of the world, revealer of the Law; but he must believe this," in Durkheim, *Journal sociologique*, p. 155.

61. Ibid., p. 243.

62. Ibid., pp. 152–53.

63. Ibid., p. 154.

64. Letter from Émile Durkheim to Marcel Mauss, June 1905, in Durkheim, *Lettres à Marcel Mauss*, pp. 355–56.

65. Letters from Émile Durkheim to Marcel Mauss, June and September 1905, in Durkheim, *Lettres à Marcel Mauss*, pp. 356–57, 365, and 369.

66. In Durkheim, *Lettres à Marcel Mauss*, p. 409.

67. Durkheim, *De la division du travail social*, p. 401.

68. Émile Durkheim, *Les règles de la méthode sociologique* (Paris: PUF, 1960), p. 5.

69. Ibid., p. 9.

70. Ibid., pp. 32–33.

71. Ibid., p. 33.

72. Ibid.

73. Émile Durkheim, "La prohibition de l'inceste et ses origines," in Durkheim, *Journal sociologique*, pp. 68–70. See also pp. 67, 71, 76–77, and 81.

74. Durkheim, *Suicide*, pp. 155–56.

75. Ibid., p. 159.

76. Ibid., pp. 159–60. In the 1899–1900 volume of *L'Année sociologique*, Durkheim emphasizes that Jews "emerge almost unscathed" from any irregular union; hence their greater family cohesion. Review of the book by Friedrich Lindner, *Die unehelichen Geburten als Sozialphaenomen*, in Durkheim, *Journal sociologique*, p. 301.

77. Émile Durkheim, review of the book by M. Mielziner, *The Jewish Law of Marriage and Divorce in Ancient and Modern Times* (1905), published in *L'Année sociologique*, 8. Émile Durkheim, *Textes* (Paris: Éditions de Minuit, 1975), vol. 3, pp. 115–16. See also "Le problème de la solidarité familiale et du totémisme chez les Hébreux," in Durkheim, *Textes*, vol. 2.

78. Durkheim, *Suicide*, p. 168.

79. Ibid., p. 156.

80. Émile Durkheim, "Antisémitisme et crise sociale," in Durkheim, *Textes*, vol. 2, p. 253.

81. Émile Durkheim, review of H. Krose, *Die Ursachen der Selbstmordhaufigkeit*, in Durkheim, *Journal sociologique*, pp. 664–65.

82. Arthur Ruppin, *Die Juden der Gegenwart*, 1904, quoted by Mitchell Hart, *Social Science and the Politics of Modern Jewish Identity* (Stanford: Stanford University Press, 2000), p. 132.

83. Durkheim, *Suicide*, p. 167.

84. Ibid., pp. 167–68 and p. 170.

85. Ibid., p. 376.

86. Maurice Halbwachs, *Les causes du suicide* (Félix Alcan, 1930), p. 258. Out of the 514 pages in this important work, fewer than two are devoted to this point: pp. 244 and 257–58. Jean-Christophe Marcel comments on this phrase by Halbwachs and thinks that "with one blow, one of the strong points of Durkheim's demonstration collapses," "Halbwachs et le suicide: de la critique de Durkheim à la fondation d'une

psychologie collective," in Massimo Borlandi and Mohamed Cherkaoui, eds., *Le suicide, un siècle après Durkheim* (Paris: PUF, 2000), p. 157. For him too, since the weakening of family solidarity brings an end to the immunity of the Jews, their religious values are thus not the origin of their resistance to suicide. In the same spirit, contemporary works demonstrate that suicide among Jews, for instance in the United States, increases beginning with the third generation, more and more secularized and less integrated into closely knit protective social networks. Bernice Pescosolido and Sharon Georgianna, "Durkheim, Suicide and Religion: Toward a Network Theory of Suicide," *American Sociological Review* 54 (February 1989): 34–35.

87. See François-André Isambert, "Durkheim et la statistique écologique," in *Une nouvelle civilisation? Hommage à Georges Friedmann* (Paris: Gallimard, 1973), p. 106. See also, by the same author, "Courants sociaux et loi des grands nombres," in Borlandi and Cherkaoui, eds., *Le suicide, un siècle après Durkheim*, pp. 97–98. See also W. S. F. Pickering, "Reading the Conclusion: *Suicide*, Morality and Religion," in W. S. F. Pickering and Geoffrey Walford, eds., *Durkheim's Suicide: A Century of Research and Debate* (London: Routledge, 2000), pp. 70 and 76.

88. Durkheim, *The Elementary Forms of Religious Life*, Karen E. Fields, trans. (New York: Free Press, 1995), p. 9.

89. Ibid., p. 44.

90. Ibid., p. 33.

91. Ibid., pp. 222 and 231.

92. Ibid., p. 379.

93. Ibid., pp. 423 and 427.

94. Ibid., p. 429.

95. Robert Bellah, Introduction to *Emile Durkheim on Morality and Society*, R. Bellah, ed. (Chicago: University of Chicago Press, 1973), p. 17.

96. Émile Durkheim, "De la définition des phénomènes religieux," in Durkheim, *Journal sociologique*, pp. 155–57.

97. Émile Durkheim, *"L'Allemagne au-dessus de tout," la mentalité allemande et la guerre* (1915; reprint, A. Colin, 1991); Émile Durkheim, with Ernest Lavisse, *Lettres à tous les Français* (1916; reprint, A. Colin, 1992).

98. Émile Durkheim, *Leçons de sociologie. Physique des moeurs et du droit* (Paris: PUF, 1950).

99. Letter from Émile Durkheim to Célestin Bouglé, November 28, 1898, in Durkheim, *Textes*, vol. 2, p. 426.

100. Ibid., March 22, 1898, in Durkheim, *Textes*, vol. 2, p. 423.

101. Émile Durkheim, letter to Paul Lapie, *Revue française de la sociologie* (January–March 1979).

102. See Birnbaum, *Jewish Destinies*, ch. 4.

103. Émile Durkheim, "L'individualisme et les intellectuels," in Émile Durkheim, *La science sociale et l'action* (Paris: PUF, 1970).

104. Émile Durkheim, "Antisémitisme et crise sociale," in Durkheim, *Textes*, vol. 2, pp. 252–54.

105. Thus, in a letter in which he reproaches his colleague and friend Camille Jullian for not supporting him locally, in Bordeaux, during the Stapfer affair, Durkheim writes, "Anti-Semitism and anti-Protestantism resist us with all their strength; they are playing their last card," *Études durkheimiennes* no. 7 (June 1982): 2.

106. Jean-Claude Filloux writes, "He had become involved for the sake of moral values and not because of strictly political considerations, or even merely as a Jew," in Durkheim, *La science sociale et l'action*, p. 257. See also Vincent Duclert, "Les intellectuels, l'antisémitisme et l'Affaire Dreyfus en France," *Revue des Études juives* (January–June 1999).

107. See Yash Nandan, "Le Maître, les doctrines, les membres et le magnum opus: Une étude critique et analytique de l'école durkheimienne et de L'Année sociologique" (PhD diss., University of Paris-Sorbonne, 1974). Philippe Besnard, "La formation de l'équipe de *L'Année sociologique*," *Revue française de sociologie* (January–March 1979). On the close contacts of Durkheim and Mauss with the Jewish intellectuals of the time, see Strenski, *Durkheim and the Jews of France*. When Robert Hertz was killed during the First World War, Durkheim wrote to Mauss, "One can do all one's duties, more than one's duties, and not offer oneself in advance to fate. He wanted to redeem the faults of Israel (in the literal sense of the word)," Letter from Durkheim to Marcel Mauss, April 1915, in Durkheim, *Lettres à Marcel Mauss*, p. 455.

108. See, for example, the letter from Durkheim to Célestin Bouglé on April 3, 1898: "This morning I saw Salomon Reinach, who had asked me to come see him. We talked for two hours about all these events and I'm beginning to see things a little more clearly. There's even more horrible duplicity than I had thought," *Revue française de sociologie* (April–June 1976): 169. See also the letter from Durkheim to Mauss on June 15, 1898, in Durkheim, *Lettres à Marcel Mauss*, p. 146.

109. On March 7, 1895, the grand rabbi of Bordeaux, Isaac Lévy, asked Durkheim to give a lecture on Judaism. We do not know Durkheim's reply, but he probably did not accept: *Lettres du consistoire israélite de Bordeaux (1894–1906)*, p. 52. On this point, see Pierre Birnbaum, Introduction to Émile Durkheim, *Le socialisme* (Paris: PUF, 1971), p. 17.

110. Thus, during a scholarly debate between Durkheim, Vidal de la Blache, Paul Desjardins, and Pécaut having to do with the links between the state, nationalism, and patriotism, since Durkheim thinks that patriotism implies the existence of a state, Pécaut, strangely, without anything having been said beforehand to lead up to this question, retorts, "You aren't going to deny 'the Jewish patriotism of the dispersed Israelites'?" And Durkheim replies: "That is the patriotism of 'nationalities,'" from "Débat sur le nationalisme et le patriotisme" (1905), in Durkheim, *Textes*, vol. 3, p. 186.

111. Durkheim gives precise details of this incident to Marcel Mauss in two letters, April 3 or April 9 and 10, 1916, in Durkheim, *Lettres à Marcel Mauss*, pp. 511–12 and 513–14.

112. The newly published text from which these quotations are taken was published by Noureddine Elkarati, "Émile Durkheim défenseur des réfugiés

russes en France. Rapport sur la situation des Russes du département de la Seine," *Genèses* (December 1990): 168–77. On the execution of Jewish Russian soldiers, see Philippe Landau, *Les Juifs de France et la Grande Guerre* (Paris: CNRS Editions, 1999).

113. Letter from Émile Durkheim to Marcel Mauss, February 5, 1916, in Durkheim, *Lettres à Marcel Mauss*, p. 99.

114. See the letters from Durkheim to Marcel Mauss, April 11 and 27 and May 4, 1916, in Durkheim, *Lettres à Marcel Mauss*, pp. 514–21.

115. See Chapter 3.

116. Letter from Émile Durkheim to Marcel Mauss on July 26, 1916, in Durkheim, *Lettres à Marcel Mauss*, pp. 537–38.

117. Émile Durkheim, "Note sur les mesures ayant pour objet d'obliger les Russes réfugiés en Angleterre à s'engager dans l'armée anglaise ou à rejoindre l'armée russe" [Note on the measures to force Russian refugees in England to enlist in the English army or join the Russian army], July 16, 1916, in *Études durkheimiennes* 5 (fall 1993).

118. Letter from Émile Durkheim to Marcel Mauss, August 1898, in Durkheim, *Lettres à Marcel Mauss*, p. 166.

119. Letters from Émile Durkheim to Marcel Mauss, in Durkheim, *Lettres à Marcel Mauss*, pp. 543–44.

120. Quoted in Fournier, *Marcel Mauss*, p. 39.

121. Letter from Durkheim to Mauss, March 19, 1916, in Durkheim, *Lettres à Marcel Mauss*, p. 509. Durkheim writes, "I won't even speak of the happy event at Épinal with which I was very pleased. Will there be a fuss about the bar mitzvah? Don't intervene. Let Henri do it. That's the best way to keep your mother from digging in her heels."

122. Letter to Marcel Mauss, October 1900[?], in Durkheim, *Lettres à Marcel Mauss*, pp. 270–71.

*Chapter Three. Georg Simmel: The Stranger, from Berlin to Chicago*

1. This text can be found in Georg Simmel, *Sociologie et épistémologie* (Paris: PUF, 1981), pp. 171ff.

2. Émile Durkheim, "Lettre à Célestin Bouglé," *Revue française de sociologie* (April–June 1976): 169.

3. S. Lozinskij, "Simmels Briefe zur jüdischen Frage," in Hannes Böhringer and Karlfried Gründer, eds., *Ästhetik und Soziologie um die Jahrhundertwende: Georg Simmel* (Frankfurt: Vittorio Klostermann, 1976), pp. 16–17.

4. For an analysis of this conjuncture, see, for example, Jehuda Reinharz and Walter Schatzberg, eds., *The Jewish Response to German Culture* (Hanover, NH: University Press of New England, 1985). See Paul Mendes-Flohr, *German Jews: A Dual Identity* (New Haven, CT: Yale University Press, 1999), ch. 1, "The Bifurcated Soul of the German Jew."

5. Ismar Schorsch, *From Text to Context: The Turn to History in Modern Judaism* (Hanover, NH: Brandeis University Press, 1994).

6. See Michael Landmann, "Bausteine zur Biographie," in Kurt Gassen and Michael Landmann, eds., *Buch des Dankes an Georg Simmel* (Berlin: Duncker and Humblot, 1958), pp. 11ff.

7. Klaus Christian Köhnke, *Der junge Simmel* (Frankfurt: Suhrkamp, 1996), p. 140. See also Alfred Laurence, "Georg Simmel: Triumph and Tragedy," in Larry Ray, ed., *Formal Sociology: The Sociology of Georg Simmel* (Aldershot, England: Elgar Reference Collection, 1991).

8. Quoted by Richard Kroner in Gassen and Landmann, eds., *Buch des Dankes an Georg Simmel*, p. 230.

9. Quoted by Köhnke, *Der junge Simmel*, pp. 128–32.

10. Ibid., p. 146.

11. Quoted in Gassen and Landmann, eds., *Buch des Dankes an Georg Simmel*, pp. 114–15. See the early article by Elias Hurwicz, "Simmel als jüdische Denker," *Neue jüdische Monatschefte* 3 (1919).

12. Quoted by Köhnke, *Der junge Simmel*, p. 115. The author thinks that Dilthey opposed Simmel's accreditation because of anti-Semitism, p. 115. This opinion is similar to the more nuanced judgment of the sociologist Albert Salomon, who was Simmel's student: Salomon thought that "although Dilthey was an implacable anti-Semite, he supported Simmel," "Georg Simmel Reconsidered," in Gary Jaworski, *Georg Simmel and the American Prospect* (Albany: State University of New York Press), p. 94.

13. Quoted by Landmann, "Bausteine zur Biographie," pp. 26–27. On this setback at Heidelberg and on Schäfer's intervention, see the very detailed commentary by Hans Liebesschütz, *Von Georg Simmel zu Franz Rosenzweig. Studien zum jüdischen Denken im deutschen Kulturbereich* (Tübingen: J. C. B. Mohr, 1970), pp. 106–12. Rudolph Weingartner quotes this letter from Schäfer as proof of the anti-Semitism experienced by Simmel, *Experience and Culture: The Philosophy of Georg Simmel* (Middletown, MA: Wesleyan Press, 1962), p. 6. Ralph Leck refutes this interpretation and downplays considerably the influence of anti-Semitism in Simmel's difficult career. In his opinion, it was more his modernist side hostile to the bourgeoisie and favorable to women, "his Archie Shepp side," that hindered his career, *Georg Simmel and Avant-Garde Sociology: The Birth of Modernity, 1880–1920* (Amherst, MA: Humanity Books, 2000), pp. 37–38 and 82–83.

14. Quoted by François Léger, *La pensée de Georg Simmel* (Kimé, 1989), p. 14.

15. On anti-Semitism in Germany at that time, see Werner Jochman, "Structure and Functions of German Anti-Semitism 1879–1914," in Herbert Strauss, ed., *Hostages of Modernization: Studies on Modern Anti-Semitism 1870–1933* (Berlin: Walter de Gruyter, 1993), vol. 3.

16. Quoted by Kurt Wolff in his introduction to *The Sociology of Georg Simmel*, Kurt Wolff, trans. and ed. (Glencoe, IL: Free Press, 1950), p. xlii.

17. Ibid., pp. 117–20 and 130.

18. Nicholas Spykman, *The Sociology of Georg Simmel* (New York: Atherton Press, 1966), p. xxviii.

19. Quoted in Gassen and Landmann, eds., *Buch des Dankes an Georg Simmel*, p. 186.

20. René König, "Die Soziologie," in Leonhard Reinisch, ed., *Die Juden und die Kultur* (Stuttgart: W. Kohlhammer Verlag, 1961), p. 62.

21. David Frisby, *Sociological Impressionism: A Reassessment of Georg Simmel's Social Theory* (London: Heinemann, 1981), p. 137. This book is probably the most complete presentation of the whole of Simmel's oeuvre. See also, by the same author, *Fragments of Modernity: Theories of Modernity in the Work of Simmel, Kracauer and Benjamin* (Cambridge, MA: MIT Press, 1986).

22. "Georg Simmel Reconsidered by Albert Salomon," in Jaworski, *Georg Simmel and the American Prospect*, p. 99. By contrast, Kurt Hiller, another of his Jewish students who founded literary expressionism, thought that Simmel was "one of the most important Jews of our century," quoted by Leck, *Georg Simmel and Avant-Garde Sociology*, p. 214.

23. According to Laurence's analysis, "Georg Simmel: Triumph and Tragedy," p. 40.

24. Simmel mentions this "tremendous rabbi" who "said to his students: When the Lord asks me in the next world: Meir, why haven't you become Moses? I will say: Lord, because I am only Meir. And when he asks me again: Meir, why haven't you become Ben Akiba? I will also say: Lord, precisely because I am Meir. But when he asks me: Meir, why haven't you become Meir? What will I say then?" G. Simmel, *La religion* (Circé, 1998), p. 82. On the nature of religion according to Simmel, see Patrick Watier, "Simmel, religion et sociologie," postscript to Simmel, *La religion*.

25. According to the remark by Liebesschütz, *Von Georg Simmel zu Franz Rosenzweig*, p. 103.

26. Quoted by Köhnke, *Der junge Simmel*, p. 26.

27. Liebesschütz, *Von Georg Simmel zu Franz Rosenzweig*, p. 122.

28. See the letter from Martin Buber to Gerhard Sholem dated November 24, 1935, published by Dominique Bourel in *Identité et cultures, Lettre d'information du Centre de recherche français de Jérusalem* no. 13 (October 1996): 33. Buber wants this chair to be called *tira ha hevra*, or "general sociology," and he intends to study "social forms," the "reciprocal relationships between people, forms, and social orders." It is easy to see why the *Encyclopedia Judaica* regards Buber as a student of Simmel: "Stimulated by Simmel, Buber described Jewish existence in is eminently relational manifestations and not in its substance. In this way the Simmelian approach to sociology has become a fundamental element of the sociology of the Jews," *Encyclopedia Judaica*, vol. 14, p. 1576. In his monumental biography of Buber, Maurice Friedman mentions several times the relationships between Simmel and Buber: Maurice Friedman, *Martin Buber's Life and Work* (New York: Dutton, 1983), vol. 1, pp. 23 and 134–35ff.

29. This anecdote is quoted by Gassen and Landmann, eds., *Buch des Dankes*

*an Georg Simmel*, pp. 222–23, by Liebesschütz, *Von Georg Simmel zu Franz Rosenzweig*, p. 122, and by Laurence, "Georg Simmel: Triumph and Tragedy," pp. 40–41. On the ephemeral relationships of Simmel and Buber, see Grete Schaeder, *Martin Buber, Hebräischer Humanismus* (1966). Several times, in his correspondence with Marianne Weber, Simmel mentions "old Jewish proverbs," quoted in Gassen and Landmann, eds., *Buch des Dankes an Georg Simmel*, p. 134.

30. Gassen and Landmann, eds., *Buch des Dankes an Georg Simmel*, "Ernst Bloch über Simmel," p. 250; Böhringer and Gründer, eds., *Ästhetik und Soziologie um die Jahrhundertwende: Georg Simmel*, p. 270.

31. Quoted by Liebesschütz, *Von Georg Simmel zu Franz Rosenzweig*, pp. 141–44.

32. Köhnke, *Der junge Simmel*, p. 144.

33. Michael Landmann, "Ernst Bloch über Simmel," in Böhringer and Gründer, eds., *Ästhetik und Soziologie um die Jahrhundertwende: Georg Simmel*, p. 270. In the same paragraph, Bloch thinks nonetheless that "Simmel's work contains no Jewish theme." For Ralph Leck, if Ernst Bloch and Franz Rosenzweig, who both frequented the Simmelian circle, could be considered Jewish thinkers who integrated the contributions of Simmel's work into their own work, Simmel on the contrary could not at all be considered a Jewish thinker, *Georg Simmel and Avant-Garde Sociology*, p. 273.

34. Landmann, "Ernst Bloch über Simmel," p. 271.

35. Quoted by Anson Rabinbach, *In the Shadow of Catastrophe: German Intellectuals Between Apocalypse and Enlightenment* (Berkeley: University of California Press, 1997), p. 51.

36. Letter from Simmel to Marianne Weber on August 14, 1914, quoted in Gassen and Landmann, eds., *Buch des Dankes an Georg Simmel*, p. 134.

37. On the contrary, according to Richard Kroner who for a long time gave courses at home to Simmel's son, Georg Simmel "belonged to that level of Jews and half-Jews who represented in the first place the German spirit, were politically liberals or even socialists, and combined an internationalist tendency with a resolute patriotism. He did not share the so common Jewish anti-Semitism, and even less the self-mockery of the Jews," quoted in Gassen and Landmann, eds., *Buch des Dankes an Georg Simmel*, p. 229.

38. The phrase is Lewis Coser's, "The Stranger in the Academy," in Lewis Coser, ed., *Georg Simmel* (New Jersey: Prentice Hall, 1965).

39. Donald Levine devoted some lines to this comparison in his introduction to *Georg Simmel: On Individuality and Social Forms* (Chicago: University of Chicago Press, 1971), p. 10. He also emphasizes the profound influence exercised by Simmel on Max Weber, Leopold von Wiese and many other German sociologists or philosophers of his time, pp. 45ff.

40. Georg Simmel, *The Sociology of Georg Simmel*, Kurt Wolff, trans. and ed. (Glencoe, IL: Free Press, 1950), p. 403.

41. Georg Simmel, *The Philosophy of Money*, Tom Bottomore and David Frisby, trans. (Boston: Routledge and Kegan Paul, 1978), pp. 223–25. .

42. Ibid., p. 245.

43. Ibid., pp. 281–82.

44. Several times Simmel returns in this book to the example of the Jews. In his systematic study of this work, Gianfranco Poggi remains curiously silent about this important aspect, Gianfranco Poggi, *Money and the Modern Mind: Georg Simmel's Philosophy of Money* (Berkeley: University of California Press, 1993).

45. Simmel, *The Philosophy of Money.*

46. Otthein Rammstedt, "L'étranger de Georg Simmel," *Revue des sciences sociales de la France de l'Est* (1994): 151. On the contrary, Freddy Raphael closely links the foreigner to the Jew in Simmel's work, "'L'étranger' de Georg Simmel," in Patrick Watier, ed., *Georg Simmel. La sociologie et l'expérience du monde moderne* (Méridiens Klincksieck, 1986). Faithful in a certain way to Simmel, he writes, "The Jew as stranger participates in distinct symbolic spheres and due to that very fact calls into question any claim of one of them to the absolute. The Hebrew, the 'Ivri,' etymologically signifies the 'one who crosses over.' The Jew is loyal to his calling when he forces cultures to renounce their attempt at establishing a universal model and, surpassing their isolation and their self-satisfaction, to enrich themselves with difference. . . He betrays his calling when he closes himself up in the narrow framework of the nation-state, and makes it a finality: worshiping the land is idolatry," p. 273.

47. Rammstedt, "L'étranger de Georg Simmel," p. 152.

48. Simmel, *The Sociology of Georg Simmel*, pp. 402–3. Translation slightly modified.

49. René König emphasizes this definition of the stranger as Jew in Simmel's thought: "Die Soziologies," in L. Reinisch, ed., *Die Juden und die Kultur*, pp. 74–75. Note that Simmel's essential phrase, "The classic example is provided by the history of the European Jews," does not figure in the translation of these pages on the stranger in *L'École de Chicago. Naissance de l'écologie urbaine*, intro. by Y. Grafmeyer and I. Joseph (Paris: Aubier, 1984), p. 55.

50. On the stranger as social form, see P. A. Lawrence, *Georg Simmel: Sociologist and European* (New York: Harper and Row, 1976), pp. 19 and 28.

51. Georg Simmel, *Sociologie* (Paris:PUF) pp. 666–67.

52. Paul Mendes-Flohr, *Divided Passions: Jewish Intellectuals and the Experience of Modernity* (Detroit, MI: Wayne State University Press, 1991), pp. 31–32.

53. Michael Walzer criticizes the position of detachment of the stranger in Simmel, *Interpretation and Social Criticism* (Cambridge, MA: Harvard University Press, 1987), p. 37. See Chapter 7.

54. Simmel, *The Sociology of Georg Simmel*, pp. 407–8.

55. Ibid., p. 404.

56. Ibid., p. 403.

57. Rammstedt, "L'étranger de Georg Simmel," pp. 148–49.

58. Simmel, *The Sociology of Georg Simmel*, p. 402.

59. Siegfried Kracauer, *Jacques Offenbach ou le secret du Second Empire* (Paris: Gallimard, "Le Promeneur," 1994). Walter Benjamin, *Paris, capitale du XIXe*

*siècle: Le livre des passages* (Paris: Le Cerf, 1989). See Olivier Agard, "Contributions juives à l'ethnographie urbaine: Simmel, Kracauer et l'École de Chicago," *Revue germanique internationale* I (2002). In his opinion, "Simmel, Kracauer or Wirth belong to those intellectuals who see in urban 'disorganization' an opening up towards a new culture, for which the Jews constitute an avantgarde, in a way . . . It is with good reason that one can say that 'the stranger' tends for Simmel to become a pure transition, he is not a content, but a position," pp. 140 and 143.

60. Simmel, "Comment les formes sociales se maintiennent," p. 196.

61. Ibid., p. 176.

62. Simmel, *Sociologie*, pp. 585–86.

63. Ibid., pp. 520–21.

64. Ibid., pp. 623–24.

65. Ibid., pp. 154 and 158.

66. Ibid., pp. 168–69. See also pp. 234 and 242.

67. Ibid., pp. 636 and 643.

68. Ibid., p. 644. See also p. 473 where he distinguishes the Hebraic God from polytheism.

69. Donald Levine, Ellwood Carter, and Eleanor Miller Gorman, "Simmel's Influence on American Sociology," *American Journal of Sociology* 81, no. 4 (1976): 813.

70. Alfred Schütz is examining the example of the Iraqi Jews who immigrated to Israel. Alfred Schütz, *On Phenomenology and Social Relations* (The Hague: Martinus Nijhoff, 1964), pp. 99–100 and 104–5.

71. Alfred Schütz, "The Stranger," in *Collected Papers: Studies in Social Theory* (The Hague: Martinus Nijhoff, 1971), pp. 91–105.

72. Ibid., p. 104.

73. See, for example, Schütz, *On Phenomenology and Social Relations*, pp. 84, 309–10ff.

74. Schütz, "The Homecomer," *Collected Papers*, pp. 106–9.

75. See the introduction to this lecture by Gary Jaworski, in Jaworski, *Georg Simmel and the American Prospect*, pp. 91–92.

76. *Universal Jewish Encyclopedia*, vol. 9 (1943), pp. 542–43. On this lecture at the Leo Baeck Institute, see *L.B.I. News* (summer 1963).

77. Salomon, "Georg Simmel Reconsidered," p. 102.

78. Ibid., pp. 103 and 105.

79. Ibid., p. 108.

80. Robert E. Park, "An Autobiographical Note," *Race and Culture* (Glencoe, IL: Free Press, 1950), p. vi.

81. Fred Matthews, *Robert Park and the Chicago School* (Montreal: McGill-Queen's University, 1977), p. 41.

82. Robert E. Park and Ernest W. Burgess, *Introduction to the Science of Sociology* (Chicago: University of Chicago Press, 1921), p. 1022.

83. Ibid., pp. 158, 277, 336, and 338.

84. This article is reprinted in Park, *Race and Culture*, pp. 354–55. See also Robert Park, "Behind Our Masks," *Survey Graphic* (May 1926).

85. Matthews, *Robert E. Park and the Chicago School*, p. 189.

86. See Jean-Michel Chapoulie, "Robert E. Park, la tradition de Chicago et l'étude des relations entre les races," *Sociétés contemporaines* nos. 33–34 (1999). I thank Jean-Michel Chapoulie for sharing with me his remarkable knowledge of the Chicago School, over the course of several interviews.

87. See the article by Park "Reflections on Communication and Culture," in *Race and Culture*, pp. 49ff. See also p. 189.

88. See, by Park, "The Career of the Africans in Brazil," originally published in 1942, in *Race and Culture*, pp. 196–203.

89. See, by Park, "Mentality of Racial Hybrids," originally published in 1929, in *Race and Culture*, pp. 377–92.

90. See, by Park, "Education in Its Relation to the Conflict and Fusion of Cultures," in *Race and Culture*, pp. 261–83.

91. See, by Park, "Immigrant Community and Immigrant Press," an article written in 1925, in *Society* (Glencoe, IL: Free Press, 1955), pp. 155 and 159.

92. See, by Park, "Foreign Language Press," dated 1923, in *Society*, pp. 169ff.

93. Robert Park and Herbert Miller, *Old World Traits Transplanted* (New York: Harper and Brothers, 1921), p. 237. This work was compiled in large part by W. I. Thomas.

94. Robert Park, review of the book by Isacque Graeber and Steuart Henderson Britt, eds., *Jews in a Gentile World: The Problem of Anti-Semitism* (New York: Macmillan, 1942); *American Sociological Review* (December 1944): 710–11. This collective book includes articles by Carl Friedrich, Talcott Parsons, Everett Stonequist, and others.

95. Commentators on Park's work insist too much on the complete metamorphosis Park supposedly imposed on Simmel's figure of the stranger. For many of them, Park is responsible for a transformation of this notion that alters its significance; it was Park who replaced "the stranger" with "the marginal man," the ethnic immigrant in need of adaptation, the *newcomer*, encouraging the majority of contemporary sociological researchers to follow him in this error. That is the interpretation of S. Dale McLemore, "Simmel's Stranger: A Critique of the Concept," article published in the *Pacific Sociological Review* and reprinted in Ray, *Formal Sociology*, pp. 265ff.; and also of Donald Levine in his article "Simmel at a Distance: On the History and Systematics of the Sociology of the Stranger," published first in *Sociological Focus* (January 1977); reprinted in Ray, *Formal Sociology*, who denounces "despite the attempt at clarification made by Stonequist, the tendency continually to confuse the marginal man with Simmel's stranger," p. 275. Donald Levine expresses the same idea in his introduction to *Georg Simmel: On Individuality and Social Forms*, pp. 49ff. The same idea is also expressed by Sando Segre, "A Simmelian Theory of Marginality, Deviance and Social Control," in

Felicitas Dörr-Backes and Ludwig Nieder, eds., *Georg Simmel Between Modernity and Postmodernity* (Munich: Königshausen and Neumann, 1995), pp. 157ff.

96. The most classical analysis of this process can be found in the book by Stanford Lyman, *The Black American in Sociological Thought* (New York: Putman, 1972).

97. Park and Miller, *Old World Traits Transplanted*, pp. 306–8.

98. Park and Burgess, *Introduction to the Science of Sociology*, p. 735.

99. See, for example, Edward Franklin Frazier, *The Negro Family in Chicago* (Chicago: Chicago University Press, 1932); or Edward Franklin Frazier, *The Black Bourgeoisie* (Glencoe, IL: Free Press, 1957).

100. See Winifred Raushenbush, *Robert Park: Biography of a Sociologist*, p. 191.

101. Louis Wirth, review of the book by Stanley Bray, *Jewish Family Solidarity: Rights or Facts?*, *Jewish Social Studies* (January 1943).

102. See Chapter 8.

103. See his testimony about his relationship with Wirth, in Edward Shils, *Portraits of a Gallery of Intellectuals*, pp. 39ff.

104. See the introduction by Albert J. Reiss Jr. to Wirth, *On Cities and Social Life*, pp. xxix and xxx. See also, in conclusion to this same book, the article by Elizabeth Wirth Marvick, "Louis Wirth: A Biographical Memorandum." One can find much autobiographical information given by Wirth and published in Howard Odum, *American Sociology: The Story of Sociology in the United States Through 1950* (New York: Longmans, Green and Co., 1951), pp. 227–33. See also Roger Salerno, *Louis Wirth: A Bio-Bibliography* (New York: Greenwood Press, 1987).

105. On Wirth's role in the Chicago School, see Jean-Michel Chapoulie, *La tradition sociologique de Chicago. 1892–1961* (Paris: Le Seuil, 2001).

106. Robert Park, Ernest Burgess, and Roderick McKenzie, *The City* (Chicago: University Press of Chicago, 1967), p. 219.

107. Louis Wirth, "Le phénomène urbain comme mode de vie," in Y. Grafmeyer and I. Joseph, eds., *L'École de Chicago*, pp. 267 and 269.

108. Ibid., pp. 275–76.

109. Robert Park, Foreword to Louis Wirth, *The Ghetto* (Chicago: University of Chicago Press, 1956), p. ix.

110. Wirth, *Ghetto*, p. 78.

111. *Historia Judaica* 6 (1944): 86.

112. Wirth, *Ghetto*, pp. 4 and 6.

113. Ibid., p. 15.

114. Ibid., p. 106.

115. Ibid., p. 193.

116. Ibid., pp. 264 and 284. For a recent analysis of this work and its reception by urban sociology, see Catherine Rhein, "Le ghetto de Louis Wirth: Forme urbaine, institution et système sociale. *The Ghetto*, 1928," in Bernard Lepetit and Christian Topalov, eds., *La ville des sciences sociales* (Paris: Belin, 2001), pp. 130ff.

117. Ibid., p. 290.

118. *Encyclopedia Judaica*, vol. 16, p. 553.

119. Seymour Martin Lipset, "The Study of Jewish Communities in a Comparative Context," *The Jewish Journal of Sociology* (December 1963): 163.

120. Marshall Sklare, "The Jew in American Sociological Thought," *Ethnicity* 1 (1974): 164. More recently, Nathan Glazer writes, "Louis Wirth, Park's successor, showed in his book on American Jews, *The Ghetto*, that he was in favor of assimilation," Nathan Glazer, *We Are All Multiculturalists Now* (Cambridge, MA: Harvard University Press, 1997), p. 116.

121. Wirth, *Ghetto*, p. 290.

122. Wirth, "The Ghetto," in *On Cities and Social Life*, pp. 97–98.

123. See Agard, "Contributions juives à l'ethnographie urbaine," pp. 133ff.

124. See the curious article by Julian Greifer, "Attitudes to the Stranger: A Study of the Attitudes of Primitive Society and Early Hebrew Culture," *American Sociological Review* (December 1945). The author is also inspired by Simmel and Park, and by Stonequist in his analysis of the way the Jews behave toward strangers, using Salo Baron's work as reference.

125. Wirth, "Some Jewish Types of Personality," in *On Cities and Social Life*, pp. 100ff.

126. Wirth, "Education for Survival: The Jews," p. 691.

127. Wirth, "The Problem of Minority Groups," in *On Cities and Social Life*, pp. 257–69.

128. Robert Park, Introduction to Everett Stonequist, *The Marginal Man* (New York: Russell and Russell, 1961), pp. xvii–xviii.

129. Stonequist, *Marginal Man*, p. 4.

130. Ibid., pp. 2–3.

131. Ibid., pp. 80–81.

132. Ibid., p. 82.

133. Ibid., pp. 102 and 119. On anti-Semitism in the United States, see p. 129.

134. Ibid., p. 133. See also pp. 140ff., 150–52. Stonequist refers to Wirth, *Marginal Man*, pp. 204, 213ff.

135. Ibid., pp. 177–78.

136. Here we are not following the interpretation of Donald Levine, Ellwood Carter, and Eleanor Miller Gorman, who think that Park's marginal man aspires to be assimilated while Simmel's stranger wanted to preserve his personality, and, in the same sense, we think that Stonequist is finally continuing this aforementioned interpretation of the marginal man although he begins by distinguishing it from the stranger. Levine, Carter, and Gorman, "Simmel's Influence on American Sociology," I, pp. 830ff.

137. Peter Rose, "Strangers in Their Midst: Small-Town Jews and Their Neighbors," cited in Peter Rose, ed., *The Study of Society* (New York: Random House, 1967).

138. Horace Kallen, *Culture and Democracy in the United States* (New York:

Transaction Publishers, 1998). See Chapter 7.

139. See David Biale, Michael Galchinsky, and Susannah Heschel, eds., *Insider/Outsider: American Jews and Multiculturalism* (Berkeley: University of California Press, 1998). See Chapter 7 below.

140. See Philip Maning, *Erving Goffman and Modern Sociology* (London: Polity Press, 1992), pp. 18ff. Other commentators think on the contrary that Goffman is more influenced by the structural perspective of Durkheim, who emphasized the control of the distribution of roles and functions. In this sense, see Randall Collins, "Theoretical Continuities in Goffman's Work," in Paul Drew and Anthony Wooton, *Erving Goffman: Exploring the Interaction Order* (Cambridge: Polity Press, 1988), p. 43. Charles Lemert, "Goffman," in Charles Lemert and Ann Branaman, *The Goffman Reader* (London: Blackwell Publishing, 1997), p. xxxix.

141. See Lewis Coser, "Georg Simmel's Style of Work: A Contribution to the Sociology of the Sociologist."

142. Lewis Coser, *Masters of Sociological Thought* (New York: Harcourt, Brace Jovanovich, 1971), pp. 177ff. See also Lewis Coser, ed., *Georg Simmel* (Englewood Cliffs, NJ: Prentice Hall, 1965). See also Lewis Coser, *The Functions of Social Conflict* (London: Routledge and Keegan Paul, 1998), which is presented as an application of Simmel's work on the question of conflict.

143. Lewis Coser, "The Alien as a Servant of Power: Court Jews and Christian Renegades," *American Sociological Review* (October 1972).

144. This description of the key universities most open in the United States to the influence of Simmel is inspired by the article by Levine, Carter, and Gorman, "Simmel's Influence on American Sociology," 1, pp. 817–21. Donald Levine himself defended a doctoral thesis at the University of Chicago in 1957 entitled "Simmel and Parsons: Two Approaches to the Study of Society."

145. Isaac Joseph, *Le passant considérable* (Paris: Librairie des Méridiens, 1984), pp. 96ff.

146. Quoted by Chapoulie, *La tradition sociologique de Chicago*, p. 286.

147. Personal interview with Howard S. Becker, Paris, April 10, 2001.

148. See the introduction by Yves Winkin to Erving Goffman, *Les moments et leurs hommes* (Paris: Seuil-Minuit, 1988), pp. 16–17.

149. See Dell Hymes, "On Erving Goffman," *Theory and Society* no. 5 (September 1984): 628.

150. See, for example, Paul Creelan, "Vicissitudes of the Sacred: Erving Goffman and the Book of Job," *Theory and Society* (September 1984).

151. Erving Goffman, *Asylums: Essays on the Social Situation of Mental Patients and Other Inmates* (Chicago: Aldine, 1961).

152. Erving Goffman, *Stigma: Notes on the Management of Spoiled Identity* (Englewood Cliffs, NJ: Prentice Hall, 1963), pp. 100 and 113.

153. Personal interview with Howard Becker.

154. See the introduction by Yves Winkin to Goffman, *Les moments et leurs*

*hommes*, pp. 13, 29, and 68–69. Here the reference is to the book by John Murray Cuddihy, *The Ordeal of Civility: Freud, Marx, Lévi-Strauss and the Jewish Struggle with Modernity* (Boston: Beacon Press, 1974), in the introduction. For Tom Burns, on the contrary, "Goffman thought, or at least said, that being Jewish, being a Russian Jew, explained much of his personality, but I doubt that," Tom Burns, *Erving Goffman* (London: Routledge, 1992), p. 9.

155. Erving Goffman, *Communication Conduct in an Island Community*, p. 103. Quoted by Winkin, Introduction to Erving Goffman, *Les moments et leurs hommes*, p. 72.

156. It seems that, in the context of the Chicago School, only little-known sociologists who did not make a career of their profession chose research subjects relating to Jewish society. That is the case for Eric Rosenthal, who undertook a demographic study of American Jews, of Ervin Rinder who, in his dissertation, wondered, to the surprise of Everett Hughes, why Jews aren't alcoholic, and of Jerome Carlin and Saul Mendelavitz, who wrote a master's thesis on the rabbis of Chicago before they both became lawyers. I thank Howard Becker for this information.

*Chapter Four. Raymond Aron:*
*An "Authentic French Jew" in Search of His Roots*

1. Jean-Paul Sartre, *Réflexions sur la question juive* (Paris: Gallimard), "Folio," p. 103. In English: *Anti-Semite and Jew*, George J. Becker, trans. (New York: Schocken Books, 1948), p. 85. For a recent, systematic, and often unforgiving analysis of *Réflexions*, see "Jean-Paul Sartre's *Anti-Semite and Jew*: A Special Issue," *October* (winter 1999).

2. Sartre, *Anti-Semite and Jew*, pp. 63–64.

3. Ibid., p. 102.

4. Ibid., p. 61.

5. Ibid., p. 138. Remember that, in Sartre's story "The Childhood of a Leader," Lucien also boasts about recognizing Jews by their noses.

6. Ibid.

7. Aline Benain, "L'itinéraire juif de Raymond Aron: hasard, déchirement et dialectique," *Pardes* 11 (1990): 164.

8. Ely Ben-Gal, *Mardi, chez Sartre. Un Hébreu à Paris (1967–1980)* (Paris: Flammarion, 1992), p. 244.

9. There is no allusion to this use of the image of Raymond Aron in the works by Annie Cohen-Solal, *Sartre* (Paris: Gallimard, 1985), who devoted only a few lines to *Anti-Semite and Jew*, or in Michael Scriven, *Jean-Paul Sartre: Politics and Culture in Postwar France* (London: Mamillan, 1999); or in John Gerassi, *Jean-Paul Sartre: Hated Conscience of his Century* (Chicago: University Press of Chicago, 1989); or in Andrew Dobson, *Jean-Paul Sartre and the Politics of Reason* (Cambridge: Cambridge University Press, 1993); or in Jeannette Colombel, *Jean-Paul*

*Sartre. Un homme en situation* (Paris: Livre de poche, 2000). Stuart Zane Charné devoted a chapter of his book on Sartre to *Anti-Semite and Jew* but does not discuss the role Raymond Aron involuntarily played in it, *Vulgarity and Authenticity: Dimensions of Otherness in the World of Jean-Paul Sartre* (Amherst: University of Massachusetts Press, 1991), ch. 4. A few lines on this subject can be found in Michel-Antoine Burnier, *L'adieu à Sartre* (Paris: Plon, 2000), p. 123.

10. Daniel Mahoney, *The Liberal Political Science of Raymond Aron* (Boston: Rowman and Littlefield, 1992). Nicolas Baverez, *Raymond Aron. Un moraliste au temps des idéologies* (Paris: Flammarion, 1993), see p. 382, however. Stephen Launay, *La pensée politique de Raymond Aron* (Paris: PUF, 1995). Brian Anderson, *Raymond Aron: The Recovery of the Political* (Boston: Rowman and Littlefield, 1997). *Raymond Aron. La philosophie de l'histoire et les sciences sociales*, Jean-Claude Chamboredon, ed. (Paris: Édition de la Rue de l'Ulm, 1999). In his study on the thinking of Raymond Aron, Father Gaston Fessard devotes long passages to its Jewish dimension, but only mentions in two lines, in a footnote, the fact that Sartre was inspired in his *Anti-Semite and Jew* by Raymond Aron in his construction of the authentic Jewish character, *La philosophie historique de Raymond Aron* (Paris: Julliard, 1980), p. 217, n. 2. In her dissertation, Ariane Chabel d'Appollonia does not mention this point either, even though she devoted some very solid and convincing pages to the question of Raymond Aron's Jewish identity, "Morale et politique chez Raymond Aron" (PhD diss. in political science Institut d'Études Politiques, 1993), vol. 1, pp. 230ff.; vol. 2, pp. 430ff. Nicolas Baverez devoted two pages of his biography to this point, writing, "It would be inexact to speak of a rediscovery by Aron of his Jewishness, since he never hid it, and since he asserted it in the 1930's, when it was most dangerous to do so. It is better to suggest the transition from a social conception, external to Judaism—somewhat close to Sartre's concepts in his *Anti-Semite and Jew*—to a more personal and internal feeling, to a more emotional solidarity with Israel and the Jews," *Raymond Aron* (Paris: Flammarion, 1993), pp. 381–82.

11. Étienne Barilier, *Les petits camarades. Essai sur Jean-Paul Sartre et Raymond Aron* (Paris: Julliard, 1987). One single allusion to this point can be found in this work, p. 15. But there isn't a word about it in Étienne Borne, "R. Aron et J.-P. Sartre, les deux camarades," *France Forum* (October 1987). Jean-François Sirinelli does not discuss this point either, even though he emphasizes the strong contrast between Aron, who immediately became involved in armed resistance during Vichy, and Sartre, who calmly pursued his career, even benefiting from successive promotions, while so many of his colleagues, both Jews and non-Jews, were excluded from teaching, *Deux intellectuels dans le siècle. Sartre et Aron* (Paris: Fayard, 1995), pp. 161ff.

12. Aron, *Memoirs*, translated by George Holoch (New York: Holmes and Meier, 1990), p. 48.

13. Sartre, *Anti-Semite and Jew*, p. 62.

14. Baverez, *Raymond Aron*, ch. 1.

15. Raymond Aron, interview published in *L'Arche* (September 1983). Published in *Essais sur la condition juive contemporaine*, texts gathered and annotated by Perrine Simon-Nahum (Paris: Éditions de Fallois, 1989) p. 269.

16. Aron, *Memoirs*, p. 6. For Annie Kriegel, "Everything in the way he led his life shows that, although he had become secularized and translated the traditional values taught and transmitted from age to age in Jewish communities into secular terms, these secularized values constituted the fabric on which he had to base his daily commitments," "Le dernier sage," *L'Arche* (December 1983), p. 126.

17. Raymond Aron, interview published in *L'Arche*, p. 274.

18. Ibid., p. 276.

19. Aron, *Memoirs*, pp. 12–13. See Jacques Hepp, "Souvenirs des années vingt," in *Raymond Aron. 1905–1983: Histoire et politique*, p. 10; and Baverez, *Raymond Aron*, ch. 1. See also Pierre Birnbaum, *Jewish Destinies*, Arthur Goldhammer, trans. (New York: Hill and Wang, 2000), ch. 4; as well as Jürg Altwegg, *Die langen Schatten von Vichy* (Munich: Hanser Verlag, 1998), ch. 11.

20. This lecture is published in Aron, *Essais sur la condition juive contemporaine*, pp. 26–29.

21. Raymond Aron, "Israël et les Juifs de France," in *Dispersion et unité* (Jerusalem, 1972), p. 165.

22. Aron, *Essais sur la condition juive contemporaine*, p. 179.

23. Raymond Aron, *Histoire et dialectique de la violence* (Paris: Gallimard, 1973), pp. 123–24.

24. Raymond Aron, *Le spectateur engagé* (Julliard, 1981), p. 104. Thus we cannot agree with Jean-Louis Missika when he writes, "Constantly, Aron will emphasize that, fundamentally, he is Jewish through the gaze of the other"; this minimizes Aron's endlessly proclaimed wish to maintain his Jewish identity and his attachments, however complex they may be with the Jewish "community," his inclusion among "us Jews," to which we will return later. "Juif par le regard de l'autre?" "Raymond Aron, Histoire et politique," *Commentaire* (February 1986): 189.

25. Sartre, *Anti-Semite and Jew*, pp. 90, 93, 107, and 137.

26. Harold Rosenberg, *Discovering the Present: Three Decades in Art, Culture and Politics* (Chicago: University of Chicago Press, 1973), pp. 281–83.

27. Aron, "Conférence prononcée au Bnai Brith de France," in *Essais sur la condition juive contemporaine*, p. 30.

28. Ibid.

29. Ibid., pp. 30–31.

30. Chabel d'Appollonia, "Morale et politique chez Raymond Aron," vol. 2, p. 431.

31. Ibid.

32. Aron, "De Gaulle, Israël et les Juifs," in *Essais sur la condition juive contemporaine*, p. 144.

33. Aron, *Memoirs*, p. 456. See also p. 465. Translation modified.

34. Ibid., p. 474.

35. Ibid., p. 336.
36. Ibid., p. 340.
37. Ibid., p. 346.
38. Ibid., p. 459.
39. Ibid., p. 470.
40. Ibid., p. 446.

41. As Jean-Louis Missika writes on this subject, "Must one hate one's country to question its past, its lies, its silences? Does silence imply oblivion? Vichy might be, for post-war generations, an enigma that must be elucidated, or even—why not?—an account that must be settled, but this question concerns all the French, Jews and non-Jews, and has nothing to do with Israel. . . . The anger and anguish that young French Jews feel about the recent past of their country are legitimate," "Juif par le regard de l'autre?" "Raymond Aron. Histoire et politique," *Commentaire*: 192.

42. One might think that "in Berlin, Aron's politicization . . . contrasts with Sartre's apolitical stance and indifference," Marie-Christine Granjon, "L'Allemagne de Raymond Aron et de Jean-Paul Sartre," in Hans Bock, Reinhart Meyer, and Michel Trebitsch, eds., *Entre Locarno et Vichy. Les relations culturelles franco-allemandes dans les années 1930* (Paris: CNRS, 1993), vol. 2, p. 469.

43. Aron, *Le spectateur engagé*, p. 101. Pierre Manent writes, "The expression 'emotional precaution' is certainly correct, but it transcribes into the language of conventional psychology a difficulty that touches the very roots of identity and human belonging. Raymond Aron, French first and foremost, is expelled as a Jew from the French community by the French. The political situation forces him to think of himself now as a Jew first of all: he is now, whatever he wants and whatever he does, for as long as the anti-Jewish government of Vichy lasts, more Jewish than French. . . . That is why Aron shows too much humility when he speaks a little flatly of 'emotional precaution' and even more when he goes so far as to say that this inner disposition, consisting of thinking as little as possible of what the French were doing to the Jews, 'is not to his honor.' Certainly Aron did not lack a sense of honor—otherwise he would not have said that—but honor is not everything. The sense of honor is not enough especially to answer the question: Who am I? It did not lie within his power to put an end to this trembling of his identity, except by an arbitrary show of force that his honesty and sincerity excluded," "Cercle de généaologie juive: Raymond Aron," February 5, 2001, Archives Raymond Aron, pp. 9–10. See also *Memoirs*, p. 150.

44. Daniel Cordier, "René Avord à Londres," in *Raymond Aron 1905–1983: Histoire et politique*, p. 27.

45. See the texts by Raymond Aron on this war in R. Aron, *Les crises. Février 1965 à avril 1977* (Éditions de Fallois), pp. 1289ff.

46. Raymond Aron, "Après l'horreur," *L'Express*, September 24, 1982. See also "Israël après Beyrouth," *L'Express*, December 17, 1982, where he dreads the future cohabitation, after Israel's conquests, "of citizens and dark-skinned foreigners.

Can we believe in the success of the reconstitution of a city of this kind in the twentieth century?"

47. Mikaël Guedj, *Les intellectuels français et la guerre des Six Jours* (thesis in history of the twentieth century, Institut d'études politiques, 2001).

48. Aron, *Memoirs*, p. 335.

49. Aron, "De Gaulle, Israël et les Juifs," in *Essais sur la condition juive contemporaine*, pp. 45 and 51. Gaston Fessard devotes many pages to this text by Raymond Aron to emphasize his "solidarity" with the Jews, *La philosophie historique de Raymond Aron*, ch. 5.

50. Ibid., pp. 67 and 70–71.

51. Aron, "Les Juifs," p. 144.

52. Aron, "De Gaulle, Israël et les Juifs," in *Essais sur la condition juive contemporaine*, pp. 66 and 180.

53. Aron, "Israël et les Juifs de France," p. 166. Aline Benain examines this dimension to conclude, "In that sense, Aron is a Jewish intellectual. Not because Judaism had a rational influence on his thinking; it does not involve a particular torsion in the definition of the concept, but it motivates certain reactions, certain emotions, that the commentator on current events that Aron also is sometimes unable to master," "L'itinéraire juif de Raymond Aron," p. 175.

54. Raymond Aron Archives. This letter is reproduced in Aron, *Mémoires*, p. 520.

55. Raymond Aron Archives. In his *Mémoires*, Aron writes, "I did not keep the text of my reply." It can be found, however, in his private archives.

56. Raymond Aron Archives. Quoted also in Aron, *Mémoires*, p. 521.

57. Raymond Aron Archives.

58. Claude Lévi-Strauss, Didier Éribon, *De près et de loin* (Odile Jacob, 1990), pp. 13–14 and 216–17.

59. Claude Lévi-Strauss, "Ce que je suis," *Le Nouvel Observateur*, July 5, 1980.

60. Aron, "De Gaulle, Israël et les Juifs," in *Essais sur la condition juive contemporaine*, p. 101.

61. Raymond Aron, "Les relations entre Israël et la Diaspora" (speech given to the World Jewish Congress, January 28, 1980), in *Essais sur la condition juive contemporaine*, p. 249.

62. Aron, "Discours de Jérusalem," in *Essais sur la condition juive contemporaine*, pp. 185–90.

63. Aron, "De Gaulle, Israël et les Juifs," in *Essais sur la condition juive contemporaine*, pp. 104, 106, 164, and 179.

64. Aron, *Mémoires*, p. 80.

65. Aron, "Les relations entre Israël et la Diaspora," p. 66. See also Aron, *Le spectateur engagé*, p. 105.

66. Ibid., pp. 178 and 272.

67. Aron, "Discours de Jérusalem," p. 189.

68. Alain Pons, "Amitiés aroniennes," in *Raymond Aron. 1905–1983. Histoire et politique*, p. 71. In this sense, isn't it a little simplistic to think no more than that

"the idea of ethnic identity, of a particularist cause, of a Jewish lobby contradicted Aron's sense of the State, his Jacobinism"? Diana Pinto, "Letter from Paris: On Raymond Aron," *Partisan Review* no. 2 (1984): 202.

69. Ibid., pp. 106–7.

70. Aron, "Conférence prononcée au Bnai Brith de France," in *Essais sur la condition juive contemporaine*, p. 26.

71. *Le Quotidien de Paris*, October 10, 1981.

72. Aron, "Conférence prononcée au Bnai Brith de France," in *Essais sur la condition juive contemporaine*, pp. 26–33.

73. Aron, "Les Juifs," p. 157.

74. Aron, "Antisémitisme et terrorisme," in *Essais sur la condition juive contemporaine*, p. 297.

75. Aron, "De Gaulle, Israël et les Juifs," in *Essais sur la condition juive contemporaine*, pp. 69, 162, 172, 175, 177, 179, and 180.

76. Aron, "Exposé: Kippour 5734," text dated 1973. *Essais sur la condition juive contemporaine*, p. 193.

77. Aron, "Antisémitisme et terrorisme," *L'Express*, October 11, 1980, in *Essais sur la condition juive contemporaine*, p. 297.

78. It is difficult to subscribe to Aline Benain's observation according to which, from 1945 to 1966, "he is a 'Sartrean Jew,' that is a Jew on whom Judaism is imposed from without," "L'itinéraire juif de Raymond Aron: Hasard, déchirement et dialectique de l'appartenance," p. 168. For Aline Benain, "none of the mental categories of Judaism influenced in any way whatever his intellectual formation," *Raymond Aron, intellectuel juif?* (master's thesis in history, Université de Paris-IV, 1987), p. 23. I thank Élisabeth Dutartre for arranging access for me to the Raymond Aron Fund.

79. Aron, "De Gaulle, Israël et les Juifs," in *Essais sur la condition juive contemporaine*, p. 64.

80. Aron, *Le Figaro littéraire*, June 12, 1967, in *Essais sur la condition juive contemporaine*, p. 101.

81. Aron, "Les Juifs," *Réalités*, September 1960, in *Essais sur la condition juive contemporaine*, p. 144.

82. Aron, "Les Juifs et l'État d'Israël," *Le Figaro littéraire*, February 24, 1962, in *Essais sur la condition juive contemporaine*, p. 179.

83. Aron, "Discours de Jérusalem," 1972, in *Essais sur la condition juive contemporaine*, p. 188.

84. Interview with Raymond Aron, "Juifs, Israélites, Français," *L'Arche*, p. 70.

85. Aron, *Memoirs*, p. 340.

86. Aron, "Israël et les Juifs de France," in *Dispersion et unité*, p. 165.

87. Aron, *Memoirs*, p. 294.

88. Ibid., p. 351. He also writes, "I see no reason on any occasion or for any reason, to claim solidarity with the community. Which I do not do," *Le Matin*, September 12, 1980.

89. Aron, *Memoirs*, p. 442.

90. Ibid., p. 443.

91. Ibid., p. 76.

92. "I don't like to break with my roots," he said in 1962, "Universalité de l'idée de nation et contestation," *Essais sur la condition juive contemporaine*, p. 248. "I don't like to extirpate my roots," he declared almost twenty years later, *Le Matin*, September 12, 1980.

93. Ady Steg, "Raymond Aron," *Les Nouveaux Cahiers* (spring 1984).

94. Raymond Aron, "Une communauté multinationale est-elle possible?" *Commentaire* (winter 1991): 55–56.

95. Bertrand Badie and Pierre Birnbaum, *The Sociology of the State*, Arthur Goldhammer, trans. (Chicago: University of Chicago Press, 1983). Pierre Birnbaum, "Sur la citoyenneté," *L'Année sociologique* no. 1 (1996).

96. See Jean-Paul Chanet, *L'école républicaine et les petites patries* (Aubier, 1996).

97. Aron, "Une communauté multinationale est-elle possible?" p. 703.

98. Aron, "Universalité de l'idée de nation et contestation," published in "Aspects du sionisme, théorie utopie-histoire," in *Essais sur la condition juive contemporaine*, p. 243.

99. Aron, "Une communauté multinationale est-elle possible?" p. 704.

100. Ibid., p. 702.

101. For Edward Shils, Aron "showed he was aware of his Jewish origin but did not regard it as an element that could separate him from other Frenchmen," "Raymond Aron," *The American Scholar* (summer 1987): 168.

102. Aron, "Les Juifs," in *Essais sur la condition juive contemporaine*, p. 153.

103. Aron, "De Gaulle, Israël et les Juifs," in *Essais sur la condition juive contemporaine*, pp. 71–72.

104. Aron, *Le Figaro littéraire*, February 24, 1962, in *Essais sur la condition juive contemporaine*, p. 164.

105. Aron, "Universalité de l'idée de nation et constestation," in *Essais sur la condition juive contemporaine*, p. 249.

106. Aron, "Israël et les Juifs de France," in *Dispersion et unité*, pp. 167–68.

107. Aron, *Memoirs*, pp. 339–41, and 350.

108. Aron, *Mémoires*, p. 169.

109. See, for example, *Essais sur la condition juive contemporaine*, pp. 168–69. Similarly in his 1976 lecture entitled "Universality of the Idea of Nation and Questioning," he writes, "For reasons that might be emotional or rational, I do not like to break off from my roots; I am animated by the sense of continuity and tradition; to express it more symbolically, if I happened to see my grandparents and great-grandparents again, I would like to be able to present myself to them without blushing," *Essais sur la condition juive contemporaine*, p. 249. In "De Gaulle, Israël et les Juifs," Aron writes, "I claim the right to be French without betraying my ancestors," *Essais sur la condition juive contemporaine*, p. 162. Finally, in his interview with *L'Arche* of September 1983, he declares that he does not want to break

with Judaism, "perhaps out of loyalty to my roots or to my ancestors," "Entretien avec *L'Arche*," in *Essais sur la condition juive contemporaine*, p. 272.

110. Raymond Aron, *Figaro-Magazine*, March 17, 1962, *Essais sur la condition juive contemporaine*, p. 179. Gaston Fessard writes, "Will we dare to say that by claiming solidarity with Isaac and Jacob, Aron has acquired along with them a contemporaneity that wins him the same title. . . . Seemingly, the *historico-philosophus* who recognizes himself as being in solidarity with Isaac and Jacob deserves to be called a 'prophet,'" *La philosophie historique de Raymond Aron*, pp. 347 and 355.

111. Aron, *Le spectateur engagé*, pp. 313–14. Annie Kriegel sees in Aron "a type that is rather frequent in the Jewish community from Alsace: although, as a sociologist, Aron was not part of the sociological lineage of Durkheim, as an individual there were many features of his personality that evoked Durkheim's—a consciousness among those of the high-ranking secular university from before 1914. . . . He also honored in his way and till his last breath the Jewish world from which he came. When he wanted to pay homage for his success to his unhappy father, wasn't it, in effect, in the same personal and discreet way that was his, paying homage at the same time to the community of his ancestors?" "Le dernier sage," p. 126.

112. Aron, "Universalité et l'idée de nation et contestation," p. 248.

113. Aron, *Introduction à la philosophie de l'histoire*, p. 475. On this aspect, see Chabel d'Appollonia, "Morale et politique chez Raymond Aron," vol. 1, pp. 230ff.

114. Aron, *Le spectateur engagé*, pp. 243–44. Already in 1967, he used exactly the same comparison. In "De Gaulle, Israël et les Juifs," he writes, in fact, "I feel less remote from an anti-Semitic Frenchman than from a Jew from the Moroccan South who speaks no other language than Arabic and who barely emerges from what seems to me the Middle Ages or, rather, from the impenetrable obscurities of radically foreign cultures," *Essais sur la condition juive contemporaine*, p. 64.

115. Aron, "De Gaulle, Israël et les Juifs," in *Essais sur la condition juive contemporaine*, p. 50.

116. Aron, *Memoirs*, p. 336. Elsewhere, however, he writes in a much subtler way: "Georges Bernanos, faithful to the values of the Ancien Regime, never understood the link between the anti-Semitism of his master Drumont that he admired till the end of his life and that of Hitler, whom he execrated," *Les Désillusions du Progrès* (Paris: Calmann-Lévy), p. 86.

117. Aron, "Les Juifs," in *Essais sur la condition juive contemporaine*, pp. 159–60.

118. See Pierre Birnbaum, *"La France aux Français." Histoire des haines nationalistes*, ch. 5.

119. Raymond Aron, "La Révolution nationale en Allemagne," *Europe* (1933): 133.

120. Raymond Aron writes that "Col. de La Rocque was not a charismatic leader liable to become a Fascist boss." These days, one section of historiography doesn't hesitate, however, to qualify Col. de La Rocque that way. See Robert

Soucy, *French Fascism: The Second Wave, 1933–1939* (New Haven, CT: Yale University Press, 1995).

121. Raymond Aron, "Du gouvernement des notables au régime policier," in *Chroniques de guerre: la France libre, 1940–1945* (Paris: Gallimard, 1990), pp. 80 and 138.

122. Aron, *Le spectateur engagé*, p. 89.

123. Ibid., p. 100. As Ariane Chabel d'Appollonia comments, "Isn't it being a little hasty to say the popular support for Pétain found its profound sources in the traumas brought about by defeat? . . . Partiality from too much impartiality? Overcompensation? Patriotism that is so sincere that it becomes abstract and leads to seeing in everything only French excellence? All these elements no doubt come into play. . . . Does that mean that from 1940 to 1942 this legend was believable, and that collaboration could find a single argument to justify it? Raymond Aron's suggestions are scarcely convincing," "Morale et politique chez Raymond Aron," vol. 2, pp. 435–36, and 439.

124. Aron, "L'imprégnation fasciste," *L'Express*, February 4, 1983, in *Essais sur la condition juive contemporaine*, p. 306. Aron still confesses, "With the hindsight of half a century, I underestimated the spread of Fascist ideas less among the voters than in the leading classes," p. 308. Curiously, in his *Memoirs*, Aron writes, "Unlike Drieu la Rochelle and Bertrand de Jouvenel, I did not run the risk of being drawn by despair into absurd commitments. I was protected not so much by my Jewishness as by the men among whom I lived," p. 107.

125. Manent, "Cercle de généaologie juive: Raymond Aron," p. 16.

126. *L'Express*, February 7, 1981, in *Essais sur la condition juive contemporaine*, p. 302. In his lecture given in 1954 to B'nai B'rith in France, he also writes, "I'm sure you can recollect a short work by Marx called *On 'The Jewish Question,'* written in his youth, where Marx's conclusion is that the Jew is precisely a man of money," in *Essais sur la condition juive contemporaine*, pp. 28–29. Aron also alludes to this text, without speaking of its anti-Semitic dimension, in *Études politiques* (Paris: Gallimard, 1972), p. 245.

127. Raymond Aron, *Le Marxisme de Marx* (Paris: Éditions de Fallois, 2002).

128. *Le Monde*, March 29, 1967.

129. Raymond Aron, *Dimensions de la conscience historique* (Paris: Plon, 1961), pp. 192, 232, 247, and 248. In "Les Juifs et l'État d'Israël," he writes, "the fact that the Israelis invoke historical rights of anteriority does not deceive anyone. . . . How can one recognize a right to property dating back more than two thousand years?" p. 176. Aron also devotes a number of pages to Israel in his studies on international strategy, in, for example, "The Disillusions of Modernity," *Encounter* (November 1970).

130. See Raymond Aron, *Les dernières années du siècle* (Paris: Julliard, 1984), pp. 158ff. and 206ff.

131. Aron, "À propos de Clausewitz: des concepts aux passions," in *Raymond Aron, 1905–1983. Histoire et politique*, pp. 501 and 505. See also Raymond Aron, *Une*

*histoire du vingtième siècle* (Paris: Plon, 1996), p. 147, and the chapters "De Sarajevo à Hiroshima" and "Les religions séculaires."

132. Raymond Aron, "De la condition historique du sociologue," *Études sociologiques* (Paris: PUF, 1988), pp. 289 and 293. Commenting on this rapprochement, Ariane Chabel d'Appollonia writes, "How does the fact of being Jewish connect with . . . the interest taken in Max Weber? . . . There are references that leave one perplexed," "Morale et politique chez Raymond Aron," vol. 2, p. 432. See also Raymond Aron, "Les philosophies d'Alain et de Maurras," *Introduction à la philosophie politique* (Paris: Le Livre de poche, 1997), p. 29.

133. Aron, *Les désillusions du progrès*, p. 100.

134. Ibid., pp. 86–87.

135. Aron, *Histoire et dialectique de la violence*, p. 126.

136. Raymond Aron, *Trois essais sur l'âge industriel* (Paris: Plon, 1966), pp. 12 and 103. This article, originally entitled "Théorie du développement et philosophie évolutionniste," appeared first in B. Hoselitz and W. Moore, *Industrialisation et société* (Paris: Mouton, 1963).

137. "Discours de Raymond Aron lors de la réception du prix Tocqueville," *Tocqueville Review*. On the comparison between the career and work of Tocqueville and that of Raymond Aron, see Hélène Meresse, *Essai sur le libéralisme français pendant la guerre froide: Aron lecteur de Tocqueville* (master's theses in political science, Institut d'études politiques, Paris, September 1995).

138. Aron, *Histoire et dialectique de la violence*, p. 124. Aron also took part, in 1981, along with various heads of Jewish institutions, industrial institutions, and also the sociologist Seymore M. Lipset, in writing a report on the economic and social commission of the World Jewish Congress. Note that Edgar Bronfman, president of the World Jewish Congress, thanked the members of this commission "for the service they did to the Jewish people," *Issues Facing World Jewry* (Washington, DC: Hershel Shanks, 1981), p. 19.

139. Aron, *Mémoires*, p. 504.

140. To explain the reasons for which he accepted giving a lecture in Israel under the auspices of the Weizmann Institute, Aron first of all invokes his memory, since Weizmann "personifies the spiritual vocation of the Jewish State," and adds, "[I would not have given this lecture], if I myself did not belong to the Diaspora," Raymond Aron, "Evening address," in Anthony Michaelis and Hugh Harvet, eds., *Scientists in Search of Their Conscience* (Berlin: Springer-Verlag, 1973), p. 122. In the same vein, see Raymond Aron, "Réflexions actuelles sur la réalité israélienne," *Dispersion et unité* no. 16 (1976): 106–7. See also "Les relations entre Israël et la diaspora," in *Essais sur la condition juive contemporaine*, p. 255.

141. Béatrice Braude, "Raymond Aron: A Jew in Spite of Himself," *Midstream* (February 1987).

142. Steg, "Raymond Aron," pp. 55 and 57.

*Chapter Five. Hannah Arendt:*
*Hannah and Rahel, "Fugitives from Palestine"*

1. Hannah Arendt, *Rahel Varnhagen: The Life of a Jewess*, Liliane Weissberg, ed., Richard and Clara Winston, trans. (Baltimore, MD: Johns Hopkins University Press, 1997), p. 85.

2. Hannah Arendt and Martin Heidegger, *Lettres et autres documents. 1925–1975* (Paris: Gallimard, 2002), p. 78. See Elzbieta Ettinger, *Hannah Arendt et Martin Heidegger* (Paris: Le Seuil, 1995), p. 87.

3. Liliane Weissberg, "Hannah Arendt, Rahel Varnhagen and the Writing of (Auto)Biography," *Rahel Varnhagen: The Life of a Jewess*, pp. 6, 13, and 16. This is the first complete version of this text, and it is accompanied by remarkable editorial work. I will mainly use this American version of the text since the French translation, as we will see later on, confuses the meaning of certain essential concepts.

4. Letter from Hannah Arendt to Karl Jaspers, September 7, 1952, in *Hannah Arendt/Karl Jaspers Correspondence 1926–1969*, Lotte Kohler and Hans Saner, eds.; Robert and Rita Kimber, trans. (New York: Harcourt Brace Jovanovich, 1992), pp. 197, 200, and 201.

5. Letter from Hannah Arendt to Karl Jaspers, February 19, 1953, in *Hannah Arendt/Karl Jaspers Correspondence*, p. 207. See Steven Aschheim, *Culture and Catastrophe: German and Jewish Confrontations with National Socialism and Other Crises* (New York: New York University Press, 1996), ch. 6.

6. Arendt, *Rahel Varnhagen*, p. 81.

7. Hannah Arendt, "De l'Humanité dans de 'sombres temps.' Réflexions sur Lessing," in Hannah Arendt, *Vies politiques* (Paris: Gallimard, "Tel," 1974), pp. 22–28. On acosmia, see Gérard Bensoussan, "Hannah Arendt, Franz Rosenzweig et le judaïsme. Acosmie et extra-historicité," *Les Temps modernes* (October–December 1998).

8. Hannah Arendt, "The Eichman Controversy," in *The Jewish Writings*, Jerome Kohn and Ron H. Feldman, eds. (New York: Schoken Books, 2007), p. 466.

9. Letter from Karl Jaspers to Hannah Arendt, October 22, 1963, in Hannah Arendt and Karl Jaspers, *Correspondance. 1926–1969* (Paris: Payot, 1955), p. 700.

10. Hannah Arendt, "Seule demeure la langue maternelle," in Hannah Arendt, *La tradition cachée* 10/18 (1987): 229 and 247–48.

11. Arendt, *Rahel Varnhagen*, p. 85.

12. Quoted by James Bernauer, "The Faith of Hannah Arendt: *Amor Mundi* and its Critique. Assimilation of Religious Experience," in *Amor Mundi: Explorations in the Faith and Thought of Hannah Arendt* (Boston: Martinus Nijhoff Publishers, 1987), p. 15.

13. Quoted by Amos Elon, "A Fugitive from Egypt and Palestine," *The New York Review of Books*, February 18, 1999. Elon points out that even Liliane Weissberg does not quote this sentence that ends Rahel's "testament."

14. Richard Berstein, *Hannah Arendt and the Jewish Question* (London: Polity

Press, 1996). This is also the perspective taken by Martine Leibovici, *Hannah Arendt, une Juive* (Desclée de Brouwer, 1998).

15. Hannah Arendt, *The Human Condition* (Chicago: University of Chicago Press, 1998). Seyla Benhabib rightly emphasizes this point in *The Recalcitrant Modernism of Hannah Arendt* (London: Sage Publications, 1996), p. 29. This is also mentioned in Sheldon Wolin, "Hannah Arendt: Democracy and the Political," in Lewis Hinchman and Sandra Hinchman, eds., *Hannah Arendt: Critical Essays* (Albany: State University of New York Press, 1994).

16. Ernest Gellner, *Culture, Identity and Politics* (Cambridge: Cambridge University Press, 1987), pp. 81–84.

17. George Steiner, "Seeing the Master Clearly," *Times Literary Supplement*, January 18, 2002. Steiner in this text takes into account the book by Richard Wolin devoted to the Jewish students of Heidegger: Richard Wolin, *Heidegger's Children: Hannah Arendt, Karl Löwith, Hans Jonas and Herbert Marcuse* (Princeton, NJ: Princeton University Press, 2002).

18. Elisabeth Young-Bruehl, *Hannah Arendt: For Love of the World* (New Haven, CT: Yale University Press, 1982), p. 119.

19. Letter from Hannah Arendt to Karl Jaspers, January 29, 1946, in *Hannah Arendt/Karl Jaspers Correspondence*, p. 32.

20. Young-Bruehl, *Hannah Arendt*, p. 435.

21. Ibid., pp. 460 and 469.

22. Letter from Hannah Arendt to Karl Jaspers, March 26, 1966, in *Hannah Arendt/Karl Jaspers Correspondence*, p. 632. On the Jaspers/Arendt dialogue, see Anson Rabinbach, "German as Pariah, Jew as Pariah: Hannah Arendt and Karl Jaspers," in Steven Aschheim, ed., *Hannah Arendt in Jerusalem* (Berkeley: University of California Press, 2002).

23. Interview with Günter Gauss, "Seule demeure la langue maternelle," *La tradition cachée*, pp. 230–33.

24. Hannah Arendt, *The Origins of Totalitarianism*, 2d enlarged ed. (New York: Meridian Books, 1958), p. xv. Soon after, her friend Kurt Blumenfeld writes to her, "It also doesn't matter at all to me to know whether the Jews, as Sartre thinks, are essentially a magnet for the hatred directed at them, as if only Judeophobia conferred a reality on them," in Hannah Arendt and Kurt Blumenfeld, *Correspondance 1933–1963* (Desclée de Brouwer, 1998), p. 81; and Hannah Arendt, *Antisemitism* (New York: Harcourt, 1968), p. xi. On Blumenfeld, Arendt's faithful friend, see the remarkable preface by Martine Leibovici to Arendt and Jaspers, *Correspondance*.

25. Hannah Arendt, "Bernard Lazare," in *The Jew as Pariah: Jewish Identity and Politics in the Modern Age*, intro. by Ron Feldman (New York: Grove Press, 1978), pp. 153 and 163.

26. Arendt, *Rahel Varnhagen*, p. 100.

27. Bernstein, *Hannah Arendt and the Jewish Question*, pp. 47ff. See also pp. 184–85.

28. Arendt, "Une patience active," *La tradition cachée*, pp. 50–54.

29. Arendt, "Moses or Washington," in *The Jewish Writings*, p. 150.

30. Arendt, "We Refugees," in *The Jewish Writings*, p. 268.

31. Ibid., pp. 271–72. These mocking remarks about Mr. Cohn, an imagined character meant to characterize the wandering Jew in search of final assimilation, become more biting if one remembers that Hannah Arendt's own maternal grandfather was named Jacob Cohn. See Young-Bruehl, *Hannah Arendt*, p. 5.

32. Arendt, "We Refugees," in *The Jewish Writings*, p. 274.

33. On this point, see Ronald Beiner, "Arendt and Nationalism," in Dana Villa, ed., *The Cambridge Companion to Hannah Arendt* (Cambridge: Cambridge University Press, 2000), p. 44.

34. Arendt, "Nous autres réfugiés," *La tradition cachée*, p. 220.

35. Letter from Hannah Arendt to Kurt Blumenfeld, July 31, 1956, in Arendt and Blumenfeld, *Correspondance*, p. 197.

36. Arendt, "Seule demeure la langue maternelle," *La tradition cachée*, p. 239.

37. Melvyn Hill, ed., *Hannah Arendt: The Recovery of the Public World* (New York: St. Martin's Press), p. 334.

38. Young-Bruehl, *Hannah Arendt*, p. 139.

39. Letter from Hannah Arendt to Kurt Blumenfeld, July 19, 1947, in Arendt and Blumenfeld, *Correspondance*, p. 65.

40. Ever critical, Walter Laqueur thinks that "most of the time, Arendt knew nothing" about the history of the Jews, Zionism, or the relationships between Arabs and Jews: her commentaries on these points are most often "wrong." "The Arendt Cult," in Ashheim, ed., *Hannah Arendt in Jerusalem*, p. 54.

41. Arendt, "Zionism Reconsidered," October 1944, in *Jew as Pariah*, pp. 156 and 163.

42. Arendt, "The Jewish State: Fifty Years After," in *Jew as Pariah*, pp. 174–77.

43. Arendt, "To Save the Jewish Homeland: There Is Still Time," in *Jew as Pariah*, pp. 182–84 and 192.

44. Arendt, "Peace or Armistice in the Near East?," in *The Jewish Writings*, p. 450.

45. Letter from Kurt Blumenfeld to Hannah Arendt, July 11, 1955, in Arendt and Blumenfeld, *Correspondance*, p. 167.

46. Arendt and Jaspers, *Correspondance*, p. 287.

47. Letter from Kurt Blumenfeld to Hannah Arendt, July 2, 1951, in Arendt and Blumenfeld, *Correspondance*, p. 81.

48. Letter from Kurt Blumenfeld to Hannah Arendt, November 13, 1955, in Arendt and Blumenfeld, *Correspondance*, p. 175.

49. Letters from Hannah Arendt to Kurt Blumenfeld, August 2, 1945, and November 28, 1955, in Arendt and Blumenfeld, *Correspondance*, pp. 36 and 177.

50. Letter from Hannah Arendt to Karl Jaspers, September 4, 1947, in *Hannah Arendt/Karl Jaspers Correspondence*, pp. 98–99.

51. In a letter to Blücher on May 6, 1961, written in Jerusalem, Arendt writes,

"And, what's more, however atrocious these crimes may have been, they are not without precedent," in Hannah Arendt and Heinrich Blücher, *Correspondance* (Paris: Calmann-Lévy, 1999), p. 485.

52. Gershon Scholem, *On Jews and Judaism in Crisis: Selected Essays* (New York: Schocken Books, 1976), p. 302.

53. Richard Cohen, "A Generation's Response to *Eichmann in Jerusalem*," in Ashheim, ed., *Hannah Arendt in Jerusalem*.

54. Letters from Hannah Arendt to Karl Jaspers, July 20, 1963, and October 20, 1963, in *Hannah Arendt/Karl Jaspers Correspondence*.

55. Letter from Hannah Arendt to Karl Jaspers, April 13, 1961, in *Hannah Arendt/Karl Jaspers Correspondence*, pp. 434–35.

56. Letter from Hannah Arendt to Heinrich Blücher, April 15, 1961, in *Within Four Walls: The Correspondence between Hannah Arendt and Heinrich Blücher, 1936–1968,* Lotte Kohler, ed., Peter Constantine, trans. (New York: Harcourt, 2000), pp. 355. In a letter written on May 6 to her husband, Arendt returns several times to the Nuremberg laws applied in Israel which she says are "enough to make you vomit," as are, on May 8, "oriental practices," in Arendt and Blücher, *Correspondance*, pp. 485 and 487.

57. In a letter to Hannah Arendt on February 1, 1957, Kurt Blumenfeld writes, "Zionism was a gift from Europe to Judaism. Present-day Israel, assuredly, is still led by Europeans or half-Europeans. . . . Centuries separate us from Eastern Jews. What these groups are learning and can learn is the Levantines into which unsavory Europeans were transformed," in Arendt and Blumenfeld, *Correspondance*, p. 235.

58. The text of Rahel's "testament" published by Liliane Weissberg is "What a History! A Fugitive from Egypt and Palestine," whereas the French translation is "a refugee from Egypt and Palestine," which underestimates the movement of flight.

59. Letters from Hannah Arendt to Heinrich Blücher, October 22, 28, and November 6, 1955, in *Within Four Walls*, p. 286.

60. Walter Laqueur, "The Arendt Cult," in Ashheim, ed., *Hannah Arendt in Jerusalem*, p. 60.

61. Arendt, "Seule demeure la langue maternelle," *La tradition cachée*, p. 230.

62. Hannah Arendt, letter to Heinrich Blücher on April 26, 1961, in Arendt and Blücher, *Correspondance*, p. 481. Hannah Arendt, *Eichmann in Jerusalem: A Report on the Banality of Evil* (New York: Penguin Classics, 1994), p. 7.

63. Letters from Karl Jaspers to Hannah Arendt, October 22 and 25, 1963, in Arendt and Jaspers, *Correspondance*, pp. 700, 702.

64. Letter from Hannah Arendt to Karl Jaspers, October 1, 1967, in *Hannah Arendt/Karl Jaspers Correspondence*, p. 675.

65. Quoted by Young-Bruehl, *Hannah Arendt*, p. 455.

66. Ibid., p. 456.

67. Hannah Arendt, *The Life of the Mind* (San Diego: Harcourt Brace Jovanovich, 1981).

68. Steven Ashheim, *Scholem, Arendt, Klemperer: Intimate Chronicles in Turbulent Times* (Bloomington: Indiana University Press, 2001), p. 67.

69. Quoted by Young-Bruehl, *Hannah Arendt*, p. 56.

70. Arendt, "Aux origines de l'assimilation. Postface à Rahel Varnhagen en commémoration du 100e anniversaire de sa mort," *La tradition cachée*.

71. Arendt, *Origins of Totalitarianism*, p. 58.

72. Ibid., pp. 59 and 60.

73. Weissberg, Introduction to Arendt, *Rahel Varnhagen*, p. 18.

74. Hannah Arendt, *Love and Saint Augustine* (Chicago: University of Chicago Press, 1996).

75. Liliane Weissberg traces the episodes of this little-known request: Introduction to *Rahel Varnhagen*, pp. 39–41.

76. Dana Villa emphasizes what he calls the preponderant influence Heidegger exercises in this work, which Arendt wanted to dedicate to Heidegger: "Apologist or Critic? On Arendt's Relation to Heidegger," in Ashheim ed., *Hannah Arendt in Jerusalem*, pp. 327ff. Unlike Gellner or Steiner, he refuses to see in the Heidegger/Arendt couple "a soap opera": Ibid., p. 337. Steven Ashheim on the contrary thinks that Heidegger does not exercise any influence over *The Human Condition*: see Ashheim, *Scholem, Arendt, Klemperer*, p. 53. For her part, Mary Dietz thinks that *The Human Condition* refers directly to the analyses of the concentration camps in *Origins of Totalitarianism*, places where the human condition was most denied: "Arendt and the Holocaust," in Villa, ed., *Cambridge Companion of Hannah Arendt*, pp. 93ff.

77. Arendt, "Aux origines de l'assimilation. Postface à Rahel Varnhagen en commémoration du 100e anniversaire de sa mort," *La tradition cachée*, p. 42.

78. Arendt, *Rahel Varnhagen*, pp. 95, 100, and 244. Arendt continually returns to the fact that Rahel is "excluded" or even "exiled" in her own country.

79. Ibid., p. 126.

80. Ibid., p. 127.

81. Letter from Rahel Varnhagen published by Arendt at the end of *Rahel Varnhagen*, p. 271.

82. Ibid., from Rahel Varnhagen's diary entry on March 11, 1810, p. 278.

83. Ibid., p. 177.

84. Ibid., pp. 196, 197, 220, 221, and 245.

85. Ibid., p. 223.

86. The English text reads "arrived" (p. 236), which is closer to the idea of parvenu than the French text, where we find "acquired," p. 239. On page 241, *arriver* is used in the French text.

87. Ibid., p. 238.

88. Ibid., p. 247.

89. Arendt, *Human Condition*, pp. 176 and 188.

90. Elzbieta Ettinger, *Hannah Arendt/Martin Heidegger* (New Haven, CT: Yale University Press, 1965), p. 15.

91. Ibid., p. 114.

92. Mark Lilla, "Ménage à Trois," *The New York Review of Books*, November 18, 1999.

93. For Norma Claire Moruzzi, "it's only when speaking and writing through Rahel that Arendt could transform the private social sufferings of the parvenu (in the feminine) and a (Jewish) pariah to a public status endowed with political independence," *Speaking Through the Mask: Hannah Arendt and the Politics of Social Identity* (Ithaca, NY: Cornell University Press, 2000), pp. 49 and 55.

94. Letter on December 16, 1957, from Hannah Arendt to Kurt Blumenfeld, in Arendt and Blumenfeld, *Correspondance*, p. 258.

95. Arendt, *Rahel Varnhagen*, pp. 90 and 93.

96. Always somewhat hostile when it comes to Arendt, Walter Laqueur contrasts Rahel's fate with Arendt's: "The Arendt Cult," in Ashheim, ed., *Hannah Arendt in Jerusalem*, p. 64.

97. Hannah Fenichel Pitkin, *The Attack of the Blob: Hannah Arendt's Concept of the Social* (Chicago: University of Chicago Press, 1998), p. 64.

98. Ibid., p. 253.

99. Arendt, "Martin Heidegger a quatre-vingts ans," in *Vies politiques*, pp. 318–20.

100. Ashheim, *Scholem, Arendt, Klemperer*, pp. 62–63.

101. Heidi Thomann Tewarson, *Rahel Lewin Varnhagen: The Life and Work of a German Jewish Intellectual* (Lincoln: University of Nebraska Press, 1998). Käte Hamburger, "Rahel et Goethe," *Revue Germanique* no. 29 (1934). On Rahel's work, see Ursula Isselstein, "Costruzione e ricostruzione di una identità: Rahel Varnhagen e i suoi diari," *Ricerche di identità* 33 (1985).

102. Lewis Coser, *Refugee Scholars in America* (New Haven, CT: Yale University Press, 1984), pp. 189ff.

103. See Deborah Hertz, "Hannah Arendt's Rahel Varnhagen," in John Fout, ed., *German Women in the Nineteenth Century: A Social History* (New York: Holmes and Meier, 1984). Joanne Cutting-Gray, "Hannah Arendt's Rahel Varnhagen," *Philosophy and Literature* no. 15 (1991). Seyla Benhabib, *Recalcitrant Modernism of Hannah Arendt*, pp. 12–14. Bat-Ami Bar On, "Women in Dark Times: Rahel Varnhagen, Rosa Luxemburg, Hannah Arendt, and Me," in Larry May and Jerome Kohn, eds., *Hannah Arendt: Twenty Years Later* (Cambridge, MA: MIT Press, 1997). On Arendt and the feminists, see Bonnie Honig, ed., *Feminist Interpretations of Hannah Arendt* (University Park: Pennsylvania State University Press, 1995). Mary Dietz tries to reconcile the perspective of *The Human Condition* with feminist visions: *Turning Operations: Feminism, Arendt and Politics* (London: Routledge and Kegan Paul, 2002). Margaret Betz Hull thinks that Arendt reproaches feminism with essentializing woman and giving her too social an interpretation, and compares this point of refusal on Arendt's part to be publicly considered as Jewish while she never stops proclaiming herself, as a private person, Jewish: "Hannah Arendt as Jew, Hannah Arendt as Woman," *Philosophy of Hannah Arendt* (New York: Routledge Curzon, 2002), pp. 123ff.

104. Tewarson, *Rahel Lewin Varnhagen*, p. 83.

105. Deborah Hertz, "Hannah Arendt's Rahel Varnhagen," in Fout, ed., *German Women in the Nineteenth Century*, p. 83.

106. Arendt, "The Jew as Pariah: A Hidden Tradition," *Jew as Pariah*, p. 71. This passage is not translated in *La tradition cachée*.

107. Arendt, "We Refugees," in *The Jewish Writings*, p. xli.

108. Letter from Hannah Arendt to Karl Jaspers, September 7, 1952, in *Hannah Arendt/Karl Jaspers Correspondence*, pp. 199–200. On this point, see Bernstein, *Hannah Arendt and the Jewish Question*, pp. 27–28 and 184–88.

109. Ibid. Letter from Hannah Arendt to Karl Jaspers, September 4, 1947, in *Hannah Arendt/Karl Jaspers Correspondence*, p. 98.

110. This is a difficulty that appears involuntarily in the following sentence by Martine Leibovici: "In this perspective we will try to show that although Arendt's thought is the thinking of a Jewish woman, it cannot in any case be regarded as Jewish thought. Or else 'Jewish' is one of the elements unique to the manifestation of Who, without however being a characteristic of Self," *Hannah Arendt, une Juive. Expérience, politique and histoire*, p. 71. One can only approve of the author writing later on, pp. 94 and 96: "If one can assert that her Jewish experience directs Arendt's thinking, it is not a matter here of Jewish thought. . . . Arendt does not envisage developing a Jewish thought. She is only trying to start with Jewish experience and from that to understand." In a rather wicked note, Heidi Thomann Tewarson thinks that Hannah Arendt "had only a limited knowledge of Jewish history," *Rahel Lewin Varnhagen*, p. 230.

111. Arendt, *Origins of Totalitarianism*, pp. 66 and 83–84.

112. Arendt, "The Eichman Controversy," in *The Jewish Writings*, p. 466.

113. Amnon Raz-Krakotzkin subtly compares the distinct perspectives of Scholem and Arendt, in Ashheim, ed., *Hannah Arendt in Jerusalem*, pp. 176ff. See also David Suchoff, "Gershom Scholem, Hannah Arendt and the Scandal of Jewish Particularity," *The Germanic Review* (winter 1997).

114. Ibid., p. 224.

115. Arendt, *Rahel Varnhagen*, p. 220.

116. Ibid., pp. 92 and 103.

117. Pitkin, *Attack of the Blob*, p. 30. On this point, see Margaret Canovan, *Hannah Arendt: A Reinterpretation of Her Political Thought* (Cambridge: Cambridge University Press, 1992), pp. 9–12.

118. Dagmar Barnow, *Visible Spaces: Hannah Arendt and the German-Jewish Experience* (Baltimore, MD: Johns Hopkins University Press, 1990), pp. 46, 50, and 56.

119. Deborah Hertz, "Hannah Arendt's Rahel Varnhagen," in Fout, ed., *German Women in the Nineteenth Century*, p. 76.

120. Letter from Hannah Arendt to Karl Jaspers, September 7, 1952, in *Hannah Arendt/Karl Jaspers Correspondence*.

121. Arendt, *Rahel Varnhagen*.

122. Ibid., pp. 175, 180, and 183.

123. Liliane Weissberg, "Stepping Out: The Writing of Difference in Rahel Varnhagen's Letters," in Sander Gilman and Steven Katz, eds., *Anti-Semitism in Times of Crisis* (New York: New York University Press, 1991), p. 144.

124. This is Deborah Hertz's standpoint in "Work, Love and Jewishness in the Life of Fanny Lewald," in Frances Malino and David Sorkin, eds., *From East and West: Jews in a Changing Europe, 1750–1870* (Oxford: Blackwell, 1991), p. 212.

125. Marion Kaplan, "Gender and Jewish History in Imperial Germany," in Jonathan Frankel and Steven Zipperstein, eds., *Assimilation and Community: The Jews in Nineteenth-Century Europe* (Cambridge: Cambridge University Press), p. 219.

126. Arendt, *Rahel Varnhagen*, p. 248. See also Weissberg, Introduction to *Rahel Varnhagen*, p. 11.

127. Weissberg, Introduction to *Rahel Varnhagen*, p. 30.

128. Quoted by Heinrich Graetz, *History of the Jews* (Philadelphia, PA: The Jewish Publication of America, 1895), vol. 5, p. 534.

129. Thus, in the French version, Rahel bewails the fact that she is "neither a daughter, nor a sister, nor a lover, nor a wife, not even a bourgeoise" (p. 256) while in the definitive American version, on p. 248, we find "*citizen.*"

130. Arendt, *Rahel Varnhagen*, p. 88.

131. Ibid., pp. 88, 103, 219, and 257. See also, for example, p. 106.

132. Ibid., pp. 91–92, 235, and 265 of the French edition.

133. Ibid., pp. 246–47.

134. Ibid., p. 81.

135. Weissberg, Introduction to *Rahel Varnhagen*, pp. 6, 14, and 18–19. Young-Bruehl, *Hannah Arendt*, p. 100. For Martine Leibovici, by contrast, "it is erroneous to regard Arendt's aim in *Rahel Varnhagen* as that of an 'autobiography by projection'": *Hannah Arendt, une Juive. Expérience, politique et histoire*, p. 34. Similarly, according to Julia Kristeva, "far from merging with her, Arendt seems to settle accounts with her heroine. . . . Arendt the puppeteer is pulling the strings," *Le génie féminin, Vol. 1, Hannah Arendt* (Paris: Fayard, 1999), pp. 87, 89, and 111. On this comparison, see also Henri Plard, "Hannah Arendt et Rahel Lewin: Illusions et pièges de l'assimilation," in Hannah Arendt, *Les Cahiers du GRIF* (Tierce, 1986).

136. Letter from Karl Jaspers to Hannah Arendt, August 23, 1952, in *Hannah Arendt/Karl Jaspers Correspondence*, p. 195.

137. Barnow, *Visible Spaces*, p. 68.

138. Letter from Karl Jaspers to Hannah Arendt, August 23, 1952, in *Hannah Arendt/Karl Jaspers Correspondence*, pp. 192 and 194. In the same sense, see Tewarson, *Rahel Lewin Varnhagen*, p. 4. This erudite biography often constitutes a severe criticism of Arendt's thesis.

139. Letter from Hannah Arendt to Karl Jaspers, September 7, 1952, in *Hannah Arendt/Karl Jaspers Correspondence*, p. 198.

140. Arendt, *Rahel Varnhagen*, p. 254.

141. Ibid., p. 257.

142. Ibid., p. 251.

143. Ibid., p. 259.

144. Graetz, *History of the Jews*, vol. 5, p. 547.

145. Simon Dubnow, *Histoire moderne du peuple juif* (Paris: Le Cerf, 1994), p. 266.

146. Michael A. Meyer, *Judaism Within Modernity: Essays on Jewish History and Religion* (Detroit, MI: Wayne State University Press, 2001), ch. 4.

147. Barnow, *Visible Spaces*, p. 77.

148. Arendt, "De l'humanité dans de sombres temps," *Vies politiques*, pp. 22–23.

149. Letter from Hannah Arendt to Karl Jaspers, September 7, 1952, in *Hannah Arendt/Karl Jaspers Correspondence*, p. 200.

150. Arendt, *Rahel Varnhagen*, p. 258.

## Chapter Six. Isaiah Berlin: The Awakening of a Wounded Nationalism

1. Quoted by Michael Ignatieff, *Isaiah Berlin, A Life* (New York: Metropolitan Books, 1998), p. 66.

2. Mario Vargas Llosa, "El hombre que sabía demasiado," *Estudios Publicos* 80 (spring 2000): 5.

3. Robert Darnton, "Free Spirit," *The New York Review of Books*, June 26, 1997.

4. Thus in the collective work published by Alan Ryan, *The Idea of Freedom: Essays in Honor of Isaiah Berlin* (Oxford: Oxford University Press, 1979), only a few lines by A. Momigliano, p. 139, briefly mention Berlin's Jewish identity. Not a word in Robert Kocis, *A Critical Appraisal of Sir Isaiah Berlin's Political Philosophy* (Lewinston: Edwin Mellen Press, 1989). John Gray almost never approaches this aspect of Berlin's work, aside from a few pages on Zionism, *Isaiah Berlin* (New York: Harper Collins, 1995), pp. 114ff. See, by contrast, the lone but remarkable chapter 7 in the book by Claude Galipeau, *Isaiah Berlin's Liberalism* (Oxford: Clarendon Press, 1994). The fine biography by Michael Ignatieff on the contrary emphasizes throughout the book the extent of his Jewish involvement, *Isaiah Berlin, A Life*. In French, the rare articles on Berlin are almost all silent on this aspect of his personal life.

5. Isaiah Berlin, "The Virtue of a Democracy," interview with Berlin by Yaël Tamir, *Globe*, May 1988, p. 102.

6. Chief Rabbi Dr. Jonathan Sacks, "In Memoriam: Sir Isaiah Berlin, 1909–1997," *Report of the Oxford Centre for Hebrew and Jewish Studies*, Academic Year 1997–1998 (Oxford, 1998), pp. 32 and 36.

7. Isaiah Berlin, *The Crooked Timber of Humanity: Chapters in the History of Ideas*, Henry Hardy, ed. (New York: Alfred A. Knopf, 1991).

8. Isaiah Berlin, "Les Juifs: de la servitude à l'émancipation," in Isaiah Berlin, *Trois essais sur la condition juive* (Paris: Calmann-Lévy, 1973), p. 144.

9. Sacks, "In Memoriam: Sir Isaiah Berlin," p. 35.

10. Ibid., p. 36.

11. Avishai Margalit, "Isaiah and the Jews," *Times Literary Supplement*, May 29,

1998, p. 19. Text reproduced in Isaiah Berlin, *The First and the Last* (New York: New York Review of Books, 1999), pp. 110 and 115.

12. Extract from the speech given by Noel Annan during that ceremony, which took place on January 14, 1998. This text is reproduced in Berlin, *First and the Last*, pp. 87–88.

13. Ramin Jahanbegloo, *Conversations with Isaiah Berlin* (London: Peter Halban, 1992), p. 87.

14. Brian Barry recently launched some lively polemics by accusing Berlin of practicing a "realism of a tribal nature," *Times Literary Supplement*, November 9, 2001. See the indignant responses by Joshua Cherniss, Ian Harris, Mario Ricciardi, John Mason, and Henry Hardy in the *Times Literary Supplement*, November 16 and December 7, 2001.

15. Ignatieff, *Isaiah Berlin, A Life*, p. 15. See the review of this book by Bernard Wasserstein, "De Mortuis," *The Jerusalem Post Magazine*, January 8, 1998.

16. Sacks, "In Memoriam: Sir Isaiah Berlin," p. 36.

17. Ignatieff, *Isaiah Berlin, A Life*, chs. 2 and 4.

18. Jahanbegloo, *Conversations with Isaiah Berlin*, pp. 85–87.

19. Ibid.

20. Quoted by Yael Tamir, "Whose History? What Ideas?" in Edna and Avishai Margalit, eds., *Isaiah Berlin: A Celebration* (Chicago: University of Chicago Press, 1991), p. 146.

21. Isaiah Berlin, *Personal Impressions* (New York: Viking Press, 1981). Ernest Gellner thinks similarly that the studies by Plamenatz on nationalism could be called "the sad peregrinations of an Oxford Montenegrin," *Nations and Nationalism* (London: Cornell University Press, 1983), p. 99.

22. Berlin, *Crooked Timber of Humanity*, pp. 38–39 and 40.

23. John Davis, "E. Gellner," *The Guardian*, November 10, 1995. Chris Hann, "A Gellner Biography," *The Independent*, November 8, 1995. Michael Rustin, "Ernest Gellner, 1925–1995," *Radical Philosophy* 76. Jiru Musil, "The Prague Roots of Ernest Gellner's Thinking," in John Hall and Ian Jarvie, eds., *The Social Philosophy of Ernest Gellner* (Amsterdam: Rodopi, 1996). See also Steven Lukes, Introduction to Ernest Gellner, *Language and Solitude* (Cambridge: Cambridge University Press, 1998). Pierre Birnbaum, "Attitudes à l'égard du nationalisme. À propos d'Ernest Gellner," in Jean-Marie Donegani, Sophie Duchesne, and Florence Haegel, eds., *Aux frontières des attitudes entre le politique et le religieux* (L'Harmattan, 2002).

24. John Skorupski, "Post-Modern Hume: Ernest Gellner's Enlightenment Fundamentalism," in Hall and Jarvie, eds., *Social Philosophy of Ernest Gellner*.

25. Gellner, *Nations and Nationalism*, p. 35.

26. Ernest Gellner, *Culture, Identity and Politics* (Cambridge: Cambridge University Press, 1987), p. 17.

27. See, however, after Berlin's death, Ernest Gellner, "The Prophet Isaiah," *The Guardian*, February 7, 1995.

28. Gellner, *Culture, Identity and Politics*, p. 17.

29. John Brueilly, *Nationalism and the State* (Chicago: University of Chicago Press, 1981), ch. 2.

30. Gellner, *Nations and Nationalism*, chs. 2 and 3. Similarly, Gellner, *Encounter with Nationalism*, pp. 29ff. See the thorough article by Brendan O'Leary, "Ernest Gellner's Diagnoses of Nationalism: A Critical Overview, or What Is Living and What is Dead in Ernest Gellner's Philosophy of Nationalism," in John A. Hall, ed., *The State of the Nation: Ernest Gellner and the Theory of Nationalism* (Chicago: Cambridge University Press, 1998). See also the article by Damien Tambini that tries to refute the idea of a link between univocal nationalism and economic modernization, "Explaining Monoculturalism: Beyond Gellner's Theory of Nationalism," *Critical Review* (summer 1996).

31. For a good discussion of these differing theories, see Anthony Smith, "Gastronomy or Geology? The Role of Nationalism in the Reconstruction of Nations," in *Nations and Nationalism* (1995). At Gellner's death, Smith, while still paying him homage, tries to justify his own position in "Memory and Modernity: Reflections on Ernest Gellner's Theory of Nationalism," in *Nations and Nationalism* (1996).

32. Ernest Gellner, "Reply to Critics," in *Social Philosophy of Ernest Gellner*, p. 625–26.

33. See, however, Ernest Gellner, "Accounting for the Horror," *Times Literary Supplement*, August 1982.

34. Ernest Gellner, *Saints of the Atlas* (London: Weidenfeld and Nicholson, 1969); or Ernest Gellner, *Muslim Society* (Cambridge: Cambridge University Press, 1981). See Henry Munson Jr., "Muslim and Jew in Morocco: Reflections on the Distinction Between Belief and Behavior," in Hall and Jarvie, eds., *Social Philosophy of Ernest Gellner*, p. 357; in the complete bibliography published as an appendix that includes several hundred titles, only one single review of a work having to do with Jewish life and concerning the Jews' situation in Muslim society can be found: it is a review of a book by Joelle Allouche-Benayoun and Doris Bensimon, *Juifs d'Algérie hier et aujourd'hui*, which Gellner published in the *Jewish Journal of Sociology*, in June 1990, the only time when, unlike Berlin, he published a text in a journal connected with Judaism.

35. Ernest Gellner, Preface to Sukumar Periwal, *Notions of Nationalism* (Budapest: Central European University Press, 1995), p. 6. See also Ernest Gellner, "Debate with Anthony Smith," in *Nations and Nationalism*, vol. 10.

36. Gellner, *Encounter with Nationalism*, pp. 14ff.

37. Gellner, *Culture, Identity and Politics*, p. 83.

38. Ibid., p. 89.

39. Jahanbegloo, *Conversations with Isaiah Berlin*, p. 82. Pursuing his attack, Berlin, in a short review of a book on Ben Gurion, thinks that the misspellings of names that appear in the work are due to Hannah Arendt; Isaiah Berlin, "Portrait of Ben-Gurion," *Jewish Chronicle*, December 25, 1964.

40. Gellner, *Nations and Nationalism*, pp. 48 and 57.

41. Isaiah Berlin, "The Life and Opinions of Moses Hess," in *Against the Current*, Henry Hardy, ed. (New York: Viking Press, 1980), p. 234.

42. The two quotes by Berlin are taken from Isaiah Berlin, "A Nation Among Nations," *Jewish Chronicle*, May 4, 1973, pp. 29 and 32.

43. Berlin, "The Virtue of a Democracy," interview with Berlin by Yael Tamir, *Globe*, May 1988, p. 100.

44. Berlin, *Against the Current*, p. 218.

45. Isaiah Berlin, *The Sense of Reality* (London: Chatto and Windus), pp. 7ff. See also "The Decline of Utopian Ideas in the West," *Crooked Timber of Humanity*, pp. 20–49.

46. Jahanbegloo, *Conversations with Isaiah Berlin*, pp. 89–90.

47. Isaiah Berlin, *The Roots of Romanticism* (Princeton, NJ: Princeton University Press, 1999), p. 60.

48. Berlin, *Crooked Timber of Humanity*, pp. 55 and 245.

49. Berlin, *Against the Current*, pp. 11 and 348.

50. See the texts in homage to Berlin published after his death by *The New York Review of Books*, December 18, 1997, especially p. 11. On Herzen, see Isaiah Berlin, *Russian Thinkers* (New York: Penguin, 1995), pp. 186–210.

51. Nathan Gardels, "Two Concepts of Nationalism: An Interview with Isaiah Berlin," *The New York Review of Books*, November 21, 1991, p. 19.

52. Berlin, *Roots of Romanticism*, pp. 64–65. See also pp. 138–39.

53. Isaiah Berlin, *The Proper Study of Mankind* (New York: Farrar, Strauss and Giroux), 1998, p. 403.

54. Ibid., p. 415.

55. Ibid., p. 397.

56. Quoted by Galipeau, *Isaiah Berlin's Liberalism*, p. 159. Private correspondence.

57. Isaiah Berlin, "My Intellectual Path," *The New York Review of Books*, May 14, 1998, p. 56.

58. Jahanbegloo, *Conversations with Isaiah Berlin*, pp. 70–71. See the commentary by Galipeau, *Isaiah Berlin's Liberalism*, ch. 3.

59. Berlin, *Crooked Timber of Humanity*, pp. 171–72.

60. Ibid., p. 109. See Pierre Birnbaum, *The Idea of France*, M.B. DeBevoise, trans. (New York: Hill and Wang, 2001), ch 3.

61. Arnaldo Momigliano, "On the Pioneer Trail," *The New York Review of Books*, November 11, 1976.

62. Berlin, *Proper Study of Mankind*, p. 390. This insistence is telling, since Berlin repeats here almost word for word an observation already formulated in *Crooked Timber of Humanity*, pp. 10–11: "This view has been called cultural or moral relativism—this is what that great scholar, my friend Arnaldo Momigliano, whom I greatly admired, supposed about both Vico and Herder. He was mistaken. It [their concepts] is not relativism. . . . It is what I describe as pluralism—that is, the conception that there are many different ends that men may seek and still be fully

rational, fully men, capable of understanding each other and sympathizing and deriving light from each other."

63. Berlin, "My Intellectual Path." See also Isaiah Berlin, *Three Critics of the Enlightenment: Vico, Hamann, Herder* (Princeton, NJ: Princeton University Press, 2000).

64. Berlin, *Crooked Timber of Humanity*, pp. 76–77.

65. Graeme Garrard, "The Counter-Enlightenment Liberalism of Isaiah Berlin," *Journal of Political Ideologies* 2 (1997): 3. The author's expression is, actually, stronger, and could be translated as "liberal reactionary."

66. Alan Ryan, "Wise Man," *The New York Review of Books*, December 17, 1998, p. 37.

67. Gray, *Isaiah Berlin*, p. 99.

68. Ibid., p. 140.

69. Michael Walzer, Introduction to Isaiah Berlin, *The Hedgehog and the Fox* (New York: Simon and Schuster, 1986), p. x.

70. Michael Walzer, "Are There Limits to Liberalism?" *The New York Review of Books*, October 19, 1995. In a very rich correspondence between Walzer and Berlin, the latter steadily reiterates his hostile position to relativism, but insists each time on dilemmas that confront individuals according to the values they have chosen. See the numerous letters between these authors exchanged from 1985 to 1996. Private archives of Michael Walzer.

71. Steven Lukes, "Berlin's Dilemma: The Distinction Between Relativism and Pluralism," *Times Literary Supplement*, March 27, 1998, p. 9. For a stance that is more favorable to Berlin's pluralism, see Stefan Collini, "Against Utopia: The Inimitable Cadence of Berlin's Writings and the Unwavering of His Thought," *Times Literary Supplement*, August 22, 1997. See also Marilyn Berger, "Isaiah Berlin, Philosopher and Pluralist, Is Dead at 88," *The New York Times*, November 7, 1997.

72. Kocis, *Critical Appraisal of Sir Isaiah Berlin's Political Philosophy*, p. 245.

73. Ibid., p. 10.

74. Jahanbegloo, *Conversations with Isaiah Berlin*, p. 89.

75. Gardels, "Two Concepts of Nationalism," p. 19.

76. Isaiah Berlin, "Nationalism: Past Neglect and Present Power," in *Against the Current*, pp. 343–44 and 351.

77. Isaiah Berlin, "The Bent Twig: On the Rise of Nationalism," in *Crooked Timber of Humanity*, p. 245.

78. Isaiah Berlin, "Nationalism: Past Neglect and Present Power," in *Against the Current*, pp. 351–52.

79. Isaiah Berlin, "Kant as an Unfamiliar Source of Nationalism," in *Sense of Reality*, pp. 368–69.

80. Gardels, "Two Concepts of Nationalism," p. 19.

81. Charles Taylor, "The Importance of Herder," in E. and A. Margalit, eds., *Isaiah Berlin: A Celebration*, p. 62.

82. Charles Taylor, "Nationalism and Modernity," in Hall, ed., *State of the Nation*, pp. 196, 208–9, and 214.

83. Isaiah Berlin, "The Three Strands in My Life," *Jewish Quarterly* (August 1979): 6.

84. Gardels, "Two Concepts of Nationalism," p. 21. On this theme, see Juan Bosco Diaz-Urmeneta, "Liberalismo y nacionalismo: Las razones de Isaiah Berlin," *Sistema* 116 (1993).

85. Berlin, *Roots of Romanticism*, pp. 35–39.

86. Gardels, "Two Concepts of Nationalism," p. 23.

87. Pierre Birnbaum, "Du multiculturalisme au nationalisme," *La pensée politique* (Paris: Gallimard-Le Seuil, "Hautes Études," May 1995), pp. 138–39.

88. Isaiah Berlin, "Les Juifs," in *Trois essais sur la condition juive*, p. 148.

89. Isaiah Berlin, "Herder and the Enlightenment," in *Proper Study of Mankind*, p. 374. And, very much a scholar of this subject, Berlin in a footnote quotes the fundamental article by F. M. Barnard, "Herder and Israel," published in *Jewish Social Studies* 28 (1966): 25–33.

90. On the French example of this anti-Semitic Zionism, see Pierre Birnbaum, *"La France aux Français." Histoire des haines nationalistes*, ch. 9.

91. Jahanbegloo, *Conversations with Isaiah Berlin*, pp. 104–5.

92. Quoted by Berlin, *Personal Impressions*, p. 37.

93. Jahanbegloo, *Conversations with Isaiah Berlin*, pp. 105–6.

94. In a vitriolic attack on the whole of Berlin's oeuvre, Norman Podhoretz accuses him not only of adhering to relativism but also of unquestioningly yielding to multiculturalist demands and of being responsible for their spread in the United States as well as in Great Britain. Podhoretz also reproaches Berlin for his criticisms of the nationalist policies in contemporary Israel that are hostile to all concessions, as symbolized by Benjamin Netanyahu. Norman Podhoretz, "A Dissent on Isaiah Berlin," *Commentary*, February 1999, pp. 36–37.

95. Isaiah Berlin, "Benjamin Disraeli and Karl Marx," in *Against the Current*, p. 257.

96. Isaiah Berlin, *Karl Marx* (Oxford: Oxford University Press, 1978), p. 198. This book was published for the first time in 1939. See also G. A. Cohen, "Isaiah's Marx, and Mine," in E. and A. Margalit, eds., *Isaiah Berlin: A Celebration*. Cohen writes, "I must confess that I am ashamed of the anti-Semitic aspects of Marx that Isaiah undeniably showed," p. 120. Similarly, see Jahanbegloo, *Conversations with Isaiah Berlin*, p. 122.

97. Berlin, "The Life and Opinions of Moses Hess," in *Against the Current*, p. 250.

98. Isaiah Berlin, "The Origins of Israel," in Walter Laqueur, ed., *The Middle East in Transition* (New York: Frederick Praeger, 1958), p. 209.

99. Berlin, "Three Strands in My Life," p. 7.

100. On this discussion, see Michael Walzer, *Thick and Thin* (Notre Dame, IL: University of Notre Dame Press, 1994). See also Sasja Tempelman,

"Constructions of Cultural Identity: Multiculturalism and Exclusion," *Political Studies* 47 (1999).

101. Isaiah Berlin, "Go There to Find Your Identity," *Jewish Chronicle*, supplement, April 16, 1974. See the observations by Galipeau, *Isaiah Berlin's Liberalism*, pp. 150ff.

102. Berlin, "Les Juifs," in *Trois essais sur la condition juive*, pp. 117–20. Berlin often uses the metaphor of the glacier in discussing Jewish history: see "Chaim Weizmann," *Personal Impressions*, p. 40, *Chaim Weizmann: Statesman of the Jewish Renaissance* (Jerusalem: The Zionist Library, 1974), p. 36. Curiously, in his article on Moses Hess, without making a comparison between these dissimilar metaphors, Berlin quotes the following text by Hess: "The superannuated productions of a fallen rationalism have left their inert residues: it is the crust that covers the Jews of the West; no inner force can break it; there must be an external shock. But the rigid crust of orthodoxy, which prevents all progress among the Jews of Eastern Europe, will be dissolved when the sparks of national sentiment, that fire that smolders beneath it, light the sacred fire, introducing the new spring of our nation to a new life," "Moïse Hess," pp. 94–95. This time, the "external crust" does not represent the Western Jews who, under the influence of the Enlightenment, are supposed to be assimilated.

103. Ibid., pp. 121–25.

104. Berlin, "Benjamin Disraeli and Karl Marx," in *Against the Current*, p. 255.

105. Berlin, "The Life and Opinions of Moses Hess," in *Against the Current*.

106. Ibid., pp. 241–42.

107. Ibid., p. 247.

108. Ibid., p. 236.

109. Ibid.

110. Isaiah Berlin, "A Nation of Nations," *Jewish Chronicle*, May 4, 1973.

111. Quoted by Anson Rabinbach, *In the Shadow of Catastrophe: German Intellectuals Between Apocalypse and Enlightenment* (Berkeley: University of California Press, 1997), p. 44.

112. Berlin, "Chaim Weizmann," in *Personal Impressions*, pp. 45 and 61. See also the lengthy and informed text that Berlin wrote on Weizmann's role in the history of Zionism, *Chaim Weizmann*. As the *Encyclopedia Judaica* notes, "He had close ties with Israel and Zionism and was the friend of many Zionist leaders like Chaim Weizmann," *Encyclopedia Judaica*, "Berlin, Sir Isaiah," p. 659.

113. Ignatieff, *Isaiah Berlin, A Life*, ch. 8.

114. H. G. Nicholas, ed., *Washington Dispatches, 1941–1945*, intro. by Isaiah Berlin (Chicago: University of Chicago Press, 1981), pp. 329, 558, and 610. See also pp. 189, 235, 239, 275, 303, 314, 316, 325, 330, 333, 362, and 479.

115. Ignatieff, *Isaiah Berlin, A Life*, ch. 12.

116. Berlin, "Les Juifs," in *Trois essais sur la condition juive*, pp. 146–47.

117. Jahanbegloo, *Conversations with Isaiah Berlin*, p. 103.

118. Stuart Hampshire, "Nationalism," in E. and A. Margalit, eds., *Isaiah Berlin: A Celebration*, p. 132.

119. See Galipeau, *Isaiah Berlin's Liberalism*, p. 162. Private correspondence with the author.

120. Berlin, "Nation of Nations," p. 34.

121. Berlin, "Origins of Israel," in Laqueur, ed., *Middle East in Transition*, pp. 215–16.

122. Berlin, "Nation of Nations," pp. 31–32.

123. Berlin, "Les Juifs," in *Trois essais sur la condition juive*, pp. 135–38.

124. Sander Gilman, *Jewish Self-Hatred* (Baltimore, MD: Johns Hopkins University Press, 1986).

125. Yael Tamir, "Whose History? What Ideas?" in E. and A. Margalit, eds., *Isaiah Berlin: A Celebration*, pp. 155ff.

126. On this process of "idealization of England" by British Jews, see Stefan Collini, *English Pasts: Essays in History and Culture* (Oxford: Oxford University Press, 1999), pp. 82ff.

## Chapter Seven. Michael Walzer: The End of Whispering

1. Michael Walzer, *Thick and Thin* (Notre Dame, IL: University of Notre Dame Press, 1994), p. 64.

2. Joseph Carens describes Michael Walzer thus in *Culture, Citizenship and Community: A Contextual Exploration of Justice as Evenhandedness* (Oxford: Oxford University Press, 2000), p. 23.

3. Michael Walzer, *What It Means to Be an American* (New York: Marsilio Publishers, 1992), p. 5.

4. See Chapter 6.

5. Michael Walzer, "Individus et communautés: Les deux pluralismes," *Esprit*, June 1995, p. 105.

6. "De la politique à la théorie: La voie de l'engagement. Entretien avec Michael Walzer," *Le Banquet*, September–October 1998, p. 278.

7. "Le multiculturalisme au coeur. Entretien avec Michael Walzer," *Critique internationale* no. 3 (spring 1999): 62.

8. Michael Walzer, "Exiles and Citizens," in Michael Walzer, Menachem Lorberbaum, and Noam Zohar, eds., *The Jewish Political Tradition* (New Haven, CT: Yale University Press, 2003), vol. 2, p. 519.

9. Michael Walzer, *The Company of Critics: Social Criticism and Political Commitment in the Twentieth Century* (New York: Basic Books, 1988), pp. ix and x.

10. Ibid., pp. 13–14.

11. Michael Walzer, *Spheres of Justice: A Defense of Pluralism and Equality* (New York: Basic Books, 1983), p. xiv.

12. Michael Walzer, *Interpretation and Social Criticism* (Cambridge, MA: Harvard University Press, 1987), p. 74.

13. Ibid., pp. 80, 81, and 94.

14. Personal interview with Michael Walzer, July 2, 2001.

15. See Mark Hunyadi, *L'art de l'exclusion. Une critique de Michael Walzer* (Paris: Le Cerf, 2000); or Justine Lacroix, *Michael Walzer. Le pluralisme et l'universalisme* (Michalon, 2001).

16. Michael Walzer, *The Revolution of the Saints: A Study in the Origins of Radical Politics* (New York: Atheneum, 1968), pp. 2–3.

17. Ibid., pp. 14–18. See François Chazel, *Du pouvoir à la contestation* (LGDJ, 2003), pp. 139ff.

18. Walzer, *Interpretation and Social Criticism*, pp. 63 and 83.

19. Walzer, *Revolution of the Saints*, p. 117. Walzer continually stresses the exile of the Puritans. See, for example, pp. 127, 130, 134, and 138.

20. Ibid., pp. 305–6.

21. Michael Walzer, *Obligations: Essays on Disobedience, War and Citizenship* (Cambridge, MA: Harvard University Press, 1970), pp. xiii, 26, 32, 210, 214, and 224. Walzer discusses these books: *Consent, Freedom and Political Obligation* by John Plamenatz; *Politics, Economics and Welfare*, by Robert Dahl and Charles Lindblom; *The People's Choice*, by Paul Lazarsfeld, Bernard Berelson, and Hazel Gaudet; and is inspired by the studies carried out by Charles Tilly on collective violence, by Grant McConnel's *Private Power and American Democracy*, and by the results—albeit debatable—found in the book by Gabriel Almond and Sidney Verba, *The Civic Culture*.

22. Walzer, *Obligations*, pp. 16ff.

23. See "Le multiculturalisme au coeur. Entretien avec Michael Walzer," p. 61.

24. Michael Walzer, *Regicide and Revolution: Speeches at the Trial of Louis XVI* (Cambridge: Cambridge University Press, 1974), pp. 69ff.

25. Ibid., p. 83.

26. Michael Walzer, "Éloge du pluralisme démocratique," *Pluralisme et démocratie* (Éditions Esprit, 1997), p. 216. Walzer criticizes the solutions proposed by Habermas, which presuppose that "the participants must be liberated from the bonds of particularism, else they will never produce the rational outcome that they require," *Interpretation and Social Criticism*, pp. 11–12.

27. See Michael Walzer, "The Politics of Rescue," *Dissent* (winter 1995): 36. See especially the seminal work in this area of Walzer's thought, *Just and Unjust Wars* (New York: Basic Books, 1977), chs. 6 and 7. Walzer declares in the same vein: "We are not the firemen of the world." See also "Un juste," *Les Inrockuptibles*, May 12, 1999, p. 49. *Just and Unjust Wars* gave rise to an immense bibliography; see the list in *Ethics and International Affairs* 11 (1997).

28. Jürgen Habermas, *L'intégration républicaine* (Paris: Fayard, 1998), pp. 143–44.

29. Michael Walzer, "Discussion," in Ronald Dworkin, Mark Lilla, and Robert Silvers, ed., *The Legacy of Isaiah Berlin* (New York: New York Review of Books, 2001), pp. 192 and 196–97.

30. Walzer, *Obligations*, p. 224.

31. Ibid., p. 227.

32. See Walzer's study on the writer Ignazio Silone who left the Communist Party of Italy, *Obligations*, pp. 191ff. Walzer returns much later to this example in *The Company of Critics*, ch. 5.

33. Walzer, *Spheres of Justice*, p. 6.

34. Ibid., p. 79.

35. Ibid., p. 319. On this debate between Rawls and Walzer, see Pierre Bouretz, "Droit et communauté: Michael Walzer," in Pierre Bouretz, ed., *La force du droit* (Éditions Esprit, 1991), pp. 105ff.

36. Michael Walzer, "La justice dans les institutions," *Pluralisme et démocratie*, p. 33.

37. Walzer, *Spheres of Justice*, p. xiv.

38. Walzer, *Interpretation and Social Criticism*, pp. 14–15. See Joël Roman, "Le pluralisme de Michael Walzer," in *Pluralisme et démocratie*, p. 15.

39. See A. Berten, ed., *Libéraux et communautariens* (Paris: PUF, 1997).

40. Walzer, *Spheres of Justice*, p. 63.

41. Ibid., pp. 32, 41, 45, 50, and 51.

42. Ibid., p. 49.

43. David Miller, *On Nationality* (Oxford: Oxford University Press, 1995).

44. Walzer, *Spheres of Justice*, p. 33.

45. See the articles by Michael Rustin, Amy Gutmann, Richard Arneson, and Adam Swift in David Miller and Michael Walzer, eds., *Pluralism, Justice and Equality*.

46. Walzer, *Spheres of Justice*, ch. 3.

47. Michael Walzer, "Sauver la société civile," *Mouvements* (March–April 2000): 109.

48. Shane O'Neill challenges the Walzer model of separation of spheres to account for justice in the framework of the civil war prevalent in the divided Northern Ireland, "Pluralist Justice and Its Limits: The Case of Northern Ireland," *Political Studies* 42 (1994). The author prefers to take his inspiration from the studies by Habermas in trying to find a fair solution to this conflict, pp. 372–73. From a similar perspective, David Bromwich follows the Enlightenment more and accuses Walzer of culturalism, "Culturalism, the Euthanasia of Liberalism," *Dissent* (winter 1995). One can find similar kinds of criticism hostile to Walzer's identitarian communitarianism in Jean-Luc Gignac, "Sur le multiculuralisme et la politique de la différence identitaire: Taylor, Walzer, Kymlicka," *Politique et Sociétés* no. 2 (1997). Likewise, see Robert Van der Veen, "The Adjudicating Citizen: On Equal Membership in Walzer's Theory of Justice," *British Journal of Political Science* 29 (1999). In a more general way, Margo Trappenberg also thinks that the theory of justice proposed by Walzer presupposes consensual societies, "In Defense of Pure Pluralism: Two Readings of Walzer's *Spheres of Justice*," *The Journal of Political Philosophy* no. 2 (2000).

49. Charles Taylor. On this point, see Pierre Birnbaum, "Du multiculuralisme

au nationalisme." Walzer writes, "I belonged, and I still belong, to those intellectuals who defend cultural pluralism in the United States, for it is, I believe, a precondition for a democratic, egalitarian society; minority identities that are underground, invisible, repressed, must be able to flourish in broad daylight. But all that requires a certain form of public space where groups can find the means to create their institutions," "Quelle démocratie pour le future?" in Jérôme Bindé, ed., *Les clefs du XXIe siècle* (UNESCO, Le Seuil, 2000), pp. 330–31.

50. Walzer, "Les deux universalismes," in *Pluralisme et démocratie*, pp. 84, 88, and 109–10.

51. Govert den Hartogh, "The Architectonic of Michael Walzer's Theory of Justice," *Political Theory* (August 1999): 517.

52. See Chapter 6.

53. Michael Walzer, "Nation and Universe," *The Tanner Lectures on Human Values*, 11 (Salt Lake City: University of Utah Press, 1990), p. 550.

54. Ibid., p. 536.

55. Walzer, *Thick and Thin*, pp. 3 and 11. For a critique of Habermas, see also p. 12.

56. Ibid., p. 16.

57. Ibid., pp. 60–61.

58. These criticisms are made by Jonathan Allen, "The Situated Critic or the Loyal Critic? Rorty and Walzer on Social Criticism," *Philosophy and Social Criticism* no. 6 (1998): 38–41; and Carens, *Culture, Citizenship and Community*, p. 26. Melissa Orlie for her part argues that universalism consists above all in recognition of the Other within our own culture and not just within that of others, which makes its transformation possible, "Beyond Identity and Difference," *Political Theory* (February 1999): 148. See also Lacroix, *Michael Walzer*, pp. 96ff. Mark Hunyadi thinks, in the same vein, that "the 'shared meanings' of Walzer are the pluralized analogue of the Taylorian theory of the inevitable priority of the good over the right," *L'art de l'exclusion*, p. 121.

59. See the critique by Norman Daniels, *Justice and Justification* (Cambridge: Cambridge University Press, 1996), pp. 112–13.

60. Walzer, *The Company of Critics*.

61. Will Kymlicka, *Multicultural Citizenship: A Liberal Theory of Minority Rights* (Oxford: Clarendon Press, 1995), p. 65.

62. Walzer, *Interpretation and Social Criticism*, p. 36.

63. Ibid., p. 37.

64. Ibid., p 39.

65. Walzer, *Thick and Thin*, p. 53.

66. Michael Walzer, "What Does It Mean to Be an American?" in *What It Means to Be an American*, pp. 23–25.

67. Ibid., pp. 42 and 49.

68. Denis Lacorne, *La crise de l'identité américaine. Du melting-pot au multiculturalisme* (Paris: Fayard, 1997).

69. "Le multiculturalisme au coeur. Entretien avec Michael Walzer," p. 63.

70. Horace Kallen, *Culture and Democracy in the United States*, intro. by Stephen Whitfield (New York: Transaction Publishers, 1998).

71. Milton Konvitz, "Horace Meyer Kallen (1882–1974): Philosopher of the Hebraic-American Idea," *American Jewish Year Book* 75 (1974). For a critique of Kallen, see Isaac Berkson, *Theories of Americanization: A Critical Study with Special Reference to the Jewish Group* (New York, 1920), pp. 149ff.

72. Kallen, *Culture and Democracy in the United States*, pp. 104 and 106.

73. Ibid., p. 54.

74. Ibid., p. 114. One can find very similar thoughts in Salo W. Baron, *Steeled by Adversity: Essays Addressed on American Jewish Life* (Philadelphia, PA: Jewish Publication Society of America, 1971), p. 547.

75. See Milton Gordon, *Assimilation in American Life* (New York: Oxford University Press, 1964); and "Models of Pluralism: The New American Dilemma," in Milton Gordon, ed., *America as a Multicultural Society* (Philadelphia: American Academy of Political and Social Science, 1981).

76. Nathan Glazer, *Ethnic Dilemmas, 1964–1982* (Cambridge, MA: Harvard University Press, 1983), pp. 106–10. See also Nathan Glazer and Daniel Moynihan, *Beyond the Melting Pot* (Cambridge, MA: Harvard University Press, 1963). John Higham, *Send These to Me: Jews and Other Immigrants in Urban America* (New York: Atheneum, 1975).

77. Nathan Glazer, *We Are All Multiculturalists Now* (Cambridge, MA: Harvard University Press, 1997). See also Nathan Glazer, "The End of Meritocracy," *The New Republic*, September 27, 1999.

78. David Biale, Michael Galchinsky, and Susannah Heschel, *Insider/Outsider: American Jews and Multiculturalism* (Berkeley: University of California Press, 1998). Seymour Martin Lipset, *The First New Nation* (New York: Doubleday, 1967). Hans Kohn, *American Nationalism: An Interpretation* (New York: Macmillan, 1957). David Riesman, *Lonely Crowd*.

79. See Dan A. Oren, *Joining the Club: A History of Jews and Yale* (New Haven, CT: Yale University Press, 1985). See also Lacorne, *La crise de l'identité américaine*, p. 319; and Daniel Sabbah, *L'égalité par le droit. Les paradoxes de la discrimination positive aux États-Unis* (Economica, 2003), pp. 368–72.

80. Biale, Galchinsky, and Heschel, eds., *Insider/Outsider*, pp. 5, 7, and 9.

81. David Biale, "The Melting Pot and Beyond," in Biale, Galchinsky, and Heschel, eds., *Insider/Outsider*, p. 26.

82. David Biale, "Intégration et citoyenneté: Le modèle américain," in Elie Barnavi and Saul Friedlander, eds., *Les Juifs et le XXe siècle* (Paris: Calmann-Lévy, 2000), p. 374. See also Biale, Galchinsky, and Heschel, eds., Introduction to *Insider/Outsider*, pp. 6–7.

83. See Marla Brettschneider, *Cornerstone of Peace: Jewish Politics and Democratic Theory* (New York: Rutgers University Press, 1996), as well as, edited by the same author, *The Narrow Bridge: Jewish Views on Multiculturalism* (New York: Rutgers University Press, 1996). Mitchell Cohen, "In Defense of Shaatnez: A Politics for

Jews in a Multicultural America," in Biale, Galchinsky, and Heschel, eds., *Insider/ Outsider.*

84. "De la politique à la théorie: la voie de l'engagement, entretien avec M. Walzer," *Le Banquet*, September–October 1998, p. 274.

85. Walzer, "Éloge du pluralisme démocratique," p. 208.

86. Walzer, "What Does It Mean to Be an American?" p. 43.

87. Ibid., p. 42.

88. Walzer, *Traité sur la tolérance*, pp. 94, 122, and 138.

89. Ibid., p. 63. For a critique, see Ryszard Legutko, "Toleration and Multiculturalism," *Critical Review* 13, nos. 1–2.

90. Ibid., p. 115. For Walzer, "once, the price to pay in a country like France was abandonment of one's former culture. One did not just become a French citizen, one was supposed to become a Frenchman," "L'Américain Michael Walzer: l'un et le multiple," *www.unesco.org/courier*, November 16, 2000.

91. Walzer, *What It Means to Be an American*, pp. 37 and 47. See also *Traité sur la tolérance*, pp. 37 and 55.

92. Michael Walzer, "Multiculturalism and the Politics of Interest," in Biale, Galchinsky, and Heschel, eds., *Insider/Outsider*, pp. 92–93 and 96. See also "Un dialogue sur l'avenir de la démocratie," a conversation between Alain Touraine and Michael Walzer, *Le Monde*, December 16, 1997.

93. Roger Smith, "America's Contents and Discontents: Reflections on Michael Sandel's America," *Critical Review* 13, nos. 1–2 (1999): 88–93.

94. Judith Shklar, *American Citizenship: The Quest for Inclusion* (Cambridge, MA: Harvard University Press, 1998).

95. See the recent summary of this by Nancy Foner, "Immigrant Commitment to America," *Citizenship Studies* (February 2001).

96. Walzer, *On Toleration*, p. xi.

97. Walzer, "Éloge du pluralisme démocratique," *Pluralisme et démocratie*, p. 208. He also writes, "I will identify with more than one single and unique tribe: I will be American, Jewish, an inhabitant of the East Coast, an intellectual, a professor . . . the multiplication of identities divides the passions," p. 128.

98. See "Un juste," *Les Inrockuptibles*, p. 48.

99. Walzer, "L'Américain Michael Walzer: L'un et le multiple," p. 4.

100. Michael Walzer, *Exodus and Revolution* (New York: Basic Books, 1985), p. ix.

101. It is within this framework that I have conversed many times with Michael Walzer.

102. Walzer, *Traité sur la tolérance*, pp. 89ff.

103. Walzer, *Interpretation and Social Criticism*, pp. 69, 77–78, and 80.

104. Ibid., pp. 79, 89, 90, and 92.

105. Ibid., p. 94.

106. Walzer, *The Company of Critics*, p. 235.

107. Ibid., p. 14.

108. Ibid., p. 13.

109. Walzer, *Interpretation and Social Criticism*, p. 63.

110. Ibid., pp. 57–61. See also *Traité sur la tolérance*, pp. 63 and 123.

111. Michael Walzer, Preface to Jean-Paul Sartre, *Anti-Semite and Jew* (New York: Schocken Books, 1995), pp. xxi–xxv. See also *The Company of Critics*.

112. Walzer, *Interpretation and Social Criticism*, p. 39.

113. Walzer, *The Company of Critics*, p. 68.

114. Ibid., pp. 74 and 79.

115. Ibid. "His detachment contributes to this incapacity: by dragging on for-ever, critical enterprise will collapse. . . . Foucault is nowhere and he cannot find any justification. Angry, he shakes the iron bars of his cage. But he has neither plans nor projects to make this cage something that would look more like a home," pp. 222–24.

116. Ibid., pp. 144, 146, and 151.

117. Walzer, *Spheres of Justice*, pp. 17, 64ff., and 172ff.

118. Walzer, *Exodus and Revolution*.

119. Ibid., pp. 66 and 68.

120. Ibid., p. 81.

121. Ibid., pp. 113 and 127. Walzer writes, "I was raised in the American Jewish community, I read the Hebrew Bible and I discovered in it that the Israelites de-veloped a kind of primitive democracy. An objective reader of the Old Testament will perhaps not see things this way but it was crucial, to help the Jews understand themselves, to imagine that it played a part in it," "Quelle démocratie pour le fu-ture?" in Jérôme Bindé, ed., *Les clefs du XXIe siècle*, p. 334.

122. Walzer, *Exodus and Revolution*, p. 87.

123. Ibid., pp. 147 and 149.

124. Ibid., p. 135.

125. Ibid., p. 5. This statement deserves to be strongly qualified.

126. Michael Walzer, *The Politics of Exile in the Hebrew Bible* (Tübingen: Mohr Siebeck, 2001), p. 10.

127. See, for example, David Biale, *Power and Powerlessness in Jewish History* (New York: Schoken Books, 1986). Walzer wants historians to recognize "the strength of stateless Jews," "History and National Liberation" (unpublished lec-ture given in New York, March 2001), p. 15.

128. Michael Walzer, Introduction to Walzer, Lorberbaum, and Zohar, eds., *Jewish Political Tradition*, p. xxx.

129. Ibid., pp. xxi–xxii.

130. See, for example, Selma Stern, *The Court Jews* (New Brunswick, NJ: Transaction Books, 1985); Fritz Stern, *Gold and Iron* (New York: Vintage Books, 1979); Richard Cohen and Vivian Mann, eds., *From Court Jews to the Rothschilds: Art, Patronage, Power* (New York: Prestel, 1996).

131. Walzer, *Politics of Exile in the Hebrew Bible*, pp. 42, 44, and 86.

132. Ibid., p. 82.

133. Michael Walzer, "A Monarchic Constitution?" in Walzer, Lorberbaum, and Zohar, eds., *Jewish Political Tradition*, p. 141.

134. Walzer, *Politics of Exile in the Hebrew Bible*, p. 44.

135. Ibid., p. 50.

136. Ibid., p. 54.

137. Pierre Birnbaum, *Sur la corde raide* (Paris: Flammarion, 2002), ch. 9.

138. Walzer, *Politics of Exile in the Hebrew Bible*, p. 58. See also "Universalism and Jewish Values" (Carnegie Council, Twentieth Morgenthau Memorial Lecture on Ethics), p. 16.

139. Menachem Lorberbaum, "Consent Theory in *Dina de Malkhuta Dina*," in Walzer, Lorberbaum, and Zohar, eds., *Jewish Political Tradition*, pp. 446ff.

140. Walzer, "Universalism and Jewish Values," p. 8.

141. Walzer, *Spheres of Justice*, pp. 52–63.

142. Walzer, "Universalism and Jewish Values," p. 8.

143. Michael Wyschogrod, *The Body of Faith: God in the People Israel* (San Francisco: Harper and Row, 1989).

144. Walzer, "Universalism and Jewish Values," pp. 7–8.

145. Ibid., p. 20.

146. David Novak, *The Image of the Non-Jew in Judaism: An Historical and Constructive Study of the Noahide Laws* (Toronto: Edwin Mellen Press, 1983).

147. Walzer, "Universalism and Jewish Values," p. 24.

148. Ibid., p. 26.

149. Michael Walzer, "Liberalism, Nationalism, Reform," in Dworkin, Lilla, and Silvers, eds., *Legacy of Isaiah Berlin*, pp. 174ff.

150. Michael Walzer, "What Kind of State is a Jewish State?" (Jerusalem: Shalom Hartman Institute, June 1989), pp. 19–20. Walzer also thinks it normal that revisionist Israeli historians describe "the dark side of the struggle for national liberation," "History and National Liberation," p. 7.

151. See also, in the same vein, the article by Yael Tamir, "A Jewish Democratic State," in Walzer, Lorberbaum, and Zohar, eds., *Jewish Political Tradition*. Close to Isaiah Berlin and Michael Walzer, Tamir argues that the State of Israel cannot be neutral, for that would undermine culture within the public space, and that it must preserve its uniquely Jewish "particular" dimension while still remaining democratic. This text, along with two others which deal with the same theme, has been translated into French in *Les Cahiers du Judaïsme* no. 12.

## Chapter Eight. Yosef Hayim Yerushalmi: A Home for "Fallen Jews"

1. Yosef H. Yerushalmi, *From Spanish Court to Italian Ghetto: Isaac Cardoso: A Study in Seventeenth-Century Marranism and Jewish Apologetics* (New York: Columbia University Press, 1971), p. 1.

2. Yosef H. Yerushalmi, *Freud's Moses: Judaism Terminable and Interminable* (New Haven, CT: Yale University Press, 1991), p. 33. Whereas *maladie* replaces

*maux* in the French translation of the first quote by Ibn Verga, in *Freud's Moses*, we find "disease," p. 32.

3. Ibid., p. 31.

4. Ibid., p. 10.

5. Yosef H. Yerushalmi, "The Purloined Kiddush Cups: Reopening the Case on Freud's Jewish Identity," published as a supplement to *Sigmund Freud and Art: His Personal Collection of Antiquities* (New York: Abrams, 1989).

6. Yerushalmi, *Freud's Moses*, p. 98.

7. Ibid., ch. 2.

8. Yosef H. Yerushalmi, *Sefardica. Essais sur l'histoire des Juifs, des marranes et des nouveaux-chrétiens d'origine hispano-portugaise* (Paris: Chandeigne, 1998), p. 182.

9. See, for example, *Zakhor: Jewish History and Jewish Memory* (Seattle: University of Washington Press, 1996), pp. 6 and 101.

10. "Entretien à Jérusalem" [Interview in Jerusalem] with Dominique Bourel, in *Zakhor. Histoire juive et mémoire juive* (Paris: La Découverte, 1984), pp. 151–53.

11. Yerushalmi, *Zakhor*, p. 101.

12. Ibid., p. 93. See also Foreword, *Sefardica*, p. 8. "I am, in fact," he says again, "a Jewish historian," "Response to Rosemary Ruether," in Eva Fleischer, ed., *Auschwitz: Beginning of a New Era?* (New York: ICTAV Publishing House, Inc., 1974), p. 97.

13. Yerushalmi, *Freud's Moses*, p. 81.

14. Yerushalmi, *Zakhor*, p. 100.

15. Yosef H. Yerushalmi, Preface to Yitzak Baer, *Galout. L'imaginaire de l'exil dans le judaïsme* (Paris: Calman-Lévy, 2000), p. 26. In English: *Galut*, translated from the Hebrew by Robert Warshow (Lanham, NH: University Press of America, 1988).

16. Yosef H. Yerushalmi, "Response to Rosemary Ruether," in Fleischer, ed., *Auschwitz*, p. 107.

17. Quoted in Yerushalmi, *Freud's Moses*, p. 12. See also pp. 13 and 64.

18. Yosef H. Yerushalmi, "Reflections on Forgetting," postscript to *Zakhor*, pp. 114 and 116.

19. "Yosef Hayim Yerushalmi," Gale Literary Databases, Document, 1998, pp. 6–7.

20. Yosef H. Yerushalmi, "A Jewish Historian in the Age of Aquarius" (Commencement Address, Hebrew College, Brookline, MA, June 1970), pp. 10–11.

21. Anthony Smith, "Nationalism and the Historians," *International Journal of Comparative Sociology* no. 32 (1992); and "Gastronomy or Geology? The Role of Nationalism in the Reconstruction of Nations," *Nations and Nationalism* 1 (1995).

22. Yosef H. Yerushalmi, "Clio and the Jews: Reflections on Jewish Historiography in the Sixteenth Century," *Jubilee Volume of the American Academy for Jewish Research Proceedings*, vols. 46–47, 1979–1980 (Jerusalem, 1980), pp. 615 and 637.

23. *Zakhor*, pp. 81 and 86. I have preferred the translation of "fallen" as *déchus* instead of *perdus* [lost], to convey the idea of the fall.

24. Personal interview with Yosef H. Yerushalmi, June 2001.

25. Before *Zakhor*, this discussion was undertaken by Lionel Kochan, who thinks on the contrary that "Jewish historiography could not exist as a discipline independent of Judaism, however one considers it; it can only express how Messianism has been interpreted. . . . Even the mystical authors who took into consideration the sense of exile should be regarded as historians," *The Jew and His History* (London: Macmillan, 1977), preface, p. ix. In Kochan's opinion, "A new, European-style historiography forms" in the modern era when the Messianic idea disappears, with Jewish history uniquely drawing its inspiration from the Enlightenment, for example, in Germany with the works of Zunz, pp. 62–64. From then on, for him, modern historians can only conceive of "fantasies" lacking all usefulness, p. 117. In the present day, almost all critiques of the works of Yosef H. Yerushalmi concern this distinction between memory and history, which we, for our part, do not place at the heart of our analysis of his work. Amos Funkenstein, first of all, gives nuance to this distinction, thinking that the historians of the Wissenschaft were themselves biased by the collective memory of the Jewish community of the time; thus he stresses that "the memory of the German Jews was in step with the works of Jost, Geiger, and Graetz," Amos Funkenstein, *Perceptions of Jewish History* (Berkeley: University of California Press, 1993), p. 254. Historians were thus connected to the "historical conscience" of their era, which "did not contradict collective memory but organized it, gave it shape," pp. 18–19. In the same vein, Michael Meyer thinks that Heinrich Graetz, for example, contributed to "retracing Jewish memory. . . . He consciously reshaped Jewish memory. . . . We cannot say that Graetz, Dubnow or Scholem were 'cut off from collective Jewish memory'": "Comments on the Last Chapter of Y. H. Yerushalmi's *Zakhor*," *AJS Newsletter* (winter 1986): 15. See also Ivan Marcus, "The Sephardic Mystique," *Orim* 1 (1985): 45–46. In a more lively way, Robert Bonfil calls into question an element not dealt with here, namely the fragile appearance of a Jewish history before the contemporary era linked with the catastrophic expulsion of Spanish Jews, in parallel with the contemporary explosion subsequent to the Shoah. For him, in an almost Zionist perspective, in the diaspora, "as long as Jews could not become the actors of their own history, they remained incapable of conceiving of a historiographical reflection about themselves": "How Golden Was the Age of the Renaissance in Jewish Historiography?" *History and Theory* 27 (1988): 92–93 and 101–2. On this last point, David Myers thinks that contemporary Israeli historians have "deliberately sought to shape a new collective memory for the Jewish people understood this time in political and national terms"; in his opinion, "the modern Jewish historian endlessly seeks to play a constructive role in the elaboration of a collective Jewish memory": "Remembering *Zakhor*: A Super Commentary," *History and Memory* (winter 1992): 138 and 141. Note that Yosef H. Yerushalmi, in a recent text, referring to the book by Myers, *Re-Inventing the Jewish Past*, writes, "Baer has, like them [Ben Zion Dinur and Gershom Scholem] the conviction that living and working in their own country, Jewish historians can finally free themselves from the apologetic and idealizing tendencies that deformed Jewish historiography in the last century,"

Preface to Baer, *Galout*, p. 15. See finally the general discussion in Michael Brenner and David Myers, eds., *Jüdische Geschichtsschreibung heute. Themen, Positionem, Kontroversen* (Munich: C. H. Beck, 2002). The distinctions proposed by *Zakhor* have entered the daily lives of American Jews, as a number of Sabbath sermons have shown. See, for example, the moving text by the secretary of the Jewish Theological Center of New York, Ismar Schorsch, on March 2, 1996, in which he mentions remembering his father's death and favorably quotes Yerushalmi's book: Parashat Hashavua, online; or the sermon by Rabbi Mark Diamond, on September 1, 2001, Jewish LA online. *Freud's Moses* has also given rise to discussions, and its influence is felt in many recent researches: Jacques Derrida, *Mal d'archive* (Paris: Galilée, 1995); Jan Assmann, *Moïse l'Égyptien. Un essai d'histoire de la mémoire* (Paris: Aubier, 2001); Jacques Le Rider, *Freud, de l'Acropole au Sinaï* (Paris: PUF, 2002).

26. Yerushalmi, *Zakhor*, p 93.

27. Ibid., p. 94.

28. Ibid., p. 101. The use of the notion of a "break," often called "radical," is constant; see p. 101. Similarly, in his *Freud's Moses*, Yerushalmi uses this idea of a "radical break," p. 2.

29. Yerushalmi, *Zakhor*, p. 100.

30. Yerushalmi, *From Spanish Court to Italian Ghetto*, p. xvi.

31. Yerushalmi, *Zakhor*, p. 81.

32. Yosef H. Yerushalmi, acceptance speech upon being awarded an honorary doctorate at the EPHE, January 14, 2003.

33. David Myers, "Of Marranos and Memory: Yosef Hayim Yerushalmi and the Writing of Jewish History," in Elisheva Carlebach, John Efron, and David Myers, eds., *Jewish History and Jewish Memory: Essays in Honor of Yosef Hayim Yerushalmi* (Hanover, NH: Brandeis University Press, 1998), p. 1.

34. On the near-impossibility of Jews obtaining employment as university professors in Germany before the Weimar Republic, see Peter Pulzer, *Jews and the German State* (Oxford: Blackwell, 1992). See also the older work by Monika Richarz, which on this point still has its importance, *Der Eintritt des Juden in die akademischen Berufe* (Tübingen: J. C. B. Mohr, 1974).

35. Schorsch, *From Text to Context*, pp. 2, 52, and 62. On Zunz, see Céline Trautman-Waller, *Philologie allemande et tradition juive. Le parcours intellectuel de Leopold Zunz* (Paris: Le Cerf, 1998).

36. Quoted by Michael Meyer, *Judaism Within Modernity: Essays on Jewish History and Religion* (Detroit, MI: Wayne State University Press, 2001), p. 135. See also, by the same author, *Response to Modernity: A History of the Reform Movement in Judaism* (Oxford: Oxford University Press, 1988), ch. 2.

37. Simon Dubnow, *Le livre de ma vie* (Paris: Le Cerf, 2001), pp. 604–5, 629ff., and 847ff.

38. Paula Hyman, "The Ideological Transformation of Modern Jewish Historiography," in Shaye Cohen and Edward Greenberg, eds., *The State of Jewish Studies* (Detroit: Wayne State University Press, 1990).

39. The American Jewish Historical Society was created in June 1892. See Nathan Kaganoff, "AJHS at 90: Reflections on the History of the Oldest Ethnic Historical Society in America," *American Jewish History* 71 (1982). Robert Liberles compares the AJHS to its British sibling, the Jewish Historical Society of England, created in June 1893, "Postemancipation Historiography and the Jewish Historical Societies of America and England," in Jonathan Frankel, ed., *Reshaping the Past: Jewish History and the Historians* (Oxford: Studies in Contemporary Jewry, 1994). The Société des Études juives was created in France in 1880.

40. Todd Endelman, "In Defense of Jewish Social History," *Jewish Social Studies* (spring–summer 2001).

41. Meyer, *Judaism Within Modernity*, p. 109.

42. Ibid., p. 335. Meyer shows that Geiger did not share this point of view.

43. For example, Elisheva Carlebach, David Myers, Aron Rodrigue, Benjamein Gampel, Michael Stanislawski, Michael Brenner, who teaches in Munich, and Nils Holger Roener, who teaches in Southampton, have all written their doctoral theses under his direction.

44. Endelman, "In Defense of Jewish Social History," p. 63.

45. Yerushalmi, *From Spanish Court to Italian Ghetto*, p. 44.

46. Yerushalmi, "Entretien à Jérusalem," p. 152.

47. Yosef H. Yerushalmi, "The Inquisition and the Jews of France in the Time of Bernard Gui," *Harvard Theological Review* (July 1970): 331ff. This text was written in 1964.

48. In the original text, we find "bifurcated," translated into French as "à la croisée de chemins" [at a crossroads], which does not convey adequately the idea of internal rupture. *Zakhor*, p. 116 of the French. See p. 99 in the American edition.

49. Yosef H. Yerushalmi, "Série Z. Une fantaisie archivistique," *Le Débat* (November–December 1996): 151.

50. Yerushalmi, *Zakhor*, p. 101.

51. "Yosef Hayim Yerushalmi," Gale Literary Databases. "Entretien à Jérusalem."

52. Yerushalmi, "Entretien à Jérusalem," pp. 154–55.

53. Joseph Blau and Salo Baron, *The Jews of the United States: 1790–1840* (New York: Columbia University Press, 1963), vol. 1, p. xxxv.

54. Yerushalmi, *Zakhor*, pp. 95, 100, and 102.

55. See Jonathan Sarna, *JPS: The Americanization of Jewish Culture, 1888–1988* (Philadelphia, PA: The Jewish Publication Society, 1989), pp. 35ff. In this book there is a photo of the publication committee of 1976 in which Yosef Yerushalmi appears, next to Edward Shils. Yerushalmi presided over this committee from 1973, when he succeeded Gerson Cohen, appointed director of the Jewish Theological Seminary. It was in this framework that Yerushalmi published his *Haggadah and History* (1975). Disagreeing with its new orientations, more literary than scientific, he resigned in 1983 and was replaced by the writer Chaim Potok. See p. 287.

56. Here we are using the interpretation that Susannah Heschel gives of the

work of Abraham Geiger, *Abraham Geiger and the Jewish Jesus* (Chicago: University of Chicago Press, 1998), pp. 3ff.

57. Nils Holger Roemer, "The Historicizing of Judaism in 19th-Century Germany: Scholarly Discipline and Popular Historical Culture" (PhD diss., Columbia University, 2000). The author thinks that "Gans is not the only member of the *Verein* to attack the Jewish proponents of the Enlightenment who had only scorn for the Jewish tradition. . . . Zunz still shared the hostility of the Enlightenment towards the Ashkenazi tradition, and its positive appreciation of the Sephardim, but he attacked the use of history by the Enlightenment. . . . Zunz attacks the *maskilim*. . . . To oppose the impact of the Enlightenment, the *Verein*, by insisting on historical studies, means to redefine Judaism," p. 42; see also p. 152.

58. We find a number of organic metaphors in *Zakhor*. The Jewish historian is "rooted in the organic life of his people"; Jewish memory was the expression of the "organic functioning" of religious and social institutions, and its decline bears witness to "the root of the malady"; "Jewish memory cannot be 'healed' unless the group itself finds healing," *Zakhor*, American edition, pp. 94 and 114. In the French edition, we find *mal* [evil, sickness] in place of *maladie* [malady, disease], p. 110.

59. Schorsch, "Wissenschaft and Values," in *From Text to Context*, p. 155, as well as, in the same book, "From Wolfenbüttel to Wissenschaft," p. 248. Schorsch points out Zunz's references to the writings of Herder and compares Graetz to Burke in the chapter "Ideology and History in the Age of Emancipation," p. 279 of the same volume.

60. Here we are following Robert Liberles, *Salo Wittmayer Baron: Architect of Jewish History* (New York: New York University Press, 1995), ch. 1. I am also basing my portrait on a long personal discussion with Robert Liberles in Beersheba in April 1999. See also David Hollinger, *Science, Jews and Secular Culture: Studies in Mid-Twentieth Century American Intellectual History* (Princeton, NJ: Princeton University Press, 1996), p. 39, n. 46.

61. Jacob Neusner meanly describes him as a "Gauleiter of Jewish studies in American universities," "Literate, Enlightened Book on Salo Wittmayer Baron," review of a book by Robert Liberles, *Jewish Spectator* (winter 1995): 40. The article is of an unusual and unacceptable violence against Baron, who is accused of being a "racist" theoretician who asserts the unicity of the Jewish people based on its innate characteristics, p. 41.

62. Unpublished letter from Arendt quoted by Liberles, *Salo Wittmayer Baron*, p. 10.

63. Salo W. Baron, *The Jewish Community* (Philadelphia, PA: Jewish Publication Society, 1942).

64. *American Journal of Sociology* 49 (1944): 319–20.

65. Salo W. Baron, "Is America Ready for Ethnic Minority Rights?" *Jewish Social Studies* (winter 1984).

66. This letter is published in Liberles, *Salo Wittmayer Baron*, p. 248.

67. Salo Baron, "Ghetto and Emancipation: Shall We Revise the Traditional View?" *The Menorah Journal* (June 1928): 516.

68. "A Conversation About Salo Baron Between Robert Liberles and Steven Zipperstein," *Jewish Social Studies* (summer 1995): 70.

69. Baron, "Ghetto and Emancipation," pp. 524–25. Salo Baron also approaches this theme in *A Social and Religious History of the Jews* (New York: Columbia University Press, 1952), vol. 1, p. 24.

70. Ibid., pp. 518–19 and 524.

71. See his article "Emphases on Jewish History," published in 1939, in Arthur Herzberg and Leon Feldman, eds., *History and Jewish Historians: Essays and Addresses by Salo Baron* (Philadelphia, PA: Jewish Publication Society of America, 1964), p. 82.

72. See also Baron's article "World Dimensions of Jewish History," published in 1963, in Herzberg and Feldman, eds., *History and Jewish Historians*, pp. 35–36, and "Newer Emphases in Jewish History," dated 1963, in this same volume, where he writes, "All my life, I have fought against the lachrymose concept of history," p. 96.

73. Roemer, "Historicizing of Judaism in 19th Century Germany," p. 109.

74. See Baron's article "Graetz and Ranke," which is dated 1918, in *History and Jewish Historians*, pp. 273–74. Robert Chazan is very favorable to the interpretation of the Middle Ages offered by Baron in his article "The Historiographical Legacy of Salo Wittmayer Baron: The Medieval Period," *AJS Review* (spring 1993): 34–35.

75. Heinrich Graetz, *History of the Jews* (Philadelphia, PA: The Jewish Publication of America, 1895), vol. 4, intro., p. 12. Graetz stresses "the unprecedented sufferings, an uninterrupted martyrdom and a constant aggravated degradation and humiliation unparalleled in history but also by mental activity, unremitting intellectual efforts and indefatigable research"; for Graetz, "if the Judaism of this era presents the most glorious martyrs . . . it has also produced eminent thinkers." See also the sixth letter of his "Correspondence of an English Lady on Judaism and Semitism," where he insists on the constancy of the "hatred" the Jews have been confronted with throughout the centuries, in Heinrich Graetz, *The Structure of Jewish History and Other Essays* (New York: Jewish Theological Seminary of America, 1975), pp. 206ff.

76. Baron, *Social and Religious History of the Jews*, vol. 9, p. 388, n. 24.

77. That is the uncharitable interpretation of Ismar Schorsch in his article "The Lacrymose Conception of Jewish History," *From Text to Context*, p. 376.

78. Baron, "Emphases on Jewish History," p. 72.

79. Ismar Schorsch, "The Last Jewish Generalist," *AJS Review* (spring 1993): 42 and 46. Lionel Kochan stresses the influence of the evolutionist thoughts of Comte and Spencer on the linear conception of history developed by Dubnow, which distinguishes several ways of approaching Jewish history: a theological age, a spiritual age, and, finally, a sociological age that allows his theory of centers: Kochan, *Jew and His History*, ch. 7.

80. See Simon Dubnow, *Lettres sur le judaïsme ancien et nouveau* (Paris: Le

Cerf, 1989), pp. 381–86.

81. Quoted by Liberles, *Salo Wittmayer Baron*, p. 314. On this point, see Arnold Eisen, *The Chosen People in America: A Study in Jewish Religious Ideology* (Bloomington: Indiana University Press, 1983).

82. Dubnow, *Le livre de ma vie*, p. 929.

83. See David Myers and David Ruderman, eds., *Re-Inventing the Jewish Past: European Jewish Intellectuals and the Zionist Return to History* (New York: Oxford University Press, 1995), pp. 183–85. We also remember that Jacob Katz challenged Baron's studies, which he considers "eclectic"; he thinks they do not place enough stress on the unity of Jewish history, in Jacob Katz, "The Concept of Social History and Its Possible Use in Jewish Historical Research," *Scripta Hierosolymitana* 3 (1956): 310.

84. Dubnow, *Le livre de ma vie*, p. 1026. On the favorable view Dubnow has of the Palestinian homeland, see Sophie Erlich-Dubnow, *Simon Dubnow. Su vida y obra* (Buenos Aires: Ediciones del YIWO, 1954), pp. 282 and 297–98.

85. See Myers and Ruderman, eds., *Re-Inventing the Jewish Past*, ch. 5. The Baer quotation is given by Liberles, *Salo Wittmayer Baron*, p. 160. Liberles shows, p. 296, the belated answer that Baron gave to Baer, which is dated 1938.

86. Yosef H. Yerushalmi, "Un champ à Anathoth: vers une histoire de l'espoir juif," *Mémoire et Histoire* (Denoël, 1986), p. 93.

87. See the magnificent introduction by Yerushalmi to *Haggadah and History* 2d ed. (Philadelphia, PA: Jewish Publication Society of America, 1996), pp. 53 and 59.

88. Yerushalmi, "Un champ à Anathoth," pp. 94 and 102–5. See David Myers, "Derrida's Yerushalmi, Yerushalmi's Freud: History, Memory and Hope in a Post-Holocaust Age," in Paolo Amodio, Romeo De Maio, and Giuseppe Lissa, eds., *La Shoah. Tra Interpretazione e Memoria* (Naples: Vivarium, 1999), pp. 506–7.

89. Yosef H. Yerushalmi, Preface to Baer, *Galout*, pp. 43 and 46.

90. Yosef H. Yerushalmi, "Exile and Expulsion in Jewish History," in Benjamin Gampel, ed., *Crisis and Creativity in the Sephardic World, 1391–1648* (New York: Columbia University Press, 1997), pp. 10–11.

91. Yerushalmi, "Exile and Expulsion in Jewish History," pp. 13–15.

92. Yerushalmi, "Un champ à Anathoth," pp. 96–98.

93. Yerushalmi, "Response to Rosemary Ruether," p. 107.

94. Yosef H. Yerushalmi, *Assimilation and Racial Antisemitism: The Iberian and the German Models*, (New York: Leo Baeck Institute, 1982), pp.23 and 26.

95. Ibid.

96. Thus, Yerushalmi writes elsewhere, "For all of one's justified mistrust of historical parallelism, it is hard to escape the feeling that the Jewish people after the Holocaust stands today at a juncture not without analogy to that of the generations following the cataclysm of the Spanish Expulsion," *Zakhor*, p. 99.

97. This fundamental text is quoted by Yosef H. Yerushalmi in "Exile and Expulsion in Jewish History," p. 6, as well as in "Serviteurs des Rois et non serviteurs

des serviteurs. Sur quelques aspects de l'histoire politique des Juifs," *Raisons politiques* (August 2002): 25.

98. Michael Walzer, *The Politics of Exile in the Hebrew Bible* (Tübingen: Mohr Siebeck, 2001), p. 50.

99. Funkestein, *Perceptions of Jewish History*, pp. 248 and 256.

100. Thus, the American rabbi Jacob Staub, director of the medieval studies department in the Reconstructionist Rabbinic College, uses several texts by Yerushalmi to validate the American Jewish home in diaspora and to oppose perspectives that, in his eyes, are too favorable to Zionism. "Interpreting Jewish History in the Light of Zionism," *The Reconstructionist: A Journal of Contemporary Jewish Thought and Practice* (February 2002).

101. Pierre Birnbaum, *La logique de l'État* (Paris: Fayard, 1982); and Pierre Birnbaum, *Sur la corde raide* (Paris: Flammarion, 2002), ch. 9.

102. Yosef H. Yerushalmi, "The Lisbon Massacre of 1506 and the Royal Image in the 'Shebet Yahudah,'" *HUCA Supplement* no. 1 (1976): 1–3.

103. More critical, Amos Funkestein thinks that "Ibn Verga lived, in the spirit of Sartre, with the desire 'to be seen.' . . . Historians and apologists based their analyses on the supposed goodness of the leading classes," *Perceptions of Jewish History*, p. 212.

104. Yerushalmi, "The Lisbon Massacre," p. 17.

105. Yerushalmi, "The Lisbon Massacre," pp. 37–39.

106. Yerushalmi, "Serviteurs des Rois et non serviteurs des serviteurs," p. 20.

107. Yerushalmi, "Inquisition and the Jews of France in the Time of Bernard Gui," pp. 320–21.

108. Selma Stern, *The Court Jews* (New Brunswick, NJ: Transaction Books, 1985). Werner Cahnman, "Pariahs, Strangers and Court Jews," in J. Maier, J. Marcus, and Z. Tarr, eds., *German Jewry* (New Brunswick, NJ: Transaction Books, 1989). Fritz Stern, *Gold and Iron* (New York: Vintage Books, 1979). Richard Cohen and Vivian Mann, eds., *From Court Jews to the Rothschilds: Arts, Patronage and Power, 1600–1800* (Munich: Prestel, 1996).

109. Yerushalmi, "Serviteurs des Rois et non serviteurs des serviteurs," pp. 17–18. Yerushalmi refers here once again explicitly to his "master Salo Baron," p. 18.

110. Quoted in Yerushalmi, "Serviteurs des Rois et non serviteurs des serviteurs," pp. 36–37.

111. Ibid., p. 38.

112. Yosef H. Yerushalmi, "Professing Jews in Post-Expulsion Spain and Portugal," *Salo Baron Jubilee Volume* (Jerusalem: American Academy for Jewish Research, 1975), p. 30.

113. Yerushalmi, *From Spanish Court to Italian Ghetto*, pp. 39–41.

114. Yosef H. Yerushalmi, "Les derniers marranes. Le temps, la peur, la mémoire," introduction to *Marranes*, with photographs by Frédéric Brenner, text by Nicole Zand (Paris: La Différence, 1992), p. 31.

115. See, for example, Alain Corbin, *Le monde retrouvé de Louis François Pinagot:*

*sur les traces d'un inconnu, 1798–1876* (Paris: Flammarion, 1998).

116. Yerushalmi, *From Spanish Court to Italian Ghetto*, pp. 56–110.

117. Ibid., p. 136.

118. Ibid., p. 172.

119. Ibid., p. 193.

120. Pierre Birnbaum, "Exile, Assimilation and Identity: From Moses to Joseph," Mark Cohen, trans., in Carlebach, Efron, and Myers, eds., *Jewish History and Jewish Memory*, pp. 249–70. This text is partially reproduced in Birnbaum, *Sur la corde raide*, ch. 1.

121. Yerushalmi, *From Spanish Court to Italian Ghetto*, p. 183.

122. Ibid., p. 388.

123. Other Marrano Jewish doctors of that era used similar themes to boast about themselves. See Yosef Kaplan, *Les Nouveaux-Juifs d'Amsterdam* (Chandeigne, 1999), pp. 74ff.

124. Yerushalmi, *From Spanish Court to Italian Ghetto*, p. 385.

125. Richard Cohen, "Nostalgia and 'Return to the Ghetto': A Cultural Phenomenon in Western and Central Europe," in Jonathan Frankel and Steven Zipperstein, eds., *Assimilation and Community: The Jews in Nineteenth-Century Europe* (Cambridge: Cambridge University Press).

126. Yerushalmi, *From Spanish Court to Italian Ghetto*, p. 469.

127. Ibid., pp. 444–47.

128. Ibid., pp. 390, 399, 441, and 469.

129. Thus, in 1936, in his inaugural lecture at the University of Jerusalem, Baer thinks that the Spanish Jews are "assimilated Jews" who "already, in many respects, resemble the Jews of Western Europe in the present era," the one that precedes the Shoah. Quoted by Maurice Kriegel, "L'alliance royale, le mythe et le mythe du mythe," *Critique* (January–February 2000): 18.

130. Yosef H. Yerushalmi, *Assimilation and Racial Antisemitism*, p. 23.

131. In another text, Yerushalmi compares in the same spirit French-style emancipation to conversion in Spain: "From the phenomenological point of view, there is an undeniable parallelism between the question of emancipation and that of the debate of the purity of blood in the Iberian peninsula. Those French who were opposed to the emancipation of the Jews were persuaded that even the granting of equal rights to Jews would not abolish their national and religious identity, and that they would not succeed in blending into the surrounding population," "Propos de Spinoza sur la survivance du peuple juif," in *Sefardica*, pp. 204–5.

132. John Efron offers the same parallel in "Interminably Maligned: The Conventional Lies about Jewish Doctors," in Carlebach, Efron, and Myers, eds., *Jewish History and Jewish Memory*, pp. 296–310.

133. Letter published by Fritz Baer and quoted by Maurice Kriegel, "La prise de décision: l'expulsion des Juifs d'Espagne en 1492," *Revue historique* CCLX/1 (1978): 49. In this article, Kriegel analyzes the reasons for this decision. See, by the same

author, "De la 'question' des 'nouveaux-chrétiens' à l'expulsion des Juifs: la double modernité des procès d'exclusion dans l'Espagne du XVe siècle," in Serge Gruzinski and Nathan Wachtel, eds., *Le Nouveau Monde, mondes nouveaux: l'expérience américaine* (Éditions de l'EHESS, 1996).

134. Yerushalmi, "Serviteurs des Rois et non serviteurs des serviteurs," p. 40.

135. Hannah Arendt, *The Origins of Totalitarianism*, 2nd enlarged ed. (New York: Meridian Books, 1958).

136. This passage, taken from the *Shebet Yehudah*, is quoted by Yerushalmi in "The Lisbon Massacre," p. 48. Maurice Kriegel insists on this point: "We can deduce that he [Ibn Verga] imagined a possible junction with the 'liberals' of Spain of his time, or in any case thought of himself aligned with them," "L'Alliance royale, le mythe et le mythe du mythe," *Critique*, p. 29.

137. Yerushalmi, "Serviteurs des Rois et non serviteurs des serviteurs," p. 47.

138. Ibid., pp. 50–51.

139. Yerushalmi, "Response to Rosemary Ruether," p. 103.

140. Yerushalmi, "Serviteurs des Rois et non serviteurs des serviteurs," p. 51.

141. Yerushalmi, "Response to Rosemary Ruether," p. 107.

142. Yerushalmi, "Serviteurs des Rois et non serviteurs des serviteurs," p. 51.

143. Pierre Birnbaum, *Dimensions du pouvoir* (Paris: PUF, 1984), ch. 9.

144. Yerushalmi, "Exile and Expulsion in Jewish History," p. 22.

145. Yosef H. Yerushalmi shows he is basically confident in the pluralistic virtues of American society as protection against the extreme forms of anti-Semitism; personal interview, June 2001. For a less optimistic interpretation, see Leonard Dinnerstein, *Uneasy at Home: Anti-Semitism and the American Jewish Experience* (New York: Columbia University Press, 1987).

146. Yerushalmi, "Le judaïsme séfarade entre la croix et le croissant," in *Sefardica*, p. 33.

## Conclusion: Exile, the Enlightenment, Disassimilation

1. Karl Marx, *On 'The Jewish Question,'* in *Karl Marx: Selected Writings* (Oxford: Oxford University Press, 1987), p. 54. See A. C. Buchanan, *Marx and Justice: The Radical Critique of Liberalism* (London: Methuen, 1982); and A. C. Buchanan, "Assessing the Communitarian Critique of Liberalism," *Ethics* no. 4 (1989). See also Vidhu Verma, *Justice, Equality and Community: An Essay in Marxist Political Theory* (London: Sage), pp. 68–76.

2. Isaiah Berlin, *Against the Current*, Henry Hardy, ed., (New York: Viking Press, 1980).

3. Leon Bramson, *The Political Context of Sociology* (Princeton, NJ: Princeton University Press, 1970), p. 14. This very debatable presentation of Durkheim's work finds its source in the studies by Robert Nisbet, "Conservatism and Sociology," *American Journal of Sociology* 58 (1952); *Emile Durkheim* (Englewood Cliffs, NJ: Prentice Hall, 1965), pp. 24ff.; and his *The Sociological Tradition* (London:

Heinemann, 1967). In the same vein, see Lewis Coser, *Continuities in the Study of Social Conflict* (New York: Free Press, 1967), ch. 8. For a refutation of this simplistic interpretation of Durkheim, see Susan Stedman Jones, *Durkheim Reconsidered* (London: Polity Press, 2001), ch. 2.

4. See Ismar Schorsch, *From Text to Context: The Turn to History in Modern Judaism* (Hanover, NH: Brandeis University Press, 1994), p. 279.

5. On this theme, see Graeme Garrard, "The Counter-Enlightenment Liberalism of Isaiah Berlin," *Journal of Political Ideologies* 2 (1997).

6. Ronald Schecter, "Rationalizing the Enlightenment: Postmodernism and Theories of Anti-Semitism," in Daniel Gordon, ed., *Postmodernism and the Enlightenment* (New York: Routledge, 2001), p. 113.

7. See Joseph Carens, *Culture, Citizenship and Community: A Contextual Exploration of Justice as Evenhandedness* (Oxford: Oxford University Press, 2000), p. 23.

8. Peter Steinfels, *The Neoconservatives: The Men Who Are Changing America's Politics* (New York: Simon and Schuster, 1979), ch. 8.

9. Jacob Talmon, "Uniqueness and Universality of Jewish History: A Mid-Century Revaluation," in *The Unique and the Universal: Some Historical Reflections* (New York: Braziller, 1965), p. 70.

10. Jacob Talmon, *The Origins of Totalitarian Democracy* (London: Secker and Warburg, 1955). Arthur Herzberg, *The French Enlightenment and the Jews* (New York: Columbia University Press, 1968). On Jacob Katz and the Enlightenment, see Richard Cohen, "How Central Was Anti-Semitism to the Historical Writing of Jacob Katz?" in Jay Harris, ed., *The Pride of Jacob: Essays on Jacob Katz and His Work* (Cambridge: Cambridge University Press, 2002). Max Horkheimer and Theodor Adorno, *Dialectic of Enlightenment* (New York: Continuum, 1987). There are many studies of this book: see, for example, Anson Rabinbach, *In the Shadow of Catastrophe: German Intellectuals Between Apocalypse and Enlightenment* (Berkeley: University of California Press, 1997), ch. 5; Dan Diner, *Beyond the Conceivable: Studies on Germany, Nazism and the Holocaust* (Berkeley: University of California Press, 2000), ch. 5; Frédéric Vandenberghe, *Une histoire critique de la sociologie allemande* (Paris: Editions La Découverte, 1998), vol. 2. Vandenberghe thinks that "the aging Horkheimer became conservative, semi-reactionary," p. 48. In this same perspective hostile to the Enlightenment, see Bauman, *Modernité et Holocauste*. We also know that Leo Strauss broke with the Enlightenment, which according to him was incapable of offering a refutation of religious beliefs. See Daniel Tanguay, *Leo Strauss, une biographie intellectuelle* (Paris: Grasset, 2003), p. 75. On this discussion and its influence over contemporary political science, see Ira Katznelson, *Desolation and Enlightenment: Political Knowledge After Total War, Totalitarianism and the Holocaust* (New York: Columbia University Press, 2003).

11. See, for example, Arthur Mitzman, *Sociology and Estrangement: Three Sociologists in Imperial Germany* (New Brunswick, NJ: Transaction Books, 1987); or Steven Seidman, *Le libéralisme et les origines de la théorie sociale en Europe* (Paris: PUF, 1987).

12. The literature on Voltaire and the Jews is immense. After Arthur Herzberg

and Léon Poliakov, *Histoire de l'antisémitisme* (Paris: Calmann-Lévy, 1968), many people stress the unbridled anti-Semitism of Voltaire. Several authors on the contrary take up his defense, and refuse any form of anachronistic judgment. See Pierre Aubery, "Voltaire and Anti-Semitism: A Reply to Herzberg," *Studies on Voltaire and the Eighteenth Century* no. 217 (1983). Bertram Schwarzbach, "Voltaire et les Juifs: bilan et plaidoyer," *Studies on Voltaire and the Eighteenth Century* no. 358 (1997). This author qualifies Voltaire's criticisms of "naïve Jews" and adds, "These reactions are natural on the part of members of a minority that remains, despite the phrase uttered by General De Gaulle after the affair of the patrol-boats, not very sure of its identity and far from unanimous about its mission in a secular Western society. . . . There is a perverse pleasure in seeing oneself a victim of the universe, to reply in the affirmative to the questioning of the Jeremiah of Lamentations," pp. 29–30. See, finally, in the same vein, Roland Mortier, "Les 'philosophes' français du XVIIIe siècle devant le judaïsme et la judéité," *Le combat des Lumières* (Ferney-Voltaire: Centre international d'études du XVIIIe siècle, 2000). Adam Sutcliffe, "Can a Jew Be a Philosophe? Isaac de Pinto, Voltaire and Jewish Participation in the European Enlightenment," *Jewish Social Studies* 3 (2000).

13. Dominique Bourel, "Les rasés et les barbus. Diderot et le judaïsme," *Revue philosophique* no. 3 (1984).

14. See, for example, the severe article by George Kateb that accuses Arendt and Strauss of being "enemies" of democracy who must be fought, "The Questionable Influence of Arendt (and Strauss)," in Peter Graf Kielmansegg, Horst Mewes, and Elisabeth Glaser-Schmidt, eds., *Hannah Arendt and Leo Strauss* (Cambridge: Cambridge University Press, 1995), p. 29. See also Kenneth Deutsch and John Murley, eds., *Leo Strauss, The Straussians and the American Regime* (Boulder, CO: Rowan and Littlefield, 1999). On the Anglo-Saxon intellectual context of this discussion, see, for example, John Gray, *Enlightenment's Wake: Politics and Culture at the Close of the Modern Age* (London: Routledge, 1995). See also Darrin McCahon, "Enemies of the Enlightenment," in *The French Counter-Enlightenment and the Making of Modernity* (Oxford: Oxford University Press, 2001).

15. Pierre Birnbaum, "La France dans la théorie politique contemporaine," in Alain Dieckhoff, ed., *La constellation des appartenances. Nationalisme, libéralisme et pluralisme* (Paris: Presses de Sciences Po, 2004). See also Robert Wokler, "The Enlightenment, the Nation-State and the Primal Patricide of Modernity," in Norman Geras and Robert Wokler, eds., *The Enlightenment and Modernity* (London: Macmillan, 2000). The author thinks on the contrary that it is the French-style nation-state that is responsible for the standardizing, repressive policies imposed during the French Revolution, not the philosophers of the Enlightenment.

16. Hannah Arendt, "Imperialism," in *The Origins of Totalitarianism*, pp. 296–97. See also pp. 123–24.

17. Ibid., pp. 299–300.

18. Hannah Arendt, *On Revolution* (New York: Viking Press, 1965), p. 38.

19. Ibid., p. 104.

20. See Robert Legros, "Hannah Arendt: Une compréhension phénoménologique des droits de l'homme," *Études phénoménologiques* no. 2 (1985); and the response by Alain Renaut and Lukas Sosoe, "H. Arendt et l'idée moderne du droit," *Philosophie du droit* (Paris: PUF, 1991), append. 1. See also, on this same Arendt-Burke conjunction, the discussion in the United States: Jean Cohen, "Rights, Citizenship and the Modern Form of the Social: Dilemmas of Arendtian Republicanism," *Constellations* no. 2 (1996); as well as Jeffrey Isaac, "A New Guarantee on Earth: Hannah Arendt on Human Dignity and the Politics of Human Rights," *American Political Science Review* (March 1996).

21. See C. P. Courtney, *Montesquieu and Burke* (Oxford: Oxford University Press, 1963), pp. 1, 17, 145, 162, and 165. Isaiah Berlin offers quite a favorable review of this book in *Modern Language Review* 60 (1965). See also the classic study by Thomas Pangle, who likens Burke to Montesquieu while still emphasizing the differences between these authors, *Montesquieu's Philosophy of Liberalism* (Chicago: University of Chicago Press, 1973), pp. 192ff. According to this book, Montesquieu did not adhere to an organic concept of the nation, and placed more emphasis on the essential role of legislators.

22. Montesquieu, *The Spirit of Laws*, Thomas Nugent, trans., 1752 (Kitchener, ON: Batoche Books, 2001), bk. 19, ch. 6.

23. Montesquieu, *Lettres persanes*, 60, *Oeuvres complètes* (Paris: Le Seuil, 1964). In English: *The Persian Letters* (Cambridge: Hackett, 1999). In the same vein, *Mes pensées*, *Oeuvres complètes*, p. 1077.

24. Montesquieu, *Spirit of Laws*, bk. 25, ch. 3.

25. Ibid., bk. 28, ch. 7, and bk. 21, ch. 20; and *Rome, secret séjour*, *Oeuvres complètes*, p. 290, where Montesquieu once again condemns "the policy of imprisoning the Jews." Studies on Montesquieu and the Jews are almost nonexistent. See, however, Allan Arkush, "Montesquieu: Un précurseur de l'Émancipation des Juifs?" *Les Cahiers du Judaïsme* (winter 2001). On diversity in Montesquieu, see Tzvetan Todorov, *Nous et les autres. La réflexion française sur la diversité humaine* (Paris: Le Seuil, 1989). Catherine Larrère, *Actualité de Montesquieu* (Paris: Presses de Sciences Po, 1999).

26. Montesquieu, *Spirit of Laws.*, bk. 25, ch. 13. Similarly, in the *Persian Letters*, Montesquieu writes, "The ever-exterminated Jews," p. 125.

27. Ibid., bk. 29, ch. 18.

28. Quoted by Norbert Col, *Burke, le contrat social et les révolutions* (Rennes: Presses universitaires de Rennes, 2002), p. 225. The author adds, p. 226, that Burke "is not in the least a rabid anti-Semite."

29. Ronald Schechter, *Obstinate Hebrews: Representations of Jews in France, 1715–1815* (Berkeley: University of California Press, 2003).

30. Jonathan Israel, *Radical Enlightenment: Philosophy and the Making of Modernity, 1650–1750* (Oxford: Oxford University Press, 2001), chs. 8 and 13. Adam Sutcliffe, *Judaism and Enlightenment* (Cambridge: Cambridge University Press, 2003), chs. 7 and 12. The literature on Spinoza and the Jews is immense. See Israël

Salvator Révah, *Des Marranes à Spinoza* (Paris: Vrin, 1995); or Yirmiahu Yovel, *Spinoza et autres hérétiques* (Paris: Le Seuil, 1991).

31. Isaiah Berlin, *Against the Current* (New York: Viking Press, 1980), pp. 139, 159, and 161. See also Isaiah Berlin, *The Crooked Timber of Humanity: Chapters in the History of Ideas*, Henry Hardy, ed. (New York: Alfred A. Knopf, 1991), pp. 30, 87, and 107. Philippe Raynaud also compares Herder to Burke; see Preface to *Réflexions sur la Révolution en France* (Paris: Hachette, "Pluriel," 1989), p. lxxxix. Similarly, Gérard Gengembre emphasizes the link between these two authors, "Burke," in François Furet and Mona Ozouf, eds., *Dictionnaire critique de la Révolution française* (Paris: Flammarion, 1988), p. 946. For Wolfgang Pross, one of the best contemporary specialists on Herder's thought, Herder "was a great reader of Montesquieu," personal communication. We know that, on her side, Arendt wrote: "Herder understands the history of the Jews as they themselves interpreted it, that is, as the history of the chosen people. . . . Herder understands that the history of this people that has its origin in Mosaic law could not be cut off from it," *La tradition cachée*, pp. 29–30. We also note that Leopold Zunz often refers to the works of Herder.

32. Arendt, *On Revolution*, pp. 120–21, 165, 176, 222–24, 263f., and 309.

33. Letters from Hannah Arendt to Karl Jaspers, January 29, 1946, and June 30, 1947, in *Hannah Arendt/Karl Jaspers Correspondence 1926–1969*, Lotte Kohler and Hans Saner, eds.; Robert and Rita Kimber, trans. (New York: Harcourt Brace Jovanovich, 1992), pp. 30 and 90. In the same period of time, she several times repeats "I am reading Tocqueville"; see Hannah Arendt and Heinrich Blücher, *Correspondance* (Paris: Calmann-Lévy, 1999), pp. 129 and 142.

34. Arendt does not do justice to the multiplicity of liberating projects engendered by the French Revolution and shows she is blind to the characteristics that distinguish the many nation-states. She does not imagine the creation of international organs of protection of human rights capable, as they are today, of imposing their mission upon the will of individual governments. She does not ask the question of protection of minorities endowed with citizenship by their respective governments, which can prove oppressive with respect to their own nationals. She also overestimates the importance of local action of citizens in the United States as well as the virtues of federalism, so many things that American political science itself tends to call into question by stressing the weight of prejudice and social control. Arendt does not see the force of fundamentalism, the violence of racism exercised against the blacks. She does not grasp the amplitude of the anti-Semitism that was, at that time in the United States, penetrating institutions like universities instead of confining itself solely to the sphere of the civil society.

35. See Annie Amiel, "Hannah Arendt, lectrice de Montesquieu," *Revue Montesquieu* no. 2 (1998).

36. Arendt declares in this sense: "The role model for this [American] republic is to a certain extent that of the Athenian *polis*," in Melvyn Hill, ed., *Hannah Arendt: The Recovery of the Public World* (New York: St. Martin's Press), p. 330. See Ernest Vollrath, "Hannah Arendt: A German-American Jewess Views the United

States—and Looks Back to Germany," in Kielmansegg, Mewes, and Glaser-Schmidt, eds., *Hannah Arendt and Leo Strauss.*

37. Arendt, "Imperialism," in *Origins of Totalitarianism*, p. 302.

38. Letter from Hannah Arendt to Karl Jaspers, April 14, 1957, in *Hannah Arendt/Karl Jaspers Correspondence*, p. 313.

39. Leon Botstein compares these two authors in a very suggestive way in "Liberating the Pariah: Politics, the Jews and Hannah Arendt," in Robert Boyers, ed., *Proceedings of History, Ethics, Politics: A Conference Based on the Work of Hannah Arendt* (New York: Empire State College, 1982), p. 210. The essential book of Mordecai Kaplan, the most important thinker of contemporary American Judaism, is *Judaism As a Civilization: Toward a Reconstruction of American Jewish Life.* On Kaplan's thought, see Emmanuel Goldsmith, Mel Scult, and Robert Seltzer, eds., *The American Judaism of Mordecai Kaplan* (New York: New York University Press, 1990). On the link between Dubnow and Kaplan, see Robert Seltzer, "From Graetz to Dubnow: The Impact of the East European Milieu on the Writing of Jewish History," in *The Legacy of Jewish Migration: 1881 and Its Impact* (New York: Social Science Monographs, Brooklyn College Press, distributed by Columbia University Press, 1983), p. 60. More than the Wissenschaft scholars, Kaplan showed he was attentive to the social sciences, and to sociology in particular, in his plan for reconstructing a real community in this new center that is the United States. See Mel Scult, *Judaism Faces the Twentieth Century: A Biography of Mordecai M. Kaplan* (Detroit, MI: Wayne State University Press, 1993), pp. 216ff.

40. Raymond Aron, *Main Currents in Sociological Thought* (New Brunswick, NJ: Transaction Publishers, 1998).

41. Raymond Boudon and François Bourricaud, *Dictionnaire critique de la sociologie* (Paris: PUF, 1982), p. 624.

42. Arnaldo Momigliano challenges Max Weber's interpretation of Jews as a pariah people, but stresses the "sympathetic comprehension" that Weber shows, on many points, towards the Jews: "Judaism As a Pariah Religion," in Arnaldo Momigliano, *Essays on Ancient and Modern Judaism,* Silvia Berti, ed. (Chicago: University of Chicago Press, 1994), p. 177.

43. Pierre Birnbaum, *The Idea of France*, M.B. DeBevoise, trans. (New York: Hill and Wang, 2001). For a recent comparison with the American model, see Frederic Cople Jaher, *The Jews and the Nation: Revolution, Emancipation, State Formation and the Liberal Paradigm in America and France* (Princeton, NJ: Princeton University Press, 2002).

44. Jürgen Habermas, *L'intégration républicaine* (Paris: Fayard, 1998), p. 77. Arnold Eisen thinks this conjuncture is unimaginable: "Habermas' thought ignores religious groups . . . his thought can scarcely be used by the Jews other than in metaphoric terms; it leaves no place for Jewish practices," *Rethinking Modern Judaism: Ritual, Commandment, Community* (Chicago: University of Chicago Press, 1998), pp. 75 and 77. See Arnold Eisen, *Galut: Modern Jewish Reflection on Homelessness and Homecoming* (Bloomington: Indiana University Press, 1986).